CHILTON'S

REPAIR MANUAL

CHEVROLET/ GMC VANS 1987-90

Covers all U.S. and Canadian models of Chevrolet/GMC 1/2, 3/4, and 1 Ton Vans, Cutaways and Motor Home Chassis

President GARY INGERSOLL
Senior Vice President, Book Publishing and Research RONALD A. HOXTER
Publisher KERRY A. FREEMAN, S.A.E.
Editor-in-Chief DEAN F. MORGANTINI, S.A.E.
Senior Editor RICHARD J. RIVELE, S.A.E.
Editor RICHARD J. RIVELE

ONE OF THE **ABC PUBLISHING COMPANIES**,
A PART OF **CAPITAL CITIES/ABC, INC.**

Radnor, Pennsylvania 19089

CONTENTS

GENERAL INFORMATION and MAINTENANCE

ENGINE PERFORMANCE and TUNE-UP

ENGINE and ENGINE OVERHAUL

EMISSION CONTROLS

FUEL SYSTEM

CHASSIS ELECTRICAL

7  DRIVE TRAIN

8  SUSPENSION and STEERING

9  BRAKES

10  BODY

11  MECHANIC'S DATA

SAFETY NOTICE

Proper service and repair procedures are vital to the safe, reliable operation of all motor vehicles, as well as the safety of those performing repairs. This book outlines procedures for serviceing and repairing vehicles using safe effective methods. The procedures contain many NOTES, CAUTIONS and WARNINGS which should be followed along with standard safety procedures to eliminate the possibility of personal injury or improper service which could damage the vehicle or compromise its safety.

It is important to note that repair procedures and techniques, tools and parts for servicing motor vehicles, as well as the skill and experience of the individual performing the work vary widely. It is not possible to anticipate all of the conceivable ways or conditions under which vehicles may be serviced, or to provide cautions as to all of the possible hazards that may result. Standard and accepted safety precautions and equipment should be used during cutting, grinding, chiseling, prying,or any other process that can cause material removal or projectiles.

Some procedures require the use of tools specially designed for a specific purpose. Before substituting another tool or procedure, you ust be com-pletely satisfied that neither your personal safety, nor the performance of the vehicle will be endangered.

Although the information in this guide is based on industry sources and is as complete as possible at the time of publication, the possibility exists that the manufacturer made later changes which could not be included here. While striving for total accuracy, Chilton Book Company cannot assume responsibilty for any errors, changes, or omissions that may occur in the compilation of this data.

PART NUMBERS

Part numbers listed in the reference are not recommendations by Chilton for any product by brand name. They are references that can be used with interchange manuals and aftermarket supplier catalogs to locate each brand supplier's discrete part number.

SPECIAL TOOLS

Special tools are recommended by the vehicle manufacturer to perform their specific job. Use has been kept to a minimum, but where absolutely neccesary, they are referred to in the text by the part number of the tool manufacturer. These tools can be purchased, under the appropiate part number, from your Service Tool Division, Kent-Moore Corporation, 1501 South Jackson Street, MI 49203. In Canada, contact Kent-Moore of Canada, Ltd., 2395 Cawthra Mississauga, Ontario, Canada L5A 3P2., or an equivalent tool can be purchased locally from a tool supplier or parts outlet. Before substituting any tool for the one recommended, read the SAFETY NOTICE at the top of this page.

ACKNOWLEDGEMENTS

Chilton Book Company expresses appreciation to Chevrolet Motor Division, General Motors Corporation, Detroit, Michigan 48202; and GMC Truck and Coach Division, General Motors Corporation, Pontiac, Michigan 48053 for their generous assistance

Information has been selected from Chevrolet and GMC shop manuals, owner's manuals, data books, brochures, service bulletins, and technical manuals.

Copyright© 1991 by Chilton Book Company
All Rights Reserved
Published in Radnor, Pennsylvania 19089 by Chilton Book Company
ONE OF THE ABC PUBLISHING COMPANIES, A PART OF CAPITAL CITIES/ABC, INC.

Manufactured in the United States of America
1234567890   0987654321

Chilton's Repair Manual: Chevy/GMC Vans 1987–90
ISBN 0–8019–8216–2 pbk.
Library of Congress Catalog Card No. 91–055222

General Information and Maintenance

HOW TO USE THIS BOOK

Chilton's Repair Manual for $\frac{1}{2}$, $\frac{3}{4}$ and 1 ton Chevrolet and GMC vans 1987 to 1990, is intended to help you learn more about the inner workings of your vehicle and save you money on its upkeep and operation. All of the operations apply to both Chevrolet and GMC vans unless specified otherwise.

The first two Chapters will be the most used, since they contain maintenance and tune-up information and procedures. Studies have shown that a properly tuned and maintained truck can get at least 10% better gas mileage (which translates into lower operating costs) and periodic maintenance will catch minor problems before they turn into major repair bills. The other Chapters deal with the more complex systems of your truck. Operating systems from engine through brakes are covered to the extent that the average do-it-yourselfer becomes mechanically involved. This book will not explain such things as rebuilding the differential for the simple reason that the expertise required and the investment in special tools make this task impractical and uneconomical. It will give you the detailed instructions to help you change your own brake pads and shoes, tune-up the engine, replace spark plugs and filters, and do many more jobs that will save you money, give you personal satisfaction and help you avoid expensive problems.

A secondary purpose of this book is a reference guide for owners who want to understand their truck and/or their mechanics better. In this case, no tools at all are required. Knowing just what a particular repair job requires in parts and labor time will allow you to evaluate whether or not you're getting a fair price quote and help decipher itemized bills from a repair shop.

Before attempting any repairs or service on your truck, read through the entire procedure outlined in the appropriate chapter. This will give you the overall view of what tools and supplies will be required. There is nothing more frustrating than having to walk to the bus stop on Monday morning because you were short one gasket on Sunday afternoon. So read ahead and plan ahead. Each operation should be approached logically and all procedures thoroughly understood before attempting any work. Some special tools that may be required can often be rented from local automotive jobbers or places specializing in renting tools and equipment. Check the yellow pages of your phone book.

All Chapters contain adjustments, maintenance, removal and installation procedures, and overhaul procedures. When overhaul is not considered practical, we tell you how to remove the failed part and then how to install the new or rebuilt replacement. In this way, you at least save the labor costs. Backyard overhaul of some components (such as the alternator or water pump) is just not practical, but the removal and installation procedure is often simple and well within the capabilities of the average truck owner.

Two basic mechanic's rules should be mentioned here. First, whenever the LEFT side of the truck or engine is referred to, it is meant to specify the DRIVER'S side of the truck. Conversely, the RIGHT side of the truck means the PASSENGER'S side. Second, all screws and bolts are removed by turning counterclockwise, and tightened by turning clockwise, unless otherwise noted.

Safety is always the most important rule. Constantly be aware of the dangers involved in working on or around an automobile and take proper precautions to avoid the risk of personal injury or damage to the vehicle. See the section in this Chapter, Servicing Your Vehicle Safely, and the SAFETY NOTICE on the acknowledgment page before attempting any service procedures and pay attention to the instructions provided. There are 3 common mistakes in mechanical work:

1. Incorrect order of assembly, disassembly or adjustment. When taking something apart or putting it together, doing things in the wrong order usually just costs you extra time; however it CAN break something. Read the entire procedure before beginning disassembly. Do everything in the order in which the instructions say you should do it, even if you can't immediately see a reason for it. When you're taking apart something that is very intricate (for example, a carburetor), you might want to draw a picture of how it looks when assembled at one point in order to make sure you get everything back in its proper position. We will supply exploded views whenever possible, but sometimes the job requires more attention to detail than an illustration provides. When making adjustments (especially tune-up adjustments), do them in order. One adjustment often affects another and you cannot expect satisfactory results unless each adjustment is made only when it cannot be changed by any other.

2. Overtorquing (or undertorquing) nuts and bolts. While it is more common for overtorquing to cause damage, undertorquing can cause a fastener to vibrate loose and cause serious damage, especially when dealing with aluminum parts. Pay attention to torque specifications and utilize a torque wrench in assembly. If a torque figure is not available remember that, if you are using the right tool to do the job, you will probably not have to strain yourself to get a fastener tight enough. The pitch of most threads is so slight that the tension you put on the wrench will be multiplied many times in actual force on what you are tightening. A good example of how critical torque is can be seen in the case of spark plug installation, especially where you are putting the plug into an aluminum cylinder head. Too little torque can fail to crush the gasket, causing leakage of combustion gases and consequent overheating of the plug and engine parts. Too much torque can damage the threads or distort the plug, which changes the spark gap at the electrode. Since more and more manufacturers are using aluminum in their engine and chassis parts to save weight, a torque wrench should be in any serious do-it-yourselfer's tool box.

There are many commercial chemical products available for ensuring that fasteners won't come loose, even if they are not torqued just right (a very common brand is Loctite®). If you're worried about getting something together tight enough to hold, but loose enough to avoid mechanical damage during assembly, one of these products might offer substantial insurance. Read the label on the package and make sure the product is compatible with the materials, fluids, etc. involved before choosing one.

3. Crossthreading. This occurs when a part such as a bolt is screwed into a nut or casting at the wrong angle and forced, causing the threads to become damaged. Crossthreading is more likely to occur if access is difficult. It helps to clean and lubricate fasteners, and to start threading with the part to be installed going straight in, using your fingers. If you encounter resistance, unscrew the part and start over again at a different angle until it can be inserted and turned several times without much effort. Keep in mind that many parts, especially spark plugs, use tapered threads so that gentle turning will automatically bring the part you're threading to the proper angle if you don't force it or resist a change in angle. Don't put a wrench on the part until it's been turned in a couple of times by hand. If you suddenly encounter resistance and the part has not seated fully, don't force it. Pull it back out and make sure it's clean and threading properly.

Always take your time and be patient; once you have some experience, working on your truck will become an enjoyable hobby.

TOOLS AND EQUIPMENT

Naturally, without the proper tools and equipment it is impossible to properly service your vehicle. It would be impossible to catalog each tool that you would need to perform each or every operation in this book. It would also be unwise for the amateur to rush out and buy an expensive set of tools an the theory that he may need one or more of them at sometime.

The best approach is to proceed slowly, gathering together a good quality set of those tools that are used most frequently. Don't be misled by the low cost of bargain tools. It is far better to spend a little more for better quality. Forged wrenches, 6- or 12-point sockets and fine tooth ratchets are by far preferable to their less expensive counterparts. As any good mechanic can tell you, there are few worse experiences than trying to work on a truck with bad tools. Your monetary savings will be far outweighed by frustration and mangled knuckles.

Certain tools, plus a basic ability to handle tools, are required to get started. A basic mechanics tool set, a torque wrench, and, a Torx® bits set. Torx® bits are hexlobular drivers

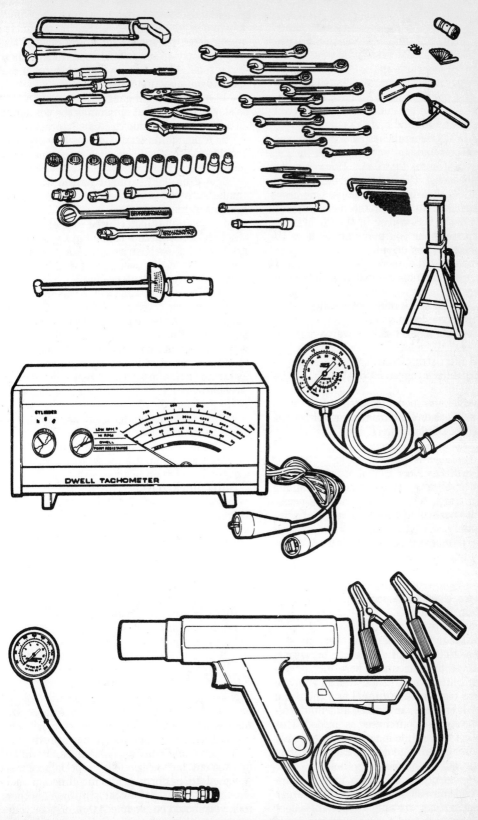

Necessary tool assortment needed for most jobs

which fit both inside and outside on special Torx® head fasteners used in various places.

Begin accumulating those tools that are used most frequently; those associated with routine maintenance and tune-up.

In addition to the normal assortment of screwdrivers and pliers you should have the following tools for routine maintenance jobs (your van uses both SAE and metric fasteners):

1. SAE/Metric wrenches, sockets and combination open end/box end wrenches in sizes from $1/8$ in. (3mm) to $3/4$ in. (19mm); and a spark plug socket ($13/16$ in.) If possible, buy various length socket drive extensions. One break in this department is that the metric sockets available in the U.S. will all fit the ratchet handles and extensions you may already have ($1/4$ in., $3/8$ in., and $1/2$ in. drive).

2. One set each of metric and S.A.E. combination (one end open and one end box) wrenches.

3. Wire-type spark plug feeler gauge.

4. Blade-type feeler gauges.

5. Slot and Phillips head screwdrivers in various sizes.

6. Oil filter strap wrench, necessary for removing oil filters (never used, though, for installing the filters).

7. Funnel, for pouring fresh oil or automatic transmission fluid from quart oil bottles.

8. Pair of slip-lock pliers.

9. Pair of vise-type pliers.

10. Adjustable wrench.

11. A hydraulic floor jack of at least $1^{1}/2$ ton capacity. If you are serious about maintaining your own truck, then a floor jack is as necessary as a spark plug socket. The greatly increased utility, strength, and safety of a hydraulic floor jack makes it pay for itself many times over through the years.

12. At least 4 sturdy jackstands for working underneath the truck. Any other type of support (bricks, wood and especially cinder blocks) is just plain dangerous.

13. An inductive timing light.

In addition to the above items there are several others that are not absolutely necessary, but handy to have around. These include oil-dry (cat box litter works just as well and may be cheaper), a transmission funnel and the usual supply of lubricants, antifreeze and fluids, although these can be purchased as needed. This is a basic list for routine maintenance, but only your personal needs and desires can accurately determine your list of necessary tools.

This is an adequate set of tools, and the more work you do yourself on your truck, the larger you'll find the set growing—a pair of pliers here, a wrench or two there. It makes more sense to have a comprehensive set of basic tools

as listed above, and then to acquire more along the line as you need them, than to go out and plunk down big money for a professional size set you may never use. In addition to these basic tools, there are several other tools and gauges you may find useful.

1. A compression gauge. The screw-in type is slower to use but it eliminates the possibility of a faulty reading due to escaping pressure.

2. A manifold vacuum gauge, very useful in troubleshooting ignition and emissions problems.

3. A drop light, to light up the work area (make sure yours is Underwriter's approved, and has a shielded bulb).

4. A volt/ohm meter, used for determining whether or not there is current in a wire. These are handy for use if a wire is broken somewhere and are especially necessary for working on today's electronics-laden vehicles.

As a final note, you will probably find a torque wrench necessary for all but the most basic work. The beam type models are perfectly adequate, although the newer click (breakaway) type are more precise, and you don't have to crane your neck to see a torque reading in awkward situations. The breakaway torque wrenches are more expensive and should be recalibrated periodically.

Torque specification for each fastener will be given in the procedure in any case that a specific torque value is required. If no torque specifications are given, use the following values as a guide, based upon fastener size:

Bolts marked 6T
6mm bolt/nut − 5–7 ft. lbs.
8mm bolt/nut − 12–17 ft. lbs.
10mm bolt/nut − 23–34 ft. lbs.
12mm bolt/nut − 41–59 ft. lbs.
14mm bolt/nut − 56–76 ft. lbs.

Bolts marked 8T
6mm bolt/nut − 6–9 ft. lbs.
8mm bolt/nut − 13–20 ft. lbs.
10mm bolt/nut − 27–40 ft. lbs.
12mm bolt/nut − 46–69 ft. lbs.
14mm bolt/nut − 75–101 ft. lbs.

Special Tools

Normally, the use of special factory tools is avoided for repair procedures, since these are not readily available for the do-it-yourself mechanic. When it is possible to perform the job with more commonly available tools, it will be pointed out, but occasionally, a special tool was designed to perform a specific function and should be used. Before substituting another tool, you should be convinced that neither your safety nor the performance of the vehicle will be compromised.

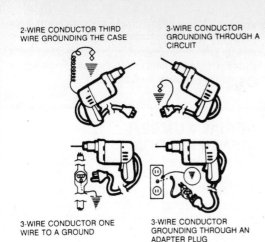

2-WIRE CONDUCTOR THIRD WIRE GROUNDING THE CASE

3-WIRE CONDUCTOR GROUNDING THROUGH A CIRCUIT

3-WIRE CONDUCTOR ONE WIRE TO A GROUND

3-WIRE CONDUCTOR GROUNDING THROUGH AN ADAPTER PLUG

When using electric tools, make sure that they are properly grounded

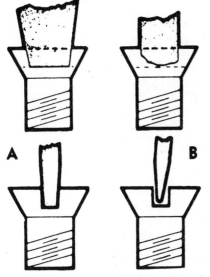

Keep screwdriver tips in good shape. They should fit in the screw head slots in the manner shown in "A". If they look like the tip shown in "B", they need grinding or replacing

Some special tools are available commercially from major tool manufacturers. Others can be purchased through your Chevy or GMC dealer.

SERVICING YOUR VAN SAFELY

It is virtually impossible to anticipate all of the hazards involved with automotive maintenance and service but care and common sense will prevent most accidents.

The rules of safety for mechanics range from "don't smoke around gasoline," to "use the proper tool for the job." The trick to avoiding injuries is to develop safe work habits and take every possible precaution.

Do's

• Do keep a fire extinguisher and first aid kit within easy reach.

• Do wear safety glasses or goggles when cutting, drilling, grinding or prying.

• Do shield your eyes whenever you work around the battery. Batteries contain sulphuric acid. In case of contact with the eyes or skin, flush the area with water or a mixture of water and baking soda and get medical attention immediately.

• Do use safety stands for any undercar service. Jacks are for raising vehicles; safety stands are for making sure the vehicle stays raised until you want it to come down. Whenever the vehicle is raised, block the wheels remaining on the ground and set the parking brake.

• Do disconnect the negative battery cable when working on the electrical system. The primary ignition system can contain up to 40,000 volts.

• Do properly maintain your tools. Loose hammerheads, mushroomed punches and chisels, frayed or poorly grounded electrical cords, excessively worn screwdrivers, spread wrenches (open end), cracked sockets, slipping

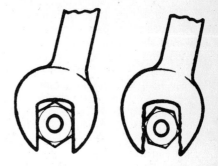

When using an open-end wrench, use the exact size needed and position it squarely on the flats of the bolt or nut

ratchets, or faulty droplight sockets can cause accidents and injuries.

• Do use the proper size and type of tool for the job being done.

• Do, when possible, pull on a wrench handle rather than push on it, and adjust your stance to prevent a fall.

• Do be sure that adjustable wrenches are tightly adjusted on the nut or bolt and pulled so that the face is on the side of the fixed jaw.

• Do select a wrench or socket that fits the nut or bolt. The wrench or socket should sit straight, not cocked.

• Do strike squarely with a hammer—avoid glancing blows.

• Do set the parking brake and block the

Always use jackstands when working under your van

drive wheels if the work requires that the engine be running.

Don'ts

• Don't run an engine in a garage or anywhere else without proper ventilation – EVER! Carbon monoxide is poisonous. It takes a long time to leave the human body and you can build up a deadly supply of it in your system by simply breathing in a little every day. Always use power vents, windows, fans or open the garage doors.

• Don't work around moving parts while wearing a necktie or other loose clothing. Short sleeves are much safer than long, loose sleeves and hard toed shoes with neoprene soles protect your toes and give a better grip on slippery surfaces. Jewelry is not safe when working around a car. Long hair should be hidden under a hat or cap.

• Don't use pockets for toolboxes. A fall or bump can drive a screwdriver deep into your body. Even a wiping cloth hanging from the back pocket can wrap around a spinning shaft or fan.

• Don't smoke when working around gasoline, cleaning solvent or other flammable material.

• Don't smoke when working around the battery. When the battery is being charged, it gives off explosive hydrogen gas.

• Don't use gasoline to wash your hands. There are excellent soaps available. Gasoline may contain lead, and lead can enter the body through a cut, accumulating in the body until you are very ill. Gasoline also removes all the natural oils from the skin so that bone dry hands will absorb oil and grease.

• Don't service the air conditioning system unless you are equipped with the necessary tools and training. The refrigerant, R-12, is extremely cold and when exposed to the air, will instantly freeze any surface it comes in contact with, including your eyes. Although the refrigerant is normally non-toxic, R-12 becomes a deadly poisonous gas in the presence of an open flame. One good whiff of the vapors from burning refrigerant can be fatal.

SERIAL NUMBER IDENTIFICATION

Vehicle

The V.I.N. plate is mounted on the driver's side of the instrument panel, and is visible through the windshield.

A 17 character code is used:

• The first character is the country of origin:

    1 = United States
    2 = Canada
    3 = Mexico

• The second character indicates the manufacturer. G = General Motors

• The third character indicates the make. Chevrolet (C) or GMC (T).

• The fourth character is the Gross Vehicle Weight range in pounds:

    B = 3,001–4,000
    C = 4,001–5,000
    D = 5,001–6,000
    E = 6,001–7,000
    F = 7,001–8,000
    G = 8,001–9,000
    H = 9,001–10,000
    J = 10,001–14,000
    K = 14,001–16,000

• The fifth character is vehicle line and chassis type: G = full-sized van.

• The sixth character is the weight code rating:

    1 = ½ ton
    2 = ¾ ton
    3 = 1 ton

• The seventh character is the body type:

    0 = chassis only

VIN label location

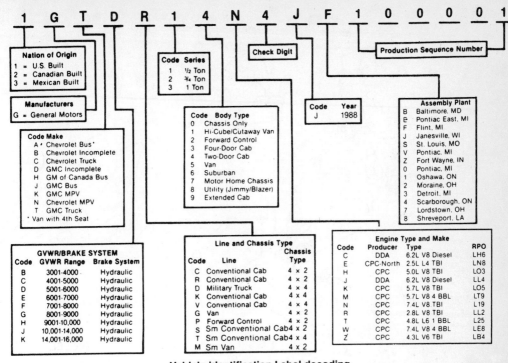

Vehicle identification Label decoding

1 = cutaway van
2 = forward control
3 = 4-door cab
4 = 2-door cab
5 = van
6 = Suburban
7 = motor home chassis
8 = Blazer/Jimmy
9 = extended cab
• The eighth character is the engine code:
C = 8–379 (6.2L) diesel
H = 8–305 (5.0L)
J = 8–379 (6.2L) diesel
K = 8–350 (5.7L) w/TBI
M = 8–350 (5.7L) w/4–bbl
N = 8–454 (7.4L) w/TBI
T = 6–292 (4.8L)
W = 8–454 (7.4L) w/4–bbl
Z = 6–262 (4.3L)
• The ninth character is a check digit.
• The tenth character is the year code. H = 1987; J = 1988; K= 1989; L = 1990.
• The eleventh character denotes the assembly plant:
B = Baltimore, MD
E = Pontiac East, MI
F = Flint, MI
J = Janesville, WI
S = St. Louis, MO
V = Pontiac, MI
Z = Fort Wayne, IN
0 = Pontiac, MI

1 = Oshawa, ON
2 = Moraine, OH
3 = Detroit, MI
4 = Scarborough, ON
7 = Lordstown, OH
8 = Shreveport, LA
• The last six numbers make up the consecutive serial number.

Engine

On V6 engines, the engine identification number is found on a machined pad on the block, at the front just below the right side cylinder head.

On V8 gasoline engines, the engine identification number is found on a machined pad on the left, rear upper side of the block, where the engine mates with the bell housing.

On V8 diesel engines, the engine identification number is found on a machined pad on the front of the block, between the left cylinder head and the thermostat housing, and/or on a machined pad on the left rear of the block, just behind the left cylinder head.

The engine number is broken down as follows:

Example – F1210TFA
• F – Manufacturing Plant. F-Flint and T-Tonawanda
• 12 – Month of Manufacture (December)
• 10 – Day of Manufacturer (Tenth)

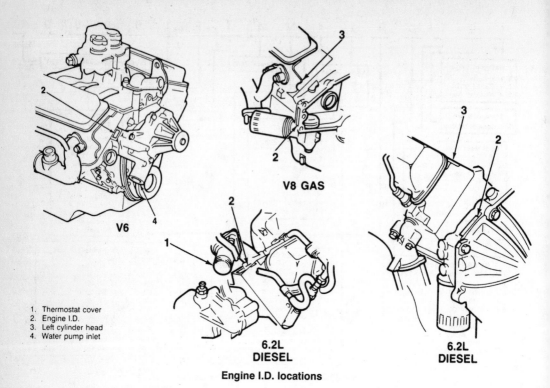

1. Thermostat cover
2. Engine I.D.
3. Left cylinder head
4. Water pump inlet

V6

V8 GAS

6.2L DIESEL

6.2L DIESEL

Engine I.D. locations

ENGINE APPLICATION CHART

Engine	Actual Displacement			Type	VIN	System	Mfg. by	Years
	Cu. In.	CC	Liters					
6–4.3	262.4	4299.7	4.3	OHV	Z	TBI	Chevrolet	1987–90
8–5.0	305.2	5001.2	5.0	OHV	H	TBI	Chevrolet	1987–90
8–5.7	349.8	5732.9	5.7	OHV	M	4-bbl	Chevrolet	1987–88
					K	TBI	Chevrolet	1987–90
8–6.2	378.2	6197.7	6.2	OHV	C,J	Diesel	DDAD	1987–90
8–7.4	453.9	7439.0	7.4	OHV	N	TBI	Chevrolet	1988–90

OHV: Overhead Valve
DDAD: Detroit Diesel Allison Division

- T – Truck engine
- FA – Transmission and Engine Combination

Transmission

The Muncie 3-speed manual transmission serial number is located on the lower left side of the case adjacent to the rear of the cover.

The New Process 4-speed transmission is numbered on the rear of the case, above the output shaft.

The Turbo Hydra-Matic is identified by a plate attached to the right side, which is stamped with the serial number.

Drive Axle

The drive axle serial number is stamped on the axle shaft housing, where it connects to the differential housing.

Service Parts Identification Plate

The service parts identification plate, commonly known as the option list, is usually located on the inside of the glove compartment door. On some vans, you may have to look for it on an inner fender panel. The plate lists the vehicle serial number, wheelbase, all regular production options (RPOs) and all special equipment. Probably, the most valuable piece of in-

MANUAL TRANSMISSION APPLICATION CHART

Transmission Types	Years	Models
Muncie 76mm 3-speed	1987	All w/6-262 or 8-305 engines
New Process 89mm 4-speed	1987–90	All models

AUTOMATIC TRANSMISSION APPLICATION CHART

Transmission Type	Years	Models
Turbo Hydra-Matic 400 3-speed	1987–90	All
Turbo Hydra-Matic 700-R4 4-speed	1987–90	All

formation on this plate is the paint code, a useful item when you have occasion to need paint.

ROUTINE MAINTENANCE

Routine maintenance is preventive medicine. It is the key to extending the life of any truck. By getting into the habit of doing some quick and simple checks once a week, you'll be sur-

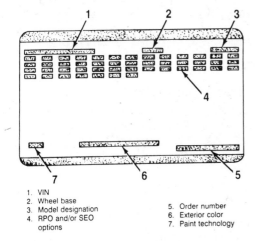

1. VIN
2. Wheel base
3. Model designation
4. RPO and/or SEO options
5. Order number
6. Exterior color
7. Paint technology

Service Parts Identification Label

prised how easy it is to keep your van in tiptop shape. It will also give you a greater awareness of the workings of your van.

By taking the time to check the engine oil, transmission fluid, battery and coolant level and the brake fluid regularly, you'll find yourself with a meticulously maintained van. You'll also be able to spot any developing problems (like a slow leak in the radiator) before they become expensive repairs. Try to check all the hinges and keep them well lubricated, too. Routine maintenance really does pay off.

The Maintenance Intervals chart gives the maintenance intervals recommended by the manufacturer.

Air Cleaner

REMOVAL AND INSTALLATION

Paper Element

Loosen the wing nut on top of the cover and remove the cover. The element should be replaced when it has become oil saturated or filled with dirt. If the filter is equipped with a foam wrapper, remove the wrapper and wash it in kerosene or similar solvent. Shake or blot dry. Saturate the wrapper in engine oil and squeeze it tightly in an absorbent towel to remove the excess oil.

REAR AXLE APPLICATION CHART

Axle Type	Years	Models
GM 8½ in. Ring Gear Semi-floating	1987–90	10/1500 series
GM 9½ in. Ring Gear Semi-floating	1987–90	10/1500 series ½ ton 20/2500 series
GM 10½ in. Ring Gear Full-floating	1987–90	20/2500 and 30/3500 series
Dana 9¾ in. Ring Gear Full-floating	1987–90	20/2500 series
Dana 10½ in. Ring Gear Full-floating	1987–90	20/2500 and 30/500 series

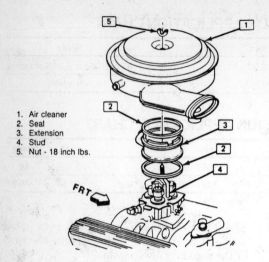

1. Air cleaner
2. Seal
3. Extension
4. Stud
5. Nut - 18 inch lbs.

Air cleaner used on all gasoline engines except the 7.4L

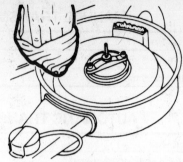

Clean out the housing before installing the new element

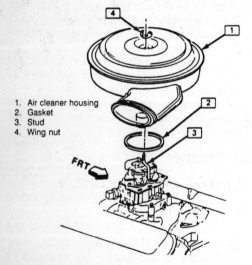

1. Air cleaner housing
2. Gasket
3. Stud
4. Wing nut

Air cleaner used on the 7.4L engine

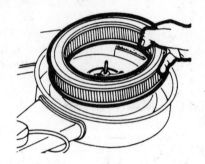

Removing the air cleaner paper element

Leave the wrapper moist. Clean the dirt from the filter by lightly tapping it against a workbench to dislodge the dirt particles. Wash the top of the air cleaner housing and wipe it dry. If equipped, replace the crankcase ventilation filter, located in the air filter housing if it appears excessively dirty. Replace the oiled wrapper on the air cleaner element and reinstall the element in the housing, repositioning it 180° from its original position.

NOTE: *Inverting the air cleaner cover for increased intake air volume is not recommended. This causes an increase in intake noise, faster dirt buildup in both the air cleaner element and the crankcase ventilation filter, and poor cold weather driveability.*

Fuel Filter

REMOVAL AND INSTALLATION

Carbureted Gasoline Engines

FILTER IN CARBURETOR

The fuel filter should be serviced at the interval given on the Maintenance Interval chart. Two types of fuel filters are used, a bronze type and a paper element type. Filter replacement should be attempted only when the engine is cold. Additionally, it is a good idea to place some absorbent rags under the fuel fittings to catch the gasoline which will spill out when the lines are loosened.

To replace the filter:

1. Disconnect the fuel line connecting at the intake fuel filter nut. Plug the opening to prevent loss of fuel.
2. Remove the intake fuel filter nut from the carburetor with a 1 in. wrench.
3. Remove the filter element and spring.
4. Check the element for restrictions by blowing on the cone end. Air should pass freely.
5. Clean or replace the element, as necessary.
6. Install the element spring, then the filter element in the carburetor. Bronze filters should have the small section of the cone facing out.
7. Install a new gasket on the intake fuel nut. Install the nut in the carburetor body and

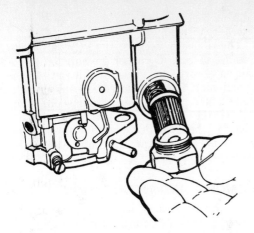

In-carburetor fuel filter

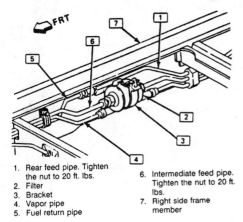

1. Rear feed pipe. Tighten the nut to 20 ft. lbs.
2. Filter
3. Bracket
4. Vapor pipe
5. Fuel return pipe
6. Intermediate feed pipe. Tighten the nut to 20 ft. lbs.
7. Right side frame member

Fuel filter location for fuel injected gasoline engines

tighten it securely, but carefully. The carburetor is made of soft metal and the threads are easily stripped!

8. Install the fuel line and tighten the connector.

INLINE FILTER

Some trucks may have an inline filter. This is a can shaped device located in the fuel line between the pump and the carburetor. It may be made of either plastic or metal. To replace the filter:

1. Place some absorbent rags under the filter. Remember, it will be full of gasoline when removed.

2. Use a pair of pliers to expand the clamp on one end of the filter, then slide the clamp down past the point to which the filter pipe extends in the rubber hose. Do the same with the other clamp.

3. Gently twist and pull the hoses free of the filter pipes. Remove and discard the old filter.

NOTE: *Most replacement filters come with new hoses that should be installed with a new filter.*

4. Install the new filter into the hoses, slide the clamps back into place, and check for leaks with the engine idling.

Fuel Injected Gasoline Engines

The inline filter on the fuel injected models is found along the frame rail.

1. Release the fuel system pressure. The 220 TBI unit contains a constant bleed feature in the pressure regulator that relieves pressure any time the engine is turned off. Therefore, no special relieve procedure is required, however, a small amount of fuel may be released when the fuel line is disconnected.

CAUTION: *To reduce the chance of personal injury, cover the fuel line with cloth to collect the fuel and then place the cloth in an approved container.*

2. Disconnect the fuel lines.

3. Remove the fuel filter from the retainer or mounting bolt.

4. To install, reverse the removal procedures. Start the engine and check for leaks.

NOTE: *The filter has an arrow (fuel flow direction) on the side of the case, be sure to install it correctly in the system, the with arrow facing away from the fuel tank.*

Diesel Engines

1. Drain the fuel from the fuel filter by opening both the air bleed and the water drain valve allowing the fuel to drain out into an appropriate container.

2. Remove the fuel tank cap to release any pressure or vacuum in the tank.

3. Unstrap both bail wires with a screwdriver and remove the filter.

4. Before installing the new filter, insure that both filter mounting plate fittings are clear of dirt.

5. Install the new filter, snap into place with the bail wires.

6. Close the water drain valve and open the air bleed valve. Connect a $1/8$ in. (3mm) I.D. hose to the air bleed port and place the other end into a suitable container.

7. Disconnect the fuel injection pump shut off solenoid wire.

8. Crank the engine for 10–15 seconds, then wait one minute for the starter motor to cool. Repeat until clear fuel is observed coming from the air bleed.

NOTE: *If the engine is to be cranked, or starting attempted with the air cleaner removed, care must be taken to prevent dirt from being pulled into the air inlet manifold which could result in engine damage.*

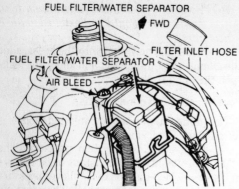

Combination fuel filter/water separator used on the diesel engine

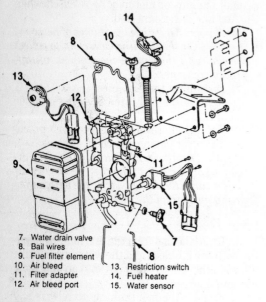

7. Water drain valve
8. Bail wires
9. Fuel filter element
10. Air bleed
11. Filter adapter
12. Air bleed port
13. Restriction switch
14. Fuel heater
15. Water sensor

Diesel fuel filter disassembled

9. Close the air bleed valve, reconnect the injection pump solenoid wire and replace the fuel tank cap.

10. Start the engine, allow it to idle for 5 minutes and check the fuel filter for leaks.

PCV Valve

OPERATION AND INSPECTION

The PCV valve is located on top of the valve cover or on the intake manifold. Its function is to purge the crankcase of harmful vapors through a system using engine vacuum to draw fresh air through the crankcase. It reburns crankcase vapors, rather than exhausting. Proper operation of the PCV valve depends on a sealed engine.

Engine operating conditions that would indicate a malfunctioning PCV system are rough idle, oil present in the air cleaner, oil leaks or excessive oil sludging.

The simplest check for the PCV valve is to remove it from its rubber grommet on top of the valve cover and shake it. If it rattles, it is functioning. If not, replace it. In any event, it should be replaced at the recommended interval whether it rattles or not. While you are about it, check the PCV hoses for breaks or restrictions. As necessary, the hoses should also be replaced.

REMOVAL AND INSTALLATION

1. Pull the valve, with the hose still attached to the valve, from the rubber grommet in the rocker cover.

2. Use a pair of pliers to release the hose clamp, remove the PCV valve from the hose.

3. Install the new valve into the hose, slide the clamp into position, and install the valve into the rubber grommet.

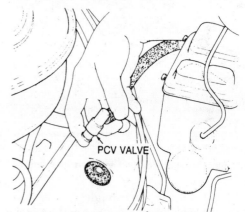

Checking the vacuum at the PCV valve

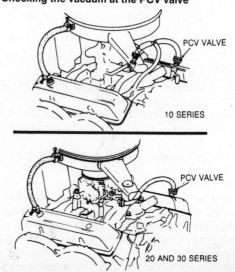

Typical PCV valve location

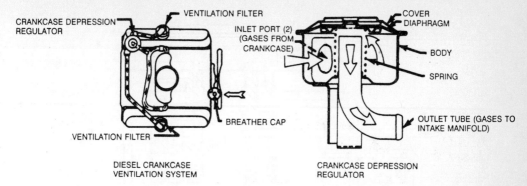

CRANKCASE DEPRESSION REGULATOR

VENTILATION FILTER

INLET PORT (2) (GASES FROM CRANKCASE)

VENTILATION FILTER

BREATHER CAP

DIESEL CRANKCASE VENTILATION SYSTEM

COVER DIAPHRAGM

BODY

SPRING

OUTLET TUBE (GASES TO INTAKE MANIFOLD)

CRANKCASE DEPRESSION REGULATOR

Diesel crankcase flow and depression regulator

Crankcase Depression Regulator and Flow Control Valve

SERVICING

Diesel Engines

The Crankcase Depression Regulator (CDR) is designed to scavenge crankcase vapors in basically the same manner as the PVC valve on gasoline engines. The valves are located either on the left rear corner of the intake manifold (CDR). On this system there are two ventilation filters, one per valve cover.

The filter assemblies should be cleaned every 15,000 miles by simply prying them carefully from the valve covers (be aware of the grommets underneath), and washing them out in solvent. The ventilation pipes and tubes should also be cleaned. The CDR valve should also be cleaned every 30,000 miles (the cover can be removed from the CDR). Dry each valve, filter, and hose with compressed air before installation.

NOTE: *Do not attempt to test the crankcase controls on these diesels. Instead, clean the valve cover filter assembly and vent pipes and check the vent pipes. Replace the breather cap assembly every 30,000 miles. Replace all rubber fittings as required every 15,000 miles.*

Evaporative Canister

SERVICING

The only regular maintenance that need be performed on the evaporative emission canister is to regularly change the filter and check the condition of the hoses. If any hoses need replacement, use only hoses which are marked EVAP. No other type should be used. Whenever the vapor vent hose is replaced, the restrictor adjacent to the canister should also be replaced.

The evaporative emission canister is located on the left side of the engine compartment, with a filter located in its bottom. Not all vans have one.

To service the canister filter:

1. Note the installed positions of the hoses, tagging them as necessary, in case any have to be removed.

2. Loosen the clamps and remove the canister.

3. Pull the filter out and throw it away.

4. Install a new canister filter.

5. Install the canister and tighten the clamps.

6. Check the hoses.

Battery

CAUTION: *Keep flame or sparks away from the battery. It gives off explosive hydrogen gas, while it is being charged.*

Check the battery fluid level (except in Maintenance Free batteries) at least once a month, more often in hot weather or during extended periods of travel. The electrolyte level should be up to the bottom of the split ring in each cell. All batteries on Chevrolet and GMC trucks are equipped with an eye in the cap of one cell. If the eye glows or has an amber color to it, this means that the level is low and only distilled water should be added. Do not add anything else to the battery. If the eye has a dark appearance the battery electrolyte level is high enough. It is wise to also check each cell individually.

At least once a year, check the specific gravity of the battery. It should be between 1.20–1.26. Clean and tighten the clamps and apply a thin coat of petroleum jelly to the terminals. This will help to retard corrosion. The terminals can be cleaned with a staff wire brush or with an inexpensive terminal cleaner designed for this purpose.

If water is added during freezing weather, the truck should be driven several miles to allow the electrolyte and water to mix. Otherwise the battery could freeze.

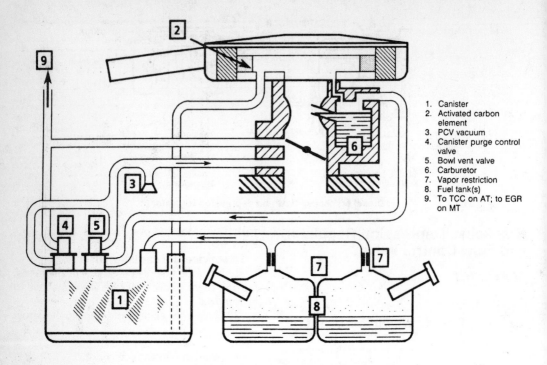

1. Canister
2. Activated carbon element
3. PCV vacuum
4. Canister purge control valve
5. Bowl vent valve
6. Carburetor
7. Vapor restriction
8. Fuel tank(s)
9. To TCC on AT; to EGR on MT

Typical evaporative canister system

If the battery becomes corroded, a solution of baking soda and water will neutralize the corrosion. This should be washed off after making sure that the caps are securely in place. Rinse the solution off with cold water.

Some batteries were equipped with a felt terminal washer. This should be saturated with engine oil approximately every 6,000 miles. This will also help to retard corrosion.

If a fast charger is used while the battery is in the truck, disconnect the battery before connecting the charger.

TESTING THE MAINTENANCE-FREE BATTERY

All later model trucks are equipped with maintenance-free batteries, which do not require normal attention as far as fluid level checks are concerned. However, the terminals require periodic cleaning, which should be performed at least once a year.

The sealed top battery cannot be checked for charge in the normal manner, since there is no provision for access to the electrolyte. To check the condition of the battery:

1. If the indicator eye on top of the battery is bright, the battery has enough fluid. If the eye is dark, the electrolyte fluid is too low and the battery must be replaced.

2. If a green dot appears in the middle of the eye, the battery is sufficiently charged. Pro-

ceed to Step 4. If no green dot is visible, charge the battery as in Step 3.

3. Charge the battery at this rate:

WARNING: *Do not charge the battery for more than 50 amp/hours! If the green dot appears, or if electrolyte squirts out of the vent hole, stop the charge and proceed to Step 4.*

It may be necessary to tip the battery from side to side to get the green dot to appear after charging.

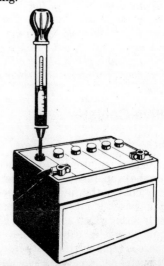

Using a hydrometer to check specific gravity

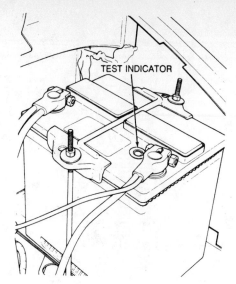

TEST INDICATOR

Indicator eye

Charging Rate Amps	Time
75	40 min
50	1 hr
25	2 hr
10	5 hr

Temperature (°F)	Minimum Voltage
70 or above	9.6
60	9.5
50	9.4
40	9.3
30	9.1
20	8.9
10	8.7
0	8.5

Battery	Test Load
Y85-4	130 amps
R85-5	170 amps
R87-5	210 amps
R89-5	230 amps

4. Connect a battery load tester and a voltmeter across the battery terminals (the battery cables should be disconnected from the battery). Apply a 300 amp load to the battery for 15 seconds to remove the surface charge. Remove the load.

5. Wait 15 seconds to allow the battery to recover. Apply the appropriate test load, as specified in the accompanying chart. Apply the load for 15 seconds while reading the voltage. Disconnect the load.

6. Check the results against the following chart. If the battery voltage is at or above the specified voltage for the temperature listed, the battery is good. If the voltage falls below what's listed, the battery should be replaced.

FILLING THE BATTERY

Batteries should be checked for proper electrolyte level at least once a month or more frequently. Keep a close eye on any cell or cells that are unusually low or seem to constantly need water – this may indicate a battery on its last legs, a leak, or a problem with the charging system.

Top up each cell to about $^3/_8$ in. (9.5mm) above the tops of the plates. Always use distilled water (available in supermarkets or auto parts stores), because most tap water contains chemicals and minerals that may slowly damage the plates of your battery.

CABLES AND CLAMPS

Twice a year, the battery terminal posts and the cable clamps should be cleaned. Loosen the

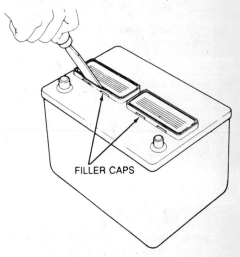

FILLER CAPS

Prying off the filler caps

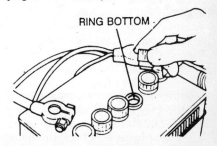

RING BOTTOM

Fill each cell to the bottom of the split ring

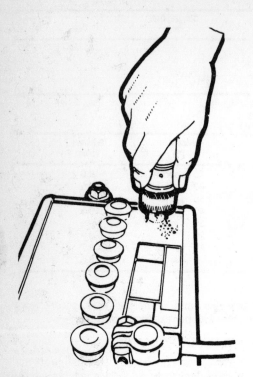

Clean the battery posts with a wire brush or the tool shown

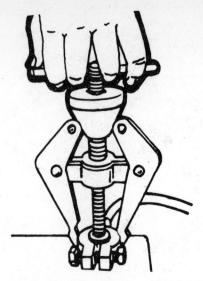

Special puller used to remove the cable end from the battery post

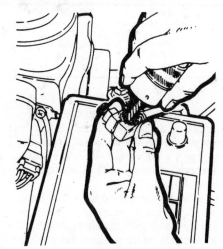

Clean the inside of the cable clamp with a wire brush

clamp bolts (you may have to brush off any corrosion with a baking soda and water solution if they are really messy) and remove the cables, negative cable first. On batteries with posts on top, the use of a battery clamp puller is recommended. It is easy to break off a battery terminal if a clamp gets stuck without the puller. These pullers are inexpensive and available in most auto parts stores or auto departments. Side terminal battery cables are secured with a bolt.

The best tool for battery clamp and terminal maintenance is a battery terminal brush. This inexpensive tool has a female ended wire brush for cleaning terminals, and a male ended wire brush inside for cleaning the insides of battery clamps. When using this tool, make sure you get both the terminal posts and the insides of the clamps nice and shiny. Any oxidation, corrosion or foreign material will prevent a sound electrical connection and inhibit either starting or charging. If your battery has side terminals, there is also a cleaning tool available for these.

Before installing the cables, remove the battery holddown clamp or strap and remove the battery. Inspect the battery casing for leaks or cracks (which unfortunately can only be fixed by buying a new battery). Check the battery tray, wash it off with warm soapy water, rinse and dry. Any rust on the tray should be sanded away, and the tray given at least two coats of a quality anti-rust paint. Replace the battery, and install the holddown clamp or strap, but do not overtighten.

Reinstall your clean battery cables, negative cable last. Tighten the cables on the terminal posts snugly; do not overtighten. Wipe a thin coat of petroleum jelly or grease all over the outsides of the clamps. This will help to inhibit corrosion.

Finally, check the battery cables themselves. If the insulation of the cables is cracked or broken, or if the ends are frayed, replace the cable with a new cable of the same length or gauge.

NOTE: *Batteries give off hydrogen gas, which is explosive. DO NOT SMOKE around the battery! The battery electrolyte contains sulfuric acid. If you should splash any into*

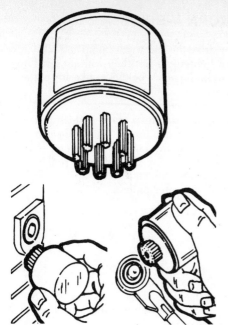

Special tools are available for cleaning the cables and terminals of side terminal batteries

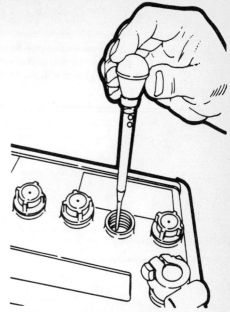

Testing the specific gravity of the battery

your eyes or skin, flush with plenty of clear water and get immediate medical help.

BATTERY CHARGING AND REPLACEMENT

Charging a battery is best done by the slow charging method (often called trickle charging), with a low amperage charger. Quick charging a battery can actually "cook" the battery, damaging the plates inside and decreasing the life of the battery drastically. Any charging should be done in a well ventilated area away from the possibility of sparks or flame. The cell caps (not found on maintenance-free batteries) should be unscrewed from their cells, but not removed.

If the battery must be quick-charged, check the cell voltages and the color of the electrolyte a few minutes after the charge is started. If cell voltages are not uniform or if the electrolyte is discolored with brown sediment, stop the quick charging in favor of a trickle charge. A common indicator of an overcharged battery is the frequent need to add water to the battery.

Drive Belts

INSPECTION

V-Belts

At the interval specified in the Maintenance Intervals chart, check the water pump, alternator, power steering pump (if equipped), air conditioning compressor (if equipped) and air pump (if equipped) drive belts for proper tension. Also look for signs of wear, fraying, separation, glazing, and so on, and replace the belts as required.

Specific Gravity Reading	Charged Condition
1.260–1.280	Fully Charged
1.230–1.250	¾ Charged
1.200–1.220	½ Charged
1.170–1.190	¼ Charged
1.140–1.160	Almost no Charge
1.110–1.130	No Charge

Serpentine Belts

Some vans are equipped with a single serpentine belt and spring loaded tensioner. The proper belt adjustment is automatically maintained by the tensioner, therefore, no periodic adjustment is needed until the pointer is past the scale on the tensioner.

BELT TENSION

Belt tension should be checked with a gauge made for the purpose. If a tension gauge is not available, tension can be checked with moderate thumb pressure applied to the belt at its longest span midway between pulleys. If the belt has a free span less than 12 in. (305mm), it should deflect approximately 1/8–1/4 in. (3–6mm). If the span is longer than 12 in. (305mm), deflection can range between 1/8 in. (3mm) and 3/8 in. (9.5mm).

If a tension gauge is available use the following procedure:

1. Place a belt tension gauge at the center

HOW TO SPOT WORN V-BELTS

V-Belts are vital to efficient engine operation—they drive the fan, water pump and other accessories. They require little maintenance (occasional tightening) but they will not last forever. Slipping or failure of the V-belt will lead to overheating. If your V-belt looks like any of these, it should be replaced.

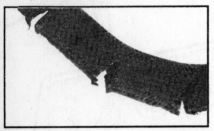

Cracking or weathering

This belt has deep cracks, which cause it to flex. Too much flexing leads to heat build-up and premature failure. These cracks can be caused by using the belt on a pulley that is too small. Notched belts are available for small diameter pulleys.

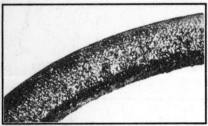

Softening (grease and oil)

Oil and grease on a belt can cause the belt's rubber compounds to soften and separate from the reinforcing cords that hold the belt together. The belt will first slip, then finally fail altogether.

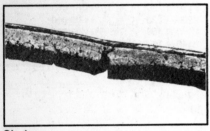

Glazing

Glazing is caused by a belt that is slipping. A slipping belt can cause a run-down battery, erratic power steering, overheating or poor accessory performance. The more the belt slips, the more glazing will be built up on the surface of the belt. The more the belt is glazed, the more it will slip. If the glazing is light, tighten the belt.

Worn cover

The cover of this belt is worn off and is peeling away. The reinforcing cords will begin to wear and the belt will shortly break. When the belt cover wears in spots or has a rough jagged appearance, check the pulley grooves for roughness.

Separation

This belt is on the verge of breaking and leaving you stranded. The layers of the belt are separating and the reinforcing cords are exposed. It's just a matter of time before it breaks completely.

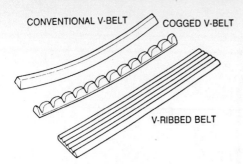

CONVENTIONAL V-BELT   COGGED V-BELT

V-RIBBED BELT

Different types of drive belts

of the greatest span of a warm not hot drive belt and measure the tension.

2. If the belt is below the specification, loosen the component mounting bracket and adjust to specification.

3. Run the engine at idle for 15 minutes to allow the belt to reseat itself in the pulleys.

4. Allow the drive belt to cool and re-meas-

ure the tension. Adjust as necessary to meet the following specifications:
   • Gasoline engines: used belt — 90 ft. lbs.; new belt — 135 ft. lbs.
   • Diesel engine: used belt — 67 ft. lbs.; new belt — 146 ft. lbs.

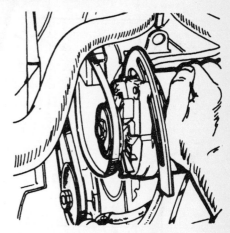

Push the component towards the engine and slip off the belt

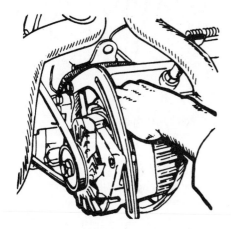

Pull outward on the component and tighten the adjusting and mounting bolts

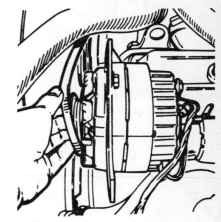

Slip the new belt over the pulley

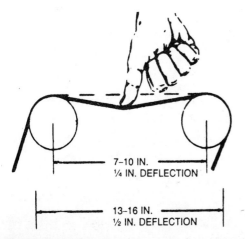

7–10 IN.
¼ IN. DEFLECTION

13–16 IN.
½ IN. DEFLECTION

A tension gauge is the most precise way to measure belt tension, but you can check it using the deflection method shown

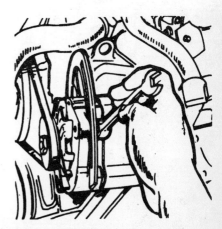

To adjust or replace a belt, first loosen the adjusting and mounting bolts

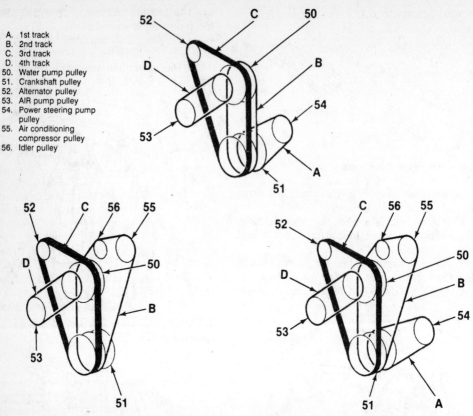

A. 1st track
B. 2nd track
C. 3rd track
D. 4th track
50. Water pump pulley
51. Crankshaft pulley
52. Alternator pulley
53. AIR pump pulley
54. Power steering pump pulley
55. Air conditioning compressor pulley
56. Idler pulley

Engine accessory drive belts for the 8-5.7L and 8-6.2L engines

NOTE: *A belt is considered "used" after 15 minutes of operation.*

REMOVAL AND INSTALLATION

V-Belts

1. Loosen the driven accessory's pivot and mounting bolts.

2. Move the accessory toward or away from the engine until the tension is correct. You can use a wooden hammer handle, or broomstick, as a lever, but do not use anything metallic, such as a prybar.

3. Tighten the bolts and recheck the tension. If new belts have been installed, run the engine for a few minutes, then recheck and readjust as necessary.

It is better to have belts too loose than too tight, because overtight belts will lead to bearing failure, particularly in the water pump and alternator. However, loose belts place an ex-

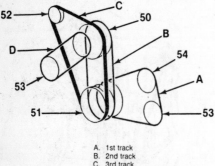

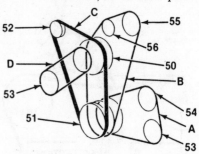

A. 1st track
B. 2nd track
C. 3rd track
D. 4th track
50. Water pump pulley
51. Crankshaft pulley
52. Alternator pulley

53. AIR pump pulley
54. Power steering pump pulley
55. Air conditioning compressor pulley
56. Idler pulley

Serpentine accessory drive belt used on the 6-4.3L, 8-5.0L, 8-5.7L and 8-7.4L engines

tremely high impact load on the driven component due to the whipping action of the belt.

Serpentine Belts

1. Insert a ¹/₂ in. breaker bar into the tensioner pulley.

2. Rotate the tensioner to the left (counterclockwise) and remove the belt.

To install:

1. Route the belt over all the pulleys except the water pump. Refer to the "Serpentine Belt" routing illustrations in this Chapter.

2. Rotate the tensioner pulley to the left (counterclockwise).

3. Install the belt over the water pump and check to see if the correct V-groove tracking is around each pulley.

WARNING: *Improper V-groove tracking will cause the belt to fail in a short period of time.*

Hoses

Radiator hoses are generally of two constructions, the preformed (molded) type, which is custom made for a particular application, and the spring-loaded type, which is made to fit several different applications. Heater hoses are all of the same general construction.

INSPECTION

Inspect the condition of the radiator and heater hoses periodically. Early spring and at the beginning of the fall or winter, when you are performing other maintenance, are good times. Make sure the engine and cooling system are cold. Visually inspect for cracking, rotting or collapsed hoses, replace as necessary. Run your hand along the length of the hose. If a weak or swollen spot is noted when squeezing the hose wall, replace the hose.

1. Drain the cooling system into a suitable container (if the coolant is to be reused).

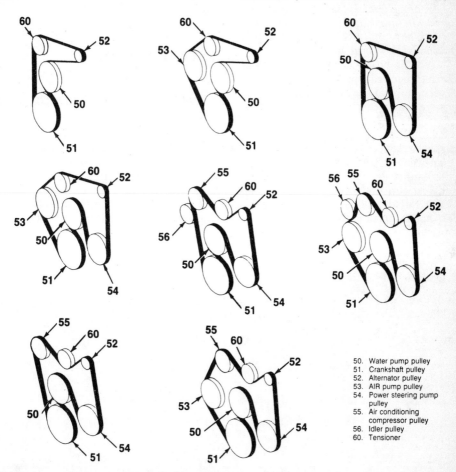

50. Water pump pulley
51. Crankshaft pulley
52. Alternator pulley
53. AIR pump pulley
54. Power steering pump pulley
55. Air conditioning compressor pulley
56. Idler pulley
60. Tensioner

Serpentine accessory drive belt used on the 6-4.3L, 8-5.0L, 8-5.7L and 8-7.4L engines

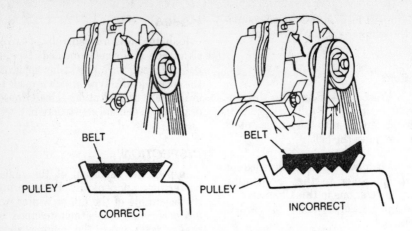

Serpentine belt installation

CAUTION: *When draining the coolant, keep in mind that cats and dogs are attracted by the ethylene glycol antifreeze, and are quite likely to drink any that is left in an uncovered container or in puddles on the ground. This will prove fatal in sufficient quantity. Always drain the coolant into a sealable container. Coolant should be reused unless it is contaminated or several years old.*

2. Loosen the hose clamps at each end of the hose that requires replacement.

3. Twist, pull and slide the hose off the radiator, water pump, thermostat or heater connection.

4. Clean the hose mounting connections. Position the hose clamps on the new hose.

5. Coat the connection surfaces with a water resistant sealer and slide the hose into position. Make sure the hose clamps are located beyond the raised bead of the connector (if equipped) and centered in the clamping area of the connection.

6. Tighten the clamps to 20–30 inch lbs. Do not overtighten.

7. Fill the cooling system.

8. Start the engine and allow it to reach normal operating temperature. Check for leaks.

AIR CONDITIONING

GENERAL SERVICING PROCEDURES

The most important aspect of air conditioning service is the maintenance of a pure and adequate charge of refrigerant in the system. A refrigeration system cannot function properly if a significant percentage of the charge is lost. Leaks are common because the severe vibration encountered in an automobile can easily cause a sufficient cracking or loosening of the air conditioning fittings; as a result, the ex-

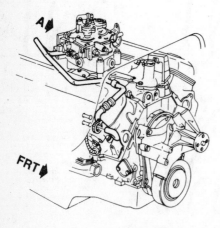
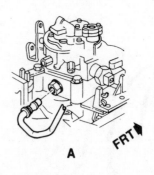

Heater inlet hose routing on 8-7.4L engines

HOW TO SPOT BAD HOSES

Both the upper and lower radiator hoses are called upon to perform difficult jobs in an inhospitable enviorment. They are subject to nearly 18 psi at under hood temperature often over 280F., and must circulate an hour-3 good reasons to have good hoses.

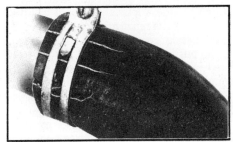

Swollen hose

A good test for any hose is to feel it for soft or spongy spots. Frequently these will appear as swollen areas of the hose. The most likely cause is oil soaking. This hose could burst at any time, when hot or under pressure.

Cracked hose

Cracked hoses can usually be seen but feel the hoses to be sure they have not hardened; a prime cause of cracking. This hose has cracked down to the reinforcing cords and could split at any of the cracks.

Frayed hose end (due to weak clamp)

Weakened clamps frequently are the cause of hose and cooling system failure. The connection between the pipe and hose has deteriorated enough to allow coolant to escape when the engine is hot.

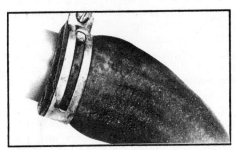

Debris in cooling system

Debris, rust and scale in the cooling system can cause the inside of a hose to weaken. This can usually be felt on the outside of the hose as soft or thinner areas.

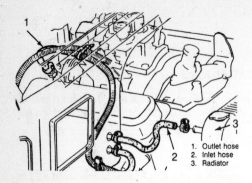

Heater hose routings on 6-4.3L, 8-5.0L and 8-5.7L engines with fuel injection

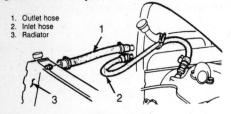

Heater house routing on 8-5.7L engines with a carburetor

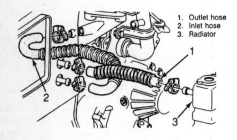

Heater hose routings on 8-6.2L diesel engines

treme operating pressures of the system force refrigerant out.

The problem can be understood by considering what happens to the system as it is operated with a continuous leak. Because the expansion valve regulates the flow of refrigerant to the evaporator, the level of refrigerant there is fairly constant. The receiver/drier stores any excess of refrigerant, and so a loss will first appear there as a reduction in the level of liquid. As this level nears the bottom of the vessel, some refrigerant vapor bubbles will begin to appear in the stream of liquid supplied to the expansion valve. This vapor decreases the capacity of the expansion valve very little as the valve opens to compensate for its presence. As the quantity of liquid in the condenser decreases, the operating pressure will drop there and throughout the high side of the system. As the R-12 continues to be expelled, the pressure

available to force the liquid through the expansion valve will continue to decrease, and, eventually, the valve's orifice will prove to be too much of a restriction for adequate flow even with the needle fully withdrawn.

At this point, low side pressure will start to drop, and severe reduction in cooling capacity, marked by freeze-up of the evaporator coil, will result. Eventually, the operating pressure of the evaporator will be lower than the pressure of the atmosphere surrounding it, and air will be drawn into the system wherever there are leaks in the low side.

Because all atmospheric air contains at least some moisture, water will enter the system and mix with the R-12 and the oil. Trace amounts of moisture will cause sludging of the oil, and corrosion of the system. Saturation and clogging of the filter/drier, and freezing of the expansion valve orifice will eventually result. As air fills the system to a greater and greater extent, it will interfere more and more with the normal flows of refrigerant and heat.

From this description, it should be obvious that much of the repairman's time will be spent detecting leaks, repairing them, and then restoring the purity and quantity of the refrigerant charge. A list of general precautions that should be observed while doing this follows:

1. Keep all tools as clean and dry as possible.

2. Thoroughly purge the service gauges and hoses of air and moisture before connecting them to the system. Keep them capped when not in use.

3. Thoroughly clean any refrigerant fitting before disconnecting it, in order to minimize the entrance of dirt into the system.

4. Plan any operation that requires opening the system beforehand, in order to minimize the length of time it will be exposed to open air. Cap or seal the open ends to minimize the entrance of foreign material.

5. When adding oil, pour it through an extremely clean and dry tube or funnel. Keep the oil capped whenever possible. Do not use oil that has not been kept tightly sealed.

6. Use only refrigerant 12. Purchase refrigerant intended for use in only automatic air conditioning systems. Avoid the use of refrigerant 12 that may be packaged for another use, such as cleaning, or powering a horn, as it is impure.

7. Completely evacuate any system that has been opened to replace a component, or that has leaked sufficiently to draw in moisture and air. This requires evacuating air and moisture with a good vacuum pump for at least one hour.   If a system has been open for a considerable length of time it may be advisable to evacuate the system for up to 12 hours (overnight).

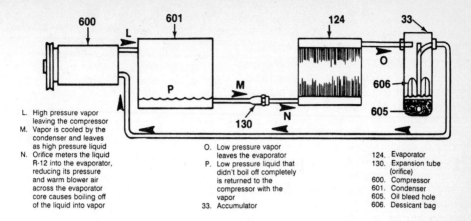

L. High pressure vapor
   leaving the compressor
M. Vapor is cooled by the
   condenser and leaves
   as high pressure liquid
N. Orifice meters the liquid
   R-12 into the evaporator,
   reducing its pressure
   and warm blower air
   across the evaporator
   core causes boiling off
   of the liquid into vapor

O. Low pressure vapor
   leaves the evaporator
P. Low pressure liquid that
   didn't boil off completely
   is returned to the
   compressor with the
   vapor
33. Accumulator

124. Evaporator
130. Expansion tube
       (orifice)
600. Compressor
601. Condenser
605. Oil bleed hole
606. Dessicant bag

Air conditioning system components

8. Use a wrench on both halves of a fitting that is to be disconnected, so as to avoid placing torque on any of the refrigerant lines.

9. When overhauling a compressor, pour some of the oil into a clean glass and inspect it. If there is evidence of dirt or metal particles, or both, flush all refrigerant components with clean refrigerant before evacuating and recharging the system. In addition, if metal particles are present, the compressor should be replaced.

10. Schrader valves may leak only when under full operating pressure. Therefore, if leakage is suspected but cannot be located, operate the system with a full charge of refrigerant and look for leaks from all Schrader valves. Replace any faulty valves.

Additional Preventive Maintenance Checks

ANTIFREEZE

In order to prevent heater core freeze-up during A/C operation, it is necessary to maintain permanent type antifreeze protection of +15°F (−9°C), or lower. A reading of −15°F (−26°C) is ideal since this protection also supplies sufficient corrosion inhibitors for the protection of the engine cooling system.

NOTE: *The same antifreeze should not be used longer than the manufacturer specifies.*

RADIATOR CAP

For efficient operation of an air conditioned van's cooling system, the radiator cap should have a holding pressure which meets manufacturer's specifications. A cap which fails to hold these pressures should be replaced.

CONDENSER

Any obstruction of or damage to the condenser configuration will restrict the air flow which is essential to its efficient operation. It is

therefore a good rule to keep this unit clean and in proper physical shape.

NOTE: *Bug screens are regarded as obstructions.*

CONDENSATION DRAIN TUBE

This single molded drain tube expels the condensation, which accumulates on the bottom of the evaporator housing, into the engine compartment. If this tube is obstructed, the air conditioning performance can be restricted and condensation buildup can spill over onto the vehicle's floor.

SAFETY PRECAUTIONS

Because of the importance of the necessary safety precautions that must be exercised when working with air conditioning systems and R-12 refrigerant, a recap of the safety precautions are outlined.

1. Avoid contact with a charged refrigeration system, even when working on another part of the air conditioning system or vehicle. If a heavy tool comes into contact with a section of copper tubing or a heat exchanger, it can easily cause the relatively soft material to rupture.

2. When it is necessary to apply force to a fitting which contains refrigerant, as when checking that all system couplings are securely tightened, use a wrench on both parts of the fitting involved, if possible. This will avoid putting torque on refrigerant tubing. (It is advisable, when possible, to use tube or line wrenches when tightening these flare nut fittings.)

3. Do not attempt to discharge the system by merely loosening a fitting, or removing the service valve caps and cracking these valves. Precise control is possible only when using the service gauges. Place a rag under the open end of the center charging hose while discharging the system to catch any drops of liquid that might

escape. Wear protective gloves when connecting or disconnecting service gauge hoses.

4. Discharge the system only in a well ventilated area, as high concentrations of the gas can exclude oxygen and act as an anesthetic. When leak testing or soldering, this is particularly important, as toxic gas is formed when R-12 contacts any flame.

5. Never start a system without first verifying that both service valves are back-seated, if equipped, and that all fittings throughout the system are snugly connected.

6. Avoid applying heat to any refrigerant line or storage vessel. Charging may be aided by using water heated to less than 125° to warm the refrigerant container. Never allow a refrigerant storage container to sit out in the sun, or near any other source of heat, such as a radiator.

7. Always wear goggles when working on a system to protect the eyes. If refrigerant contacts the eyes, it is advisable in all cases to see a physician as soon as possible.

8. Frostbite from liquid refrigerant should be treated by first gradually warming the area with cool water, and then gently applying petroleum jelly. A physician should be consulted.

9. Always keep refrigerant drum fittings capped when not in use. Avoid sudden shock to the drum, which might occur from dropping it, or from banging a heavy tool against it. Never carry a drum in the passenger compartment of a van.

10. Always completely discharge the system before painting the vehicle (if the paint is to be baked on), or before welding anywhere near refrigerant lines.

Air Conditioning Tools and Gauges

Test Gauges

Most of the service work performed in air conditioning requires the use of a set of two gauges, one for the high (head) pressure side of the system, the other for the low (suction) side.

The low side gauge records both pressure and vacuum. Vacuum readings are calibrated from 0 to 30 inches and the pressure graduations read from 0 to no less than 60 psi.

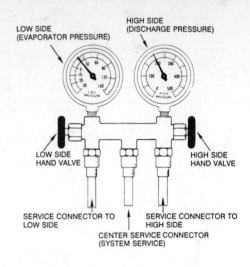

Manifold gauge set

The high side gauge measures pressure from 0 to at least 600 psi.

Both gauges are threaded into a manifold that contains two hand shut-off valves. Proper manipulation of these valves and the use of the attached test hoses allow the user to perform the following services:

1. Test high and low side pressures.
2. Remove air, moisture, and contaminated refrigerant.
3. Purge the system (of refrigerant).
4. Charge the system (with refrigerant).

The manifold valves are designed so they have no direct effect on gauge readings, but serve only to provide for, or cut off, flow of refrigerant through the manifold. During all testing and hook-up operations, the valves are kept in a closed position to avoid disturbing the refrigeration system. The valves are opened only to purge the system of refrigerant or to charge it.

When purging the system, the center hose is uncapped at the lower end, and both valves are cracked open slightly. This allows refrigerant pressure to force the entire contents of the system out through the center hose. During charging, the valve on the high side of the manifold is closed, and the valve on the low side is cracked open. Under these conditions, the low pressure in the evaporator will draw refrigerant from the relatively warm refrigerant storage container into the system.

Service Valves

For the user to diagnose an air conditioning system he or she must gain "entrance" to the system in order to observe the pressures. There are two types of terminals for this purpose, the hand shut off type and the familiar Schrader valve.

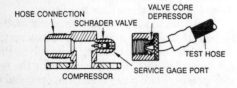

Typical Schraeder valve

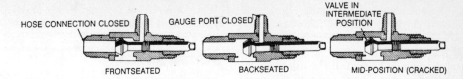

Manual service valve positions

The Schrader valve is similar to a tire valve stem and the process of connecting the test hoses is the same as threading a hand pump outlet hose to a bicycle tire. As the test hose is threaded to the service port the valve core is depressed, allowing the refrigerant to enter the test hose outlet. Removal of the test hose automatically closes the system.

Extreme caution must be observed when removing test hoses from the Schrader valves as some refrigerant will normally escape, usually under high pressure. (Observe safety precautions.)

Some systems have hand shut-off valves (the stem can be rotated with a special ratcheting box wrench) that can be positioned in the following three ways:

1. FRONT SEATED – Rotated to full clockwise position.

a. Refrigerant will not flow to compressor, but will reach test gauge port. COMPRESSOR WILL BE DAMAGED IF SYSTEM IS TURNED ON IN THIS POSITION.

b. The compressor is now isolated and ready for service. However, care must be exercised when removing service valves from the compressor as a residue of refrigerant may still be present within the compressor. Therefore, remove service valves slowly observing all safety precautions.

2. BACK SEATED – Rotated to full counter clockwise position. Normal position for system while in operation. Refrigerant flows to compressor but not to test gauge.

3. MID-POSITION (CRACKED) – Refrigerant flows to entire system. Gauge port (with hose connected) open for testing.

USING THE MANIFOLD GAUGES

The following are step-by-step procedures to guide the user to correct gauge usage.

1. WEAR GOGGLES OR FACE SHIELD DURING ALL TESTING OPERATIONS. BACKSEAT HAND SHUT-OFF TYPE SERVICE VALVES.

2. Remove caps from high and low side service ports. Make sure both gauge valves are closed.

3. Connect low side test hose to service valve that leads to the evaporator (located be-

tween the evaporator outlet and the compressor).

4. Attach high side test hose to service valve that leads to the condenser.

5. Mid-position hand shutoff type service valves.

6. Start engine and allow for warm-up. All testing and charging of the system should be done after engine and system have reached normal operation temperatures (except when using certain charging stations).

7. Adjust air conditioner controls to maximum cold.

8. Observe gauge readings.

When the gauges are not being used it is a good idea to:

a. Keep both hand valves in the closed position.

b. Attach both ends of the high and low service hoses to the manifold, if extra outlets are present on the manifold, or plug them if not. Also, keep the center charging hose attached to an empty refrigerant can. This extra precaution will reduce the possibility of moisture entering the gauges. If air and moisture have gotten into the gauges, purge the hoses by supplying refrigerant under pressure to the center hose with both gauge valves open and all openings unplugged.

SYSTEM CHECKS

CAUTION: *Do not attempt to charge or discharge the refrigerant system unless you are thoroughly familiar with its operation and the hazards involved. The compressed refrigerant used in the air conditioning system expands and evaporates (boils) into the atmosphere at a temperature of –21.7°F (–29.8°C) or less. This will freeze any surface that it comes in contact with, including your eyes. In addition, the refrigerant decomposes into a poisonous gas in the presence of flame.*

These air conditioning systems have no sight glass for checking.

1. Warm the engine to normal operating temperature.

2. Open the hood and doors.

3. Set the selector lever at A/C.

4. Set the temperature lever at the first detent to the right of COLD (outside air).

5. Set the blower on HI.

6. Idle the engine at 1,000 rpm.

7. Feel the temperature of the evaporator inlet and the accumulator outlet with the compressor engaged.

Both lines should be cold. If the inlet pipe is colder than the outlet pipe the system is low on charge.

DISCHARGING THE SYSTEM

CAUTION: *Perform operation in a well ventilated area.*

When it is necessary to remove (purge) the refrigerant pressurized in the system, follow this procedure:

1. Operate air conditioner for at least 10 minutes.

2. Attach gauges, shut off engine and air conditioner.

3. Place a container or rag at the outlet of the center charging hose on the gauge. The refrigerant will be discharged there and this precaution will avoid its uncontrolled exposure.

4. Open low side hand valve on gauge slightly.

5. Open high side hand valve slightly.

NOTE: *Too rapid a purging process will be identified by the appearance of an oily foam. If this occurs, close the hand valves a little more until this condition stops.*

6. Close both hand valves on the gauge set when the pressures read 0 and all the refrigerant has left the system.

EVACUATING THE SYSTEM

Before charging any system it is necessary to purge the refrigerant and draw out the trapped moisture with a suitable vacuum pump. Failure to do so will result in ineffective charging and possible damage to the system.

Use this hook-up for the proper evacuation procedure:

1. Connect both service gauge hoses to the high and low service outlets.

2. Open high and low side hand valves on gauge manifold.

3. Open both service valves a slight amount (from back seated position), allow refrigerant to discharge from system.

4. Install center charging hose of gauge set to vacuum pump.

5. Operate vacuum pump for at least one hour. (If the system has been subjected to open conditions for a prolonged period of time it may be necessary to "pump the system down" overnight. Refer to "System Sweep" procedure.)

NOTE: *If low pressure gauge does not show at least 28 in.Hg within 5 minutes, check the system for a leak or loose gauge connectors.*

6. Close hand valves on gauge manifold.

7. Shut off pump.

8. Observe low pressure gauge to determine if vacuum is holding. A vacuum drop may indicate a leak.

SYSTEM SWEEP

An efficient vacuum pump can remove all the air contained in a contaminated air conditioning system very quickly, because of its vapor state. Moisture, however, is far more difficult to remove because the vacuum must force the liquid to evaporate before it will be able to remove it from the system. If a system has become severely contaminated, as, for example, it might become after all the charge was lost in conjunction with vehicle accident damage, moisture removal is extremely time consuming. A vacuum pump could remove all of the moisture only if it were operated for 12 hours or more.

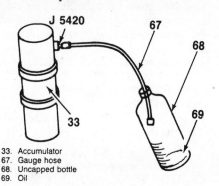

33. Accumulator
67. Gauge hose
68. Uncapped bottle
69. Oil

Discharging the system

Under these conditions, sweeping the system with refrigerant will speed the process of moisture removal considerably. To sweep, follow the following procedure:

1. Connect vacuum pump to gauges, operate it until vacuum ceases to increase, then continue operation for ten more minutes.

2. Charge system with 50% of its rated refrigerant capacity.

3. Operate system at fast idle for ten minutes.

4. Discharge the system.

5. Repeat twice the process of charging to 50% capacity, running the system for ten minutes, and discharging it, for a total of three sweeps.

6. Replace drier.

7. Pump system down as in Step 1.

8. Charge system.

CHARGING THE SYSTEM

CAUTION: *Never attempt to charge the system by opening the high pressure gauge control while the compressor is operating.*

A. To ECM, exc. 7.4L
   engine
B. To ECM with 7.4L
   engine
103. Fuse block
104. Mode selector
105. Relay assembly
106. Evaporator
     pressure control switch
108. Fast idle solenoid
     — 5.7L carbureted
     engine
110. Head pressure cut-
     out switch for 7.4L
     engine
111. Compressor for
     7.4L engine
112. Blower motor
113. Junction block
114. Resistor
115. Blower speed
     switch
600. Compressor, exc.
     7.4L engine

Air conditioning system wiring diagram

The compressor accumulating pressure can burst the refrigerant container, causing sever personal injuries.

Basic System

In this procedure the refrigerant enters the suction side of the system as a vapor while the compressor is running. Before proceeding, the system should be in a partial vacuum after adequate evacuation. Both hand valves on the gauge manifold should be closed.

1. Attach both test hoses to their respective service valve ports. Mid-position manually operated service valves, if present.

2. Install dispensing valve (closed position) on the refrigerant container. (Single and multiple refrigerant manifolds are available to accommodate one to four 15 oz. cans.)

3. Attach center charging hose to the refrigerant container valve.

4. Open dispensing valve on the refrigerant can.

5. Loosen the center charging hose coupler where it connects to the gauge manifold to allow the escaping refrigerant to purge the hose of contaminants.

6. Tighten center charging hose connection.

7. Purge the low pressure test hose at the gauge manifold.

8. Start the van's engine, roll down the windows and adjust the air conditioner to maximum cooling. The engine should be at normal operating temperature before proceeding. The heated environment helps the liquid vaporize more efficiently.

9. Crack open the low side hand valve on the manifold. Manipulate the valve so that the refrigerant that enters the system does not cause the low side pressure to exceed 40 psi.

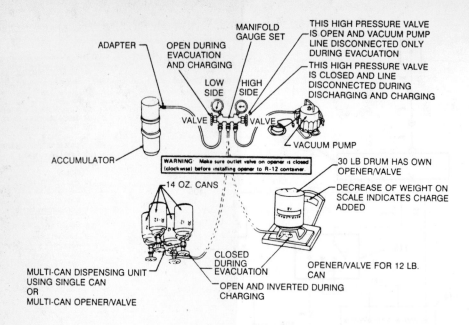

Typical gauge connections

Too sudden a surge may permit the entrance of unwanted liquid to the compressor. Since liquids cannot be compressed, the compressor will suffer damage if compelled to attempt it. If the suction side of the system remains in a vacuum the system is blocked. Locate and correct the condition before proceeding any further.

NOTE: *Placing the refrigerant can in a container of warm water, no hotter than 125°F (51°C) will speed the charging process. Slight agitation of the can is helpful too, but be careful not to turn the can upside down.*

Some manufacturers allow for a partial charging of the A/C system in the form of a liquid (can inverted and compressor off) by opening the high side gauge valve only, and putting the high side compressor service valve in the middle position (if so equipped). The remainder of the refrigerant is then added in the form of a gas in the normal manner, through the suction side only.

When charging the CCOT system, attach only the low pressure line to the low pressure gauge port, located on the accumulator. Do not attach the high pressure line to any service port or allow it to remain attached to the vacuum pump after evacuation. Be sure both the high and the low pressure control valves are closed on the gauge set. To complete the charging of the system, follow the outline supplied.

1. Start the engine and allow to run at idle, with the cooling system at normal operating temperature.

2. Attach the center gauge hose to a single or multi-can dispenser.

3. With the multi-can dispenser inverted, allow one pound or the contents of one or two 14 oz. cans to enter the system through the low pressure side by opening the gauge low pressure control valve.

4. Close the low pressure gauge control valve and turn the A/C system on to engage the compressor. Place the blower motor in its high mode.

5. Open the low pressure gauge control valve and draw the remaining charge into the system. Refer to the capacity chart at the end of this Chapter for the individual vehicle or system capacity.

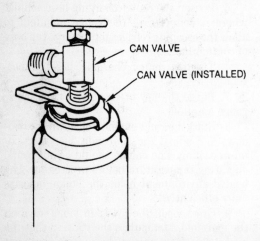

1 lb. R-12 can with opener/valve connected

Troubleshooting Basic Air Conditioning Problems

Problem	Cause	Solution
There's little or no air coming from the vents (and you're sure it's on)	• The A/C fuse is blown • Broken or loose wires or connections • The on/off switch is defective	• Check and/or replace fuse • Check and/or repair connections • Replace switch
The air coming from the vents is not cool enough	• Windows and air vent wings open • The compressor belt is slipping • Heater is on • Condenser is clogged with debris • Refrigerant has escaped through a leak in the system • Receiver/drier is plugged	• Close windows and vent wings • Tighten or replace compressor belt • Shut heater off • Clean the condenser • Check system • Service system
The air has an odor	• Vacuum system is disrupted • Odor producing substances on the evaporator case • Condensation has collected in the bottom of the evaporator housing	• Have the system checked/repaired • Clean the evaporator case • Clean the evaporator housing drains
System is noisy or vibrating	• Compressor belt or mountings loose • Air in the system	• Tighten or replace belt; tighten mounting bolts • Have the system serviced
Sight glass condition Constant bubbles, foam or oil streaks Clear sight glass, but no cold air Clear sight glass, but air is cold Clouded with milky fluid	• Undercharged system • No refrigerant at all • System is OK • Receiver drier is leaking dessicant	• Charge the system • Check and charge the system • Have system checked
Large difference in temperature of lines	• System undercharged	• Charge and leak test the system
Compressor noise	• Broken valves • Overcharged • Incorrect oil level • Piston slap • Broken rings • Drive belt pulley bolts are loose	• Replace the valve plate • Discharge, evacuate and install the correct charge • Isolate the compressor and check the oil level. Correct as necessary. • Replace the compressor • Replace the compressor • Tighten with the correct torque specification
Excessive vibration	• Incorrect belt tension • Clutch loose • Overcharged • Pulley is misaligned	• Adjust the belt tension • Tighten the clutch • Discharge, evacuate and install the correct charge • Align the pulley
Condensation dripping in the passenger compartment	• Drain hose plugged or improperly positioned • Insulation removed or improperly installed	• Clean the drain hose and check for proper installation • Replace the insulation on the expansion valve and hoses
Frozen evaporator coil	• Faulty thermostat • Thermostat capillary tube improperly installed • Thermostat not adjusted properly	• Replace the thermostat • Install the capillary tube correctly • Adjust the thermostat
Low side low—high side low	• System refrigerant is low • Expansion valve is restricted	• Evacuate, leak test and charge the system • Replace the expansion valve
Low side high—high side low	• Internal leak in the compressor—worn	• Remove the compressor cylinder head and inspect the compressor. Replace the valve plate assembly if necessary. If the compressor pistons, rings or

Troubleshooting Basic Air Conditioning Problems (cont.)

Problem	Cause	Solution
Low side high—high side low (cont.)		cylinders are excessively worn or scored replace the compressor
	• Cylinder head gasket is leaking	• Install a replacement cylinder head gasket
	• Expansion valve is defective	• Replace the expansion valve
	• Drive belt slipping	• Adjust the belt tension
Low side high—high side high	• Condenser fins obstructed	• Clean the condenser fins
	• Air in the system	• Evacuate, leak test and charge the system
	• Expansion valve is defective	• Replace the expansion valve
	• Loose or worn fan belts	• Adjust or replace the belts as necessary
Low side low—high side high	• Expansion valve is defective	• Replace the expansion valve
	• Restriction in the refrigerant hose	• Check the hose for kinks—replace if necessary
	• Restriction in the receiver/drier	• Replace the receiver/drier
	• Restriction in the condenser	• Replace the condenser
Low side and high side normal (inadequate cooling)	• Air in the system	• Evacuate, leak test and charge the system
	• Moisture in the system	• Evacuate, leak test and charge the system

6. Close the low pressure gauge control valve and the refrigerant source valve, on the multi-can dispenser. Remove the low pressure hose from the accumulator quickly to avoid loss of refrigerant through the Schrader valve.

7. Install the protective cap on the gauge port and check the system for leakage.

8. Test the system for proper operation.

Refrigerant Capacities
- 1987 Front Only: 3 lb. 8 oz.
- 1987 Rear: 4 lb. 8 oz.
- 1988–89 Front Only, exc. w/7.4L engine: 3 lb. 8 oz.
- 1988–89 Front Only, w/7.4L engine: 2 lb. 12 oz.
- 1988–89 Rear, exc. w/7.4L engine: 4 lb. 8 oz.
- 1988–89 Rear w/7.4L engine: 4 lb.
- 1990 Front Only, exc. w/7.4L engine: 3 lb.
- 1990 Front Only, w/7.4L engine: 2 lb. 8 oz.
- 1990 Rear, exc. w/7.4L engine: 4 lb. 5 oz.
- 1990 Rear w/7.4L engine: 4 lb.

Leak Testing the System

There are several methods of detecting leaks in an air conditioning system; among them, the two most popular are (1) halide leak-detection or the "open flame method," and (2) electronic leak-detection.

The halide leak detection is a torch like device which produces a yellow-green color when refrigerant is introduced into the flame at the burner. A purple or violet color indicates the presence of large amounts of refrigerant at the burner.

An electronic leak detector is a small portable electronic device with an extended probe. With the unit activated the probe is passed along those components of the system which contain refrigerant. If a leak is detected, the unit will sound an alarm signal or activate a display signal depending on the manufacturer's design. It is advisable to follow the manufacturer's instructions as the design and function of the detection may vary significantly.

CAUTION: *Care should be taken to operate either type of detector in well ventilated areas, so as to reduce the chance of personal injury, which may result from coming in contact with poisonous gases produced when R-12 is exposed to flame or electric spark.*

Windshield Wipers

Intense heat from the sun, snow and ice, road oils and the chemicals used in windshield washer solvents combine to deteriorate the rubber wiper refills.

For maximum effectiveness and longest element life, the windshield and wiper blades should be kept clean. Dirt, tree sap, road tar and so on will cause streaking, smearing and blade deterioration if left on the windshield. It is advisable to wash the windshield carefully with a commercial glass cleaner at least once a month. Wipe off the rubber blades with a wet rag afterwards. Do not attempt to move the wipers back and forth by hand! Damage to the motor and drive mechanism will result.

If the blades are found to be cracked, broken or torn they should be replaced immediately. Replacement intervals will vary with usage, although ozone deterioration usually limits blade lift to about one year. If the wiper pattern is smeared or streaked, or if the blade chatters across the glass, the blades should be replaced. It is easiest and most sensible to replace them in pairs.

WIPER REFILL REPLACEMENT

Normally, if the wipers are not cleaning the windshield properly, only the refill has to be replaced. The blade and arm usually require replacement only in the event of damage. It is not necessary to remove the arm or the blade to replace the refill (rubber part), though you may have to position the arm higher on the glass. You can do this by turning the key on and operating the wipers. When they are positioned where they are accessible, turn the key off.

There are several types of refills and your vehicle could have any kind, since aftermarket blades and arms may not use exactly the same type refill as the original equipment.

Most Trico® styles use a release button that is pushed down to allow the refill to slide out of the yoke jaws. The new refill slides in an locks in place. Some Trico® refills are removed by locating where the metal backing strip or the refill is wider and inserting a small screwdriver blade between the frame and metal backing strip. Press down to release the refill from the retaining tab.

The Anco® style is unlocked at one end by squeezing the metal tabs, and the refill is slid out of the frame jaws. When the new refill is installed, the tabs will click into place, locking the refill.

The polycarbonate type is held in place by a locking lever that is pushed downward out of the groove in the arm to free the refill. When

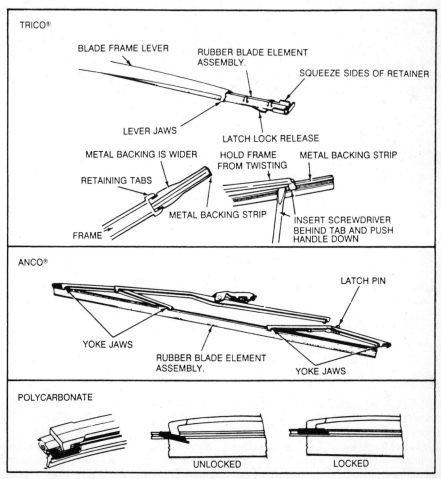

Windshield wiper blade refills

the new refill is installed, it will lock in place automatically.

No matter which type of refill you use, be sure that all of the frame claws engage the refill. Before operating the wipers, be sure that no part of the metal frame is contacting the windshield.

Tires and Wheels

INSPECTION

The tires on your truck should have built-in tread wear indicators, which appear as $1/2$ in. (12.7mm) bands when the tread depth gets as low as $1/16$ in. (1.6mm). When the indicators appear in 2 or more adjacent grooves, it's time for new tires.

For optimum tire life, you should keep the tires properly inflated, rotate them often and have the wheel alignment checked periodically.

Some models have the maximum load pressures listed in the V.I.N. plate on the left door frame. In general, pressure of 28–32 psi would be suitable for highway use with moderate loads and passenger car type tires (load range B, non-flotation) of original equipment size. Pressures should be checked before driving, since pressure can increase as much as 6 psi due to heat. It is a good idea to have an accurate gauge and to check pressures weekly. Not all gauges on service station air pumps are to be trusted. In general, truck type tires require higher pressures and flotation type tires, lower pressures.

TIRE ROTATION

It is recommended that you have the tires rotated every 6,000 miles. There is no way to give a tire rotation diagram for every combination of tires and vehicles, but the accompanying diagrams are a general rule to follow. Radial tires should not be cross-switched. They last longer if their direction of rotation is not changed. Truck tires sometimes have directional tread, indicated by arrows on the sidewalls. The arrow shows the direction of rotation. They will wear very rapidly if reversed. Studded snow tires will lose their studs if their direction of rotation is reversed.

NOTE: *Mark the wheel position or direction of rotation on radial tires or studded snow tires before removing them.*

If your truck is equipped with tires having different load ratings on the front and the rear, the tires should not be rotated front to rear. Rotating these tires could affect tire life (the tires with the lower rating will wear faster, and could become overloaded), and upset the handling of the truck.

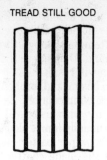
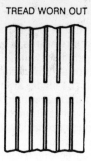

TREAD STILL GOOD   TREAD WORN OUT

Tread wear indicators appear as solid bands when the tread is worn

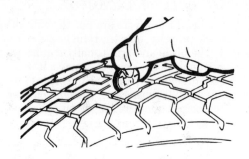

Tread depth can be check with a penny; when the top of Lincoln's head is visible, it time for new tires

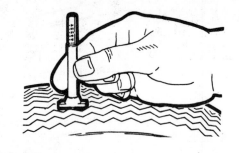

Tread depth can also be check with an inexpensive gauge made for the purpose

TIRE USAGE

The tires on your truck were selected to provide the best all around performance for normal operation when inflated as specified. Oversize tires (Load Range D) will not increase the maximum carrying capacity of the vehicle, although they will provide an extra margin of tread life. Be sure to check overall height before using larger size tires which may cause interference with suspension components or wheel wells. When replacing conventional tire sizes with other tire size designations, be sure to check the manufacturer's recommendations. Interchangeability is not always possible because of differences in load ratings, tire dimen-

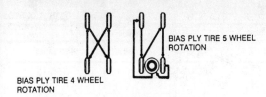

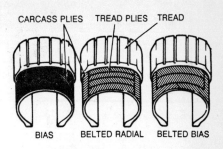

This rotation is for bias-belted tires only

Types of tire construction

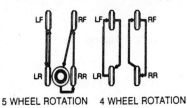

This rotation is for radial tires

sions, wheel well clearances, and rim size. Also due to differences in handling characteristics, 70 Series and 60 Series tires should be used only in pairs on the same axle. Radial tires should be used only in sets of four.

The wheels must be the correct width for the tire. Tire dealers have charts of tire and rim compatibility. A mismatch can cause sloppy handling and rapid tread wear. The old rule of thumb is that the tread width should match the rim width (inside bead to inside bead)

within 1 in. (25.4mm). For radial tires, the rim width should be 80% or less of the tire (not tread) width.

The height (mounted diameter) of the new tires can greatly change speedometer accuracy, engine speed at a given road speed, fuel mileage, acceleration, and ground clearance. Tire manufacturers furnish full measurement specifications. Speedometer drive gears are available for correction.

NOTE: *Dimensions of tires marked the same size may vary significantly, even among tires from the same manufacturer.*

The spare tire should be usable, at least for low speed operation, with the new tires.

Troubleshooting Basic Wheel Problems

Problem	Cause	Solution
The car's front end vibrates at high speed	• The wheels are out of balance • Wheels are out of alignment	• Have wheels balanced • Have wheel alignment checked/adjusted
Car pulls to either side	• Wheels are out of alignment • Unequal tire pressure • Different size tires or wheels	• Have wheel alignment checked/adjusted • Check/adjust tire pressure • Change tires or wheels to same size
The car's wheel(s) wobbles	• Loose wheel lug nuts • Wheels out of balance • Damaged wheel • Wheels are out of alignment • Worn or damaged ball joint • Excessive play in the steering linkage (usually due to worn parts) • Defective shock absorber	• Tighten wheel lug nuts • Have tires balanced • Raise car and spin the wheel. If the wheel is bent, it should be replaced • Have wheel alignment checked/adjusted • Check ball joints • Check steering linkage • Check shock absorbers
Tires wear unevenly or prematurely	• Incorrect wheel size • Wheels are out of balance • Wheels are out of alignment	• Check if wheel and tire size are compatible • Have wheels balanced • Have wheel alignment checked/adjusted

Tire Size Comparison Chart

"60 Series"	"70 Series"	"78 Series"	1965–77	"60 Series"	"70 Series"	"80 Series"
			5.50-12, 5.60-12	165/60-12	165/70-12	155-12
		Y78-12	6.00-12			
		W78-13	5.20-13	165/60-13	145/70-13	135-13
		Y78-13	5.60-13	175/60-13	155/70-13	145-13
			6.15-13	185/60-13	165/70-13	155-13, P155/80-13
A60-13	A70-13	A78-13	6.40-13	195/60-13	175/70-13	165-13
B60-13	B70-13	B78-13	6.70-13	205/60-13	185/70-13	175-13
			6.90-13			
C60-13	C70-13	C78-13	7.00-13	215/60-13	195/70-13	185-13
D60-13	D70-13	D78-13	7.25-13			
E60-13	E70-13	E78-13	7.75-13			195-13
			5.20-14	165/60-14	145/70-14	135-14
			5.60-14	175/60-14	155/70-14	145-14
			5.90-14			
A60-14	A70-14	A78-14	6.15-14	185/60-14	165/70-14	155-14
	B70-14	B78-14	6.45-14	195/60-14	175/70-14	165-14
	C70-14	C78-14	6.95-14	205/60-14	185/70-14	175-14
D60-14	D70-14	D78-14				
E60-14	E70-14	E78-14	7.35-14	215/60-14	195/70-14	185-14
F60-14	F70-14	F78-14, F83-14	7.75-14	225/60-14	200/70-14	195-14
G60-14	G70-14	G77-14, G78-14	8.25-14	235/60-14	205/70-14	205-14
H60-14	H70-14	H78-14	8.55-14	245/60-14	215/70-14	215-14
J60-14	J70-14	J78-14	8.85-14	255/60-14	225/70-14	225-14
L60-14	L70-14		9.15-14	265/60-14	235/70-14	
	A70-15	A78-15	5.60-15	185/60-15	165/70-15	155-15
B60-15	B70-15	B78-15	6.35-15	195/60-15	175/70-15	165-15
C60-15	C70-15	C78-15	6.85-15	205/60-15	185/70-15	175-15
	D70-15	D78-15				
E60-15	E70-15	E78-15	7.35-15	215/60-15	195/70-15	185-15
F60-15	F70-15	F78-15	7.75-15	225/60-15	205/70-15	195-15
G60-15	G70-15	G78-15	8.15-15/8.25-15	235/60-15	215/70-15	205-15
H60-15	H70-15	H78-15	8.45-15/8.55-15	245/60-15	225/70-15	215-15
J60-15	J70-15	J78-15	8.85-15/8.90-15	255/60-15	235/70-15	225-15
	K70-15		9.00-15	265/60-15	245/70-15	230-15
L60-15	L70-15	L78-15, L84-15	9.15-15			235-15
	M70-15	M78-15				255-15
		N78-15				

Note: Every size tire is not listed and many size comparisons are approximate, based on load ratings. Wider tires than those supplied new with the vehicle, should always be checked for clearance.

TIRE DESIGN

For maximum satisfaction, tires should be used in sets of five. Mixing or different types (radial, bias/belted, fiberglass belted) should be avoided. Conventional bias tires are constructed so that the cords run bead-to-bead at an angle. Alternate plies run at an opposite angle. This type of construction gives rigidity to both tread and sidewall. Bias/belted tires are similar in construction to conventional bias ply tires. Belts run at an angle and also at a 90° angle to the bead, as in the radial tire. Tread life is improved considerably over the conventional bias tire. The radial tire differs in construction, but instead of the carcass plies running at an angle of 90° to each other, they run at an angle of 90° to the bead. This gives the tread a great deal of rigidity and the sidewall a great deal of flexibility and accounts for the characteristic bulge associated with radial tires.

Chevrolet and GMC trucks are capable of using radial tires and they are recommended in some years. If they are used, tire sizes and wheel diameters should be selected to maintain ground clearance and tire load capacity equivalent to the minimum specified tire. Radial tires should always be used in sets of five, but in an emergency radial tires can be used with caution on the rear axle only. If this is done, both tires on the rear should be of radial design.

NOTE: *Radial tires should never be used on only the front axle.*

Troubleshooting Basic Tire Problems

Problem	Cause	Solution
The car's front end vibrates at high speeds and the steering wheel shakes	• Wheels out of balance • Front end needs aligning	• Have wheels balanced • Have front end alignment checked
The car pulls to one side while cruising	• Unequal tire pressure (car will usually pull to the low side) • Mismatched tires • Front end needs aligning	• Check/adjust tire pressure • Be sure tires are of the same type and size • Have front end alignment checked
Abnormal, excessive or uneven tire wear See "How to Read Tire Wear"	• Infrequent tire rotation • Improper tire pressure • Sudden stops/starts or high speed on curves	• Rotate tires more frequently to equalize wear • Check/adjust pressure • Correct driving habits
Tire squeals	• Improper tire pressure • Front end needs aligning	• Check/adjust tire pressure • Have front end alignment checked

FLUIDS AND LUBRICANTS

Fuel Recommendations

GASOLINE ENGINES

Chevrolet and GMC trucks with Gross Vehicle Weight Ratings (GVWR) which place them in the heavy duty emissions class do not require a catalytic converter. However, almost all 1975 and later light duty emissions trucks have a catalytic converter. The light duty classification applies to all trucks with a GVWR under 6,000 lbs. through 1978, except for 1978 trucks sold in California. 1978 California models and all 1979 models with GVWR's under 8,500 lbs. fall into the light duty category. In 1980 and later, the light duty classification applies to all trucks with GVWR's under 8,600 lbs.

The catalytic converter is a muffler shaped device installed in the exhaust system. It contains platinum and palladium coated pellets which, through catalytic action, oxidize hydrocarbon and carbon monoxide gases into hydrogen, oxygen, and carbon dioxide.

The design of the converter requires the exclusive use of unleaded fuel. Leaded fuel renders the converter inoperative, raising exhaust emissions to legal levels. In addition, the lead in the gasoline coats the pellets in the converter, blocking the flow of exhaust gases. This raises exhaust back pressure and severely reduces engine performance. In extreme cases, the exhaust system becomes so clocked that the engine will not run.

Converter equipped trucks are delivered with the label "Unleaded Fuel Only" placed next to the fuel gauge on the instrument panel and next to the gas tank filler opening. In general, any unleaded fuel is suitable for use in these trucks as long as the gas has an octane rating or 87 or more. Octane ratings are posted on the gas pumps. However, in some cases, knocking may occur even though the recommended fuel is being used. The only practical solution for this is to switch to a slightly higher grade of unleaded fuel, or to switch brands of unleaded gasoline.

DIESEL ENGINES

Diesel engined vans require the use of diesel fuel. Two grades of diesel fuel are manufactured, #1 and #2, although #2 grade is generally the only grade available. Better fuel economy results from the use of #2 grade fuel. In some northern parts of the U.S., and in most parts of Canada, #1 grade fuel is available in winter, or a winterized blend of #2 grade is supplied in winter months. If #1 grade is available, it should be used whenever temperatures fall below +20°F (-7°C). Winterized #2 grade may also be used at these temperatures. However, unwinterized #2 grade should not be used below +20°F (-7°C). Cold temperatures cause unwinterized #2 grade to thicken (it actually gels), blocking the fuel lines and preventing the engine from running.

WARNING: *Do not use home heating oil or gasoline in the diesel engine. Do not attempt to thin unwinterized #2 diesel fuel with gasoline. Gasoline line or home heating oil will damage the engine and void the manufacturer's warranty.*

Engine OIL RECOMMENDATIONS

The SAE grade number indicates the viscosity of the engine oil, or its ability to lubricate under a given temperature. The lower the SAE grade number, the lighter the oil; the lower the viscosity, the easier it is to crank the engine in cold weather.

The API (American Petroleum Institute) designation indicates the classification of engine oil for use under given operating conditions. Only oils designated for "Service SF or SG" should be used. These oils provide maximum engine protection. Both the SAE grade number and the API designation can be found on the top of a can of oil.

NOTE: *Non-detergent oils should not be used.*

Oil viscosities should be chosen from those oils recommended for the lowest anticipated temperatures during the oil change interval.

The multi-viscosity oils offer the important advantage of being adaptable to temperature extremes. They allow easy starting at low temperatures, yet give good protection at high speeds and engine temperatures. This is a decided advantage in changeable climates or in long distance driving.

Diesel engines also require SF or SG engine oil. In addition, the oil must qualify for a CC and/or CD rating. The API has a number of different diesel engine ratings, including CB, CC, and CD.

For recommended oil viscosities, refer to the chart. 10W–30 grade oils are not recommended for sustained high speed driving.

Single viscosity oil (SAE 30) is recommended for sustained high speed driving.

SYNTHETIC OIL

There are excellent synthetic and fuel-efficient oils available that, under the right circumstances, can help provide better fuel mileage and better engine protection. However, these advantages come at a price, which can be three or four times the price per quart of conventional motor oils.

Before pouring any synthetic oils into your van's engine, you should consider the condition of the engine and the type of driving you do. Also, check the truck's warranty conditions regarding the use of synthetics.

Generally, it is best to avoid the use of synthetic oil in both brand new and older, high mileage engines. New engines require a proper break-in, and the synthetics are so slippery that they can prevent this. Most manufacturers recommend that you wait at least 5,000 miles before switching to a synthetic oil. Conversely, older engines are looser and tend to use

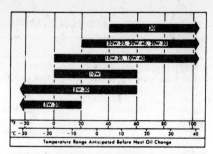

NOTES: 1. SAE 5W and 5W-20 are not recommended for sustained high speed driving.
2. SAE 5W-30 is recommended for all seasons in Canada

Gasoline engine oil viscosity chart

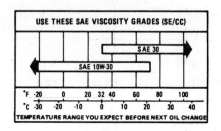

Diesel engine oil viscosity chart

more oil. Synthetics will slip past worn parts more readily than regular oil, and will be used up faster. If your van already leaks and/or uses oil (due to worn parts and bad seals or gaskets), it will leak and use more with a slippery synthetic inside.

Consider your type of driving. If most of your accumulated mileage is on the highway at higher, steadier speeds, a synthetic oil will reduce friction and probably help deliver fuel mileage. Under such ideal highway conditions, the oil change interval can be extended, as long as the oil filter will operate effectively for the extended life of the oil. If the filter can't do its job for this extended period, dirt and sludge will build up in your engine's crankcase, sump, oil pump and lines, no matter what type of oil is used. If using synthetic oil in this manner, you should continue to change the oil filter at the recommended intervals.

Trucks used under harder, stop-and-go, short hop circumstances should always be serviced more frequently, and for these vans, synthetic oil may not be a wise investment. Because of the necessary shorter change interval needed for this type of driving, you cannot take advantage of the long recommended change interval of most synthetic oils.

Finally, most synthetic oil are not compatible with conventional oils and cannot be added to them. This means you should always carry a

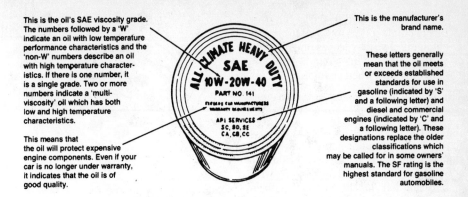

This is the oil's SAE viscosity grade. The numbers followed by a 'W' indicate an oil with low temperature performance characteristics and the 'non-W' numbers describe an oil with high temperature character-istics. If there is one number, it is a single grade. Two or more numbers indicate a 'multi-viscosity' oil which has both low and high temperature characteristics.

This means that the oil will protect expensive engine components. Even if your car is no longer under warranty, it indicates that the oil is of good quality.

This is the manufacturer's brand name.

These letters generally mean that the oil meets or exceeds established standards for use in gasoline (indicated by 'S' and a following letter) and diesel and commercial engines (indicated by 'C' and a following letter). These designations replace the older classifications which may be called for in some owners' manuals. The SF rating is the highest standard for gasoline automobiles.

The oil can or bottle will tell you all you need to know about engine oil

couple of quarts of synthetic oil with you while on a long trip, as not all service stations carry this oil.

Engine Oil Level Check

The engine oil should be checked on a regular basis, ideally at each fuel stop. If the van is used for trailer towing or for heavy duty use, it would be safer to check it more often.

When checking the oil level it is best that the oil be at operating temperature, although check-ing the level immediately after stopping will give a false reading because all of the oil will not yet have drained back into the crankcase. Be sure that the van is resting on a level surface, allowing time for the oil to drain back into the crankcase.

1. Open the hood or engine compartment and locate the dipstick. Remove it from the tube. The oil dipstick is located on the driver's side.

2. Wipe the dipstick with a clean rag.

3. Insert the dipstick fully into the tube, and remove it again. Hold the dipstick horizon-tally and read the oil level. The level should be between the "FULL" and "ADD OIL" marks. If the oil level is at or below the "ADD OIL" mark, oil should be added as necessary. Oil is added through the capped opening on the valve cover(s). See Oil and Fuel Recommendations for proper viscosity and oil to use.

4. Replace the dipstick and check the level after adding oil. Be careful not to overfill the crankcase. There is about 1 quart between the marks.

Engine Oil and Filter Change

Engine oil should be changed according to the schedule in the Maintenance Interval Chart. Under conditions such as:

• Driving in dusty conditions

• Continuous trailer pulling or RV use
• Extensive or prolonged idling
• Extensive short trip operation in freez-ing temperatures (when the engine is not thor-oughly warmed up)
• Frequent long runs at high speeds and high ambient temperatures
• Stop-and-go service such as delivery trucks, the oil change interval and filter replace-ment interval should be cut in half. Operation of the engine in severe conditions such as a dust storm may require an immediate oil and filter change.

Chevrolet and GMC recommended changing both the oil and filter during the first oil change and the filter every other oil change thereafter. HOWEVER, For the small price of an oil filter, it's cheap insurance to replace the

Check the engine oil level with the dipstick

The oil level should be between the ADD and FULL marks

filter at every oil change. One of the larger filter manufacturers points out in its advertisements that not changing the filter leaves one quart of dirty oil in the engine. This claim is true and should be kept in mind when changing your oil.

NOTE: *The oil filter on the diesel engines must be changed every oil change.*

To change the oil, the truck should be on a level surface, and the engine should be at operating temperature. This is to ensure that the foreign matter will be drained away along with the oil, and not left in the engine to form sludge. You should have available a container that will hold a minimum of 8 quarts of liquid, a wrench to fit the old drain plug, a spout for pouring in new oil, and a rag or two, which you will always need. If the filter is being replaced, you will also need a band wrench or filter wrench to fit the end of the filter.

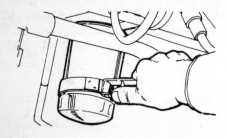

Use a strap wrench to loosen the oil filter, but, tighten it by hand

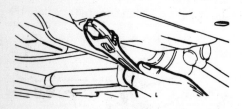

The oil drain plug is located at the lowest point of the oil pan

Add oil through the opening in the valve cover

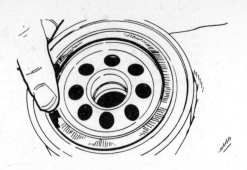

Coat the gasket on the new oil filter with clean engine oil

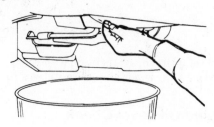

After loosening the plug with a wrench, unscrew the plug by hand, keeping an inward pressure on the plug, so that the hot oil won't escape until you pull the plug away

NOTE: *If the engine is equipped with an oil cooler, this will also have to be drained, using the drain plug. Be sure to add enough oil to fill the cooler in addition to the engine.*

1. Position the truck on a level surface and set the parking brake or block the wheels. Slide a drain pan under the oil drain plug.

2. From under the truck, loosen, but do not remove the oil drain plug. Cover your hand with a rag or glove and slowly unscrew the drain plug.

CAUTION: *The engine oil will be HOT! Keep your arms, face and hands clear of the oil as it drains out!*

3. Remove the plug and let the oil drain into the pan.

NOTE: *Do not drop the plug into the drain pan.*

4. When all of the oil has drained, clean off the drain plug and put it back into the hole. Remember to tighten the plug 20 ft. lbs. (30 ft. lbs. for diesel engines).

5. Loosen the filter with a band wrench or special oil filter cap wrench. On most Chevrolet engines, especially the V8s, the oil filter is next to the exhaust pipes. Stay clear of these, since even a passing contact will result in a painful burn.

CAUTION: *On trucks equipped with catalytic converters stay clear of the converter. The outside temperature of a hot catalytic converter can approach 1,200°F (650°C)!*

Install the filter by hand only! Do not use a strap wrench!

6. Cover your hand with a rag, and spin the filter off by hand.

7. Coat the rubber gasket on a new filter with a light film of clean engine oil. Screw the filter onto the mounting stud and tighten according to the directions on the filter (usually hand tight one turn past the point where the gasket contacts the mounting base). Don't overtighten the filter.

8. Refill the engine with the specified amount of clean engine oil.

9. Run the engine for several minutes, checking for leaks. Check the level of the oil and add oil if necessary.

When you have finished this job, you will notice that you now possess four or five quarts of dirty oil. The best thing to do with it is to pour it into plastic jugs, such as milk or antifreeze containers. Then, find a gas station or service garage which accepts waste oil for recycling and dispose of it there.

Manual Transmission

FLUID RECOMMENDATION

The 3-speed unit uses SAE 80W-90 GL-5. For vehicles normally operated in cold climates, use SAE 80W GL-5 gear lubricant.

The 4-speed unit uses Dexron®II ATF.

FLUID LEVEL CHECK

Check the lubricant level at the interval specified in the maintenance chart.

1. With the truck parked on a level surface, remove the filler plug from the side of the transmission case. Be careful not to take out the drain plug at the bottom.

2. If lubricant begins to trickle out of the hole, there is enough. If not, carefully insert a finger (watch out for sharp threads) and check that the level is up to the edge of the hole.

3. If not, add sufficient lubricant with a funnel and tube, or a squeeze bulb to bring it to the proper level.

4. Replace the plug and check for leaks.

DRAIN AND REFILL

No intervals are specified for changing the transmission lubricant, but it is a good idea on a used vehicle, one that has been worked hard, or one driven in deep water. The vehicle should be on a level surface and the lubricant should be at operating temperature.

1. Position the truck on a level surface.

2. Place a pan of sufficient capacity under the transmission drain plug.

3. Remove the upper (fill) plug to provide a vent opening.

4. Remove the lower (drain) plug and let the lubricant drain out.

5. Replace the drain plug.

6. Add lubricant with a suction gun or squeeze bulb.

7. Reinstall the filler plug. Run the engine and check for leaks.

Automatic Transmission

FLUID RECOMMENDATIONS

Use only high quality automatic transmission fluids that are identified by the name DEXRON®II.

LEVEL CHECK

Check the level of the fluid at the specified interval. The fluid level should be checked with the engine at normal operating temperature and running. If the truck has been running at high speed for a long period, in city traffic on a hot day, or pulling a trailer, let it cool down for about thirty minutes before checking the level.

1. Park on the level with the engine running and the shift lever in Park.

2. Remove the dipstick at the rear of the engine compartment. Cautiously feel the end of the dipstick with your fingers. Wipe it off and replace it, then pull it again and check the level of the fluid on the dipstick.

3. If the fluid felt cool, the level should be between the two dimples below ADD. If it was too hot to hold, the level should be between the ADD and FULL marks.

4. If the fluid is at or below the ADD mark, add fluid through the dipstick tube. One pint raises the level from ADD to FULL when the fluid is hot. The correct fluid to use is DEXRON®II. Be certain that the transmission is not over filled, this will cause foaming, fluid loss, and slippage.

PAN AND FILTER SERVICE DRAIN AND REFILL

The fluid should be drained with the transmission warm. It is easier to change the fluid if the truck is raised somewhat from the ground,

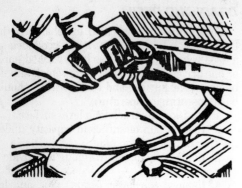

Add automatic transmission fluid through the dipstick tube

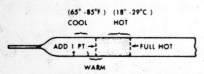

NOTE: <u>DO NOT OVERFILL</u>. It takes only one pint to raise level from ADD to FULL with a hot transmission.

Automatic transmission dipstick markings

Install a new gasket on the pan

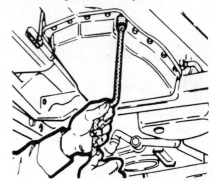

Removing the transmission drain pan

but this is not always easy without a lift. The transmission must be level for it to drain properly.

1. Place a shallow pan underneath to catch the transmission fluid (about 5 pints). Loosen all the pan bolts, then pull one corner down to drain most of the fluid. If it sticks, VERY CARE-FULLY pry the pan loose. You can buy aftermarket drain plug kits that makes this operation a bit less messy, once installed.

NOTE: *If the fluid removed smells burnt, serious transmission troubles, probably due to overheating, should be suspected.*

2. Remove the pan bolts and empty out the pan. On some models, there may not be much room to get at the screws at the front of the pan.

3. Clean the pan with solvent and allow it to air dry. If you use a rag to wipe it out, you risk leaving bits of lint and threads in the transmission.

4. Remove the filter or strainer retaining bolts. On the Turbo Hydra-Matic 400, there are two screws securing the filter or screen to the valve body. A reusable strainer may be found on some models. The strainer may be cleaned in solvent and air dried thoroughly. The filter and gasket must be replaced.

5. Install a new gasket and filter.

6. Install a new gasket on the pan, and tighten the bolts evenly to 12 foot pounds in a criss-cross pattern.

7. Add DEXRON®II transmission fluid

through the dipstick tube. The correct amount is in the Capacities Chart. Do not overfill.

8. With the gearshift lever in PARK, start the engine and let it idle. Do not race the engine.

9. Move the gearshift lever through each position, holding the brakes. Return the lever to PARK, and check the fluid level with the engine idling. The level should be between the two dimples on the dipstick, about 1/4 in. (6mm) below the ADD mark. Add fluid, if necessary.

10. Check the fluid level after the truck has been driven enough to thoroughly warm up the transmission. Details are given under Fluid Level Checks earlier in the Chapter. If the transmission is over filled, the excess must be

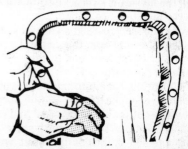

Clean the pan with a non-flammable solvent and dry it thoroughly

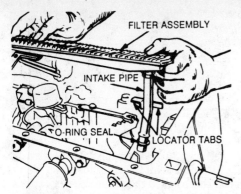

FILTER ASSEMBLY

INTAKE PIPE

O-RING SEAL   LOCATOR TABS

The Turbo Hydra-Matic 400 has an O-ring on the intake pipe. Check the condition of this O-ring and replace it as necessary

drained off. Overfilling causes aerated fluid, resulting in transmission slippage and probable damage.

Rear Axle Differential

FLUID RECOMMENDATION

Rear axles use SAE 80W–90 GL-5 gear oil. Positraction® axles must use special lubricant available from dealers. If the special fluid is not used, noise, uneven operation, and damage will result. There is also a Positraction® additive used to cure noise and slippage. Positraction® axles have an identifying tag, as well as a warning sticker near the jack or on the rear wheel well.

FLUID LEVEL CHECK

Lubricant levels in the rear axle should be checked as specified in the Maintenance chart. To check the lubricant level:

1. Park on level ground.
2. Remove the filler plug from the differential housing cover.
3. If lubricant trickles out, there is enough. If not, carefully insert a finger and check that the level is up to the bottom of the hole. Front axles should be full up to the level of the hole when warm, and ¹/₂ in. (12.7mm) below when cool.
4. Lubricant may be added with a funnel or a squeeze bulb. Rear axles use SAE 80W–90 GL-5 gear lubricant.

Positraction® limited slip axles must use a special lubricant available from dealers. If the special fluid is not used, noise, uneven operation, and damage will result. There is also a Positraction® additive to cure noise and slippage. Positraction® axles have an identifying tag, as well as a warning sticker near the jack or on the rear wheel well.

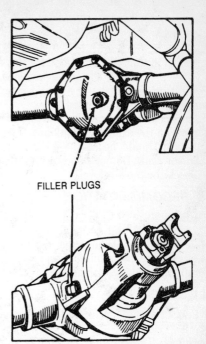

FILLER PLUGS

The rear axle filler plug may be in either of these two locations

REAR AXLE DRAIN AND REFILL

No intervals are specified for changing axle lubricant, but it is a good idea, especially if you have driven in water over the axle vents.

1. Park the vehicle on the level with the axles at normal operating temperature.
2. Place a pan of at least 6 pints capacity under the differential housing.
3. Remove the filler plug.
4. If you have a drain plug, remove it. If not, unbolt and remove the differential cover.
5. Replace the drain plug, or differential cover. Use a new gasket if the differential cover has been removed.
6. Lubricant may be added with a suction gun or squeeze bulb. Rear axles use SAE 80W–90 gear oil. Positraction® axles must use special lubricant available from dealers. If the special fluid is not used, noise, uneven operation, and damage will result. There is also a Positraction® additive used to cure noise and slippage. Positraction® axles have an identifying tag, as well as a warning sticker near the jack or on the rear wheel well. Rear axle lubricant level should be up to the bottom of the filler plug opening.

Cooling System

The coolant level should be checked at each fuel stop, ideally, to prevent the possibility of overheating and serious engine damage. If not, it should at least be checked once each month.

The cooling system was filled at the factory

with a high quality coolant solution that is good for year around operation and protects the system from freezing down to –20°F (–29°C) (–32°F [–36°C] in Canada). It is good for two full calendar years or 24,000 miles, whichever occurs first, provided that the proper concentration of coolant is maintained.

The hot coolant level should be at the FULL HOT mark on the expansion tank and the cold coolant level should be at the FULL COLD mark on the tank. Do not remove the radiator cap to check the coolant level.

FLUID RECOMMENDATION

Coolant mixture in Chevy/GMC Vans is 50/50 ethylene glycol and water for year round use. Use a good quality antifreeze with water pump lubricants, rust inhibitors and other corrosion inhibitors along with acid neutralizers.

LEVEL CHECK

1. Check the level on the see-through expansion tank.

CAUTION: *The radiator coolant is under pressure when hot. To avoid the danger of physical harm, coolant level should be checked or replenished only when the engine is cold. To remove the radiator cap when the engine is hot, first cover the cap with a thick rag, or wear a heavy glove for protection. Press down on the cap slightly and slowly turn it counterclockwise until it reaches the first stop. Allow all the pressure to vent (indicated when the hissing sound stops). When the pressure is released, press down on the cap and continue to rotate it counterclockwise. Some radiator caps have a lever for venting the pressure, but you should still exercise extreme caution when removing the cap.*

2. Check the level and, if necessary, add coolant to the proper level. Use a 50/50 mix of ethylene glycol antifreeze and water. Alcohol or methanol base coolants are not recommended. Antifreeze solutions should be used, even in summer, to prevent rust and to take advantage of the solution's higher boiling point compared to plain water. This is imperative on air conditioned trucks; the heater core can freeze if it isn't protected. Coolant should be added through the coolant recovery tank, not the radiator filler neck.

LIFT LEVER

Some radiator caps have a pressure relief lever

WARNING: *Never add large quantities of cold coolant to a hot engine! A cracked engine block may result!*

3. Replace the plug.

Each year the cooling system should be serviced as follows:

• Wash the radiator cap and filler neck with clean water.

• Check the coolant for proper level and freeze protection.

• Have the system pressure tested (15 psi). If a replacement cap is installed, be sure that it conforms to the original specifications.

• Tighten the hose clamps and inspect all hoses. Replace hoses that are swollen, cracked or otherwise deteriorated.

• Clean the frontal area of the radiator core and the air conditioning condenser, if so equipped.

DRAINING, FLUSHING AND TESTING THE
COOLING SYSTEM AND COOLANT

The cooling system in you van accumulates some internal rust and corrosion in its normal operation. A simple method of keeping the system clean is known as flushing the system. It is performed by circulating a can of radiator flush through the system, and then draining and refilling the system with the normal coolant. Radiator flush is marketed by several different manufacturers, and is available in cans at auto departments, parts stores, and many hardware stores. This operation should be performed every 30,000 miles or once a year.

To flush the cooling system:

CAUTION: *When draining the coolant, keep in mind that cats and dogs are attracted by the ethylene glycol antifreeze, and are quite likely to drink any that is left in an uncovered container or in puddles on the ground. This will prove fatal in sufficient quantity. Always drain the coolant into a sealable container. Coolant should be reused unless it is contaminated or several years old.*

1. Drain the existing antifreeze and coolant. Open the radiator and engine drain petcocks (located near the bottom of the radiator and engine block, respectively), or disconnect the bottom radiator hose at the radiator outlet.

NOTE: *Before opening the radiator petcock, spray it with some penetrating oil. Be aware that if the engine has been run up to operating temperature, the coolant emptied will be HOT.*

2. Close the petcock or reconnect the lower hose and fill the system with water—hot water if the system has just been run.

3. Add a can of quality radiator flush to the

The system should be pressure-tested once a year

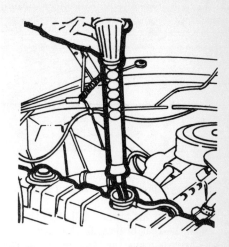

Coolant condition can be checked with an inexpensive tester

radiator or recovery tank, following any special instructions on the can.

4. Idle the engine as long as specified on the can of flush, or until the upper radiator hose gets hot.

5. Drain the system again. There should be quite a bit of scale and rust in the drained water.

6. Repeat this process until the drained water is mostly clear.

7. Close all petcocks and connect all hoses.

8. Flush the coolant recovery reservoir with water and leave empty.

9. Determine the capacity of your van's cooling system (see Capacities specifications in this guide. Add a 50/50 mix of ethylene glycol antifreeze and water to provide the desired protection.

10. Run the engine to operating temperature, then stop the engine and check for leaks. Check the coolant level and top up if necessary.

11. Check the protection level of your antifreeze mix with an antifreeze tester (a small, inexpensive syringe type device available at any auto parts store). The tester has five or six small colored balls inside, each of which signify a certain temperature rating. Insert the tester in the recovery tank and suck just enough coolant into the syringe to float as many individual balls as you can (without sucking in too much coolant and floating all the balls at once). A table supplied with the tester will explain how many floating balls equal protection down to a certain temperature (three floating balls might mean the coolant will protect your engine down to +5°F (−15°C), for example.

Master Cylinder

FLUID RECOMMENDATIONS

Only high quality brake fluids, such as General Motors Supreme No. 11 Hydraulic Brake Fluid, Delco Supreme No. 11 Hydraulic Brake Fluid or fluids meeting DOT-3 specifications should be used.

LEVEL CHECK

Chevrolet and GMC vans are equipped with a dual braking system, allowing a vehicle to be brought to a safe stop in the event of failure in either front or rear brakes. The dual master cylinder has 2 entirely separate reservoirs, one con-

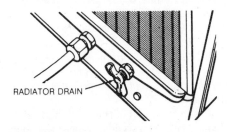

Radiator drain cock

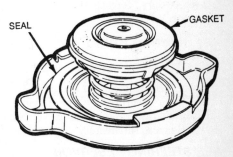

Check the condition of the radiator cap gasket and seal

Remove any debris from the radiator's cooling fins

nected to the front brakes and the other connected to the rear brakes. In the event of failure in either portion, the remaining part is not affected.

The master cylinder is mounted to the left side of the firewall.

1. Clean all of the dirt from around the cover of the master cylinder.

2. Be sure that the vehicle is resting on a level surface.

3. Carefully pry the clip from the top of the master cylinder to release the cover.

4. The fluid level should be approximately 1/4 in. (6mm) from the top of the master cylinder. If not, add fluid until the level is correct. Replacement fluid should be Delco Supreme No. 11, DOT 3, or its equivalent. It is normal for the fluid level to fall as the disc brake ads wear.

WARNING: *Brake fluid dissolves paint! It also absorbs moisture from the air. Never leave a container or the master cylinder uncovered any longer than necessary!*

5. Install the cover of the master cylinder. On most models there is a rubber gasket under the cover, which fits into 2 slots on the cover. Be sure that this is seated properly.

6. Push the clip back into place and be sure that it seats in the groove on the top of the cover.

7. As necessary, replace the access cover and floor mat.

Power Steering Pump

FLUID RECOMMENDATION

The power steering reservoir should be filled with GM Power Steering fluid, or its equivalent. Automatic Transmission Fluid DEXRON®II is also satisfactory.

POWER STEERING RESERVOIR LEVEL CHECK

Check the dipstick in the pump reservoir when the fluid is at operating temperature.

The fluid should be between the HOT and COLD marks. If the fluid is at room temperature, the fluid should be between the ADD and COLD marks. The fluid does not require periodic changing.

On systems with a remote reservoir, the level should be maintained approximately 1/2–1 in. (12.7–25.4mm) from the top with the wheels in the full left turn position.

Steering Gear

FLUID RECOMMENDATION

No lubrication is needed for the life of the gear, except in the event of seal replacement or overhaul, when the gear should be refilled with a 13 oz. container of Steering Gear Lubricant (Part No. 1051052) which meets GM Specification GM 4673M, or its equivalent.

NOTE: *On these models do not use EP Chassis Lubricant.*

FLUID LEVEL CHECK

The steering gear is factory filled with a lubricant which does not require seasonal change. The housing should not be drained. No lubricant is required for the life of the gear.

The gear should be inspected for seal leakage. Look for solid grease, not an oily film. If a seal is replaced or the gear overhauled, the gear should be filled with Part No. 1051052, which is a 13 oz. container of Steering Gear lubricant which meets GM Specifications. Do not use EP Chassis Lube to lubricate the gear and do not overfill.

Chassis Greasing

Refer to the diagrams for chassis points to be lubricated. Not all vehicles have all the fittings illustrated. Water resistant EP chassis lubricant (grease) conforming to GM specification 6031-M should be used for all chassis grease points.

Every year or 7,500 miles the front suspension ball points, both upper and lower on each side of the truck, must be greased. Most trucks covered in this guide should be equipped with grease nipples on the ball joints, although some may have plugs which must be removed and nipples fitted.

WARNING: *Do not pump so much grease into the ball joint that excess grease squeezes out of the rubber boot. This destroys the watertight seal.*

Jack up the front end of the truck and safely support it with jackstands. Block the rear wheels and firmly apply the parking brake. If the truck has been parked in temperatures below 20°F for any length of time, park it in a

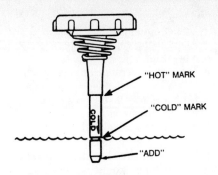

"HOT" MARK

"COLD" MARK

"ADD"

Master cylinder fluid level

heated garage for an hour or so until the ball joints loosen up enough to accept the grease.

Depending on which front wheel you work on first, turn the wheel and tire outward, either full-lock right or full-lock left. You now have the ends of the upper and lower suspension control arms in front of you; the grease nipples are visible pointing up (top ball joint) and down (lower ball joint) through the end of each control arm. If the nipples are not accessible enough, remove the wheel and tire. Wipe all dirt and crud from the nipples or from around the plugs (if installed). If plugs are on the truck, remove them and install grease nipples in the holes (nipples are available in various thread sizes at most auto parts stores). Using a hand operated, low pressure grease gun loaded with a quality chassis grease, grease the ball joint only until the rubber joint boot begins to swell out.

Steering Linkage

The steering linkage should be greased at the same interval as the ball joints. Grease nipples are installed on the steering tie rod ends on most models. Wipe all dirt and crud from around the nipples at each tie rod end. Using a hand operated, low pressure grease gun loaded with a suitable chassis grease, grease the linkage until the old grease begins to squeeze out around the tie rod ends. Wipe off the nipples and any excess grease. Also grease the nipples on the steering idler arms.

Parking Brake Linkage

Use chassis grease on the parking brake cable where it contacts the cable guides, levers and linkage.

Automatic Transmission Linkage

Apply a small amount of clean engine oil to the kickdown and shift linkage points at 7,500 mile intervals.

OUTSIDE VEHICLE MAINTENANCE

Lock Cylinders

Apply graphite lubricant sparingly through the key slot. Insert the key and operate the lock several times to be sure that the lubricant is worked into the lock cylinder.

Hood Latch and Hinges

Clean the latch surfaces and apply clean engine oil to the latch pilot bolts and the spring anchor. Also lubricate the hood hinges with engine oil. Use a chassis grease to lubricate all the pivot points in the latch release mechanism.

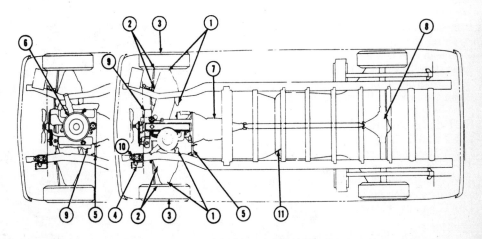

Chassis lubrication points

Door Hinges

The gas tank filler door and truck doors should be wiped clean and lubricated with clean engine oil once a year. The door lock cylinders and latch mechanisms should be lubricated periodically with a few drops of graphite lock lubricant or a few shots of silicone spray.

Body Drain Holes

Be sure that the drain holes in the doors and rocker panels are cleared of obstruction. A small screwdriver can be used to clear them of any debris.

FRONT WHEEL BEARINGS

Only the front wheel bearings require periodic maintenance. A premium high melting point grease meeting GM specification 6031–M must be used. Long fiber type greases must not be used. This service is recommended at the intervals in the Maintenance Intervals Chart or whenever the van has been driven in water up to the hubs.

Before handling the bearings, there are a few things that you should remember to do and not to do.

Remember to DO the following:
• Remove all outside dirt from the housing before exposing the bearing.
• Treat a used bearing as gently as you would a new one.
• Work with clean tools in clean surroundings.
• Use clean, dry canvas gloves, or at least clean, dry hands.
• Clean solvents and flushing fluids are a must.
• Use clean paper when laying out the bearings to dry.
• Protect disassembled bearings from rust and dirt. Cover them up.
• Use clean rags to wipe bearings.
• Keep the bearings in oil-proof paper when they are to be stored or are not in use.
• Clean the inside of the housing before replacing the bearing.

Do NOT do the following:
• Don't work in dirty surroundings.
• Don't use dirty, chipped or damaged tools.
• Try not to work on wooden work benches or use wooden mallets.
• Don't handle bearings with dirty or moist hands.
• Do not use gasoline for cleaning; use a safe solvent.
• Do not spin-dry bearings with com-pressed air. They will be damaged.
• Do not spin dirty bearings.
• Avoid using cotton waste or dirty cloths to wipe bearings.
• Try not to scratch or nick bearing surfaces.
• Do not allow the bearing to come in contact with dirt or rust at any time.

1. Remove the wheel and tire assembly, and the brake drum or brake caliper.

2. Remove the hub and disc as an assembly. Remove the caliper mounting bolts and insert a block between the brake pads as the caliper is removed. Remove the caliper and wind it out of the way. Do not allow the caliper to hang from the brake hose

3. Pry out the grease cap, cotter pin, spindle nut, and washer, then remove the hub. Do not drop the wheel bearings.

4. Remove the outer roller bearing assembly from the hub. The inner bearing assembly will remain in the hub and may be removed after prying out the inner seal. Discard the seal.

5. Clean all parts in solvent (air dry) and check for excessive wear and damage.

6. Using a hammer and drift, remove the bearing races from the hub. When installing new races, make sure that they are not cocked and that they are fully seated against the hub shoulder.

7. Pack both wheel bearings using high melting point wheel bearing grease for disc brakes. Ordinary grease will melt and ooze out ruining the pads. Place a healthy glob of grease in the

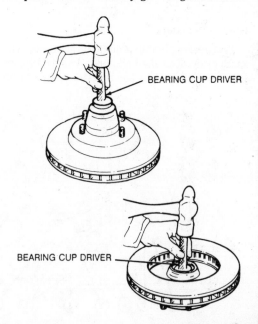

Install front wheel bearing races

palm of one hand and force the edge of the bearing into it so that the grease fills the bearing. Do this until the whole bearing is packed. Grease packing tools are available to make this job a lot less messy. There are also tools that also make it possible to grease the inner bearing without removing it from the spindle.

8. Place the inner bearing in the hub and install a new inner seal, making sure that the seal flange faces the bearing race.

9. Carefully install the wheel hub over the spindle.

10. Using your hands, firmly press the outer bearing into the hub. Install the spindle washer and nut.

11. Spin the wheel hub by hand and tighten the nut until it is just snug (12 ft. lbs.). Back off the nut until it is loose, then tighten it finger tight. Loosen the nut until either hole in the spindle lines up with a slot in the nut and

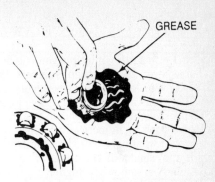

Packing the wheel bearing by hand

insert a new cotter pin. There should be 0.001–0.005 in. (0.025–0.127mm) endplay. This can be measured with a dial indicator, if you wish.

12. Replace the dust cap, wheel and tire.

TRAILER TOWING

Chevrolet and GMC vans have long been popular as trailer towing vehicles. Their strong construction, and wide range of engine/transmission combinations make them ideal for towing campers, boat trailers and utility trailers.

Factory trailer towing packages are available on most Chevrolet and GMC vans, if you are installing a trailer hitch and wiring on your van, there are a few thing that you ought to know.

Trailer Weight

Trailer weight is the first, and most important, factor in determining whether or not your vehicle is suitable for towing the trailer you have in mind. The horsepower-to-weight ratio

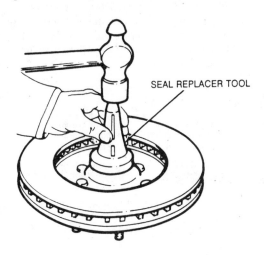

Install the inner seal

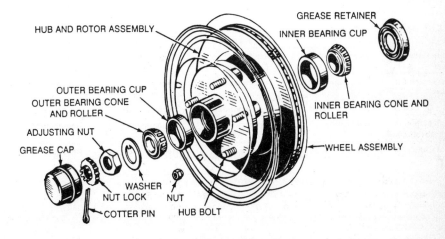

Front hub and bearing components

should be calculated. The basic standard is a ratio of 35:1. That is, 35 pounds of GVW for every horsepower.

To calculate this ratio, multiply you engine's rated horsepower by 35, then subtract the weight of the vehicle, including passengers and luggage. The resulting figure is the ideal maximum trailer weight that you can tow. One point to consider: a numerically higher axle ratio can offset what appears to be a low trailer weight. If the weight of the trailer that you have in mind is somewhat higher than the weight you just calculated, you might consider changing your rear axle ratio to compensate.

Hitch Weight

There are three kinds of hitches: bumper mounted, frame mounted, and load equalizing.

Bumper mounted hitches are those which attach solely to the vehicle's bumper. Many states prohibit towing with this type of hitch, when it attaches to the vehicle's stock bumper, since it subjects the bumper to stresses for which it was not designed. Aftermarket rear step bumpers, designed for trailer towing, are acceptable for use with bumper mounted hitches.

Frame mounted hitches can be of the type which bolts to two or more points on the frame, plus the bumper, or just to several points on the frame. Frame mounted hitches can also be of the tongue type, for Class I towing, or, of the receiver type, for classes II and III.

Load equalizing hitches are usually used for large trailers. Most equalizing hitches are welded in place and use equalizing bars and chains to level the vehicle after the trailer is hooked up.

The bolt-on hitches are the most common, since they are relatively easy to install.

Check the gross weight rating of your trailer. Tongue weight is usually figured as 10% of gross trailer weight. Therefore, a trailer with a maximum gross weight of 2,000 lb. will have a maximum tongue weight of 200 lb. Class I trailers fall into this category. Class II trailers are those with a gross weight rating of 2,000–3,500 lb., while Class III trailers fall into the 3,500–6,000 lb. category. Class IV trailers are those over 6,000 lb. and are for use with fifth wheel trucks, only.

Recommended Equipment Checklist

Equipment	Class I Trailers Under 2,000 pounds	Class II Trailers 2,000-3,500 pounds	Class III Trailers 3,500-6,000 pounds	Class IV Trailers 6,000 pounds and up
Hitch	Frame or Equalizing	Equalizing	Equalizing	Fifth wheel Pick-up truck only
Tongue Load Limit**	Up to 200 pounds	200-350 pounds	350-600 pounds	600 pounds and up
Trailer Brakes	Not Required	Required	Required	Required
Safety Chain	3/16" diameter links	1/4" diameter links	5/16" diameter links	–
Fender Mounted Mirrors	Useful, but not necessary	Recommended	Recommended	Recommended
Turn Signal Flasher	Standard	Constant Rate or heavy duty	Constant Rate or heavy duty	Constant Rate or heavy duty
Coolant Recovery System	Recommended	Required	Required	Required
Transmission Oil Cooler	Recommended	Recommended	Recommended	Recommended
Engine Oil Cooler	Recommended	Recommended	Recommended	Recommended
Air Adjustable Shock Absorbers	Recommended	Recommended	Recommended	Recommended
Flex or Clutch Fan	Recommended	Recommended	Recommended	Recommended
Tires	•••	•••	•••	•••

NOTE The information in this chart is a guide. Check the manufacturer's recommendations for your car if in doubt.

 *Local laws may require specific equipment such as trailer brakes or fender mounted mirrors. Check your local laws
   Hitch weight is usually 10-15% of trailer gross weight and should be measured with trailer loaded
 **Most manufacturer's do not recommend towing trailers of over 1,000 pounds with compacts. Some intermediates cannot tow Class III trailers
 ***Check manufacturer's recommendations for your specific car trailer combination
 —Does not apply

When you've determined the hitch that you'll need, follow the manufacturer's installation instructions, exactly, especially when it comes to fastener torques. The hitch will subjected to a lot of stress and good hitches come with hardened bolts. Never substitute an inferior bolt for a hardened bolt.

Wiring

Wiring the van for towing is fairly easy. There are a number of good wiring kits available and these should be used, rather than trying to design your own. All trailers will need brake lights and turn signals as well as tail lights and side marker lights. Most states require extra marker lights for overly wide trailers. Also, most states have recently required back-up lights for trailers, and most trailer manufacturers have been building trailers with back-up lights for several years.

Additionally, some Class I, most Class II and just about all Class III trailers will have electric brakes.

Add to this number an accessories wire, to operate trailer internal equipment or to charge the trailer's battery, and you can have as many as seven wires in the harness.

Determine the equipment on your trailer and buy the wiring kit necessary. The kit will contain all the wires needed, plus a plug adapter set which included the female plug, mounted on the bumper or hitch, and the male plug, wired into, or plugged into the trailer harness.

When installing the kit, follow the manufacturer's instructions. The color coding of the wires is standard throughout the industry.

One point to note, some domestic vehicles, and most imported vehicles, have separate turn signals. On most domestic vehicles, the brake lights and rear turn signals operate with the same bulb. For those vehicles with separate turn signals, you can purchase an isolation unit so that the brake lights won't blink whenever the turn signals are operated, or, you can go to your local electronics supply house and buy four diodes to wire in series with the brake and turn signal bulbs. Diodes will isolate the brake and turn signals. The choice is yours. The isolation units are simple and quick to install, but far more expensive than the diodes. The diodes, however, require more work to install properly, since they require the cutting of each bulb's wire and soldering in place of the diode.

One, final point, the best kits are those with a spring loaded cover on the vehicle mounted socket. This cover prevent dirt and moisture from corroding the terminals. Never let the vehicle socket hang loosely. Always mount it securely to the bumper or hitch.

Cooling

ENGINE

One of the most common, if not THE most common, problem associated with trailer towing is engine overheating.

With factory installed trailer towing packages, a heavy duty cooling system is usually included. Heavy duty cooling systems are available as optional equipment on most GM vehicles, with or without a trailer package. If you have one of these extra capacity systems, you shouldn't have any overheating problems.

If you have a standard cooling system, without an expansion tank, you'll definitely need to get an aftermarket expansion tank kit, preferably one with at least a 2 quart capacity. These kits are easily installed on the radiator's overflow hose, and come with a pressure cap designed for expansion tanks.

Another helpful accessory is a Flex Fan. These fan are large diameter units are designed to provide more airflow at low speeds, with blades that have deeply cupped surfaces. The blades then flex, or flatten out, at high speed, when less cooling air is needed. These fans are far lighter in weight than stock fans, requiring less horsepower to drive them. Also, they are far quieter than stock fans.

If you do decide to replace your stock fan with a flex fan, note that if your van has a fan clutch, a spacer between the flex fan and water pump hub will be needed.

Aftermarket engine oil coolers are helpful for prolonging engine oil life and reducing overall engine temperatures. Both of these factors increase engine life.

While not absolutely necessary in towing Class I and some Class II trailers, they are recommended for heavier Class II and all Class III towing.

Engine oil cooler systems consist of an adapter, screwed on in place of the oil filter, a remote filter mounting and a multi-tube, finned heat exchanger, which is mounted in front of the radiator or air conditioning condenser.

TRANSMISSION

An automatic transmission is usually recommended for trailer towing. Modern automatics have proven reliable and, of course, easy to operate, in trailer towing.

The increased load of a trailer, however, causes an increase in the temperature of the automatic transmission fluid. Heat is the worst enemy of an automatic transmission. As the temperature of the fluid increases, the life of the fluid decreases.

It is essential, therefore, that you install an automatic transmission cooler. The cooler, which consists of a multi-tube, finned heat exchanger, is usually installed in front of the radiator or air conditioning compressor, and hooked inline with the transmission cooler tank inlet line. Follow the cooler manufacturer's installation instructions.

Select a cooler of at least adequate capacity, based upon the combined gross weights of the van and trailer.

Cooler manufacturers recommend that you use an aftermarket cooler in addition to, and not instead of, the present cooling tank in your vans radiator. If you do want to use it in place of the radiator cooling tank, get a cooler at least two sizes larger than normally necessary.

One note: transmission cooler can, sometimes, cause slow or harsh shifting in the transmission during cold weather, until the fluid has a chance to come up to normal operating temperature. Some coolers can be purchased with or retrofitted with a temperature bypass valve which will allow fluid flow through the cooler only when the fluid has reached operating temperature, or above.

PUSHING

Chevrolet and GMC vans with manual transmissions can be push started, but this is not recommended if you value the appearance of your van.

To push start, make sure that both bumpers are in reasonable alignment. Bent sheet metal and inflamed tempers are both common results from misaligned bumpers when push starting. Turn the ignition key to ON and engage High gear. Depress the clutch pedal. When a speed of about 10 mph is reached, slightly depress the gas pedal and slowly release the clutch. The engine should start.

WARNING: *Never get an assist by having your vehicle towed! Automatic transmission equipped vans cannot be started by pushing.*

TOWING

Chevrolet and GMC vans can be towed on all four wheels (flat towed) at speeds of less than 35 mph for distances less than 50 miles, providing that the axle, driveline and engine/transmission are normally operable. The transmission should be in Neutral, the engine off, the steering unlocked, and the parking brake released.

The rear wheels must be raised off the ground or the driveshaft disconnected when

the transmission if not operating properly, or when speeds of over 35 mph will be used or when towing more than 50 miles.

Do not attach chains to the bumpers or bracketing. All attachments must be made to the structural members. Safety chains should be used. It should also be remembered that power steering and brake assists will not be working with the engine off.

JUMP STARTING A DUAL BATTERY DIESEL

All GM V8 diesels are equipped with two 12 volt batteries. The batteries are connected in parallel circuit (positive terminal to positive terminal, negative terminal to negative terminal). Hooking the batteries up in parallel circuit increases battery cranking power without increasing total battery voltage output (12 volts). On the other hand, hooking two 12 volt batteries up in a series circuit (positive terminal to negative terminal, positive terminal to negative terminal) increases total battery output to 24 volts (12 volts + 12 volts).

CAUTION: *NEVER hook the batteries up in a series circuit or the entire electrical system will go up in smoke.*

In the event that a dual battery diesel must be jump started, use the following procedure.

1. Open the hood and locate the batteries. On GM diesels, the manufacturer usually suggests using the battery on the driver's side of the van to make the correction.

2. Position the donor vehicle so that the jumper cables will reach from its battery (must be 12 volt, negative ground) to the appropriate battery in the diesel. Do not allow the vehicles to touch.

3. Shut off all electrical equipment on both vehicles. Turn off the engine of the donor vehicle, set the parking brakes on both vehicles and block the wheels. Also, make sure both vehicles

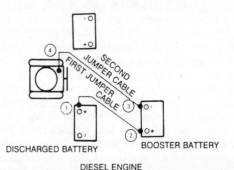

DISCHARGED BATTERY   BOOSTER BATTERY

DIESEL ENGINE

Dual battery jump-starting diagram

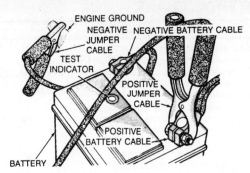

Jumper cable installation

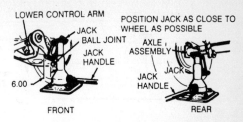

Jacking points for 20, 30, 2500 and 3500 Series

are in Neutral (manual transmission models) or Park (automatic transmission models).

4. Using the jumper cables, connect the positive (+) terminal of the donor vehicle's battery to the positive terminal of one (not both) of the diesel batteries.

5. Using the second jumper cable, connect the negative (–) terminal of the donor battery to a solid, stationary, metallic point on the diesel (alternator bracket, engine block, etc.). Be very careful to keep the jumper cables away

from moving parts (cooling fan, alternator belt, etc.) on both vehicles.

6. Start the engine of the donor can and run it at moderate speed.

7. Start the engine of the diesel.

8. When the diesel starts, disconnect the battery cables in the reverse order of attachment.

JACKING

The jack supplied with the van was meant for changing tires. It was not meant to support a van while you crawl under it and work. Whenever it is necessary to get under a van to perform service operations, always be sure that it is adequately supported, preferably by jackstands at the proper points.

If your van is equipped with a Positraction® or locking rear axle, do not run the engine for any reason with one rear wheel off the ground. Power will be transmitted through the rear wheel remaining on the ground, possibly causing the vehicle to drive itself off the jack.

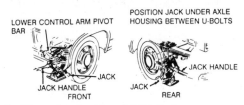

Jacking points for 10 and 1500 Series

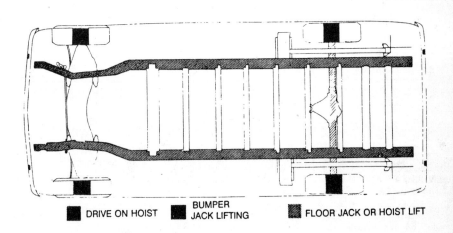

Lifting and hoisting points

MAINTENANCE INTERVAL CHART

Maintenance Item	Interval
Air cleaner element	Replace every 30,000 miles
Automatic transmission fluid and filter	Check once a month. Change every 30,000 miles
Battery	Check fluid level twice a month. Clean terminals as necessary
Brake fluid	Check once a month. Add as necessary
Chassis lubrication	Every 6 months
Coolant level	Check once a week. Add as necessary
Drive belts	Check every month. Adjust as necessary
Engine oil	Check at every fuel stop. Change every 3,000 miles
Engine oil filter	Change every oil change
Evaporative canister filter	Replace every 24 mos./30,000 miles
Front wheel bearings	Clean and repack every 30,000 miles
Fuel filter	Replace every 6,000 miles
Manual transmission fluid	Check twice a year. Add as necessary
PCV valve	Replace every 12 mos./15,000 miles
Power steering reservoir	Check once a month. Add as necessary
Rear axle	Check twice a year. Add as necessary
Tires	Check pressure once a week. Rotate every 6,000 miles

CAPACITIES CHART

Years	Models	Engines	Crankcase Incl. Filter (qt.)	Transmission (pt.)*			Drive Axle (pt.)	Fuel Tank (gal.)	Cooling System (qt.)	
				3-sp	4-sp	Auto.			w/AC	wo/AC
1987	All	6–4.3L	5.0	3.0	8.0	③	②	22.0 ①	11.0	11.0
		8–5.0L	5.0	3.0	8.0	③	②	22.0 ①	17.0	17.0
		8–5.7L	5.0	—	—	③	②	22.0 ①	17.0	17.0
		8–6.2L	7.0	—	8.0	③	②	22.0 ①	25.5	25.5
1988	All	6–4.3L	5.0	—	8.0	③	②	22.0 ①	11.0	11.0
		8–5.0L	5.0	—	8.0	③	②	22.0 ①	17.0	17.0
		8–5.7L	5.0	—	—	③	②	22.0 ①	17.0	17.0
		8–6.2L	7.0	—	8.0	③	②	22.0 ①	25.5	25.5
		8–7.4L	6.0	—	—	③	②	22.0 ①	23.0	23.0
1989	All	6–4.3L	5.0	—	8.0	③	②	22.0 ①	11.0	11.0
		8–5.0L	5.0	—	8.0	③	②	22.0 ①	17.0	17.0
		8–5.7L	5.0	—	—	③	②	22.0 ①	17.0	17.0
		8–6.2L	7.0	—	8.0	③	②	22.0 ①	25.5	25.5
		8–7.4L	6.0	—	—	③	②	22.0 ①	23.0	23.0
1990	All	6–4.3L	5.0	—	8.0	③	②	22.0 ①	11.0	11.0
		8–5.0L	5.0	—	8.0	③	②	22.0 ①	17.5	18.0
		8–5.7L	5.0	—	—	③	②	22.0 ①	17.5	18.0
		8–6.2L	7.0	—	8.0	③	②	22.0 ①	25.0	25.0
		8–7.4L	6.0	—	—	③	②	22.0 ①	23.0	25.0

*Drain and refill only
① Optional: 33.0
② 8½ in. ring gear: 4.2
9¾ in. ring gear: 6.0
Dana 10½ in. ring gear: 7.2
Chevrolet 10½ in. ring gear: 6.5

③ Turbo Hydra-Matic 400: 9.0
Turbo Hydra-Matic 700-R4: 10.0

Engine Performance and Tune-Up

2

TUNE-UP PROCEDURES

In order to extract the full measure of performance and economy from your engine it is essential that it be properly tuned at regular intervals. A regular tune-up will keep your vehicle's engine running smoothly and will prevent the annoying minor breakdowns and poor performance associated with an untuned engine.

Neither tune-up nor troubleshooting can be considered independently since each has a direct relationship with the other.

It is advisable to follow a definite and thorough tune-up procedure. Tune-up consists of three separate steps: Analysis, the process of determining whether normal wear is responsible for performance loss, and whether parts require replacement or service; parts replacement or service; and adjustment, where engine adjustments are performed.

The manufacturer's recommended interval for tune-ups is every 22,500 miles or 18 months, except for heavy duty emission models, which use the 12 mo/12,000 miles schedule in all years. These intervals should be shortened if the truck is subjected to severe operating conditions such as trailer pulling, or if starting and running problems are noticed. It is assumed that the routine maintenance described in Section 1 has been kept up, as this will have an effect on the results of the tune-up. All the applicable tune-up steps should be followed, as each adjustment complements the effects of the others. If the tune-up (emission control) sticker in the engine compartment disagrees with the information presented in the Tune-up Specifications chart in this Chapter, the sticker figures must be followed. The sticker information reflects running changes made by the manufacturer during production. The light duty

sticker is usually found on the underhood sheet metal above the grille. The heavy duty sticker is usually on top of the air cleaner.

Diesel engines do not require tune-ups per say, as there is no ignition system.

Troubleshooting is a logical sequence of procedures designed to locate a particular cause of trouble.

It is advisable to read the entire Chapter before beginning a tune-up, although those who are more familiar with tune-up procedures may wish to go directly to the instructions.

Spark Plugs

A typical spark plug consists of a metal shell surrounding a ceramic insulator. A metal electrode extends downward through the center of the insulator and protrudes a small distance. Located at the end of the plug and attached to the side of the outer metal shell is the side electrode. The side electrode bends in at a 90° angle so that its tip is even with, and parallel to, the tip of the center electrode. The distance between these two electrodes (measured in thousandths of an inch) is called the spark plug gap. The spark plug in no way produces a spark but merely provides a gap across which the current can arc. The coil produces anywhere from 20,000 to 40,000 volts which travels to the distributor where it is distributed through the spark plug wires to the spark plugs. The current passes along the center electrode and jumps the gap to the side electrode, and, in doing, ignites the air/fuel mixture in the combustion chamber.

Rough idle, hard starting, frequent engine miss at high speeds and physical deterioration are all indications that the plugs should be replaced.

The electrode end of a spark plug is a good

Troubleshooting Engine Performance

Problem	Cause	Solution
Hard starting (engine cranks normally)	• Binding linkage, choke valve or choke piston	• Repair as necessary
	• Restricted choke vacuum diaphragm	• Clean passages
	• Improper fuel level	• Adjust float level
	• Dirty, worn or faulty needle valve and seat	• Repair as necessary
	• Float sticking	• Repair as necessary
	• Faulty fuel pump	• Replace fuel pump
	• Incorrect choke cover adjustment	• Adjust choke cover
	• Inadequate choke unloader adjustment	• Adjust choke unloader
	• Faulty ignition coil	• Test and replace as necessary
	• Improper spark plug gap	• Adjust gap
	• Incorrect ignition timing	• Adjust timing
	• Incorrect valve timing	• Check valve timing; repair as necessary
Rough idle or stalling	• Incorrect curb or fast idle speed	• Adjust curb or fast idle speed
	• Incorrect ignition timing	• Adjust timing to specification
	• Improper feedback system operation	• Refer to Chapter 4
	• Improper fast idle cam adjustment	• Adjust fast idle cam
	• Faulty EGR valve operation	• Test EGR system and replace as necessary
	• Faulty PCV valve air flow	• Test PCV valve and replace as necessary
	• Choke binding	• Locate and eliminate binding condition
	• Faulty TAC vacuum motor or valve	• Repair as necessary
	• Air leak into manifold vacuum	• Inspect manifold vacuum connections and repair as necessary
	• Improper fuel level	• Adjust fuel level
	• Faulty distributor rotor or cap	• Replace rotor or cap
	• Improperly seated valves	• Test cylinder compression, repair as necessary
	• Incorrect ignition wiring	• Inspect wiring and correct as necessary
	• Faulty ignition coil	• Test coil and replace as necessary
	• Restricted air vent or idle passages	• Clean passages
	• Restricted air cleaner	• Clean or replace air cleaner filler element
	• Faulty choke vacuum diaphragm	• Repair as necessary
Faulty low-speed operation	• Restricted idle transfer slots	• Clean transfer slots
	• Restricted idle air vents and passages	• Clean air vents and passages
	• Restricted air cleaner	• Clean or replace air cleaner filter element
	• Improper fuel level	• Adjust fuel level
	• Faulty spark plugs	• Clean or replace spark plugs
	• Dirty, corroded, or loose ignition secondary circuit wire connections	• Clean or tighten secondary circuit wire connections
	• Improper feedback system operation	• Refer to Chapter 4
	• Faulty ignition coil high voltage wire	• Replace ignition coil high voltage wire
	• Faulty distributor cap	• Replace cap
Faulty acceleration	• Improper accelerator pump stroke	• Adjust accelerator pump stroke
	• Incorrect ignition timing	• Adjust timing
	• Inoperative pump discharge check ball or needle	• Clean or replace as necessary
	• Worn or damaged pump diaphragm or piston	• Replace diaphragm or piston

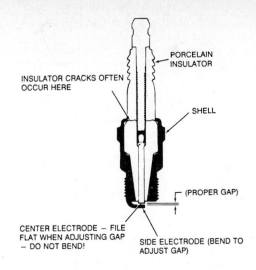

PORCELAIN INSULATOR

INSULATOR CRACKS OFTEN OCCUR HERE

SHELL

(PROPER GAP)

CENTER ELECTRODE — FILE FLAT WHEN ADJUSTING GAP — DO NOT BEND!

SIDE ELECTRODE (BEND TO ADJUST GAP)

Cutaway of a spark plug

indicator of the internal condition of your engine. If a spark plug is fouled, causing the engine to misfire, the problem will have to be found and corrected. Often, reading the plugs will lead you to the cause of the problem.

There are several reasons why a spark plug will foul and you can learn which reason by just looking at the plug. The two most common problems are oil fouling and pre-ignition/detonation.

Oil fouling is easily noticed as dark, wet oily deposits on the plug's electrodes. Oil fouling is caused by internal engine problems, the most common of which are worn valve seals or guides and worn or damaged piston rings. These problems can be corrected only by engine repairs.

Pre-ignition or detonation problems are characterized by extensive burning and/or damage to the plug's electrodes. The problem is caused by incorrect ignition timing or faulty spark control. Check the timing and/or diagnose the spark control system.

NOTE: *A small amount of light tan or rust red colored deposits at the electrode end of the plug is normal. These plugs need not be renewed unless they are severely worn.*

SPARK PLUG HEAT RANGE

Spark plug heat range is the ability of the plug to dissipate heat. The longer the insulator (or the farther it extends into the engine), the hotter the plug will operate; the shorter the insulator the cooler it will operate. A plug that absorbs little heat and remains too cool will quickly accumulate deposits of oil and carbon since it is not hot enough to burn them off. This leads to plug fouling and consequently to misfiring. A plug that absorbs too much heat will have no deposits, but, due to the excessive

heat, the electrodes will burn away quickly and in some instances, pre-ignition may result. Pre-ignition takes place when plug tips get so hot that they glow sufficiently to ignite the fuel/air mixture before the actual spark occurs. This early ignition will usually cause a pinging during low speeds and heavy loads.

The general rule of thumb for choosing the correct heat range when picking a spark plug is: if most of your driving is long distance, high speed travel, use a colder plug; if most of your driving is stop and go, use a hotter plug. Original equipment plugs are compromise plugs, but most people never have occasion to change their plugs from the factory recommended heat range.

REPLACEMENT

A set of spark plugs usually requires replacement after about 20,000 to 30,000 miles, depending on your style of driving. In normal operation, plug gap increases about 0.001 in. for every 1,000–2,500 miles. As the gap increases, the plug's voltage requirement also increases. It requires a greater voltage to jump the wider gap and about two to three times as much voltage to fire a plug at high speeds than at idle.

When you're removing spark plugs, you should work on one at a time. Don't start by removing the plug wires all at once, because unless you number them, they may become mixed up. Take a minute before you begin and number the wires with tape. The best location for numbering is near where the wires come out of the cap.

1. Disconnect each spark plug wire by twisting and pulling on the rubber cap, not on the wire. Carbon core wires can be internally broken rather easily.

2. If the wires are dirty or oily, wipe them clean with a cloth dampened in kerosene and then wipe them dry. If the wires are cracked, they should be replaced. Make sure to get the radio noise suppression type.

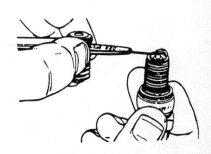

Use a wire gauge to check the plug's electrode gap

Adjusting the gap

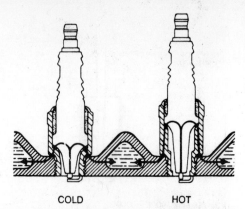

COLD   HOT

Spark plug heat range. The plug with the higher heat range is on the right. It has a longer heat flow path and thus operates at a higher tip temperature. It should be used for low speed driving and light load conditions

3. Blow or brush the dirt away from each of the spark plugs. This can be done by loosening the plugs and cranking the engine with the starter.

4. Remove each spark plug with a spark plug socket — $^5/_8$ in. or $^{13}/_{16}$ in. Make sure that the socket is all the way down on the plug to prevent it from slipping and cracking the porcelain insulator. On some V8s, the plugs are more accessible from under the truck.

5. In general, a tan or medium gray color (rust red with some unleaded fuels) on the business end of the plug indicates normal combustion conditions. A spark plug's useful life is at least 12,000 miles. Thus it would make sense to throw away the plugs if it has been 12,000 miles or more since the last tune-up. Most professional mechanics won't waste their time cleaning used plugs. There is too much chance of unsatisfactory performance and a customer comeback. Refer to the Tune-Up Specifications chart for the proper spark plug type.

The letter codes on the General Motors original equipment type plus are read this way:

- R — resistor
- S — extended tip
- T — tapered seat
- X — wide gap

The numbers indicate heat range. Hotter running plugs have higher numbers.

6. If the plugs are to be reused, file the center and side electrodes flat with a small, fine file. Heavy or baked on deposits can be carefully scraped off with a small knife blade or the scraper tool on a combination spark plug tool. Check the gap between the two electrodes with a spark plug gap gauge. The round wire type is the most accurate. If the gap is not as specified, use the adjusting device on the gap gauge to bend the outside electrode to correct.

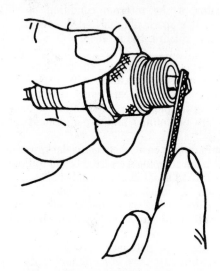

Filing the electrodes on a used plug

Twist and pull the boot to remove a spark plug wire

NOTE: *Always check the gap on new plugs.*

CAUTION: *Be careful not to bend the electrode too far or too often, because excessive bending may cause it to break off and fall into the combustion chamber. This would require cylinder head removal to reach the broken piece, and could result in cylinder wall, ring, or valve damage.*

7. Clean the plug threads with a wire brush. If you choose to lubricate the threads, use only one drop of engine oil.

8. Screw the plugs in finger tight. Tighten them with the plug socket. If a torque wrench is available, tighten them to 15 ft. lbs. for plug designation with a T, and 25 ft. lbs. for the rest.

9. Reinstall the wires. If there is any doubt as to their proper locations, refer to the Firing Order illustrations.

Spark Plug Wires

Every 10,000 miles, inspect the spark plug wires for burns, cuts, or breaks in the insulation. Check the boots and the nipples on the distributor cap. Replace any damaged wiring.

Every 30,000 miles or so, the resistance of the wires should be checked with an ohmmeter. Wires with excessive resistance will cause misfiring, and may make the engine difficult to start in damp weather. Generally, the useful life of the cables is 45,000–60,000 miles.

To check resistance, remove the distributor cap, leaving the wires in place. Connect one lead of an ohmmeter to an electrode within the cap. Connect the other lead to the corresponding spark plug terminal (remove it from the spark plug for this test). Replace any wire which shows a resistance over 30,000Ω. Generally speaking, however, resistance should not be over 25,000Ω, and 30,000Ω must be considered the outer limit of acceptability.

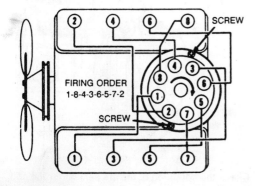

V8 firing order

It should be remembered that resistance is also a function of length. The longer the wire, the greater the resistance. Thus, if the wires on your van are longer than the factory originals, the resistance will be higher, possibly outside these limits.

When installing new wires, replace them one at a time to avoid mixups. Start by replacing the longest one first. Install the boot firmly over the spark plug. Route the wire over the same path as the original. Insert the nipple firmly onto the tower on the distributor cap, then install the cap cover and latches to secure the wires.

FIRING ORDERS

Always label each wire before removing it!

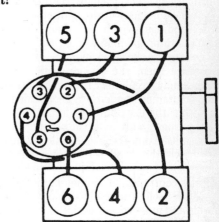

6-4.3L firing order

ELECTRONIC IGNITION SYSTEM

All engines use the breakerless HEI (High Energy Ignition) system. Since there is no mechanical contact, there is no wear or need for periodic service. There is an item in the distributor that resembles a condenser. It is a radio interference suppression capacitor which requires no service.

Description

The General Motors HEI system is a pulse-triggered, transistorized controlled, inductive discharge ignition system. The entire HEI system is contained within the distributor cap.

The distributor, in addition to housing the mechanical and vacuum advance mechanisms, contains the ignition coil, the electronic control module, and the magnetic triggering device. The magnetic pick-up assembly contains a permanent magnet, a pole piece with internal teeth, and a pick-up coil (not to be confused with the ignition coil).

In the HEI system, as in other electronic ignition systems, the breaker points have been replaced with an electronic switch—a transistor—which is located within the control module. This switching transistor performs the same function the points did in a conventional ignition system. It simply turns coil primary current on and off at the correct time. Essentially then, electronic and conventional ignition systems operate on the same principle.

The module which houses the switching transistor is controlled (turned on and off) by a magnetically generated impulse induced in the pick-up coil. When the teeth of the rotating timer align with the teeth of the pole piece, the induced voltage in the pick-up coil signals the electronic module to open the coil primary circuit. The primary current then decreases, and a high voltage is induced in the ignition coil secondary windings which is then directed through the rotor and high voltage leads (spark plug wires) to fire the spark plugs.

In essence then, the pick-up coil module system simply replaces the conventional breaker points and condenser. The condenser found within the distributor is for radio suppression purposes only and had nothing to do with the ignition process. The module automatically controls the dwell period, increasing it with increasing engine speed. Since dwell is automatically controlled, it cannot be adjusted. The module itself is non-adjustable and non-repairable and must be replaced if found defective.

HEI SYSTEM PRECAUTIONS

Before going on to troubleshooting, it might be a good idea to take note of the following precautions:

Timing Light Use

Inductive pick-up timing lights are the best kind to use if your van is equipped with HEI. Timing lights which connect between the spark plug and the spark plug wire occasionally (not always) give false readings.

Spark Plug Wires

The plug wires used with HEI systems are of a different construction than conventional wires. When replacing them, make sure you get the correct wires, since conventional wires won't carry the voltage. Also, handle them carefully to avoid cracking or splitting them and never pierce them.

Tachometer Use

Not all tachometers will operate or indicate correctly when used on a HEI system. While some tachometers may give a reading, this does not necessarily mean the reading is correct. In addition, some tachometers hook up differently from others. If you can't figure out whether or not your tachometer will work on your van, check with the tachometer manufacturer. Dwell readings, of course, have no significance at all.

HEI Systems Testers

Instruments designed specifically for testing HEI systems are available from several tool manufacturers. Some of these will even test the module itself. However, the tests given in the following section will require only a ohmmeter and a voltmeter.

TROUBLESHOOTING THE HEI SYSTEM

The symptoms of a defective component within the HEI system are exactly the same as those you would encounter in a conventional system.

Some of these symptoms are:
- Hard or no Starting
- Rough Idle
- Fuel Poor Economy
- Engine misses under load or while accelerating

If you suspect a problem in the ignition

Wire Length	Minimum	Maximum
0–15 inches	3000 ohms	10,000 ohms
15–25 inches	4000 ohms	15,000 ohms
25–35 inches	6000 ohms	20,000 ohms
Over 35 inches		25,000 ohms

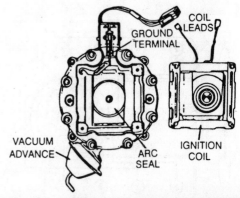

Check the condition of the arc seal under the coil

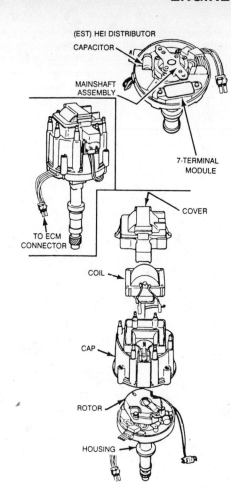

HEI distributor components

Labels: (EST) HEI DISTRIBUTOR CAPACITOR, MAINSHAFT ASSEMBLY, 7-TERMINAL MODULE, COVER, COIL, CAP, ROTOR, HOUSING, TO ECM CONNECTOR

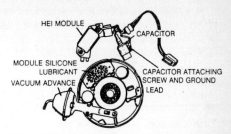

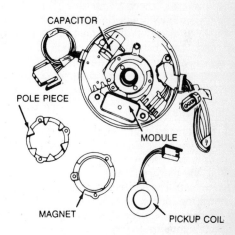

Module replacement. Be sure to coat the mating surfaces with silicone lubricant

Labels: HEI MODULE, CAPACITOR, MODULE SILICONE LUBRICANT, VACUUM ADVANCE, CAPACITOR ATTACHING SCREW AND GROUND LEAD

Labels: CAPACITOR, POLE PIECE, MODULE, MAGNET, PICKUP COIL

Pickup coil removed and disassembled

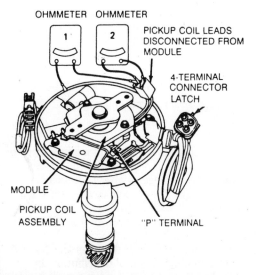

Ohmmeter 1 shows the connections for testing the pickup coil. Ohmmeter 2 shows the connections for testing the pickup coil continuity

Labels: OHMMETER 1, OHMMETER 2, PICKUP COIL LEADS DISCONNECTED FROM MODULE, 4-TERMINAL CONNECTOR LATCH, MODULE, PICKUP COIL ASSEMBLY, "P" TERMINAL

system, there are certain preliminary checks which you should carry out before you begin to check the electronic portions of the system. First, it is extremely important to make sure the vehicle battery is in a good state of charge. A defective or poorly charged battery will cause the various components of the ignition system to read incorrectly when they are being tested. Second, make sure all wiring connections are clean and tight, not only at the battery, but also at the distributor cap, ignition coil, and at the electronic control module.

Since the only change between electronic and conventional ignition systems is in the distributor component area, it is imperative to check the secondary ignition circuit first. If the secondary circuit checks out properly, then the engine condition is probably not the fault of the

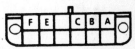

A. Ground
B. Diagnostic terminal
C. A.I.R. (if used)
D. Serial data (see special tools)
E. T.C.C. (if used)

Terminal identification of the ALCL connector

ignition system. To check the secondary ignition system, perform a simple spark test. Remove one of the plug wires and insert some sort of extension in the plug socket. An old spark plug with the ground electrode removed makes a good extension. Hold the wire and extension about $1/4''$ away from the block and crank the engine. If a normal spark occurs, then the problem is most likely not in the ignition system. Check for fuel system problems, or fouled spark plugs.

If, however, there is no spark or a weak spark, then further ignition system testing will have to be done. Troubleshooting techniques fall into two categories, depending on the nature of the problem. The categories are (1) Engine cranks, but won't start or (2) Engine runs, but runs rough or cuts out.

Engine Fails to Start

If the engine won't start, perform a spark test as described earlier. If no spark occurs, check for the presence of normal battery voltage at the battery (BAT) terminal in the distributor cap. The ignition switch must be in the **on** position for this test. Either a voltmeter or a test light may be used for this test. Connect the test light wire to ground and the probe end to the BAT terminal at the distributor. If the light comes on, you have voltage to the distributor. If the light fails to come on, this indicates an open circuit in the ignition primary wiring leading to the distributor. In this case, you will have to check wiring continuity back to the ignition switch using a test light. If there is battery voltage at the BAT terminal, but no spark at the plugs, then the problem lies within the distributor assembly. Go on to the distributor components test section.

Engine Runs, but Runs Rough or Cuts Out

1. Make sure the plug wires are in good shape first. There should be no obvious cracks or breaks. You can check the plug wires with an ohmmeter, but do not pierce the wires with a probe. Check the chart for the correct plug wire resistance.

2. If the plug wires are OK, remove the cap assembly, and check for moisture, cracks, chips, or carbon tracks, or any other high voltage leaks or failures. Replace the cap if you find any defects. Make sure the timer wheel rotates when the engine is cranked. If everything is all right so far, go on to the distributor components test section.

Distributor Components Testing

If the trouble has been narrowed down to the units within the distributor, the following tests can help pinpoint the defective component. An ohmmeter with both high and low ranges should be used. These tests are made with the cap assembly removed and the battery wire disconnected.

1. Connect an ohmmeter between the TACH and BAT terminals in the distributor cap. The primary coil resistance should be less than one ohm (zero or nearly zero).

2. To check the coil secondary resistance, connect an ohmmeter between the rotor button and the BAT terminal. Then connect the ohmmeter between the ground terminal and the rotor button. The resistance in both cases should be between 6,000 and 30,000 ohms.

3. Replace the coil only if the readings in step one and two are infinite.

NOTE: *These resistance checks will not disclose shorted coil windings. This condition can be detected only with scope analysis or a suitably designed coil tester. If these instruments are unavailable, replace the coil with a known good coil as a final coil test.*

4. To test the pick-up coil, first disconnect the white and green module leads. Set the ohmmeter on the high scale and connect it between a ground and either the white or green lead. Any resistance measurement less than infinity requires replacement of the pick-up coil.

5. Pick-up coil continuity is tested by connecting the ohmmeter (on low range) between the white and green leads. Normal resistance is between 500 and 1500 ohms. Move the vacuum advance arm while performing this test. This will detect any break in coil continuity. Such a condition can cause intermittent misfiring. Replace the pick-up coil if the reading is outside the specified limits.

6. If no defects have been found at this time, and you still have a problem, then the module will have to be checked. If you do not have access to a module tester, the only possible alternative is a substitution test. If the module fails the substitution test, replace it.

COMPONENT REPLACEMENT

Ignition Coil

1. Disconnect the feel and module wire terminal connectors from the distributor cap.

2. Remove the ignition set retainer.

3. Remove the 4 coil cover-to-distributor cap screws and coil cover.

4. Remove the 4 coil-to-distributor cap screws.

5. Using a blunt drift, press the coil wire spade terminals up out of distributor cap.

6. Lift the coil up out of the distributor cap.

7. Remove and clean the coil spring, rubber seal washer and coil cavity of the distributor cap.

8. Coat the rubber seal with a dielectric lubricant furnished in the replacement ignition coil package.

9. Reverse the above procedures to install.

Distributor Cap

1. Remove the feel and module wire terminal connectors from the distributor cap.

2. Remove the retainer and spark plug wires from the cap.

3. Depress and release the 4 distributor cap-to-housing retainers and lift off the cap assembly.

4. Remove the 4 coil cover screws and cover.

5. Using a finger or a blunt drift, push the spade terminals up out of the distributor cap.

6. Remove all 4 coil screws and lift the coil, coil spring and rubber seal washer out of the cap coil cavity.

7. Using a new distributor cap, reverse the above procedures to assemble, being sure to clean and lubricate the rubber seal washer with dielectric lubricant.

Rotor

1. Disconnect the feel and module wire connectors from the distributor.

2. Depress and release the 4 distributor cap to housing retainers and lift off the cap assembly.

3. Remove the two rotor attaching screws and rotor.

4. Reverse the above procedure to install.

Vacuum Advance

1. Remove the distributor cap and rotor as previously described.

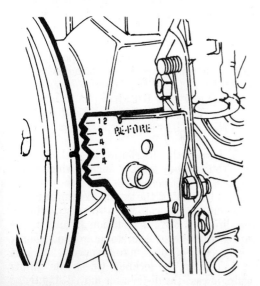

Typical timing marks

2. Disconnect the vacuum hose from the vacuum advance unit.

3. Remove the two vacuum advance retaining screws, pull the advance unit outward, rotate and disengage the operating rod from its tang.

4. Reverse the above procedure to install.

Module

1. Remove the distributor cap and rotor as previously described.

2. Disconnect the harness connector and pick-up coil spade connectors from the module. Be careful not to damage the wires when removing the connector.

3. Remove the two screws and module from the distributor housing.

4. Coat the bottom of the new module with dielectric lubricant supplies with the new module. Reverse the above procedure to install.

IGNITION TIMING

Ignition timing is the measurement, in degrees of crankshaft rotation, of the point at which the spark plugs fire in each of the cylinders. It is measured in degrees before or after Top Dead Center (TDC) of the compression stroke. Ignition timing is controlled by turning the distributor in the engine.

Ideally, the air/fuel mixture in the cylinder will be ignited by the spark plug just as the piston passes TDC of the compression stroke. If this happens, this piston will be beginning the power stroke just as the compressed and ignited air/fuel mixture starts to expand. The expansion of the air/fuel mixture then forces the piston down on the power stroke and turns the crankshaft.

Because it takes a fraction of a second for the spark plug to ignite the gases in the cylinder, the spark plug must fire a little before the piston reaches TDC. Otherwise, the mixture will not be completely ignited as the piston passes TDC and the full benefit of the explosion will not be used by the engine. The timing measurement is given in degrees of crankshaft rotation before the piston reaches TDC (BTDC). If the setting for the ignition timing is 5 degrees BTDC, the spark plug must fire 5 degrees before that piston reaches TDC. This only holds true, however, when the engine is at idle speed.

As the engine speed increases, the pistons go faster. The spark plugs have to ignite the fuel even sooner if it is to be completely ignited when the piston reaches TDC. To do this, the distributor has a means to advance the timing of the spark as the engine speed increases.

If the ignition is set too far advanced (BTDC), the ignition and expansion of the fuel in the cylinder will occur too soon and tend to force the piston down while it is still traveling up. This causes engine ping. If the engine is too far retarded after TDC (ATDC), the piston will have already passed TDC and started on its way down when the fuel is ignited. This will cause the piston to be forced down for only a portion of its travel. This will result in poor engine performance and lack of power.

Timing should be checked at each tune-up and any time the points are adjusted or replaced. It isn't likely to change much with HEI. The timing marks consist of a notch on the rim of the crankshaft pulley or vibration damper and a graduated scale attached to the engine front (timing) cover. A stroboscopic flash (dynamic) timing light must be used, as a static light is too inaccurate for emission controlled engines.

There are three basic types of timing light available. The first is a simple neon bulb with two wire connections. One wire connects to the spark plug terminal and the other plugs into the end of the spark plug wire for the No. 1 cylinder, thus connecting the light in series with the spark plug. This type of light is pretty dim and must be held very closely to the timing marks to be seen. Sometimes a dark corner has to be sought out to see the flash at all. This type of light is very inexpensive. The second type operates from the vehicle battery—two alligator clips connect to the battery terminals, while an adapter enables a third clip to be connected between No. 1 spark plug and wire. This type is a bit more expensive, but it provides a nice bright flash that you can see even in bright sunlight. It is the type most often seen in professional shops. The third type replaces the battery power source with 100 volt current.

Some timing lights have other features built into them, such as dwell meters, or tachometers. These are convenient, in that they reduce the tangle of wires under the hood when you're working, but may duplicate the functions of tools you already have. One worthwhile feature, which is becoming more of a necessity with higher voltage ignition systems, is an inductive pickup. The inductive pickup clamps around the No. 1 spark plug wire, sensing the surges of high voltage electricity as they are sent to the plug. The advantage is that no mechanical connection is inserted between the wire and the plug. The advantage is that no mechanical connection is inserted between the wire and the plug, which eliminates false signals to the timing light. A timing light with an inductive pickup should be used on HEI systems.

To check and adjust the timing:

1. Warm up the engine to normal operating temperature. Stop the engine and connect the timing light to the No. 1 (left front) spark plug wire, at the plug or at the distributor cap. You can also use the No. 6 wire, if it is more convenient. Numbering is illustrated earlier in this Chapter.

NOTE: *Do not pierce the plug wire insulation with HEI; it will cause a miss. The best method is an inductive pickup timing light.*

Clean off the timing marks and mark the pulley or damper notch and timing scale with white chalk.

2. Disconnect and plug the vacuum line at the distributor. This is done to prevent any distributor vacuum advance. Check the underhood emission sticker for any other hoses or wires which may need to be disconnected.

3. Start the engine and adjust the idle speed to that specified in the Tune-up Specifications chart. With automatic transmission, set the specified idle speed in Park. It will be too high, since it is normally (in most cases) adjusted in Drive. You can disconnect the idle solenoid, if any, to get the speed down. Otherwise, adjust the idle speed screw. This is done to prevent any centrifugal (mechanical) advance.

The tachometer connects to the TACH terminal on the distributor and to a ground. Some tachometers must connect to the TACH terminal and to the positive battery terminal. Some tachometers won't work with HEI.

WARNING: *Never ground the HEI TACH terminal; serious system damage will result.*

4. Aim the timing light at the pointer marks. Be careful not to touch the fan, because it may appear to be standing still. If the pulley or damper notch isn't aligned with the proper timing mark (see the Tune-up Specifications chart), the timing will have to be adjusted.

NOTE: *TDC or Top Dead Center corresponds to 0°B, or BTDC, or Before Top Dead Center may be shown as BEFORE. A, or ATDC, or After Top Dead Center may be shown as AFTER.*

5. Loosen the distributor base clamp locknut. You can buy trick wrenches which make this task a lot easier on V8s. Turn the distributor slowly to adjust the timing, holding it by the body and not the cap. Turn the distributor in the direction of rotor rotation (found in the Firing Order illustration) to retard, and against the direction of rotation to advance.

6. Tighten the locknut. Check the timing again, in case the distributor moved slightly as you tightened it.

7. Replace the distributor vacuum line. Correct the idle speed.

8. Stop the engine and disconnect the timing light.

DIESEL INJECTION TIMING

For the engine to be properly timed, the marks on the top of the engine front cover must be aligned with the marks on the injection pump flange. The engine must be OFF when the timing is reset.

NOTE: *On 49-state engines, the marks are scribe lines. On California engines, the marks are half circles.*

1. Loosen the three pump retaining nuts. If the marks are not aligned, adjustment is necessary.

2. Loosen the three pump retaining nuts.

3. Align the mark on the injection pump with the mark on the front cover. Tighten the nuts to 30 ft. lbs.

NOTE: *Use a $^3/_4$ in. open end wrench on the nut at the front of the injection pump to aid in rotating the pump to align the marks.*

4. Adjust the throttle linkage if necessary.

VALVE LASH

All engines covered in this guide are equipped with hydraulic valve lifters. Engines so equipped operate with zero clearance in the valve train. Because of this the rocker arms are non-adjustable. The hydraulic lifters themselves do not require any adjustment as part of the normal tune-up, although they occasionally become noisy (especially on high mileage engines) and need to be replaced. In the event of cylinder head removal or any operation that re-

quires disturbing or removing the rocker arms, the rocker arms have to be adjusted. Please refer to Chapter 3. Hydraulic lifter service is also covered in Chapter 3.

FUEL SYSTEM

Adjustments

In most cases, the mixture screws have limiter caps, but in later years the mixture screws are concealed under staked-in plugs. Idle mixture is adjustable only during carburetor overhaul, and requires the addition of propane as an artificial mixture enricher. For these reasons, mixture adjustments are not covered here for affected models.

See the emission control label in the engine compartment for procedures and specifications not supplied here.

NOTE: *See Carburetor Identification in Section 5 for carburetor I.D. specifics.*

IDLE SPEED AND MIXTURE ADJUSTMENT

These procedures require the use of a tachometer. Tachometer hookup was explained earlier under Ignition Timing, Step 3. In some cases, the degree of accuracy required is greater than that available on a hand-held unit; a shop tachometer would be required to follow the instructions exactly. If the idle speed screws have plastic limiter caps, it is not recommended that they be removed unless a satisfactory idle cannot be obtained with them in place. If the caps are removed, exhaust emissions may go beyond the specified legal limits. This can be checked on an exhaust gas analyzer.

NOTE: *Most 4-bbl carburetors have an internal fuel passage restriction. Beyond a certain*

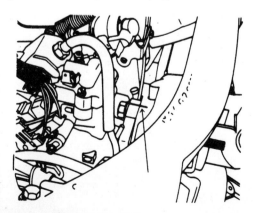

Diesel injection timing marks

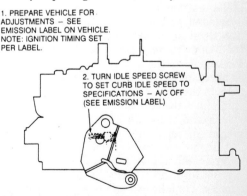

Idle speed adjustment points on the 4-bbl without a solenoid

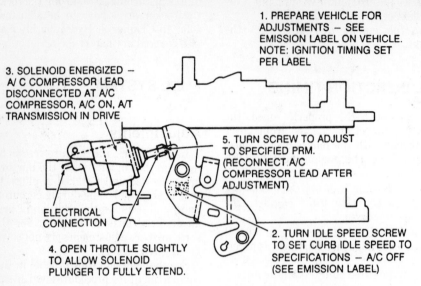

1. PREPARE VEHICLE FOR ADJUSTMENTS − SEE EMISSION LABEL ON VEHICLE. NOTE: IGNITION TIMING SET PER LABEL

3. SOLENOID ENERGIZED − A/ C COMPRESSOR LEAD DISCONNECTED AT A/C COMPRESSOR, A/C ON, A/T TRANSMISSION IN DRIVE

5. TURN SCREW TO ADJUST TO SPECIFIED PRM. (RECONNECT A/C COMPRESSOR LEAD AFTER ADJUSTMENT)

ELECTRICAL CONNECTION

4. OPEN THROTTLE SLIGHTLY TO ALLOW SOLENOID PLUNGER TO FULLY EXTEND.

2. TURN IDLE SPEED SCREW TO SET CURB IDLE SPEED TO SPECIFICATIONS − A/C OFF (SEE EMISSION LABEL)

Idle speed adjustment points on the 4-bbl with a solenoid

limited point, turning the idle mixture screws out has no further richening effect.

Idle speed and mixture are set with the engine at normal running temperature. The automatic transmission should be in Drive, except when specified otherwise. The air conditioner should be off for adjusting mixture and off unless otherwise specified in the text or specifications chart for setting idle speed.

CAUTION: *Block the wheels, set the parking brake, and don't stand in front of the truck.*

Idle Speed Adjustment

1. All adjustments should be made with the engine at normal operating temperature, air cleaner on, choke open, and air conditioning off, unless otherwise noted. Set the parking brake and block the rear wheels. Automatic transmissions should be set in Drive, manuals in Neutral, unless otherwise noted in the procedures or on the emission control label.

2. Refer to the underhood emission sticker and prepare the vehicle for adjustment as specified on the sticker. On models without a solenoid, turn the idle speed to obtain the idle speed listed in the Tune-Up chart. On models with a solenoid, turn the idle speed screw to obtain the idle speed listed in the Tune-Up chart. Disconnect the wire at the A/C compressor and turn the A/C On. Rev the engine momentarily to fully extend the solenoid plunger. Turn the solenoid screw to obtain the solenoid idle speed listed on the underhood emission sticker. Reconnect the A/C wire at the compressor.

Mixture Adjustments

1. The engine must be at normal operating temperature, choke open, parking brake applied, and the transmission in Park or Neutral. Block the rear wheels and do not stand in from of the truck when making adjustments.

2. Remove the air cleaner. Connect a tachometer and a vacuum gauge to the engine.

3. Turn the idle mixture screws in lightly until they seat, then back them out two turns. Be careful not to tighten the mixture screw against its seat, or damage may result.

4. Adjust the idle speed screw to obtain the engine rpm figure specified on the emission control label.

5. Adjust the idle mixture screws equally to obtain the highest engine speed.

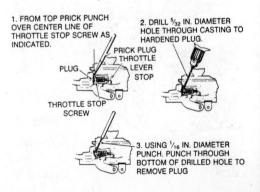

1. FROM TOP PRICK PUNCH OVER CENTER LINE OF THROTTLE STOP SCREW AS INDICATED.

2. DRILL 5/32 IN. DIAMETER HOLE THROUGH CASTING TO HARDENED PLUG.

PRICK PLUG THROTTLE LEVER STOP

PLUG

THROTTLE STOP SCREW

3. USING 1/16 IN. DIAMETER PUNCH. PUNCH THROUGH BOTTOM OF DRILLED HOLE TO REMOVE PLUG

Removing the throttle stop screw form the throttle body

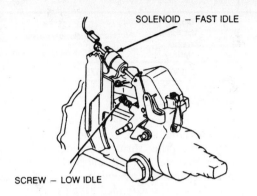

Idle speed adjustment points on the diesel injection pump

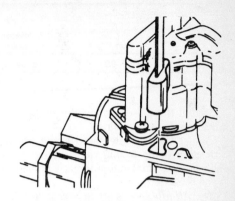

Using GM tool J-33047 to plug the idle air passage of the throttle body

6. Repeat Steps 4 and 5 until the best idle is obtained.

7. Shut off the engine, remove the tachometer and vacuum gauge, and install the air cleaner.

Throttle Body Injection (TBI)

The throttle body injected vehicles are controlled by a computer which supplies the correct amount of fuel during all engine operating conditions; no adjustment is necessary.

Diesel Fuel Injection

IDLE SPEED ADJUSTMENT

NOTE: *A special tachometer suitable for diesel engines must be used. A gasoline engine type tach will not work with the diesel engine.*

1. Set the parking brake and block the drive wheels.

2. Run the engine up to normal operating temperature. The air cleaner must be mounted and all accessories turned off.

GASOLINE ENGINE TUNE-UP SPECIFICATIONS

Years	Engine	Spark Plugs Type	Gap (in.)	Ignition Timing (deg.) Man. Trans.	Auto. Trans.	Fuel Pump Pressure (psi)	Idle Speed Man. Trans.	Auto. Trans.
1987	6–4.3L	R43TS	0.045	①	①	4.5–6.0	Not Adjustable	
	8–5.0L	R43TS	0.045	①	①	7.5–9.0	Not Adjustable	
	8–5.7L	R44T	0.045	①	①	7.5–9.0	①	①
1988	6–4.3L	R43TS	0.045	①	①	4.5–6.0	Not Adjustable	
	8–5.0L	R43TS	0.045	①	①	7.5–9.0	Not Adjustable	
	8–5.7L	R44T	0.045	①	①	7.5–9.0	①	①
	8–7.4L	CR43TS	0.045	①	①	7.5–9.0	Not Adjustable	
1989	6–4.3L	CR43TS	0.045	①	①	4.5–6.0	Not Adjustable	
	8–5.0L	CR43TS	0.045	①	①	7.5–9.0	Not Adjustable	
	8–5.7L	CR43TS	0.045	①	①	7.5–9.0	①	①
	8–7.4L	CR43TS	0.045	①	①	7.5–9.0	Not Adjustable	
1990	6–4.3L	CR43TS	0.045	①	①	4.5–6.0	Not Adjustable	
	8–5.0L	CR43TS	0.045	①	①	7.5–9.0	Not Adjustable	
	8–5.7L	CR43TS	0.045	①	①	7.5–9.0	①	①
	8–7.4L	CR43TS	0.045	①	①	7.5–9.0	Not Adjustable	

① See underhood sticker

DIESEL ENGINE TUNE-UP SPECIFICATIONS

Engine	Years	Injection Timing	Nozzle Opening Pressure (psi)	Idle Speed (rpm)	
				MT	AT
8–6.2L	1987–90	scribe mark	1,500	575	550

3. Install the diesel tachometer as per the manufacturer's instructions.

4. Adjust the low idle speed screw on the fuel injection pump to 650 rpm in Neutral or Park for both manual and automatic transmissions.

NOTE: *All idle speeds are to be set within 25 rpm of the specified values.*

5. Adjust the fast idle speed as follows:

a. Remove the connector from the fast idle solenoid. Use an insulated jumper wire from the battery positive terminal to the solenoid terminal to energize the solenoid.

b. Open the throttle momentarily to ensure that the fast idle solenoid plunger is energized and fully extended.

c. Adjust the extended plunger by turning the hex-head screw to an engine sped of 800 rpm in Neutral.

d. Remove the jumper wire and reinstall the connector to the fast idle solenoid.

6. Disconnect and remove the tachometer.

ENGINE ELECTRICAL

Understanding the Engine Electrical System

The engine electrical system can be broken down into three separate and distinct systems:

1. The starting system.
2. The charging system.
3. The ignition system.

BATTERY AND STARTING SYSTEM

Basic Operating Principles

The battery is the first link in the chain of mechanisms which work together to provide cranking of the automobile engine. In most modern vans, the battery is a lead/acid electrochemical device consisting of six 2v subsections connected in series so the unit is capable of producing approximately 12v of electrical pressure. Each subsection, or cell, consists of a series of positive and negative plates held a short distance apart in a solution of sulfuric acid and water. The two types of plates are of dissimilar metals. This causes a chemical reaction to be set up, and it is this reaction which produces current flow from the battery when its positive and negative terminals are connected to an electrical appliance such as a lamp or motor. The continued transfer of electrons would eventually convert the sulfuric acid in the electrolyte to water, and make the two plates identical in chemical composition. As electrical energy is removed from the battery, its voltage output tends to drop. Thus, measuring battery voltage and battery electrolyte composition are two ways of checking the ability of the unit to supply power. During the starting of the engine, electrical energy is removed from the battery. However, if the charging circuit is in good condition and the operating conditions are normal, the power removed from the battery will be replaced by the generator (or alternator) which will force electrons back through the battery, reversing the normal flow, and restoring the battery to its original chemical state.

The battery and starting motor are linked by very heavy electrical cables designed to minimize resistance to the flow of current. Generally, the major power supply cable that leaves the battery goes directly to the starter, while other electrical system needs are supplied by a smaller cable. During starter operation, power flows from the battery to the starter and is grounded through the van's frame and the battery's negative ground strap.

The starting motor is a specially designed, direct current electric motor capable of producing a very great amount of power for its size. One thing that allows the motor to produce a great deal of power is its tremendous rotating speed. It drives the engine through a tiny pinion gear (attached to the starter's armature), which drives the very large flywheel ring gear at a greatly reduced speed. Another factor allowing it to produce so much power is that only intermittent operation is required of it. This, little allowance for air circulation is required, and the windings can be built into a very small space.

The starter solenoid is a magnetic device which employs the small current supplied by the starting switch circuit of the ignition switch. This magnetic action moves a plunger which mechanically engages the starter and electrically closes the heavy switch which connects it to the battery. The starting switch circuit consists of the starting switch contained within the ignition switch, a transmission neutral safety switch or clutch pedal switch, and the wiring necessary to connect these in series with the starter solenoid or relay.

A pinion, which is a small gear, is mounted to a one-way drive clutch. This clutch is splined to the starter armature shaft. When the ignition switch is moved to the **start** position, the solenoid plunger slides the pinion toward the flywheel ring gear via a collar and spring. If the teeth on the pinion and flywheel match properly, the pinion will engage the flywheel immediately. If the gear teeth butt one another, the spring will be compressed and will force the gears to mesh as soon as the starter turns far enough to allow them to do so. As the solenoid plunger reaches the end of its travel, it closes the contacts that connect the battery and starter and then the engine is cranked.

As soon as the engine starts, the flywheel ring gear begins turning fast enough to drive the pinion at an extremely high rate of speed. At this point, the one-way clutch begins allowing the pinion to spin faster than the starter shaft so that the starter will not operate at excessive speed. When the ignition switch is released from the starter position, the solenoid is de-energized, and a spring contained within the solenoid assembly pulls the gear out of mesh and interrupts the current flow to the starter.

Some starter employ a separate relay, mounted away from the starter, to switch the motor and solenoid current on and off. The relay thus replaces the solenoid electrical switch, buy does not eliminate the need for a solenoid mounted on the starter used to mechanically engage the starter drive gears. The relay is used to reduce the amount of current the starting switch must carry.

THE CHARGING SYSTEM

Basic Operating Principles

The automobile charging system provides electrical power for operation of the vehicle's ignition and starting systems and all the electrical accessories. The battery services as an electrical surge or storage tank, storing (in chemical form) the energy originally produced by the engine driven generator. The system also provides a means of regulating generator output to protect the battery from being overcharged and to avoid excessive voltage to the accessories.

The storage battery is a chemical device incorporating parallel lead plates in a tank containing a sulfuric acid/water solution. Adjacent plates are slightly dissimilar, and the chemical reaction of the two dissimilar plates produces electrical energy when the battery is connected to a load such as the starter motor. The chemical reaction is reversible, so that when the generator is producing a voltage (electrical pressure) greater than that produced by the battery, electricity is forced into the battery, and the battery is returned to its fully charged state.

The vehicle's generator is driven mechanically, through V-belts, by the engine crankshaft. It consists of two coils of fine wire, one stationary (the stator), and one movable (the rotor). The rotor may also be known as the armature, and consists of fine wire wrapped around an iron core which is mounted on a shaft. The electricity which flows through the two coils of wire (provided initially by the battery in some cases) creates an intense magnetic field around both rotor and stator, and the interaction between the two fields creates voltage, allowing the generator to power the accessories and charge the battery.

There are two types of generators: the earlier is the direct current (DC) type. The current produced by the DC generator is generated in the armature and carried off the spinning armature by stationary brushes contacting the commutator. The commutator is a series of smooth metal contact plates on the end of the armature. The commutator is a series of smooth metal contact plates on the end of the armature. The commutator plates, which are separated from one another by a very short gap, are connected to the armature circuits so that current will flow in one directions only in the wires carrying the generator output. The generator stator consists of two stationary coils of wire which draw some of the output current of the generator to form a powerful magnetic field and create the interaction of fields which generates the voltage. The generator field is wired in series with the regulator.

Newer automobiles use alternating current generators or alternators, because they are more efficient, can be rotated at higher speeds, and have fewer brush problems. In an alternator, the field rotates while all the current produced passes only through the stator winding. The brushes bear against continuous slip rings rather than a commutator. This causes the current produced to periodically reverse the direction of its flow. Diodes (electrical one-way switches) block the flow of current from traveling in the wrong direction. A series of diodes is wired together to permit the alternating flow of the stator to be converted to a pulsating, but unidirectional flow at the alternator output. The alternator's field is wired in series with the voltage regulator.

The regulator consists of several circuits. Each circuit has a core, or magnetic coil of wire, which operates a switch. Each switch is connected to ground through one or more resistors. The coil of wire responds directly to system voltage. When the voltage reaches the required level, the magnetic field created by the winding of wire closes the switch and inserts a resistance into the generator field circuit, thus reducing the output. The contacts of the switch cycle open and close many times each second to precisely control voltage.

While alternators are self-limiting as far as maximum current is concerned, DC generators employ a current regulating circuit which responds directly to the total amount of current flowing through the generator circuit rather than to the output voltage. The current regulator is similar to the voltage regulator except that all system current must flow through the energizing coil on its way to the various accessories.

HIGH ENERGY IGNITION (HEI) SYSTEM

The HEI system operates in basically the same manner as the conventional ignition system, with the exception of the type of switching device used. A toothed iron timer core is mounted on the distributor shaft which rotates inside of an electronic pole piece. The pole piece has internal teeth (corresponding to those on the timer core) which contains a permanent magnet and pick-up coil (not to be confused with the ignition coil). The pole piece senses the magnetic field of the timer core teeth and sends a signal to the ignition module which electronically controls the primary coil voltage. The ignition coil operates in basically the same manner as a conventional ignition coil (though the ignition coils DO NOT interchange).

NOTE: *The HEI systems uses a capacitor within the distributor which is primarily used for radio interference purposes.*

None of the electrical components used in the HEI systems are adjustable. If a component is found to be defective, it must be replaced.

Timing Light Use

Inductive pick-up timing lights are the best kind to use. Timing lights which connect between the spark plug and the spark plug wire occasionally give false readings.

Some engines incorporate a magnetic timing probe terminal (at the damper pulley) for use of special electronic timing equipment. Refer to the manufacturer's instructions when using this equipment.

Spark Plug Wires

The plug wires are of a different construction than conventional wires. When replacing them, make sure to use the correct wires, since conventional wires won't carry the higher voltage. Also, handle them carefully to avoid cracking or splitting them and never pierce them.

Tachometer Use

Not all tachometers will operate or indicate correctly. While some tachometers may give a reading, this does not necessarily mean the reading is correct. In addition, some tachometers connect differently than others. If you can't figure out whether or not your tachometer will work on your vehicle, check with the tachometer manufacturer.

System Testers

Instruments designed specifically for testing the HEI system are available from several tool manufacturers. Some of these will even test the module.

Ignition Coil

TESTING, REMOVAL AND INSTALLATION

1. Detach the wiring connector from the distributor cap.
2. Turn the four latches and remove the cap and coil assembly from the lower housing.
3. Connect an ohmmeter. Test 1.
4. Reading should be zero, or nearly zero. If not replace the coil.
5. Connect the ohmmeter both ways. Test 2. Use the high scale. Replace the coil only if both readings are infinite.
6. If the coil is good, go to step 13.
7. Remove the coil cover attaching screws and lift off the cover.
8. Remove the ignition coil attaching screws and lift the coil, with the leads, from the cap.
9. Remove the ignition coil arc seal.
10. Clean with a soft cloth and inspect the cap for defects. Replace if necessary.
11. Assemble the new coil and cover to the cap.
12. On all distributors, including distributors with a Hall Effect Switch identified in step 27, remove the rotor and pick-up coil leads from the module.
13. Connect the ohmmeter Test 1 and then Test 2. 14. If a vacuum unit is used, connect a vacuum source to the vacuum unit. Replace the vacuum unit if inoperative. Observe the ohmmeter throughout the vacuum range: flex the leads by hand without vacuum to check for intermittent opens.
15. Test 1 should read infinite at all times. Test 2 should read steady at one value within 500–1,500Ω range.

NOTE: *Ohmmeter may deflect if operating vacuum unit causes teeth to align. This is not a defect.*

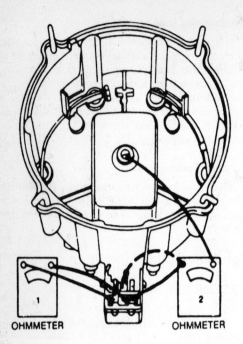

Testing the coil

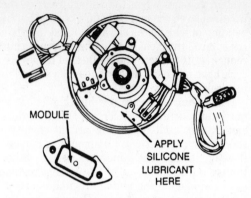

Module removal

16. If the pickup coil is defective go to step 17. If the coil is okay, go to step 22. 17. Mark the distributor shaft and gear so they can be reassembled in the same position.

18. Drive out the roll pin.

19. Remove the gear and pull the shaft assembly from the distributor.

20. Remove the three attaching screws and remove the magnetic shield.

21. Remove the retaining ring and remove the pickup coil, magnet and pole piece.

22. Remove the two module attaching screws, and the capacitor attaching screw. Lift the module, capacitor and harness assembly from the base.

23. Disconnect the wiring harness from the module.

24. Check the module with an approved module tester.

25. Install the module, wiring harness, and capacitor assembly. Use silicone lubricant on the housing under the module.

26. The procedures previously covered, Steps 1–25, also apply to distributors with Hall Effect Switches.

Ignition Module

REMOVAL AND INSTALLATION

1. Remove the distributor cap and rotor.

2. Remove the two module attaching screws, and capacitor attaching screw. Lift the module, capacitor and harness assembly from the base.

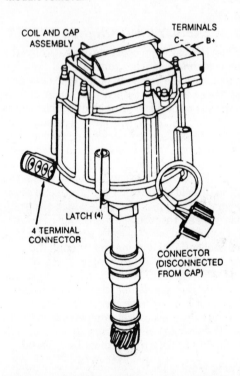

Coil-in-cap distributor used on carbureted V8 engines

3. Disconnect the wiring harness from the module.

4. Check the module with an approved module tester.

5. Install the module, wiring harness, and capacitor assembly. Use silicone lubricant on the housing under module.

Distributor

REMOVAL AND INSTALLATION

1. Disconnect the wiring harness connectors at the side of the distributor cap.

2. Remove the distributor cap and set it aside.

3. Disconnect the vacuum advance line.

4. Scribe a mark on the engine in line with the rotor and note the approximate position of the vacuum advance unit in relation to the engine.

5. Remove the distributor holddown clamp and nut.

6. Lift the distributor from the engine.

To install the distributor with the crankshaft not turned:

7. Reinsert the distributor into its opening, aligning the previously made marks on the housing and the engine block.

8. The rotor may have to be turned either way a slight amount before inserting the distributor to align the rotor-to-housing marks.

9. Install the retaining clamp and bolt. Install the distributor cap, primary wire, and the vacuum hose.

10. Start the engine and check the ignition timing.

To install the distributor with the crankshaft turned, or to install a new distributor:

11. Turn the engine to bring the No. 1 piston to the top of its compression stroke. This may be determined by covering the No. 1 spark plug hole with your thumb and slowly turning the engine over. When the timing mark on the crankshaft pulley aligns with the 0 on the timing scale and your thumb is pushed out by compression, No. 1 piston is at top dead center (TDC). If you don't feel compression, you've No. 6 at TDC.

12. Install the distributor to the engine block so that the vacuum advance unit points in the correct direction.

13. Turn the rotor so that it will point to the No. 1 terminal in the cap. Some distributors have a punch mark on the gear facing the same way as the rotor tip.

14. Install the distributor into the engine block. It may be necessary to turn the rotor a little in either direction in order to engage the gears.

15. Tap the starter switch a few times to ensure that the oil pump shaft is mated to the distributor shaft.

16. Bring the engine to No. 1 TDC again and check to see that the rotor is indeed pointing toward the No. 1 terminal of the cap.

17. After correct positioning is assured, turn the distributor housing so that the points are just opening. Tighten the retaining clamp.

18. Install the cap and primary wire. Check the ignition timing. Install the vacuum hose.

Alternator

The alternator charging system is a negative (–) ground system which consists of an alternator, a regulator, a charge indicator, a storage battery and wiring connecting the components, and fuse link wire.

The alternator is belt-driven from the engine. Energy is supplied from the alternator/regulator system to the rotating field through two brushes to two slip-rings. The slip-rings are mounted on the rotor shaft and are connected to the field coil. This energy supplied to the rotating field from the battery is called excitation current and is used to initially energize the field to begin the generation of electricity. Once the alternator starts to generate electricity, the excitation current comes from its own output rather than the battery.

The alternator produces power in the form of alternating current. The alternating current is rectified by 6 diodes into direct current. The direct current is used to charge the battery and power the rest of the electrical system.

When the ignition key is turned on, current flows from the battery, through the charging system indicator light on the instrument panel, to the voltage regulator, and to the alternator. Since the alternator is not producing any current, the alternator warning light comes on. When the engine is started, the alternator begins to produce current and turns the alternator light off. As the alternator turns and produces current, the current is divided in two ways: part to the battery to charge the battery and power the electrical components of the vehicle, and part is returned to the alternator to enable it to increase its output. In this situation, the alternator is receiving current from the battery and from itself. A voltage regulator is wired into the current supply to the alternator to prevent it from receiving too much current which would cause it to put out too much current. Conversely, if the voltage regulator does not allow the alternator to receive enough current, the battery will not be fully charged and will eventually go dead.

The battery is connected to the alternator at all times, whether the ignition key is turned on or not. If the battery were shorted to ground, the alternator would also be shorted. This would damage the alternator. To prevent this, a fuse link is installed in the wiring between the battery and the alternator. If the battery is shorted, the fuse link is melted, protecting the alternator.

ALTERNATOR PRECAUTIONS

Some precautions should be taken when working on this, or any other, AC charging system.

1. Never switch battery polarity.

2. When installing a battery, always connect the grounded terminal first.

3. Never disconnect the battery while the engine is running.

4. If the molded connector is disconnected from the alternator, never ground the hot wire.

5. Never run the alternator with the main output cable disconnected.

6. Never electric weld around the truck without disconnecting the alternator.

7. Never apply any voltage in excess of battery voltage while testing.

8. Never jump a battery for starting purposes with more than 12v.

CHARGING SYSTEM TROUBLESHOOTING

There are many possible ways in which the charging system can malfunction. Often the source of a problem is difficult to diagnose, requiring special equipment and a good deal of experience. This is usually not the case, however, where the charging system fails completely and causes the dash board warning light to come on or the battery to become dead. To troubleshoot a complete system failure only two pieces of equipment are needed: a test light, to determine that current is reaching a certain point; and a current indicator (ammeter), to determine the direction of the current flow and its measurement in amps.

This test works under three assumptions:

1. The battery is known to be good and fully charged.

2. The alternator belt is in good condition and adjusted to the proper tension.

3. All connections in the system are clean and tight.

NOTE: *In order for the current indicator to give a valid reading, the van must be equipped with battery cables which are of the same gauge size and quality as original equipment battery cables.*

1. Turn off all electrical components on the van.

2. Make sure the doors of the van are closed.

3. If the van is equipped with a clock, disconnect the clock by removing the lead wire from the rear of the clock.

4. Disconnect the positive battery cable from the battery and connect the ground wire on a test light to the disconnected positive battery cable.

5. Touch the probe end of the test light to the positive battery post. The test light should not light. If the test light does light, there is a short or open circuit on the van.

6. Disconnect the voltage regulator wiring

harness connector at the voltage regulator.

7. Turn on the ignition key.

8. Connect the wire on a test light to a good ground (engine bolt).

9. Touch the probe end of a test light to the ignition wire connector into the voltage regulator wiring connector. This wire corresponds to the **I** terminal on the regulator. If the test light goes on, the charging system warning light circuit is complete. If the test light does not come on and the warning light on the instrument panel is on, either the resistor wire, which is parallel with the warning light, or the wiring to the voltage regulator, is defective. If the test light does not come on and the warning light is not on, either the bulb is defective or the power supply wire form the battery through the ignition switch to the bulb has an open circuit. Connect the wiring harness to the regulator.

10. Examine the fuse link wire in the wiring harness from the starter relay to the alternator. If the insulation on the wire is cracked or split, the fuse link may be melted.

11. Connect a test light to the fuse link by attaching the ground wire on the test light to an engine bolt and touching the probe end of the light to the bottom of the fuse link wire where it splices into the alternator output wire. If the bulb in the test light does not light, the fuse link is melted.

12. Start the engine and place a current indicator on the positive battery cable.

13. Turn off all electrical accessories and make sure the doors are closed. If the charging system is working properly, the gauge will show a draw of less than 5 amps. If the system is not working properly, the gauge will show a draw of more than 5 amps. A charge moves the needle toward the battery, a draw moves the needle away from the battery. Turn the engine off.

14. Disconnect the wiring harness from the voltage regulator at the regulator at the regulator connector.

15. Connect a male spade terminal (solderless connector) to each end of a jumper wire.

16. Insert one end of the wire into the wiring harness connector which corresponds to the **A** terminal on the regulator.

17. Insert the other end of the wire into the wiring harness connector which corresponds to the **F** terminal on the regulator.

18. Position the connector with the jumper wire installed so that it cannot contact any metal surface under the hood.

19. Position a current indicator gauge on the positive battery cable. Have an assistant start the engine. Observe the reading on the current indicator. Have your assistant slowly raise the speed of the engine to about 2,000 rpm or until

the current indicator needle stops moving, whichever comes first. Do not run the engine for more than a short period of time in this condition. If the wiring harness connector or jumper wire becomes excessively hot during this test, turn off the engine and check for a grounded wire in the regulator wiring harness. If the current indicator shows a charge of about three amps less than the output of the alternator, the alternator is working properly. If the previous tests showed a draw, the voltage regulator is defective. If the gauge does not show the proper charging rate, the alternator is defective.

Three basic alternators are used: the 5.5 in. (140mm) Series 1D Delcotron, the 6.2 in. (158mm) Series 150 Delcotron and the integral regulator 10 SI Delcotron.

PRELIMINARY CHARGING SYSTEM TESTS

1. If you suspect a defect in your charging system, first perform these general checks before going on to more specific tests.

2. Check the condition of the alternator belt and tighten it if necessary.

3. Clean the battery cable connections at the battery. Make sure the connections between the battery wires and the battery clamps are good. Reconnect the negative terminal only and proceed to the next step.

4. With the key off, insert a test light between the positive terminal on the battery and the disconnected positive battery terminal clamp. If the test light comes on, there is a short in the electrical system of the van. The short must be repaired before proceeding. If the light does not come on, proceed to the next step.

NOTE: *If the van is equipped with an electric shock, the clock must be disconnected.*

5. Check the charging system wiring for any obvious breaks or shorts.

6. Check the battery to make sure it is fully charged and in good condition.

CHARGING SYSTEM OPERATIONAL TEST

NOTE: *You will need a current indicator to perform this test. If the current indicator is to give an accurate reading, the battery cables must be the same gauge and length as the original equipment.*

1. With the engine running and all electrical systems turned off, place a current indicator over the positive battery cable.

2. If a charge of roughly five amps is recorded, the charging system is working. If a draw of about five amps is recorded, the system is not working. The needle moves toward the

battery when a charge condition is indicated, and away from the battery when a draw condition is indicated.

3. If a draw is indicated, proceed with further testing. If an excessive charge (10–15 amps) is indicated, the regulator may be at fault.

OUTPUT TEST

1. You will need an ammeter for this test.

2. Disconnect the battery ground cable.

3. Disconnect the wire from the battery terminal on the alternator.

4. Connect the ammeter negative lead to the battery terminal wire removed in step three, and connect the ammeter positive lead to the battery terminal on the alternator.

5. Reconnect the battery ground cable and turn on all electrical accessories. If the battery is fully charged, disconnect the coil wire and bump the starter a few times to partially discharge it.

6. Start the engine and run it until you

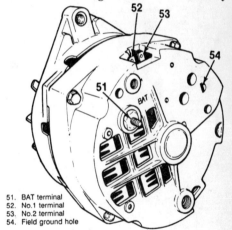

51. BAT terminal
52. No.1 terminal
53. No.2 terminal
54. Field ground hole

17-SI alternator

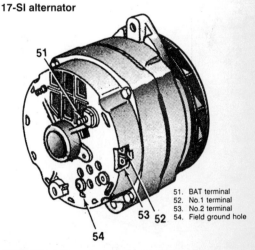

51. BAT terminal
52. No.1 terminal
53. No.2 terminal
54. Field ground hole

12-SI alternator

obtain a maximum current reading on the ammeter.

7. If the current is not within ten amps of the rated output of the alternator, the alternator is working properly. If the current is not within ten amps, insert a screwdriver in the test hole in the end frame of the alternator and ground the tab in the test hole against the side of the hole.

8. If the current is now within ten amps of

the rated output, remove the alternator and have the voltage regulator replaced. If it is still below ten amps of rated output, have the alternator repaired.

REMOVAL AND INSTALLATION

1. Disconnect the battery ground cable to prevent diode damage.

2. Disconnect and tag all wiring to the alternator.

3. Remove the alternator brace bolt.

4. Remove the drive belt.

5. Support the alternator and remove the mounting bolts. Remove the alternator.

6. Install the unit using the reverse procedure of removal. Adjust the belt to have $1/2$ in. (12.7mm) depression under thumb pressure on its longest run.

Regulator

REMOVAL AND INSTALLATION

The regulator on these models is an integral part of the alternator. Alternator disassembly is required to replace it.

Battery

REMOVAL AND INSTALLATION

1. Disconnect the negative (ground) cable terminal and then the positive cable terminal. Special pullers are available to remove clamp type battery terminals.

NOTE: *To avoid sparks, always disconnect the battery ground cable first, and connect it last.*

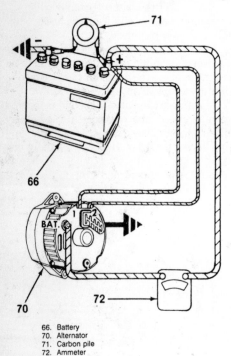

66. Battery
70. Alternator
71. Carbon pile
72. Ammeter

Connectors for the alternator output test

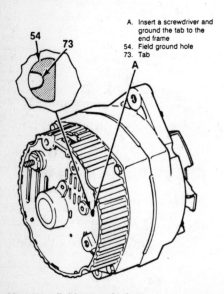

A. Insert a screwdriver and ground the tab to the end frame
54. Field ground hole
73. Tab

Alternator field ground tab

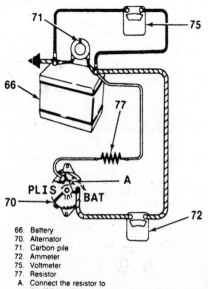

66. Battery
70. Alternator
71. Carbon pile
72. Ammeter
75. Voltmeter
77. Resistor
A. Connect the resistor to the "L" terminal

Connections for a bench text

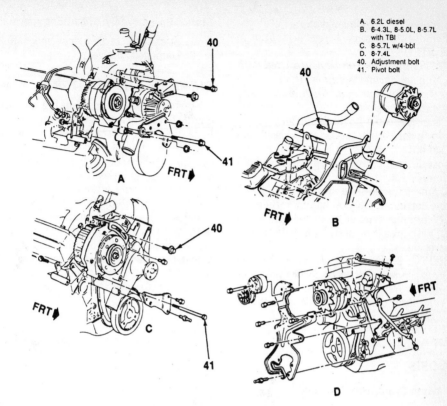

A. 6.2L diesel
B. 6-4.3L, 8-5.0L, 8-5.7L
   with TBI
C. 8-5.7L w/4-bbl
D. 8-7.4L
40. Adjustment bolt
41. Pivot bolt

Alternator mounting positions

Troubleshooting Basic Charging System Problems

Problem	Cause	Solution
Noisy alternator	• Loose mountings • Loose drive pulley • Worn bearings • Brush noise • Internal circuits shorted (High pitched whine)	• Tighten mounting bolts • Tighten pulley • Replace alternator • Replace alternator • Replace alternator
Squeal when starting engine or accelerating	• Glazed or loose belt	• Replace or adjust belt
Indicator light remains on or ammeter indicates discharge (engine running)	• Broken fan belt • Broken or disconnected wires • Internal alternator problems • Defective voltage regulator	• Install belt • Repair or connect wiring • Replace alternator • Replace voltage regulator
Car light bulbs continually burn out—battery needs water continually	• Alternator/regulator overcharging	• Replace voltage regulator/alternator
Car lights flare on acceleration	• Battery low • Internal alternator/regulator problems	• Charge or replace battery • Replace alternator/regulator
Low voltage output (alternator light flickers continually or ammeter needle wanders)	• Loose or worn belt • Dirty or corroded connections • Internal alternator/regulator problems	• Replace or adjust belt • Clean or replace connections • Replace alternator or regulator

2. Remove the holddown clamp.

3. Remove the battery, being careful not to spill the acid.

NOTE: *Spilled acid can be neutralized with a backing soda/water solution. If you somehow get acid in your eyes, flush with lots of water and visit a doctor.*

4. Clean the cable terminals of any corrosion, using a wire brush tool or an old jackknife inside and out.

5. Install the battery. Replace the hold down clamp.

6. Connect the positive and then the negative cable terminal. Do not hammer them in place. The terminals should be coated lightly (externally) with grease or petroleum jelly to prevent corrosion.

WARNING: *Make absolutely sure that the battery is connected properly before you start the engine! Reversed polarity can destroy your alternator and regulator in a matter of seconds!*

Starter

DIAGNOSIS

Starter Won't Crank The Engine

1. Dead battery.
2. Open starter circuit, such as:
   a. Broken or loose battery cables.
   b. Inoperative starter motor solenoid.
   c. Broken or loose wire from ignition switch to solenoid.
   d. Poor solenoid or starter ground.
   e. Bad ignition switch.
3. Defective starter internal circuit, such as:
   a. Dirty or burnt commutator.
   b. Stuck, worn or broken brushes.
   c. Open or shorted armature.
   d. Open or grounded fields.
4. Starter motor mechanical faults, such as:
   a. Jammed armature end bearings.
   b. Bad bearings, allowing armature to rub fields.
   c. Bent shaft.
   d. Broken starter housing.
   e. Bad starter drive mechanism.
   f. Bad starter drive or flywheel-driven gear.
5. Engine hard or impossible to crank, such as:
   a. Hydrostatic lock, water in combustion chamber.
   b. Crankshaft seizing in bearings.
   c. Piston or ring seizing.
   d. Bent or broken connecting rod.
   e. Seizing of connecting rod bearings.
   f. Flywheel jammed or broken.

Starter Spins Freely, Won't Engage

1. Sticking or broken drive mechanism.
2. Damaged ring gear.

SHIMMING THE STARTER

Starter noise during cranking and after the engine fires is often a result of too much or too little distance between the starter pinion gear and the flywheel. A high pitched whine during cranking (before the engine fires) can be caused by the pinion and flywheel being too far apart. Likewise, a whine after the engine starts (as the key is released) is often a result of the pinion-flywheel relationship being too close. In both cases flywheel damage can occur. Shims are available in 0.015 in. sizes to properly adjust the starter on its mount. You will also need a flywheel turning tool, available at most auto parts stores or from any auto tool store or salesperson.

If your van's starter emits the above noises, follow the shimming procedure below:

1. Disconnect the negative battery cable.

2. Remove the flywheel inspection cover on the bottom of the bell housing.

3. Using the flywheel turning tool, turn the flywheel and examine the flywheel teeth. If damage is evident, the flywheel should be replaced.

4. Insert a screwdriver into the small hole in the bottom of the starter and move the starter pinion and clutch assembly so the pinion and flywheel teeth mesh. If necessary, rotate the flywheel so that a pinion tooth is directly in the center of the two flywheel teeth and on the centerline of the two gears, as shown in the accompanying illustration.

5. Check the pinion-to-flywheel clearance

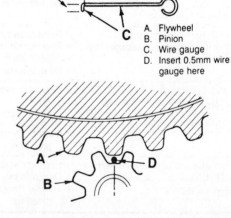

6.355-12.7mm (1/4"-1/2") |— 76.2mm (3")—| APPROXIMATE

A. Flywheel
B. Pinion
C. Wire gauge
D. Insert 0.5mm wire gauge here

Pinion-to-flywheel clearance

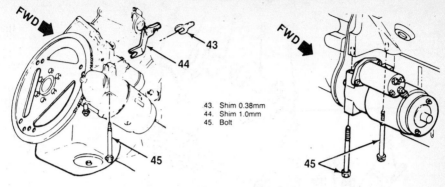

43. Shim 0.38mm
44. Shim 1.0mm
45. Bolt

Shimming the gasoline engine starter

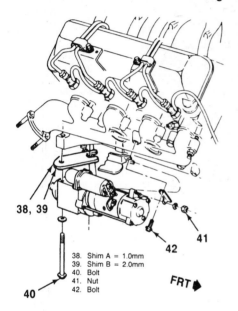

38, 39

38. Shim A = 1.0mm
39. Shim B = 2.0mm
40. Bolt
41. Nut
42. Bolt

40

41

42

FRT ▶

Shimming the diesel starter

by using a 0.020 in. wire gauge (a spark plug wire gauge may work here, or you can make your own). Make sure you center the pinion tooth between the flywheel teeth and the gauge—NOT in the corners, as you may get a false reading. If the clearance is under this minimum, shim the starter away from the flywheel by adding shim(s) one at a time to the starter mount. Check clearance after adding each shim.

6. If the clearance is a good deal over 0.020 in. (in the vicinity of 0.050 in. plus), shim the starter towards the flywheel. Broken or severely mangled flywheel teeth are also a good indicator that the clearance here is too great. Shimming the starter towards the flywheel is done by adding shims to the outboard starter mounting pad only. Check the clearance after each shim is added. A shim of 0.015 in. at this location will decrease the clearance about 0.010 in.

REMOVAL AND INSTALLATION

The following is a general procedure for all vans, and may vary slightly depending on model and series.

1. Disconnect the battery ground cable at the battery.

2. Raise and support the vehicle.

3. Disconnect and tag all wires at the solenoid terminal.

4. Reinstall all nuts as soon as they are removed, since the thread sizes are different.

5. Remove the front bracket from the starter and the two mounting bolts. On engines with a solenoid heat shield, remove the front bracket upper bolt and detach the bracket from the starter.

6. Remove the front bracket bolt or nut. Lower the starter front end first, and then remove the unit from the van.

7. Reverse the removal procedures to install the starter. Torque the two mounting bolts to 25–35 ft. lbs.

STARTER OVERHAUL

Solenoid Replacement

1. Remove the screw and washer from the field strap terminal.

2. Remove the two solenoid-to-housing retaining screws and the motor terminal bolt.

3. Remove the solenoid by twisting the unit 90 degrees.

4. To replace the solenoid, reverse the above procedure. Make sure the return spring is on the plunger, and rotate the solenoid unit into place on the starter.

Brush Replacement

1. Disconnect the field coil connectors from the starter motor solenoid terminal.

2. Remove the through bolts.

3. Remove the end frame and the field frame from the drive housing.

4. Disassemble the brush assembly from

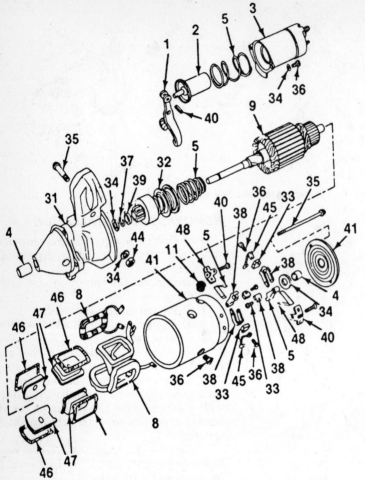

1.	Lever
2.	Plunger
3.	Solenoid
4.	Bushing
5.	Spring
8.	Coil
9.	Armature
11.	Grommet
31.	Housing
32.	Drive
33.	Brushes
34.	Washers
35.	Bolt
36.	Screw
37.	Ring
38.	Holder
39.	Collar
40.	Pin
41.	Frame
44.	Nut
45.	Lead
46.	Insulator
47.	Shoe
48.	Plate

Gasoline engine starter

the field frame by releasing the spring and removing the supporting pin. Pull the brushes and the brush holders out and disconnect the wiring.

5. Install the new brushes into the holders.

6. Assemble the brush holder using the spring and position the unit on the supporting pin.

7. Install the unit in the starter motor and attach the wiring.

8. Position the field frame over the armature.

9. Install the through bolts.

10. Connect the field coil connectors to the solenoid.

Starter Drive Replacement

1. Disconnect the field coil straps from the solenoid.

2. Remove the through-bolts (usually 2), and separate the commutator end frame, field frame assembly, drive housing, and armature assembly from each other.

NOTE: *On the diesel starters, remove the insulator from the end frame. The armature on the diesel starter remains in the drive end frame.*

3. On diesel starters, remove the shift lever pivot bolt. On the diesel 25 MT starter only, remove the center bearing screws and remove the drive gear housing from the armature shaft. The shift lever and plunger assembly will now fall away from the starter clutch.

4. Slide the two-piece thrust collar off the end of the armature shaft.

5. Slide a $5/8$in. deep socket, piece of pipe or an old pinion onto the shaft so that the end of the pipe, socket, or pinion butts up against the edge of the pinion retainer.

6. Place the lower end of the armature securely on a soft surface, such as a wooden block or thick piece of foam rubber. Tap the end of

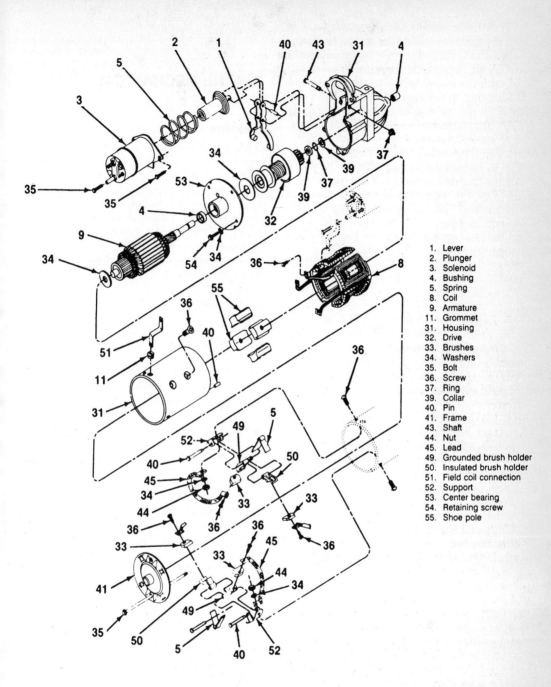

1. Lever
2. Plunger
3. Solenoid
4. Bushing
5. Spring
8. Coil
9. Armature
11. Grommet
31. Housing
32. Drive
33. Brushes
34. Washers
35. Bolt
36. Screw
37. Ring
39. Collar
40. Pin
41. Frame
43. Shaft
44. Nut
45. Lead
49. Grounded brush holder
50. Insulated brush holder
51. Field coil connection
52. Support
53. Center bearing
54. Retaining screw
55. Shoe pole

Diesel engine starter

the socket, pipe or pinion, driving the retainer towards the armature end of the snapring.

7. Remove the snapring from the groove in the armature shaft with a pair of pliers. If the snapring is distorted, replace it with a new one during reassembly. Slide the retainer and starter drive from the shaft; on diesel starters, remove the fiber washer and the center bearing from the armature shaft. On gasoline engine

starters, the shift lever and plunger may be disassembled at this time (if necessary) by removing the roll pin.

8. To reassemble, lubricate the drive end of the armature shaft with silicone lubricant. On diesel starters, install the center bearing with the bearing toward the armature winding, then install the fiber washer on the armature shaft.

9. Slide the starter drive onto the armature

shaft with the pinion facing outward (away from the armature). Slide the retainer onto the shaft with the cupped surface facing outward.

10. Again support the armature on a soft surface, with the pinion on the upper end. Center the snapring on the top of the shaft (use a new ring if the old one was misshapen or damaged). Gently place a block of wood on top of the snapring so as not to move it from a centered position. Tap the wooden block with a hammer in order to force the snapring around the shaft. Slide the ring down into the snap groove.

11. Lay the armature down flat on your work surface. Slide the retainer close up onto the shaft and position it and the thrust collar next to the snapring. Using two pairs of pliers on opposite ends of the shaft, squeeze the thrust collar and the retainer together until the snapring is forced into the retainer.

12. Lube the drive housing bushing with a silicone lubricant.

13. Engage the shift lever yoke with the clutch. Position the front of the armature shaft into the bushing, then slide the complete drive assembly into the drive gear housing.

NOTE: *On non-diesel starters the shift lever may be installed in the drive gear housing first.*

14. On the 25 MT diesel starter only, install the center bearing screws and the shift lever pivot bolt, and tighten securely.

15. Apply a sealing compound approved for this application onto the drive housing, to the solenoid flange where the field frame contacts it. Position the field frame around the armature shaft and against the drive housing. Work carefully and slowly to prevent damaging the starter brushes.

16. Lubricate the bushing in the commutator end frame with a silicone lubricant, place the leather washer onto the armature shaft, and then slide the commutator end frame over the shaft and into position against the field frame. On diesel starters, install the insulator and then the end frame onto the shaft. Line up the bolt holes, then install and tighten the through-bolts (make sure they pass through the bolt holes in the insulator).

17. Connect the field coil straps to the **motor** terminal of the solenoid.

NOTE: *If replacement of the starter drive fails to cure improper engagements of the starter pinion to the flywheel, there may be defective parts in the solenoid and/or shift lever. The best procedure is to take the assembly to a shop where a pinion clearance check can be made by energizing the solenoid on a test bench. If the pinion clearance check can be made by energizing the solenoid on a test bench. If the pinion clearance is incorrect, dis-* assemble the solenoid and shift lever, inspect, and replace the worn parts.

ENGINE MECHANICAL

Design

All Chevrolet and GMC van engines are water cooled, overhead valve powerplants, using cast iron cylinder blocks and heads.

The 4.3 Liter engines are 90° V6 type, overhead valve, water cooled, with cast iron block and heads. The crankshaft is supported by four precision insert main bearings, with crankshaft thrust taken at the number 4 (rear) bearing. The camshaft is supported by four plain bearings and is chain driven. Motion from the camshaft is transmitted to the valves by hydraulic lifters, pushrods, and ball type rocker arms. The valve guides are integral in the cylinder head. The connecting rods are forged steel, with precision insert type crankpin bearings. The piston pins are a press fit in the connecting rods. The pistons are cast aluminum alloy and the piston pins are a floating fit in the piston.

The small block family of V8 engines, 5.0L and 5.7L cu. in., are derived from the innovative design of the original 1955 265 cu. in. Chevrolet V8. This engine introduced the ball mounted rocker arm design, replacing the once standard shaft mounted rocker arms. There is extensive interchangeability of components among these engines, extending to the several other small block displacement sizes available.

The 8-7.4L engine is known as the Mark IV engine or big block. This engine features unusual cylinder heads, in that the intake and exhaust valves are canted at the angle at which their respective port enters the cylinder. The big block cylinder heads use ball joint rockers similar to those on the small block engines.

The 8-6.2L cu. in. (6.2L) diesel was introduced for the vans in 1983. This engine is built by GM's Detroit Diesel Division. Designed "from the block up" as a diesel, it utilizes robust features such as four-bolt main bearing caps.

Engine Overhaul Tips

Most engine overhaul procedures are fairly standard. In addition to specific parts replacement procedures and complete specifications for your individual engine, this section also is a guide to accept rebuilding procedures. Examples of standard rebuilding practice are shown and should be used along with specific details concerning your particular engine.

Competent and accurate machine shop serv-

Troubleshooting Basic Starting System Problems

Problem	Cause	Solution
Starter motor rotates engine slowly	• Battery charge low or battery defective	• Charge or replace battery
	• Defective circuit between battery and starter motor	• Clean and tighten, or replace cables
	• Low load current	• Bench-test starter motor. Inspect for worn brushes and weak brush springs.
	• High load current	• Bench-test starter motor. Check engine for friction, drag or coolant in cylinders. Check ring gear-to-pinion gear clearance.
Starter motor will not rotate engine	• Battery charge low or battery defective	• Charge or replace battery
	• Faulty solenoid	• Check solenoid ground. Repair or replace as necessary.
	• Damage drive pinion gear or ring gear	• Replace damaged gear(s)
	• Starter motor engagement weak	• Bench-test starter motor
	• Starter motor rotates slowly with high load current	• Inspect drive yoke pull-down and point gap, check for worn end bushings, check ring gear clearance
	• Engine seized	• Repair engine
Starter motor drive will not engage (solenoid known to be good)	• Defective contact point assembly	• Repair or replace contact point assembly
	• Inadequate contact point assembly ground	• Repair connection at ground screw
	• Defective hold-in coil	• Replace field winding assembly
Starter motor drive will not disengage	• Starter motor loose on flywheel housing	• Tighten mounting bolts
	• Worn drive end busing	• Replace bushing
	• Damaged ring gear teeth	• Replace ring gear or driveplate
	• Drive yoke return spring broken or missing	• Replace spring
Starter motor drive disengages prematurely	• Weak drive assembly thrust spring	• Replace drive mechanism
	• Hold-in coil defective	• Replace field winding assembly
Low load current	• Worn brushes	• Replace brushes
	• Weak brush springs	• Replace springs

ices will ensure maximum performance, reliability and engine life.

In most instances it is more profitable for the do-it-yourself mechanic to remove, clean and inspect the component, buy the necessary parts and deliver these to a shop for actual machine work.

On the other hand, much of the rebuilding work (crankshaft, block, bearings, piston rods, and other components) is well within the scope of the do-it-yourself mechanic.

TOOLS

The tools required for an engine overhaul or parts replacement will depend on the depth of your involvement. With a few exceptions, they will be the tools found in a mechanic's tool kit (see Chapter 1). More in-depth work will require any or all of the following:
   • a dial indicator (reading in thousandths)
mounted on a universal base
   • micrometers and telescope gauges
   • jaw and screw type pullers
   • scraper
   • valve spring compressor
   • ring groove cleaner
   • piston ring expander and compressor
   • ridge reamer
   • cylinder hone or glaze breaker
   • Plastigage®
   • engine stand

Use of most of these tools is illustrated in this section. Many can be rented for a one time use from a local parts jobber or tool supply house specializing in automotive work.

Occasionally, the use of special tools is called for. See the information on Special Tools and Safety Notice in the front of this book before substituting another tool.

Troubleshooting Engine Mechanical Problems

Problem	Cause	Solution
External oil leaks	• Fuel pump gasket broken or improperly seated	• Replace gasket
	• Cylinder head cover RTV sealant broken or improperly seated	• Replace sealant; inspect cylinder head cover sealant flange and cylinder head sealant surface for distortion and cracks
	• Oil filler cap leaking or missing	• Replace cap
	• Oil filter gasket broken or improperly seated	• Replace oil filter
	• Oil pan side gasket broken, improperly seated or opening in RTV sealant	• Replace gasket or repair opening in sealant; inspect oil pan gasket flange for distortion
	• Oil pan front oil seal broken or improperly seated	• Replace seal; inspect timing case cover and oil pan seal flange for distortion
	• Oil pan rear oil seal broken or improperly seated	• Replace seal; inspect oil pan rear oil seal flange; inspect rear main bearing cap for cracks, plugged oil return channels, or distortion in seal groove
	• Timing case cover oil seal broken or improperly seated	• Replace seal
	• Excess oil pressure because of restricted PCV valve	• Replace PCV valve
	• Oil pan drain plug loose or has stripped threads	• Repair as necessary and tighten
	• Rear oil gallery plug loose	• Use appropriate sealant on gallery plug and tighten
	• Rear camshaft plug loose or improperly seated	• Seat camshaft plug or replace and seal, as necessary
	• Distributor base gasket damaged	• Replace gasket
Excessive oil consumption	• Oil level too high	• Drain oil to specified level
	• Oil with wrong viscosity being used	• Replace with specified oil
	• PCV valve stuck closed	• Replace PCV valve
	• Valve stem oil deflectors (or seals) are damaged, missing, or incorrect type	• Replace valve stem oil deflectors
	• Valve stems or valve guides worn	• Measure stem-to-guide clearance and repair as necessary
	• Poorly fitted or missing valve cover baffles	• Replace valve cover
	• Piston rings broken or missing	• Replace broken or missing rings
	• Scuffed piston	• Replace piston
	• Incorrect piston ring gap	• Measure ring gap, repair as necessary
	• Piston rings sticking or excessively loose in grooves	• Measure ring side clearance, repair as necessary
	• Compression rings installed upside down	• Repair as necessary
	• Cylinder walls worn, scored, or glazed	• Repair as necessary
	• Piston ring gaps not properly staggered	• Repair as necessary
	• Excessive main or connecting rod bearing clearance	• Measure bearing clearance, repair as necessary
No oil pressure	• Low oil level	• Add oil to correct level
	• Oil pressure gauge, warning lamp or sending unit inaccurate	• Replace oil pressure gauge or warning lamp
	• Oil pump malfunction	• Replace oil pump
	• Oil pressure relief valve sticking	• Remove and inspect oil pressure relief valve assembly
	• Oil passages on pressure side of pump obstructed	• Inspect oil passages for obstruction

Troubleshooting Engine Mechanical Problems (cont.)

Problem	Cause	Solution
No oil pressure (cont.)	• Oil pickup screen or tube obstructed	• Inspect oil pickup for obstruction
	• Loose oil inlet tube	• Tighten or seal inlet tube
Low oil pressure	• Low oil level	• Add oil to correct level
	• Inaccurate gauge, warning lamp or sending unit	• Replace oil pressure gauge or warning lamp
	• Oil excessively thin because of dilution, poor quality, or improper grade	• Drain and refill crankcase with recommended oil
	• Excessive oil temperature	• Correct cause of overheating engine
	• Oil pressure relief spring weak or sticking	• Remove and inspect oil pressure relief valve assembly
	• Oil inlet tube and screen assembly has restriction or air leak	• Remove and inspect oil inlet tube and screen assembly. (Fill inlet tube with lacquer thinner to locate leaks.)
	• Excessive oil pump clearance	• Measure clearances
	• Excessive main, rod, or camshaft bearing clearance	• Measure bearing clearances, repair as necessary
High oil pressure	• Improper oil viscosity	• Drain and refill crankcase with correct viscosity oil
	• Oil pressure gauge or sending unit inaccurate	• Replace oil pressure gauge
	• Oil pressure relief valve sticking closed	• Remove and inspect oil pressure relief valve assembly
Main bearing noise	• Insufficient oil supply	• Inspect for low oil level and low oil pressure
	• Main bearing clearance excessive	• Measure main bearing clearance, repair as necessary
	• Bearing insert missing	• Replace missing insert
	• Crankshaft end play excessive	• Measure end play, repair as necessary
	• Improperly tightened main bearing cap bolts	• Tighten bolts with specified torque
	• Loose flywheel or drive plate	• Tighten flywheel or drive plate attaching bolts
	• Loose or damaged vibration damper	• Repair as necessary
Connecting rod bearing noise	• Insufficient oil supply	• Inspect for low oil level and low oil pressure
	• Carbon build-up on piston	• Remove carbon from piston crown
	• Bearing clearance excessive or bearing missing	• Measure clearance, repair as necessary
	• Crankshaft connecting rod journal out-of-round	• Measure journal dimensions, repair or replace as necessary
	• Misaligned connecting rod or cap	• Repair as necessary
	• Connecting rod bolts tightened improperly	• Tighten bolts with specified torque
Piston noise	• Piston-to-cylinder wall clearance excessive (scuffed piston)	• Measure clearance and examine piston
	• Cylinder walls excessively tapered or out-of-round	• Measure cylinder wall dimensions, rebore cylinder
	• Piston ring broken	• Replace all rings on piston
	• Loose or seized piston pin	• Measure piston-to-pin clearance, repair as necessary
	• Connecting rods misaligned	• Measure rod alignment, straighten or replace
	• Piston ring side clearance excessively loose or tight	• Measure ring side clearance, repair as necessary
	• Carbon build-up on piston is excessive	• Remove carbon from piston

Troubleshooting Engine Mechanical Problems (cont.)

Problem	Cause	Solution
Valve actuating component noise	• Insufficient oil supply	• Check for: (a) Low oil level (b) Low oil pressure (c) Plugged push rods (d) Wrong hydraulic tappets (e) Restricted oil gallery (f) Excessive tappet to bore clearance
	• Push rods worn or bent	• Replace worn or bent push rods
	• Rocker arms or pivots worn	• Replace worn rocker arms or pivots
	• Foreign objects or chips in hydraulic tappets	• Clean tappets
	• Excessive tappet leak-down	• Replace valve tappet
	• Tappet face worn	• Replace tappet; inspect corresponding cam lobe for wear
	• Broken or cocked valve springs	• Properly seat cocked springs; replace broken springs
	• Stem-to-guide clearance excessive	• Measure stem-to-guide clearance, repair as required
	• Valve bent	• Replace valve
	• Loose rocker arms	• Tighten bolts with specified torque
	• Valve seat runout excessive	• Regrind valve seat/valves
	• Missing valve lock	• Install valve lock
	• Push rod rubbing or contacting cylinder head	• Remove cylinder head and remove obstruction in head
	• Excessive engine oil (four-cylinder engine)	• Correct oil level

INSPECTION TECHNIQUES

Procedures and specifications are given in this section for inspecting, cleaning and assessing the wear limits of most major components. Other procedures such as Magnaflux® and Zyglo® can be used to locate material flaws and stress cracks. Magnaflux® is a magnetic process applicable only to ferrous materials. The Zyglo® process coats the material with a fluorescent dye penetrant and can be used on any material Check for suspected surface cracks can be more readily made using spot check dye. The dye is sprayed onto the suspected area, wiped off and the area sprayed with a developer. Cracks will show up brightly.

OVERHAUL TIPS

Aluminum has become extremely popular for use in engines, due to its low weight. Observe the following precautions when handling aluminum parts:

• Never hot tank aluminum parts (the caustic hot tank solution will eat the aluminum.

• Remove all aluminum parts (identification tag, etc.) from engine parts prior to the tanking.

• Always coat threads lightly with engine oil or anti-seize compounds before installation, to prevent seizure.

• Never over torque bolts or spark plugs especially in aluminum threads.

Stripped threads in any component can be repaired using any of several commercial repair kits (Heli-Coil®, Microdot®, Keenserts®, etc.).

When assembling the engine, any parts that will be frictional contact must be prelubed to provide lubrication at initial start-up. Any product specifically formulated for this purpose can be used, but engine oil is not recommended as a prelube.

When semi-permanent (locked, but removable) installation of bolts or nuts is desired, threads should be cleaned and coated with Loctite® or other similar, commercial non-hardening sealant.

REPAIRING DAMAGED THREADS

Several methods of repairing damaged threads are available. Heli-Coil®, Keenserts® and Microdot® are among the most widely used. All involve basically the same principle—drilling out stripped threads, tapping the hole and installing a prewound insert—making

Troubleshooting the Cooling System

Problem	Cause	Solution
High temperature gauge indication—overheating	• Coolant level low	• Replenish coolant
	• Fan belt loose	• Adjust fan belt tension
	• Radiator hose(s) collapsed	• Replace hose(s)
	• Radiator airflow blocked	• Remove restriction (bug screen, fog lamps, etc.)
	• Faulty radiator cap	• Replace radiator cap
	• Ignition timing incorrect	• Adjust ignition timing
	• Idle speed low	• Adjust idle speed
	• Air trapped in cooling system	• Purge air
	• Heavy traffic driving	• Operate at fast idle in neutral intermittently to cool engine
	• Incorrect cooling system component(s) installed	• Install proper component(s)
	• Faulty thermostat	• Replace thermostat
	• Water pump shaft broken or impeller loose	• Replace water pump
	• Radiator tubes clogged	• Flush radiator
	• Cooling system clogged	• Flush system
	• Casting flash in cooling passages	• Repair or replace as necessary. Flash may be visible by removing cooling system components or removing core plugs.
	• Brakes dragging	• Repair brakes
	• Excessive engine friction	• Repair engine
	• Antifreeze concentration over 68%	• Lower antifreeze concentration percentage
	• Missing air seals	• Replace air seals
	• Faulty gauge or sending unit	• Repair or replace faulty component
	• Loss of coolant flow caused by leakage or foaming	• Repair or replace leaking component, replace coolant
	• Viscous fan drive failed	• Replace unit
Low temperature indication—undercooling	• Thermostat stuck open	• Replace thermostat
	• Faulty gauge or sending unit	• Repair or replace faulty component
Coolant loss—boilover	• Overfilled cooling system	• Reduce coolant level to proper specification
	• Quick shutdown after hard (hot) run	• Allow engine to run at fast idle prior to shutdown
	• Air in system resulting in occasional "burping" of coolant	• Purge system
	• Insufficient antifreeze allowing coolant boiling point to be too low	• Add antifreeze to raise boiling point
	• Antifreeze deteriorated because of age or contamination	• Replace coolant
	• Leaks due to loose hose clamps, loose nuts, bolts, drain plugs, faulty hoses, or defective radiator	• Pressure test system to locate source of leak(s) then repair as necessary
	• Faulty head gasket	• Replace head gasket
	• Cracked head, manifold, or block	• Replace as necessary
	• Faulty radiator cap	• Replace cap
Coolant entry into crankcase or cylinder(s)	• Faulty head gasket	• Replace head gasket
	• Crack in head, manifold or block	• Replace as necessary
Coolant recovery system inoperative	• Coolant level low	• Replenish coolant to FULL mark
	• Leak in system	• Pressure test to isolate leak and repair as necessary
	• Pressure cap not tight or seal missing, or leaking	• Repair as necessary
	• Pressure cap defective	• Replace cap
	• Overflow tube clogged or leaking	• Repair as necessary
	• Recovery bottle vent restricted	• Remove restriction

Troubleshooting the Cooling System (cont.)

Problem	Cause	Solution
Noise	• Fan contacting shroud	• Reposition shroud and inspect engine mounts
	• Loose water pump impeller	• Replace pump
	• Glazed fan belt	• Apply silicone or replace belt
	• Loose fan belt	• Adjust fan belt tension
	• Rough surface on drive pulley	• Replace pulley
	• Water pump bearing worn	• Remove belt to isolate. Replace pump.
	• Belt alignment	• Check pulley alignment. Repair as necessary.
No coolant flow through heater core	• Restricted return inlet in water pump	• Remove restriction
	• Heater hose collapsed or restricted	• Remove restriction or replace hose
	• Restricted heater core	• Remove restriction or replace core
	• Restricted outlet in thermostat housing	• Remove flash or restriction
	• Intake manifold bypass hole in cylinder head restricted	• Remove restriction
	• Faulty heater control valve	• Replace valve
	• Intake manifold coolant passage restricted	• Remove restriction or replace intake manifold

NOTE: *Immediately after shutdown, the engine enters a condition known as heat soak. This is caused by the cooling system being inoperative while engine temperature is still high. If coolant temperature rises above boiling point, expansion and pressure may push some coolant out of the radiator overflow tube. If this does not occur frequently it is considered normal.*

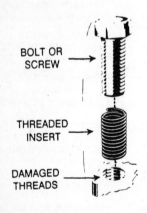

Damaged bolt holes can be repair with thread inserts

Drill out the damaged threads with the specified bit. Drill completely through an open hole, or to the bottom of a blind hole

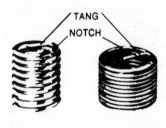

Standard thread insert (left) and spark plug insert

welding, plugging and oversize fasteners unnecessary.

Two types of thread repair inserts are usually supplied—a standard type for most Inch Coarse, Inch Fine, Metric Course and Metric Fine thread sizes and a spark lug type to fit most spark plug port sizes. Consult the individual manufacturer's catalog to determine exact applications. Typical thread repair kits will contain a selection of prewound threaded inserts, a tap (corresponding to the outside diameter threads of the insert) and an installation tool. Spark plug inserts usually differ because they require a tap equipped with pilot threads and a combined reamer/tap section. Most manufacturers also supply blister-packed thread repair inserts separately in addition to a master kit con-

Troubleshooting the Serpentine Drive Belt

Problem	Cause	Solution
Tension sheeting fabric failure (woven fabric on outside circumference of belt has cracked or separated from body of belt)	• Grooved or backside idler pulley diameters are less than minimum recommended	• Replace pulley(s) not conforming to specification
	• Tension sheeting contacting (rubbing) stationary object	• Correct rubbing condition
	• Excessive heat causing woven fabric to age	• Replace belt
	• Tension sheeting splice has fractured	• Replace belt
Noise (objectional squeal, squeak, or rumble is heard or felt while drive belt is in operation)	• Belt slippage	• Adjust belt
	• Bearing noise	• Locate and repair
	• Belt misalignment	• Align belt/pulley(s)
	• Belt-to-pulley mismatch	• Install correct belt
	• Driven component inducing vibration	• Locate defective driven component and repair
	• System resonant frequency inducing vibration	• Vary belt tension within specifications. Replace belt.
Rib chunking (one or more ribs has separated from belt body)	• Foreign objects imbedded in pulley grooves	• Remove foreign objects from pulley grooves
	• Installation damage	• Replace belt
	• Drive loads in excess of design specifications	• Adjust belt tension
	• Insufficient internal belt adhesion	• Replace belt
Rib or belt wear (belt ribs contact bottom of pulley grooves)	• Pulley(s) misaligned	• Align pulley(s)
	• Mismatch of belt and pulley groove widths	• Replace belt
	• Abrasive environment	• Replace belt
	• Rusted pulley(s)	• Clean rust from pulley(s)
	• Sharp or jagged pulley groove tips	• Replace pulley
	• Rubber deteriorated	• Replace belt
Longitudinal belt cracking (cracks between two ribs)	• Belt has mistracked from pulley groove	• Replace belt
	• Pulley groove tip has worn away rubber-to-tensile member	• Replace belt
Belt slips	• Belt slipping because of insufficient tension	• Adjust tension
	• Belt or pulley subjected to substance (belt dressing, oil, ethylene glycol) that has reduced friction	• Replace belt and clean pulleys
	• Driven component bearing failure	• Replace faulty component bearing
	• Belt glazed and hardened from heat and excessive slippage	• Replace Belt
"Groove jumping" (belt does not maintain correct position on pulley, or turns over and/or runs off pulleys)	• Insufficient belt tension	• Adjust belt tension
	• Pulley(s) not within design tolerance	• Replace pulley(s)
	• Foreign object(s) in grooves	• Remove foreign objects from grooves
	• Excessive belt speed	• Avoid excessive engine acceleration
	• Pulley misalignment	• Align pulley(s)
	• Belt-to-pulley profile mismatched	• Install correct belt
	• Belt cordline is distorted	• Replace belt
Belt broken (Note: identify and correct problem before replacement belt is installed)	• Excessive tension	• Replace belt and adjust tension to specification
	• Tensile members damaged during belt installation	• Replace belt
	• Belt turnover	• Replace belt
	• Severe pulley misalignment	• Align pulley(s)
	• Bracket, pulley, or bearing failure	• Replace defective component and belt

Troubleshooting the Serpentine Drive Belt (cont.)

Problem	Cause	Solution
Cord edge failure (tensile member exposed at edges of belt or separated from belt body)	• Excessive tension • Drive pulley misalignment • Belt contacting stationary object • Pulley irregularities • Improper pulley construction • Insufficient adhesion between tensile member and rubber matrix	• Adjust belt tension • Align pulley • Correct as necessary • Replace pulley • Replace pulley • Replace belt and adjust tension to specifications
Sporadic rib cracking (multiple cracks in belt ribs at random intervals)	• Ribbed pulley(s) diameter less than minimum specification • Backside bend flat pulley(s) diameter less than minimum • Excessive heat condition causing rubber to harden • Excessive belt thickness • Belt overcured • Excessive tension	• Replace pulley(s) • Replace pulley(s) • Correct heat condition as necessary • Replace belt • Replace belt • Adjust belt tension

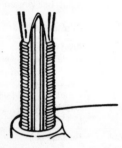

With the tap supplied, tap the hole to receive the thread insert. Keep the tap well oiled and back it out frequently to avoid clogging the threads

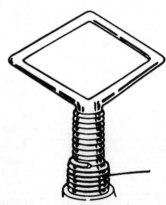

Screw the thread insert onto the installation tool until the tang engages the slot. Screw the insert into the taped hole until it is 1/4–1/2 turn below the top surface. After installation, break off the tang with a hammer and punch

taining a variety of taps and inserts plus installation tools.

Before effecting a repair to a threaded hole, remove any snapped, broken or damaged bolts or studs. Penetrating oil can be used to free frozen threads. The offending item can be removed with locking pliers or with a screw or stud extractor. After the hole is clear, the thread can be repaired, as follows:

Checking Engine Compression

A noticeable lack of engine power, excessive oil consumption and/or poor fuel mileage measured over an extended period are all indicators of internal engine war. Worn piston rings, scored or worn cylinder bores, blown head gaskets, sticking or burnt valves and worn valve seats are all possible culprits here. A check of each cylinder's compression will help you locate the problems.

As mentioned in the Tools and Equipment section of Chapter 1, a screw-in type compression gauge is more accurate that the type you simply hold against the spark plug hole, although it takes slightly longer to use. It's worth it to obtain a more accurate reading. Follow the procedures below for gasoline and diesel engined trucks.

GASOLINE ENGINES

1. Warm up the engine to normal operating temperature.
2. Remove all spark plugs.
3. Disconnect the high tension lead from the ignition coil.
4. On fully open the throttle either by operating the throttle linkage by hand or by having an assistant floor the accelerator pedal.
5. Screw the compression gauge into the no.1 spark plug hole until the fitting is snug.

NOTE: *Be careful not to crossthread the plug hole. On aluminum cylinder heads use*

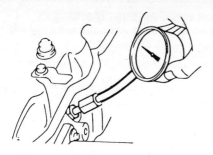

The screw-in type of compression gauge is much more accurate than the push-in type

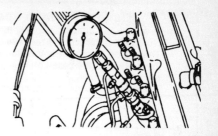

Diesel engines require a special gauge adapter

extra care, as the threads in these heads are easily ruined.

6. Ask an assistant to depress the accelerator pedal fully on both carbureted and fuel injected trucks. Then, while you read the compression gauge, ask the assistant to crank the engine two or three times in short bursts using the ignition switch.

7. Read the compression gauge at the end of each series of cranks, and record the highest of these readings. Repeat this procedure for each of the engine's cylinders. Compare the highest reading of each cylinder to the compression pressure specification in the Tune-Up Specifications chart in Chapter 2. The specs in this chart are maximum values.

A cylinder's compression pressure is usually acceptable if it is not less than 80% of maximum. The difference between each cylinder should be no more than 12–14 pounds.

8. If a cylinder is unusually low, pour a tablespoon of clean engine oil into the cylinder through the spark plug hole and repeat the compression test. If the compression comes up after adding the oil, it appears that the cylinder's piston rings or bore are damaged or worn. If the pressure remains low, the valves may not be seating properly (a valve job is needed), or the head gasket may be blown near that cylinder. If compression in any two adjacent cylinders is low, and if the addition of oil doesn't help the compression, there is leakage past the head gasket. Oil and coolant water in the combustion chamber can result from this problem. There may be evidence of water droplets on the engine dipstick when a head gasket has blown.

DIESEL ENGINES

Checking cylinder compression on diesel engines is basically the same procedure as on gasoline engines except for the following:

1. A special compression gauge adaptor suitable for diesel engines (because these engines have much greater compression pressures) must be used.

2. Remove the injector tubes and remove the injectors from each cylinder.

NOTE: *Don't forget to remove the washer underneath each injector; otherwise, it may get lost when the engine is cranked.*

3. When fitting the compression gauge adaptor to the cylinder head, make sure the bleeder of the gauge (if equipped) is closed.

4. When reinstalling the injector assemblies, install new washers underneath each injector.

Engine

REMOVAL AND INSTALLATION

6–4.3L

1. Disconnect the battery cables.
2. Remove the glove box.
3. Drain the cooling system.
CAUTION: *When draining the coolant, keep in mind that cats and dogs are attracted by the ethylene glycol antifreeze, and are quite likely to drink any that is left in an uncovered container or in puddles on the ground. This will prove fatal in sufficient quantity. Always drain the coolant into a sealable container. Coolant should be reused unless it is contaminated or several years old.*
4. Remove the engine cover.
5. Remove the outside air duct.
6. Remove the power steering reservoir.
7. Remove the hood release cable.
8. Remove the upper fan shroud bolts.
9. Remove the fan and pulley.
10. Remove the air cleaner.
11. Remove the cruise control servo, servo bracket and transducer.
12. Tag and disconnect all vacuum hoses.
13. Disconnect the accelerator linkage and TVS cables.
14. Remove the TBI unit.
15. Remove the distributor cap.
16. Disconnect the heater hoses at the engine.

Standard Torque Specifications and Fastener Markings

In the absence of specific torques, the following chart can be used as a guide to the maximum safe torque of a particular size/grade of fastener.
- There is no torque difference for fine or coarse threads.
- Torque values are based on clean, dry threads. Reduce the value by 10% if threads are oiled prior to assembly.
- The torque required for aluminum components or fasteners is considerably less.

U.S. Bolts

SAE Grade Number	1 or 2			5			6 or 7		
Number of lines always 2 less than the grade number.									
Bolt Size (Inches)—(Thread)	**Maximum Torque**			**Maximum Torque**			**Maximum Torque**		
	Ft./Lbs.	Kgm	Nm	Ft./Lbs.	Kgm	Nm	Ft./Lbs.	Kgm	Nm
¼ — 20	5	0.7	6.8	8	1.1	10.8	10	1.4	13.5
— 28	6	0.8	8.1	10	1.4	13.6			
⁵/₁₆ — 18	11	1.5	14.9	17	2.3	23.0	19	2.6	25.8
— 24	13	1.8	17.6	19	2.6	25.7			
³/₈ — 16	18	2.5	24.4	31	4.3	42.0	34	4.7	46.0
— 24	20	2.75	27.1	35	4.8	47.5			
⁷/₁₆ — 14	28	3.8	37.0	49	6.8	66.4	55	7.6	74.5
— 20	30	4.2	40.7	55	7.6	74.5			
½ — 13	39	5.4	52.8	75	10.4	101.7	85	11.75	115.2
— 20	41	5.7	55.6	85	11.7	115.2			
⁹/₁₆ — 12	51	7.0	69.2	110	15.2	149.1	120	16.6	162.7
— 18	55	7.6	74.5	120	16.6	162.7			
⅝ — 11	83	11.5	112.5	150	20.7	203.3	167	23.0	226.5
— 18	95	13.1	128.8	170	23.5	230.5			
¾ — 10	105	14.5	142.3	270	37.3	366.0	280	38.7	379.6
— 16	115	15.9	155.9	295	40.8	400.0			
⅞ — 9	160	22.1	216.9	395	54.6	535.5	440	60.9	596.5
— 14	175	24.2	237.2	435	60.1	589.7			
1 — 8	236	32.5	318.6	590	81.6	799.9	660	91.3	894.8
— 14	250	34.6	338.9	660	91.3	849.8			

Metric Bolts

Relative Strength Marking	4.6, 4.8			8.8		
Bolt Markings						
Bolt Size Thread Size x Pitch (mm)	**Maximum Torque**			**Maximum Torque**		
	Ft./Lbs.	Kgm	Nm	Ft./Lbs.	Kgm	Nm
6 x 1.0	2–3	.2–.4	3–4	3–6	.4–.8	5–8
8 x 1.25	6–8	.8–1	8–12	9–14	1.2–1.9	13–19
10 x 1.25	12–17	1.5–2.3	16–23	20–29	2.7–4.0	27–39
12 x 1.25	21–32	2.9–4.4	29–43	35–53	4.8–7.3	47–72
14 x 1.5	35–52	4.8–7.1	48–70	57–85	7.8–11.7	77–110
16 x 1.5	51–77	7.0–10.6	67–100	90–120	12.4–16.5	130–160
18 x 1.5	74–110	10.2–15.1	100–150	130–170	17.9–23.4	180–230
20 x 1.5	110–140	15.1–19.3	150–190	190–240	26.2–46.9	160–320
22 x 1.5	150–190	22.0–26.2	200–260	250–320	34.5–44.1	340–430
24 x 1.5	190–240	26.2–46.9	260–320	310–410	42.7–56.5	420–550

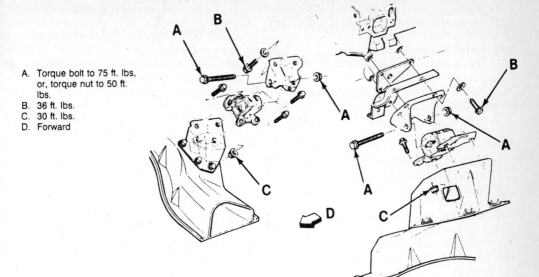

A. Torque bolt to 75 ft. lbs,
   or, torque nut to 50 ft.
   lbs.
B. 36 ft. lbs.
C. 30 ft. lbs.
D. Forward

Front engine mounts for the 6-4.3L in R and V series trucks

17. Remove the PCV valve.

18. Discharge the air conditioning system and remove the air conditioning vacuum reservoir.

CAUTION: *Discharging the air conditioning refrigerant should only be attempted by those who have the proper tools and training to do so, as serious personal injury may result. The refrigerant will instantly freeze any surface it comes in contact with, including your eyes.*

19. Remove the air conditioning compressor and bracket.

20. Remove the upper half of the engine dipstick tube.

21. Remove the oil filler tube.

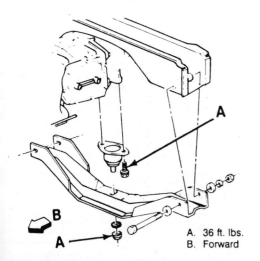

A. 36 ft. lbs.
B. Forward

Rear engine mounts for the 6-4.3L in R and V series trucks

22. Remove the transmission dipstick tube and the accelerator cable at the tube.

23. Remove the fuel line at the fuel pump.

24. Remove the power steering pump.

25. Remove the head light bezels and the grille.

26. Remove the upper radiator support.

27. Remove the lower fan shroud and filler panel.

28. Remove the hood latch support.

29. Remove the condenser. Cap all openings at once!

30. Raise and support the van on jackstands.

31. Drain the engine oil.

32. Disconnect the exhaust pipes at the manifolds.

33. Remove the strut rods at the torque converter or flywheel underpan.

34. Remove the torque converter or flywheel cover.

35. Remove the starter.

36. Remove the flex plate-to-torque converter bolts (automatic transmissions).

37. Remove the bell housing-to-engine bolts.

38. Remove the engine mounting through bolts.

39. Lower the van support the transmission on a floor jack.

40. Attach an engine crane to the engine, pull the engine forward and upward and remove it from the van.

To install:

41. Raise the engine into position.

42. Install the engine mount through bolts. Torque the bolts to 75 ft. lbs.

43. Install the bell housing-to-engine bolts. Torque the bolts to 50 ft. lbs.

44. Install the flex plate-to-torque converter bolts (automatic transmissions). Torque the bolts to 40 ft. lbs.

45. Install the starter.

46. Install the torque converter or flywheel cover.

47. Install the strut rods at the torque converter or flywheel underpan.

48. Connect the exhaust pipes at the manifolds.

49. Install the fuel line at the fuel pump.

50. Install the condenser.

51. Install the hood latch support.

52. Install the lower fan shroud and filler panel.

53. Install the transmission dipstick tube and the accelerator cable at the tube.

54. Install the PCV valve.

55. Install the distributor cap.

56. Install the cruise control servo, servo bracket and transducer.

57. Install the oil filler pipe and the engine dipstick tube.

58. Install the thermostat housing.

59. Connect the heater hoses at the engine.

60. Connect the engine wiring harness from the firewall connection.

61. Install the air conditioning compressor mounting bracket.

62. Install the radiator and the shroud.

63. Install the radiator support bracket.

64. Install the TBI unit.

65. Connect the accelerator linkage and TVS cable.

66. Install the windshield wiper jar and bracket.

67. Install the air conditioning compressor.

68. Install the air conditioning vacuum reservoir.

69. Charge the air conditioning system. See Chapter 1.

CAUTION: *Charging the air conditioning refrigerant should only be attempted by those who have the proper tools and training to do so, as serious personal injury may result. The refrigerant will instantly freeze any surface it comes in contact with, including your eyes.*

70. If the van is equipped with an automatic transmission, install the fluid cooler lines at the radiator.

71. Install the power steering reservoir.

72. Install the hood release cable.

73. Connect the radiator hoses at the radiator.

74. Install the head light bezels and the grille.

75. Install the air cleaner.

76. Install the outside air duct.

77. Install the engine cover.

78. Fill the cooling system.

79. Fill the crankcase.

80. Connect the battery cables.

81. Install the glove box.

8–5.0L
8–5.7L

1. Disconnect the negative battery cable, then the positive battery cable, at the battery.

2. Drain the cooling system.

CAUTION: *When draining the coolant, keep in mind that cats and dogs are attracted by the ethylene glycol antifreeze, and are quite likely to drink any that is left in an uncovered container or in puddles on the ground. This will prove fatal in sufficient quantity. Always drain the coolant into a sealable container. Coolant should be reused unless it is contaminated or several years old.*

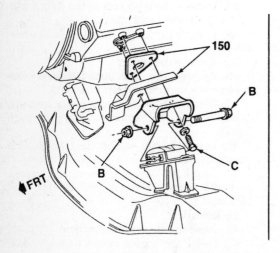
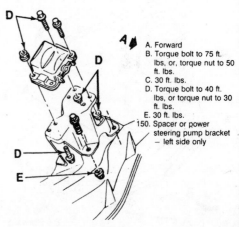

A. Forward
B. Torque bolt to 75 ft. lbs, or torque nut to 50 ft. lbs.
C. 30 ft. lbs.
D. Torque bolt to 40 ft. lbs, or torque nut to 30 ft. lbs.
E. 30 ft. lbs.
150. Spacer or power steering pump bracket – left side only

Front engine mounts for the 8-5.0L and 8-5.7L

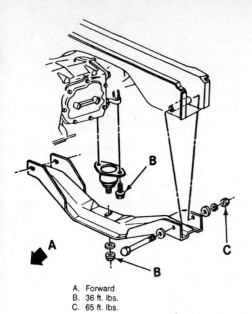

A. Forward
B. 36 ft. lbs.
C. 65 ft. lbs.

Rear engine mount for the 8-5.0L and 8-5.7L

3. Remove the radiator coolant reservoir bottle.

4. Remove the upper radiator support.

5. Remove the grille and the lower grille valance.

CAUTION: *Discharging the air conditioning refrigerant should only be attempted by those who have the proper tools and training to do so, as serious personal injury may result. The refrigerant will instantly freeze any surface it comes in contact with, including your eyes.*

6. Discharge the air conditioning system and remove the air conditioning vacuum reservoir.

7. Remove the air conditioning condenser from in front of the radiator.

8. If the van is equipped with an automatic transmission, remove the fluid cooler lines from the radiator.

9. Disconnect the radiator hoses at the radiator.

10. Remove the radiator support bracket and remove the radiator and the shroud.

11. Remove the engine cover.

12. Remove the air cleaner.

13. Disconnect the accelerator linkage.

14. Disconnect all hoses and wires at the carburetor or TBI unit.

15. Remove the carburetor or TBI unit.

16. Disconnect the engine wiring harness from the firewall connection.

17. Tag and disconnect all vacuum lines.

18. Remove the power steering pump. It's not necessary to disconnect the hoses; just lay it aside.

19. Disconnect the heater hoses at the engine.

20. Remove the thermostat housing.

21. Remove the oil filler tube.

22. Raise and support the van on jackstands.

23. Remove the cruise control servo, servo bracket and transducer.

4. Drain the engine oil.

25. Disconnect the exhaust pipes at the manifolds.

26. Remove the driveshaft and plug the end of the transmission.

27. Disconnect the transmission shift linkage and the speedometer cable.

28. Remove the fuel line from the fuel tank and at the fuel pump.

29. Remove the transmission mounting bolts.

30. Lower the van, support the transmission and engine.

31. Remove the engine mount bracket-to-frame bolts.

32. Remove the engine mount through bolts.

33. Raise the engine slightly and remove the engine mounts. Support the engine with wood between the oil pan and the crossmember.

34. Remove the manual transmission and clutch as follows:

a. Remove the clutch housing rear bolts.

b. Remove the bolts attaching the clutch housing to the engine and remove the transmission and clutch as a unit.

NOTE: *Support the transmission as the last bolt is being removed to prevent damaging the clutch.*

c. Remove the starter and clutch housing rear cover.

d. Loosen the clutch mounting bolts a little at a time to prevent distorting the disc until spring pressure is released. Remove all of the bolts, the clutch disc and the pressure plate.

35. Remove the automatic transmission as follows:

a. Lower the engine and support it on blocks.

b. Remove the starter and converter housing underpan.

c. Remove the flywheel-to-converter attaching bolts.

d. Support the transmission on blocks.

e. Disconnect the detent cable on the Turbo Hydra-Matic.

f. Remove the transmission-to-engine mounting bolts.

g. Remove the blocks from the engine only and glide the engine away from the transmission.

To install:

36. Raise the engine slightly and install the

engine mounts. Torque the bolts to 40 ft. lbs.

37. Install the manual transmission and clutch as follows:

a. Install the clutch disc and the pressure plate. Tighten the clutch mounting bolts a little at a time to prevent distorting the disc.

b. Install the starter and clutch housing rear cover.

c. Install the bolts attaching the clutch housing to the engine and install the transmission and clutch as a unit. Torque the bolts to 40 ft. lbs.

d. Install the clutch housing rear bolts.

38. To install the automatic transmission:

a. Position the transmission.

b. Install the transmission-to-engine mounting bolts.

c. Connect the throttle linkage and detent cable.

d. Install the flywheel-to-converter attaching bolts. Torque the bolts to 40 ft. lbs.

e. Install the starter and converter housing underpan.

39. Install the engine mount through bolts. Torque the bolts to 40 ft. lbs.

40. Install the engine mount bracket-to-frame bolts. Torque the bolts to 40 ft. lbs.

41. Install the clutch cross-shaft.

42. Install the transmission mounting bolts. Torque the bolts to 40 ft. lbs.

43. Connect the transmission shift linkage and the speedometer cable.

44. Install the driveshaft.

45. Install the condenser.

46. Install the hood latch support.

47. Install the lower fan shroud and filler panel.

48. Install the transmission dipstick tube and the accelerator cable at the tube.

49. Install the coolant hose at the intake manifold and the PCV valve.

50. Install the distributor cap.

51. Install the cruise control servo, servo bracket and transducer.

52. Install the oil filler pipe and the engine dipstick tube.

53. Install the thermostat housing.

54. Connect the heater hoses at the engine.

55. Connect the engine wiring harness from the firewall connection.

56. Install the radiator and the shroud.

57. Install the radiator support bracket.

58. Install the carburetor or TBI unit.

59. Connect the accelerator linkage.

60. Install the windshield wiper jar and bracket.

61. Install the air conditioning condenser.

62. Install the air conditioning vacuum reservoir.

63. Charge the air conditioning system.

CAUTION: *Charging the air conditioning refrigerant should only be attempted by those who have the proper tools and training to do so, as serious personal injury may result. The refrigerant will instantly freeze any surface it comes in contact with, including your eyes.*

64. If the van is equipped with an automatic transmission, install the fluid cooler lines at the radiator.

65. Install the radiator coolant reservoir bottle.

66. Connect radiator hoses to the radiator.

67. Install the upper radiator support the grille and the lower grille valance.

68. Install the air cleaner.

69. Install the air stove pipe.

70. Install the engine cover.

71. Fill the cooling system.

72. Connect the battery cables.

8–6.2L Diesel

1. Disconnect the negative battery cable, then the positive battery cable, at the battery.

2. Remove the upper radiator support.

3. Remove the grille.

4. Remove the bumper.

5. Remove the lower grille valance.

6. Remove the hood latch.

7. Drain the cooling system.

CAUTION: *When draining the coolant, keep in mind that cats and dogs are attracted by the ethylene glycol antifreeze, and are quite likely to drink any that is left in an uncovered container or in puddles on the ground. This will prove fatal in sufficient quantity. Always drain the coolant into a sealable container. Coolant should be reused unless it is contaminated or several years old.*

8. Remove the radiator coolant reservoir bottle.

9. Remove the radiator support bracket.

10. Remove the radiator and the fan shroud.

11. Remove the engine cover.

12. Remove the air cleaner.

13. Discharge the air conditioning system.

CAUTION: *Discharging the air conditioning refrigerant should only be attempted by those who have the proper tools and training to do so, as serious personal injury may result. The refrigerant will instantly freeze any surface it comes in contact with, including your eyes.*

14. Remove the air conditioning condenser. Cap all openings at once!

15. Disconnect the air cleaner bracket at the valve cover.

16. Remove the crankcase ventilator bracket and move it aside.

17. Disconnect the secondary fuel filter lines.

18. Remove the secondary fuel filter adapter.

19. Loosen the vacuum pump holddown clamp and rotate the pump in order to gain access to the intake manifold bolt.

20. Remove the intake manifold bolts. The injection line clips are retained by the same bolts.

21. Remove the injection line clips at the loom brackets.

22. Remove the injection lines at the nozzles and cover the nozzles with protective caps.

23. Remove the injection lines at the pump and tag the lines for later installation.

24. Remove the fuel line from the injection pump.

25. Disconnect the alternator cable at the injection pump, and the detent cable where applicable.

26. Tag and disconnect the necessary wires and hoses at the injection pump.

27. Remove the air conditioning hose retainer bracket if equipped with air conditioning.

28. Remove the oil fill tube, including the crankcase depression valve vent hose assembly.

29. Remove the grommet.

30. Scribe or paint a matchmark on the front cover and on the injection pump flange.

31. The crankshaft must be rotated in order to gain access to the injection pump drive gear bolts through the oil filler neck hole.

32. Remove the injection pump-to-front cover attaching nuts.

33. Remove the pump and cap all open lines and nozzles.

34. Remove the intake manifold.

35. Raise and support the van on jackstands.

36. Disconnect the exhaust pipes at the manifolds.

37. Disconnect the radiator hoses at the radiator.

38. If the van is equipped with an automatic transmission, remove the fluid cooler lines from the radiator.

39. Remove the windshield wiper jar and bracket.

40. Disconnect the engine wiring harness from the firewall connection.

41. Disconnect the heater hoses at the engine.

42. Remove the oil filler pipe.

43. Remove the engine dipstick tube.

44. Remove the cruise control servo, servo bracket and transducer.

45. Remove the glow plug relay.

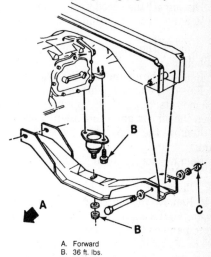

A. Forward
B. 36 ft. lbs.
C. 65 ft. lbs.

Rear engine mounts for the 8-6.2L

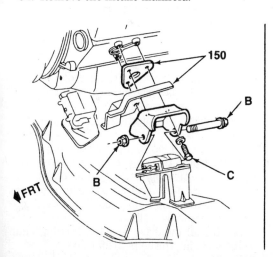

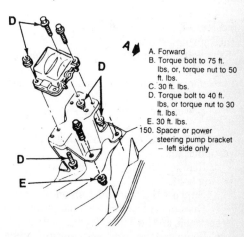

A. Forward
B. Torque bolt to 75 ft. lbs, or, torque nut to 50 ft. lbs.
C. 30 ft. lbs.
D. Torque bolt to 40 ft. lbs, or torque nut to 30 ft. lbs.
E. 30 ft. lbs.
150. Spacer or power steering pump bracket — left side only

Front engine mounts for the 8-6.2L

46. Remove the alternator upper bracket.

47. Remove the coolant crossover/thermostat assembly.

48. Disconnect the block heater wires.

49. Remove the coolant hose at the intake manifold.

50. Remove the transmission dipstick tube and the accelerator cable.

51. Remove the air conditioning idler pulley.

52. Remove the lower fan shroud and filler panel.

53. Raise the vehicle.

54. Drain the engine oil.

55. Remove the fuel line from the fuel tank and at the fuel pump.

56. Remove the driveshaft and plug the end of the transmission.

57. Disconnect the transmission shift linkage.

58. Disconnect the speedometer cable.

59. Remove the transmission mounting bolts.

60. Remove the engine mount bracket-to-frame bolts.

61. Remove the engine mount through bolts.

62. Raise the engine slightly and remove the engine mounts. Support the engine with wood between the oil pan and the crossmember.

63. Remove the engine and transmission as one unit.

64. Remove the manual transmission and clutch as follows:

    a. Remove the clutch housing rear bolts.

    b. Remove the bolts attaching the clutch housing to the engine and remove the transmission and clutch as a unit.

NOTE: *Support the transmission as the last bolt is being removed to prevent damaging the clutch.*

    c. Remove the starter and clutch housing rear cover.

    d. Loosen the clutch mounting bolts a little at a time to prevent distorting the disc until spring pressure is released. Remove all of the bolts, the clutch disc and the pressure plate.

65. Remove the automatic transmission as follows:

    a. Lower the engine and support it on blocks.

    b. Remove the starter and converter housing underpan.

    c. Remove the flywheel-to-converter attaching bolts.

    d. Support the transmission on blocks.

    e. Disconnect the throttle linkage and the detent cable on the Turbo Hydra-Matic.

    f. Remove the transmission-to-engine mounting bolts.

    g. Remove the blocks from the engine

only and glide the engine away from the transmission.

To install:

66. Raise the engine into position.

67. Raise the engine slightly and install the engine mounts. Torque the bolts to 36 ft. lbs.

68. Install the manual transmission and clutch as follows:

    a. Install the clutch disc and the pressure plate. Tighten the clutch mounting bolts a little at a time to prevent distorting the disc.

    b. Install the starter and clutch housing rear cover.

    c. Install the bolts attaching the clutch housing to the engine and install the transmission and clutch as a unit. Torque the bolts to 30 ft. lbs.

    d. Install the clutch housing rear bolts.

69. Install the automatic transmission as follows:

    a. Position the transmission.

    b. Install the transmission-to-engine mounting bolts. Torque the bolts to 30 ft. lbs.

    c. Connect the throttle linkage and the detent cable on the Turbo Hydra-Matic.

    d. Install the flywheel-to-converter attaching bolts. Torque the bolts to 40 ft. lbs.

    e. Install the starter and converter housing underpan.

70. Install the engine mount through bolts. Torque the bolt to 75 ft. lbs.

71. Install the engine mount bracket-to-frame bolts. Torque the bolts to 40 ft. lbs. and the nuts to 30 ft. lbs.

72. Install the clutch cross-shaft.

73. Install the transmission mounting bolts. Torque the bolts to 36 ft. lbs.

74. Connect the transmission shift linkage.

75. Connect the speedometer cable.

76. Install the driveshaft.

77. Install the condenser.

78. Install the hood latch support.

79. Install the lower fan shroud and filler panel.

80. Install the air conditioning idler pulley.

81. Install the transmission dipstick tube and the accelerator cable.

82. Replace the injection pump gasket. This is important!

83. Align the locating pin on the pump hub with the slot in the injection pump driven gear. At the same time, align the timing marks.

84. Attach the injection pump to the front cover, aligning the timing marks before torquing the nuts to 30 ft. lbs.

85. Install the drive gear to injection pump bolts, torquing the bolts to 20 ft. lbs.

86. The crankshaft must be rotated in order to gain access to the injection pump drive gear bolts through the oil filler neck hole.

87. Install the air conditioning hose retainer bracket if equipped with air conditioning.

88. Connect the fuel feed line at the injection pump. Torque the fuel feed line at the injection pump to 20 ft. lbs.

89. Connect the fuel return line at the top of the injection pump.

90. Connect the necessary wires and hoses at the injection pump.

91. Connect the alternator cable at the injection pump, and the detent cable where applicable.

92. Install the intake manifold.

93. Install the fuel line at the injection pump.

94. Install the injection lines at the pump.

95. Install the injection lines at the nozzles.

96. Install the injection line clips at the loom brackets.

97. Install the secondary fuel filter adapter.

98. Connect the secondary fuel filter lines.

99. Install the crankcase ventilator bracket.

100. Connect the air cleaner bracket at the valve cover.

101. Connect the coolant hose at the intake manifold.

102. Install the cruise control servo, servo bracket and transducer.

103. Install the oil filler pipe.

104. Install the engine dipstick tube.

105. Install the glow plug relay.

106. Install the alternator upper bracket.

107. Install the coolant crossover/thermostat assembly.

108. Connect the block heater wires.

109. Connect the heater hoses at the engine.

110. Connect the engine wiring harness at the firewall connection.

111. Install the radiator and the shroud.

112. Install the radiator support bracket.

113. Install the windshield wiper jar and bracket.

114. Install the air conditioning vacuum reservoir.

115. Charge the air conditioning system. See Chapter 1.

116. If the van is equipped with an automatic transmission, install the fluid cooler lines at the radiator.

117. Install the radiator coolant reservoir bottle.

118. Connect the radiator hoses at the radiator.

119. Install the upper radiator support.

120. Install the grille.

121. Install the lower grille valance.

122. Install the air cleaner.

123. Install the engine cover.

124. Fill the cooling system.

125. Connect the battery cables.

8–7.4L

1. Disconnect the battery cables.

2. Drain the cooling system.

CAUTION: *When draining the coolant, keep in mind that cats and dogs are attracted by the ethylene glycol antifreeze, and are quite likely to drink any that is left in an uncovered container or in puddles on the ground. This will prove fatal in sufficient quantity. Always drain the coolant into a sealable container. Coolant should be reused unless it is contaminated or several years old.*

3. Remove the engine cover.

4. Remove the air cleaner.

5. Remove the cruise control servo, servo bracket and transducer.

6. Remove the grille and the lower grille valance.

7. Remove the upper radiator support.

CAUTION: *Discharging the air conditioning refrigerant should only be attempted by those who have the proper tools and training to do so, as serious personal injury may result. The refrigerant will instantly freeze any surface it comes in contact with, including your eyes.*

8. Discharge the air conditioning system and remove the air conditioning vacuum reservoir.

9. Remove the air conditioning condenser from in front of the radiator. Cap all openings at once!

10. Disconnect the radiator hoses at the radiator.

11. Remove the fluid cooler lines from the radiator.

12. Remove the radiator coolant reservoir bottle.

13. Remove the radiator support bracket and remove the radiator and the shroud.

14. Remove the power steering pump.

15. Remove the air conditioning compressor. Cap all openings at once!

16. Disconnect the wiring fuel lines and linkage at the TBI unit.

17. Remove the TBI unit.

18. Disconnect the engine wiring harness from the firewall connection.

19. Disconnect the starter wires.

20. Disconnect the alternator wires.

21. Disconnect the temperature sensor wire.

22. Disconnect the oil pressure sender.

23. Disconnect the distributor and coil wiring.

24. Disconnect and plug the fuel supply and vapor lines.

25. Tag and disconnect all vacuum hoses.

26. Disconnect the heater hoses at the engine.

27. Remove the thermostat housing.

28. Remove the windshield wiper jar and bracket.

29. Remove the oil filler pipe and the engine dipstick tube.

30. Raise and support the van on jackstands.

31. Disconnect the exhaust pipes at the manifolds.

32. Remove the driveshaft and plug the end of the transmission.

33. Disconnect the transmission shift linkage and the speedometer cable.

34. Drain the engine oil.

35. Support the engine with a floor jack. DO NOT position the jack under the oil pan, crankshaft pulley or any sheet metal!

36. Attach an engine crane to the engine and take up its weight.

37. Remove the transmission mounting bolts.

38. Raise the engine slightly and remove the engine mounts. Support the engine with wood between the oil pan and the crossmember.

39. Lower the van.

40. Raise the engine as necessary and maneuver the engine/transmission assembly from the van.

41. Separate the engine and transmission as follows:

   a. Support the engine on blocks.

   b. Remove the starter and converter housing underpan.

   c. Remove the flywheel-to-converter attaching bolts.

   d. Support the transmission on blocks.

   e. Disconnect the detent cable.

   f. Remove the transmission-to-engine mounting bolts.

   g. Remove the blocks from the engine only and guide the engine away from the transmission.

42. Mount the engine on a work stand.

To install:

43. Install the automatic transmission as follows:

   a. Position the transmission.

   b. Install the transmission-to-engine mounting bolts. Torque the bolts to 40 ft. lbs.

   c. Connect the throttle linkage detent cable on the Turbo Hydra-Matic.

   d. Install the flywheel-to-converter attaching bolts. Torque the bolts to 40 ft. lbs.

   e. Install the starter and converter housing underpan.

44. Raise the engine/transmission and guide the assembly into position in the van.

45. Raise the engine slightly and install the engine mounts. Torque the mount-to-block bolts to 36 ft. lbs.

46. Install the engine mount through bolts. Torque the bolts to 75 ft. lbs.

47. Install the engine mount bracket-to-frame bolts. Torque the front mount bolts to 30 ft. lbs.; the rear mount bolts to 40 ft. lbs.

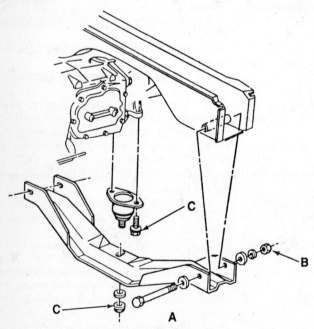

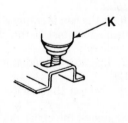

A. Front
B. 65 ft. lbs.
C. 36 ft. lbs.
K. With 700-R4 the mount must be in the maximum rearward position

Rear engine mounts for the 8-7.4L

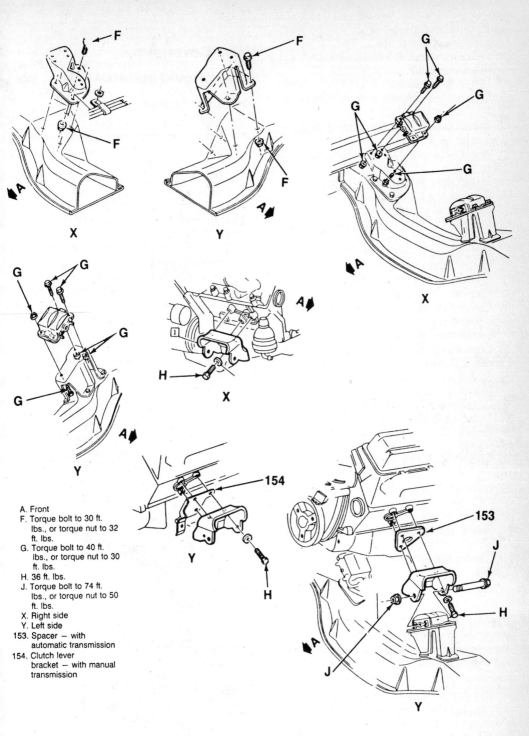

A. Front
F. Torque bolt to 30 ft.
   lbs., or torque nut to 32
   ft. lbs.
G. Torque bolt to 40 ft.
   lbs., or torque nut to 30
   ft. lbs.
H. 36 ft. lbs.
J. Torque bolt to 74 ft.
   lbs., or torque nut to 50
   ft. lbs.
X. Right side
Y. Left side
153. Spacer — with
     automatic transmission
154. Clutch lever
     bracket — with manual
     transmission

Front engine mounts for the 8-7.4L

48. Install the transmission mounting bolts. Torque the nuts to 36 ft. lbs.

49. Connect the transmission shift linkage and the speedometer cable.

50. Install the driveshaft.

51. Connect the exhaust pipes at the manifolds.

52. Install the oil filler pipe and the engine dipstick tube.

53. Install the windshield wiper jar and bracket.

54. Install the thermostat housing.

55. Connect the heater hoses at the engine.

56. Connect all vacuum hoses.

57. Connect the fuel supply and vapor lines.

58. Connect the distributor and coil wiring.

59. Connect the oil pressure sender.

60. Connect the temperature sensor wire.

61. Connect the alternator wires.

62. Connect the starter wires.

63. Connect the engine wiring harness at the firewall connection.

64. Install the TBI unit.

65. Connect the wiring, fuel lines and linkage at the TBI unit.

66. Install the air conditioning compressor.

67. Install the power steering pump.

68. Install the radiator and the shroud.

69. Install the radiator support bracket.

70. Install the radiator coolant reservoir bottle.

71. Install the fluid cooler lines at the radiator.

72. Connect the radiator hoses at the radiator.

73. Install the air conditioning condenser.

74. Install the air conditioning vacuum reservoir.

75. Charge the air conditioning system. See Chapter 1.

CAUTION: *Charging the air conditioning refrigerant should only be attempted by those who have the proper tools and training to do so, as serious personal injury may result! The refrigerant will instantly freeze any surface it comes in contact with, including your eyes!*

76. Install the upper radiator support.

77. Connect the radiator hoses at the radiator.

78. Install the grille and the lower grille valance.

79. Install the cruise control servo, servo bracket and transducer.

80. Fill the crankcase.

81. Install the air cleaner.

82. Install the engine cover.

83. Fill the cooling system.

84. Connect the battery cables.

Valve Cover(s)

REMOVAL AND INSTALLATION

All Gasoline Engines

1. Remove air cleaner.

2. Disconnect and reposition as necessary any vacuum or PCV hoses that obstruct the valve covers.

3. Disconnect electrical wire(s) (spark plug, etc.) from the valve cover clips.

4. Unbolt and remove the valve cover(s).

NOTE: *Do not pry the covers off if they seem stuck. Instead, gently tap around each cover with a rubber mallet until the old gasket or sealer breaks loose.*

5. To install, use a new valve cover gasket or RTV (or any equivalent) sealer. If using sealer, follow directions on the tube. Install valve cover and tighten cover bolts to 36 inch lbs.

6. Connect and reposition all vacuum and PCV hoses, and reconnect electrical and/or spark plug wires at the cover clips. Install the air cleaner.

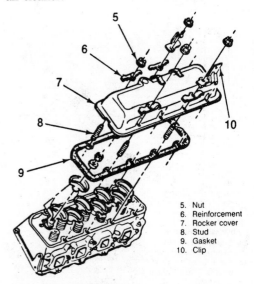

5. Nut
6. Reinforcement
7. Rocker cover
8. Stud
9. Gasket
10. Clip

Valve cover for the 8-7.4L

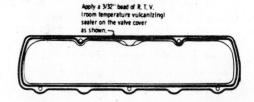

Apply a 3/32'' bead of R.T.V. (room temperature vulcanizing) sealer on the valve cover as shown.

Correct RTV application on the rocker cover

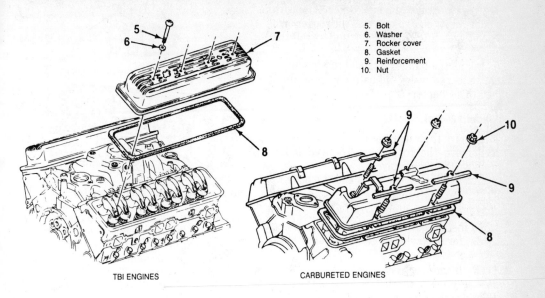

5. Bolt
6. Washer
7. Rocker cover
8. Gasket
9. Reinforcement
10. Nut

TBI ENGINES   CARBURETED ENGINES

Valve covers for the 6-4.3L, 8-5.0L and 8-5.7L

8–6.2L Diesel

RIGHT SIDE

1. Remove the intake manifold.
2. Remove the fuel injection lines for all except the Nos. 5 and 7 injectors.
3. Disconnect the glow plug wires.
4. Remove the wiring harness from the clip.
5. Remove the cover bolts.
6. Remove the cover. If the cover sticks, jar it loose with a plastic or rubber mallet. NEVER pry it loose!
7. Installation is the reverse of removal. Clean all old RTV gasket material from the mating surfaces. Apply a $5/16$ in. bead of sealer to the head mating surfaces. Tighten the cover bolts to 16 ft. lbs.

LEFT SIDE

1. Remove the intake manifold.
2. Remove the fuel injection lines.
3. On vans with air conditioning, remove the upper fan shroud.
4. On vans with air conditioning, remove the compressor drive belt.
5. On vans with air conditioning, remove the left exhaust manifold.
6. On vans with air conditioning, dismount the compressor and move it out of the way. It may be possible to avoid disconnecting the refrigerant lines. If not, Discharge the system

and disconnect the lines. Cap all openings at once. See Chapter 1 for discharging procedures.
7. Remove the dipstick tube front bracket from the stud.
8. Remove the wiring harness brackets.
9. Remove the rocker arm cover bolts and fuel return bracket.
10. Remove the cover. If the cover sticks, jar it loose with a plastic or rubber mallet. NEVER pry it loose!
11. Installation is the reverse of removal. Clean all old RTV gasket material from the mating surfaces. Apply a $5/16$ in. bead of sealer to the head mating surfaces. Tighten the cover bolts to 16 ft. lbs.

Rocker Arms

REMOVAL AND INSTALLATION

8–5.0L
8–5.7L

1. Remove the valve cover.
2. Remove the rocker arm flanged bolts, and remove the rocker pivots.
3. Remove the rocker arms.
NOTE: *Remove each set of rocker arms (one set per cylinder) as a unit.*
4. To install, position a set of rocker arms (for one cylinder) in the proper location.
NOTE: *Install the rocker arms for each cylinder only when the lifters are off the cam lobe and both valves are closed.*

5. Coat the replacement rocker arm with Molycoat® or its equivalent, and the rocker arm and pivot with SAE 90 gear oil, and install the pivots.

6. Install the flange bolts and tighten alternately. See the valve adjustment procedure later in this Chapter.

6–4.3L and 8–7.4L

1. Remove the valve cover.

2. Remove the rocker arm flanged bolts, and remove the rocker pivots.

3. Remove the rocker arms and the balls.

NOTE: *Remove each set of rocker arms and balls (one set per cylinder) as a unit.*

4. To install, position a set of rocker arms, and balls (for one cylinder) in the proper location.

NOTE: *Install the rocker arms for each cylinder only when the lifters are off the cam lobe and both valves are closed.*

5. Coat the replacement rocker arms and balls with Molycoat® or its equivalent, and install the pivots.

6. Install the flange bolts and tighten alternately. See the valve adjustment procedure later in this Chapter.

8–6.2L Diesel

1. Remove the valve cover as previously explained.

2. The rocker assemblies are mounted on two short rocker shafts per cylinder head, with each shaft operating four rockers. Remove the two bolts which secure each rocker shaft assembly, and remove the shaft.

3. The rocker arms can be removed from the shaft by removing the cotter pin on the end of each shaft. The rocker arms and springs slide off.

4. To install, make sure first that the rocker arms and springs go back on the shafts in the exact order in which they were removed.

NOTE: *Always install new cotter pins on the rocker shaft ends.*

5. Install the rocker shaft assemblies, torquing the bolts to 41 ft. lbs.

Thermostat

REMOVAL AND INSTALLATION

All Gasoline Engines

1. Drain the radiator until the level is below the thermostat level (below the level of the intake manifold).

CAUTION: *When draining the coolant, keep in mind that cats and dogs are attracted by*

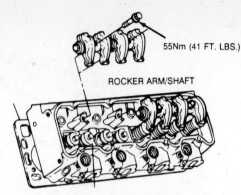

55Nm (41 FT. LBS.)

ROCKER ARM/SHAFT

8-6.2L diesel rocker shaft assembly

the ethylene glycol antifreeze, and are quite likely to drink any that is left in an uncovered container or in puddles on the ground. This will prove fatal in sufficient quantity. Always drain the coolant into a sealable container. Coolant should be reused unless it is contaminated or several years old.

2. Remove the water outlet elbow assembly from the engine. Remove the thermostat from inside the elbow.

3. Install new thermostat in the reverse order of removal, making sure the spring side is inserted into the engine. Clean the gasket surfaces on the water outlet elbow and the intake manifold. Use a new gasket when installing the elbow to the manifold. Torque the thermostat housing bolts to 20 ft. lbs.

4. Refill the cooling system.

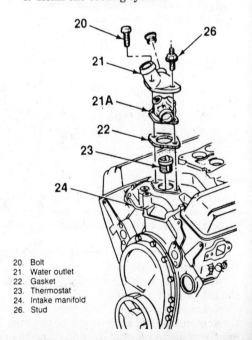

20. Bolt
21. Water outlet
22. Gasket
23. Thermostat
24. Intake manifold
26. Stud

Thermostat for the 8-5.0L and 8-5.7L

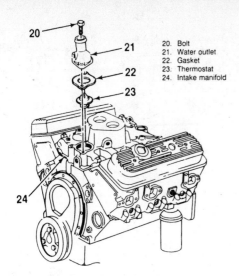

20.	Bolt
21.	Water outlet
22.	Gasket
23.	Thermostat
24.	Intake manifold

Thermostat for the 6-4.3L

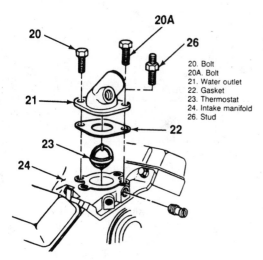

20.	Bolt
20A.	Bolt
21.	Water outlet
22.	Gasket
23.	Thermostat
24.	Intake manifold
26.	Stud

Thermostat for the 8-7.4L

8–6.2L Diesel

1. Remove the upper fan shroud.
2. Drain the cooling system to a point below the thermostat.

CAUTION: *When draining the coolant, keep in mind that cats and dogs are attracted by the ethylene glycol antifreeze, and are quite likely to drink any that is left in an uncovered container or in puddles on the ground. This will prove fatal in sufficient quantity. Always drain the coolant into a sealable container. Coolant should be reused unless it is contaminated or several years old.*

3. Remove the engine oil dipstick tube brace and the oil fill brace.
4. Remove the upper radiator hose.

5. Remove the water outlet.
6. Remove the thermostat and gasket.
7. Installation is the reverse of removal. Use a new gasket coated with sealer, Make sure that the spring end of the thermostat is in the engine. Torque the bolts to 35 ft. lbs.

De-Aeration Tank

REMOVAL AND INSTALLATION

1. Drain the cooling system to a point below the level of the tank.

CAUTION: *When draining the coolant, keep in mind that cats and dogs are attracted by the ethylene glycol antifreeze, and are quite likely to drink any that is left in an uncovered container or in puddles on the ground. This will prove fatal in sufficient quantity. Always drain the coolant into a sealable container. Coolant should be reused unless it is contaminated or several years old.*

2. Disconnect the overflow hose from the radiator.
3. Disconnect the return hose from the tank.
4. Remove the tank's mounting screw and bolt and lift the tank from the van.
5. Installation is the reverse of removal.
6. Fill the cooling system.

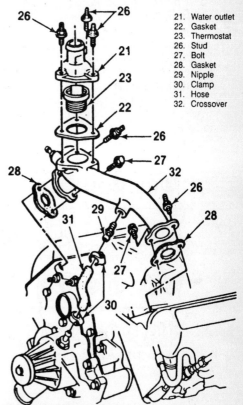

21.	Water outlet
22.	Gasket
23.	Thermostat
26.	Stud
27.	Bolt
28.	Gasket
29.	Nipple
30.	Clamp
31.	Hose
32.	Crossover

Thermostat for the 8-6.2L

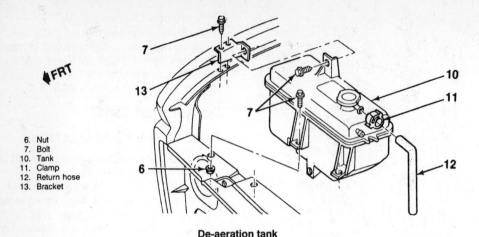

♦FRT

6. Nut
7. Bolt
10. Tank
11. Clamp
12. Return hose
13. Bracket

De-aeration tank

Intake Manifold

REMOVAL AND INSTALLATION

6–4.3L

1. Drain the cooling system.
CAUTION: *When draining the coolant, keep in mind that cats and dogs are attracted by the ethylene glycol antifreeze, and are quite likely to drink any that is left in an uncovered container or in puddles on the ground. This will prove fatal in sufficient quantity. Always drain the coolant into a sealable container. Coolant should be reused unless it is contaminated or several years old.*

2. Remove the air cleaner assembly.
3. Remove the thermostat housing and the bypass hose. It is not necessary to remove the top radiator hose from the thermostat housing.
4. Disconnect the heater hose at the rear of the manifold.
5. Disconnect all electrical connections and

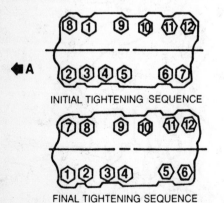

INITIAL TIGHTENING SEQUENCE

FINAL TIGHTENING SEQUENCE

A. Front of Engine

Intake manifold bolt tightening sequence for the 6-4.3L

vacuum lines from the manifold. Remove the EGR valve if necessary.

6. On vehicles equipped with power brakes remove the vacuum line from the vacuum booster to the manifold.
7. Remove the distributor (if necessary).
8. Remove the fuel line at the TBI unit.
9. Remove the accelerator linkage.
10. Remove the TBI unit.
11. Remove the intake manifold bolts. Remove the manifold and the gaskets. Remember to reinstall the O-ring between the intake manifold and timing chain cover during assembly, if so equipped.

To install:

NOTE: *Before installing the intake manifold, be sure that the gasket surfaces are thoroughly clean.*

13. Use plastic gasket retainers to prevent the manifold gasket from slipping out of place, if so equipped.
14. Install the manifold and the gaskets. Remember to reinstall the O-ring between the intake manifold and timing chain cover, if so equipped.
15. Install the intake manifold bolts.
16. Install the TBI unit.
17. Install the TBI linkage.
18. Install the fuel line.
19. Install the distributor (if necessary).
20. On vehicles equipped with power brakes install the vacuum line between the vacuum booster and manifold.
21. Connect all electrical connections and vacuum lines at the manifold. Install the EGR valve if necessary.
22. Connect the heater hose at the rear of the manifold.
23. Install the thermostat housing and the bypass hose.
24. Install the air cleaner assembly.
25. Fill the cooling system.

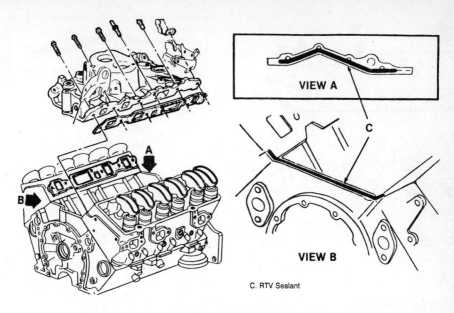

C. RTV Sealant

6-4.3L intake manifold

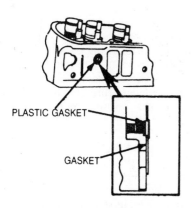

PLASTIC GASKET

GASKET

Plastic manifold gasket retainers on gasoline V8 engines

8–5.0L
8–5.7L

1. Drain the cooling system.

CAUTION: *When draining the coolant, keep in mind that cats and dogs are attracted by the ethylene glycol antifreeze, and are quite likely to drink any that is left in an uncovered container or in puddles on the ground. This will prove fatal in sufficient quantity. Always drain the coolant into a sealable container. Coolant should be reused unless it is contaminated or several years old.*

2. Remove the air cleaner assembly.

3. Remove the thermostat housing and the bypass hose. It is not necessary to remove the top radiator hose from the thermostat housing.

4. Disconnect the heater hose at the rear of the manifold.

5. Disconnect all electrical connections and vacuum lines from the manifold. Remove the EGR valve if necessary.

6. On vehicles equipped with power brakes remove the vacuum line from the vacuum booster to the manifold.

7. Remove the distributor (if necessary).

8. Remove the fuel line at the carburetor or TBI unit.

9. Remove the accelerator linkage.

10. Remove the carburetor or TBI unit.

11. Remove the intake manifold bolts. Remove the manifold and the gaskets. Remember to reinstall the O-ring between the intake manifold and timing chain cover during assembly, if so equipped.

To install:

NOTE: *Before installing the intake manifold, be sure that the gasket surfaces are thoroughly clean.*

13. Use plastic gasket retainers to prevent the manifold gasket from slipping out of place, if so equipped. Place a $\frac{3}{16}$ in. (4.8mm) bead of RTV type silicone sealer on the front and rear

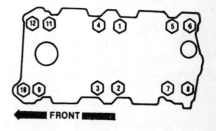

Intake manifold bolt tightening sequence for the 8-5.0L and 8-5.7L

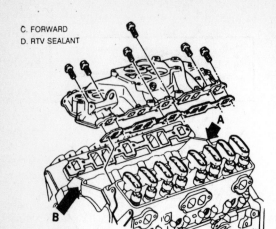

C. FORWARD
D. RTV SEALANT

A

B

C

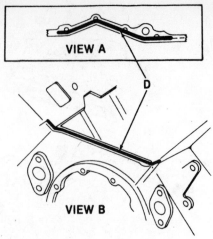

VIEW A

D

VIEW B

Intake manifold for the 8-5.0L or 8-5.7L

ridges of the cylinder block-to-manifold mating surfaces. Extend the bead ½ in. (12.7mm) up each cylinder head to seal and retain the manifold side gaskets.

14. Install the manifold and the gaskets. Remember to reinstall the O-ring between the intake manifold and timing chain cover, if so equipped.

15. Install the intake manifold bolts.

16. Install the carburetor or TBI unit.

17. Install the carburetor or TBI linkage.

18. Install the fuel line.

19. Install the distributor (if necessary).

20. On vehicles equipped with power brakes install the vacuum line between the vacuum booster and manifold.

21. Connect all electrical connections and vacuum lines at the manifold. Install the EGR valve if necessary.

22. Connect the heater hose at the rear of the manifold.

23. Install the thermostat housing and the bypass hose.

24. Install the air cleaner assembly.

25. Fill the cooling system.

8–6.2L Diesel

1. Disconnect both batteries.

2. Remove the air cleaner assembly.

3. Remove the crankcase ventilator tubes, and disconnect the secondary fuel filter lines. Remove the secondary filter and adaptor.

4. Loosen the vacuum pump holddown clamp and rotate the pump to gain access to the nearest manifold bolt.

5. Remove the EPR/EGR valve bracket, if equipped.

6. Remove the rear air conditioning bracket, if equipped.

7. Remove the intake manifold bolts. The injection line clips are retained by these bolts.

8. Remove the intake manifold.

NOTE: *If the engine is to be further serviced with the manifold removed, install protective covers over the intake ports.*

LEFT SIDE

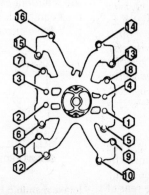

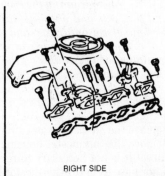

RIGHT SIDE

Intake manifold for the 6.2L diesel

To install:

9. Clean the manifold gasket surfaces on the cylinder heads and install new gaskets before installing the manifold.

NOTE: *The gaskets have an opening for the EGR valve on light duty installations. An insert covers this opening on heavy duty installations.*

10. Install the manifold. Torque the bolts in the sequence illustrated.

11. The secondary filter must be filled with clean diesel fuel before it is reinstalled.

12. Install the rear air conditioning bracket, if equipped.

13. Install the EPR/EGR valve bracket, if equipped.

14. Tighten the vacuum pump holddown clamp.

15. Install the secondary filter and adaptor.

16. Connect the secondary fuel filter lines.

17. Install the crankcase ventilator tubes.

18. Install the air cleaner assembly.

19. Connect both batteries.

8–7.4L

1. Disconnect the battery.

2. Drain the cooling system.

CAUTION: *When draining the coolant, keep in mind that cats and dogs are attracted by the ethylene glycol antifreeze, and are quite likely to drink any that is left in an uncovered container or in puddles on the ground. This will prove fatal in sufficient quantity. Always drain the coolant into a sealable container. Coolant should be reused unless it is contaminated or several years old.*

3. Remove the air cleaner assembly.

4. Remove the upper radiator hose, thermostat housing and the bypass hose.

5. Disconnect the heater hose and pipe.

6. Tag and disconnect all electrical connections and vacuum lines from the manifold.

7. Disconnect the accelerator linkage.

8. Disconnect the cruise control cable.

9. Disconnect the TVS cable.

10. Remove the fuel line at the TBI unit.

11. Remove the TBI unit.

12. Remove the distributor.

13. Remove the cruise control transducer.

14. Disconnect the ignition coil wires.

15. Remove the EGR solenoid and bracket.

16. Remove the MAP sensor and bracket.

17. Remove the air conditioning compressor rear bracket.

18. Remove the front alternator/AIR pump bracket.

19. Remove the intake manifold bolts.

20. Remove the manifold and the gaskets and seals.

NOTE: *Remember to reinstall the O-ring between the intake manifold and timing chain cover during assembly, if so equipped.*

To install:

NOTE: *Before installing the intake manifold, be sure that the gasket surfaces are thoroughly clean.*

21. Install the manifold and the gaskets and seals.

22. Install the intake manifold bolts. Torque the bolts, in sequence, to 30 ft. lbs.

23. Install the front alternator/AIR pump bracket.

24. Install the air conditioning compressor rear bracket.

25. Install the MAP sensor and bracket.

26. Install the EGR solenoid and bracket.

27. Connect the ignition coil wires.

28. Install the cruise control transducer.

29. Install the distributor.

30. Install the TBI unit.

31. Install the fuel line at the TBI unit.

32. Connect the TVS cable.

33. Connect the cruise control cable.

34. Connect the accelerator linkage.

35. Connect all electrical connections and vacuum lines at the manifold.

36. Connect the heater hose and pipe.

37. Install the upper radiator hose, thermostat housing and the bypass hose.

38. Install the air cleaner assembly.

39. Fill the cooling system.

40. Connect the battery.

Exhaust Manifold

REMOVAL AND INSTALLATION

6–4.3L
8–5.0L
8–5.7L

Tab locks are used on the front and rear pairs of bolts on each exhaust manifold. When removing the bolts, straighten the tabs from beneath the van using a suitable tool. When installing the tab locks, bend the tabs against the sides of the bolt, not over the top of the bolt.

1. Remove the air cleaner.

2. Remove the hot air shroud, (if so equipped).

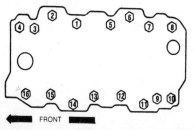

8-7.4L intake manifold bolt tightening sequence

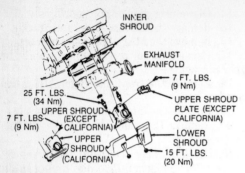

8-5.0L and 8-5.7L exhaust manifold

3. Loosen the alternator and remove its lower bracket.

4. Jack up your van and support it with jackstands.

5. Disconnect the crossover pipe from both manifolds.

NOTE: *On models with air conditioning it may be necessary to remove the compressor, and tie it out of the way. Do not disconnect the compressor lines.*

6. Remove the manifold bolts and remove the manifold(s). Some models have lock tabs on the front and rear manifold bolts which must be removed before removing the bolts. These tabs can be bent with a drift pin.

7. Installation is the reverse of removal.

8–7.4L

RIGHT SIDE

1. Disconnect the battery.
2. Remove the heat stove pipe.
3. Remove the dipstick tube.
4. Disconnect the AIR hose at the check valve.

5. Remove the park plugs.
6. Disconnect the exhaust pipe at the manifold.
7. Remove the manifold bolts and spark plug heat shields.
8. Remove the manifold.

To install:

9. Clean the mating surfaces.
10. Clean the stud threads.
11. Install the manifold and bolts. Tighten the bolts to 40 ft. lbs. starting from the center bolts and working towards the outside.
12. Connect the exhaust pipe at the manifold.
13. Install the park plugs.
14. Connect the AIR hose at the check valve.
15. Install the dipstick tube.
16. Install the heat stove pipe.
17. Connect the battery.

LEFT SIDE

1. Disconnect the battery.
2. Disconnect the oxygen sensor wire.
3. Disconnect the AIR hose at the check valve.
4. Remove the park plugs.
5. Disconnect the exhaust pipe at the manifold.
6. Remove the manifold bolts and spark plug heat shields.
7. Remove the manifold.

To install:

8. Clean the mating surfaces.
9. Clean the stud threads.
10. Install the manifold and bolts. Tighten the bolts to 40 ft. lbs. starting from the center bolts and working towards the outside.
11. Connect the exhaust pipe at the manifold.

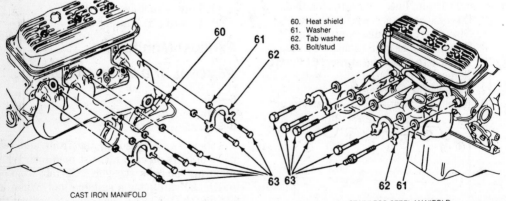

60. Heat shield
61. Washer
62. Tab washer
63. Bolt/stud

CAST IRON MANIFOLD

STAINLESS STEEL MANIFOLD RETAINERS

6-4.3L exhaust manifold

12. Install the park plugs.
13. Connect the AIR hose at the check valve.
14. Connect the oxygen sensor wire.
15. Connect the battery.

8–6.2L Diesel

RIGHT SIDE

1. Disconnect the batteries.
2. Jack up the truck and safely support it with jackstands.
3. Disconnect the exhaust pipe from the manifold flange and lower the truck.
4. Disconnect the glow plug wires.
5. Remove the air cleaner duct bracket.
6. Remove the glow plug wires.
7. Remove the manifold bolts and remove the manifold.
8. To install, reverse the above procedure and torque the bolts to 25 ft. lbs.

LEFT SIDE

1. Disconnect the batteries.
2. Remove the dipstick tube nut, and remove the dipstick tube.
3. Disconnect the glow plug wires.
4. Jack up the truck and safely support it with jackstands.
5. Disconnect the exhaust pipe at the manifold flange.
6. Remove the manifold bolts. Remove the manifold from underneath the truck.
7. Reverse the above procedure to install. Start the manifold bolts while the truck is jacked up first. Torque the bolts to 25 ft. lbs.

Vacuum Pump

REMOVAL AND INSTALLATION

Diesel Engine Only

1. Disconnect the battery ground cable.
2. Remove the alternator belt.
3. Remove the upper pump attaching bolts.
4. Raise and support the front end on jackstands.
5. Drain the cooling system.
CAUTION: *When draining the coolant, keep in mind that cats and dogs are attracted by the ethylene glycol antifreeze, and are quite likely to drink any that is left in an uncovered container or in puddles on the ground. This will prove fatal in sufficient quantity. Always drain the coolant into a sealable container. Coolant should be reused unless it is contaminated or several years old.*
6. Remove the lower radiator hose.
7. Disconnect the vacuum hose at the pump.
8. Remove the lower pump attaching bolt.

9. Remove the pump/pulley assembly. If the pulley is being removed, use puller J-25034-B or its equivalent. DO NOT pry on the pulley or pump body.
To install:
10. Position the pump on the engine and install the lower attaching bolt. Torque the bolt to 20 ft. lbs.
11. Connect the vacuum hose.
12. Connect the lower radiator hose.
13. Lower the van.
14. Install the upper attaching bolts. Torque them to 20 ft. lbs.
15. Install and adjust the belt.
16. Connect the battery.
17. Fill the cooling system.

Air Conditioning Compressor

REMOVAL AND INSTALLATION

1. Disconnect the negative battery cable.
2. Disconnect the compressor clutch connector.
3. Purge the system of refrigerant.
CAUTION: *Discharging the air conditioning refrigerant should only be attempted by those who have the proper tools and training to do so, as serious personal injury may result. The refrigerant will instantly freeze any surface it comes in contact with, including your eyes.*
4. Remove the belt by releasing the belt tension at the idler pulley.
NOTE: *On some models it will be necessary to remove the crankshaft pulley to remove the belt.*
5. Remove the engine cover (if necessary).
6. Remove the air cleaner.
7. Remove the fitting and muffler assembly. Cap and plug all open connections.
8. Remove the compressor bracket.
9. Remove the engine oil tube support bracket bolt and nut.
10. Disconnect the clutch ground lead.
11. Remove the compressor.
12. Drain and measure the oil in the compressor and check for contamination.
To install:
13. Install the compressor.
14. Install the measured amount of oil in the compressor.
15. Connect the clutch ground lead.
16. Install the engine oil tube support bracket bolt and nut.
17. Install the compressor bracket.
18. Install the fitting and muffler assembly.
19. Install the air cleaner.
20. Install the engine cover (if necessary).
21. Install the crankshaft pulley.
22. Install the belt.

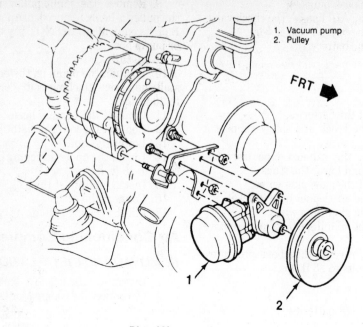

1. Vacuum pump
2. Pulley

Diesel Vacuum pump

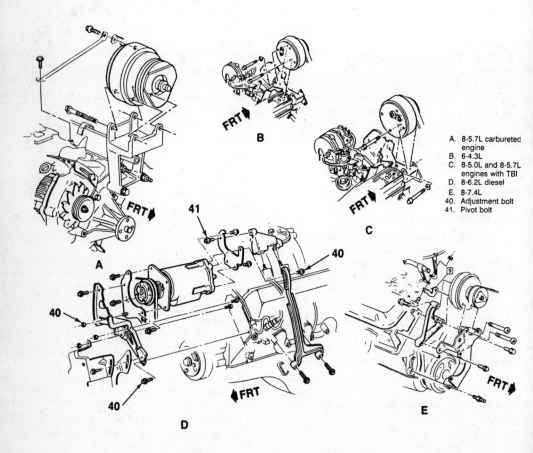

A. 8-5.7L carbureted engine
B. 6-4.3L
C. 8-5.0L and 8-5.7L engines with TBI
D. 8-6.2L diesel
E. 8-7.4L
40. Adjustment bolt
41. Pivot bolt

Air conditioning compressor mountings

23. Charge refrigerant system. See Chapter 1.

24. Connect the compressor clutch connector.

25. Connect the negative battery cable.

Radiator

REMOVAL AND INSTALLATION

Gasoline Engines

1. Drain the cooling system.

CAUTION: *When draining the coolant, keep in mind that cats and dogs are attracted by the ethylene glycol antifreeze, and are quite likely to drink any that is left in an uncovered container or in puddles on the ground. This will prove fatal in sufficient quantity. Always drain the coolant into a sealable container. Coolant should be reused unless it is contaminated or several years old.*

2. Disconnect the radiator upper and lower hoses and, if applicable, the transmission coolant lines. Remove the coolant recovery system line, if so equipped.

3. Remove the radiator upper panel if so equipped.

4. If there is a radiator shroud in front of the radiator, the radiator and shroud are removed as an assembly.

5. If there is a fan shroud, remove the shroud attaching screws and let the shroud hang on the fan.

6. Remove the radiator attaching bolts and remove the radiator.

7. Installation is the reverse of the removal procedure.

Diesel Engine

1. Drain the cooling system.

CAUTION: *When draining the coolant, keep in mind that cats and dogs are attracted by the ethylene glycol antifreeze, and are quite likely to drink any that is left in an uncovered container or in puddles on the ground. This will prove fatal in sufficient quantity. Always drain the coolant into a sealable container. Coolant should be reused unless it is contaminated or several years old.*

2. Remove the air intake snorkel.

3. Remove the windshield washer bottle.

4. Remove the hood release cable.

5. Remove the upper fan shroud.

6. Disconnect the upper radiator hose.

7. Disconnect the transmission cooler lines.

8. Disconnect the low coolant sensor wire.

9. Disconnect the overflow hose.

10. Disconnect the engine oil cooler lines.

11. Disconnect the lower radiator hose.

12. Remove the brake master cylinder. See Chapter 9.

13. Unbolt and remove the radiator.

To install:

14. Install the radiator.

15. Install the brake master cylinder.

16. Connect the lower radiator hose.

17. Connect the engine oil cooler lines.

18. Connect the overflow hose.

19. Connect the low coolant sensor wire.

20. Connect the transmission cooler lines.

21. Connect the upper radiator hose.

22. Install the upper fan shroud.

23. Install the hood release cable.

24. Install the windshield washer bottle.

25. Install the air intake snorkel.

26. Fill the cooling system.

Air Conditioning Condenser

REMOVAL AND INSTALLATION

1. Disconnect the battery ground cable.

2. Discharge the system. See Chapter 1.

3. Remove the grille, hood lock and center hood lock support. See Chapter 10.

4. Using a back-up wrench, disconnect the refrigerant lines at the condenser. Cap all openings at once!

5. Remove the condenser mounting bolts and lift out the condenser.

6. Installation is the reverse of removal. Evacuate, charge and leak-test the system. Use new O-rings, coated with clean refrigerant oil, at the refrigerant line connections. When install a new condenser, add 1 oz. of clean refrigerant oil.

Thermostat Housing Crossover

REMOVAL AND INSTALLATION

Diesel Engine

1. Drain the cooling system.

CAUTION: *When draining the coolant, keep in mind that cats and dogs are attracted by the ethylene glycol antifreeze, and are quite likely to drink any that is left in an uncovered container or in puddles on the ground. This will prove fatal in sufficient quantity. Always drain the coolant into a sealable container. Coolant should be reused unless it is contaminated or several years old.*

2. Remove the engine cover.

3. Remove the air cleaner.

4. Remove the air cleaner resonator and bracket.

5. Remove the upper fan shroud.

6. Remove the upper alternator bracket.

7. Remove the bypass hose.

8. Remove the upper radiator hose.

2. Radiator
3. Radiator cap
4. Upper insulator
9. Upper shroud
10. Lower shroud
11. Hose
12. Reservoir cap
13. Reservoir
15. Drain cock
16. Lower insulator
26. Left baffle
27. Nut
29. Screw
30. Screw
31. Screw
32. Screw
33. Panel
34. Bracket
35. Screw
36. Bracket
37. Screw
38. Surge tank
39. Cap
40. Hose
42. Nut
43. Screw
44. Lower hose
45. Clamp
46. Nut
47. Right baffle
48. Upper hose
49. Screw
50. Mounting panels
51. Cross sill
52. Mounting brackets
53. Screw
54. Nut
55. Nut
56. Clip
58. Hose

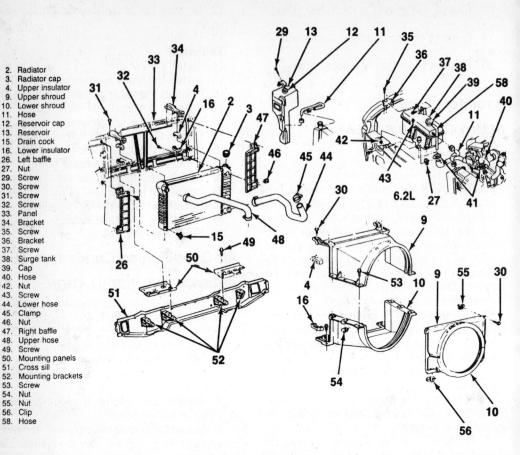

Radiator and related parts

9. Disconnect the heater hose.

10. Remove the attaching bolts and lift out the crossover.

To install:

11. Thoroughly clean the mating surfaces.

12. Position the crossover, using new gaskets coated with sealer.

13. Install the attaching bolts and torque them to 35 ft. lbs.

14. Connect the heater hose.

15. Install the upper radiator hose.

16. Install the bypass hose.

17. Install the upper alternator bracket.

18. Install the upper fan shroud.

19. Install the air cleaner resonator and bracket.

20. Install the air cleaner.

21. Install the engine cover.

22. Fill the cooling system.

Auxiliary Cooling Fan

REMOVAL AND INSTALLATION

1. Remove the grille.

2. Unplug the fan harness connector.

3. Remove the fan-to-brace bolts and lift out the fan.

4. Installation is the reverse of removal. Torque the bolts to 53 ft. lbs.

Water Pump

REMOVAL AND INSTALLATION

6–4.3L
8–5.0L, 5.7L, 7.4L

1. Disconnect the battery.

2. Drain the radiator.

CAUTION: *When draining the coolant, keep in mind that cats and dogs are attracted by the ethylene glycol antifreeze, and are quite likely to drink any that is left in an uncovered container or in puddles on the ground. This will prove fatal in sufficient quantity. Always drain the coolant into a sealable container. Coolant should be reused unless it is contaminated or several years old.*

3. Loosen the alternator and other accessories at their adjusting points, and remove the fan belts from the fan pulley.

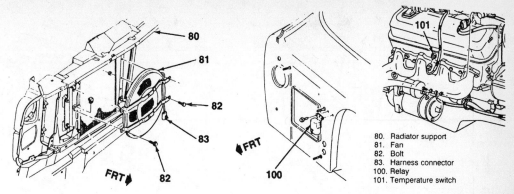

80. Radiator support
81. Fan
82. Bolt
83. Harness connector
100. Relay
101. Temperature switch

Auxiliary cooling fan

4. Remove the fan and pulley.

5. Remove any accessory brackets that might interfere with water pump removal.

6. Disconnect the hose from the water pump inlet and the heater hose from the nipple on the pump. Remove the bolts, pump assembly and old gasket from the timing chain cover.

7. Check the pump shaft bearings for end play or roughness in operation. Water pump bearings usually emit a squealing sound with the engine running when the bearings need to be replaced. Replace the pump if the bearings are not in good shape or have been noisy.

To install:

8. Make sure the gasket surfaces on the pump and timing chain cover are clean.

9. Install the pump assembly with a new gasket. Tighten the bolts to 30 ft. lbs.

10. Connect the hose between the water pump inlet and the nipple on the pump.

11. Install any accessory brackets.

12. Install the fan and pulley.

13. Install and adjust the alternator and other accessories.

14. Install the fan belts from the fan pulley.

15. Fill the cooling system.

16. Connect the battery.

8–6.2L Diesel

1. Disconnect the batteries.

2. Remove the fan and fan shroud.

3. Drain the radiator.

CAUTION: *When draining the coolant, keep in mind that cats and dogs are attracted by the ethylene glycol antifreeze, and are quite likely to drink any that is left in an uncovered container or in puddles on the ground. This will prove fatal in sufficient quantity. Always drain the coolant into a sealable container. Coolant should be reused unless it is contaminated or several years old.*

4. If the truck is equipped with air conditioning, remove the air conditioning hose bracket nuts.

5. Remove the oil filler tube.

6. Remove the generator pivot bolt and remove the generator belt.

7. Remove the generator lower bracket.

8. Remove the power steering belt and secure it out of the way.

9. Remove the air conditioning belt if equipped.

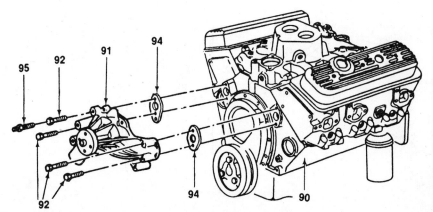

90. Engine block
91. Water pump
92. Bolt
94. Gasket
95. Stud

6-4.3L water pump

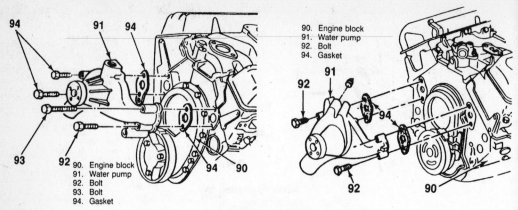

90. Engine block
91. Water pump
92. Bolt
94. Gasket

90. Engine block
91. Water pump
92. Bolt
93. Bolt
94. Gasket

8-7.4L water pump

10. Disconnect the by-pass hose and the lower radiator hose.

11. Remove the water pump bolts. Remove the water pump plate and gasket and water pump. If the pump gasket is to be replaced, remove the plate attaching bolts to the water pump and remove (and replace) the gasket.

To install:

12. When installing the pump, the flanges must be free of oil. Apply an anaerobic sealer (GM part No.1052357 or equivalent) as shown in the accompanying illustration.

NOTE: *The sealer must be wet to the touch when the bolts are torqued.*

13. Attach the water pump and plate assembly. Torque the bolts to 35 ft. lbs.

14. Connect the by-pass hose and the lower radiator hose.

15. Install the air conditioning belt if equipped.

16. Install the power steering belt.

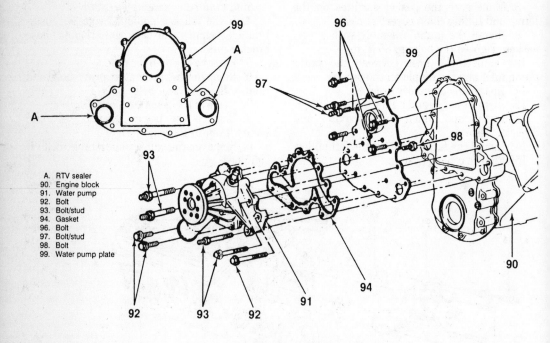

A. RTV sealer
90. Engine block
91. Water pump
92. Bolt
93. Bolt/stud
94. Gasket
96. Bolt
97. Bolt/stud
98. Bolt
99. Water pump plate

8-6.2L diesel water pump

17. Install the generator lower bracket.
18. Install the generator pivot bolt.
19. Install the generator belt.
20. Install the oil filler tube.
21. If the truck is equipped with air conditioning, install the air conditioning hose bracket nuts.
22. Fill the radiator.
23. Install the fan and fan shroud.
24. Connect the batteries.

Hydraulic Lifters

REMOVAL AND INSTALLATION

6–4.3L

1. Remove the rocker cover.
2. Remove the intake manifold.
3. Back off the rocker arm adjusting nuts and remove the pushrods. Keep them in order for installation.
4. Remove the lifter retainer bolts, retainer and restrictor.
5. Remove the lifters. If your are going to re-use the lifters, remove them one at a time and mark each one for installation. They *must* be re-installed in the same locations.   If a lifter is stuck, it can be removed with a grasping-type lifter tool, available form most auto parts stores.
6. Inspect each lifter thoroughly. If any of

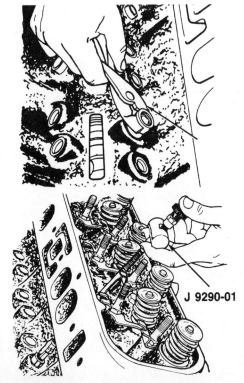

Removing hydraulic lifters from V6 or V8 engines

them shows any signs of wear, heat bluing or damage, replace the whole set.
7. Installation is the reverse of removal. Coat each lifter with engine oil supplement prior to installation. Torque the retainer bolts to 12 ft. lbs. Adjust the valves as described below.

8–5.0L
8–5.7L
8–7.4L

1. Remove the rocker cover.
2. Remove the intake manifold.
3. Back off the rocker arm adjusting nuts and remove the pushrods. Keep them in order for installation.
4. Remove the lifters. If your are going to re-use the lifters, remove them one at a time and mark each one for installation. They *must* be re-installed in the same locations.   If a lifter is stuck, it can be removed with a grasping-type lifter tool, available form most auto parts stores.
5. Inspect each lifter thoroughly. If any of them shows any signs of wear, heat bluing or damage, replace the whole set.
6. Installation is the reverse of removal. Coat each lifter with engine oil supplement prior to installation. Adjust the valves as described below.

8–6.2L Diesel

1. Remove the rocker cover.
2. Remove the rocker arm shaft, rocker arms and pushrods. Keep all parts in order and properly identified for installation.
3. Remove the clamps and lifter guide plates.
4. Remove the lifters by reaching through the access holes in the cylinder head with a magnetic lifter tool. If your are going to re-use the lifters, remove them one at a time and mark each one for installation. They *must* be re-installed in the same locations.   If a lifter is stuck, it can be removed with a grasping-type lifter tool, available form most auto parts stores.
5. Inspect each lifter thoroughly. If any of them shows any signs of wear, heat bluing or damage, replace the whole set.

NOTE: *Some engines will have both standard and 0.010 in. oversize lifters. The oversized lifters will have "10" etched into the side. The block will be stamped "OS" on the cast pad next to the lifter bore. and on the top rail of the crankcase above the lifter bore.*

To install:

WARNING: *New lifters must be primed before installation. Damage to the lifters and*

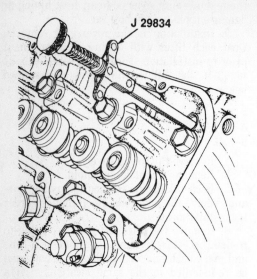

Removing the hydraulic lifters from the diesel engine

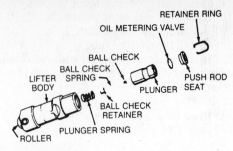

Diesel engine lifter

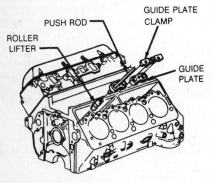

Diesel lifter retaining parts

engine will result if new lifters are installed dry!

6. Prime new lifters by immersing them in clean kerosene or diesel fuel and working the lifter plunger while the unit is submerged.

7. Prior to installation, coat the lifter roller with engine oil supplement. Re-used lifters must be installed in their original positions!

8. Install the lifters.

9. Install the guide plates and clamps. Torque the clamp bolts to 18 ft. lbs.

10. After all the clamps are installed, turn the crankshaft by hand, 2 full turns (720°) to ensure free movement of the lifters in the guide plates. If the crankshaft won't turn, one or more lifters may be jamming in the guide plates.

11. The remainder of assembly the reverse of disassembly.

Rocker Stud

REPLACEMENT

NOTE: *The following tools will be necessary for this procedure: Rocker stud replacement tool J–5802–01, Reamer J–5715 (0.003 in. os) or Reamer J–6036 (0.013 in. os) and In-staller J–6880, or their equivalents.*

6–4.3L
8–5.0L
8–5.7L

1. Remove the rocker cover.

2. Remove the rocker arm.

3. Place the tool over the stud. Install the nut and flat washer.

4. Tighten the nut to remove the stud.

To install:

5. Using one of the reamers, ream the stud hole as necessary.

6. Coat the lower end of the new stud with SAE 80W–90 gear oil.

7. Using the installing tool, install the new stud. The stud is properly installed when the tool bottoms on the cylinder head.

8. Install the rocker arm(s) and adjust the valves.

9. Install the cover.

8–7.4L

1. Remove the rocker cover.

2. Remove the rocker arm.

3. Using a deep socket, unscrew the stud.

4. Installation is the reverse of removal. Tighten the stud to 50 ft. lbs. Adjust the valves.

Cylinder Head

REMOVAL AND INSTALLATION

6–4.3L

1. Disconnect the negative battery cable.

2. Remove the engine cover.

3. Remove the intake manifold as described later.

4. Remove the exhaust manifold as de-scriber later.

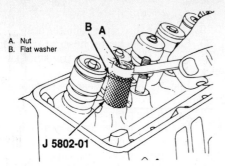

A. Nut
B. Flat washer

J 5802-01

Rocker stud removal

5. Remove the air pipe at the rear of the head (right cylinder head).

6. Remove the generator mounting bolt at the cylinder head (right cylinder head).

7. Remove the power steering pump and brackets from the cylinder head, and lay them aside (left cylinder head).

8. Remove the air conditioner compressor, and lay it aside (left cylinder head).

9. Remove the rocker arm cover as outlined previously.

10. Remove the spark plugs.

11. Remove the pushrods, as outlined previously.

12. Remove the cylinder head bolts.

13. Remove the cylinder head.

To install:

14. Clean all gasket mating surfaces, install a new gasket and reinstall the cylinder head.

15. Install the cylinder heads using new gaskets. Install the gaskets with the head up.

NOTE: *Coat a steel gasket on both sides with sealer. If a composition gasket is used, do not use sealer.*

16. Clean the bolts, apply sealer to the threads, and install them hand tight.

17. Tighten the head bolts a little at a time in the sequence shown. Head bolt torque is listed in the Torque Specifications chart.

18. Install the intake and exhaust manifolds.

19. Adjust the rocker arms.

20. Install the pushrods.

21. Install the spark plugs.

22. Install the rocker arm cover.

23. Install the air conditioner compressor.

24. Install the power steering pump and brackets.

25. Install the generator mounting bolt at the cylinder head.

26. Install the air pipe at the rear of the head.

27. Install the exhaust manifold.

28. Install the intake manifold.

29. Install the engine cover.

30. Connect the negative battery cable.

8–5.0L
8–5.7L

1. Remove the intake manifold.

2. Remove the exhaust manifolds as described later and tie out of the way.

3. If the van is equipped with air conditioning, remove the air conditioning compressor and the forward mounting bracket and lay the compressor aside. Do not disconnect any of the refrigerant lines.

4. Back off the rocker arm nuts and pivot the rocker arms out of the way so that the pushrods can be removed. Identify the pushrods so that they can be installed in their original positions.

5. Remove the cylinder head bolts and remove the heads.

6. Install the cylinder heads using new gaskets. Install the gaskets with the word **HEAD** up.

NOTE: *Coat a steel gasket on both sides with sealer. If a composition gasket is used, do not use sealer.*

7. Clean the bolts, apply sealer to the threads, and install them hand tight.

8. Tighten the head bolts a little at a time in the sequence shown. Head bolt torque is listed in the Torque Specifications chart.

9. Install the intake and exhaust manifolds.

10. Adjust the rocker arms as explained later.

8–6.2L Diesel

RIGHT SIDE

1. Remove the intake manifold.

2. Remove the fuel injection lines. See Chapter 5.

3. Remove the cruise control transducer.

4. Remove the upper fan shroud.

5. Remove the air conditioning compressor belt.

6. Remove the exhaust manifold.

7. Disconnect and label the glow plug wiring.

8. Remove the oil dipstick tube.

9. Remove the oil fill tube upper bracket.

10. Remove the rocker arm cover(s), after re-

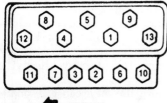

FRONT

6-4.3L head bolt torque sequence

moving any accessory brackets which interfere with cover removal.

11. Remove the rocker arm assemblies. It is a good practice to number or mark the parts to avoid interchanging them.

12. Remove the pushrods. Keep them in order.

13. Remove the air cleaner resonator and bracket.

14. Remove the automatic transmission dipstick and tube.

15. Drain the cooling system.

CAUTION: *When draining the coolant, keep in mind that cats and dogs are attracted by the ethylene glycol antifreeze, and are quite likely to drink any that is left in an uncovered container or in puddles on the ground. This will prove fatal in sufficient quantity. Always drain the coolant into a sealable container. Coolant should be reused unless it is contaminated or several years old.*

16. Disconnect the heater hoses at the head.

17. Disconnect the upper radiator hose.

18. Disconnect the bypass hose.

19. Remove the alternator upper bracket.

20. Remove the coolant crossover pipe and thermostat.

21. Remove the head bolts.

22. Remove the cylinder head.

To install:

23. Clean the mating surfaces of the head and block thoroughly.

24. Install a new head gasket on the engine block. Do NOT coat the gaskets with any sealer on either engine. The gaskets have a special coating that eliminates the need for sealer. The use of sealer will interfere with this coating and cause leaks. Install the cylinder head onto the block.

25. Clean the head bolts thoroughly. The left rear head bolt must be installed into the head prior to head installation. Coat the threads and heads of the head bolts with sealing compound (GM part No.1052080 or equivalent) before installation. Tighten the head bolts as explained in the Torque Specifications Chart.

26. Install the coolant crossover pipe and thermostat.

27. Install the alternator upper bracket.

28. Connect the bypass hose.

29. Connect the upper radiator hose.

30. Connect the heater hoses at the head.

31. Install the automatic transmission dipstick and tube.

32. Install the air cleaner resonator and bracket.

33. Install the pushrods.

34. Install the rocker arm assemblies.

35. Adjust the valves.

36. Install the rocker arm cover(s).

37. Install the oil fill tube upper bracket.

38. Install the oil dipstick tube.

39. Connect the glow plug wiring.

40. Install the exhaust manifold.

41. Install the air conditioning compressor belt.

42. Install the upper fan shroud.

43. Install the cruise control transducer.

44. Install the fuel injection lines. See Chapter 5.

45. Install the intake manifold.

46. Fill the cooling system.

LEFT SIDE

1. Remove the intake manifold.

2. Remove the fuel injection lines. See Chapter 5.

3. Remove the cruise control transducer.

4. Remove the upper fan shroud.

5. Remove the air conditioning compressor belt.

6. Remove the exhaust manifold.

7. Remove the power steering pump lower adjusting bolts.

8. Disconnect and label the glow plug wiring.

9. Remove the air conditioning compressor and position it out of the way. DO NOT DISCONNECT ANY REFRIGERANT LINES!

10. Remove the power steering pump and position it out of the way. DO NOT DISCONNECT THE FLUID LINES!

11. Remove the oil dipstick tube.

12. Disconnect the transmission detent cable.

13. Remove the glow plug controller and bracket.

14. Remove the rocker arm cover(s), after removing any accessory brackets which interfere with cover removal.

15. Remove the rocker arm assemblies. It is a good practice to number or mark the parts to avoid interchanging them.

16. Remove the pushrods. Keep them in order.

17. Remove the air cleaner resonator and bracket.

18. Remove the automatic transmission dipstick and tube.

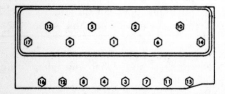

8-5.0L and 8-5.7L head bolt torque sequence

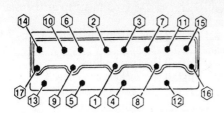

8-6.2L diesel head bolt torque sequence

19. Drain the cooling system.

CAUTION: *When draining the coolant, keep in mind that cats and dogs are attracted by the ethylene glycol antifreeze, and are quite likely to drink any that is left in an uncovered container or in puddles on the ground. This will prove fatal in sufficient quantity. Always drain the coolant into a sealable container. Coolant should be reused unless it is contaminated or several years old.*

20. Remove the alternator upper bracket.

21. Remove the coolant crossover pipe and thermostat.

22. Remove the head bolts.

23. Remove the cylinder head.

To install:

24. Clean the mating surfaces of the head and block thoroughly.

25. Install a new head gasket on the engine block. Do NOT coat the gaskets with any sealer on either engine. The gaskets have a special coating that eliminates the need for sealer. The use of sealer will interfere with this coating and cause leaks. Install the cylinder head onto the block.

26. Clean the head bolts thoroughly. The left rear head bolt must be installed into the head prior to head installation. Coat the threads and heads of the head bolts with sealing compound (GM part No.1052080 or equivalent) before installation. Tighten the head bolts as explained in the Torque Specifications Chart.

27. Install the coolant crossover pipe and thermostat.

28. Install the alternator upper bracket.

29. Install the automatic transmission dipstick and tube.

30. Install the air cleaner resonator and bracket.

31. Install the pushrods.

32. Install the rocker arm assemblies.

33. Adjust the valves.

34. Install the rocker arm cover(s).

35. Install the oil fill tube upper bracket.

36. Install the oil dipstick tube.

37. Connect the glow plug wiring.

38. Install the compressor.

39. Install the power steering pump.

40. Install the glow plug controller.

41. Install the exhaust manifold.

42. Connect the detent cable.

43. Install the air conditioning compressor belt.

44. Install the upper fan shroud.

45. Install the cruise control transducer.

46. Install the fuel injection lines. See Chapter 5.

47. Install the intake manifold.

48. Fill the cooling system.

8–7.4L

RIGHT SIDE

1. Remove the intake manifold.

2. Remove the exhaust manifolds.

3. Remove the alternator.

4. Remove the AIR pump.

5. If the van is equipped with air conditioning, remove the air conditioning compressor and the forward mounting bracket and lay the compressor aside. Do not disconnect any of the refrigerant lines.

6. Remove the rocker arm cover.

7. Remove the spark plugs.

8. Remove the AIR pipes at the rear of the head.

9. Disconnect the ground strap at the rear of the head.

10. Disconnect the sensor wire.

11. Back off the rocker arm nuts and pivot the rocker arms out of the way so that the pushrods can be removed. Identify the pushrods so that they can be installed in their original positions.

12. Remove the cylinder head bolts and remove the heads.

13. To install, Thoroughly clean the mating surfaces of the head and block. Clean the bolt holes thoroughly.

14. Install the cylinder heads using new gaskets. Install the gaskets with the word **HEAD** up.

NOTE: *Coat a steel gasket on both sides with sealer. If a composition gasket is used, do not use sealer.*

15. Clean the bolts, apply sealer to the threads, and install them hand tight.

16. Tighten the head bolts a little at a time in the sequence shown. Head bolt torque is listed in the Torque Specifications chart.

17. Install the intake and exhaust manifolds.

18. Install the pushrods.

19. Install the rocker arms and adjust them as described in this Chapter.

20. Connect the sensor wire.

21. Connect the ground strap at the rear of the head.

22. Install the AIR pipes at the rear of the head.

23. Install the spark plugs.
24. Install the rocker arm cover.
25. Install the air conditioning compressor and the forward mounting bracket.
26. Install the AIR pump.
27. Install the alternator.

LEFT SIDE

1. Remove the intake manifold.
2. Remove the exhaust manifolds.
3. Remove the alternator.
4. If the van is equipped with air conditioning, remove the air conditioning compressor and the forward mounting bracket and lay the compressor aside. Do not disconnect any of the refrigerant lines.
5. Remove the rocker arm cover.
6. Remove the spark plugs.
7. Remove the AIR pipes at the rear of the head.
8. Disconnect the ground strap at the rear of the head.
9. Disconnect the sensor wire.
10. Back off the rocker arm nuts and pivot the rocker arms out of the way so that the pushrods can be removed. Identify the pushrods so that they can be installed in their original positions.
11. Remove the cylinder head bolts and remove the heads.
To install:
12. Thoroughly clean the mating surfaces of the head and block. Clean the bolt holes thoroughly.
13. Install the cylinder heads using new gaskets. Install the gaskets with the word **HEAD** up.
NOTE: *Coat a steel gasket on both sides with sealer. If a composition gasket is used, do not use sealer.*
14. Clean the bolts, apply sealer to the threads, and install them hand tight.
15. Tighten the head bolts a little at a time in the sequence shown. Head bolt torque is listed in the Torque Specifications chart.
16. Install the intake and exhaust manifolds.
17. Install the pushrods.
18. Install the rocker arms and adjust them as described in this Chapter.
19. Connect the sensor wire.

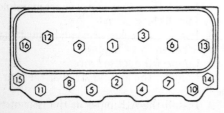

8-7.4L head bolt torque sequence

20. Connect the ground strap at the rear of the head.
21. Install the AIR pipes at the rear of the head.
22. Install the spark plugs.
23. Install the rocker arm cover.
24. Install the air conditioning compressor and the forward mounting bracket.
25. Install the alternator.

CLEANING AND INSPECTION

Gasoline Engines

NOTE: *Any diesel cylinder head work should be handled by a reputable machine shop familiar with diesel engines. Disassembly, valve lapping, and assembly can be completed by the following engine procedures.*

One the complete valve train has been removed from the cylinder head(s), the head itself can be inspected, cleaned and machined (if necessary). Set the head(s) on a clean work space, so the combustion chambers are facing up. Begin cleaning the chambers and ports with a hardwood chisel or other non-metallic tool (to avoid nicking or gouging the chamber, ports, and especially the valve seats). Chip away the major carbon deposits, then remove the remainder of carbon with a wire brush fitted to an electric drill.

NOTE: *Be sure that the carbon is actually removed, rather than just burnished.*

After decarbonizing is completed, take the head(s) to a machine shop and have the head hot tanked. In this process, the head is lowered into a hot chemical bath that very effectively cleans all grease, corrosion, and scale from all internal and external head surfaces. Also have the machinist check the valve seats and recut them if necessary. When you bring the clean head(s) home, place them on a clean surface. Completely clean the entire valve train with solvent.

CHECKING FOR HEAD WARPAGE

Lay the head down with the combustion chambers facing up. Place a straight edge across the gasket surface of the head, both diagonally and straight across the center. Using a flat feeler gauge, determine the clearance at the center of the straight edge. If warpage exceeds 0.003 in. (0.0762mm) in a 6 in. (152mm) span, or 0.006 in. (0.152mm) over the total length, the cylinder head must be resurfaced (which is akin to planing a piece of wood). Resurfacing can be performed at most machine shops.

NOTE: *When resurfacing the cylinder head(s) of V8 engines, the intake manifold mounting position is altered, and must be cor-*

rected by machining a proportionate amount from the intake manifold flange.

RESURFACING

Cylinder head resurfacing should be done by a qualified machine shop.

Valves and Springs

REMOVAL AND INSTALLATION

Cylinder Heads Removed

1. Remove the head(s), and place on a clean surface.

2. Using a suitable spring compressor (for pushrod type overhead valve engines), compress the valve spring and remove the valve spring cap key. Release the spring compressor and remove the valve spring and cap (and valve rotator on some engines).

NOTE: *Use care in removing the keys. They are easily lost.*

3. Remove the valve seals from the intake valve guides. Throw these old seals away, as you'll be installing new seals during reassembly.

4. Slide the valves out of the head from the combustion chamber side.

5. Make a holder for the valves out of a piece of wood or cardboard, as outlined for the pushrods in gasoline engine Cylinder Head Removal. Make sure you number each hole in the cardboard to keep the valves in proper order. Slide the valves out of the head from the combustion chamber side. They MUST be installed as they were removed.

Cylinder Head(s) Installed

It is often not necessary to remove the cylinder head(s) in order to service the valve train. Such is the case when valve seals need to be replaced. Valve seals can be easily replaced with the head(s) on the engine. The only special equipment needed for this job are an air line adapter (sold in most auto parts stores), which screws a compressed air line into the spark plug hole of the cylinder on which you are working,

and a valve spring compressor. A source of compressed air is needed, of course.

1. Remove the valve cover as previously detailed.

2. Remove the spark plug, rocker arm and pushrod on the cylinder(s) to be serviced.

3. Install the air line adapter (GM tool #J-23590 or equivalent) into the spark plug hole. Turn on the air compressor to apply compressed air into the cylinder. This keeps the valves up in place.

NOTE: *Set the regulator of the air compressor at least 50 pounds to ensure adequate pressure.*

4. Using the valve spring compressor, compress the valve spring and remove the valve keys and keepers, the valve spring and damper.

5. Remove the valve stem seal.

6. To reassemble, oil the valve stem and new seal. Install a new seal over the valve stem. Set the spring, damper and keeper in place. Compress the spring. Coat the keys with grease

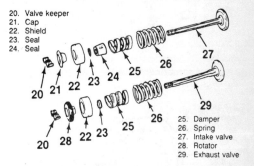

20. Valve keeper
21. Cap
22. Shield
23. Seal
24. Seal
25. Damper
26. Spring
27. Intake valve
28. Rotator
29. Exhaust valve

Valves and related components for the 6-4.3L, 6-4.8L, 8-5.0L and 8-5.7L engines

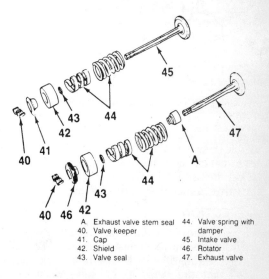

A. Exhaust valve stem seal
40. Valve keeper
41. Cap
42. Shield
43. Valve seal
44. Valve spring with damper
45. Intake valve
46. Rotator
47. Exhaust valve

Valves and components for the 6.2L diesel engine

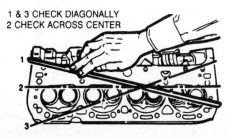

1 & 3 CHECK DIAGONALLY
2 CHECK ACROSS CENTER

Check the cylinder head mating surface for warpage with a machinist's straightedge

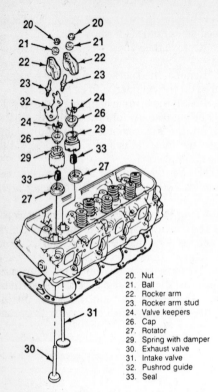

20.	Nut
21.	Ball
22.	Rocker arm
23.	Rocker arm stud
24.	Valve keepers
26.	Cap
27.	Rotator
29.	Spring with damper
30.	Exhaust valve
31.	Intake valve
32.	Pushrod guide
33.	Seal

Valves and components for the 7.4L engine

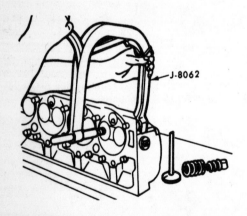

Removing the valve springs with the head off the engine

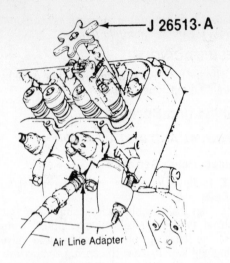

Valve spring removal with the head installed, on diesel engines

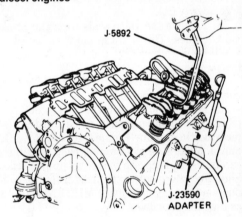

Valve spring removal with the head installed, on gasoline engines

to hold them onto the valve stem and install the keys, making sure they are seated fully in the keeper. Reinstall the valve cover after adjusting the valves, as outlined in this Chapter.

INSPECTION

Inspect the valve faces and seats (in the head) for pits, burned spots and other evidence of poor seating. If a valve face is in such bad shape that the head of the valve must be ground in order to true up the face, discard the valve because the sharp edge will run too hot.

The correct angle for valve faces is 45°. We recommend the refacing be done at a reputable machine shop.

Check the valve stem for scoring and burned spots. If not noticeably scored or damaged, clean the valve stem with solvent to remove all gum and varnish. Clean the valve guides using solvent and an expanding wire type valve guide cleaner. If you have access to a dial indicator for measuring valve stem-to-guide clearance, mount it so that the stem of the indicator is at 90° to the valve stem, and as close to the valve guide as possible. Move the valve off its seat, and measure the valve guide-to-stem clearance by rocking the stem back and forth to actuate the dial indicator. Measure the valve stems using a micrometer, and compare to specifications to determine whether stem or guide wear is responsible for the excess clearance. If a dial indicator and micrometer are not available to

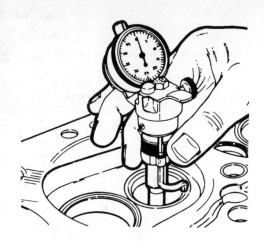

Checking the valve seal concentricity

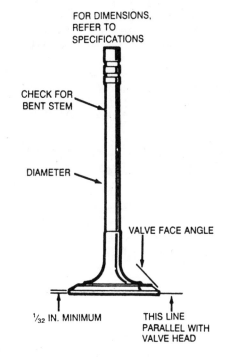

FOR DIMENSIONS,
REFER TO
SPECIFICATIONS

CHECK FOR
BENT STEM

DIAMETER

VALVE FACE ANGLE

1/32 IN. MINIMUM

THIS LINE
PARALLEL WITH
VALVE HEAD

Critical valve dimensions

you, take your cylinder head and valves to a reputable machine shop for inspection.

Some of the engines covered in this guide are equipped with valve rotators, which double as valve spring caps. In normal operation the rotators put a certain degree of wear on the tip of the valve stem. This wear appears as concentric rings on the stem tip. However, if the rotator is not working properly, the wear may appear as straight notches or $\mathbf{X}$ patterns across the valve stem tip. Whenever the valves are removed from the cylinder head, the tips should be in-

spected for improper pattern, which could indicate valve rotator problems. Valve stem tips will have to be ground flat if rotator patterns are severe.

Valve Seats

REMOVAL AND INSTALLATION

The valve seats in Chevrolet engines are not removable. Refer all servicing of the valve seats to a qualified machine shop.

Valve Guides

The engines covered in this guide use integral valve guides. That is, they are a part of the cylinder head and cannot be replaced. The guides can, however, be reamed oversize if they are found to be worn past an acceptable limit. Occasionally, a valve guide bore will be oversize as manufactured. These are marked on the inboard side of the cylinder heads on the machined surface just above the intake manifold.

If the guides must be reamed (this service is available at most machine shops), then valves with oversize stems must be fitted. Valves are usually available in 0.001 in. (0.0254mm), 0.003 in. (0.0762mm) and 0.005 in. (0.127mm) stem oversizes. Valve guides which are not excessively worn or distorted may, in some cases, be knurled rather than reamed. Knurling is a process in which the metal on the valve guide bore is displaced and raised, thereby reducing clearance. Knurling also provides excellent oil control. The option of knurling rather than reaming valve guides should be discussed with a reputable machinist or engine specialist.

LAPPING THE VALVES

When valve faces and seats have been refaced and recut, or if they are determined to be in good condition, the valves must be lapped in to ensure efficient sealing when the valve closes against the seat.

1. Invert the cylinder head so that the combustion chambers are facing up.

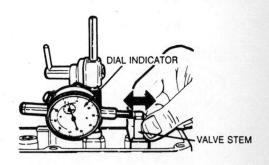

DIAL INDICATOR

VALVE STEM

Check the stem-to-guide clearance

PROPER TIP
PATTERN

NO ROTATION
PATTERN

PARTIAL ROTATION
TIP PATTERN

ROTATOR
FUNCTIONING
PROPERLY

REPLACE ROTATOR
AND CHECK
ROTATION

REPLACE ROTATOR
AND CHECK ROTATION

Valve stem wear

2. Lightly lubricate the valve stems with clean oil, and coat the valve seats with valve grinding compound. Install the valves in the head as numbered.

3. Attach the suction cup of a valve lapping tool to a valve head. You'll probably have to moisten the cup to securely attach the tool to the valve.

4. Rotate the tool between the palms. changing position and lifting the tool often to prevent grooving. Lap the valve until a smooth, polished seat is evident (you may have to add a bit more compound after some lapping is done).

5. Remove the valve and tool, and remove ALL traces of grinding compound with solvent soaked rag, or rinse the head with solvent.

NOTE: *Valve lapping can also be done by fastening a suction cup to a piece of drill rod in a hand eggbeater type drill. Proceed as above, using the drill as a lapping tool. Due to the higher speeds involved when using the hand drill, care must be exercised to avoid grooving the seat. Lift the tool and change direction of rotation often.*

Valve Springs

HEIGHT AND PRESSURE CHECK

1. Place the valve spring on a flat, clean surface next to a square.

2. Measure the height of the spring, and rotate it against the edge of the square to measure distortion (out-of-roundness). If spring height varies between springs by more than $\frac{1}{16}$ in. (1.5875mm) replace the spring.

A valve spring tester is needed to test spring test pressure, so the valve springs must usually be taken to a professional machine shop for this test. Spring pressure at the installed and compressed heights is checked, and a tolerance of plus or minus 5 lbs. is permissible on the springs covered in this guide.

VALVE INSTALLATION

NOTE: *For installing new valve stem seals without removing the cylinder head(s), see the procedure under Valves and Springs — Cylinder Head(s) Installed earlier in this Chapter.*

New valve seals must be installed when the valve train is put back together. Certain seals slip over the valve stem and guide boss, while others require that the boss be machined. Teflon® guide seals are available. Check with a machinist and/or automotive parts store for a suggestion on the proper seals to use.

NOTE: *Remember that when installing valve seals, a small amount of oil must be*

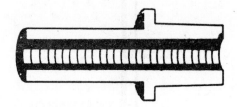

Cutaway view of a knurled guide

Lapping the valves by hand

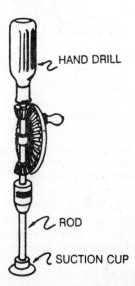

HAND DRILL

ROD

SUCTION CUP

Homemade lapping tool

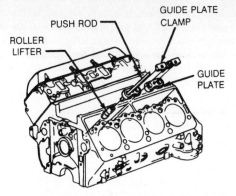

Checking valve spring free length and squareness

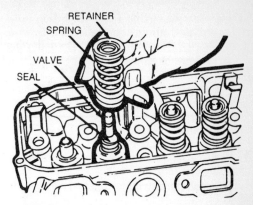

Installing valve stem seal

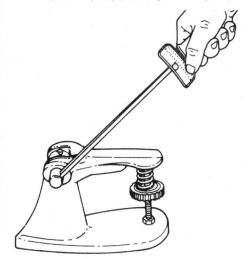

Checking valve spring pressure

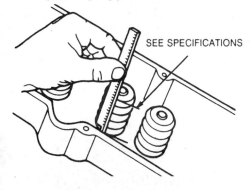

Checking valve spring installed height

able to pass the seal to lubricate the valve guides; otherwise, excessive wear will result.

To install the valves and rocker assembly:

1. Lubricate the valve stems with clean engine oil.

2. Install the valves in the cylinder head, one at a time, as numbered.

3. Lubricate and position the seals and valve springs, again a valve at a time.

4. Install the spring retainers, and compress the springs.

5. With the valve key groove exposed above the compressed valve spring, wipe some wheel bearing grease around the groove. This will retain the keys as you release the spring compressor.

6. Using needle nose pliers (or your fingers), place the keys in the key grooves. The grease should hold the keys in place. Slowly release the spring compressor. The valve cap or rotator will raise up as the compressor is released, retaining the keys.

7. Install the rocker assembly, and install the cylinder head(s).

VALVE LASH ADJUSTMENT

All engines described in this book use hydraulic lifters, which require no periodic adjustment. In the event of cylinder head removal or any operation that requires disturbing the rocker arms, the rocker arms will have to be adjusted.

1. Remove the rocker covers and gaskets.

2. Crank the engine until the mark on the damper aligns with the **TDC** or **0** mark on the timing tab and the engine is in No. 1 firing position. This can be determined by placing the fingers on the No. 1 cylinder valves as the marks align. If the valves do not move, it is in No. 1 firing position. If the valves move, it is in No. 6 firing position (No. 4 on the V6) and the crankshaft should be rotated 1 more revolution to the No. 1 firing position.

3. With the engine in No. 1 firing position, the following valves can be adjusted:

V6 Engines
- Exhaust — 1, 5, 6,
- Intake — 1, 2, 3,

V8 Engines
- Exhaust — 1,3,4,8
- Intake — 1,2,5,7

4. Crank the engine 1 full revolution until the marks are again in alignment. This is No. 6 firing position (No. 4 on the V6). The following valves can now be adjusted:

V6 Engines
- Exhaust — 2, 3, 4
- Intake — 4, 5, 6

V8 Engines
- Exhaust — 2,5,6,7
- Intake — 3,4,6,8

5. Reinstall the rocker arm covers using new gaskets.

6. Install the distributor cap and wire assembly.

Oil Pan

REMOVAL AND INSTALLATION

6–4.3L

A one piece type oil pan gasket is used.

1. Disconnect the negative battery cable. Raise the vehicle, support it safely, and drain the engine oil.

2. Remove the exhaust crossover pipe.

3. Remove the torque converter cover (on models with automatic transmission).

4. Remove the strut rods at the flywheel cover.

5. Remove the strut rod brackets at the front engine mountings.

6. Remove the starter.

7. Remove the oil pan bolts, nuts and reinforcements.

8. Remove the oil pan and gaskets.

To install:

9. Thoroughly clean all gasket surfaces and install a new gasket, using only a small amount of sealer at the front and rear corners of the oil pan.

10. Install the oil pan and new gaskets.

11. Install the oil pan bolts, nuts and reinforcements. Torque the pan bolts to 100 inch lbs.

12. Install the starter.

13. Install the strut rod brackets at the front engine mountings.

14. Install the strut rods at the flywheel cover.

15. Install the torque converter cover (on models with automatic transmission).

16. Install the exhaust crossover pipe.

17. Connect the negative battery cable.

18. Fill the crankcase.

8–5.0L
8–5.7L

1. Drain the engine oil.

2. Remove the oil dipstick and tube.

3. If necessary remove the exhaust pipe crossover.

4. If equipped with automatic transmission, remove the converter housing pan.

5. Remove the starter brace and bolt and swing the starter aside.

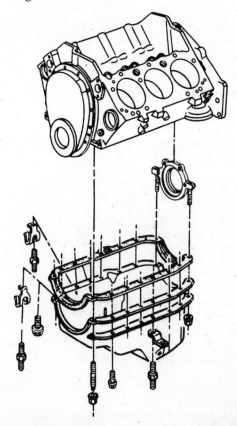

6-4.3L engine oil pan

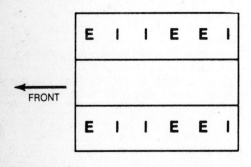

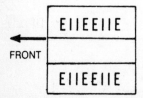

Valve arrangement: V6 top; V8 bottom

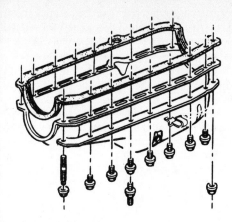

8-5.0L/5.7L oil pan

6. Remove the oil pan and discard the gaskets.

7. Installation is the reverse of removal. Clean all gasket surfaces and use new gaskets to assemble. Use gasket sealer to retain side gaskets to the cylinder block. Install a new oil pan rear seal in the rear main bearing cap slot with the ends butting the side gaskets. Install a new front seal in the crankcase front cover with the ends butting the side gaskets. Torque the pan bolts to 65 inch lbs. Fill the engine with oil and check for leaks.

8-7.4L

1. Disconnect the battery.
2. Remove the fan shroud.
3. Remove the air cleaner.
4. Remove the distributor cap.
5. Raise and support the front end on jackstands.
6. Drain the engine oil.
7. Remove the converter housing pan.
8. Remove the oil filter.
9. Remove the oil pressure line.
10. Support the engine with a floor jack.
WARNING: *Do not place the jack under the pan, sheet metal or pulley!*
11. Remove the engine mount through-bolts.
12. Raise the engine just enough to remove the pan.
13. Remove the oil pan and discard the gaskets.
To install:
14. Clean all mating surfaces thoroughly.
15. Apply RTV gasket material to the front and rear corners of the gaskets.
16. Coat the gaskets with adhesive sealer and position them on the block.
17. Install the rear pan seal in the pan with the seal ends mating with the gaskets.
8. Install the front seal on the bottom of

the front cover, pressing the locating tabs into the holes in the cover.
19. Install the oil pan.
20. Install the pan bolts, clips and reinforcements. Torque the pan-to-cover bolts to 70 inch lbs.; the pan-to-block bolts to 13 ft. lbs.
21. Lower the engine onto the mounts.
22. Install the engine mount through-bolts.
23. Install the oil pressure line.
24. Install the oil filter.
25. Install the converter housing pan.
26. Install the distributor cap.
27. Install the air cleaner.
28. Install the fan shroud.
29. Connect the battery.
30. Fill the crankcase.

8-6.2L Diesel

1. Remove the vacuum pump and drive (with air conditioning) or the oil pump drive (without air conditioning).
2. Disconnect the batteries and remove the dipstick.
3. Remove the upper radiator support and fan shroud.
4. Raise and support the car. Drain the oil.
5. Remove the flywheel cover.
6. Disconnect the exhaust and crossover pipes.
7. Remove the oil cooler lines at the filter base.
8. Remove the starter assembly. Support the engine with a jack.
9. Remove the engine mounts from the block.
10. Raise the front of the engine and remove the oil pan.
To install:
11. Using new gaskets coated with sealer, position the oil pan on the block and install the bolts. Torque the bolts to 84 inch lbs., except for the two rear bolts. Torque them to 17 ft. lbs.

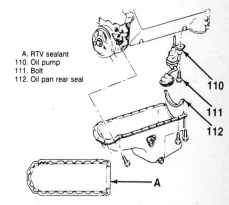

A. RTV sealant
110. Oil pump
111. Bolt
112. Oil pan rear seal

6.2 diesel engine oil pan

12. Install the engine mounts.

13. Remove the jack.

14. Install the starter assembly.

15. Install the oil cooler lines at the filter base.

16. Connect the exhaust and crossover pipes.

17. Install the flywheel cover.

18. Install the upper radiator support and fan shroud.

19. Connect the batteries.

20. Install the dipstick.

21. Install the vacuum pump and drive (with air conditioning) or the oil pump drive (without air conditioning).

22. Fill the crankcase.

Oil Pump

REMOVAL AND INSTALLATION

6–4.3L

1. Remove the oil pan.

2. Remove the bolt attaching the pump to the rear main bearing cap. Remove the pump and the extension shaft, which will come out behind it.

3. If the pump has been disassembled, is being replaced, or for any reason oil has been removed from it, it must be primed. It can either be filled with oil before installing the cover plate (and oil kept within the pump during handling), or the entire pump cavity can be filled with petroleum jelly. IF THE PUMP IS NOT PRIMED, THE ENGINE COULD BE DAMAGED BEFORE IT RECEIVES ADEQUATE LUBRICATION WHEN YOU START IT!

4. Engage the extension shaft with the oil pump shaft. Align the slot on the top of the extension shaft with the drive tang on the lower end of the distributor driveshaft, and then position the pump at the rear main bearing cap so the mounting bolt can be installed. Install the bolt, torquing to 65 ft. lbs.

5. Install the oil pan.

8–5.0L
8–5.7L
8–7.4L

1. Drain the oil and remove the oil pan.

2. Remove the bolt holding the pump to the rear main bearing cap.

3. Remove the pump and extension shaft.

4. To install, assemble the pump and extension shaft to the rear main bearing cap aligning the slot on the top of the extension shaft with the drive tang on the distributor driveshaft. The installed position of the oil pump screen is with the bottom edge parallel to the oil pan rails. Further installation is the reverse of removal.

8–6.2L Diesel

1. Drain the oil.

2. Lower the oil pan enough to gain access to the pump.

2. Rotate the crankshaft so that the forward crankshaft throw and Nos. 1 and 2 connecting rod journals are up.

3. Remove the bolt retaining the pump to the main bearing cap. Let the pump and extension shaft fall into the pan.

To install:

4. Maneuver the pan, pump and extension shaft into position.

5. Position the pump on the bearing cap.

6. Align the extension shaft with the oil pump drive or vacuum pump. The pump should push easily into place. Install the pump and tighten the bolt to 65 ft. lbs.

7. Install the pan as described above.

OVERHAUL

6–4.3L

1. Remove the oil pump driveshaft extension.

2. Remove the cotter pin, spring and pressure regulator valve.

NOTE: *Place your thumb over the pressure regulator bore before removing the cotter pin, as the spring is under pressure.*

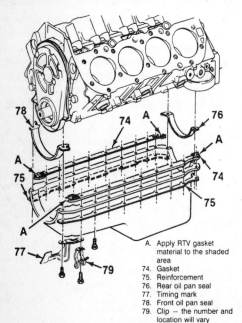

A. Apply RTV gasket material to the shaded area
74. Gasket
75. Reinforcement
76. Rear oil pan seal
77. Timing mark
78. Front oil pan seal
79. Clip — the number and location will vary

7.4L engine oil pan

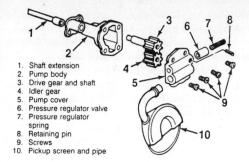

1. Shaft extension
2. Pump body
3. Drive gear and shaft
4. Idler gear
5. Pump cover
6. Pressure regulator valve
7. Pressure regulator spring
8. Retaining pin
9. Screws
10. Pickup screen and pipe

4.3L engine oil pump

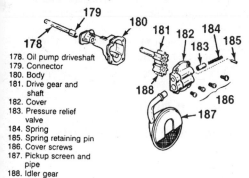

178. Oil pump driveshaft
179. Connector
180. Body
181. Drive gear and shaft
182. Cover
183. Pressure relief valve
184. Spring
185. Spring retaining pin
186. Cover screws
187. Pickup screen and pipe
188. Idler gear

5.0L/5.7L oil pump

178. Oil pump driveshaft
179. Connector
180. Body
181. Drive gear and shaft
182. Cover
183. Pressure relief valve
184. Spring
185. Spring retaining pin
186. Cover screws
187. Pickup screen and pipe
188. Idler gear
189. Washer
190. Gasket

7.4L oil pump

3. Remove the oil pump cover attaching screws and remove the oil pump cover and gasket. Clean the pump in solvent or kerosene, and wash out the pickup screen.

4. Remove the drive gear and the idler gear from the pump body.

5. Check the gears for scoring and other damage. Install the gears if in good condition or replace them if damaged. Check gear end clearance by placing a straight edge over the gears and measuring the clearance between the straight edge and the gasket surface with a feeler gauge. End clearance is 0.002 in. (0.051mm) to 0.0065 in. (0.165mm). If end clear-

ance is excessive, check for scores in the cover that would bring the total clearance over the specs.

6. Check the gear side clearance by inserting the feeler gauge between the gear teeth and the side of the pump body. Clearance should be between 0.002 in. (0.051mm) and 0.005 in. (0.127mm).

7. Pack the inside of the pump completely with petroleum jelly. DO NOT USE ENGINE OIL. The pump MUST be primed this way or it will not produce any oil pressure when the engine is started.

8. Install the cover screws and tighten alternately and evenly to 96 inch lbs.

9. Position the pressure valve into the pump cover, closed end first, then install the spring and retaining pin.

NOTE: *When assembling the driveshaft extension into the driveshaft, the end of the extension nearest the washers must be inserted into the driveshaft.*

10. Insert the driveshaft extension through the opening in the main bearing cap and block until the shaft mates into the distributor drive gear.

11. Install the pump onto the rear main bearing cap and install the attaching bolts. Torque the bolts to 35 ft. lbs.

12. Install the pan.

8–5.0L
8–5.7L
8–7.4L

1. Remove the oil pump driveshaft extension.

2. Remove the cotter pin, spring and the pressure regulator valve.

NOTE: *Place your thumb over the pressure regulator bore before removing the cotter pin, as the spring is under pressure.*

3. Remove the oil pump cover attaching screws and remove the oil pump cover and gasket. Clean the pump in solvent or kerosene, and wash out the pickup screen.

4. Remove the drive gear and the idler gear from the pump body.

5. Check the gears for scoring and other damage. Install the gears if in good condition or replace them if damaged. Check gear end clearance by placing a straight edge over the gears and measuring the clearance between the straight edge and the gasket surface with a feeler gauge. End clearance is 0.002 in. (0.051mm) to 0.0065 in. (0.165mm). If end clearance is excessive, check for scores in the cover that would bring the total clearance over the specs.

6. Check the gear side clearance by inserting the feeler gauge between the gear teeth and

the side of the pump body. Clearance should be between 0.002 in. (0.051mm) and 0.005 in. (0.127mm).

7. Pack the inside of the pump completely with petroleum jelly. DO NOT USE ENGINE OIL. The pump MUST be primed this way or it will not produce any oil pressure when the engine is started.

8. Install the cover screws and tighten alternately and evenly to 8 ft. lbs.

9. Position the pressure valve into the pump cover, closed end first, then install the spring and retaining pin.

NOTE: *When assembling the driveshaft extension into the driveshaft, the end of the extension nearest the washers must be inserted into the driveshaft.*

10. Insert the driveshaft extension through the opening in the main bearing cap and block until the shaft mates into the distributor drive gear.

11. Install the pump onto the rear main bearing cap and install the attaching bolts. Torque the bolts to 35 ft. lbs.

12. Install the pan.

8–6.2L Diesel

1. Remove the oil pump driveshaft extension.

2. Remove the cotter pin, spring and the pressure regulator valve.

NOTE: *Place your thumb over the pressure regulator bore before removing the cotter pin, as the spring is under pressure.*

3. Remove the oil pump cover attaching screws and remove the oil pump cover and gasket. Clean the pump in solvent or kerosene, and wash out the pickup screen.

4. Remove the drive gear and the idler gear from the pump body.

5. Check the gears for scoring and other damage. Install the gears if in good condition or replace them if damaged. Check gear end clearance by placing a straight edge over the gears and measuring the clearance between the straight edge and the gasket surface with a feeler gauge. End clearance is 0.002 in. (0.051mm) to 0.0065 in. (0.165mm). If end clearance is excessive, check for scores in the cover that would bring the total clearance over the specs.

6. Check the gear side clearance by inserting the feeler gauge between the gear teeth and the side of the pump body. Clearance should be between 0.002 in. (0.051mm) and 0.005 in. (0.127mm).

7. Pack the inside of the pump completely with petroleum jelly. DO NOT USE ENGINE OIL. The pump MUST be primed this way or it

will not produce any oil pressure when the engine is started.

8. Install the cover screws and tighten alternately and evenly to 96 inch lbs.

9. Position the pressure valve into the pump cover, closed end first, then install the spring and retaining pin.

NOTE: *When assembling the driveshaft extension into the driveshaft, the end of the extension nearest the washers must be inserted into the driveshaft.*

10. Insert the driveshaft extension through the opening in the main bearing cap and block until the shaft mates into the distributor drive gear.

11. Install the pump onto the rear main bearing cap and install the attaching bolts. Torque the bolts to 35 ft. lbs.

12. Install the pan.

Crankshaft Damper

REMOVAL AND INSTALLATION

NOTE: *Torsional damper puller tool No.J–23523–E is required to perform this procedure.*

1. Remove the fan belts, fan and pulley.

2. Remove the fan shroud assembly.

3. Remove the accessory drive pulley.

4. Remove the torsional damper bolt.

5. Remove the torsional damper using tool No.J–23523–E.

NOTE: *Make sure you do not loose the crankshaft key, if it has been removed.*

To install:

6. Coat the crankshaft stub with engine oil.

7. Position the damper on the shaft and tap it into place with a plastic mallet. Make sure the key is in place.

8. Make sure the damper is all the way on, then install the bolt. Torque the bolt to the figure given in the Torque Specifications Chart.

Timing Chain Cover and Front Oil Seal

REMOVAL AND INSTALLATION

6–4.3L

1. Drain the cooling system.

CAUTION: *When draining the coolant, keep in mind that cats and dogs are attracted by the ethylene glycol antifreeze, and are quite likely to drink any that is left in an uncovered container or in puddles on the ground. This will prove fatal in sufficient quantity. Always drain the coolant into a sealable container. Coolant should be reused unless it is contaminated or several years old.*

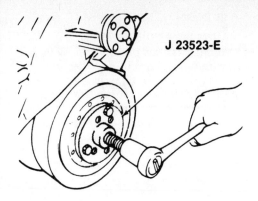

J 23523-E

Removing the crankshaft damper

2. Remove the crankshaft pulley and damper. Remove the water pump. Remove the screws holding the timing case cover to the block and remove the cover and gaskets.

3. Use a suitable tool to pry the old seal out of the front face of the cover.

4. Install the new seal so that the open end is toward the inside of the cover.

NOTE: *Coat the lip of the new seal with oil prior to installation.*

5. Check that the timing chain oil slinger is in place against the crankshaft sprocket.

6. Apply sealer to the front cover as shown in the accompanying illustration. Install the cover carefully onto the locating dowels.

7. Tighten the attaching screws to 72–96 inch lbs.

8–5.0L
8–5.7L

1. Drain the cooling system.

CAUTION: *When draining the coolant, keep in mind that cats and dogs are attracted by the ethylene glycol antifreeze, and are quite likely to drink any that is left in an uncovered container or in puddles on the ground. This will prove fatal in sufficient quantity. Always drain the coolant into a sealable container. Coolant should be reused unless it is contaminated or several years old.*

2. Remove the crankshaft pulley and damper. Remove the water pump. Remove the screws holding the timing case cover to the block and remove the cover and gaskets.

3. Use a suitable tool to pry the old seal out of the front face of the cover.

4. Install the new seal so that the open end is toward the inside of the cover.

NOTE: *Coat the lip of the new seal with oil prior to installation.*

5. Check that the timing chain oil slinger is in place against the crankshaft sprocket.

6. Apply sealer to the front cover as shown

in the accompanying illustration. Install the cover carefully onto the locating dowels.

7. Tighten the attaching screws to 72–96 inch lbs.

8–7.4L

1. Disconnect the battery.

2. Drain the cooling system.

CAUTION: *When draining the coolant, keep in mind that cats and dogs are attracted by the ethylene glycol antifreeze, and are quite likely to drink any that is left in an uncovered container or in puddles on the ground. This will prove fatal in sufficient quantity. Always drain the coolant into a sealable container. Coolant should be reused unless it is contaminated or several years old.*

3. Remove the water pump.

4. Remove the crankshaft pulley and damper.

5. Remove the oil pan-to-front cover bolts.

6. Remove the screws holding the timing case cover to the block, pull the cover forward enough to cut the front oil pan seal. Cut the seal flush with the block on both sides.

7. Pull off the cover and gaskets.

8. Use a suitable tool to pry the old seal out of the front face of the cover.

To install:

9. Using seal driver J-22102, or equivalent, install the new seal so that the open end is toward the inside of the cover.

NOTE: *Coat the lip of the new seal with oil prior to installation.*

10. Install a new front pan seal, cutting the tabs off.

11. Coat a new cover gasket with adhesive sealer and position it on the block.

12. Apply a $1/8$ in. bead of RTV gasket material to the front cover. Install the cover carefully onto the locating dowels.

13. Tighten the attaching screws to 96 inch lbs.

Seal installation with the cover removed

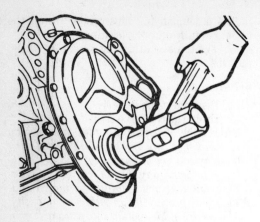

Seal installation with the cover installed

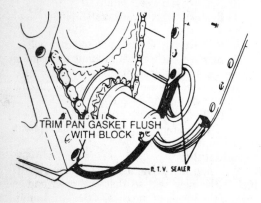

TRIM PAN GASKET FLUSH WITH BLOCK

R.T.V. SEALER

Sealer application

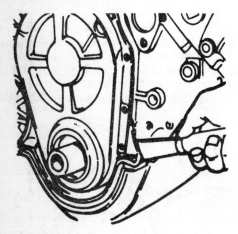

Cutting the seal

14. Tighten the cover-to-pan bolts to 70 inch lbs.
15. Install the damper.
16. Install the water pump.
17. Connect the battery cables.
18. Fill the cooling system.

8–6.2L Diesel

1. Drain the cooling system.

CAUTION: *When draining the coolant, keep in mind that cats and dogs are attracted by the ethylene glycol antifreeze, and are quite likely to drink any that is left in an uncovered container or in puddles on the ground. This will prove fatal in sufficient quantity. Always drain the coolant into a sealable container. Coolant should be reused unless it is contaminated or several years old.*

2. Remove the water pump as outlined elsewhere in this Chapter.

3. Rotate the crankshaft to align the marks on the injection pump driven gear and the camshaft gear as shown in the illustration.

4. Scribe a mark aligning the injection pump flange and the front cover.

5. Remove the crankshaft pulley and torsional damper.

6. Remove the 4 front cover-to-oil pan bolts.

7. Remove the two fuel return line clips.

8. Remove the injection pump retaining nuts from the front cover.

9. Remove the baffle. Remove the remaining cover bolts, and remove the front cover.

10. If the front cover oil seal is to be replaced, it can now be pried out of the cover with a suitable prying tool. Press the new seal into the cover evenly.

NOTE: *The oil seal can also be replaced with the front cover installed. Remove the torsional damper first, then pry the old seal out of the cover using a suitable prying tool. Use care not to damage the surface of the crankshaft. Install the new seal evenly into the cover and install the damper.*

11. To install the front cover, first clean both sealing surfaces until all traces of old sealer are gone. Apply a 2mm bead of sealant (GM sealant #1052357 or equivalent) to the sealing surface as shown in the illustration. Apply a bead of RTV type sealer to the bottom portion of the front cover which attached to the oil pan. Install the front cover.

12. Install the baffle.

13. Install the injection pump, making sure the scribe marks on the pump and front cover are aligned.

14. Install the injection pump driven gear, making sure the marks on the cam gear and pump are aligned. Be sure the dowel pin and the three holes on the pump flange are also aligned.

15. Install the fuel line clips, the front cover-to-oil bolts, and the torsional damper and crankshaft pulley. Torque the pan bolts to 4–7 ft. lbs., and the damper bolt to 140–162 ft. lbs.

Timing Chain

REMOVAL AND INSTALLATION

All Gasoline Engines

1. Remove the radiator, water pump, the harmonic balancer and the crankcase front cover. This will allow access to the timing chain.

2. Crank the engine until the timing marks on both sprockets are nearest each other and in line between the shaft centers.

3. Take out the three bolts that hold the camshaft gear to the camshaft. This gear is a light press fit on the camshaft and will come off easily. It is located by a dowel. The chain comes off with the camshaft gear.

NOTE: *A gear puller will be required to remove the crankshaft gear.*

4. Without disturbing the position of the engine, mount the new crankshaft gear on the shaft, and mount the chain over the camshaft gear. Arrange the camshaft gear in such a way that the timing marks will line up between the shaft centers and the camshaft locating dowel will enter the dowel hole in the cam sprocket.

5. Place the cam sprocket, with its chain mounted over it, in position on the front of the van and pull up with the three bolts that hold it to the camshaft.

6. After the gears are in place, turn the engine two full revolutions to make certain that the timing marks are in correct alignment between the shaft centers.

End play of the camshaft is zero.

8–6.2L Diesel

1. Remove the front cover as previously detailed.

2. Remove the bolt and washer attaching the camshaft gear. Remove the injection pump gear.

3. Remove the camshaft sprocket, timing chain and crankshaft sprocket as a unit.

To install:

4. Install the cam sprocket, timing chain and crankshaft sprocket as a unit, aligning the timing marks on the sprockets as shown in the illustration.

5. Rotate the crankshaft 360° so that the camshaft gear and the injection pump gear are aligned as shown in the illustration (accompanying the 6.2L Diesel Front Cover Removal Procedure).

6. Install the front cover as previously detailed. The injection pump must be retimed since the timing chain assembly was removed. See Chapter 5 for this procedure.

Camshaft

REMOVAL AND INSTALLATION

6–4.3L

1. Disconnect the battery.

2. Drain and remove the radiator.

CAUTION: *When draining the coolant, keep in mind that cats and dogs are attracted by the ethylene glycol antifreeze, and are quite likely to drink any that is left in an uncovered container or in puddles on the ground. This will prove fatal in sufficient quantity.*

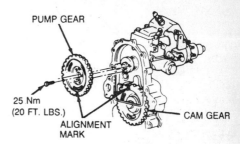

Injection pump and cam gear alignment

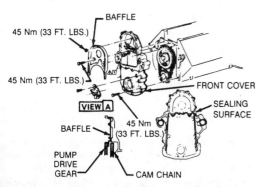

Diesel front cover installation showing sealer application

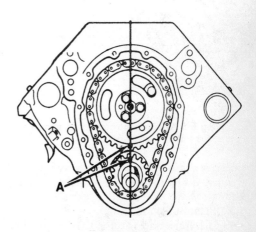

Timing marks alignment for all engines

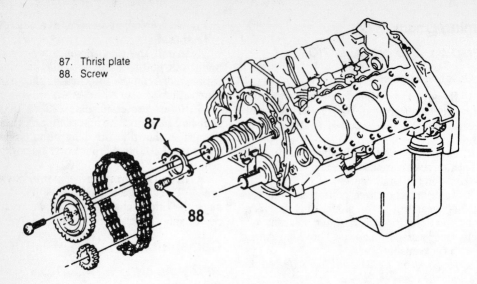

87. Thrist plate
88. Screw

6-4.3L camshaft and timing chain

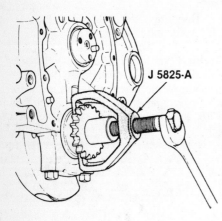

J 5825-A

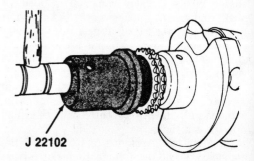

J 22102

Removing and installing the crankshaft sprocket on the 7.4L engines

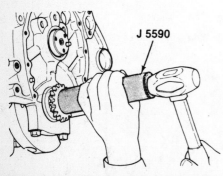

J 5590

Removing and installing the crankshaft sprocket on the 4.3, 5.0 and 5.7L engines

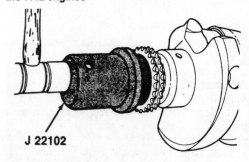

J 22102

Diesel timing chain installation

Always drain the coolant into a sealable container. Coolant should be reused unless it is contaminated or several years old.

3. Remove the fuel pump.

4. Disconnect the throttle cable and the air cleaner.

5. Remove the alternator belt, loosen the al-ternator bolts and move the alternator to one side.

6. Remove the power steering pump from its brackets and move it out of the way.

7. Remove the air conditioning compressor from its brackets and move the compressor out of the way without disconnecting the lines.

8. Disconnect the hoses from the water pump.

9. Disconnect the electrical and vacuum connections.

10. Mark the distributor as to location in the block. Remove the distributor.

11. Raise the van and drain the oil pan.

12. Remove the exhaust crossover pipe and starter motor.

13. Disconnect the exhaust pipe at the manifold.

14. Remove the harmonic balancer and pulley.

15. Support the engine and remove the front motor mounts.

16. Remove the flywheel inspection cover.

17. Remove the engine oil pan.

18. Support the engine by placing wooden blocks between the exhaust manifolds and the front crossmember.

19. Remove the engine front cover.

20. Remove the valve covers.

21. Remove the intake manifold, oil filler pipe, and temperature sending switch.

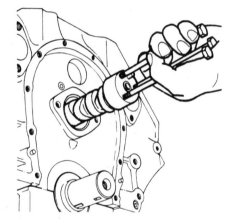

Removing the camshaft

22. Mark the lifters, pushrods, and rocker arms as to location so that they may be installed in the same position. Remove these parts.

23. If the van is equipped with air conditioning, discharge the air conditioning system and remove the condenser.

24. Remove the fuel pump eccentric, camshaft gear, oil slinger, and timing chain. Remove the camshaft thrust plate (on front of camshaft) if equipped.

25. Carefully remove the camshaft from the engine.

26. Inspect the shaft for signs of excessive wear or damage.

27. Liberally coat camshaft and bearing with heavy engine oil or engine assembly lubricant and insert the cam into the engine.

28. Align the timing marks on the camshaft and crankshaft gears. See Timing Chain Replacement for details.

29. Install the distributor using the locating marks made during removal. If any problems are encountered, see Distributor Installation.

30. Install the camshaft thrust plate (on front of camshaft) if equipped.

31. Install the timing chain, oil slinger, camshaft gear, and fuel pump eccentric.

32. Install the condenser. If the van is equipped with air conditioning, charge the air conditioning system. See Chapter 1.

33. Install the lifters, pushrods, and rocker arms.

34. Install the temperature sending switch.

35. Install the oil filler pipe.

36. Install the intake manifold.

37. Install the valve covers.

38. Install the engine front cover.

39. Install the engine oil pan.

40. Install the front motor mounts.

41. Remove the wood blocks.

42. Install the flywheel inspection cover.

43. Install the harmonic balancer and pulley.

44. Connect the exhaust pipe at the manifold.

45. Install the exhaust crossover pipe.

46. Install the starter motor.

47. Install the flywheel inspection cover.

48. Install the distributor.

49. Connect the electrical wiring.

50. Connect all vacuum connections.

51. Connect the hoses at the water pump.

52. Install the air conditioning compressor.

53. Install the timing indicator.

54. Install the power steering pump.

55. Install the alternator and belt.

56. Connect the throttle cable.

57. Install the air cleaner.

58. Install the fuel pump.

59. Install the radiator.

60. Connect the battery.

61. Fill the crankcase.

62. Fill the cooling system.

8–5.0L
8–5.7L

1. Disconnect the battery.

2. Drain and remove the radiator.

CAUTION: *When draining the coolant, keep in mind that cats and dogs are attracted by the ethylene glycol antifreeze, and are quite likely to drink any that is left in an uncovered container or in puddles on the ground. This will prove fatal in sufficient quantity. Always drain the coolant into a sealable container. Coolant should be reused unless it is contaminated or several years old.*

3. Disconnect the fuel line at the fuel pump. Remove the pump.

4. Disconnect the throttle cable and the air cleaner.

5. Remove the alternator belt, loosen the alternator bolts and move the alternator to one side.

6. Remove the power steering pump from its brackets and move it out of the way.

7. Remove the air conditioning compressor from its brackets and move the compressor out of the way without disconnecting the lines.

8. Disconnect the hoses from the water pump.

9. Disconnect the electrical and vacuum connections.

10. Mark the distributor as to location in the block. Remove the distributor.

11. Raise the van and drain the oil pan.

12. Remove the exhaust crossover pipe and starter motor.

13. Disconnect the exhaust pipe at the manifold.

14. Remove the harmonic balancer and pulley.

15. Support the engine and remove the front motor mounts.

16. Remove the flywheel inspection cover.

17. Remove the engine oil pan.

18. Support the engine by placing wooden blocks between the exhaust manifolds and the front crossmember.

19. Remove the engine front cover.

20. Remove the valve covers.

21. Remove the intake manifold, oil filler pipe, and temperature sending switch.

22. Mark the lifters, pushrods, and rocker arms as to location so that they may be installed in the same position. Remove these parts.

23. If the van is equipped with air conditioning, discharge the air conditioning system and remove the condenser.

24. Remove the fuel pump eccentric, camshaft gear, oil slinger, and timing chain. Remove the camshaft thrust plate (on front of camshaft) if equipped.

25. Carefully remove the camshaft from the engine.

26. Inspect the shaft for signs of excessive wear or damage.

To install:

27. Liberally coat camshaft and bearing with heavy engine oil or engine assembly lubricant and insert the cam into the engine.

28. Align the timing marks on the camshaft and crankshaft gears. See Timing Chain Replacement for details.

29. Install the distributor using the locating marks made during removal. If any problems are encountered, see Distributor Installation.

30. Install the camshaft thrust plate (on front of camshaft) if equipped.

31. Install the timing chain, oil slinger,, cam-

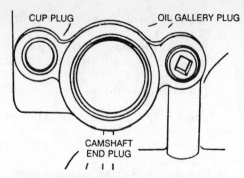

Camshaft oil gallery plugs at the rear of the block

shaft gear, and fuel pump eccentric.

32. Install the condenser. If the van is equipped with air conditioning, charge the air conditioning system. See Chapter 1.

33. Install the lifters, pushrods, and rocker arms.

34. Install the temperature sending switch.

35. Install the oil filler pipe.

36. Install the intake manifold.

37. Install the valve covers.

38. Install the engine front cover.

39. Install the engine oil pan.

40. Install the front motor mounts.

41. Remove the wood blocks.

42. Install the flywheel inspection cover.

43. Install the harmonic balancer and pulley.

44. Connect the exhaust pipe at the manifold.

45. Install the exhaust crossover pipe.

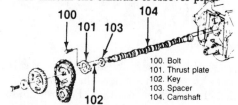

100. Bolt
101. Thrust plate
102. Key
103. Spacer
104. Camshaft

V8 gasoline engine camshaft and related parts

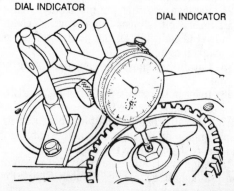

Check camshaft endplay

46. Install the starter motor.
47. Install the flywheel inspection cover.
48. Install the distributor.
49. Connect the electrical wiring.
50. Connect all vacuum connections.
51. Connect the hoses at the water pump.
52. Install the air conditioning compressor.
53. Install the timing indicator.
54. Install the power steering pump.
55. Install the alternator and belt.
56. Connect the throttle cable.
57. Install the air cleaner.
58. Connect the fuel line at the fuel pump. Install the pump.
59. Install the radiator.
60. Connect the battery.
61. Fill the crankcase.
62. Fill the cooling system.

8–7.4L

1. Disconnect the battery.
2. Remove the air cleaner.
3. Remove the grille.
4. Remove the air conditioning compressor from its brackets and move the compressor out of the way without disconnecting the lines.
5. Drain the cooling system.
6. Remove the fan shroud and radiator.
7. Remove the alternator belt, loosen the alternator bolts and move the alternator to one side.
8. Remove the valve covers.
9. Disconnect the hoses from the water pump.
10. Remove the water pump.
11. Remove the harmonic balancer and pulley.
12. Remove the engine front cover.
13. Mark the distributor as to location in the block. Remove the distributor.
14. Remove the intake manifold.
15. Mark the lifters, pushrods, and rocker arms as to location so that they may be installed in the same position. Remove these parts.
16. Rotate the camshaft so that the timing marks align.
17. Remove the camshaft sprocket bolts.
18. Pull the camshaft sprocket and timing chain off. The sprocket is a tight fit, so you'll have to tap it loose with a plastic mallet.
19. Install two $5/16$–18 bolts in the holes in the front of the camshaft and carefully pull the camshaft from the block.
To install:
20. Liberally coat camshaft and bearing with heavy engine oil or engine assembly lubricant and insert the cam into the engine.
21. Install the distributor using the locating

marks made during removal. If any problems are encountered, see Distributor Installation.
22. Install the camshaft sprocket bolts.
23. Install the lifters, pushrods, and rocker.
24. Install the intake manifold.
25. Install the distributor.
26. Install the engine front cover.
27. Install the harmonic balancer and pulley.
28. Install the water pump.
29. Connect the hoses at the water pump.
30. Install the valve covers.
31. Install the alternator.
32. Install the fan shroud and radiator.
33. Fill the cooling system.
34. Install the air conditioning compressor.
35. Install the grille.
36. Install the air cleaner.
37. Connect the battery.

8–6.2L Diesel

1. Disconnect the battery.
2. Jack up the truck and safely support it with jackstands.
3. Drain the cooling system, including the block.

CAUTION: *When draining the coolant, keep in mind that cats and dogs are attracted by the ethylene glycol antifreeze, and are quite likely to drink any that is left in an uncovered container or in puddles on the ground. This will prove fatal in sufficient quantity. Always drain the coolant into a sealable container. Coolant should be reused unless it is contaminated or several years old.*

4. Disconnect the exhaust pipes at the manifolds. Remove the fan shroud.
5. Lower the truck.
6. Remove the radiator and fan.
7. Remove the vacuum pump, and remove the intake manifolds as previously detailed.
8. Remove the injection pump and lines as outlined in Chapter 5. Make sure you cap all injection lines to prevent dirt from entering the system, and tag the lines for later installation.
9. Remove the water pump.
10. Remove the injection pump drive gear.
11. Scribe a mark aligning the line on the injection pump flange to the front cover.
12. Remove the injection pump from the cover.
13. Remove the power steering pump and the generator and lay them aside.
14. If the truck is equipped with air conditioning, remove the compressor (with the lines attached) and position it out of the way.

CAUTION: *DO NOT disconnect the air conditioning lines unless you are familiar with this procedure.*

15. Remove the valve covers.

16. Remove the rocker shaft assemblies and pushrods. Place the pushrods in order in a rack (easily by punching holes in a piece of heavy cardboard and numbering the holes) so that they can be installed in correct order.

17. Remove the thermostat housing and the crossover from the cylinder heads.

18. Remove the cylinder heads as previously detailed, with the exhaust manifolds attached.

19. Remove the valve lifter clamps, guide plates and valve lifters. Place these parts in a rack so they can be installed in the correct order.

20. Remove the front cover.

21. Remove the timing chain assembly.

22. Remove the fuel pump.

23. Remove the camshaft retainer plate.

24. If the truck is equipped with air conditioning, remove the air conditioning condenser mounting bolts. Have an assistant help in lifting the condenser out of the way.

25. Remove the camshaft by carefully sliding it out of the block.

NOTE: *Whenever a new camshaft installed, GM recommends replacing all the valve lifters, as well as the oil filter. The engine oil must be changed. These measures will help ensure proper wear characteristics of the new camshaft.*

To install:

26. Coat the camshaft lobes with Molykote® or an equivalent lube. Liberally tube the camshaft journals with clean engine oil and install the camshaft carefully.

27. Install the camshaft retainer plate and torque the bolts to 20 ft. lbs.

28. Install the fuel pump.

29. Install the timing chain assembly as previously detailed.

30. Install the front cover as previously detailed.

31. Install the valve lifters, guide plates and clamps, and rotate the crankshaft as previously outlined so that the lifters are free to travel.

32. Install the cylinder heads.

33. Install the pushrods in their original order. Install the rocker shaft assemblies, then install the valve covers.

34. Install the injection pump to the front cover, making sure the lines on the pump and the scribe line on the front cover are aligned.

35. Install the injection pump driven gear, making sure the gears are aligned. Retime the injection pump.

36. Install the air conditioning condenser. Charge the system. See Chapter 1.

37. Install the thermostat housing and the crossover.

38. Install the compressor.

39. Install the power steering pump.

40. Install the alternator.

41. Install the water pump.

42. Install the vacuum pump.

43. Install the intake manifolds.

44. Install the radiator and fan.

45. Install the fan shroud.

46. Connect the exhaust pipes at the manifolds.

47. Fill the cooling system.

48. Connect the battery.

CAMSHAFT INSPECTION

Completely clean the camshaft with solvent, paying special attention to cleaning the oil holes. Visually inspect the cam lobes and bearing journals for excessive wear. If a lobe is questionable, have the cam checked at a reputable machine shop. If a journal or lobe is worn, the camshaft must be reground or replaced. Also have the camshaft checked for straightness on a dial indicator.

NOTE: *If a cam journal is worn, there is a good chance that the bushings are worn.*

Camshaft Bearings

REMOVAL AND INSTALLATION

If excessive camshaft wear is found, or if the engine is completely rebuilt, the camshaft bearings should be replaced.

NOTE: *The front and rear bearings should be removed last, and installed first. Those bearings act as guides for the other bearings and pilot.*

1. Drive the camshaft rear plug from the block.

2. Assemble the removal puller with its shoulder on the bearing to be removed. Gradually tighten the puller nut until the bearing is removed.

3. Remove the remaining bearings, leaving the front and rear for last. To remove these, reverse the position of the puller, so as to pull the bearings towards the center of the block. Leave the tool in this position, pilot the new front and rear bearings on the installer, and pull them into position.

4. Return the puller to its original position and pull the remaining bearings into position.

NOTE: *You must make sure that the oil holes of the bearings and block align when installing the bearings. If they don't align, the camshaft will not get proper lubrication and may seize or at least be seriously damaged. To check for correct oil hole alignment, use a piece of brass rod with a 90° bend in the end as shown in the illustration. Check all oil hole openings. The wire must enter each hole, or the hole is not properly aligned.*

5. Replace the camshaft rear plug, and stake it into position. On the 8–6.2L diesel, coat the outer diameter of the new plug with GM sealant #1052080 or equivalent, and install it flush to $\frac{1}{32}$ in. (0.794mm) deep.

Pistons and Connecting Rods

REMOVAL AND INSTALLATION

Before removing the pistons, the top of the cylinder bore must be examined for a ridge. A ridge at the top of the bore is the result of normal cylinder wear, caused by the piston

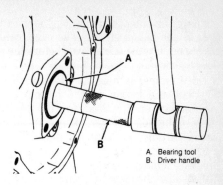

A. Bearing tool
B. Driver handle

Install outer camshaft bearings

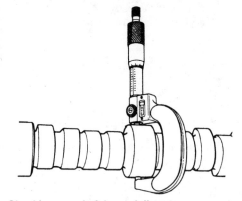

Checking camshaft journal diameter

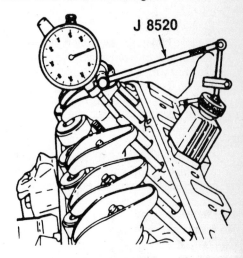

J 8520

Measuring camshaft lobe lift

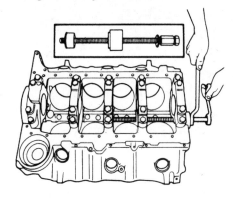

Removing camshaft bearings

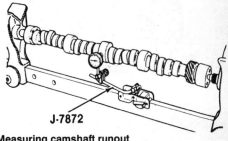

J-7872

Measuring camshaft runout

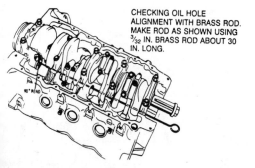

CHECKING OIL HOLE ALIGNMENT WITH BRASS ROD. MAKE ROD AS SHOWN USING $\frac{3}{32}$ IN. BRASS ROD ABOUT 30 IN. LONG.

Make this simple tool to check camshaft bearing oil hole alignment

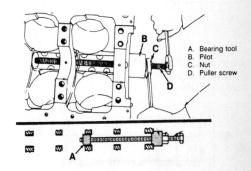

A. Bearing tool
B. Pilot
C. Nut
D. Puller screw

Replacing the inner camshaft bearings

rings only traveling so far up the bore in the course of the piston stroke. The ridge can be felt by hand. It must be removed before the pistons are removed.

A ridge reamer is necessary for this operation. Place the piston at the bottom of its stroke, and cover it with a rag. Cut the ridge away with the ridge reamer, using extreme care to avoid cutting too deeply. Remove the rag, and remove the cuttings that remain on the piston with a magnet and a rag soaked in clean oil. Make sure the piston top and cylinder bore are absolutely clean before moving the piston.

1. Remove intake manifold and cylinder head or heads.

2. Remove oil pan.

3. Remove oil pump assembly if necessary.

4. Matchmark the connecting rod cap to the connecting rod with a scribe. Each cap must be reinstalled on its proper rod in the proper direction. Remove the connecting rod bearing cap and the rod bearing. Number the top of each piston with silver paint or a felt tip pen for later assembly.

5. Cut lengths of ³/₈ in. (9.53mm) diameter hose to use as rod bolt guides. Install the hose over the threads of the rod bolts, to prevent the bolt threads from damaging the crankshaft journals and cylinder walls when the piston is removed.

6. Squirt some clean engine oil onto the cylinder wall from above, until the wall is coated. Carefully push the piston and rod assembly up and out of the cylinder by tapping on the bottom of the connecting rod with a wooden hammer handle.

7. Place the rod bearing and cap back on the connecting rod, and install the nuts temporarily. Using a number stamp or punch, stamp the cylinder number on the side of the connecting rod and cap. This will help keep the proper piston and rod assembly on the proper cylinder.

NOTE: *On all V8s, starting at the front the right bank cylinders are 2–4–6–8 and the left bank 1–3–5–7. On the V6 engine even number cylinders 2–4–6 are in the right bank, odd number cylinders 1–3–5 are in the left bank, when viewed from the rear of the engine.*

8. Remove remaining pistons in similar manner.

On all gasoline engines, the notch on the piston will face the front of the engine for assembly. The chamfered corners of the bearing caps should face toward the front of the left

A. Ridge reamer
B. Cloth

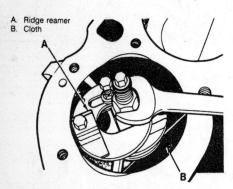

Removing the ridge at the top of the cylinder

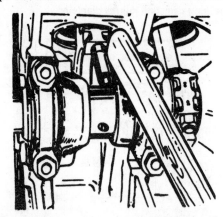

Push the piston and rod assembly out with a hammer handle

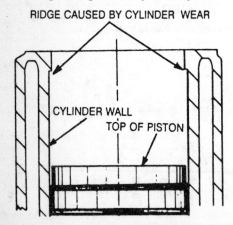

RIDGE CAUSED BY CYLINDER WEAR

CYLINDER WALL

TOP OF PISTON

Ridge formed by pistons at the top of their travel

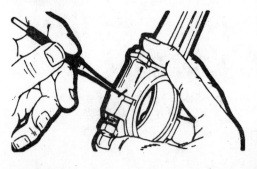

Match the connecting rods to their caps with a scribe mark

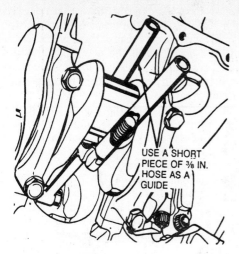

USE A SHORT PIECE OF ⅜ IN. HOSE AS A GUIDE

Connecting rod bolt guide

RING COMPRESSOR

Using a hammer handle, tap the piston down, through the ring compressor, and into the cylinder

bank and toward the rear of the right bank, and the boss on the connecting rod should face toward the front of the engine for the right bank and to the rear of the engine on the left bank.

On the 6.2L diesel, install the piston and rod assemblies with the rod bearing tang slots on the side opposite the camshaft.

On various engines, the piston compression rings are marked with a dimple, a letter **T**, a letter **O**, **GM** or the word **TOP** to identify the side of the ring which must face toward the top of the piston.

Piston Ring and Wrist Pin

REMOVAL

Some of the engines covered in this guide utilize pistons with pressed in wrist pins. These must be removed by a special press designed for this purpose. Other pistons have their wrist pins secured by snaprings, which are easily removed with snapring pliers. Separate the piston from the connecting rod.

A piston ring expander is necessary for removing piston rings without damaging them. Any other method (screwdriver blades, pliers. etc.) usually results in the rings being bent, scratched or distorted, or the piston itself being damaged. When the rings are removed, clean the ring grooves using an appropriate ring groove cleaning tool, using care not to cut too deeply. Thoroughly clean all carbon and varnish from the piston with solvent.

Do not use a wire brush or caustic solvent (acids, etc.) on pistons.

Inspect the pistons for scuffing, scoring, cracks, pitting, or excessive ring groove wear. If these are evident, the piston must be replaced.

The piston should also be checked in relation to the cylinder diameter. Using a telescoping gauge and micrometer, or a dial gauge, measure the cylinder bore diameter perpendicular (90°) to the piston pin, $2^1/_2$ in. (63.5mm) below the cylinder block deck (surface where the block mates with the heads). Then, with the micrometer, measure the piston perpendicular to its wrist pin on the shirt. The difference between the two measurements is the piston clearance. If the clearance is within specifications or slightly below (after the cylinders have been bored or honed), finish honing is all that is necessary. If the clearance is excessive, try to obtain a slightly larger piston to bring clearance to within specifications. If this is not possible, obtain the first oversize piston and hone (if necessary, bore) the cylinder to size. Generally, if the cylinder bore is tapered 0.005 in. (0.127mm) or more or is out-of-round 0.003 in. (0.0762mm) or more, it is advisable to rebore for the smallest possible oversize piston and rings.

After measuring, mark pistons with a felt tip pen for reference and for assembly.

NOTE: *Cylinder honing and/or boring should be performed by a reputable, professional mechanic with the proper equipment. In some cases, cleanup honing can be done with the cylinder block in the car, but most excessive honing and all cylinder boring must be done with the block stripped and removed from the car.*

PISTON RING END GAP

Piston ring end gap should be checked while the rings are removed from the pistons. Incorrect end gap indicates that the wrong size rings are being used; ring breakage could occur.

Compress the piston rings to be used in a cylinder, one at a time, into that cylinder. Squirt clean oil into the cylinder, so that the rings and the top 2 in. (51mm) of cylinder wall are coated. Using an inverted piston, press the rings approximately 1 in. (25.4mm) below the deck of the block (on diesels, measure ring gap clearance with the ring positioned at the bottom of ring travel in the bore). Measure the ring end gap with a feeler gauge, and compare to the Ring Gap chart in this Chapter. Carefully pull the ring out of the cylinder and file the ends squarely with a fine file to obtain the proper clearance.

PISTON RING SIDE CLEARANCE CHECK AND INSTALLATION

Check the piston to see that the ring grooves and oil return holes have been properly cleaned. Slide a piston ring into its groove, and check the side clearance with a feeler gauge. On gasoline engines, make sure you insert the gauge between the ring and its lower land (lower edge of the groove), because any wear that occurs forms a step at the inner portion of the lower land. On diesels, insert the gauge between the ring and the upper land. If the piston

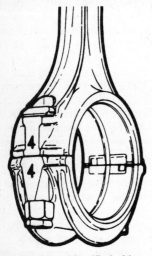

Some caps and rods are identified with corresponding numbers

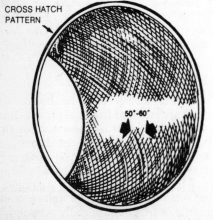

A properly honed cylinder bore

grooves have worn to the extent that relatively high steps exist on the lower land, the piston should be replaced, because these will interfere with the operation of the new rings and ring clearances will be excessive. Pistons rings are not furnished in oversize widths to compensate for ring groove wear.

Install the rings on the piston, lowest ring first, using a piston ring expander. There is a high risk of breaking or distorting the rings, or scratching the piston, if the rings are installed by hand or other means.

Position the rings on the piston as illustrated. Spacing of the various piston ring gaps is crucial to proper oil retention and even cylinder wear. When installing new rings, refer to the illustration diagram furnished with the new parts.

Connecting Rod Bearings

Connecting rod bearings for the engine covered in this guide consist of two halves or shells which are interchangable in the rod and cap. When the shells are placed in position, the ends extend slightly beyond the rod and cap surfaces so that when the rod bolts are torqued the shells will be capped tightly in place to insure positive seating and to prevent turning. A tang holds the shells in place.

NOTE: *The ends of the bearing shell must never be filed flush with the mating surface of the rod and cap.*

If a rod bearing becomes noisy or is worn so that its clearance on the crank journal is sloppy, a new bearing of the correct undersize must be selected and installed since there is a provision for adjustment.

Under no circumstances should the rod end or cap be filed to adjust the bearing clearance, nor should shims of any kind be used.

Inspect the rod bearings while the rod assemblies are out of the engine. If the shells are scored or show flaking, they should be replaced. If they are in good shape check for proper clear-

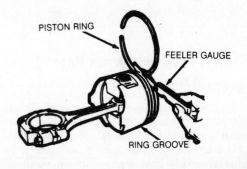

Checking piston ring side clearance

Removing the piston rings

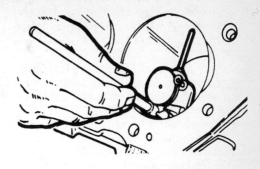

Measuring cylinder bore with a dial gauge

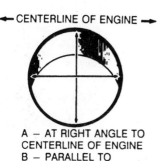

Cleaning the piston ring grooves with a ring groove cleaner

Installing the piston pin lock rings

◄— CENTERLINE OF ENGINE —►

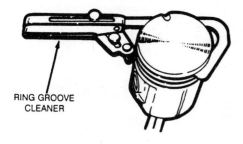

A — AT RIGHT ANGLE TO
CENTERLINE OF ENGINE
B — PARALLEL TO
CENTERLINE OF ENGINE

Cylinder bore measuring points

Measuring piston diameter

ance on the crank journal (see below). Any scoring or ridges on the crank journal means the crankshaft must be replaced, or reground and fitted with undersized bearings.

CHECKING BEARING CLEARANCE AND REPLACING BEARINGS

NOTE: *Make sure connecting rods and their caps are kept together, and that the caps are installed in the proper direction.*

Replacement bearings are available in standard size, and in undersizes for reground crankshafts. Connecting rod-to-crankshaft bearing clearance is checked using Plastigage® at either the top or bottom of each crank journal. The Plastigage® has a range of 0.001–0.003 in. (0.0254–0.0762mm).

1. Remove the rod cap with the bearing

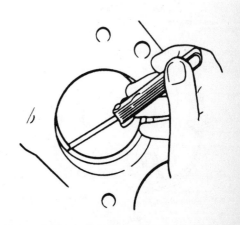

Checking piston ring end gap

shell. Completely clean the bearing shell and the crank journal, and blow any oil from the oil hole in the crankshaft; Plastigage® is soluble in oil.

2. Place a piece of Plastigage® lengthwise along the bottom center of the lower bearing shell, then install the cap with shell and torque the bolt or nuts to specification. DO NOT turn the crankshaft with Plastigage® in the bearing.

3. Remove the bearing cap with the shell. The flattened Plastigage® will be found sticking to either the bearing shell or crank journal. Do not remove it yet.

4. Use the scale printed on the Plastigage® envelope to measure the flattened material at its widest point. The number within the scale

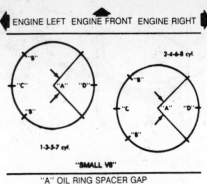

"A" OIL RING SPACER GAP
(TANG IN HOLE OR SLIT
WITHIN ARC)
"B" OIL RING RAIL GAPS
"C" 2ND COMPRESSION RING GAP
"D" TOP COMPRESSION RING GAP

Ring gap locations for all gasoline engines

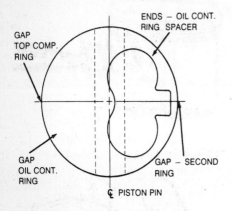

Ring gap positioning for diesel engines

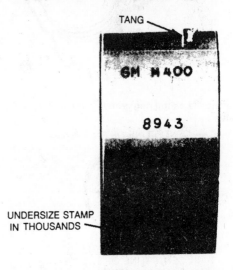

UNDERSIZE STAMP
IN THOUSANDS

Undersize marks are stamped on the bearing shells. The tang fits in the notches in the rod and cap

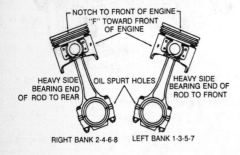

Piston and rod positioning for the 6-4.3L, 8-5.0L and 8-5.7L engines

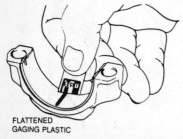

FLATTENED
GAGING PLASTIC

Checking rod bearing clearance with a Plastigage®

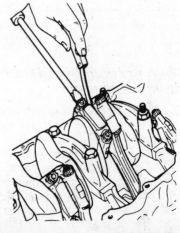

Checking connecting rod side clearance. Use a small prybar to carefully spread the rods

which most closely corresponds to the width of the Plastigage® indicates bearing clearance in thousandths of an inch.

5. Check the specifications chart in this Chapter for the desired clearance. It is advisable to install a new bearing if clearance exceeds 0.003 in. (0.0762mm). However, if the bearing is in good condition and is not being checked because of bearing noise, bearing replacement is not necessary.

6. If you are installing new bearings, try a standard size, then each undersize in order until one is found that is within the specified limits when checked for clearance with Plastigage®. Each undersize shell has its size stamped on it.

7. When the proper size shell is found, clean off the Plastigage®, oil the bearing thoroughly, reinstall the cap with its shell and torque the rod bolt nuts to specification.

NOTE: *With the proper bearing selected and the nuts torqued, it should be possible to move the connecting rod back and forth freely on the crank journal as allowed by the specified connecting rod and clearance. If the rod cannot be moved, either the rod bearing is too far undersize or the rod is misaligned.*

PISTON AND CONNECTING ROD ASSEMBLY AND INSTALLATION

NOTE: *Most engines are equipped with silicone coated pistons. If your engine has these pistons, if replaced, they must be replaced with silicone coated pistons. Substituting another type of piston could reduce the life of the engine.*

Install the connecting rod to the piston, making sure piston installation notches and any marks on the rod are in proper relation to one another. Lubricate the wrist pin with clean engine oil, and install the pin into the rod and piston assembly, either by hand or by using a wrist pin press as required. Install snaprings if equipped, and rotate them in their grooves to make sure they are seated. To install the piston and connecting rod assembly:

1. Make sure connecting rod big end bearings (including end cap) are of the correct size and properly installed.

2. Fit rubber hoses over the connecting rod bolts to protect the crankshaft journals, as in the Piston Removal procedure. Coat the rod bearings with clean oil.

3. Using the proper ring compressor, insert the piston assembly into the cylinder so that the notch in the top of the piston faces the front of the engine (this assumes that the dimple(s) or other markings on the connecting rods are in correct relation to the piston notch(es).

4. From beneath the engine, coat each crank journal with clean oil. Pull the connecting rod, with the bearing shell in place, into position against the crank journal.

5. Remove the rubber hoses. Install the bearing cap and cap nuts and torque to specification.

NOTE: *When more than one rod and piston assembly is being installed, the connecting rod cap attaching nuts should only be tightened enough to keep each rod in position until all have been installed. This will ease the installation of the remaining piston assemblies.*

6. Check the clearance between the sides of the connecting rods and the crankshaft using a feeler gauge. Spread the rods slightly with a screwdriver to insert the gauge. If clearance is below the minimum tolerance, the rod may be machined to provide adequate clearance. If clearance is excessive, substitute an unworn rod, and recheck. If clearance is still outside specifications, the crankshaft must be welded and reground or replaced.

7. Replace the oil pump if removed and the oil pan.

8. Install the cylinder head(s) and intake manifold.

Rear Main Oil Seal

REMOVAL AND INSTALLATION

6–4.3L
8–5.0L
8–5.7L

1. Remove the transmission.

2. With manual transmission, remove the clutch.

3. Remove the flywheel or flexplate.

4. Insert a small prying tool in the notches provided in the seal retainer and pry out the old seal. Be VERY CAREFUL to avoid nicking or scratching the sealing surfaces of the crankshaft.

To install:

5. Coat the inner and outer diameters of the new seal with clean engine oil.

6. Using seal tool J–35621, or equivalent, position the seal on the tool.

7. Thread the attaching screws into the holes in the crankshaft end and tighten them securely with a screwdriver.

8. Turn the installer handle until it bottoms.

9. Remove the tool.

10. Install the flywheel/flexplate, clutch and transmission.

8–7.4L

1. Remove the oil pan, oil pump and rear main bearing cap.

2. Remove the oil seal from the bearing cap by prying it out with a suitable tool.

3. Remove the upper half of the seal with a small punch. Drive it around far enough to be gripped with pliers.

To install:

4. Clean the crankshaft and bearing cap.

5. Coat the lips and bead of the seal with

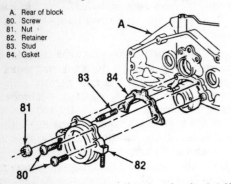

A. Rear of block
80. Screw
81. Nut
82. Retainer
83. Stud
84. Gsket

Crankshaft rear oil seal and retainer for the 6-4.3L, 8-5.0L and 8-5.7L engines

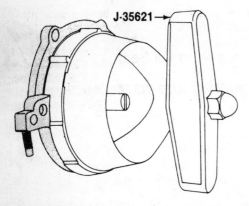

Installing the rear oil seal on the 6-4.3L, 8-5.0L and 8-5.7L engines

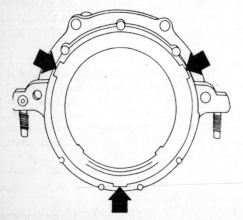

Seal removal notches

light engine oil, keeping oil from the ends of the seal.

6. Position the fabricated tool between the crankshaft and seal seat.

7. Position the seal between the crankshaft and tip of the tool so that the seal bead contacts the tip of the tool. The oil seal lip should face forward.

8. Roll the seal around the crankshaft using the tool to protect the seal bead from the sharp corners of the crankcase.

9. The installation tool should be left installed until the seal is properly positioned with both ends flush with the block.

10. Remove the tool.

11. Install the other half of the seal in the bearing cap using the tool in the same manner as before. Light thumb pressure should install the seal.

12. Install the bearing cap with sealant applied to the mating areas of the cap and block. Keep sealant from the ends of the seal.

13. Torque the main bearing cap retaining bolts to 10–12 ft. lbs. Tap the end of the crankshaft first rearward, then forward with a lead hammer. This will line up the rear main bearing and the crankshaft thrust surfaces. Tighten the main bearing cap to specification.

14. Install the oil pump.

15. Install the oil pan.

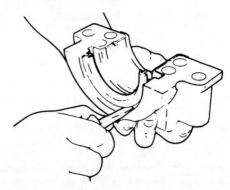

Removing the rear seal half from the bearing cap on the 7.4L, 6.2L and 4.8L engine

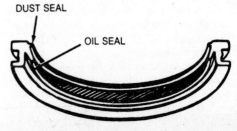

DUST SEAL

OIL SEAL

7.4L, 6.2L and 4.8L engine rear main seal half - bearing cap side

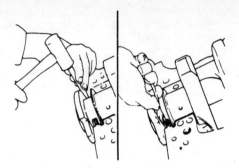

Removing the upper rear seal half from the 7.4L and 6.2L engine

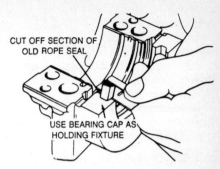

CUT OFF SECTION OF OLD ROPE SEAL

USE BEARING CAP AS HOLDING FIXTURE

Cutting the lower seal ends on the 7.4L, 6.2L and 4.8L engine

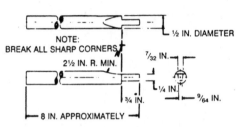

NOTE: BREAK ALL SHARP CORNERS

½ IN. DIAMETER

2½ IN. R. MIN.

$^7/_{32}$ IN.

¼ IN.

¾ IN.

$^9/_{64}$ IN.

8 IN. APPROXIMATELY

Homemade rear main seal packing tool, using a wood dowel, for the 7.4L, 6.2L and 4.8L engine

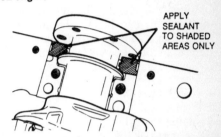

APPLY SEALANT TO SHADED AREAS ONLY

Sealing the bearing cap before final torquing, on the 7.4L, 6.2L and 4.8L. Apply a bit of oil to the crank journal just before installing the cap

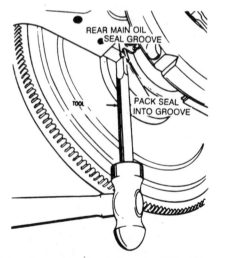

REAR MAIN OIL SEAL GROOVE

TOOL

PACK SEAL INTO GROOVE

Packing the upper rear seal on the 7.4L, 6.2L and 4.8L engine

8–6.2L Diesel

The crankshaft need not be removed to replace the rear main bearing upper oil seal. The lower seal is installed in the bearing cap.

NOTE: *The production seal is a rope-type. This seal should be replaced with the service lip-type seal.*

1. Drain the crankcase oil and remove the oil pan and rear main bearing cap.

2. Using a special main seal tool or a tool that can be made from a dowel (see illustra-

tion), drive the upper seal into its groove on each side until it is tightly packed. This is usually ¼–¾ in. (6.35–19.05mm).

3. Measure the amount the seal was driven up on one side. Add ¹/₁₆ in. (1.5875mm) and cut another length from the old seal. Use the main bearing cap as a holding fixture when cutting the seal as illustrated. Carefully trim protruding seal.

4. Work these two pieces of seal up into the cylinder block on each side with two nailsets or small screwdrivers. Using the packing tool again, pack these pieces into the block, then trim the flush with a razor blade or hobby knife as shown. Do not scratch the bearing surface with the razor.

NOTE: *It may help to use a bit of oil on the short pieces of the rope seal when packing it into the block.*

5. Apply Loctite® # 496 sealer or equivalent to the rear main bearing cap and install the rope seal. Cut the ends of the seal flush with the cap.

6. Check to see if the rear main cap with the new seal will seat properly on the block. Place a piece of Plastigage® on the rear main journal, install the cap and torque to 70 ft. lbs. Remove the cap and check the Plastigage® against specifications. If out of specs, recheck the end of the seal for fraying that may be preventing the cap from seating properly.

7. Make sure all traces of Plastigage® are re-

moved from the crankshaft journal. Apply a thin film of sealer (GM part # 1052357 or equivalent) to the bearing cap. Keep the sealant off of both the seal and the bearing.

8. Just before assembly, apply a light coat of clean engine oil on the crankshaft surface that will contact the seal.

9. Install the bearing cap and torque to specification.

10. Install the oil pump and oil pan.

Crankshaft and Main Bearings

CRANKSHAFT REMOVAL

1. Drain the engine oil and remove the engine from the car. Mount the engine on a work stand in a suitable working area. Invert the engine, so the oil pan is facing up.

2. Remove the engine front (timing) cover.

3. Remove the timing chain and gears.

4. Remove the oil pan.

5. Remove the oil pump.

6. Stamp the cylinder number on the machined surfaces of the bolt bosses of the connecting rods and caps for identification when reinstalling. If the pistons are to be removed eventually from the connecting rod, mark the cylinder number on the pistons with silver paint or felt tip pen for proper cylinder identification and cap-to-rod location.

7. Remove the connecting rod caps. Install lengths of rubber hose on each of the connecting rod bolts, to protect the crank journals when the crank is removed.

8. Mark the main bearing caps with a number punch or punch so that they can be reinstalled in their original positions.

9. Remove all main bearing caps.

10. Note the position of the keyway in the crankshaft so it can be installed in the same position.

11. Install rubber bands between a bolt on each connecting rod and oil pan bolts that have been reinstalled in the block (see illustration). This will keep the rods from banging on the block when the crank is removed.

12. Carefully lift the crankshaft out of the block. The rods will pivot to the center of the engine when the crank is removed.

MAIN BEARING INSPECTION

Like connecting rod big end bearings, the crankshaft main bearings are shell type inserts that do not utilize shims and cannot be adjusted. The bearings are available in various standard and undersizes. If main bearing clearance is found to be too sloppy, a new bearing (both upper and lower halves) is required.

NOTE: *Factory undersized crankshafts are marked, sometimes with a 9 and/or a large*

spot of *light green paint. The bearing caps also will have the paint on each side of the undersized journal.*

Generally, the lower half of the bearing shell (except No. 1 bearing) shows greater wear and fatigue. If the lower half only shows the effects of normal wear (no heavy scoring or discoloration), it can usually be assumed that the upper half is also in good shape. Conversely, if the lower half is heavily worn or damaged, both halves should be replaced. Never replace one bearing half without replacing the other.

CHECKING CLEARANCE

Main bearing clearance can be checked both with the crankshaft in the van and with the engine out of the car. If the engine block is still in the car, the crankshaft should be supported both front and rear (by the damper and to remove clearance from the upper bearing. Total clearance can then be measured between the lower bearing and journal. If the block has been removed from the car, and is inverted, the crank will rest on the upper bearings and the total clearance can be measured between the lower bearing and journal. Clearance is checked in the same manner as the connecting rod bearings, with Plastigage®.

NOTE: *Crankshaft bearing caps and bearing shells should NEVER be filed flush with the cap-to-block mating surface to adjust for wear in the old bearings. Always install new bearings.*

1. If the crankshaft has been removed, install it (block removed from car). If the block is still in the car, remove the oil pan and oil pump. Starting with the rear bearing cap, remove the

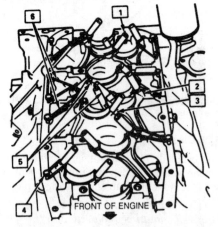

1. Rubber hose
2. #4 rod
3. #3 rod
4. Oil pan bolt
5. Note overlap of adjacent rods
6. Rubber bands

Crankshaft removal, showing hose lengths on the rod belts

cap and wipe all oil from the crank journal and bearing cap.

2. Place a strip of Plastigage® the full width of the bearing, (parallel to the crankshaft), on the journal.

WARNING: *Do not rotate the crankshaft while the gaging material is between the bearing and the journal!*

3. Install the bearing cap and evenly torque the cap bolts to specification.

4. Remove the bearing cap. The flattened Plastigage® will be sticking to either the bearing shell or the crank journal.

5. Use the graduated scale on the Plastigage® envelope to measure the material at its widest point.

NOTE: *If the flattened Plastigage® tapers toward the middle or ends, there is a differ-*ence in clearance indicating the bearing or journal has a taper, low spot or other irregularity. If this is indicated, measure the crank journal with a micrometer.

6. If bearing clearance is within specifications, the bearing insert is in good shape. Replace the insert if the clearance is not within specifications. Always replace both upper and lower inserts as a unit.

7. Standard, 0.001 in. (0.0254mm) or 0.002 in. (0.051mm) undersize bearings should produce the proper clearance. If these sizes still produce too sloppy a fit, the crankshaft must be reground for use with the next undersize bearing. Recheck all clearances after installing new bearings.

8. Replace the rest of the bearings in the

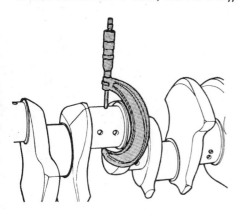

Measuring crankshaft bearing journals

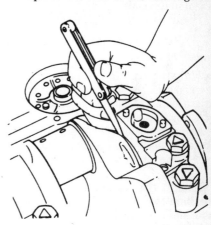

Measuring crankshaft endplay

Measuring crankshaft runout

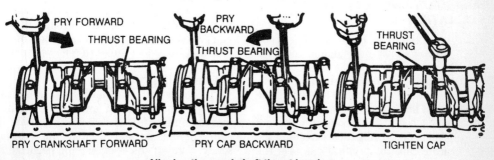

Aligning the crankshaft thrust bearing

same manner. After all bearings have been checked, rotate the crankshaft to make sure there is no excessive drag. When checking the No. 1 main bearing, loosen the accessory drive belts (engine in car) to prevent a tapered reading with the Plastigage®.

MAIN BEARING REPLACEMENT

Engine Out of Van

1. Remove and inspect the crankshaft.
2. Remove the main bearings from the bearing saddles in the cylinder block and main bearing caps.
3. Coat the bearing surfaces of the new, correct size main bearings with clean engine oil and install them in the bearing saddles in the block and in the main bearing caps.
4. Install the crankshaft. See Crankshaft Installation.

Engine in Van

1. With the oil pan, oil pump and spark plugs removed, remove the cap from the main bearing needing replacement and remove the bearing from the cap.
2. Make a bearing roll out pin, using a bent cotter pin as shown in the illustration. Install the end of the pin in the oil hole in the crankshaft journal.
3. Rotate the crankshaft clockwise as viewed from the front of the engine. This will roll the upper bearing out of the block.
4. Lube the new upper bearing with clean engine oil and insert the plain (unnotched) end between the crankshaft and the indented or notched side of the block. Roll the bearing into place, making sure that the oil holes are aligned. Remove the roll pin from the oil hole.
5. Lube the new lower bearing and install the main bearing cap. Install the main bearing cap, making sure it is positioned in proper direction with the matchmarks in alignment.
6. Torque the main bearing cap bolts to specification.

NOTE: *See Crankshaft Installation for thrust bearing alignment.*

CRANKSHAFT END PLAY AND INSTALLATION

When main bearing clearance has been checked, bearings examined and/or replaced, the crankshaft can be installed. Thoroughly clean the upper and lower bearing surfaces, and lube them with clean engine oil. Install the crankshaft and main bearing caps.

Dip all main bearing cap bolts in clean oil, and torque all main bearing caps, excluding the thrust bearing cap, to specifications (see the Crankshaft and Connecting Rod chart in this Chapter to determine which bearing is the thrust bearing). Tighten the thrust bearing bolts finger tight. To align the thrust bearing, pry the crankshaft the extent of its axial travel several times, holding the last movement toward the front of the engine. Add thrust washers if required for proper alignment. Torque the thrust bearing cap to specifications.

To check crankshaft end play, pry the crankshaft to the extreme rear of its axial travel, then to the extreme front of its travel. Using a feeler gauge, measure the end plate at the front of the rear main bearing. End play may also be measured at the thrust bearing. Install a new rear main bearing oil seal in the cylinder block and main bearing cap. Continue to reassemble the engine.

Engine Block Heater and Freeze Plugs

REMOVAL AND INSTALLATION

CAUTION: *Removing the block heater or freeze plug may cause personal injury if the engine is not completely cooled down. Even after the radiator has been drained, there will be engine coolant still in the block. Use care when removing assembly from the block.*

To remove an engine freeze plug or block heater, accessories may have to be removed, such as the starter motor, motor mount, etc. Remove an obstruction before attempting to remove the freeze plug.

1. Disconnect the negative (–) battery cable.
2. **To remove the block heater, drain the engine coolant, disconnect the electrical connector, loosen the retaining screw and remove the heater from the block.**

CAUTION: *When draining the coolant, keep in mind that cats and dogs are attracted by the ethylene glycol antifreeze, and are quite likely to drink any that is left in an uncovered container or in puddles on the ground. This will prove fatal in sufficient quantity. Always drain the coolant into a sealable container. Coolant should be reused unless it is contaminated or several years old.*

3. **To remove the freeze plug,** drain the engine coolant, drive chisel through the plug and pry outward. Or drill an $1/8$ in. hole into the plug and use a dent puller to remove the freeze plug.

To install:

1. **To install the block heater,** coat the O-ring with engine oil and clean the block mating surface free of rust and corrosion. Install the heater and tighten the retaining screw. Connect the electrical and negative battery cable.

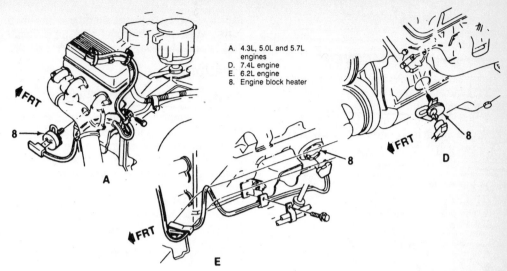

A. 4.3L, 5.0L and 5.7L
   engines
D. 7.4L engine
E. 6.2L engine
8. Engine block heater

Engine block heater locations

2. **To install the freeze plug,** coat the new plug with silicone sealer and clean the block mating surface free of rust and corrosion. Using a deep socket the size of the interior of the plug, drive the plug into the block until the plug lip is flush with the cylinder block. Run silicone sealer around the mating area.

3. Fill the engine with coolant and check for leaks.

Flywheel and Ring Gear

REMOVAL AND INSTALLATION

The ring gear is an integral part of the flywheel and is not replaceable.

1. Remove the transmission.

2. Remove the six bolts attaching the flywheel to the crankshaft flange. Remove the flywheel.

3. Inspect the flywheel for cracks, and inspect the ring gear for burrs or worn teeth. Replace the flywheel if any damage is apparent. Remove burrs with a mill file.

4. Install the flywheel. The flywheel will only attach to the crankshaft in one position, as the bolt holes are unevenly spaced. Install the bolts and torque to specification.

EXHAUST SYSTEM

Safety Precautions

For a number of reasons, exhaust system work can be the most dangerous type of work you can do on your van. Always observe the following precautions:

1. Support the van extra securely. Not only will you often be working directly under it, but you'll frequently be using a lot of force, say, heavy hammer blows, to dislodge rusted parts. This can cause a van that's improperly supported to shift and possibly fall.

2. Wear goggles. Exhaust system parts are always rusty. Metal chips can be dislodged, even when you're only turning rusted bolts. Attempting to pry pipes apart with a chisel makes the chips fly even more frequently.

3. If you're using a cutting torch, keep it a great distance from either the fuel tank or lines. Stop what you're doing and feel the temperature of the fuel bearing pipes on the tank frequently. Even slight heat can expand and/or vaporize fuel, resulting in accumulated vapor, or even a liquid leak, near your torch.

4. Watch where your hammer blows fall. You could easily tap a brake or fuel line when you hit an exhaust system part with a glancing blow. Inspect all lines and hoses in the area where you've been working.

Special Tools

A number of special exhaust system tools can be rented from auto supply houses or local stores that rent special equipment. A common one is a tail pipe expander, designed to enable you to join pipes of identical diameter.

It may also be quite helpful to use solvents designed to loosen rusted bolts or flanges. Soaking rusted parts the night before you do the job can speed the work of freeing rusted parts considerably. Remember that these solvents are often flammable. Apply only to parts after they are cool!

Crossover Pipe

REMOVAL AND REPLACEMENT

The crossover pipe (used on V-type engines only) is typically connected to the manifolds by flanged connections or collars. In some cases, bolts that are unthreaded for part of their length are used in conjunction with springs. Make sure you install the springs and that they

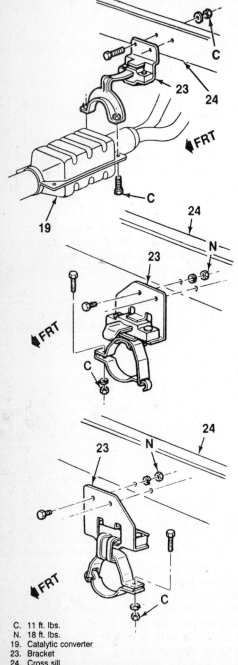

C. 11 ft. lbs.
N. 18 ft. lbs.
19. Catalytic converter
23. Bracket
24. Cross sill

Front and rear muffler hangers

are in good mechanical condition (no broken coils) when installing the new pipe. Replace ring type seals, also.

Headpipe

REMOVAL AND REPLACEMENT

The headpipe is typically attached to the rear of one exhaust manifold with a flange or collar type connector and flagged to the front of the catalytic converter. Remove nuts and bolts and, if springs are used to maintain the seal, the springs. The pipe may then be separated from the rest of the system at both flanges.

Replace ring seals; inspect springs and replace them if any coils are broken.

Catalytic Converter

REMOVAL AND REPLACEMENT

CAUTION: *Be very careful when working on or near the converter! External temperatures can reach +1,500°F (+816°C) and more, causing severe burns! Removal or installation should only be performed on a cold exhaust system.*

Remove bolts at the flange at the rear end. Then, loosen nuts and remove U-clamp to remove the catalyst. Slide the catalyst out of the outlet pipe. Replace all ring seals. In some cases, you'll have to disconnect an air line coming from the engine compartment before catalyst removal. In some cases, a hanger supports the converter via one of the flange bolts. Make sure the hanger gets properly reconnected. Also, be careful to retain all parts used to heat shield the converter and reinstall them. Make sure the converter is replaced for proper direction of flow and air supply connections.

Muffler and Tailpipes

REMOVAL AND INSTALLATION

These units are typically connected by flanges at the rear of the converter and at either end of mufflers either by an original weld or by U-clamps working over a pipe connection in which one side of the connection is slightly larger than the other. You may have to cut the original connection and use the pipe expander to allow the original equipment exhaust pipe to be fitted over the new muffler. In this case, you'll have to purchase new U-clamps to fasten the joints. GM recommends that whenever you replace a muffler, all parts to the rear of the muffler in the exhaust system must be replaced. Also, all slip joints rearward of the converter should be coated with sealer before they are assembled.

Be careful to connect all U-clamps or other

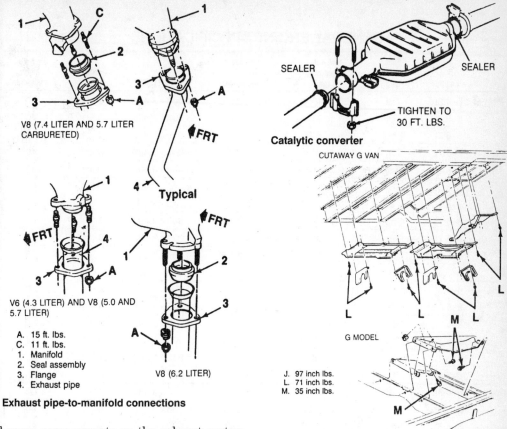

V8 (7.4 LITER AND 5.7 LITER CARBURETED)

Typical

V6 (4.3 LITER) AND V8 (5.0 AND 5.7 LITER)

A. 15 ft. lbs.
C. 11 ft. lbs.
1. Manifold
2. Seal assembly
3. Flange
4. Exhaust pipe

V8 (6.2 LITER)

Exhaust pipe-to-manifold connections

Catalytic converter

SEALER   SEALER

TIGHTEN TO 30 FT. LBS.

CUTAWAY G VAN

G MODEL

J. 97 inch lbs.
L. 71 inch lbs.
M. 35 inch lbs.

Exhaust heat shields

hanger arrangements so the exhaust system will not flex. Assemble all parts loosely and rotate parts inside one another or clamps on the pipes to ensure proper routing of all exhaust system parts to avoid excessive heating of the floorpan, fuel lines and tank, etc. Also, make sure there is clearance to prevent the system from rattling against spring shackles, the differential, etc. You may be able to bend long pipes slightly by hand to help get enough clearance, if necessary.

While disassembling the system, keep your eye open for any leaks or for excessively close clearance to any brake system parts. Inspect the brake system for any sort of heat damage and repair as necessary.

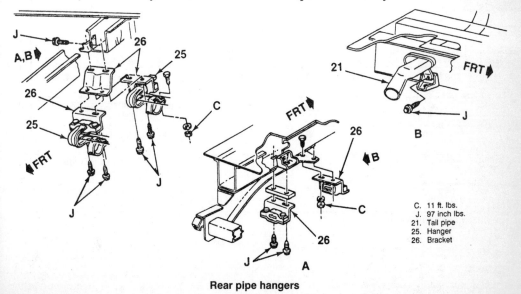

C. 11 ft. lbs.
J. 97 inch lbs.
21. Tail pipe
25. Hanger
26. Bracket

Rear pipe hangers

GENERAL ENGINE SPECIFICATIONS

Years	Engine	Fuel System Type	SAE net Horsepower @ rpm	SAE net Torque ft. lbs. @ rpm	Bore × Stroke	Comp. Ratio	Oil Press. (psi.) @ 2000 rpm
1987	6–4.3L	TBI	155 @ 4000	235 @ 2400	4.000 × 3.480	9.3:1	50
	8–5.0L	TBI	170 @ 4400	250 @ 2400	3.736 × 3.480	8.5:1	40
	8–5.7L	4-bbl	165 @ 3800	275 @ 1600	4.000 × 3.480	8.2:1	40
	8–5.7L	TBI	185 @ 4000	285 @ 2400	4.000 × 3.480	8.2:1	40
	8–6.2L	Diesel	140 @ 3600	240 @ 2000	3.980 × 3.800	21.5:1	45
1988	6–4.3L	TBI	155 @ 4000	235 @ 2400	4.000 × 3.480	9.3:1	50
	8–5.0L	TBI	170 @ 4400	250 @ 2400	3.736 × 3.480	8.5:1	40
	8–5.7L	4-bbl	165 @ 3800	275 @ 1600	4.000 × 3.480	8.2:1	40
	8–5.7L	TBI	185 @ 4000	285 @ 2400	4.000 × 3.480	8.2:1	40
	8–6.2L	Diesel	140 @ 3600	240 @ 2000	3.980 × 3.800	21.5:1	45
	8–7.4L	TBI	240 @ 3800	375 @ 3200	4.250 × 4.000	8.0:1	45
1989	6–4.3L	TBI	155 @ 4000	235 @ 2400	4.000 × 3.480	9.3:1	50
	8–5.0L	TBI	170 @ 4400	250 @ 2400	3.736 × 3.480	8.5:1	40
	8–5.7L	4-bbl	165 @ 3800	275 @ 1600	4.000 × 3.480	8.2:1	40
	8–5.7L	TBI	185 @ 4000	285 @ 2400	4.000 × 3.480	8.2:1	40
	8–6.2L	Diesel	140 @ 3600	240 @ 2000	3.980 × 3.800	21.5:1	45
	8–7.4L	TBI	240 @ 3800	375 @ 3200	4.250 × 4.000	8.0:1	45
1990	6–4.3L	TBI	150 @ 4000	235 @ 2400	4.000 × 3.480	9.3:1	50
	8–5.0L	TBI	170 @ 4400	250 @ 2400	3.736 × 3.480	8.5:1	40
	8–5.7L	4-bbl	165 @ 3800	275 @ 1600	4.000 × 3.480	8.2:1	40
	8–5.7L	TBI	185 @ 4000	285 @ 2400	4.000 × 3.480	8.2:1	40
	8–6.2L	Diesel	140 @ 3600	240 @ 2000	3.980 × 3.800	21.5:1	45
	8–7.4L	TBI	240 @ 3800	375 @ 3200	4.250 × 4.000	8.0:1	45

TBI: Throttle Body Injection

VALVE SPECIFICATIONS

Engine	Years	Seat Angle (deg.)	Face Angle (deg.)	Spring Test Pressure (lbs. @ in.)	Spring Installed Height (in.)	Stem-to-Guide Clearance (in.) Intake	Stem-to-Guide Clearance (in.) Exhaust	StemDiameter (in.) Intake	StemDiameter (in.) Exhaust
6–4.3L	1987–90	46	45	200 @ 1.25	1.72	0.0010–0.0027	0.0010–0.0027	0.3414	0.3414
8–5.0L	1987–90	46	45	200 @ 1.25	1.71	0.0010–0.0027	0.0010–0.0027	0.3414	0.3414
8–5.7L	1987–90	46	45	200 @ 1.25	1.71	0.0010–0.0027	0.0010–0.0027	0.3414	0.3414
8–6.2L	1987–90	46	45	230 @ 1.39	1.81	0.0010–0.0027	0.0010–0.0027	NA	NA
8–7.4L	1988–90	46	45	205 @ 1.40	1.80	0.0010–0.0027	0.0012–0.0029	0.3719	0.3719

NA: Information Not Available

PISTON AND RING SPECIFICATIONS
(All specifications in inches)

Engine	Years	Ring Gap			Ring Side Clearance			Piston-to-Bore Clearance
		No. 1 Compr.	No. 2 Compr.	Oil Control	No. 1 Compr.	No. 2 Compr.	Oil Control	
6–4.3L	1987–90	0.010–0.020	0.010–0.025	0.015–0.055	0.0012–0.0032	0.0012–0.0032	0.002–0.007	0.0007–0.0017
8–5.0L	1987–90	0.010–0.020	0.010–0.025	0.015–0.055	0.0012–0.0032	0.0012–0.0032	0.002–0.007	0.0007–0.0017
8–5.7L	1987–90	0.010–0.020	0.010–0.025	0.015–0.055	0.0012–0.0032	0.0012–0.0032	0.002–0.007	0.0007–0.0017
8–6.2L	1987–90	0.012–0.022	0.030–0.040	0.010–0.020	0.0030–0.0070	0.0015–0.0031	0.0016–0.0038	①
8–7.4L	1988–90	0.010–0.020	0.010–0.020	0.015–0.055	0.0017–0.0032	0.0017–0.0032	0.0050–0.0065	0.0030–0.0040

① Bohn pistons
   Bores 1, 2, 3, 4, 5, 6: 0.0035–0.0045
   Bores 6 & 7: 0.0040–0.0050

Zollner Pistons
   Bores 1, 2, 3, 4, 5, 6: 0.0044–0.0054
   Bores 6 & 7: 0.0049–0.0059

TORQUE SPECIFICATIONS
(All specifications in ft. lbs.)

Engine	Years	Cyl. Head	Conn. Rod	Main Bearing	Crankshaft Damper	Flywheel	Manifold	
							Intake	Exhaust
6–4.3L	1987	65	45	75	70	75	35	②
	1988–90	65	45	80	70	75	35	②
8–5.0L	1987–90	65	45	③	70	75	35	④
8–5.7L	1987–90	65	45	③	70	75	35	④
8–6.2L	1987–90	⑤	48	①	200	65	30	26
8–7.4L	1988	80	48	110	85	65	30	40
	1989–90	80	48	100	85	65	30	40

① Inner: 111
   Outer: 100
② Center two bolts: 26
   All others: 20
③ Outer bolts on Nos. 2, 3, 4: 70
   All others: 80

⑤ Cast iron manifold
   Center two bolts: 26
   All others: 20
   Stainless steel manifold: 26

⑥ Tighten bolts in sequence to
   Step 1: 20
   Step 2: 50
   Step 3: ¼ turn (90 degrees) more

CAMSHAFT SPECIFICATIONS

(All specifications in inches)

| Engine | Years | Journal Diameter | Lobe Lift | | End Play |
			Int.	Exh.	
6–4.3L	1987–90	1.8682–1.8692	0.3570	0.3900	0.004–0.012
8–5.0L	1987–90	1.8682–1.8692	0.2336	0.2565	0.004–0.012
8–5.7L	1987–90	1.8682–1.8692	0.2565	0.2690	0.004–0.012
8–6.2L	1987–90	①	0.2808	0.2808	0.002–0.012
8–7.4L	1988–90	1.9482–1.9492	0.2343	0.2530	0

① Nos. 1, 2, 3, 4: 2.1642–2.1663
No. 5: 2.0067–2.0089

CRANKSHAFT AND CONNECTING ROD SPECIFICATIONS

(All specifications in inches)

| Engine | Years | Crankshaft | | | | Connecting Rod | | |
		Main Bearing Journal Dia.	Main Bearing Oil Clearance	Shaft End Play	Thrust on No.	Journal Dia.	Oil Clearance	Side Clearance
6–4.3L	1987	①	②	0.002–0.006	3	2.2487–2.2497	0.0010–0.0032	0.007–0.015
	1988–90	①	②	0.002–0.006	3	2.2487–2.2497	0.0013–0.0035	0.006–0.014
8–5.0L	1987–90	③	④	0.002–0.006	5	2.0988–2.0998	0.0013–0.0035	0.006–0.014
8–5.7L	1987–90	③	④	0.002–0.006	5	2.0988–2.0998	0.0013–0.0035	0.006–0.014
8–6.2L	1987–88	⑤	⑥	0.002–0.007	5	2.3980–2.3990	0.0018–0.0039	0.007–0.024
	1989–90	⑤	⑥	0.004–0.010	5	2.3981–2.3992	0.0018–0.0039	0.006–0.025
8–7.4L	1988–90	⑦	⑧	0.006–0.010	5	2.1990–2.2000	0.0009–0.0025	0.013–0.023

① No. 1: 2.4484–2.4493
Nos. 2 and 3: 2.4481–2.4990
No. 4: 2.4479–2.4488
② No. 1: 0.0008–0.0020
Nos. 2 and 3: 0.0011–0.0023
No. 3: 0.0017–0.0032
③ No. 1: 2.4484–2.4493
Nos. 2, 3, 4: 2.4481–2.4490
No. 5: 2.4479–2.4488

④ No. 1: 0.0008–0.0020
Nos. 2, 3, 4: 0.0011–0.0023
No. 5: 0.0017–0.0033
⑤ Nos. 1, 2, 3, 4: 2.9495–2.9504
No. 5: 2.9493–2.9502
⑥ Nos. 1, 2, 3, 4: 0.0018–0.0032
No. 5: 0.0022–0.0037

⑦ Nos. 1, 2, 3, 4: 2.7481–2.7490
No. 5: 2.7476–2.7486
⑧ Nos. 1, 2, 3, 4: 0.0013–0.0025
No. 5: 0.0024–0.0040

EMISSION CONTROLS

Positive Crankcase Ventilation

PCV is the earliest form of emission control. Prior to its use, crankcase vapors were vented into the atmosphere through a road draft tube or crankcase breather. The PCV system first appeared in 1955.

This system draws crankcase vapors that are formed through normal combustion into the intake manifold and subsequently into the combustion chambers to be burned. Fresh air is introduced to the crankcase by way of a hose connected to the air cleaner. Manifold vacuum is used to draw the vapors from the crankcase through a PCV valve and into the intake manifold. Non-vented filler caps are used on all models.

SERVICE

Other than checking and replacing the PCV valve and associated hoses, there is not service required. Engine operating conditions that would direct suspicion to the PCV system are rough idle, oil present in the air cleaner, oil leaks and excessive oil sludging or dilution. If any of the above conditions exist, remove the PCV valve and shake it. A clicking sound indicates that the valve is free. If no clicking sound is heard, replace the valve. Inspect the PCV breather in the air cleaner. Replace the breather if it is so dirty that it will not allow gases to pass through. Check all the PCV hoses for condition and tight connections. Replace any hoses that have deteriorated.

Air Injector Reactor (Air Pump)

The AIR system injects compressed air into the exhaust system, near enough to the exhaust valves to continue the burning of the normally unburned segment of the exhaust gases. To do this it employs an air injection pump and a system of hoses, valves, tubes, etc., necessary to carry the compressed air from the pump to the exhaust manifolds.

A diverter valve is used to prevent backfiring. The valve senses sudden increases in manifold vacuum and ceases the injection of air during dual rich periods. During coasting, this valve diverts the entire air flow through a muffler and during high engine speeds, expels it through a relief valve. Check valves in the system prevent exhaust gases from entering the pump.

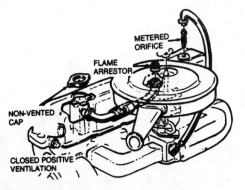

Closed and positive crankcase ventilation systems

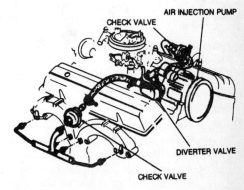

AIR system components

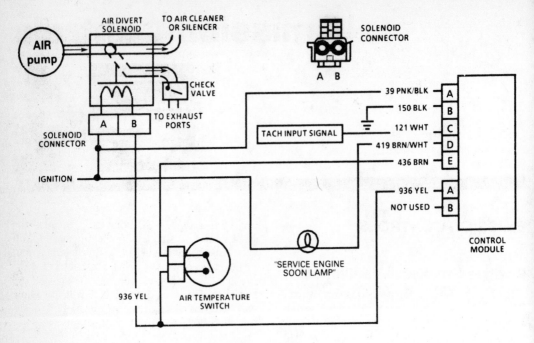

AIR schematic

Air management system component installation

TESTING

Check Valve

To test the check valve, disconnect the hose at the diverter valve. Blow into the hose and suck on it. Air should flow only into the engine.

Diverter Valve

Pull off the vacuum line to the top of the valve with the engine running. There should be vacuum in the line. Replace the line. No air should be escaping with the engine running at a steady idle. Open and quickly close the throttle. A blast of air should come out of the valve muffler for at least one second.

Air Pump

Disconnect the hose from the diverter valve. Start the engine and accelerate it to about 1,500 rpm. The air flow should increase as the engine is accelerated. If no air flow is noted or it remains constant, check the following:

1. Drive belt tension.
2. Listen for a leaking pressure relief valve. If it is defective, replace the whole relief/diverter valve.
3. Foreign matter in pump filter openings. If the pump is defective or excessively noisy, it must be replaced.

SERVICE

All hoses and fittings should be inspected for condition and tightness of connections. Check the drive belt for wear and tension periodically.

NOTE: *The A.I.R. system is not completely silent under normal conditions. Noises will rise in pitch as engine speed increases. If the noise is excessive, eliminate the air pump itself by disconnecting the drive belt. If the noise disappears, the air pump is not at fault.*

Air Pump

REMOVAL AND INSTALLATION

1. Disconnect the output hose.
2. Hold the pump from turning by squeezing the drive belt.
3. Loosen the pulley bolts.

1. Check valve — tighten
   to 74 ft. lbs.
2. Hose — valve-to-check
   valve
3. Air control valve —
   tighten mounting screws
   to 98 inch lbs.
4. Air pump — tighten
   mounting screws to 24
   ft. lbs.
5. Hose — valve-to-air
   cleaner
6. Air injection pipe —
   tighten nuts to 44 ft. lbs.
   — right side is similar

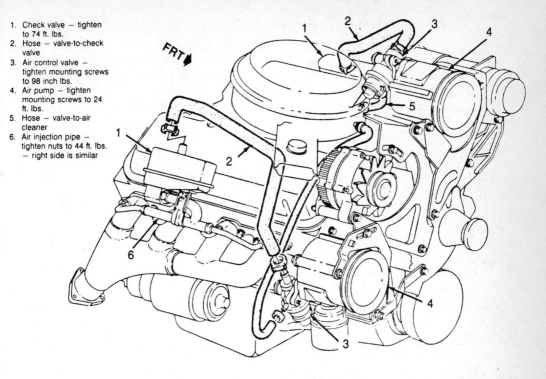

AIR system components for the 8-7.4L engine

4. Loosen the alternator so the belt can be removed.
5. Remove the pulley.
6. Remove the pump mounting bolts and the pump.
7. Install the pump with the mounting bolts loose.
8. Install the pulley and tighten the bolts finger tight.
9. Install and adjust the drive belt.
10. Squeeze the drive belt to prevent the pump from turning.
11. Torque the pulley bolts to 25 ft. lbs. Tighten the pump mountings.
12. Check and adjust the belt tension again, if necessary.
13. Connect the hose.
14. If any hose leaks are suspected, pour soapy water over the suspected area with the engine running. Bubbles will form wherever air is escaping.

FILTER REPLACEMENT

1. Disconnect the air and vacuum hoses from the diverter valve.
2. Loosen the pump pivot and adjusting bolts and remove the drive belt.
3. Remove the pivot and adjusting bolts from the pump. Remove the pump and the diverter valve as an assembly.

WARNING: *Do not clamp the pump in a vise or use a hammer or pry bar on the pump housing!*

4. To change the filter, break the plastic fan from the hub. It is seldom possible to remove the fan without breaking it.
5. Remove the remaining portion of the fan filter from the pump hub. Be careful that filter fragments do not enter the air intake hole.
6. Position the new centrifugal fan filter on the pump hub. Place the pump pulley against the fan filter and install the securing screws. Torque the screws alternately to 95 inch lbs. and the fan filter will be pressed onto the pump hub.
7. Install the pump on the engine and adjust its drive belt.

Controlled Combustion System

SERVICE

Refer to the CHA, TCS, CEC or EGR Sections for maintenance and service (if applicable).

Air Management System

The Air Management System is used to provide additional oxygen to continue the combustion process after the exhaust gases leave the combustion chamber; much the same as the

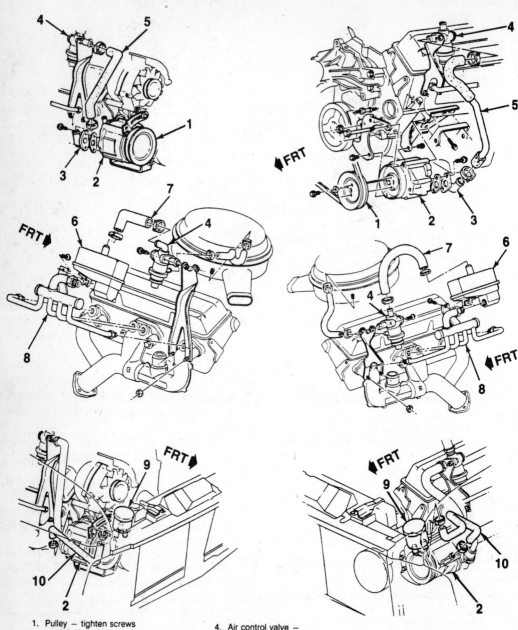

1. Pulley — tighten screws to 18 ft. lbs.; tighten again, within 10 minutes, to 18 ft. lbs.
2. AIR pump — tighten mounting screws to 22 ft. lbs.
3. Adapter — tighten screws to 98 inch lbs.
4. Air control valve — tighten screws to 18 ft. lbs.
5. Hose — pump-to-air control valve
6. Check valve — tighten nut to 74 ft. lbs.
7. Hose — air control valve-to-check valve
8. Air injection pipe — tighten nuts to 44 ft. lbs.
9. Filter — drain hole in inlet hose MUST point downward
10. Hose — filter-to-pump

AIR system components for the 8-5.7L engine

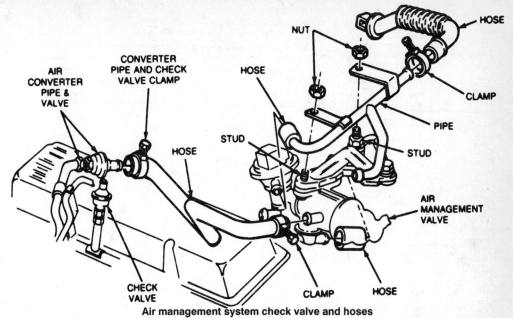

Air management system check valve and hoses

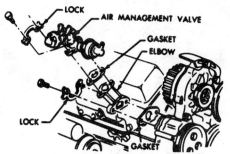

Air management system component installation -typical

AIR system described earlier in this Chapter. Air is injected into either the exhaust port(s), the exhaust manifold(s) or the catalytic converter by an engine driven air pump. The system is in operating at all times and will bypass air only momentarily during deceleration and at high speeds. The bypass function is performed by the Air Management Valve, which the check valve protects the air pump by preventing any backflow of exhaust gases.

The AIR system helps to reduce HC and CO content in the exhaust gases by injecting air into the exhaust ports during cold engine operation. This air injection also helps the catalytic converter to reach the proper temperature quicker during warm-up. When the engine warm (closed loop), the AIR system injects air into the beds of a 3-way converter to lower the HC and CO content in the exhaust.

The Air Management System utilizes the following components:

1. An engine driven air pump.
2. Air management valves (Air Control and Air Switching)

3. Air flow and control hoses
4. Check valves
5. A dual bed, 3-way catalytic converter

The belt driven, vane type air pump is located at the front of the engine and supplies clean air to the system for purposes already stated. When the engine is cold, the Electronic Control Module (ECM) energizes an air control solenoid. This allows air to flow to the air switching valve. The air switching valve is then energized to direct air into the exhaust ports.

When the engine is warm, the ECM de-energizes the air switching valve, thus directing the air between the beds of the catalytic converter. This then provides additional oxygen for the oxidizing catalyst in the second bed to decrease HC and CO levels, while at the same time keeping oxygen levels low in the first bed, enabling the reducing catalyst to effectively decrease the levels of NOx.

If the air control valve detects a rapid increase in manifold vacuum (deceleration), certain operating modes (wide open throttle, etc.) or if the ECM self diagnostic system detects any problems in the system, air is diverted to the air cleaner or directly into the atmosphere.

The primary purpose of the ECM's divert mode is to prevent backfiring. Throttle closure at the beginning of deceleration will temporarily create air/fuel mixtures which are too rich to burn completely. These mixtures will be come burnable when they reach the exhaust if they are combined with injection air. The next firing of the engine will ignite the mixture causing an exhaust backfire. Momentary diverting of the injection air from the exhaust prevents this.

The Air Management System check valves

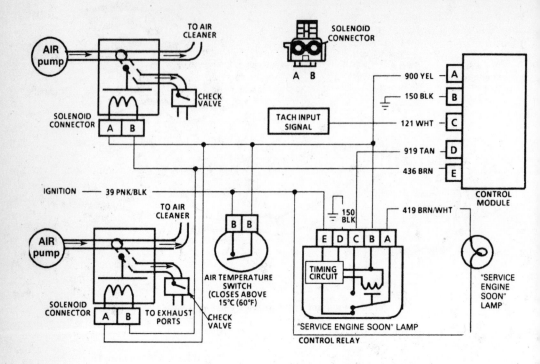

Air Management System schematic for the 8-7.4L engine

and hoses should be checked periodically for any leaks, cracks or deterioration.

REMOVAL AND INSTALLATION

Air Pump

1. Remove the valves and/or adapter at the air pump.
2. Loosen the air pump adjustment bolt and remove the drive belt.
3. Unscrew the three mounting bolts and then remove the pump pulley.
4. Unscrew the pump mounting bolts and then remove the pump.
5. Installation is in the reverse order of removal. Be sure to adjust the drive bolt tension after installing it.

Check Valve

1. Release the clamp and disconnect the air hoses from the valve.
2. Unscrew the check valve from the air injection pipe.
3. Installation is in the reverse order of removal.

Air Management Valve

1. Disconnect the negative battery cable.
2. Remove the air cleaner.
3. Tag and disconnect the vacuum hose from the valve.

4. Tag and disconnect the air outlet hoses from the valve.
5. Bend back the lock tabs and then remove the bolts holding the elbow to the valve.
6. Tag and disconnect any electrical connections at the valve and then remove the valve from the elbow.
7. Installation is in the reverse order of removal.

Thermostatic Air Cleaner

The use of carburetor heated air dates back to 1960 when it was first used on heavy trucks.

This system is designed to warm the air entering the intake manifold when underhood temperatures are low. This allows more precise combustion.

The thermostatically controlled air cleaner is composed of the air cleaner body, a filter, sensor unit, vacuum diaphragm, damper door and associated hoses and connections. Heat radiating from the exhaust manifold is trapped by a heat stove and is ducted to the air cleaner to supply heated air to the carburetor. A movable door in the air cleaner snorkel allows air to be drawn in from the heat stove (cold operation) or from the underhood air (warm operation). Periods of extended idling, climbing a grade or high speed operation are followed by a considerable increase in engine compartment temperature. Excessive fuel vapors enter the intake manifold causing an over-rich mixture, resulting in a rough idle. To overcome this, some engines may be equipped with a hot idle compensator.

SERVICE

1. Either start with a cold engine or remove the air cleaner from the engine for at least half an hour. While cooling the air cleaner, leave the engine compartment hood open.
2. Tape a thermometer, of known accuracy, to the inside of the air cleaner so that it is near the temperature sensor unit. Install the air cleaner on the engine but do not fasten its securing nut.
3. Start the engine. With the engine cold and the outside temperature less than +90°F (+32°C), the door should be in the HEAT ON position (closed to outside air).

NOTE: *Due to the position of the air cleaner on some trucks, a mirror may be necessary when observing the position of the air door.*

4. Operate the throttle lever rapidly to 1/2–3/4 of its opening and release it. The air door should open to allow outside air to enter and then close again.
5. Allow the engine to warm up to normal temperature. Watch the door. When it opens to the outside air, remove the cover from the air cleaner. The temperature should be over +90°F (+32°C) and no more than +130°F (+54°C); +115°F (+46°C) is about normal. If the door does not work within these temperature ranges, or fails to work at all, check for linkage or door binding.

If binding is not present and the air door is not working, proceed with the vacuum tests, given below. If these indicate no faults in the vacuum motor and the door is not working, the temperature sensor is defective and must be replaced.

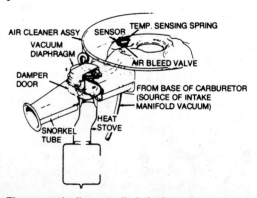

Thermostatically controlled air cleaner

Vacuum Motor Test

NOTE: *Be sure that the vacuum hose which runs between the temperature switch and the vacuum motor is not pinched by the retaining clip under the air cleaner. This could prevent the air door from closing.*

1. Check all of the vacuum lines and fittings for leaks. Correct any leaks. If none are found, proceed with the test.
2. Remove the hose which runs from the sensor to the vacuum motor. Run a hose directly from the manifold vacuum source to the vacuum motor.
3. If the motor closes the air door, it is functioning properly and the temperature sensor is defective.
4. If the motor does not close the door and no binding is present in its operation, the vacuum motor is defective and must be replaced.

NOTE: *If an alternate vacuum source is applied to the motor, insert a vacuum gauge in the line by using a T-fitting. Apply at least 9 in.Hg of vacuum in order to operate the motor.*

Engine Control Systems

The 6–4.3L, 8–5.0L, and 8–5.7L engines have a Computer Command Control system which controls:
- Fuel control system.
- Air injection reaction (AIR).
- Exhaust gas recirculation (EGR).
- Evaporative Emission Control System (EECS).
- Electronic Spark Timing (EST).
- Electronic Spark Control (ESC) (4.3L CAL.).
- Transmission Converter Clutch (TCC).

An Electronic Control Module (ECM) is the heart of the Computer Command Control System. The ECM uses sensors to get information about engine operation which it uses to vary systems it controls.

The ECM has the ability to do some diagnosis of itself. When it recognizes a problem, it lights a "Service Engine Soon" lamp on the instrument panel. When this occurs, the cause of the light coming on should be checked as soon as reasonably possible, and the malfunction corrected.

All diagnosis and repair of the Computer Command Control system, the Electronic Control Module, and the components they control, should be referred to a qualified technician possessing the proper diagnostic equipment.

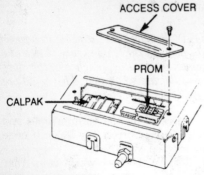

Access cover removal

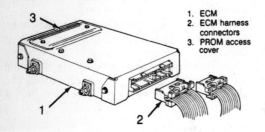

1. ECM
2. ECM harness connectors
3. PROM access cover

Electronic control module for V6 and V8 engines

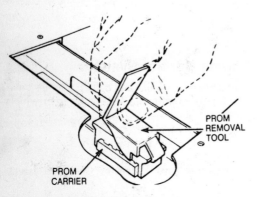

Removing PROM carrier

TESTING

If there is a TCS system malfunction, first connect a vacuum gauge in the hose between the solenoid valve and the distributor vacuum unit. Drive the vehicle or raise it on a frame lift and observe the vacuum gauge. If full vacuum is available in all gears, check for the following:

1. Blown fuse.
2. Disconnected wire at solenoid operated vacuum valve.
3. Disconnected wire at transmission switch.
4. Temperature override switch energized due to low engine temperature.
5. Solenoid failure.

If no vacuum is available in any gear, check the following:

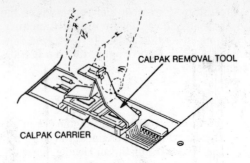

Removing the CALPAK

PROM carrier

1. Solenoid valve vacuum lines switched.
2. Clogged solenoid vacuum valve.
3. Distributor or manifold vacuum lines leaking or disconnected.
4. Transmission switch or wire grounded.

Tests for individual components are as follows:

Idle Stop Solenoid

This unit may be checked simply by observing it while an assistant switches the ignition on and off. It should extend further with the current switched on. The unit is not repairable.

Solenoid Vacuum Valve

Check that proper manifold vacuum is available. Connect the vacuum gauge in the line between the solenoid valve and the distributor. Apply 12 volts to the solenoid. If vacuum is still not available, the valve is defective, either mechanically or electrically. The unit is not repairable. If the valve is satisfactory, check the relay next.

Relay

1. With the engine at normal operating temperature and the ignition on, ground the solenoid vacuum valve terminal with the black lead. The solenoid should energize (no vacuum) if the relay is satisfactory.
2. With the solenoid energized as in Step 1, connect a jumper from the relay terminal with the green/white stripe lead to ground. The solenoid should de-energize (vacuum available) if the relay is satisfactory.
3. If the relay worked properly in Steps 1 and 2, check the temperature switch. The relay unit is not repairable.

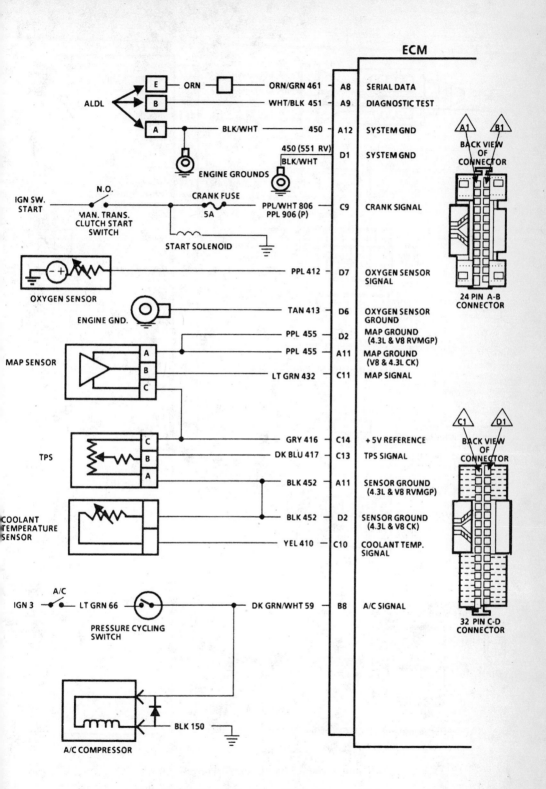

ECM wiring diagram for V6 and V8 engines - part 1

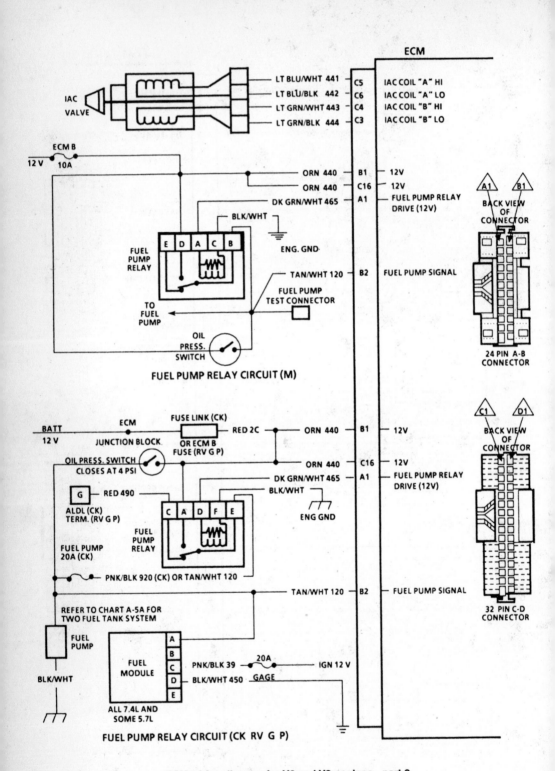

ECM wiring diagram for V6 and V8 engines - part 2

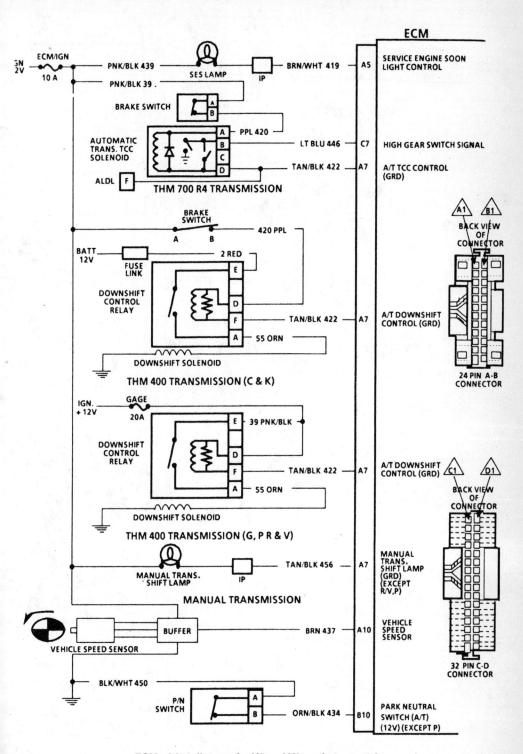

ECM wiring diagram for V6 and V8 engines - part 3

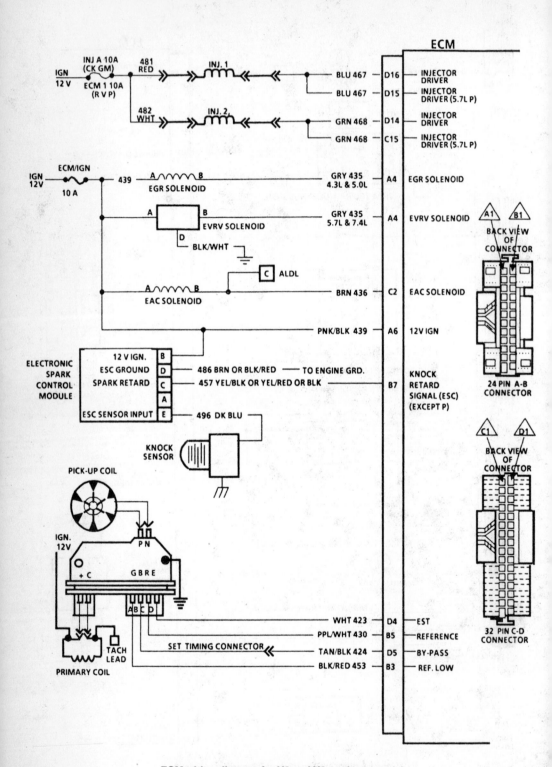

ECM wiring diagram for V6 and V8 engines - part 4

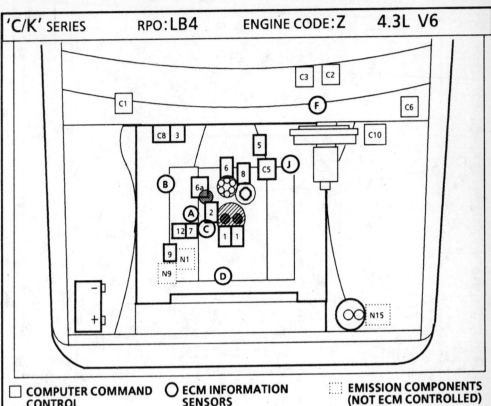

'C/K' SERIES   RPO: LB4   ENGINE CODE: Z   4.3L V6

☐ COMPUTER COMMAND CONTROL

C1   Electronic Control Module (E.C.M.)
C2   ALDL diagnostic connector
C3   "SERVICE ENGINE SOON" light
C5   ECM harness ground
C6   Fuse panel
C8   Fuel pump test connector

☐ ECM CONTROLLED COMPONENTS

1   Fuel injector
2   Idle air control
3   Fuel pump relay
5   Transmission Converter Clutch Connector
6   Electronic Spark Timing Distributor (E.S.T.)
6a   Remote ignition coil
7   Electronic Spark Control module (E.S.C.)
8   Oil pressure switch
9   Electric Air Control solenoid (E.A.C.)
12   Exhaust Gas Recirculation Vacuum Solenoid

◯ ECM INFORMATION SENSORS

A   Manifold Absolute Pressure (M.A.P.)
B   Exhaust oxygen
C   Throttle position (T.P.S.)
D   Coolant temperature
F   Vehicle speed (V.S.S.)
J   Electronic Spark Control Knock (E.S.C.)

⬚ EMISSION COMPONENTS (NOT ECM CONTROLLED)

N1   Crankcase vent valve (PCV)
N9   Air Pump
N15   Fuel Vapor Canister

V8 electronic engine control component locator

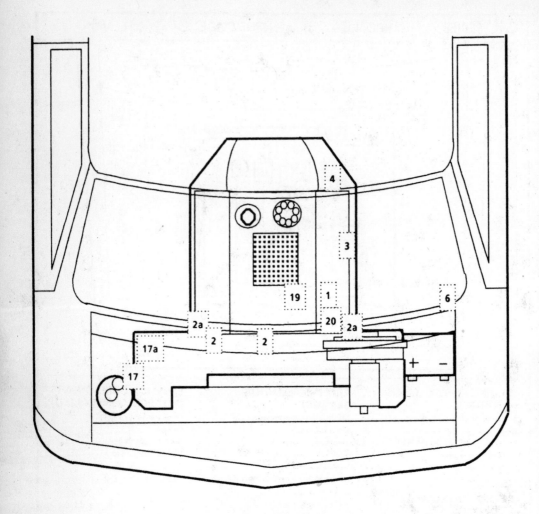

EMISSIONS DEVICES

1   Crankcase vent valve (PCV)
2   Air injection pump
2a   Air injection divert valve
3   Deceleration valve
4   EFE valve
6   Fuse panel
17   Fuel vapor canister
17a   Fuel vapor canister solenoid
19   Throttle return control
20   Throttle valve relay

Exhaust Gas Recirculation valve

V6 electronic engine control component locator

Temperature Switch

The vacuum valve solenoid should be de-energized (vacuum available) with the engine cold. If it is not, ground the green/white stripe wire from the switch. If the solenoid now de-energizes, replace the switch. If the switch was satisfactory, check the transmission switch.

Transmission Switch

With the engine at normal operating temperature and the transmission in one of the no vacuum gears, the vacuum valve solenoid should be energized (no vacuum). If not, remove and ground the switch electrical lead. If the solenoid energizes, replace the switch.

Exhaust Gas Recirculation

The EGR system's purpose is to control oxides of nitrogen which are formed during the peak combustion temperatures. The end products of combustion are relatively inert gases derived from the exhaust gases which are directed into the EGR valve to help lower peak combustion temperatures.

The EGR valve contains a vacuum diaphragm operated by manifold vacuum. The

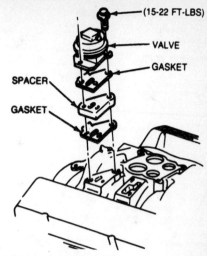

(15-22 FT-LBS)
VALVE
GASKET
SPACER
GASKET

V8 EGR valve installation

vacuum signal port is located in the carburetor body and is exposed to engine vacuum in the off/idle and part throttle operation. A thermal delay switch delays operation of the valve during engine warmup, when NOx levels are already at a minimum.

The valve is located on the right rear side of the intake manifold adjacent to the rocker arm cover.

SERVICE

The EGR valve is not serviceable, except for replacement. To check the valve, proceed as follows:

1. Connect a tachometer to the engine.

2. With the engine running at normal operating temperature, with the choke valve fully open, set the engine rpm at 2000. The transmission should be in Park (automatic) or Neutral (manual) with the parking brake On and the wheels blocked.

3. Disconnect the vacuum hose at the valve. Make sure that vacuum is available at the valve and look at the tachometer to see if the engine speed increases. If it does, a malfunction of the valve is indicated.

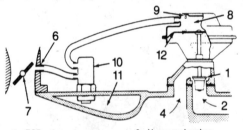

1. EGR valve	8. Vacuum chamber
2. Exhaust gas	9. Valve return spring
4. Intake flow	10. Thermal vacuum switch
6. Vacuum port	11. Coolant
7. Throttle valve	12. Diaphragm

EGR system with TVS

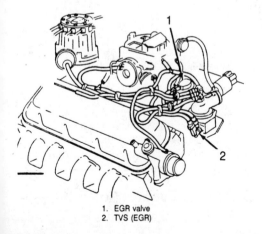

1. EGR valve
2. TVS (EGR)

TVS location on the 8-7.4L engine

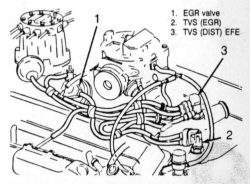

1. EGR valve
2. TVS (EGR)
3. TVS (DIST) EFE

TVS location on the 8-5.7L engine

3. Actuator
4. Manifold
5. Nut — tighten to 18 ft. lbs.
6. Actuator rod clip
7. EFE valve lever
8. TVS switch

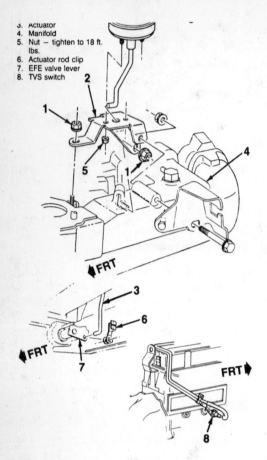

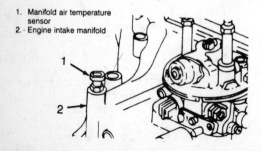

Valve, actuator and TVS location on the 6-4.8L engine

4. If necessary, replace the valve.

Evaporation Control System

This system reduces the amount of escaping gasoline vapors. The venting of fuel tank vapors into the air has been stopped. Fuel vapors are now directed through lines to a canister containing an activated charcoal filter. Unburned vapors are trapped here until the engine is started. When the engine is running,

1. Manifold air temperature sensor
2. Engine intake manifold

MAT sensor

2. Tension spring
3. Right exhaust pipe

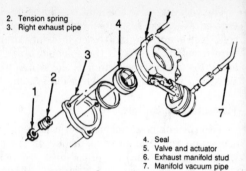

4. Seal
5. Valve and actuator
6. Exhaust manifold stud
7. Manifold vacuum pipe

Valve and actuator on the 8-5.7L engine

1. Nut — tighten to 15 ft. lbs.
2. Tension spring
3. Right exhaust pipe
4. Seal
5. Valve and actuator
6. Exhaust manifold
7. Manifold vacuum pipe

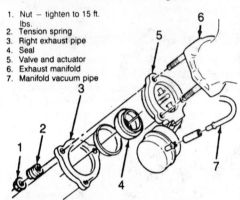

Valve and actuator on the 8-7.4L engine

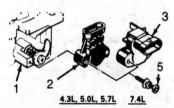

4.3L, 5.0L, 5.7L   7.4L

1. Throttle body assembly
2. Throttle position sensor – non-adjustable
3. Throttle position sensor – non-adjustable

Throttle position sensor

the canister is purged by air drawn in by manifold vacuum. The air and fuel vapors are directed into the engine to be burned.

SERVICE

Replace the filter in the engine compartment canister at the intervals shown in the Maintenance Intervals Chart in Chapter 1. If the fuel tank cap requires replacement, ensure that the new cap is the correct part for your truck.

Early Fuel Evaporation System

This system is used on some light duty models.

The EFE system consists of an EFE valve at

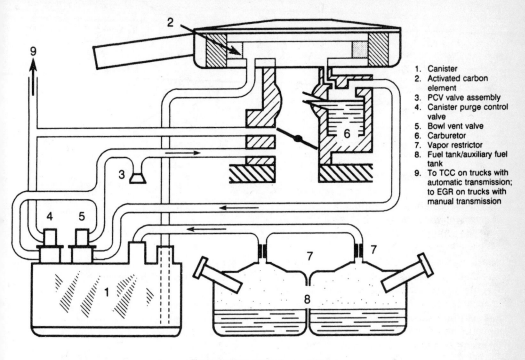

1. Canister
2. Activated carbon element
3. PCV valve assembly
4. Canister purge control valve
5. Bowl vent valve
6. Carburetor
7. Vapor restrictor
8. Fuel tank/auxiliary fuel tank
9. To TCC on trucks with automatic transmission; to EGR on trucks with manual transmission

Evaporative emission system

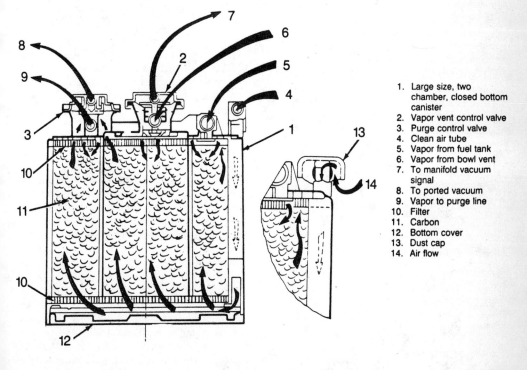

1. Large size, two chamber, closed bottom canister
2. Vapor vent control valve
3. Purge control valve
4. Clean air tube
5. Vapor from fuel tank
6. Vapor from bowl vent
7. To manifold vacuum signal
8. To ported vacuum
9. Vapor to purge line
10. Filter
11. Carbon
12. Bottom cover
13. Dust cap
14. Air flow

Fuel vapor canister

1. EFE/TVS switch
2. EGR/TVS switch

EFE coolant TVS - except on the 6-4.8L engine

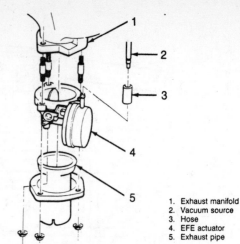

1. Exhaust manifold
2. Vacuum source
3. Hose
4. EFE actuator
5. Exhaust pipe

Vacuum servo type EFE system

the flange of the exhaust manifold, an actuator, and a thermal vacuum switch. The TVS is located in the coolant outlet housing and directly controls vacuum.

In both systems, manifold vacuum is applied to the actuator, which in turn, closes the EFE valve. This routes hot exhaust gases to the base of the carburetor. When coolant temperatures reach a set limit, vacuum is denied to the actuator allowing an internal spring to return the actuator to its normal position, opening the EFE valve.

Throttle Return Control

The system consists of a throttle lever actuator, a solenoid vacuum control valve, and an electronic speed sensor. The throttle lever actuator, mounted on the carburetor, opens the primary throttle plates a present amount, above normal engine idle speed, in response to a signal from the solenoid vacuum control valve. The valve is mounted on the thermostat housing mounting stud. It is held open in response to a signal from the electronic speed sensor. When open, the valve allows a vacuum signal to be sent to the throttle lever actuator. The speed sensor monitors engine speed at the distributor. It supplies an electrical signal to the solenoid valve, as long as a preset engine speed is exceeded. The object of this system is the same as that of the earlier system.

THROTTLE LEVER ACTUATOR

The checking procedure is the same as for earlier years. Follow Steps 1–9 of the Throttle Valve procedure. Adjustment procedures are covered in the carburetor adjustments section in Chapter 5.

TRC SYSTEM CHECK

1. Connect a tachometer to the distributor TACH terminal. Start the engine and raise the engine speed to 1890 rpm. The throttle lever actuator on the carburetor should extend.

2. Reduce the engine speed to 1700 rpm. The lever actuator should retract.

3. If the actuator operates outside of the speed limits, the speed switch is faulty and must be replaced. It cannot be adjusted.

4. If the actuator does not operate at all:

a. Check the voltage at the vacuum solenoid and the speed switch with a voltmeter. Connect the negative probe of the voltmeter to the engine ground and the positive probe to the voltage source wire on the component. The positive probe can be inserted on the connector body at the wire side; it is not necessary to unplug the connector. Voltage should be 12 to 14 volts in both cases.

b. If the correct voltage is present at one component but not the other, the engine wiring harness is faulty.

c. If the voltage is not present at all, check the engine harness connections at the distributor and the bulkhead connector and repair as necessary.

d. If the correct voltage is present at both components, check the solenoid operation: ground the solenoid-to-speed switch connecting wire terminal at the solenoid connector with a jumper wire. This should cause the throttle lever actuator to extend, with the engine running.

e. If the lever actuator does not extend, remove the hose from the solenoid side port which connects the actuator hose. Check the port for obstructions or blockage. If the port is not plugged, replace the solenoid.

f. If the actuator extends in Step d, ground the solenoid-to-speed switch wire terminal at the switch. If the actuator does not extend, the wire between the speed switch and the solenoid is open and must be repaired. If the actuator does extend, check the

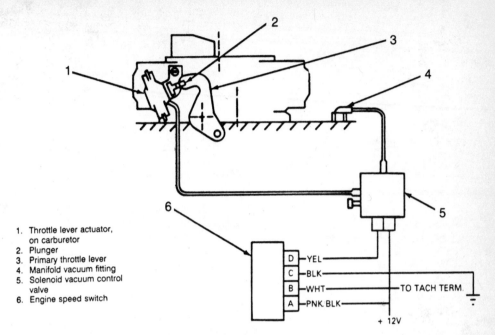

1. Throttle lever actuator, on carburetor
2. Plunger
3. Primary throttle lever
4. Manifold vacuum fitting
5. Solenoid vacuum control valve
6. Engine speed switch

Throttle Return Control System

speed switch ground wire for a ground; it should read zero volts with the engine running. Check the speed switch-to-distributor wire for a proper connection. If the ground and distributor wires are properly connected and the actuator still does not extend when the engine speed is above 1,890 rpm, replace the speed switch.

5. If the actuator is extended at all speeds:

a. Remove the connector from the vacuum solenoid.

b. If the actuator remains extended, check the solenoid side port orifice for blockage. If plugged, clear and reconnect the system and recheck. If the actuator is still extended, remove the solenoid connector; if the actuator does not retreat, replace the vacuum solenoid.

c. If the actuator retracts with the solenoid connector off, reconnect it and remove the speed switch connector. If the actuator retracts, the problem is in the speed switch, which should be replaced. If the actuator does not retract, the solenoid-to-speed switch wire is shorted to ground in the wiring harness. Repair the short.

Oxygen Sensor

The oxygen sensor is a spark plug shaped device that is screwed into the exhaust manifold. It monitors the oxygen content of the exhaust gases and sends a voltage signal to the Electronic Control Module (ECM). The ECM

monitors this voltage and, depending on the value of the received signal, issues a command to the mixture control solenoid on the carburetor to adjust for rich or lean conditions.

The proper operation of the oxygen sensor depends upon four basic conditions:

1. Good electrical connections. Since the sensor generates low currents, good clean electrical connections at the sensor are a must.

2. Outside air supply. Air must circulate to the internal portion of the sensor. When servicing the sensor, do not restrict the air passages.

3. Proper operating temperatures. The ECM will not recognize the sensor's signals until the sensor reaches approximately $+600°F$ $(+316°C)$.

4. Non-leaded fuel. The use of leaded gasoline will damage the sensor very quickly.

NOTE: *No attempt should be made to measure the output voltage of the sensor. The current drain of any conventional voltmeter would be enough to permanently damage the sensor. No jumpers, test leads, or other electrical connections should ever be made to the sensor. Use these tool ONLY on the ECM side of the harness connector AFTER the oxygen sensor has been disconnected.*

REMOVAL AND INSTALLATION

CAUTION: *The sensor uses a permanently attached pigtail and connector. This pigtail should not be removed from the sensor. Damage or removal of the pigtail or connector could affect the proper operation of the*

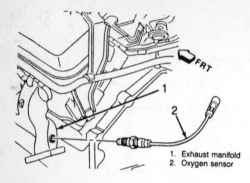

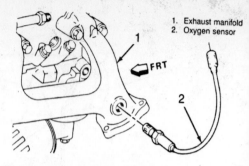

Oxygen sensor on the 6-4.3L

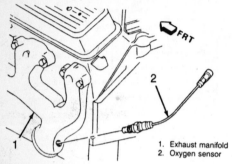

Oxygen sensor on the 8-7.4L engine

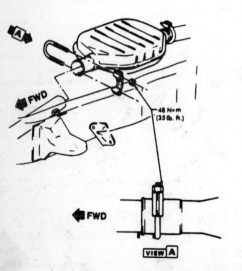

Oxygen sensor on the 8-5.0L and 8-5.7L engines

sensor. Keep the electrical connector and lou-vered end of the sensor clean and free of grease. NEVER use cleaning solvents of any type on the sensor!

NOTE: *The oxygen sensor may be difficult to remove when the temperature of the engine is below +120°F (+49°C). Excessive force may damage the threads in the exhaust manifold or exhaust pipe.*

1. Disconnect the electrical connector and any attaching hardware.

2. Remove the sensor.

3. Coat the threads of the sensor with a GM antiseize compound (No. 5613695) before installation. New sensors are precoated with this compound.

NOTE: *The GM antiseize compound is NOT a conventional anti-seize paste. The sue of a regular paste may electrically insulate the sensor, rendering it useless. The threads MUST be coated with the proper electrically conductive anti-seize compound.*

4. Install the sensor and torque to 30 ft. lbs. Use care in making sure the silicone boot is in the correct position to avoid melting it during operation.

5. Connect the electrical connector and attaching hardware if used.

Oxidizing Catalytic Converter

An underfloor oxidizing catalytic converter is used to control hydrocarbon and carbon mon-

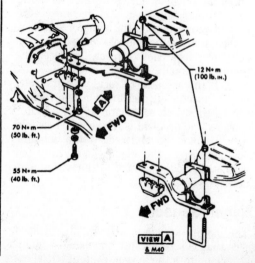

Typical catalytic converter installation

oxide emissions. Control is accomplished by placing a catalyst in the exhaust system to enable all exhaust gas flow to pass through it and undergo a chemical reaction before passing into the atmosphere. The chemical reaction involved is the oxidizing of hydrocarbons and carbon monoxide into water vapor and carbon dioxide.

REMOVAL AND INSTALLATION

CAUTION: *Catalytic converter operating temperatures are extremely high. Outside converter temperatures can go well over +1,000°F (+538°C). Use extreme care when working on or around the catalytic converter.*

1. Raise and support the truck.
2. Remove the clamps at the front and rear of the converter.
3. Cut the converter pipes at the front and rear of the converter and remove it.
4. Remove the support from the transmission.
5. Remove the converter pipe-to-exhaust pipe and the converter pipe-to-tailpipe.

To install the converter:

6. Install the exhaust pipe and tailpipe into the converter with sealer.
7. Loosely install the support on the transmission.
8. Install new U-bolts and clamps, check all clearances and tighten the clamps.
9. Lower the truck.

NOTE: *Dealers have equipment to remove and replace the converter contents (pellets) without removing the converter from the exhaust system.*

Pulse Air Injection Reactor System

This system consists of four air valves which inject fresh air into the exhaust system in order to further the combustion process of the exhaust gases. The firing of the engine creates a pulsating flow of exhaust gases, which are of either positive or negative pressure. Negative pressure at the pulse air valve will result in air being injected into the exhaust system. Positive pressure will force the check valve closed and no exhaust gases will flow into the fresh air supply.

Regularly inspect the pulse air valves, pipes, grommets and hose for cracks and leaks. Replace the necessary part if any are found. If a check valve fails, exhaust gases will get into the carburetor through the air cleaner and cause the engine to surge and perform poorly.

If exhaust gases pass through a pulse air valve, the paint will be burned off the rocker arm cover plenum as a result of the excessive heat. The rubber grommets and hose will also deteriorate. Failure of the pulse air valve can also be indicated by a hissing sound.

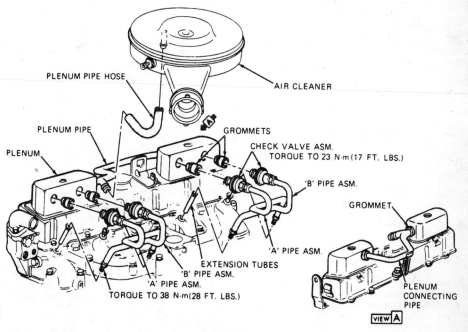

PAIR system

REMOVAL AND INSTALLATION

1. Remove the air cleaner. Disconnect the rubber hose from the plenum connecting pipe. (See illustration).

2. Disconnect the four check valve fittings at the cylinder head and remove the check valve pipes from the plenum grommets.

3. Disconnect the check valve from the check valve pipe.

4. Assemble the replacement check valve to the check valve pipe.

5. Attach the check valve assembly to the cylinder head as illustrated. Hand tighten the fittings.

6. Using a 1 in. (25.4mm) open end wrench as a lever, align the check valve on pipe A with the plenum grommet. Using the palm of your left hand, press the check valve into the grommet. Using a silicone lubricant on the grommet will make thing a little easier. Repeat this procedure for pipe **B** using your left hand for the tool and your right hand for installing the valve in the grommet.

DIESEL ENGINE EMISSIONS CONTROLS

Crankcase Ventilation

A Crankcase Depression Regulator Valve (CDRV) is used to regulate (meter) the flow of crankcase gases back into the engine to be burned. The CDRV is designed to limit vacuum in the crankcase as the gases are drawn from the valve covers through the CDRV and into the intake manifold (air crossover).

Fresh air enters the engine through the combination filter, check valve and oil fill cap. The fresh air mixes with blow-by gases and enters both valve covers. The gases pass through a filter installed on the valve covers and are drawn into connecting tubing.

Intake manifold vacuum acts against a spring loaded diaphragm to control the flow of crankcase gases. Higher intake vacuum levels pull the diaphragm closer to the top of the outlet tube. This reduces the amount of gases being drawn from the crankcase and decreases the vacuum level in the crankcase. As the intake vacuum decreases, the spring pushes the diaphragm away from the top of the outlet tube allowing more gases to flow to the intake manifold.

NOTE: *Do not allow any solvent to come in contact with the diaphragm of the Crankcase Depression Regulator Valve because the diaphragm will fail.*

Exhaust Gas Recirculation (EGR)

To lower the formation of nitrogen oxides (NOx) in the exhaust, it is necessary to reduce combustion temperatures. This is done in the diesel, as in the gasoline engine, by introducing exhaust gases into the cylinders through the EGR valve.

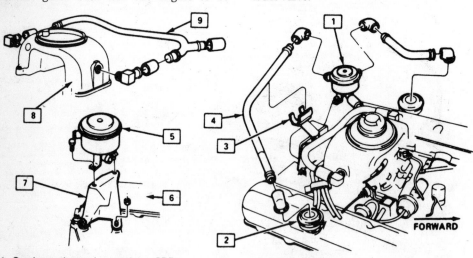

1. Crankcase depression regulator (CDR)
2. Ventilation filter
3. Brace clip
4. Ventilation pipes
5. Crankcase depression regulator (CDR)
6. L.H. valve cover
7. Bracket
8. Air crossover
9. Air crossover to regulator valve pipe

FORWARD

Diesel engine crankcase ventilation system

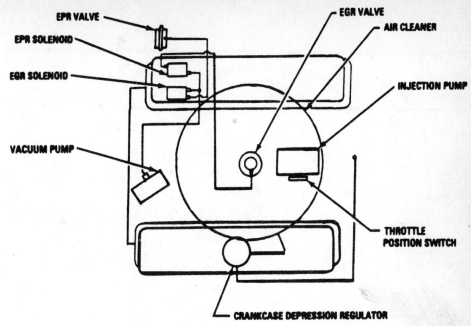

Diesel engine emission control component locator

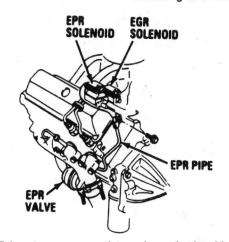

Exhaust pressure regulator valve and solenoid

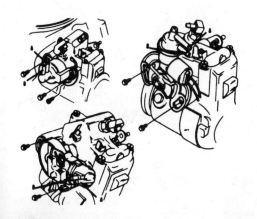

Diesel vacuum regulator valve, mounted on the injection pump

On the 6.2L diesel, and Exhaust Pressure Regulator (EPR) valve and solenoid operate in conjunction with the EGR valve. The EPR valve's job is to increase exhaust backpressure in order to increase EGR flow (to reduce nitrous oxide emissions). The EPR valve is usually open, and the solenoid is normally closed. When energized by the **B**+ wire from the Throttle Position Switch (TPS), the solenoid opens, allowing vacuum to the EPR valve, closing it. This occurs at idle. As the throttle is opened, at a calibrated throttle angle, the TPS de-energizes the EPR solenoid, cutting off vacuum to the EPR valve, closing the valve.

FUNCTIONAL TESTS OF COMPONENTS

Vacuum Regulator Valve (VRV)

The Vacuum Regulator Valve is attached to the side of the injection pump and regulates vacuum in proportion to throttle angle. Vacuum from the vacuum pump is supplied to port **A** and vacuum at port **B** is reduced as the throttle is opened. At closed throttle, the vacuum is 15 in.; at half throttle, 6 in.; at wide open throttle there is zero vacuum.

Exhaust Gas Recirculation (EGR) Valve

Apply vacuum to vacuum port. The valve should be fully open at 10.5 in. and closed below 6 in.

Response Vacuum Reducer (RVR)

Connect a vacuum gauge to the port marked **To EGR** valve to T.C.C. solenoid. Connect a

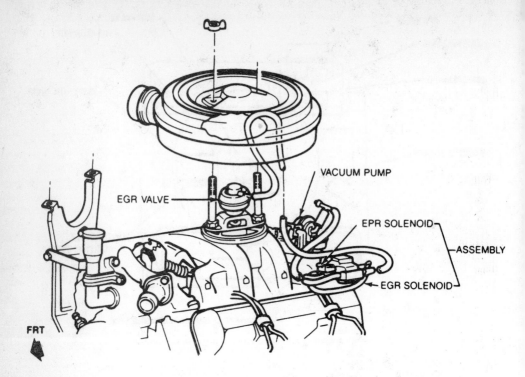

EGR VALVE

VACUUM PUMP

EPR SOLENOID

ASSEMBLY

EGR SOLENOID

FRT

Diesel EGR valve and related components

hand operated vacuum pump to the VRV port. Draw a 50.66 kPa (15 in.Hg) vacuum on the pump and the reading on the vacuum gauge should be lower than the vacuum pump reading as follows:

- 0.75 in. Except High Altitude
- 2.5 in. High Altitude

Torque Converter Clutch Operated Solenoid

When the torque converter clutch is engaged, an electrical signal energizes the solenoid allowing ports 1 and 2 to be interconnected. When the solenoid is not energized, port 1 is closed and ports 2 and 3 are interconnected.

Solenoid Energized

- Ports 1 and 3 are connected.

Solenoid De-Energized

- Ports 2 and 3 are connected.

Vacuum Pump Diesel Engines

Since the air crossover and intake manifold in a diesel engine is unrestricted (unlike a gasoline engine which has throttle plates creating a venturi effect) there is no vacuum source. To provide vacuum, a vacuum pump is mounted in the location occupied by the distributor in a gasoline engine. This pump supplies the air conditioning servos, the cruise control servos, and the transmission vacuum modulator where required.

The pump is a diaphragm type which needs no maintenance. It is driven by a drive gear on its lower end which meshes with gear teeth on the end of the engine's camshaft.

REMOVAL AND INSTALLATION

1. Disconnect the batteries.
2. Remove the air cleaner, and cover the intake manifold.
3. Remove the vacuum pump clamp, disconnect the vacuum line and remove the pump.
4. Install a new gasket. Install the pump and reverse the removal procedures for installation.

GENERAL MOTORS FEEDBACK CARBURETOR AND COMPUTER COMMAND CONTROL (CCC) SYSTEMS

General Information

The CCC System monitors up to nineteen engine/vehicle operating conditions which it uses to control up to nine engine and emission control systems. This system controls engine operation and lowers the exhaust emissions while maintaining good fuel economy and driveability. The "Electronic Control Module (ECM) is the brain of the CCC system. The ECM controls as many as 12 engine related systems constantly adjusting the engine operation. In addition to maintaining the ideal air/fuel ratio for the catalytic converter and adjusting ignition timing, the CCC System also controls the Air Management System so that the catalytic converter can operate at the highest efficiency possible. The system also controls the lockup on the transmission torque converter clutch (certain automatic transmission models only), adjusts idle speed over a wide range of conditions, purges the evaporative emissions charcoal canister, controls the EGR valve operation and operates the early fuel evaporative (EFE) system. Not all engines use all of the above sub-systems.

The CCC system is primarily an emission control system, designed to maintain a 14.7:1 air/fuel ratio under all operating conditions. When this ideal air/fuel ratio is maintained the catalytic converter can control oxides of nitrogen (NOx), hydrocarbon (HC) and carbon monoxide (CO) emissions.

There are two operation modes for CCC System: closed loop and open loop fuel control. Closed loop fuel control means the oxygen sensor is controlling the carburetor's air/fuel mixture ratio. Under open loop fuel control operating conditions (wide open throttle, engine and/or oxygen sensor cold), the oxygen sensor has no effect on the air/fuel mixture.

NOTE: *On some engines, the oxygen sensor will cool off while the engine is idling, putting the system into open loop operation. To restore closed loop operation, run the engine at part throttle and accelerate from idle to part throttle a few times.*

This basic system block diagram shows the catalytic converter located in the exhaust system close to the engine. It is ahead of the muffler and tailpipe. If the converter is to do its job effectively, the engine must receive an air-fuel mixture of approximately 14.7 to 1.

The carburetor mixes air and gasoline into a combustible mixture before delivering it to the engine. However, carburetors have reached a point where they can no longer control the air-fuel mixture sufficiently close to the ideal 14.7 to 1 ratio for most operating conditions. Therefore, a different type of control must be used on the carburetor, something that has never been used before.

An electric solenoid in the carburetor controls the air-fuel ratio. The solenoid is connected to an electronic module (ECM) which is an on board computer. The ECM provides a controlling signal to the solenoid. The solenoid controls the metering rod(s) and an idle air bleed valve to closely control the air-fuel ration throughout the operating range of the engine. However, since the engine operates under a wide variety of conditions, the computer must be told what those conditions are. This is so that it will know what to tell the carburetor solenoid to do.

A sensor is located in the exhaust stream close to the engine. It's known as an oxygen sensor or simply an O_2 sensor. This sensor functions when the engine's exhaust temperature rises above 600°F (316°C). There is a direct relationship between the mixture delivered by the carburetor and the amount of oxygen left in the exhaust gases. The O_2 sensor can determine whether the exhaust is too rich or too lean. It sends a varying voltage signal to the ECM.

The ECM will then signal the mixture control solenoid to deliver richer or leaner mixture for the current engine operating conditions. As the carburetor makes a change, the O_2 sensor will sense that change and signal the ECM whether or not it's too rich or too lean. The ECM will then make a correction, if necessary. This goes on continually and is what we refer to as Closed Loop operation. Closed loop conditions deliver a 14.7 to 1 air/fuel mixture to the engine. This makes it possible for the converter to act upon all three of the major pollutants in an efficient and effective manner. consider, however, what happens in the morning when it's cold and the car is started. If the system where to keep the air/fuel mixture to the 14.7 to 1 air/fuel ratio when it's cold the chances are that the engine wouldn't run very well. When the engine is cold, it has to have a richer mixture. An automatic choke is used to give the engine a richer mixture until it is up to normal operating temperature. during this time, the O_2 sensor signals are ignored by the ECM.

A temperature sensor is located in the water jacket of the engine and connected to the electronic control module. When the engine is cold, the temperature sensor will tell the ECM to ignore the oxygen sensor signal, since the sensor is too cold to operate. The electronic control module then tells the carburetor to deliver a richer mixture based upon what has already been programmed into the ECM. The ECM will also use information from other sensors during cold start operation.

After the engine has been running for some time and has reached normal operating temperature, the temperature sensor will signal the ECM that the engine is warm, and it can accept the oxygen sensor signal. If other system requirements are met, closed loop operations begins. The oxygen sensor will then influence the ECM as to what mixture it should deliver to the engine. In addition to these two conditions, there are three other conditions which affect the air/fuel mixture delivered to the engine. First is the load that is placed upon the engine. When an engine is working hard, such as pulling a heavy load up a long grade, it requires a richer air/fuel mixture. This is different from a vehicle that is operating in a cruise condition on a level highway at a constant rate of speed.

Manifold vacuum is used to determine engine load. A manifold pressure sensor is located in the intake manifold. It detects changes in the manifold pressure which are signaled to the ECM. As changes occur, the load placed upon the engine varies. The ECM takes this varying signal into account when determining what mixture the carburetor should be delivering to the engine. The next condition in determining what air/fuel mixture should be is the amount of throttle opening. The more throttle opening at any given time, the richer the mixture required by the engine. On most applications a TPS (throttle position sensor) in the carburetor sends a signal to the ECM. It tells the ECM the position of the throttle, whether it it at idle, part throttle, wide open or whatever condition that exists in between.

The last condition, which has a bearing on the mixture that the engine would require, is the speed the engine is running. Certainly when an engine is operating at 600 rpm, it doesn't need as much gasoline as it does when it is operating at 4000 rpm. Therefore, a tachometer signal from the distributor is delivered to the electronic control module. This tells the ECM how fast the engine is running. This signal will also be taken into consideration when the ECM decides what mixture the carburetor should be delivering to the engine. In the typical CCC system, the ECM will use various inputs to make decisions that will best control the operation of the mixture control solenoid for maximum system efficiency.

SYSTEM COMPONENTS

Electronic Control Module (ECM)

The ECM is a reliable solid state computer, protected in a metal box. It is used to monitor and control all the functions of the CCC System and is located in one of several places in the passenger compartment. The ECM can perform several on-car functions at the same time

and has the ability to diagnose itself as well as other CCC System circuits.

The ECM performs the functions of an on and off switch. It can send a voltage signal to a circuit or connect a circuit to ground at a precise time. Programmed into the ECM's memory are voltage and time values. These valves will differ from one engine to another. As an example then, if the ECM "sees" a proper voltage value for the correct length of time it will perform a certain function. This could be turning the EGR system on as the engine warms up. If however, the voltage or the time interval is not correct, the ECM will also recognize this. It will not perform its function and in most cases turn the CHECK ENGINE or SERVICE ENGINE SOON Light ON.

The other CCC components include the oxygen sensor, an electronically controlled variable-mixture carburetor, a three-way catalytic converter, throttle position and coolant sensors, a barometric pressure (BARO) sensor, a manifold absolute pressure (MAP) sensor, a "Check Engine" light on the instrument cluster, and an Electronic Spark Timing (EST), which is linked to an Electronic Spark Control system for all engines except the 8-7.4L.

Other components used by the CCC System include the Air Injection Reaction (AIR) Management System, charcoal canister purge solenoid, EGR valve control, vehicle speed sensor (located in the instrument cluster), transmission torque converter clutch solenoid (automatic transmission models only), idle speed control, and early fuel evaporative (EFE) system.

The CCC System ECM, in addition to monitoring sensors and sending a control signal to the carburetor, also controls the charcoal canister purge, AIR Management System, fuel control, idle speed control, idle air control, automatic transmission converter clutch lockup, distributor ignition timing, EGR valve control, EFE control, air conditioner compressor clutch operation, electric fuel pump and the CHECK ENGINE light.

• The AIR Management System is an emission control which provides additional oxygen either to the catalyst or the cylinder head ports (in some cases exhaust manifold). An AIR Management System, composed of an air switching valve and/or an air control valve, controls the air pump flow and is itself controlled by the ECM. A complete description of the AIR system is given towards the front of this section. The major difference between the CCC AIR System and the systems used on other cars is that the flow of air from the air pump is controlled electrically by the ECM, rather than by vacuum signal.

NOTE: *On some models the Air Management System may not be controlled by the ECM.*

• The charcoal canister purge control is an electrically operated solenoid valve controlled by the ECM. When energized, the purge control solenoid blocks vacuum from reaching the canister purge valve. When the ECM de-energizes the purge control solenoid, vacuum is allowed to reach the canister and operate the purge valve. This releases the fuel vapors collected in the canister into the induction system.

• The EGR valve control solenoid is activated by the ECM in similar fashion to the canister purge solenoid. When the engine is cold, the ECM energizes the solenoid, which blocks the vacuum signal to the EGR valve. When the engine is warm, the ECM de-energizes the solenoid and the vacuum signal is allowed to reach and activate the EGR valve.

• The Transmission Converter Clutch (TCC) lock is controlled by the ECM through an electrical solenoid in the automatic transmission. When the vehicle speed sensor in the instrument panel signals the ECM that the vehicle has reached the correct speed, the ECM energizes the solenoid which allows the torque converter to mechanically couple the engine to the transmission. When the brake pedal is pushed or during deceleration, passing, etc., the ECM returns the transmission to fluid drive.

• The idle speed control adjusts the idle speed to load conditions, and will lower the idle speed under no-load or low-load conditions to conserve gasoline.

• The Early Fuel Evaporative (EFE) system is used on most engines to provide rapid heat to the engine induction system to promote smooth start-up and operation. There are two types of system: vacuum servo and electrically heated. They use different means to achieve the same end, which is to pre-heat the incoming air/fuel mixture. They may or may not be controlled by the ECM.

• A/C Wide Open Throttle (WOT) Control, on this system the ECM controls the A/C compressor clutch to disengage the clutch during hard acceleration. On some engines, the ECM disengages the clutch during the engine start-up on a warm engine. The WOT control is not installed on all engines.

• Electronic Spark Control (ESC) system controls the spark timing on certain engines to allow the engine to have maximum spark advance without spark knock. This improves the driveability and fuel economy. This system is not used on the 8–7.4L engine.

• Shift Light Control: the ECM controls the shift light on the manual transmission to indicate the best shift point for maximum fuel economy. This control is not used on all engines.

• Electric Cooling Fan Control, under certain conditions, the ECM may control the electric cooling fan to cool the engine and the A/C condenser. At cruising speed, the ECM may turn the fan off for better fuel economy. This control is on most transverse engine front wheel drive vehicles.

Basic Troubleshooting

NOTE: *The following explains how to activate the Trouble Code signal light in the instrument cluster and gives an explanation of what each code means. This is not a full CCC System troubleshooting and isolation procedure.*

Before suspecting the CCC System or any of its components as faulty, check the ignition system including distributor, timing, spark plugs and wires. Check the engine compression, air cleaner, and emission control components not controlled by the ECM. Also check the intake manifold, vacuum hoses and hose connectors for leaks and the carburetor bolts for tightness.

The following symptoms could indicate a possible problem with the CCC System.

1. Detonation
2. Stalls or rough idle-cold
3. Stalls or rough idle-hot
4. Missing
5. Hesitation
6. Surges
7. Poor gasoline mileage
8. Sluggish or spongy performance
9. Hard starting-cold
10. Objectionable exhaust odors (that "rotten egg" smell)
11. Cuts out
12. Improper idle speed

As a bulb and system check, the CHECK ENGINE light will come on when the ignition switch is turned to the ON position but the engine is not started. The CHECK ENGINE light will also produce the trouble code or codes by a series of flashes which translate as follows. When the diagnostic test terminal under the dash is grounded, with the ignition in the ON position and the engine not running, the CHECK ENGINE light will flash once, pause, then flash twice in rapid succession. This is a code 12, which indicates that the diagnostic system is working. After a long pause, the code 12 will repeat itself two more times. The cycle will then repeat itself until the engine is started or the ignition is turned off.

When the engine is started, the CHECK ENGINE light will remain on for a few seconds, then turn off. If the CHECK ENGINE light remains on, the self-diagnostic system has detected a problem. If the test terminal is then grounded, the trouble code will flash three times. If more than one problem is found, each trouble code will flash three times. Trouble codes will flash in numerical order (lowest code number to highest). The trouble codes series will repeat as long as the test terminal is grounded.

A trouble code indicates a problem with a given circuit. For example, trouble code 14 indicates a problem in the cooling sensor circuit. This includes the coolant sensor, its electrical harness, and the Electronic Control Module (ECM) Since the self-diagnostic system cannot diagnose every possible fault in the system, the absence of a trouble code does not mean the system is trouble-free. To determine problems within the system which do not activate a trouble code, a system performance check must be made.

In the case of an intermittent fault in the system, the CHECK ENGINE light will go out when the fault goes away, but the trouble code will remain in the memory of the ECM. Therefore, it a trouble code can be obtained even though the CHECK ENGINE light is not on, the trouble code must be evaluated. It must be determined if the fault is intermittent or if the engine must be at certain operating conditions (under load, etc.) before the CHECK ENGINE light will come on. Some trouble codes will not be recorded in the ECM until the engine has been operated at part throttle for about 5–18 minutes. On the CCC System, a trouble code will be stored until terminal **R** of the ECM has been disconnected from the battery for 10 seconds.

An easy way to erase the computer memory on the CCC System is to disconnect the battery terminals from the battery. If this method is used, don't forget to reset clocks and electronic preprogrammable radios. Another method is to remove the fuse marked ECM in the fuse panel. Not all models have such a fuse.

CCC SYSTEM CIRCUIT DIAGNOSIS

For in-depth diagnosis of the CCC system, refer to Chilton's Electronic Engine Controls Manual.

ELECTRONIC SPARK TIMING SYSTEM (EST)

General Description

The High Energy Ignition (HEI) system controls fuel combustion by providing the spark to ignite the compressed air/fuel mixture, in the combustion chamber, at the correct time. To provide improved engine performance, fuel economy and control of the exhaust emissions, the ECM controls distributor spark advance (timing) with the Electronic Spark Timing (EST) system.

The standard High Energy Ignition (HEI) system has a modified distributor module which is used in conjunction with the EST system. The module has seven terminals instead of the four used without EST. Two different terminal arrangements are used, depending upon the distributor used with a particular engine application.

To properly control ignition/combustion timing, the ECM needs to know the following information:

1. Crankshaft position.
2. Engine speed (rpm).
3. Engine load (manifold pressure or vacuum).
4. Atmospheric (barometric) pressure.
5. Engine temperature.
6. Transmission gear position (certain models)

The EST system consists of the distributor module, ECM and its connecting wires. The distributor has four wires from the HEI module connected to a four terminal connector, which mates with a four wire connector from the ECM.

These circuits perform the following functions:

1. Distributor reference at terminal B –

This provides the ECM with rpm and crankshaft position information.

2. Reference ground at terminal D – This wire is grounded in the distributor and makes sure the ground circuit has no voltage drop, which could affect performance. If this circuit is open, it could cause poor performance.

3. By-pass at terminal C – At approximately 400 rpm, the ECM applies 5 volts to this circuit to switch the spark timing control from the HEI module to the ECM. An open or grounded bypass circuit will set a Code 42 and the engine will run at base timing, plus a small amount of advance built into the HEI module.

4. EST at terminal A – This triggers the HEI module. The ECM does not know what the actual timing is, but it does know when it gets its reference signal. It then advances or retards the spark timing from that point. Therefore, if the base timing is set incorrectly, the entire spark curve will be incorrect.

An open circuit in the EST circuit will set a Code 42 and cause the engine to run on the HEI module timing. This will cause poor performance and poor fuel economy. A ground may set a Code 42, but the engine will not run.

The ECM uses information from the MAP or VAC and coolant sensors, in addition to rpm, in order to calculate spark advance as follows:

1. Low MAP output voltage (high VAC sensor output voltage) would require MORE spark advance.

2. Cold engine would require MORE spark advance.

3. High MAP output voltage (low VAC sensor output voltage) would require LESS spark advance.

4. Hot engine would require LESS spark advance.

RESULTS OF INCORRECT EST OPERATION

Detonation could be caused by low MAP output (high VAC sensor output), or high resistance in the coolant sensor circuit.

Poor performance could be caused by high MAP output (low VAC sensor output) or low resistance in the coolant sensor circuit.

HOW CODE 42 IS DETERMINED

When the systems is operating on the HEI module with no voltage in the by-pass line, the HEI module grounds the EST signal. The ECM expects to sense no voltage on the EST line during this condition. If it senses voltage, it sets Code 42 and will not go into the EST mode.

When the rpm for EST is reached (approximately 400 rpm), the ECM applies 5 volts to the by-pass line and the EST should no longer be grounded in the HEI module, so the EST voltage should be varying.

If the by-pass line is open, the HEI module will not switch to the EST mode, so the EST voltage will be low and Code 42 will be set.

If the EST line is grounded, the HEI module will switch to the EST, but because the line is grounded, there will be no EST signal and the engine will not operate. A Code 42 may or may not be set.

NOTE: *For in-depth diagnosis of the EST system, refer to Chilton's Electronic Engine Controls Manual.*

ELECTRONIC SPARK CONTROL SYSTEM (ESC)

General Description

The Electronic Spark Control (ESC) operates in conjunction with the Electronic Spark Timing (EST) system and modifies (retards) the spark advance when detonation occurs. The retard mode is held for approximately 20 seconds after which the spark control will again revert to the Electronic Spark Timing (EST) system. There are three basic components of the Electronic Spark Control (ESC) system.

SENSOR

The Electronic Spark Control (ESC) sensor detects the presence (or absence) and intensity of the detonation by the vibration characteristics of the engine. The output is an electrical signal that goes to the controller. A sensor failure would allow no spark retard.

DISTRIBUTOR

The distributor is an HEI/EST unit with an electronic module, modified so it can respond to the ESC controller signal. This command is delayed when detonation is occurring, thus providing the level of spark retard required. The amount of spark retard is a function of the degree of detonation.

CONTROLLER

The Electronic Spark Control (ESC) controller processes the sensor signal into a command signal to the distributor, to adjust the spark timing. The process is continuous, so that the presence of detonation is monitored and controlled. The controller is a hard wired signal processor and amplifier which operates from 6–16 volts. Controller failure would be no ignition, no retard or full retard. The controller has no memory storage.

CODE 43

Should a Code 43 be set in the ECM memory, it would indicate that the ESC system retard signal has been sensed by the ECM for too long a period of time. When voltage at terminal **L** of the ECM is low, spark timing is retarded.

Normal voltage in the non-retarded mode is approximately 7.5 volts or more.

BASIC IGNITION TIMING

Basic ignition timing is critical to the proper operation of the ESC system. Always follow the Vehicle Emission Control Information label procedures when adjusting ignition timing.

Some engines will incorporate a magnetic timing probe hole for use with special electronic timing equipment. Consult the manufacturer's instructions for the use of this electronic timing equipment.

NOTE: *For an in-depth diagnosis of the ESC system, refer to Chilton's Electronic Engine Controls manual.*

CHILTON'S
FUEL ECONOMY
& TUNE-UP TIPS

Tune-up • Spark Plug Diagnosis • Emission Controls

Fuel System • Cooling System • Tires and Wheels

General Maintenance

CHILTON'S FUEL ECONOMY & TUNE-UP TIPS

Fuel economy is important to everyone, no matter what kind of vehicle you drive. The maintenance-minded motorist can save both money and fuel using these tips and the periodic maintenance and tune-up procedures in this Repair and Tune-Up Guide.

There are more than 130,000,000 cars and trucks registered for private use in the United States. Each travels an average of 10-12,000 miles per year, and, and in total they consume close to 70 billion gallons of fuel each year. This represents nearly ⅔ of the oil imported by the United States each year. The Federal government's goal is to reduce consumption 10% by 1985. A variety of methods are either already in use or under serious consideration, and they all affect you driving and the cars you will drive. In addition to "down-sizing", the auto industry is using or investigating the use of electronic fuel delivery, electronic engine controls and alternative engines for use in smaller and lighter vehicles, among other alternatives to meet the federally mandated Corporate Average Fuel Economy (CAFE) of 27.5 mpg by 1985. The government, for its part, is considering rationing, mandatory driving curtailments and tax increases on motor vehicle fuel in an effort to reduce consumption. The government's goal of a 10% reduction could be realized — and further government regulation avoided — if every private vehicle could use just 1 less gallon of fuel per week.

How Much Can You Save?

Tests have proven that almost anyone can make at least a 10% reduction in fuel consumption through regular maintenance and tune-ups. When a major manufacturer of spark plugs sur-

TUNE-UP

1. Check the cylinder compression to be sure the engine will really benefit from a tune-up and that it is capable of producing good fuel economy. A tune-up will be wasted on an engine in poor mechanical condition.

2. Replace spark plugs regularly. New spark plugs alone can increase fuel economy 3%.

3. Be sure the spark plugs are the correct type (heat range) for your vehicle. See the Tune-Up Specifications.

Heat range refers to the spark plug's ability to conduct heat away from the firing end. It must conduct the heat away in an even pattern to avoid becoming a source of pre-ignition, yet it must also operate hot enough to burn off conductive deposits that could cause misfiring.

The heat range is usually indicated by a number on the spark plug, part of the manufacturer's designation for each individual spark plug. The numbers in bold-face indicate the heat range in each manufacturer's identification system.

Periodically, check the spark plugs to be sure they are firing efficiently. They are excellent indicators of the internal condition of your engine.

Manufacturer	Typical Designation
AC	R **45** TS
Bosch (old)	WA **145** T30
Bosch (new)	HR **8** Y
Champion	RBL **15** Y
Fram/Autolite	41**5**
Mopar	P-**62** PR
Motorcraft	BRF-**42**
NGK	BP **5** ES-15
Nippondenso	W **16** EP
Prestolite	14GR **5** 2A

On AC, Bosch (new), Champion, Fram/Autolite, Mopar, Motorcraft and Prestolite, a higher number indicates a hotter plug. On Bosch (old), NGK and Nippondenso, a higher number indicates a colder plug.

4. Make sure the spark plugs are properly gapped. See the Tune-Up Specifications in this book.

5. Be sure the spark plugs are firing efficiently. The illustrations on the next 2 pages show you how to "read" the firing end of the spark plug.

6. Check the ignition timing and set it to specifications. Tests show that almost all cars have incorrect ignition timing by more than 2°.

veyed over 6,000 cars nationwide, they found that a tune-up, on cars that needed one, increased fuel economy over 11%. Replacing worn plugs alone, accounted for a 3% increase. The same test also revealed that 8 out of every 10 vehicles will have some maintenance deficiency that will directly affect fuel economy, emissions or performance. Most of this mileage-robbing neglect could be prevented with regular maintenance.

Modern engines require that all of the functioning systems operate properly for maximum efficiency. A malfunction anywhere wastes fuel. You can keep your vehicle running as efficiently and economically as possible, by being aware of your vehicle's operating and performance characteristics. If your vehicle suddenly develops performance or fuel economy problems it could be due to one or more of the following:

PROBLEM	POSSIBLE CAUSE
Engine Idles Rough	Ignition timing, idle mixture, vacuum leak or something amiss in the emission control system.
Hesitates on Acceleration	Dirty carburetor or fuel filter, improper accelerator pump setting, ignition timing or fouled spark plugs.
Starts Hard or Fails to Start	Worn spark plugs, improperly set automatic choke, ice (or water) in fuel system.
Stalls Frequently	Automatic choke improperly adjusted and possible dirty air filter or fuel filter.
Performs Sluggishly	Worn spark plugs, dirty fuel or air filter, ignition timing or automatic choke out of adjustment.

Check spark plug wires on conventional point type ignition for cracks by bending them in a loop around your finger.

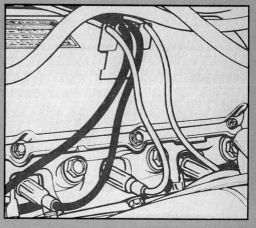

Be sure that spark plug wires leading to adjacent cylinders do not run too close together. (Photo courtesy Champion Spark Plug Co.)

7. If your vehicle does not have electronic ignition, check the points, rotor and cap as specified.

8. Check the spark plug wires (used with conventional point-type ignitions) for cracks and burned or broken insulation by bending them in a loop around your finger. Cracked wires decrease fuel efficiency by failing to deliver full voltage to the spark plugs. One misfiring spark plug can cost you as much as 2 mpg.

9. Check the routing of the plug wires. Misfiring can be the result of spark plug leads to adjacent cylinders running parallel to each other and too close together. One wire tends to pick up voltage from the other causing it to fire "out of time".

10. Check all electrical and ignition circuits for voltage drop and resistance.

11. Check the distributor mechanical and/or vacuum advance mechanisms for proper functioning. The vacuum advance can be checked by twisting the distributor plate in the opposite direction of rotation. It should spring back when released.

12. Check and adjust the valve clearance on engines with mechanical lifters. The clearance should be slightly loose rather than too tight.

SPARK PLUG DIAGNOSIS

Normal

APPEARANCE: This plug is typical of one operating normally. The insulator nose varies from a light tan to grayish color with slight electrode wear. The presence of slight deposits is normal on used plugs and will have no adverse effect on engine performance. The spark plug heat range is correct for the engine and the engine is running normally.

CAUSE: Properly running engine.

RECOMMENDATION: Before reinstalling this plug, the electrodes should be cleaned and filed square. Set the gap to specifications. If the plug has been in service for more than 10-12,000 miles, the entire set should probably be replaced with a fresh set of the same heat range.

Oil Deposits

APPEARANCE: The firing end of the plug is covered with a wet, oily coating.

CAUSE: The problem is poor oil control. On high mileage engines, oil is leaking past the rings or valve guides into the combustion chamber. A common cause is also a plugged PCV valve, and a ruptured fuel pump diaphragm can also cause this condition. Oil fouled plugs such as these are often found in new or recently overhauled engines, before normal oil control is achieved, and can be cleaned and reinstalled.

RECOMMENDATION: A hotter spark plug may temporarily relieve the problem, but the engine is probably in need of work.

Incorrect Heat Range

APPEARANCE: The effects of high temperature on a spark plug are indicated by clean white, often blistered insulator. This can also be accompanied by excessive wear of the electrode, and the absence of deposits.

CAUSE: Check for the correct spark plug heat range. A plug which is too hot for the engine can result in overheating. A car operated mostly at high speeds can require a colder plug. Also check ignition timing, cooling system level, fuel mixture and leaking intake manifold.

RECOMMENDATION: If all ignition and engine adjustments are known to be correct, and no other malfunction exists, install spark plugs one heat range colder.

Photos Courtesy Fram Corporation

Carbon Deposits

APPEARANCE: Carbon fouling is easily identified by the presence of dry, soft, black, sooty deposits.

CAUSE: Changing the heat range can often lead to carbon fouling, as can prolonged slow, stop-and-start driving. If the heat range is correct, carbon fouling can be attributed to a rich fuel mixture, sticking choke, clogged air cleaner, worn breaker points, retarded timing or low compression. If only one or two plugs are carbon fouled, check for corroded or cracked wires on the affected plugs. Also look for cracks in the distributor cap between the towers of affected cylinders.

RECOMMENDATION: After the problem is corrected, these plugs can be cleaned and reinstalled if not worn severely.

MMT Fouled

APPEARANCE: Spark plugs fouled by MMT (Methycyclopentadienyl Maganese Tricarbonyl) have reddish, rusty appearance on the insulator and side electrode.

CAUSE: MMT is an anti-knock additive in gasoline used to replace lead. During the combustion process, the MMT leaves a reddish deposit on the insulator and side electrode.

RECOMMENDATION: No engine malfunction is indicated and the deposits will not affect plug performance any more than lead deposits (see Ash Deposits). MMT fouled plugs can be cleaned, regapped and reinstalled.

High Speed Glazing

APPEARANCE: Glazing appears as shiny coating on the plug, either yellow or tan in color.

CAUSE: During hard, fast acceleration, plug temperatures rise suddenly. Deposits from normal combustion have no chance to fluff-off; instead, they melt on the insulator forming an electrically conductive coating which causes misfiring.

RECOMMENDATION: Glazed plugs are not easily cleaned. They should be replaced with a fresh set of plugs of the correct heat range. If the condition recurs, using plugs with a heat range one step colder may cure the problem.

Ash (Lead) Deposits

APPEARANCE: Ash deposits are characterized by light brown or white colored deposits crusted on the side or center electrodes. In some cases it may give the plug a rusty appearance.

CAUSE: Ash deposits are normally derived from oil or fuel additives burned during normal combustion. Normally they are harmless, though excessive amounts can cause misfiring. If deposits are excessive in short mileage, the valve guides may be worn.

RECOMMENDATION: Ash-fouled plugs can be cleaned, gapped and reinstalled.

Detonation

APPEARANCE: Detonation is usually characterized by a broken plug insulator.

CAUSE: A portion of the fuel charge will begin to burn spontaneously, from the increased heat following ignition. The explosion that results applies extreme pressure to engine components, frequently damaging spark plugs and pistons.

Detonation can result by over-advanced ignition timing, inferior gasoline (low octane) lean air/fuel mixture, poor carburetion, engine lugging or an increase in compression ratio due to combustion chamber deposits or engine modification.

RECOMMENDATION: Replace the plugs after correcting the problem.

Photos Courtesy Champion Spark Plug Co.

EMISSION CONTROLS

13. Be aware of the general condition of the emission control system. It contributes to reduced pollution and should be serviced regularly to maintain efficient engine operation.

14. Check all vacuum lines for dried, cracked or brittle conditions. Something as simple as a leaking vacuum hose can cause poor performance and loss of economy.

15. Avoid tampering with the emission control system. Attempting to improve fuel econ-

FUEL SYSTEM

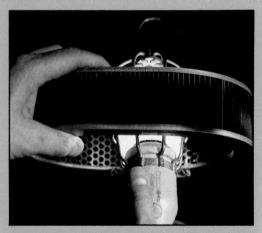

Check the air filter with a light behind it. If you can see light through the filter it can be reused.

Extremely clogged filters should be discarded and replaced with a new one.

18. Replace the air filter regularly. A dirty air filter richens the air/fuel mixture and can increase fuel consumption as much as 10%. Tests show that ⅓ of all vehicles have air filters in need of replacement.

19. Replace the fuel filter at least as often as recommended.

20. Set the idle speed and carburetor mixture to specifications.

21. Check the automatic choke. A sticking or malfunctioning choke wastes gas.

22. During the summer months, adjust the automatic choke for a leaner mixture which will produce faster engine warm-ups.

COOLING SYSTEM

29. Be sure all accessory drive belts are in good condition. Check for cracks or wear.

30. Adjust all accessory drive belts to proper tension.

31. Check all hoses for swollen areas, worn spots, or loose clamps.

32. Check coolant level in the radiator or expansion tank.

33. Be sure the thermostat is operating properly. A stuck thermostat delays engine warm-up and a cold engine uses nearly twice as much fuel as a warm engine.

34. Drain and replace the engine coolant at least as often as recommended. Rust and scale

TIRES & WHEELS

38. Check the tire pressure often with a pencil type gauge. Tests by a major tire manufacturer show that 90% of all vehicles have at least 1 tire improperly inflated. Better mileage can be achieved by over-inflating tires, but never exceed the maximum inflation pressure on the side of the tire.

39. If possible, install radial tires. Radial tires deliver as much as ½ mpg more than bias belted tires.

40. Avoid installing super-wide tires. They only create extra rolling resistance and decrease fuel mileage. Stick to the manufacturer's recommendations.

41. Have the wheels properly balanced.

omy by tampering with emission controls is more likely to worsen fuel economy than improve it. Emission control changes on modern engines are not readily reversible.

16. Clean (or replace) the EGR valve and lines as recommended.

17. Be sure that all vacuum lines and hoses are reconnected properly after working under the hood. An unconnected or misrouted vacuum line can wreak havoc with engine performance.

23. Check for fuel leaks at the carburetor, fuel pump, fuel lines and fuel tank. Be sure all lines and connections are tight.

24. Periodically check the tightness of the carburetor and intake manifold attaching nuts and bolts. These are a common place for vacuum leaks to occur.

25. Clean the carburetor periodically and lubricate the linkage.

26. The condition of the tailpipe can be an excellent indicator of proper engine combustion. After a long drive at highway speeds, the inside of the tailpipe should be a light grey in color. Black or soot on the insides indicates an overly rich mixture.

27. Check the fuel pump pressure. The fuel pump may be supplying more fuel than the engine needs.

28. Use the proper grade of gasoline for your engine. Don't try to compensate for knocking or "pinging" by advancing the ignition timing. This practice will only increase plug temperature and the chances of detonation or pre-ignition with relatively little performance gain.

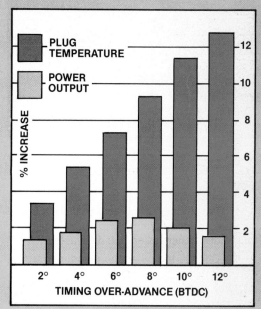

Increasing ignition timing past the specified setting results in a drastic increase in spark plug temperature with increased chance of detonation or preignition. Performance increase is considerably less. (Photo courtesy Champion Spark Plug Co.)

that form in the engine should be flushed out to allow the engine to operate at peak efficiency.

35. Clean the radiator of debris that can decrease cooling efficiency.

36. Install a flex-type or electric cooling fan, if you don't have a clutch type fan. Flex fans use curved plastic blades to push more air at low speeds when more cooling is needed; at high speeds the blades flatten out for less resistance. Electric fans only run when the engine temperature reaches a predetermined level.

37. Check the radiator cap for a worn or cracked gasket. If the cap does not seal properly, the cooling system will not function properly.

42. Be sure the front end is correctly aligned. A misaligned front end actually has wheels going in differed directions. The increased drag can reduce fuel economy by .3 mpg.

43. Correctly adjust the wheel bearings. Wheel bearings that are adjusted too tight increase rolling resistance.

Check tire pressures regularly with a reliable pocket type gauge. Be sure to check the pressure on a cold tire.

GENERAL MAINTENANCE

Check the fluid levels (particularly engine oil) on a regular basis. Be sure to check the oil for grit, water or other contamination.

A vacuum gauge is another excellent indicator of internal engine condition and can also be installed in the dash as a mileage indicator.

44. Periodically check the fluid levels in the engine, power steering pump, master cylinder, automatic transmission and drive axle.

45. Change the oil at the recommended interval and change the filter at every oil change. Dirty oil is thick and causes extra friction between moving parts, cutting efficiency and increasing wear. A worn engine requires more frequent tune-ups and gets progressively worse fuel economy. In general, use the lightest viscosity oil for the driving conditions you will encounter.

46. Use the recommended viscosity fluids in the transmission and axle.

47. Be sure the battery is fully charged for fast starts. A slow starting engine wastes fuel.

48. Be sure battery terminals are clean and tight.

49. Check the battery electrolyte level and add distilled water if necessary.

50. Check the exhaust system for crushed pipes, blockages and leaks.

51. Adjust the brakes. Dragging brakes or brakes that are not releasing create increased drag on the engine.

52. Install a vacuum gauge or miles-per-gallon gauge. These gauges visually indicate engine vacuum in the intake manifold. High vacuum = good mileage and low vacuum = poorer mileage. The gauge can also be an excellent indicator of internal engine conditions.

53. Be sure the clutch is properly adjusted. A slipping clutch wastes fuel.

54. Check and periodically lubricate the heat control valve in the exhaust manifold. A sticking or inoperative valve prevents engine warm-up and wastes gas.

55. Keep accurate records to check fuel economy over a period of time. A sudden drop in fuel economy may signal a need for tune-up or other maintenance.

CARBURETED GASOLINE ENGINE FUEL SYSTEM

Only the 8–5.7L is equipped with a carburetor. The model used is the M4ME/M4MEF 4-bbl. The difference between the two models is that the M4MEF has a wide open throttle mixture control. The M4ME is used only on some 1987 models. Only the M4MEF is used for 1988–90.

Mechanical Fuel Pump

The fuel pump is a single action AC diaphragm type.

The pump is operated by an eccentric on the camshaft. A pushrod between the camshaft eccentric and the fuel pump operates the pump rocker arm.

TESTING THE FUEL PUMP

Fuel pumps should always be tested on the vehicle. The larger line between the pump and tank is the suction side of the system and the smaller line, between the pump and carburetor, is the pressure side. A leak in the pressure side would be apparent because of dripping fuel. A leak in the suction side is usually only apparent because of a reduced volume of fuel delivered to the pressure side.

1. Tighten any loose line connections and look for any kinks or restrictions.

2. Disconnect the fuel line at the carburetor. Disconnect the distributor-to-coil primary wire. Place a container at the end of the fuel line and crank the engine a few revolutions. If little or no fuel flows from the line, either the fuel pump is inoperative or the line is plugged. Blow through the lines with compressed air and try the test again. Reconnect the line.

3. If fuel flows in good volume, check the fuel pump pressure to be sure.

4. Attach a pressure gauge to the pressure side of the fuel line. On trucks equipped with a vapor return system, squeeze off the return hose.

5. Run the engine at idle and note the reading on the gauge. Stop the engine and compare the reading with the specifications listed in the Tune-Up Specifications chart. If the pump is operating properly, the pressure will be as specified and will be constant at idle speed. If pressure varies sporadically or is too high or low, the pump should be replaced.

6. Remove the pressure gauge.

The following flow test can also be performed:

1. Disconnect the fuel line from the carburetor. Run the fuel line into a suitable measuring container.

2. Run the engine at idle until there is one pint of fuel in the container. One pint should be pumped in 30 seconds or less.

3. If the flow is below minimum, check for a restriction in the line.

The only way to check fuel pump pressure is by connecting an accurate pressure gauge to the fuel line at the carburetor level. Never replace a fuel pump without performing this simple test. If the engine seems to be starving out, check the ignition system first. Also check for a plugged fuel filter or a restricted fuel line before replacing the pump.

REMOVAL AND INSTALLATION

CAUTION: *Never smoke when working around gasoline! Avoid all sources of sparks or ignition. Gasoline vapors are EXTREMELY volatile!*

NOTE: *When you connect the fuel pump outlet fitting, always use 2 wrenches to avoid damaging the pump.*

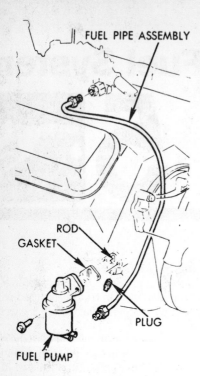

Mechanical fuel pump installation

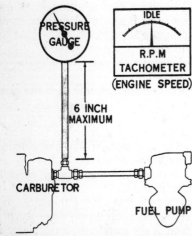

Pressure testing the mechanical fuel pump

1. Disconnect the fuel intake and outlet lines at the pump and plug the pump intake line.

2. You can remove the upper bolt from the right front engine mounting boss (on the front of the block) and insert a long bolt ($3/8$ in.–16 × 2 in.) to hold the fuel pump pushrod.

3. Remove the two pump mounting bolts and lock washers; remove the pump and its gasket.

4. If the rocker arm pushrod is to be removed, remove the two adapter bolts and lock washers and remove the adapter and its gasket.

5. Install the fuel pump with a new gasket reversing the removal procedure. Heavy grease can be used to hold the fuel pump pushrod up when installing the pump, if you didn't install the long bolt in Step 2. Coat the mating surfaces with sealer.

6. Connect the fuel lines an check for leaks.

Carburetor

DESCRIPTION AND OPERATING PRINCIPALS

These Rochester models are four barrel, two stage carburetors with three major assemblies: the air horn, float bowl, and throttle body. They have six basic operating systems:
1. Float
2. Idle
3. Main Metering
4. Power
5. Pump
6. Choke

The first "M" in the model identification number indicates that the carburetor is of a Modified primary metering "open loop" design. The "4M" is the model designation, indicating it is a four barrel carburetor. The remaining letters designate specific features as follows:

• C – It has an integral Hot Air Choke.

• D – Dual capacity pump valve and a combined mixture control/dual capacity pump solenoid assembly.

• E – Has an electric choke.

• F – Has an adjustable wide open throttle mixture control.

The carburetor identification number is stamped vertically on the float bowl near the secondary throttle lever. Refer to this number before servicing the carburetor. If replacing the float bowl assembly, follow the instructions in the service package and stamp or engrave the number on the new float bowl.

A single float chamber supplies fuel to all carburetor bores. A float, float needle with pull clip and a float needle seat are used to control the level of fuel in the float chamber. A vacuum-operated power piston and metering rods control the air/fuel metering in the primary bores of the carburetor. Tapered metering rods are attached to the power valve piston assembly and move in fixed metering jets to provide the fuel flow for varying engine demands. A factory-set adjustable part throttle screw, used on all models, precisely positions the tapered portion of the metering rods in the jets. On M4MEF models, the factory-set rich stop adjusting bushing precisely positions the enrichment portion of the metering rods in the jets.

Air valves and tapered metering rods control the air/fuel mixture in the secondary bores during increased engine air flow at wide open throttle. On M4MEF models, the factory-set secondary well air bleed adjusting screw provides additional control of the air/fuel mixture during wide open throttle (WOT).

The accelerator pump system on all models uses a throttle actuated pump plunger, operating in the pump well. The pump provides extra fuel during quick throttle openings.

An electrically heated choke coil provides the choke valve closing force for cold startup and for correct opening time during warm-up. A vacuum break assembly(ies) controls initial choke valve opening at startup to provide sufficient air flow to the engine. An unloader tang on the throttle lever forces the choke valve to open to purge a flooded engine when the accelerator is pressed to the floor. The fast idle cam, following choke valve movement, acts as a graduated throttle stop to provide increased idle speed during warm-up.

The electric Idle Stop Solenoid (ISS) on Federal V8 engines with manual transmission provides the desired engine idle speed, and prevents dieseling when the ignition is switched off. A vacuum-operated Throttle Kicker assembly on California V8 engines retards throttle closing during deceleration to improve emission control. Vacuum to the kicker is controlled by the Throttle Return Control system.

FUNCTIONAL TESTS

Float Level External Test

This procedure requires the use of an external float level gauge tool No. J–34935–1 or equivalent.

1. With the engine idling and the choke valve wide open, insert tool J–34935–1 in the vent slot or vent hole. Allow the gauge to float freely.

NOTE: *Do not press down on the gauge. Flooding or float damage could result.*

2. Observe the mark on the gauge that lines up with the top of the casting. The setting should be within $\frac{1}{16}$ in. (1.6mm) of the specified float level setting. Incorrect fuel pressure will adversely affect the fuel level.

3. If not within specification, remove the air horn and adjust the float.

Choke Checking Procedure (Engine Off)

1. Remove the air cleaner assembly.
2. Hold the throttle half way down.
3. Open and close the choke several times. Be sure all links are connected and not damaged. Choke valve, linkage, and fast idle cam must operate freely.
4. If the choke valve, linkage or fast idle cam is sticking due to varnish, clean with choke cleaner.
5. Do not lubricate linkage, as lubricant will collect dust and cause sticking.

Checking Electric Choke (On Vehicle)

1. Allow the choke thermostat to stabilize at about 70°F (21°C).
2. Open the throttle to allow the choke valve to close.
3. Start the engine and determine the length of time for the choke valve to reach full open position:
   a. If longer than five minutes, check the voltage at the choke stat connector, with the engine running.
   b. If voltage is between 12 and 15 volts, check for proper ground between choke cover and choke housing. If correct, replace choke cover assembly.
   c. If the voltage is low or zero, check all wires and connections.

Checking Vacuum Break

A hand-operated vacuum pump such as J–23738–A or equivalent will be needed for this procedure.

1. If the vacuum break has an air bleed hole, plug it during this checking procedure.
2. Apply 15 in. Hg vacuum to the vacuum break with the hand pump.
   a. Apply finger pressure to see if the plunger has moved through full travel. If not, replace the vacuum break.
   b. Observe the vacuum gauge. Vacuum should hold vacuum for at least twenty seconds. If not, replace the vacuum break.
3. Replace vacuum break hoses that are cracked, cut or hardened.

Checking Idle Stop Solenoid (ISS)

A non-functioning idle stop solenoid (if equipped) could cause stalling or rough idle.

1. Turn the ignition ON, but do not start the engine.
2. Open the throttle momentarily to allow the solenoid plunger to extend.
3. Disconnect the wire at the solenoid. The plunger should drop back from the throttle lever.
4. Connect the solenoid wire. The plunger should move out and contact the throttle lever.
5. If the plunger does not move in and out as the wire is disconnected and connected, check the voltage across the feed wire:
   a. If 12–15 volts are present in the feed wire, replace the solenoid.
   b. If the voltage is low, locate the cause of the open circuit in the solenoid feed wire and repair as necessary.

Checking Throttle Kicker

A hand-operated vacuum pump such as J-23738–A or equivalent will be needed for this procedure.

1. Hold the throttle half way open to allow the plunger to extend fully.

2. Apply 20 in. Hg vacuum to the throttle kicker with the hand vacuum pump.

    a. Apply finger pressure to the plunger to see if it has extended fully. If not, replace the throttle kicker.

    b. Observe the vacuum gauge. Vacuum should hold for at least twenty seconds. If not, replace the throttle kicker.

3. Release the vacuum to the throttle kicker.

4. If the plunger does not retract to its starting position, replace kicker.

ADJUSTMENTS

Float Adjustment

A float level T-scale such as J-9789–90 or equivalent and float positioning tool kit J-34817 or equivalent will be needed for this adjustment.

1. Remove the air horn, gasket, power piston and metering rod assembly, and the float bowl insert.

2. Attach float adjustment tool J-34817–1 or equivalent to the float bowl.

3. Place float adjustment tool J-34817–3 or equivalent into float adjustment tool J-34817–1 or equivalent, with the contact pin resting on the outer edge of the float lever.

4. Measure the distance from the top of the casting to the top of the float at a point $3/16$ in. from the large end of the float using the float adjustment tool J-9789–90 or equivalent.

5. If more than $\pm 1/16$ in. from specification, use the float gauge adjusting tool J-34817–

25 or equivalent to bend the lever up or down. Remove the gauge adjusting tool and measure, repeating until within specifications.

6. Check the float alignment and reassemble the carburetor.

Pump Adjustment

Float Level T-scale J-9789–90 or equivalent will be needed for this adjustment.

1. The pump link must be in the specified hole to make this adjustment.

2. With the fast idle cam off the cam follower lever, turn the throttle stop screw out so it does not touch the throttle lever.

3. Measure the distance from the top of the choke valve wall to the top of the pump stem.

4. Adjust, if necessary, by supporting the pump lever with a screwdriver and bending it at the notch.

Air Valve Return Spring Adjustment

1. Loosen the setscrew.

2. Turn spring fulcrum pin counterclockwise until the air valves open.

3. Turn the pin clockwise until the air valves close, then the additional turns specified.

4. Tighten the setscrew. Apply lithium grease to the spring contact area.

Choke Stat Lever Adjustment

Linkage Bending Tool J-9789–111 or equivalent will be needed for this adjustment.

1. Drill out and remove the choke cover attaching rivets. Remove choke cover and thermostat assembly.

2. Place fast idle cam on high step against the cam follower lever.

3. Push up on the choke stat lever to close the choke valve.

4. Check the stat lever for correct orientation by inserting a 3mm (0.120 in.) plug gauge

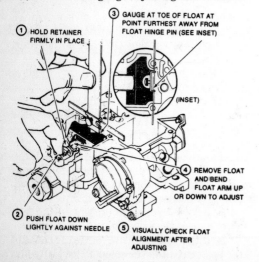

Float adjustment - 4-bbl

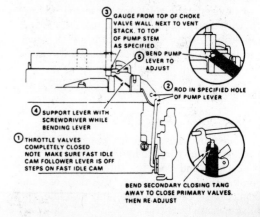

Pump adjustment - 4-bbl

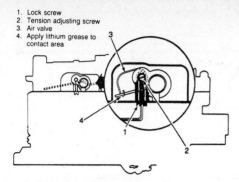

1. Lock screw
2. Tension adjusting screw
3. Air valve
4. Apply lithium grease to contact area

Air valve spring adjustment

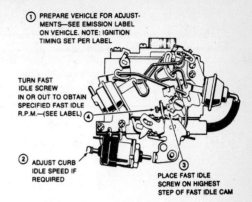

① PREPARE VEHICLE FOR ADJUSTMENTS—SEE EMISSION LABEL ON VEHICLE. NOTE: IGNITION TIMING SET PER LABEL

TURN FAST IDLE SCREW IN OR OUT TO OBTAIN SPECIFIED FAST IDLE R.P.M.—(SEE LABEL)

② ADJUST CURB IDLE SPEED IF REQUIRED

PLACE FAST IDLE SCREW ON HIGHEST STEP OF FAST IDLE CAM

Fast idle adjustment, on vehicle

hole in the choke housing. The gauge should fit in the hole and touch the edge of the lever.

5. Adjust, if necessary, by bending the choke link with J–9789–111 or equivalent.

Choke Link and Fast Idle Cam Adjustment

Choke Valve Angle Gauge J–26701–A or equivalent will be needed for this adjustment.

1. Attach a rubber band to the vacuum break lever of the intermediate choke shaft.

2. Open the throttle to allow the choke valve to close.

3. Set up J–26701–A or equivalent and set the angle to specification as follows:

　a. Rotate the degree scale until zero is opposite the pointer.

　b. Center the leveling bubble.

　c. Rotate the scale to the specified angle.

4. Place the fast idle cam on the second step against the cam follower lever, with the lever contacting the rise of the high step. If the lever does not contact the cam, turn the fast idle adjusting screw in additional turn(s).

NOTE: *Final fast idle speed adjustment must be performed according to the underhood emission control information label.*

5. Adjust, if bubble is not recentered, by bending the fast idle cam kick lever with pliers.

Primary Side Vacuum Break Adjustment

Choke Valve Angle Gauge J–26701–A and Hand Operated Vacuum Pump J–23738–A or equivalents, will be needed for this adjustment.

1. Attach rubber band to the vacuum break

lever of the intermediate choke shaft.

2. Open the throttle to allow the choke valve to close.

3. Set up J–26701–A or equivalent and set angle to specifications.

4. Plug the vacuum break bleed holes, if applicable. Apply 15 in. Hg vacuum to seat the vacuum break plunger.

5. Seat the bucking spring, if so equipped. If necessary, bend the air valve link to permit full plunger travel, then re-apply vacuum to fully retract plunger.

6. Adjust, if bubble is not re-centered, by turning the vacuum break adjusting screw.

Secondary Side Vacuum Break Adjustment

Choke Valve Angle Gauge J–26701–A, Hand Operated Vacuum Pump J–23738–A and Linkage Bending Tool J–9789–111 or equivalents will be needed for this adjustment.

1. Attach a rubber band to the vacuum break lever of the intermediate choke shaft.

2. Open the throttle to allow the choke valve to close.

3. Set up J–26701–A or equivalent and set angle to specification.

4. Plug vacuum break bleed holes, if so equipped. Apply 15 in. Hg vacuum to seat the vacuum break plunger.

5. Compress the plunger bucking spring, if

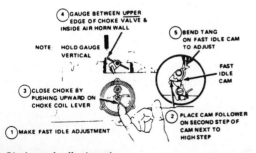

④ GAUGE BETWEEN UPPER EDGE OF CHOKE VALVE & INSIDE AIR HORN WALL

NOTE HOLD GAUGE VERTICAL

⑤ BEND TANG ON FAST IDLE CAM TO ADJUST

FAST IDLE CAM

③ CLOSE CHOKE BY PUSHING UPWARD ON CHOKE COIL LEVER

① MAKE FAST IDLE ADJUSTMENT

② PLACE CAM FOLLOWER ON SECOND STEP OF CAM NEXT TO HIGH STEP

Choke rod adjustment

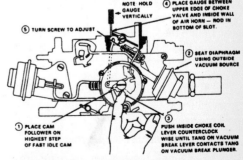

NOTE HOLD GAUGE VERTICALLY

④ PLACE GAUGE BETWEEN UPPER EDGE OF CHOKE VALVE AND INSIDE WALL OF AIR HORN — ROD IN BOTTOM OF SLOT.

⑤ TURN SCREW TO ADJUST

② SEAT DIAPHRAGM USING OUTSIDE VACUUM SOURCE

① PLACE CAM FOLLOWER ON HIGHEST STEP OF FAST IDLE CAM

③ PUSH INSIDE CHOKE COIL LEVER COUNTERCLOCKWISE UNTIL TANG ON VACUUM BREAK LEVER CONTACTS TANG ON VACUUM BREAK PLUNGER

Primary side vacuum break adjustment

so equipped. If necessary, bend the air valve link to permit full plunger travel, then re-apply vacuum to fully retract the plunger.

6. Adjust, if bubble is not re-centered, by either supporting the link where shown and bending it with J–9789–111 or equivalent, or by turning the screw with a ⅛ in. hex wrench.

Air Valve Link Adjustment

Hand Operated Vacuum Pump J–23738–A and Linkage Bending Tool J–9789–111 or equivalents will be needed for this adjustment.

1. Plug vacuum break bleed holes, if applicable. With the air valves closed, apply 15 in. Hg vacuum to seat the vacuum break plunger.

2. Gauge the clearance between the air valve link and the end of the slot in the air valve lever. Clearance should be 0.6mm (0.025 in.)

3. Adjust, if necessary, by bending the link with J–9789–111 or equivalent.

Unloader Adjustment

Choke Valve Angle Gauge J–26701–A and Linkage Bending Tool J–9789–111 or equivalents will be needed for this adjustment.

1. Attach rubber band to the vacuum break lever of the intermediate choke shaft.

2. Open the throttle to allow the choke valve to close.

3. Set up J–26701–A or equivalent and set angle to specifications.

4. Hold the secondary lockout lever away from the pin.

5. Hold the throttle lever in wide open position.

6. Adjust, if bubble is not re-centered, by bending fast idle lever with J–9789–111 or equivalent.

Secondary Throttle Lockout Adjustment

1. Place the fast idle cam on the high step against the cam follower lever.

2. Hold the throttle lever closed.

3. Gauge the clearance between the lockout lever and pin. It must be 0.015 inch ± 0.005 in.

4. Adjust, if necessary, by bending pin.

5. Push down on tail of fast idle cam to move lockout lever away from pin.

6. Rotate the throttle lever to bring the lockout pin to the position of minimum clearance with the lockout lever.

7. Gauge the clearance between the lockout lever and pin. The minimum must be 0.015 in.

8. Adjust, if necessary, by filing the end of the pin.

Idle Speed and Mixture Adjustment

In case of a major carburetor overhaul, throttle body replacement, or high idle CO (when in-

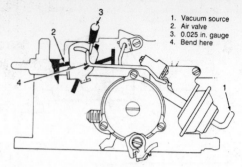

1. Vacuum source
2. Air valve
3. 0.025 in. gauge
4. Bend here

Front air valve rod adjustment

1. Vacuum source
2. Air valve
3. 0.025 in. gauge
4. Bend here

Rear air valve rod adjustment

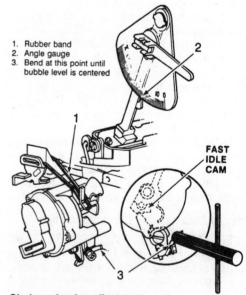

1. Rubber band
2. Angle gauge
3. Bend at this point until bubble level is centered

FAST IDLE CAM

Choke unloader adjustment

dicated by an emissions inspection), the idle mixture may be adjusted. Adjusting the mixture by other than the following method may violate Federal and/or state laws. Idle mixture needle socket J–29030–B or equivalent is required for this adjustment.

1. Set the parking brake and block the drive wheels.

2. Remove the carburetor from the engine.

3. Drain the fuel from the carburetor into a container. Dispose of the fuel in an approved container.

4. Remove the idle mixture needle plugs as follows:

    a. Invert the carburetor and support it to avoid damaging external components.

    b. Make two parallel hacksaw cuts in the throttle body, between the locator points near one idle mixture needle plug. The distance between the cuts depends on the size of the punch to be used.

    c. Cut down to the plug, but not more than $1/8$ in. beyond the locator point.

    d. Place a flat punch at a point near the ends of the saw marks. Hold the punch at a 45° angle and drive it into the throttle body until the casting breaks away, exposing the steel plug.

    e. Use a center punch to break the plug apart, uncover idle mixture needle. Remove all loose pieces of plug.

    f. Repeat the previous steps for the other needle plug.

5. Use idle mixture needle socket J–29030–B or equivalent to lightly seat the idle mixture needles, then back them out three turns.

6. Reinstall the carburetor on the engine.

7. Place the transmission in Park (automatic transmission) or Neutral (manual transmission).

8. Start the engine and bring it to a normal operating temperature, choke valve open, and air conditioning off.

9. Connect a known accurate tachometer to the engine.

10. Check ignition timing, and adjust if necessary, by following the procedure described on the Emission Control Information Label located under the hood on the vehicle.

11. Use idle mixture needle socket J–29030–B or equivalent to turn the mixture needles equally ($1/8$ turn at a time), in or out, to obtain the highest rpm (best idle).

12. Adjust the idle speed screw (throttle stop) to obtain the base idle speed specified on the underhood emission control information label.

13. Again try to readjust mixture needles to obtain the highest idle rpm. The adjustment is correct when the highest rpm (best idle) is reached with the minimum number of mixture needle turns from the seated position.

14. If necessary, readjust the idle speed screw (throttle stop) to obtain the specified base idle speed.

15. Check (and if necessary adjust) the idle speed solenoid activated speed and fast idle speed. Refer to the underhood emission control information label.

16. Check the throttle kicker and adjust if necessary.

17. Turn off the engine, remove all test equipment and remove the block from the drive wheels.

REMOVAL AND INSTALLATION

1. Disconnect the negative battery terminal. Remove the air cleaner assembly and gasket.

2. Disconnect the electrical connectors from the choke and idle stop solenoid.

3. Disconnect and tag the vacuum hoses.

4. Disconnect the accelerator linkage, downshift cable (automatic transmission only) and cruise control linkage (if equipped).

5. Disconnect the fuel line connection at the fuel inlet nut.

6. Remove the carburetor attaching bolts and the carburetor with the flange insulator.

CAUTION: *Clean the sealing surfaces on the intake manifold and carburetor. Be sure to extinguish all open flames while filling and testing carburetor with gasoline to avoid the risk of fire.*

7. Install the carburetor with a new flange gasket. It is good shop practice to fill the carburetor float bowl before installing the carburetor. This reduces the strain on starting motor and battery and reduces the possibility of backfiring while attempting to start the engine. Operate the throttle several times and check the discharge from pump jets before installing the carburetor.

8. Install the carburetor attaching bolts and torque them to 12 ft. lbs. (16 Nm). Be sure to torque the bolts in a criss-cross pattern.

9. Install the fuel line to the fuel inlet nut, cruise control cable (if equipped), downshift cable (automatic transmission only), accelerator linkage, vacuum hoses, electrical connectors to the choke and idle stop solenoid, air cleaner assembly with gasket and the negative battery terminal.

NOTE: *After servicing the carburetor, tighten the mounting bolts in a clockwise direction to 12 ft. lbs. (16 Nm). When tightening the carburetor at recommended maintenance intervals, check the bolt torque. If less than 5 ft. lbs. (7 Nm), retighten to 8 ft. lbs. (11 Nm); but if greater than 5 ft. lbs. (7 Nm), do not retighten.*

Refer to exploded view for parts identification. Always replace internal gaskets that are removed. Base gasket should be inspected and replaced, only if damaged.

Idle Speed Solenoid Removal

Remove the attaching screws, then remove the Idle Speed Solenoid. The Idle Speed Solenoid should not be immersed in any carburetor cleaner, and should always be removed before complete carburetor overhaul, as carburetor cleaner will damage the internal components.

Idle Mixture Needle Plug Removal

1. Use hacksaw to make two parallel cuts in the throttle body, one on each side of the locator points near one idle mixture needle plug. The distance between the cuts will depend on the size of the punch to be used. Cuts should reach down to the steel plug, but should but extend more than $1/8$ in. beyond the locator points.

2. Place a flat punch at a point near the ends of the saw marks in the throttle body. Hold the punch at a 45° angle, and drive it into the throttle body until the casting breaks away, exposing the hardened steel plug. The plug will break, rather than remaining intact. Remove all the loose pieces.

3. Repeat the procedure for the other idle mixture needle plug.

Idle Air Bleed Valve Removal

1. Cover internal bowl vents and air inlets to the bleed valve with masking tape.

2. Carefully align a $7/64$ in. drill bit on rivet head. Drill only enough to remove head of each rivet holding the idle air bleed valve cover.

3. Use a suitably sized punch to drive out the remainder of the rivet from the castings. Repeat procedure with other rivet.

CAUTION: *For the next operation, safety glasses must be worn to protect eyes from possible metal shaving damage.*

4. Lift off cover and remove any pieces of rivet still inside tower. Use shop air to blow out any remaining chips.

5. Remove idle air bleed valve from the air horn.

6. Remove and discard O-ring seals from valve. New O-ring seals are required for reassembly. The idle air bleed valve is serviced as a complete assembly only.

Air Horn Removal

1. Remove upper choke lever from the end of choke shaft by removing retaining screw. Rotate upper choke lever to remove choke rod from slot in lever.

2. Remove choke rod from lower lever inside the float bowl casting. Remove rod by holding lower lever outward with small screwdriver and twisting rod counterclockwise.

3. Remove secondary metering rods by removing the small screw in the top of the metering rod hanger. Lift upward on the metering rod hanger until the secondary metering rods are completely out of the air horn. Metering rods may be disassembled from the hanger by

rotating the ends out of the holes in the end of the hanger.

4. Remove pump link retainer and remove link from pump lever.

NOTE: *Do not attempt to remove the lever, as damage to the air horn could result.*

5. Remove front vacuum break hose from tube on float bowl.

6. Remove eleven air horn-to-bowl screws; then remove the two countersunk attaching screws located next to the venturi. If used, remove secondary air baffle deflector from beneath the two center air horn screws.

7. Remove air horn from float bowl by lifting it straight up. The air horn gasket should remain on the float bowl for removal later.

NOTE: *When removing air horn from float bowl, use care to prevent damaging the mixture control solenoid connector, Throttle Position Sensor (TPS) adjustment lever, and the small tubes protruding from the air horn. These tubes are permanently pressed into the air horn casting. DO NOT remove them.*

8. Remove front vacuum break bracket attaching screws. The vacuum break assembly may now be removed from the air valve dashpot rod, and the dashpot rod from the air valve lever.

NOTE: *Do not place vacuum break assembly in carburetor cleaner, as damage to vacuum break will occur.*

9. Remove Throttle Position Sensor (TPS) plunger by pushing plunger down through seal in air horn.

10. Remove TPS seal and pump plunger stem seal by inverting air horn and using a small screwdriver to remove staking holding seal retainers in place. Remove and discard retainers and seals.

NOTE: *Use care in removing the TPS plunger seal retainer and pump plunger stem seal retainer to prevent damage to air horn casting. New seals and retainers are required for reassembly.*

11. Invert air horn, and use Tool J–28696–4, BT–7967A, or equivalent, to remove rich mixture stop screw and spring.

12. Use a suitable punch to drive the lean mixture screw plug and rich mixture stop screw plug out of the air horn. Discard the plugs.

13. Further disassembly of the air horn is not required for cleaning purposes.

The choke valve and choke valve screws, the air valves and air valve shaft should not be removed. However, if it is necessary to replace the air valve closing springs or center plastic eccentric cam, a repair kit is available. Instructions for assembly are included in the repair kit.

Float Bowl Disassembly

1. Remove solenoid metering rod plunger by lifting straight up.

2. Remove air horn gasket by lifting it from the dowel locating pins on float bowl. Discard gasket.

3. Remove pump plunger from pump well.

4. Remove staking holding Throttle Position Sensor (TPS) in bowl as follows:

a. Lay a flat tool or metal piece across bowl casting to protect gasket sealing surface.

b. Use a small screwdriver to depress TPS sensor lightly and hold against spring tension.

c. Observing safety precautions, pry upward with a small chisel or equivalent to remove bowl staking, making sure prying force is exerted against the metal piece and not against the bowl casting. Use care not to damage the TPS sensor.

d. Push up from bottom on electrical connector and remove TPS and connector assembly from bowl. Use care in removing sensor

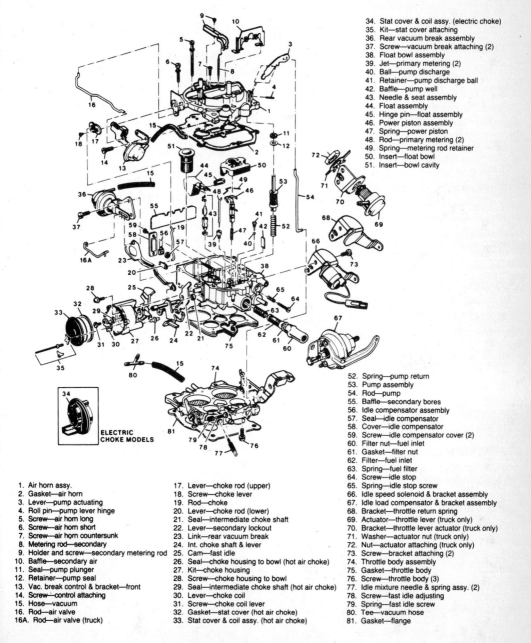

34. Stat cover & coil assy. (electric choke)
35. Kit—stat cover attaching
36. Rear vacuum break assembly
37. Screw—vacuum break attaching (2)
38. Float bowl assembly
39. Jet—primary metering (2)
40. Ball—pump discharge
41. Retainer—pump discharge ball
42. Baffle—pump well
43. Needle & seat assembly
44. Float assembly
45. Hinge pin—float assembly
46. Power piston assembly
47. Spring—power piston
48. Rod—primary metering (2)
49. Spring—metering rod retainer
50. Insert—float bowl
51. Insert—bowl cavity

52. Spring—pump return
53. Pump assembly
54. Rod—pump
55. Baffle—secondary bores
56. Idle compensator assembly
57. Seal—idle compensator
58. Cover—idle compensator
59. Screw—idle compensator cover (2)
60. Filter nut—fuel inlet
61. Gasket—filter nut
62. Filter—fuel inlet
63. Spring—fuel filter
64. Screw—idle stop
65. Spring—idle stop screw
66. Idle speed solenoid & bracket assembly
67. Idle load compensator & bracket assembly
68. Bracket—throttle return spring
69. Actuator—throttle lever (truck only)
70. Bracket—throttle lever actuator (truck only)
71. Washer—actuator nut (truck only)
72. Nut—actuator attaching (truck only)
73. Screw—bracket attaching (2)
74. Throttle body assembly
75. Gasket—throttle body
76. Screw—throttle body (3)
77. Idle mixture needle & spring assy. (2)
78. Screw—fast idle adjusting
79. Spring—fast idle screw
80. Tee—vacuum hose
81. Gasket—flange

ELECTRIC CHOKE MODELS

1. Air horn assy.
2. Gasket—air horn
3. Lever—pump actuating
4. Roll pin—pump lever hinge
5. Screw—air horn long
6. Screw—air horn short
7. Screw—air horn countersunk
8. Metering rod—secondary
9. Holder and screw—secondary metering rod
10. Baffle—secondary air
11. Seal—pump plunger
12. Retainer—pump seal
13. Vac. break control & bracket—front
14. Screw—control attaching
15. Hose—vacuum
16. Rod—air valve
16A. Rod—air valve (truck)

17. Lever—choke rod (upper)
18. Screw—choke lever
19. Rod—choke
20. Lever—choke rod (lower)
21. Seal—intermediate choke shaft
22. Lever—secondary lockout
23. Link—rear vacuum break
24. Int. choke shaft & lever
25. Cam—fast idle
26. Seal—choke housing to bowl (hot air choke)
27. Kit—choke housing
28. Screw—choke housing to bowl
29. Seal—intermediate choke shaft (hot air choke)
30. Lever—choke coil
31. Screw—choke coil lever
32. Gasket—stat cover (hot air choke)
33. Stat cover & coil assy. (hot air choke)

M4ME/M4MEF exploded view

and connector assembly to prevent damage to this critical electrical part.

  e. Remove spring from bottom of TPS well in float bowl.

5. Remove plastic bowl insert from float bowl.

6. Carefully lift each metering rod out of the guided metering jet, checking to be sure the return spring is removed with each metering rod.

NOTE: *Use extreme care when handling these critical parts to avoid damage to the metering rod and spring.*

7. Remove the mixture control solenoid from the float bowl as follows:

  a. Remove screw attaching solenoid connector to float bowl. Do not remove solenoid connector from float bowl until called for in text.

  b. Use Tool J-28696-10, BT-7928, or equivalent, to remove lean mixture (solenoid) screw. Do not remove plunger return spring or connector and wires from the solenoid body. The mixture control solenoid, with plunger and connector, is only serviced as a complete assembly.

  c. Remove rubber gasket from top of solenoid connector and discard.

  d. Remove solenoid screw tension spring (next to float hanger pin).

8. Remove float assembly and float needle by pulling up on retaining pin. Remove needle and seat and gasket using set remover Tool J-22769, BT-3006M, or equivalent.

9. Remove large mixture control solenoid tension spring from boss on bottom of float bowl located between guided metering jets.

10. If necessary, remove the primary main metering jets using special Tool J-28696-4, BT-7928, or equivalent.

NOTE: *Use care installing tool on jet, to prevent damage to the metering rod guide (upper area), and locating tool over vertical float sections on lower area of jet. Also, no attempt should be made to remove the secondary metering jets (metering orifice plates). These jets are fixed and, if damaged, entire bowl replacement is required.*

11. Remove pump discharge check ball retainer and turn bowl upside down, catching discharge ball as if falls.

12. Remove secondary air baffle, if replaced is required.

13. Remove pump well fill slot baffle only if necessary.

Choke Disassembly

The tamper-resistant choke cover is used to discourage unnecessary readjustment of the choke thermostatic cover and coil assembly. However, if it is necessary to remove the cover

and coil assembly during normal carburetor disassembly for cleaning and normal carburetor disassembly for cleaning and overhaul, the procedures below should be followed.

1. Support float bowl and throttle body, as an assembly, on a suitable holding fixture such as Tool J-9789-118, BT-30-15, or equivalent.

2. Carefully align a $5/32$ in. drill (.159 in.) on rivet head and drill only enough to remove rivet head. Drill the two remaining rivet heads, then use a drift and small hammer to drive the remainder of the rivets out of the choke housing.

NOTE: *Use care in drilling to prevent damage to the choke cover or housing.*

3. Remove the two conventional retainers, retainer with tab, and choke cover assembly from choke housing.

4. Remove choke housing assembly from float bowl by removing retaining screw and washer inside the choke housing. The complete choke assembly can be removed from the float bowl by sliding outward.

5. Remove secondary throttle valve lockout lever from float bowl.

6. Remove lower choke lever from inside float bowl cavity by inverting bowl.

7. To disassemble intermediate choke shaft from choke housing, remove coil lever retaining screw at end of shaft inside the choke housing. Remove thermostatic coil lever from flats on intermediate choke shaft.

8. Remove intermediate choke shaft from the choke housing by sliding it outward. The fast idle cam can now be removed from the intermediate choke shaft. Remove the cup seal from the float bowl cleaning purposes. DO NOT ATTEMPT TO REMOVE THE INSERT!

9. Remove fuel inlet nut, gasket, check valve, filter assembly and spring. Discard Check valve filter assembly and gasket.

10. Remove three throttle body-to-bowl attaching screws and lock washers and remove throttle body assembly.

11. Remove throttle body-to-bowl insulator gasket.

Throttle Body Disassembly

Place throttle body assembly on carburetor holding fixture to avoid damage to throttle valves.

1. Remove pump rod from the throttle lever by rotating the rod until the tang on the rod aligns with the slot in the lever.

2. Use Tool J-29030-B, BT-7610B, or equivalent, to remove idle mixture needles for thorough throttle body cleaning.

3. Further disassembly of the throttle body is not required for cleaning purposes. The throttle valve screws are permanently staked in

place and should not be removed. The throttle body is serviced as a complete assembly.

Carburetor Reassembly

1. Install the lower end of the pump rod in the throttle lever by aligning the tang on the rod with the slot in the lever. The end of the rod should point outward toward the throttle lever.

2. Install idle mixture needles and springs using Tool J–29030–B, BT–7610B, or equivalent. Lightly seat each needle and then turn counterclockwise the number of specified turns, the final idle mixture adjustment is made on the vehicle.

3. If a new float bowl assembly is used, stamp or engrave the model number on the new float bowl. Install new throttle body-to-bowl insulator gasket over two locating dowels on bowl.

4. Install throttle body making certain throttle body is properly located over dowels on float bowl. Install three throttle body-to-bowl screws and lock washers and tighten evenly and securely.

5. Place carburetor on proper holding fixture such as J–9789–118, BT–30–15 or equivalent.

6. Install fuel inlet filter spring, a new check valve filter assembly, new gasket and inlet nut. Tighten nut to 18 ft. lbs. (24 Nm).

NOTE: *When installing a service replacement filter, make sure the filter is the type that includes the check valve to meet government safety standard. New service replacement filters with check valve meet this requirement. When properly installed, the hole in the filter faces toward the inlet nut. Ribs on the closed end of the filter element prevent it from being installed incorrectly, unless forced. Tightening beyond the specified torque can damage the nylon gasket.*

7. Install a new cup seal into the insert on the side of the float bowl for the intermediate choke shaft. The lip on the cup seal faces outward.

8. Install the secondary throttle valve lockout lever on the boss of the float bowl, with the recess hole in the lever facing inward.

9. Install the fast idle cam on the intermediate choke shaft (steps on cam face downward).

10. Carefully install fast idle cam and intermediate choke shaft assembly in the choke housing. Install the thermostatic coil lever on the flats on the intermediate choke shaft. Inside thermostatic choke coil lever is properly aligned when both inside and outside levers face toward the fuel inlet. Install inside lever retain-

ing screw into the end of the intermediate choke shaft.

11. Install lower choke rod (inner) lever into cavity in float bowl.

12. Install choke housing to bowl, sliding intermediate choke shaft into lower (inner) lever. Tool J–23417, BT–6911 or equivalent, can be used to hold the lower choke lever in correct position while installing the choke housing. The intermediate choke shaft lever and fast idle cam are in correct position when the tang on lever is beneath the fast idle cam.

13. Install choke housing retaining screws and washers. Check linkage for freedom of movement. Do not install choke cover and coil assembly until inside coil lever is adjusted.

14. If removed, install air baffle in secondary side of float bowl with notches toward the top. Top edge of baffle must be flush with bowl casting.

15. If removed, install baffle inside of the pump well with slot toward the bottom.

16. Install pump discharge check ball and retainer screw in the passage next to the pump well.

17. If removed, carefully install primary main metering jets in bottom of float bowl using Tool J–28696–4, BT–7928, or equivalent.

NOTE: *Use care in installing jets to prevent damage to metering rod guide.*

18. Install large mixture control solenoid tension spring over boss on bottom of float bowl.

19. Install needle seat assembly, with gasket, using seat installer J–22769, BT–3006M, or equivalent.

20. To make adjustment easier, carefully bend float arm before assembly.

21. Install float needle onto float arm by sliding float lever under needle pull clip. Proper installation of the needle pull clip is to hook the clip over the edge of the float on the float arm facing the float pontoon.

22. Install float hinge pin into float arm with end of loop of pin facing pump well. Install float assembly by aligning needle in the seat, and float hinge pin into locating channels in float bowl. DO NOT install float needle pull clip into holes in float arm.

23. Make a float level adjustment as necessary.

24. Install mixture control solenoid screw tension spring between raised bosses next to float hanger pin.

25. Install mixture control solenoid and connector assembly as follows:

   a. Install new rubber gasket on top of solenoid connector.

   b. Install solenoid carefully in the float chamber, aligning pin on end of solenoid with hole in raised boss at bottom of bowl. Align solenoid connector wires to fit in slot in bowl.

c. Install lean mixture (solenoid) screw through hole in solenoid bracket and tension spring in bowl, engaging first six screw threads to assure proper thread engagement.

d. Install mixture control solenoid gauging Tool J–33815–1, BT–8253–A, or equivalent over the throttle side metering jet rod guide, and temporarily install solenoid plunger.

e. Holding the solenoid plunger against the Solenoid Stop, use Tool J–28696–10, BT–7928, or equivalent, to turn the lean mixture (solenoid) screw slowly clockwise, until the solenoid plunger just contacts the gauging tool. The adjustment is correct when the solenoid plunger is contacting BOTH the Solenoid Stop and the Gauging Tool.

f. Remove solenoid plunger and gauging tool.

26. Install connector attaching screw, but DO NOT over tighten, as that could cause damage to the connector.

27. Install Throttle Position Sensor return spring in bottom of well in float bowl.

28. Install Throttle Position Sensor and connector assembly in float bowl by aligning groove in electrical connector with slot in float bowl casting. Push down on connector and sensor assembly so that connector and wires are located below bowl casting surface.

29. Install plastic bowl insert over float valve, pressing downward until properly seated (flush with bowl casting surface).

30. Slide metering rod return spring over metering rod tip until small end of spring stops against shoulder on rod. Carefully install metering rod and spring assembly through holding in plastic bowl insert and gently lower the metering rod into the guided metering jet, until large end of spring seats on the recess on end of jet guide.

CAUTION: *Do not force metering rod down in jet. Use extreme care when handling these critical parts to avoid damage to rod and spring. if service replacement metering rods, springs and jets are installed, they must be installed in matched sets.*

31. Install pump return spring in pump well.

32. Install pump plunger assembly in pump well.

33. Holding down on pump plunger assembly against return spring tension, install air horn gasket by aligning pump plunger stem with hole in gasket, and aligning holes in gasket over TPS plunger, solenoid plunger return spring metering rods, solenoid attaching screw and electrical connector. Position gasket over the two dowel locating pins on the float bowl.

34. Holding down on air horn gasket and pump plunger assembly, install the solenoid-metering rod plunger in the solenoid, aligning slot in end of plunger with solenoid attaching screw. Be sure plunger arms engage top of each metering.

35. If a service replacement Mixture Control Solenoid package is installed, the solenoid and plunger MUST be installed as a matched set.

Air Horn Assembly

1. If removed, install TPS adjustment screw in air horn using Tool J–28696–10, BT–7967A, or equivalent. Final adjustment of the Throttle Position Sensor is made on the vehicle.

2. Inspect the air valve shaft pin for lubrication. Apply a liberal quantity of lithium base grease to the air valve shaft pin, especially in the area contacted by the air valve spring.

3. Install new pump plunger and TPS plunger seals and retainers in air horn casting. The lip on the seal faces outward, away from the air horn mounting surface. Lightly stake seal retainer in three places, choosing locations different from the original staking.

4. Install rich mixture stop screw and rich authority adjusting spring from bottom side of the air horn. Use Tool J–2869–4, BT–7967A, or equivalent, to bottom the stop screw lightly, then back out 1/4 turn. Final adjustment procedure will be covered later in this section.

5. Install TPS actuator plunger in the seal.

6. Carefully lower the air horn assembly onto the float bowl while positioning the TPS Adjustment Lever over the TPS sensor and guiding pump plunger stem through the seal in the air horn casting. To ease installation, insert a thin screwdriver between the air horn gasket and float bowl to raise the TPS Adjustment Lever, positioning it over the TPS sensor.

7. Make sure that the bleed tubes and accelerating well tubes are positioned properly through the holes in the air horn gasket. Do not force the air horn assembly onto the bowl, but lower it lightly into place over the two dowel locating pins.

8. Install two long air horn screws and lock washers, nine short screws and lock washers and two countersunk screws located next to the carburetor venturi area. Install secondary air baffle beneath the No. 3 and 4 screws. Tighten all screws evenly and securely.

9. Install air valve rod into slot in the lever on the end of the air valve shaft. Install the other end of the rod in hole in front vacuum break plunger. Install front vacuum break and bracket assembly on the air horn, using two at-

taching screws. Tighten screw securely. Connect pump link to pump lever and install retainer.

NOTE: *Use care installing the roll pin to prevent damage to the pump lever bearing surface and casting bosses.*

10. Install two secondary metering rods into the secondary metering rod hanger (upper end of rods point toward each other). Install secondary metering rod holder, with rods, onto air valve cam follower. Install retaining screw and tighten securely. Work air valves up and down several times to make sure they remove freely in both directions.

11. Connect choke rod into lower choke lever inside bowl cavity. Install choke rod in slot in upper choke lever, and position lever on end of choke shaft, making sure flats on end of shaft align with flats in lever. Install attaching screw and tighten securely. When properly installed, the number on the lever will face outward.

12. Adjust the rich mixture stop screw:

a. Insert external float gauging Tool J–34935–1,BT–8420A, or equivalent, in the vertical D–shaped vent hole in the air horn casting (next to the idle air bleed valve) and allow it to float freely.

b. Read (at eye level) the mark on the gauge, in inches, that lines up with the tip of the air horn casting.

c. Lightly press down on gauge, and again read and record the mark on the gauge that lines up with the top of the air horn casting.

d. Subtract gauge UP dimension, found in Step b, from gauge DOWN dimension, found in Step c, and record the difference in inches. This difference in dimension is the total solenoid plunger travel.

e. Insert Tool J–28696–10, BT–7928, or equivalent, in the access hole in the air horn, and adjust the rich mixture stop screw to obtain $1/8$ in. total solenoid plunger travel.

13. With the solenoid plunger travel correctly set, install the plugs supplied in the service kit into the air horn to retain the setting and prevent fuel vapor loss:

a. Install the plug, hollow end down, into the access hole to the lean mixture (solenoid) screw and use a suitably sized punch to drive the plug into the air horn until top of plug is even with the lower edge of the hole chamber.

b. In a similar manner, install the plug over the rich mixture screw access hole and drive the plug into place so that the tip of the plug is $1/16$ in. below the surface of the air horn casting.

14. Install the Idle Air Bleed Valve as follows:

a. Lightly coat two new O-ring seals with automatic transmission fluid, to aid in their installation on the idle air bleed valve body. The thick seal goes in the upper groove and the thin seal goes in the lower groove.

b. Install the idle air bleed valve in the air horn, making sure that there is proper thread engagement.

c. Insert idle air bleed valve gauging Tool J–33815–2, BT–8353B, or equivalent, in throttle side D-shaped vent hole of the air horn casting. The upper end of the tool should be positioned over the open cavity next to the idle air bleed valve.

d. Hold the gauging tool down lightly so that the solenoid plunger is against the solenoid stop, then adjust the idle air bleed valve so that the gauging tool will pivot over and just contact the top of the valve.

e. Remove the gauging tool.

f. The final adjustment of the idle air bleed valve is made on the vehicle to obtain idle mixture control.

15. Perform the Air Valve Spring Adjustment and Choke coil Lever Adjustment as previously described.

16. Install the cover and coil assembly in the choke housing, as follows:

a. Place the cam follower on the highest step of the fast idle cam.

b. Install the thermostatic cover and coil assembly in the choke housing, making sure the coil tang engages the inside coil pickup lever. Ground contact for the electric choke is provided by a metal plate located at the rear of the choke cover assembly. DO NOT install a choke cover gasket between the electric choke assembly and the choke housing.

c. A choke cover retainer kit is required to attach the choke cover to the choke housing. Follow the instructions found in the kit and install the proper retainer and rivets using a suitable blind rivet tool.

d. It may be necessary to use an adapter (tube) if the installing tool interferes with the electrical connector tower on the choke cover.

17. Install the hose on the front vacuum brake and on the tube on the float bowl.

18. Position the idle speed solenoid and bracket assembly on the float bowl, retaining it with two large countersunk screws.

19. Perform the Choke Rod-Fast Idle Cam Adjustment, Primary (Front) Vacuum Break Adjustment, Air Valve Rod Adjustment-Front, Unloader Adjustment and the Secondary Lockout Adjustment as previously described.

20. Reinstall the carburetor on the vehicle with a new flange gasket.

GASOLINE FUEL INJECTION SYSTEM

General Information

The electronic fuel injection system is a fuel metering system with the amount of fuel delivered by the throttle body injectors (TBI) determined by an electronic signal supplied by the Electronic Control Module (ECM). The ECM monitors various engine and vehicle conditions to calculate the fuel delivery time (pulse width) of the injectors. The fuel pulse may be modified by the ECM to account for special operating conditions, such as cranking, cold starting, altitude, acceleration, and deceleration.

The ECM controls the exhaust emissions by modifying fuel delivery to achieve, as near as possible, and air/fuel ratio of 14.7 to 1. The injector "ON" time is determined by various inputs to the ECM. By increasing the injector pulse, more fuel is delivered, enriching the air/fuel ratio. Decreasing the injector pulse, leans the air/fuel ratio. Pulses are sent to the injector in two different modes: synchronized and nonsynchronized.

Synchronized Mode

In synchronized mode operation, the injector is pulsed once for each distributor reference pulse.

Nonsynchronized Mode

In nonsynchronized mode operation, the injector is pulsed once every 12.5 milliseconds or 6.25 milliseconds depending on calibration. This pulse time is totally independent of distributor reference pulses.

Nonsynchronized mode results only under the following conditions.

1. The fuel pulse width is too small to be delivered accurately by the injector (approximately 1.5 milliseconds).
2. During the delivery of prime pulses (prime pulses charge the intake manifold with fuel during or just prior to engine starting).
3. During acceleration enrichment.
4. During deceleration leanout.

The basic TBI unit is made up of two major casting assemblies: (1) a throttle body with a valve to control airflow and (2) a fuel body assembly with an integral pressure regulator and fuel injector to supply the required fuel. An electronically operated device to control the idle speed and a device to provide information regarding throttle valve position are included as part of the TBI unit.

The fuel injector(s) is a solenoid-operated device controlled by the ECM. The incoming fuel is directed to the lower end of the injector assembly which has a fine screen filter surrounding the injector inlet. The ECM actuates the solenoid, which lifts a normally closed ball valve off a seat. The fuel under pressure is injected in a conical spray pattern at the walls of the throttle body bore above the throttle valve. The excess fuel passes through a pressure regulator before being returned to the vehicle fuel tank.

The pressure regulator is a diaphragm-operated relief valve with injector pressure on one side and air cleaner pressure on the other. The function of the regulator is to maintain a constant pressure drop across the injector throughout the operating load and speed range of the engine.

The throttle body portion of the TBI may contain ports located at, above, or below the throttle valve. These ports generate the vacuum signals for the EGR valve, MAP sensor, and the canister purge system.

The throttle position sensor (TPS) is a variable resistor used to convert the degree of throttle plate opening to an electrical signal to the ECM. The ECM uses this signal as a reference point of throttle valve position. In addition, an idle air control assembly (IAC), mounted in the throttle body is used to control idle speeds. A cone-shaped valve in the IAC assembly is located in an air passage in the throttle body that leads from the point beneath the air cleaner to below the throttle valve. The ECM monitors idle speeds and, depending on engine load, moves the IAC cone in the air passage to increase or decrease air bypassing the throttle valve to the intake manifold for control of idle speeds.

COMPONENTS AND OPERATION

The throttle body injection (TBI) system provides a means of fuel distribution for controlling exhaust emissions within legislated limits by precisely controlling the air/fuel mixture and under all operating conditions for, as near as possible, complete combustion.

This is accomplished by using an Electronic Control Module (ECM) – a small "on-board" microcomputer – that receives electrical inputs from various sensors about engine operating conditions. An oxygen sensor in the main exhaust stream functions to provide "feedback" information to the ECM as to the oxygen content, lean or rich, in the exhaust. The ECM uses this information from the oxygen sensor, and other sensors, to modify fuel delivery to achieve, as near as possible, an ideal air/fuel ratio of 14.7:1. This air/fuel ratio allows the three-way catalytic converter to be more efficient in the conversion process of reducing exhaust emissions while at the same time providing acceptable levels of driveability and fuel economy.

The ECM program electronically signals the fuel injector in the TBI assembly to provide the correct quantity of fuel for a wide range of operating conditions. Several sensors are used to determine existing operating conditions and the ECM then signals the injector to provide the precise amount of fuel required.

The ECM used on EFI vehicles has a "learning" capability. If the battery is disconnected to clear diagnostic codes, or for repair, the "learning" process has to begin all over again. A change may be noted in vehicle performance. To "teach" the vehicle, make sure the vehicle is at operating temperature and drive at part throttle, under moderate acceleration and idle conditions, until performance returns.

With the EFI system the TBI assembly is centrally located on the intake manifold where air and fuel are distributed through a single bore in the throttle body, similar to a carbureted engine. Air for combustion is controlled by a single throttle valve which is connected to the accelerator pedal linkage by a throttle shaft and lever assembly. A special plate is located directly beneath the throttle valve to aid in mixture distribution.

Fuel for combustion is supplied by a single fuel injector, mounted on the TBI assembly, whose metering tip is located directly above the throttle valve. The injector is "pulsed" or "timed" open or closed by an electronic output signal received from the ECM. The ECM receives inputs concerning engine operating conditions from the various sensors (coolant temperature sensor, oxygen sensor, etc.). The ECM, using this information, performs high speed calculations of engine fuel requirements and "pulses" or "times" the injector , open or closed, thereby controlling fuel and air mixtures to achieve, as near as possible, ideal air/fuel mixture ratios.

When the ignition key is turned on, the ECM will initialize (start program running) and energize the fuel pump relay. The fuel pump pressurizes the system to approximately 10 psi. If the ECM does not receive a distributor reference pulse (telling the ECM the engine is turning) within two seconds, the ECM will then de-energize the fuel pump relay, turning off the fuel pump. If a distributor reference pulse is later received, the ECM will turn the fuel pump back on.

Cranking Mode

During engine crank, for each distributor reference pulse the ECM will deliver an injector pulse (synchronized). The crank air/fuel ratio will be used if the throttle position is less than 80% open. Crank air fuel is determined by the ECM and ranges from 1.5:1 at –33°F (–36°C) to 14.7:1 at 201°F (94°C).

The lower the coolant temperature, the longer the pulse width (injector on-time) or richer the air/fuel ratio. The higher the coolant temperature, the less pulse width (injector on-time) or the leaner the air/fuel ratio.

Clear Flood Mode

If for some reason the engine should become flooded, provisions have been made to clear this condition. To clear the flood, the driver must depress the accelerator pedal enough to open to wide-open throttle position. The ECM then issues injector pulses at a rate that would be equal to an air/fuel ratio of 20:1. The ECM maintains this injector rate as long as the throttle remains wide open and the engine RPM is below 600. If the throttle position becomes less than 80%, the ECM then would immediately start issuing crank pulses to the injector calculated by the ECM based on the coolant temperature.

Run Mode

There are two different run modes. When the engine RPM is above 600, the system goes into open loop operation. In open loop operation, the ECM will ignore the signal from the oxygen (O_2) sensor and calculate the injector on-time based upon inputs from the coolant and MAP sensors.

During open loop operation, the ECM analyzes the following items to determine when the system is ready to go to the closed loop mode.

1. The oxygen sensor varying voltage output. (This is dependent on temperature).

2. The coolant sensor must be above specified temperature.

3. A specific amount of time must elapse after starting the engine. These values are stored in the PROM.

When these conditions have been met, the system goes into closed loop operation In closed loop operation, the ECM will modify the pulse width (injector on-time) based upon the signal from the oxygen sensor. The ECM will decrease the on-time if the air/fuel ratio is too rich, and will increase the on-time if the air/fuel ratio is too lean.

The pulse width, thus the amount of enrichment, is determined by manifold pressure change, throttle angle change, and coolant temperature. The higher the manifold pressure and the wider the throttle opening, the wider the pulse width. The acceleration enrichment pulses are delivered nonsynchronized.

Any reduction in throttle angle will cancel the enrichment pulses. This way, quick movements of the accelerator will not over-enrich the mixture.

Acceleration Enrichment

When the engine is required to accelerate, the opening of the throttle valve(s) causes a rapid increase in manifold absolute pressure (MAP). This rapid increase in MAP causes fuel to condense on the manifold walls. The ECM senses this increase in throttle angle and MAP, and supplies additional fuel for a short period of time. This prevents the engine from stumbling due to too lean a mixture.

Deceleration Leanout

Upon deceleration, a leaner fuel mixture is required to reduce emission of hydrocarbons (H) and carbon monoxide (CO). To adjust the injection on-time, the ECM uses the decrease in MAP and the decrease in throttle position to calculate a decrease in pulse width. To maintain an idle fuel ratio of 14.7:1, fuel output is momentarily reduced. This is done because of the fuel remaining in the intake manifold.

Deceleration Fuel Cut-Off

The purpose of deceleration fuel cut-off is to remove fuel from the engine during extreme deceleration conditions. Deceleration fuel cut-off is based on values of manifold pressure, throttle position, and engine RPM stored in the calibration PROM. Deceleration fuel cut-off overrides the deceleration enleanment mode.

Battery Voltage Correction

The purpose of battery voltage correction is to compensate for variations in battery voltage to fuel pump and injector response. The ECM modifies the pulse width by a correction factor in the PROM. When battery voltage decreases, pulse width increases.

Battery voltage correction takes place in all operating modes. When battery voltage is low, the spark delivered by the distributor may be low. To correct this low battery voltage problem, the ECM can do any or all of the following:

a. Increase injector pulse width (increase fuel).

b. Increase idle RPM.

c. Increase ignition dwell time.

Fuel Cut-Off

When the ignition is off, the ECM will not energize the injector. Fuel will also be cut off if the ECM does not receive a reference pulse from the distributor. To prevent dieseling, fuel delivery is completely stopped as soon as the engine is stopped. The ECM will not allow any fuel supply until it receives distributor reference pulses which prevents flooding.

ELECTRONIC FUEL INJECTION SUBSYSTEMS

Electronic fuel injection (EFI) is the name given to the entire fuel injection system. Various "subsystems" are combined to form the overall system. These subsystems are:

1. Fuel Supply System.
2. Throttle Body Injector Assembly (TBI).
3. Idle Air Control (IAC).
4. Electronic Control Module (ECM).
5. Data Sensors.
6. Electronic Spark Timing (EST).
7. Emission Controls.

Each subsystem is described in the following paragraphs.

Fuel Supply System

Fuel, supplied by an electric fuel pump mounted in the fuel tank, passes through an in-line fuel filter to the TBI assembly. To control fuel pump operation, a fuel pump rely is used.

When the ignition switch is turned to the ON position the fuel pump relay activates the electric fuel pump for 1.5–2.0 seconds to prime the injector. If the ECM does not receive reference pulses from the distributor after this time, the ECM signals the relay to turn the fuel pump off. The relay will once again activate the fuel pump when the ECM receives distributor reference pulses.

The oil pressure sender is the backup for the fuel pump relay. The sender has two circuits, one for the instrument cluster light or gauge, the other to activate the fuel pump if the relay fails. If the fuse relay has failed, the sender activates the fuel pump when oil pressure reaches 4 psi. Thus a failed fuel pump relay would cause a longer crank, especially in cold weather. If the fuel pump fails, a no start condition exists.

Throttle Body Injector (TBI) Assembly

The basic TBI unit is made up of two major casting assemblies:

1. A throttle body with a valve to control airflow and

2. A fuel body assembly with an integral pressure regulator and fuel injector to supply the required fuel. A device to control idle speed (IAC) and a device to provide information about throttle valve position (TPS) are included as part of the TBI unit.

The throttle body portion of the TBI unit may contain ports located at, above, or below the throttle valve. These ports generate the vacuum signals for the EGR valve, MAP sensor, and the canister purge system.

The fuel injector is a solenoid-operated device controlled by the ECM. The incoming fuel is directed to the lower end of the injector assembly which has a fine screen filter surrounding the injector inlet. The ECM turns on the solenoid, which lifts a normally closed ball valve off a seat. The fuel, under pressure, is injected in a conical spray pattern at the walls of the throttle body bore above the throttle valve. The excess fuel passes through a pressure regulator before being returned to the vehicle fuel tank.

The pressure regulator is a diaphragm-operated relief valve with the injector pressure on one side, and the air cleaner pressure on the other. The function of the regulator is to maintain constant pressure (approximately 11 psi) to the injector throughout the operating loads and speed ranges of the engine. If the regulator pressure is too low, below 9 psi, it can cause poor performance. Too high a pressure could cause detonation and a strong fuel odor.

Idle Air Control (IAC)

The purpose of the idle air control (IAC) system is to control engine idle speeds while preventing stalls due to changes in engine load. The IAC assembly, mounted on the throttle body, controls bypass air around the throttle plate. By extending or retracting a conical valve, a controlled amount of air can move around the throttle plate. If RPM is too low, more air is diverted around the throttle plate to increase RPM.

During idle, the proper position of the IAC valve is calculated by the ECM based on battery voltage, coolant temperature, engine load, and engine RPM. If the RPM drops below a specified rate, the throttle plate is closed. The ECM will then calculate a new valve position.

Three different designs are used for the IAC conical valve. The first design used is single 35 taper while the second design used is a dual taper. The third design is a blunt valve. Care should be taken to insure use of the correct design when service replacement is required.

The IAC motor has 255 different positions or steps. The zero, or reference position, is the fully extended position at which the pintle is seated in the air bypass seat and no air is allowed to bypass the throttle plate. When the motor is fully retracted, maximum air is allowed to bypass the throttle plate. When the motor is fully retracted, maximum air is allowed to bypass the throttle plate.

The ECM always monitors how many steps it has extended or retracted the pintle from the zero or reference position; thus, it always calculates the exact position of the motor. Once the engine has started and the vehicle has reached approximately 40 MPH, the ECM will extend the motor 255 steps from whatever position it is in. This will bottom out the pintle against the seat. The ECM will call this position "0" and thus keep its zero reference updated.

The IAC only affects the engine's idle characteristics. If it is stuck fully open, idle speed is too high (too much air enters the throttle bore) If it is stuck closed, idle speed is too low (not enough air entering). If it is stuck somewhere in the middle, idle may be rough, and the engine won't respond to load changes.

Idle Speed Control

Incorrect diagnosis and/or misunderstanding of the idle speed control systems used on EFI engines may lead to unnecessary replacement of the IAC valve. Engine idle speed is controlled by the ECM which changes the idle speed by moving the IAC valve. The ECM adjusts idle speed in response to fluctuations in engine load (A/C, power steering, electrical loads, etc.) to maintain acceptable idle quality and proper exhaust emission performance.

The following is provided to assist the technician to better understand the system and correctly respond to the following customer concerns:

   1. Rough Idle/Low Idle Speed.
   2. High Idle Speed/Warm-up Idle Speed; No "Kickdown".

Rough Idle/Low Idle Speed

The ECM will respond to increases in engine load, which would cause a drop in idle speed, by moving the IAC valve to maintain proper idle speed. After the induced load is removed the ECM will return the idle speed to the proper level.

During A/C compressor operation. (MAX, BI-LEVEL, NORM or DEFROST mode) the ECM will increase idle speed in response to an "A/C-ON" signal, thereby compensating for any drop in idle speed due to compressor load. The ECM will also increase the idle speed models in response to high power steering loads.

During periods of especially heavy loads (A/C-ON plus parking maneuvers) significant effects on idle quality may be experienced. Abnormally low idle, rough idle and idle shake may occur if the ECM does not receive the proper signals from the monitored systems.

High Idle Speed/Warm-Up Idle Speed (No "Kickdown")

Engine idle speeds as high as 2,100 RPM may be experienced during cold starts to quickly raise the catalytic converter to operating temperature for proper exhaust emissions performance. The idle speed attained after a cold start is ECM-controlled and will not drop for 45 seconds regardless of diver attempts to "kickdown."

It is important to recognize the EFI engines have no accelerator pump or choke. Idle speed during warm-up is entirely ECM-controlled and cannot be changed by accelerator "kickdown" or "pumping".

DIAGNOSIS

Abnormally low idle speeds are usually caused by an ECM system-controlled or monitored irregularity, while the most common cause for abnormally high idle speed is an induction (intake air) leak. The idle air control valve may occasionally lose its memory function, and it has an ECM-programmed method of "relearning" the correct idle position. This reset, when required, will occur the next time the car exceeds 35 MPH. At this time the ECM seats the pintle of the IAC valve in the throttle body to determine a reference point. Then it backs out a fixed distance to maintain proper idle speed.

Electronic Control Module (ECM)

The ECM, located in the passenger compartment, is the control center of the fuel injection system. The ECM constantly monitors the input information, processes this information from various sensors, and generates output commands to the various systems that affect vehicle performance.

The ability of the ECM to recognize and adjust for vehicle variations (engine transmission, vehicle weight, axle ratio, etc.) is provided by a removable calibration unit (PROM) that is programmed to tailor the ECM for the particular vehicle. There is a specific ECM/PROM combination for each specific vehicle, and the combinations are not interchangeable with those of other vehicles.

The ECM also performs the diagnostic function of the system. It can recognize operational problems, alert the driver through the "CHECK ENGINE" light, and store a code or codes which identify the problem areas to aid the technician in making repairs.

DATA SENSORS

A variety of sensors provide information to the ECM regarding engine operating characteristics. These sensors and their functions are described below.

Engine Coolant Temperature

The coolant sensor is a thermistor (a resistor which changes value based on temperature) mounted on the engine coolant stream. As the temperature of the engine coolant changes, the resistance of the coolant sensor changes. Low coolant temperature produces a high resistance (100,000 ohms at −40°C/−40°F), while high temperature causes low resistance (70 ohms at 130°C/266°F).

The ECM supplies a 5-volt signal to the coolant sensor and measures the voltage that returns. By measuring the voltage change, the ECM determines the engine coolant temperature. This information is used to control fuel management, IAC, spark timing, EGR, canister purge and other engine operating conditions.

Oxygen Sensor

The exhaust oxygen sensor is mounted in the exhaust system where it can monitor the oxygen content of the exhaust gas stream. The oxygen content in the exhaust reacts with the oxygen sensor to produce a voltage output. This voltage ranges from approximately 100 millivolts (high oxygen - lean mixture) to 900 millivolts (low oxygen - rich mixture).

By monitoring the voltage output of the oxygen sensor, the ECM will determine what fuel mixture command to give to the injector (lean mixture-low voltage-rich command, rich mixture-high voltage lean command).

Remember that oxygen sensor indicates to the ECM what is happening in the exhaust. It does not cause things to happen. It is a type of gauge: high oxygen content = lean mixture; low oxygen content = rich mixture. The ECM adjust fuel to keep the system working.

MAP Sensor

The manifold absolute pressure (MAP) sensor measures the changes in the intake manifold pressure which result from engine load and speed changes. The pressure measured by the MAP sensor is the difference between barometric pressure (outside air) and manifold pressure (vacuum). A closed throttle engine coastdown would produce a relatively low MAP value (approximately 20–35 kPa), while wide-open throttle would produce a high value (100 kPa). This high value is produced when the pressure inside the manifold is the same as outside the manifold, and 100% of outside air (or 100 kPa) is being measured. This MAP output is the opposite of what you would measure on a vacuum gauge. The use of this sensor also allows the ECM to adjust automatically for different altitude.

The ECM sends a 5-volt reference signal to

the MAP sensor. As the MAP changes, the electrical resistance of the sensor also changes. By monitoring the sensor output voltage the ECM can determine the manifold pressure. A higher pressure, lower vacuum (high voltage) requires more fuel, while a lower pressure, higher vacuum (low voltage) requires less fuel.

Vehicle Speed Sensor (VSS)

NOTE: *Vehicle should not be driven without a VSS as idle quality may be affected.*

The vehicle speed sensor (VSS) is mounted behind the speedometer in the instrument cluster. It provides electrical pulses to the ECM from the speedometer head. The pulses indicate the road speed. The ECM uses this information to operate the IAC, canister purge, and TCC.

Some vehicles equipped with digital instrument clusters use a permanent magnet (PM) generator to provide the VSS signal. The PM generator is located in the transmission and replaces the speedometer cable. The signal from the PM generator drives a stepper motor which drives the odometer.

Throttle Position Sensor (TPS)

The throttle position sensor (TPS) is connected to the throttle shaft and is controlled by the throttle mechanism. A 5-volt reference signal is sent to the TPS from the ECM. As the throttle valve angle is changed (accelerator pedal moved), the resistance of the TPS also changes. At a closed throttle position, the resistance of the TPS is high, so the output voltage to the ECM will be low (approximately 0.5 volt). As the throttle plate opens, the resistance decreases so that, at wide open throttle, the output voltage should be approximately 5 volts.

By monitoring the output voltage from the TPS, the ECM can determine fuel delivery based on throttle valve angle (driver demand). The TPS can either be misadjusted, shorted, open or loose. Misadjustment might result in poor idle or poor wide-open throttle performance. An open TPS signals the ECM that the throttle is always closed, resulting in poor performance. This usually sets a Code 22. A shorted TPS gives the ECM a constant wide-open throttle signal and should set a Code 21. A loose TPS indicates to the ECM that the throttle is moving. This causes intermittent bursts of fuel from the injector and an unstable idle.

Park/Neutral Switch

NOTE: *Vehicle should not be driven with the Park/Neutral switch disconnected as idle quality may be affected in Park or Neutral.*

This switch indicates to the ECM when the transmission is in Park or Neutral.

A/C Compressor Clutch Engagement. This signal indicates to the ECM that the A/C compressor clutch is engaged.

CAUTION: *The 220 TBI unit has a bleed in the pressure regulator to relieve pressure any time the engine is turned off, however a small amount of fuel may be released when the fuel line is disconnected. As a precaution, cover the fuel line with a cloth and dispose of properly.*

Electric Fuel Pump

REMOVAL AND INSTALLATION

1. With the engine turned OFF, relieve the fuel pressure at the pressure regulator. See Warning above.
2. Disconnect the negative battery cable.
3. Raise and support the rear of the vehicle on jackstands.
4. Drain the fuel tank, then remove it.
5. Using a hammer and a drift punch, drive the fuel lever sending device and pump assembly locking ring (located on top of the fuel tank) counterclockwise, Lift the assembly from the tank and remove the pump from the fuel lever sending device.
6. Pull the pump up into the attaching hose while pulling it outward away from the bottom support. Be careful not to damage the rubber insulator and strainer during removal. After the pump assembly is clear of the bottom support, pull it out of the rubber connector.
7. To install, reverse the removal procedures.

Testing

1. Secure two sections of $3/8$ in. x 10 in. (steel tubing), with a double-flare on one end of each section.
2. Install a flare nut on each section of tubing, then connect each of the sections into the flare nut-to-flare nut adapter, while care included in the Gauge Adapter tool No. J–29658–82.
3. Attach the pipe and the adapter assembly to the Gauge tool No. J–29658.
4. Raise and support the vehicle on jackstands.
5. Remove the air cleaner and plug the THERMAC vacuum port on the TBI.
6. Disconnect the fuel feed hose between the fuel tank and the filter, then secure the other ends of the $3/8$ in. tubing into the fuel hoses with hose clamps.
7. Start the engine, check for leaks and observe the fuel pressure, it should be 9–13 psi.
8. Depressurize the fuel system, remove the testing tool, remove the plug from the TH-

ERMAC vacuum port, reconnect the fuel line, start the engine and check for fuel leaks.

Throttle Body

REMOVAL AND INSTALLATION

1. Release the fuel pressure at the pressure regulator (see Warning above).

2. Disconnect the THERMAC hose from the engine fitting and remove the air cleaner.

3. Disconnect the electrical connectors at the idle air control, throttle position sensor and the injector.

4. Disconnect the throttle linkage, return spring and cruise control (if equipped).

5. Disconnect the throttle body vacuum hoses, the fuel supply and fuel return lines.

6. Disconnect the bolts securing the throttle body, then remove it.

7. To install, reverse the removal procedures. Replace the manifold gaskets and O-rings.

Injector

REPLACEMENT

WARNING: *When removing the injectors, be careful not to damage the electrical connector pins (on top of the injector), the injector fuel filter and the nozzle. The fuel injector is serviced as a complete assembly ONLY. The injector is an electrical component and should not be immersed in any kind of cleaner.*

1. Remove the air cleaner. Relieve the fuel pressure (see Warning above).

2. At the injector connector, squeeze the two tabs together and pull straight up.

3. Remove the fuel meter cover and leave the cover gasket in place.

4. Using a small pry bar or tool No. J–

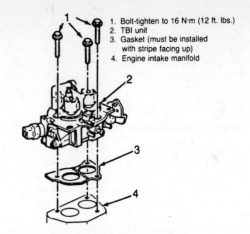

1. Bolt-tighten to 16 N·m (12 ft. lbs.)
2. TBI unit
3. Gasket (must be installed with stripe facing up)
4. Engine intake manifold

Throttle body installation on the V6

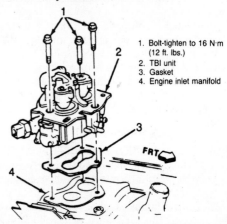

1. Bolt-tighten to 16 N·m (12 ft. lbs.)
2. TBI unit
3. Gasket
4. Engine inlet manifold

Throttle body installation on the 8-5.0L and 8-5.7L

26868, carefully lift the injector until it is free from the fuel meter body.

5. Remove the small O-ring from the nozzle end of the injector. Carefully rotate the injector's fuel filter back and forth to remove it from the base of the injector.

6. Discard the fuel meter cover gasket.

7. Remove the large O-ring and back-up washer from the top of the counterbore of the fuel meter body injector cavity.

8. To install, lubricate the O-rings with automatic transmission fluid and reverse the removal procedures.

Fuel Meter Cover

REPLACEMENT

1. Depressurize the fuel system.

2. Raise the hood, install fender covers and remove the air cleaner assembly.

3. Disconnect the negative battery cable.

4. Disconnect electrical connector at the injector by squeezing the two tabs and pulling straight up.

5. Remove the five screws securing the fuel

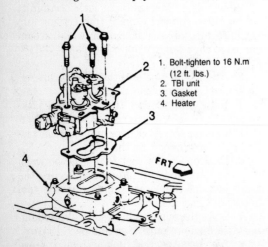

1. Bolt-tighten to 16 N.m (12 ft. lbs.)
2. TBI unit
3. Gasket
4. Heater

Throttle body installation on the 8-7.4L

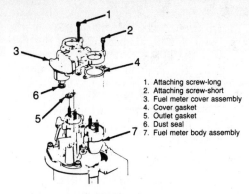

1. Attaching screw-long
2. Attaching screw-short
3. Fuel meter cover assembly
4. Cover gasket
5. Outlet gasket
6. Dust seal
7. Fuel meter body assembly

Replacing the fuel meter cover

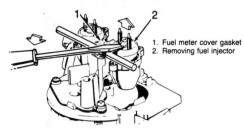

1. Fuel meter cover gasket
2. Removing fuel injector

Removing the TBI injector

meter cover to the fuel meter body. Notice the location of the two short screws during removal.

CAUTION: *Do not remove the four screws securing the pressure regulator to the fuel meter cover! The fuel pressure regulator includes a large spring under heavy tension which, if accidentally released, could cause personal injury! The fuel meter cover is serviced only as a complete assembly and includes the fuel pressure regulator preset and plugged at the factor.*

6. Remove the fuel meter cover assembly from the throttle body.

WARNING: *DO NOT immerse the fuel meter cover (with pressure regulator) in any type of cleaner! Immersion of cleaner will damage the internal fuel pressure regulator diaphragms and gaskets.*

7. Installation is the reverse of removal. Be sure to use new gaskets and torque the fuel meter cover attaching screws to 28 in. lbs.

NOTE: *The service kits include a small vial of thread locking compound with directions for use. If the material is not available, use part number 1052624, Loctite® 262, or equivalent. Do not use a higher strength locking compound than recommended, as this may prevent attaching screw removal or breakage of the screwhead if removal is again required.*

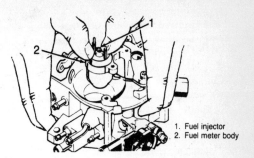

1. Fuel injector
2. Fuel meter body

Installing the TBI injector

Fuel Meter Body

REMOVAL AND INSTALLATION

1. Depressurize the fuel system.
2. Raise the hood, install fender covers and remove the air cleaner assembly.
3. Disconnect the negative battery cable.
4. Remove the fuel meter cover assembly.
5. Remove the fuel meter cover gasket, fuel meter outlet gasket and pressure regulator seal.
6. Remove the fuel injectors.
7. Remove the fuel inlet and fuel outlet nuts and gaskets from the fuel meter body.
8. Remove the three screws and lock washers, then remove the fuel meter body from the throttle assembly.

NOTE: *DO not remove the center screw and staking at each end holding the fuel distribution skirt in the throttle body. The skirt is an integral part of the throttle body and is not serviced separately.*

9. Remove the fuel meter body insulator gasket.
10. Installation is the reverse order of the removal procedure. Be sure to install new gaskets and O-rings where ever necessary. Apply thread-locking compound, Threadlock Sealer 262 or equivalent to the fuel meter retaining screws.

Throttle Position Sensor (TPS)

NOTE: *The throttle position sensor on some 1987–88 models is not adjustable. If the sensor is found out of specifications and the sensor is at fault it cannot be adjusted and should be replaced.*

REMOVAL

The Throttle Position Sensor (TPS) is an electrical unit and must not be immersed in any type of liquid solvent or cleaner. The TPS is factory adjusted and the retaining screws are spot welded in place to retain the critical setting. With these considerations, it is possible to clean the throttle body assembly without removing the TPS if care is used. Should TPS replacement be required however, proceed using the following steps:

NOTE: *On some of the earlier models, the TPS retaining screws may be removed from the outside of the throttle body, from the side of the sensor.*

1. Remove the throttle body as previously outlined in this Chapter. Invert the throttle body and place it on a clean, flat surface.

2. Using a $5/16$ in. drill bit, drill completely through the 2 TPS screw access holes in the base of the throttle body to be sure of removing the spot welds holding the TPS screws in place.

3. Remove the two TPS attaching screws, lock washers, and retainers. Then, remove the TPS sensor from the throttle body. DISCARD THE SCREWS! New screws are supplied in the service kits.

4. If necessary, remove the screw holding the Throttle Position Sensor actuator lever to the end of the throttle shaft.

5. Remove the Idle Air Control assembly and gasket from the throttle body.

NOTE: *DO NOT immerse the Idle Air Control motor in any type of cleaner and it should always be removed before throttle body cleaning. Immersion in cleaner will damage the IAC assembly. It is replaced only as a complete assembly. Further disassembly of the throttle body is not required for cleaning purposes. The throttle valve screws are permanently staked in place and should not be removed. The throttle body is serviced as a complete assembly.*

INSTALLATION

1. Place the throttle body assembly on a holding fixture to avoid damaging the throttle valve.

2. Using a new sealing gasket, install the Idle Air Control motor in the throttle body. Tighten the motor securely. DO NOT over tighten it, to prevent damage to valve.

3. If it was removed, install the Throttle Position Sensor actuator lever by aligning the flats on the lever with the flats on the end of the shaft. Install the retaining screw and tighten it securely.

NOTE: *Install the Throttle Position Sensor after completing the assembly of the throttle body unit. Use the thread locking compound supplied in the service kit on the attaching screws.*

ADJUSTMENT

1. After installing the TPS on the throttle body, install the throttle body unit on the engine.

2. Remove the EGR valve and the heat

shield from engine.

3. Disconnect the TPS harness from the TPS. Using 3, 6 in. jumpers, connect the TPS harness to the TPS.

4. With the ignition ON and the engine stopped, use a digital voltmeter to measure the voltage between the TPS terminals A and B.

5. Loosen the 2 TPS attaching screws and rotate the throttle position sensor to obtain a voltage reading of 0.525 ± 0.75 volts.

6. With the ignition OFF, remove the jumpers and reconnect the TPS harness to the TPS.

7. Install the EGR valve and heat shield on the engine, using a new gasket as necessary.

8. Install the air cleaner gasket and air cleaner on the throttle body unit.

Non-Adjustable TPS Output Check

This check should only be performed, when the throttle body or the TPS has been replaced or after the minimum idle speed has been adjusted.

1. Remove the air cleaner.

2. Disconnect the TPS harness from the TPS.

3. Using suitable jumper wires, connect a digital voltmeter J–29125–A or equivalent to TPS terminals A and B (a suitable ALDL scanner can also be used to read the TPS output voltage).

4. With the ignition ON and the engine running, the TPS voltage should be 0.450–1.25 volts at base idle to approximately 4.5 volts at wide open throttle.

5. If the reading on the TPS is out of specification, check the minimum idle speed before replacing the TPS.

6. If the voltage reading is correct, remove the voltmeter and jumper wires and reconnect the TPS connector to the sensor. Re-install the air cleaner.

Idle Air Control Valve

NOTE: *All engines except the 7.4L use a thread type IAC valve. The 7.4L is equipped with a flange type IAC valve which is attached with screws.*

REPLACEMENT

1. Remove the air cleaner.

2. Disconnect the electrical connector from the idle air control valve.

3. On the threaded type, use a $1^1/4$ in. (32mm) wrench or tool J–33031, remove the idle air control valve.

4. On the 8–7.4L engine, remove the retaining screws and remove the IAC valve.

WARNING: *Before install a new idle air control valve, measure the distance that the*

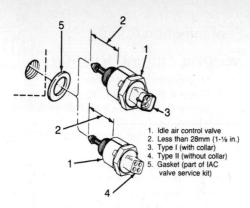

1. Idle air control valve
2. Less than 28mm (1-⅛ in.)
3. Type I (with collar)
4. Type II (without collar)
5. Gasket (part of IAC valve service kit)

Threaded type IAC valve

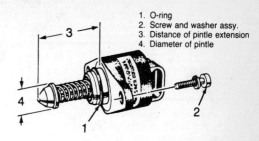

1. O-ring
2. Screw and washer assy.
3. Distance of pintle extension
4. Diameter of pintle

Flange type IAC valve

valve extends (from the motor housing to the end of the cone); the distance should be no greater than 1⅛ in. (28mm). If it extends too far, damage will occur to the valve when it is installed.

4. To adjust the threaded type without a collar compress the valve retaining spring, while turning the valve "in". On all others, exert firm pressure, with slight side to side movement, on the pintle to retract it.

5. To complete the installation, use a new gasket and reverse the removal procedures. Start the engine and allow it to reach operating temperature.

NOTE: *The ECM will reset the idle speed when the vehicle is driven at 30 mph.*

Fuel Pump Relay

REPLACEMENT

The fuel pump relay is located in the engine compartment. Other than checking for loose electrical connections, the only service necessary is to replace the relay.

Oil Pressure Switch

REPLACEMENT

The oil pressure switch is mounted to the top rear of the engine.

1. Remove the electrical connector from the switch.
2. Remove the oil pressure switch.
3. To install, reverse the removal procedures.

Minimum Idle Speed

ADJUSTMENT

Only if parts of the throttle body have been replaced should this procedure be performed; the engine should be at operating temperature.

1. Remove the air cleaner, adapter and gaskets. Discard the gaskets. Plug any vacuum line ports, as necessary.

2. Leave the idle air control (IAC) valve connected and ground the diagnostic terminal (ALDL connector).

3. Turn the ignition switch to the on position, do not start the engine. Wait for at least 30 seconds (this allows the IAC valve pintle to extend and seat in the throttle body).

4. With the ignition switch still in the on position, disconnect IAC electrical connector.

5. Remove the ground from the diagnostic terminal and start the engine. Let the engine reach normal operating temperature.

6. Apply the parking brake and block the drive wheels. Remove the plug from the idle stop screw by piercing it first with a suitable tool, then applying leverage to the tool to lift the plug out.

7. With the engine in the drive position adjust the idle stop screw to obtain the following specifications:
• 500–550 rpm in drive on models equipped with automatic transmissions.
• 600–650 rpm in neutral on models equipped with manual transmissions.

8. Turn the ignition off and reconnect the IAC valve connector. Unplug any plugged vacuum line ports and install the air cleaner, adapter and new gaskets.

DIESEL ENGINE FUEL SYSTEM

Fuel Supply Pump

REMOVAL AND INSTALLATION

The diesel fuel supply pump is serviced in the same manner as the fuel pump on the gasoline engines.

Fuel Filter

See Diesel Fuel Filter in Chapter 1 for service procedures.

WATER IN FUEL

Water is the worst enemy of the diesel fuel injection system. The injection pump, which is

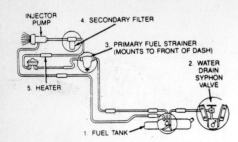

Anti-water system used on diesel engines

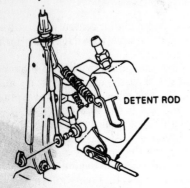

Diesel accelerator cable linkage

designed and constructed to extremely close tolerances, and the injectors can be easily damaged if enough water if forced through them in the fuel. Engine performance will also be drastically affected, and engine damage can occur.

Diesel fuel is much more susceptible than gasoline to water contamination. Diesel engined trucks are equipped with an indicator lamp system that turns on an instrument panel lamp if water (1 to $2\frac{1}{2}$ gallons) is detected in the fuel tank. The lamp will come on for 2 to 5 seconds each time the ignition is turned on, assuring the driver the lamp is working. If there is water in the fuel, the light will come back on after a 15 to 20 second off delay, and then remain on.

PURGING THE FUEL TANK

The 6.2L diesel equipped vans also have a water-in-fuel warning system. The fuel tank is equipped with a filter which screens out the water and lets it lay in the bottom of the tank below the fuel pickup. When the water level reaches a point where it could be drawn into the system, a warning light flashes in the cab. A built-in siphoning system starting at the fuel tank and going to the rear spring hanger on some models, and at the midway point of the right frame rail on other models permits you to attach a hose at the shut-off and siphon out the water.

If it becomes necessary to drain water from the fuel tank, also check the primary fuel filter for water. This procedure is covered under Diesel Fuel Filter in Chapter 1.

Fuel Injection Pump

REMOVAL AND INSTALLATION

1. Disconnect both batteries.
2. Remove the fan and fan shroud.
3. Remove the intake manifold as described in Chapter 3.
4. Remove the fuel lines as described in this Chapter.
5. Disconnect the alternator cable at the injection pump, and the detent cable (see illustration) where applicable.
6. Tag and disconnect the necessary wires and hoses at the injection pump.
7. Disconnect the fuel return line at the top of the injection pump.
8. Disconnect the fuel feed line at the injection pump.
9. Remove the air conditioning hose retainer bracket if equipped with A/C.
10. Remove the oil fill tube, including the crankcase depression valve vent hose assembly.
11. Remove the grommet.
12. Scribe or paint a match mark on the front cover and on the injection pump flange.
13. The crankshaft must be rotated in order to gain access to the injection pump drive gear bolts through the oil filler neck hole.
14. Remove the injection pump-to-front cover attaching nuts. Remove the pump and cap all open lines and nozzles.
    To install:
15. Replace the gasket. This is important.
16. Align the locating pin on the pump hub with the slot in the injection pump driven gear. At the same time, align the timing marks.
17. Attach the injection pump to the front cover, aligning the timing marks before torquing the nuts to 30 ft. lbs.
18. Install the drive gear to injection pump bolts, torquing the bolts to 20 ft. lbs.
19. Install the remaining components in the reverse order of removal. Torque the fuel feed line at the injection pump to 20 ft. lbs. Start the engine and check for leaks.

Injection Pump Fuel Lines

REMOVAL AND INSTALLATION

NOTE: *When the fuel lines are to be removed, clean all fuel line fittings thoroughly before loosening. Immediately cap the lines, nozzles and pump fittings to maintain cleanliness.*

1. Disconnect both batteries.
2. Disconnect the air cleaner bracket at the valve cover.
3. Remove the crankcase ventilator bracket and move it aside.

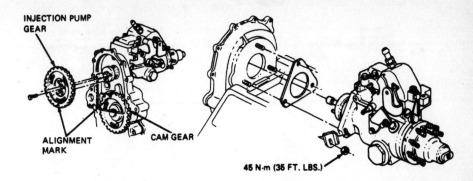

Diesel injection pump mounting

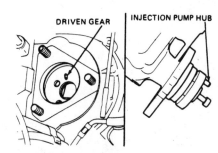

Injection pump locating pin

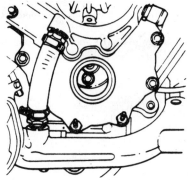

Rotate the crankshaft so that the injection pump drive gear bolts become accessible through the hole

4. Disconnect the secondary filter lines.

5. Remove the secondary filter adapter.

6. Loosen the vacuum pump holddown clamp and rotate the pump in order to gain access to the intake manifold bolt. Remove the intake manifold bolts. The injection line clips are retained by the same bolts.

7. Remove the intake manifold. Install a protective cover (GM part No. J–29664–1 or equivalent) so no foreign material falls into the engine.

8. Remove the injection line clips at the loom brackets.

9. Remove the injection lines at the nozzles and cover the nozzles with protective caps.

10. Remove the injection lines at the pump

and tag the lines for later installation.

11. Remove the fuel line from the injection pump.

12. Install all components in the reverse order of removal. Follow the illustrations for injection line connection.

Fuel Injectors

REMOVAL AND INSTALLATION

1. Disconnect the truck's batteries.

2. Disconnect the fuel line clip, and remove the fuel return hose.

3. Remove the fuel injection line as previously detailed.

4. Using GM special tool J–29873, remove the injector. Always remove the injector by turning the 30mm hex portion of the injector; turning the round portion will damage the injector. Always cap the injector and fuel lines when disconnected, to prevent contamination.

5. Install the injector with new gasket and torque to 50 ft. lbs. Connect the injection line and torque the nut to 20 ft. lbs. Install the fuel return hose, fuel line clips, and connect the batteries.

Injection Timing Adjustment

For the engine to be properly timed, the lines on the top of the injection pump adapter and the flange of the injection pump must be aligned.

1. The engine must be off for resetting the timing.

2. Loosen the three pump retaining nuts with tool J–26987, an injection pump intake manifold wrench, or its equivalent.

3. Align the mark on the injection pump with the marks on the adapter and tighten the nuts. Torque to 35 ft. lbs. Use a ³/₄ in. open-end wrench on the boss at the front of the injection pump to aid in rotating the pump to align the marks.

4. Adjust the throttle rod. See step 22, Fuel Injection Pump Removal and Installation.

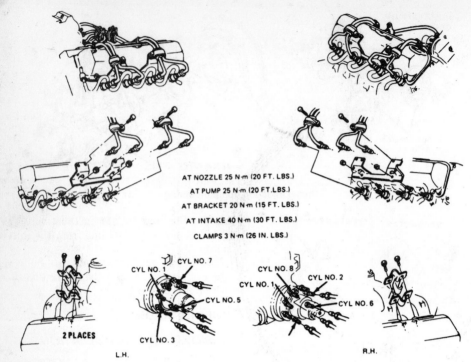

AT NOZZLE 25 N·m (20 FT. LBS.)

AT PUMP 25 N·m (20 FT.LBS.)

AT BRACKET 20 N·m (15 FT. LBS.)

AT INTAKE 40 N·m (30 FT. LBS.)

CLAMPS 3 N·m (26 IN. LBS.)

CYL NO. 7

CYL NO. 1

CYL NO. 5

CYL NO. 3

2 PLACES

L.H.

CYL NO. 8

CYL NO. 1

CYL NO. 2

CYL NO. 6

R.H.

Torque specifications and fuel line routing

FUEL TANK

DRAINING

CAUTION: *Disconnect the battery before beginning the draining operation.*

If the vehicle is not equipped with a drain plug, use the following procedure to remove the fuel.

1. Using a 10 ft. (305cm) piece of ³/₈ in. (9.525mm) hose cut a flap slit 18 in. (457mm) from one end.

2. Install a pipe nipple, of slightly larger diameter than the hose, into the opposite end of the hose.

3. Install the nipple end of the hose into the fuel tank with the natural curve of the hose pointing downward. Keep feeding the hose in until the nipple hits the bottom of the tank.

4. Place the other end of the hose in a suitable container and insert a air hose pointing it in the downward direction of the slit and inject air into the line.

NOTE: *If the vehicle is to be stored, always drain the fuel from the complete fuel system including the carburetor or throttle body, fuel pump supply, fuel injection pump, fuel lines, and tank.*

REMOVAL AND INSTALLATION

1. Drain the tank.

2. Jack up your vehicle and support it with jackstands.

3. Remove the clamp on the filler neck and the vent tube hose.

4. Remove the gauge hose which is attached to the frame.

5. While supporting the tank securely, remove the support straps.

6. Lower the tank until the gauge wiring can be removed.

7. Remove the tank.

8. Install the unit by reversing the removal procedure. Make certain that the anti-squeak material is replaced during installation.

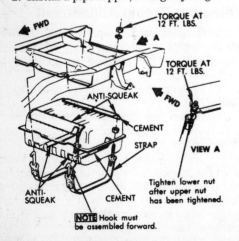

FWD

TORQUE AT 12 FT. LBS.

A

TORQUE AT 12 FT. LBS.

ANTI-SQUEAK

FWD

CEMENT

STRAP

VIEW A

ANTI-SQUEAK

CEMENT

Tighten lower nut after upper nut has been tightened.

NOTE Hook must be assembled forward.

Standard fuel tank installation

Chassis Electrical

6

UNDERSTANDING AND TROUBLESHOOTING ELECTRICAL SYSTEMS

For any electrical system to operate, it must make a complete circuit. This simply means that the power flow from the battery must make a complete circle. When an electrical component is operating, power flows from the battery to the component, passes through the component causing it to perform its function (lighting a light bulb, for example) and then returns to the battery through the ground of the circuit. This ground is usually (but not always) the metal part of the vehicle on which the electrical component is mounted.

Perhaps the easiest way to visualize this is to think of connecting a light bulb with two wires attached to it to your vehicle battery. The battery in your vehicle has two posts (negative and positive). If one of the two wires attached to the light bulb was attached to the negative post of the battery and the other wire was attached to the positive post of the battery, you would have a complete circuit. Current from the battery would flow out one post, through the wire attached to it and then to the light bulb, causing it to light. It would then leave the light bulb, travel through the other wire, and return to the other post of the battery.

The normal automotive circuit differs from this simple example in two ways. First, instead of having a return wire from the bulb to the battery, the light bulb returns the current to the battery through the chassis of the vehicle. Since the negative battery cable is attached to the chassis and the chassis is made of electrically conductive metal, the chassis of the vehicle can serve as a ground wire to complete the circuit. Secondly, most automotive circuits contain switches to turn components on and off as required.

There are many types of switches, but the most common simply serves to prevent the passage of current when it is turned off. Since the switch is a part of the circle necessary for a complete circuit, it operates to leave an opening in the circuit, and thus an incomplete or open circuit, when it is turned off.

Some electrical components which require a large amount of current to operate also have a relay in their circuit. Since these circuits carry a large amount of current, the thickness of the wire (gauge size) in the circuit is also greater. If this large wire were connected from the component to the control switch on the instrument panel, and then back to the component, a voltage drop would occur in the circuit. To prevent this potential drop in voltage, an electromagnetic switch (relay) is used. The large wires in the circuit are connected from the vehicle battery to one side of the relay, and from the opposite side of the relay to the component. The relay is normally open, preventing current from passing through the circuit. An additional, smaller, wire is connected from the relay to the control switch to the circuit. When the control switch is turned on, it completes the circuit. This closes the relay and allows current to flow from the battery to the component. The horn, headlight, and starter circuits are three which use relays.

You have probably noticed how the vehicle's instrument panel lights get brighter the faster you rev the engine. This happens because you alternator (which supplies the battery) puts out more current at speeds above idle. This is normal. However, it is possible for larger surges of current to pass through the electrical system of your car. If this surge of current were to reach an electrical component, it could burn the component out. To prevent this from happening, fuses are connected into the current supply wires of most of the major electrical systems of your vehicle. The fuse serves to head off the surge at the pass. When an electrical current of excessive power passes through the component's fuse, the fuse blows out and breaks the circuit, saving it from destruction.

The fuse also protects the component from damage if the power supply wire to the component is grounded before the current reaches the component.

There is another important rule to the complete circle circuit. Every complete circuit from a power source must include a component which is using the power from the power source. If you were to disconnect the light bulb (from the previous example of a light bulb being connected to the battery by two wires together (take our word for it-don't try it) the result would literally be shocking. A similar thing happens (on a smaller scale) when the power supply wire to a component or the electrical component itself becomes grounded before the normal ground connection for the circuit. To prevent damage to the system, the fuse for the circuit blows to interrupt the circuit, protecting the components from damage. Because grounding a wire from a power source makes a complete circuit, less the required component to use the power, this phenomenon is called a short circuit. The most common causes of short circuits are: the rubber insulation on a wire breaking or rubbing through to expose the current carrying core of the wire to a metal part of the vehicle, or a short switch.

Some electrical systems on the vehicle are protected by a circuit breaker which is, basically, a self-repairing fuse. When either of the above described events takes place in a system which is protected by a circuit breaker, the circuit breaker opens the circuit the same way a fuse does. However, when either the short is removed from the circuit or the surge subsides, the circuit breaker resets itself and does not have to be replaced as a fuse does.

The final protective device in the chassis electrical system is a fuse link. A fuse link is a wire that acts as a fuse. It is connected between the starter relay and the main wiring harness for the car. This connection is under the hood, very near a similar fuse link which protects all the chassis electrical components. It is the probable cause of trouble when none of the electrical components function, unless the battery is disconnected or dead.

Electrical problems generally fall into one of three areas:

1. The component that is not functioning is not receiving current.

2. The component itself is not functioning.

3. The component is not properly grounded.

Problems that fall into the first category are by far the most complicated. It is the current supply system to the component which contains all the switches, relays, fuses, etc.

The electrical system can be checked with a test light and a jumper wire. A test light is a device that looks like a pointed screwdriver with a wire attached to it. It has a light bulb in its handle. A jumper wire is a piece of insulated wire with an alligator clip attached to each end.

If a light bulb is not working, you must follow a systematic plan to determine which of the three causes is the villain.

1. Turn on the switch that controls the inoperable bulb.

2. Disconnect the power supply wire from the bulb.

3. Attach the ground wire on the test light to a good metal ground.

4. Touch the probe end of the test light to the end of the power supply wire that was disconnected from the bulb. If the bulb is receiving current, the test light will go on.

NOTE: *If the bulb is one which works only when the ignition key is turned on (turn signal), make sure the key is turned on.*

If the test light does not go on, then the problem is in the circuit between the battery and the bulb. As mentioned before, this includes all the switches, fuses, and relays in the system. The problem is an open circuit between the battery and the bulb. If the fuse is blown and, when replaced, immediately blows again, there is a short circuit in the system which must be located and repaired. If there is a switch in the system, bypass it with a jumper wire. This is done by connecting one end of the jumper wire to the power supply wire into the switch, and the other end of the jumper wire to the wire coming out of the switch. If the test light lights with the jumper wire installed, the switch or whatever was bypassed is defective.

NOTE: *Never substitute the jumper wire for the bulb, as the bulb is the component required to use the power from the power source.*

5. If the bulb in the test light goes on, then the current is getting to the bulb that is not working in the vehicle. This eliminates the first of the three possible causes. Connect the power supply wire and connect a jumper wire from the bulb to a good metal ground. Do this with the switch which controls the bulb turned on, and also the ignition switch turned on if it is required for the light to work. If the bulb works with the jumper wire installed, then it has a

bad ground. This is usually caused by the metal area on which the bulb mounts to the car being coated with some type of foreign matter or rust.

6. If neither test located the source of the trouble, then the light bulb itself is defective.

The above test procedure can be applied to any of the components of the chassis electrical system by substituting the component that is not working for the light bulb. Remember that for any electrical system to work, all connections must be clean and tight.

HEATING AND AIR CONDITIONING

Heater/Air Conditioner Blower Motor

REMOVAL AND INSTALLATION

1987–90 Without Air Conditioning

1. Disconnect the battery ground cable.
2. Remove the coolant overflow bottle.
3. Unplug the motor wiring.
4. Remove the attaching screws and lift out the blower motor.

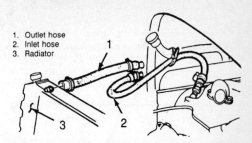

1. Outlet hose
2. Inlet hose
3. Radiator

Heater hose routing for the 8-5.7L (carbureted) engines

5. Installation is the reverse of removal.

1987–89 With Air Conditioning

1. Disconnect the battery ground cable.
2. Remove the power antenna, if so equipped.
3. Remove the coolant overflow bottle.
4. Unplug the motor wiring.
5. Remove the attaching screws and lift out the blower motor.
6. Installation is the reverse of removal.

1990 With Air Conditioning

1. Disconnect the battery ground cable.
2. Remove the coolant overflow bottle.
3. Unplug the motor wiring.
4. Remove the attaching screws and lift out the blower motor.

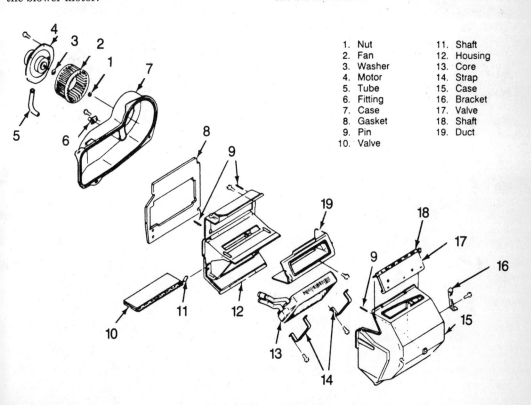

1. Nut	11. Shaft
2. Fan	12. Housing
3. Washer	13. Core
4. Motor	14. Strap
5. Tube	15. Case
6. Fitting	16. Bracket
7. Case	17. Valve
8. Gasket	18. Shaft
9. Pin	19. Duct
10. Valve	

Heater case exploded view

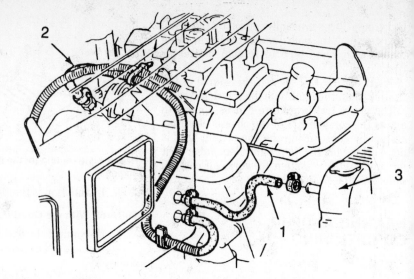

1. Outlet hose
2. Inlet hose
3. Radiator

Heater hose routing for the 6-4.3L, 8-5.0L and 8-5.7L (TBI) engines

5. Installation is the reverse of removal.

Core

REMOVAL AND INSTALLATION

1987–90 Without Air Conditioning

1. Disconnect the negative battery cable.
2. Remove the coolant recovery bottle.
3. Place a pan under the van and disconnect the heater intake and outlet hoses. Quickly remove and plug the hoses and support them in an upright position. Drain the coolant from the heater core into the pan.

CAUTION: *When draining the coolant, keep in mind that cats and dogs are attracted by the ethylene glycol antifreeze, and are quite likely to drink any that is left in an uncovered container or in puddles on the ground. This will prove fatal in sufficient quantity.*

Always drain the coolant into a sealable container. Coolant should be reused unless it is contaminated or several years old.

4. Remove the heater distributor duct-to-case attaching screws and the duct-to-engine cover screw. Remove the duct.

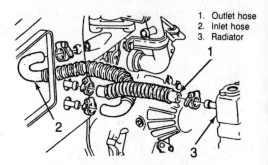

1. Outlet hose
2. Inlet hose
3. Radiator

Heater hose routing for the 8-6.2L diesel engines

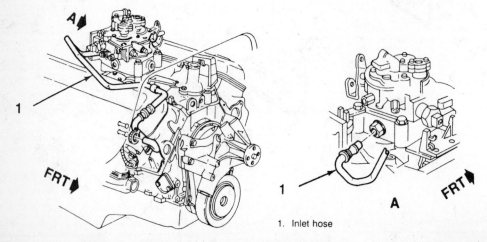

1. Inlet hose

Heater hose routing for the 8-7.L engines

5. Remove the engine cover.

6. Remove all the instrument panel attaching screws.

7. Carefully lower the steering column. Raise and support the right side of the instrument panel. See Chapter 8.

8. Remove the defroster duct-to-case attaching screws and the two screws attaching the distributor to the heater case.

9. Disconnect the temperature door cable. Carefully fold the cable back and out of the way.

10. Remove the three nuts from the engine compartment side of the distributor case and the screw from the passenger compartment side.

11. Remove the heater case and core assembly.

12. Remove the core retaining straps and remove the core.

To install:

13. Install the core.

14. Install the core retaining straps.

15. Install the heater case and core assembly.

16. Install the three nuts on the engine compartment side of the distributor case and the screw on the passenger compartment side.

17. Connect the temperature door cable.

18. Install the defroster duct-to-case attaching screws and the two screws attaching the distributor to the heater case.

19. Install the steering column.

20. Install all the instrument panel attaching screws.

21. Install the engine cover.

22. Install the duct. Install the heater distributor duct-to-case attaching screws and the duct-to-engine cover screw.

23. Connect the heater intake and outlet hoses.

24. Fill the cooling system.

25. Install the coolant recovery bottle.

26. Connect the negative battery cable.

1987–89 With Air Conditioning

1. Disconnect the battery ground cable.

2. Remove the engine cover.

3. Remove the steering column to instrument panel bolts. Lower the column carefully.

4. Remove the upper and lower instrument panel attaching screws. Remove the radio support bracket screw.

5. Raise and support the right side of the instrument panel.

6. Remove the lower right instrument panel bracket.

7. Remove the vacuum actuator from the kick panel.

8. Disconnect the temperature cable and

vacuum hoses at the case. Remove the heater distributor duct from over the engine hump.

9. Remove the two defroster duct to firewall attaching screws below the windshield.

10. Under the hood, disconnect and plug the heater hoses at the firewall.

11. Remove the three nuts and one screw (inside) holding the heater case to the firewall.

12. Remove the case from the truck. Remove the gasket for access to the screws holding the case together. Remove the temperature cable support bracket. Remove the screws and separate the case. Remove the heater core.

To install:

13. Install the heater core.

14. Install the screws and separate the case.

15. Install the temperature cable support bracket.

16. Install the gasket.

17. Install the case in the truck.

18. Install the three nuts and one screw (inside) holding the heater case to the firewall.

19. Connect and plug the heater hoses at the firewall.

20. Install the two defroster duct-to-firewall attaching screws below the windshield.

21. Install the heater distributor duct.

22. Connect the temperature cable and vacuum hoses at the case.

23. Install the vacuum actuator at the kick panel.

24. Install the lower right instrument panel bracket.

25. Install the radio support bracket screw.

26. Install the upper and lower instrument panel attaching screws.

27. Install the steering column to instrument panel bolts.

28. Install the engine cover.

29. Connect the battery ground cable.

30. Refill the cooling system as necessary.

1990 With Air Conditioning

1. Disconnect the battery ground cable.

2. Remove the engine cover.

3. Remove the steering column to instrument panel bolts. Lower the column carefully.

4. Remove the upper and lower instrument panel attaching screws. Remove the radio support bracket screw.

5. Raise and support the right side of the instrument panel.

6. Remove the lower right instrument panel bracket.

7. Remove the vacuum actuator from the kick panel.

8. Disconnect the temperature cable and vacuum hoses at the case. Remove the heater distributor duct from over the engine hump.

9. Remove the two defroster duct to fire-

wall attaching screws below the windshield.

10. Under the hood, disconnect and plug the heater hoses at the firewall.

11. Remove the three nuts and one screw (inside) holding the heater case to the firewall.

12. Remove the case from the truck. Remove the gasket for access to the screws holding the case together. Remove the temperature cable support bracket. Remove the screws and separate the case. Remove the heater core.

To install:

13. Install the heater core.

14. Install the screws and separate the case.

15. Install the temperature cable support bracket.

16. Install the gasket.

17. Install the case in the truck.

18. Install the three nuts and one screw (inside) holding the heater case to the firewall.

19. Connect and plug the heater hoses at the firewall.

20. Install the two defroster duct-to-firewall attaching screws below the windshield.

21. Install the heater distributor duct.

22. Connect the temperature cable and vacuum hoses at the case.

23. Install the vacuum actuator at the kick panel.

24. Install the lower right instrument panel bracket.

25. Install the radio support bracket screw.

26. Install the upper and lower instrument panel attaching screws.

27. Install the steering column to instrument panel bolts.

28. Install the engine cover.

29. Connect the battery ground cable.

30. Refill the cooling system as necessary.

Control Head

REMOVAL AND INSTALLATION

1. Disconnect the negative battery cable.

2. Remove the headlamp switch control knob.

3. Remove the instrument panel bezel.

4. Remove the control screws.

5. Disconnect the temperature cable eyelet clip and retainer.

6. Remove the control lower right mounting tab through the dash opening.

7. Remove the upper tab and the lower right tab.

8. Disconnect the electrical harness.

9. Disconnect the vacuum harness.

10. Remove the control assembly.

To install:

11. Install the control assembly.

12. Connect the vacuum harness.

13. Connect the electrical harness.

14. Install the upper tab and the lower right tab.

15. Install the control lower right mounting tab through the dash opening.

16. Connect the temperature cable eyelet clip and retainer.

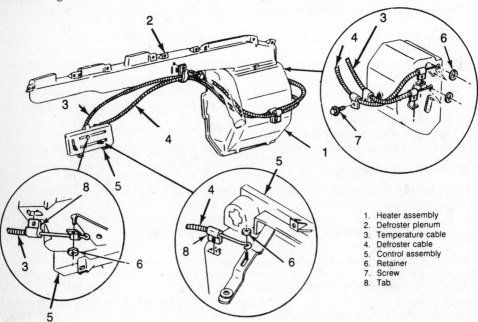

1. Heater assembly
2. Defroster plenum
3. Temperature cable
4. Defroster cable
5. Control assembly
6. Retainer
7. Screw
8. Tab

Control cables

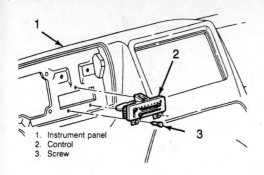

1. Instrument panel
2. Control
3. Screw

Control assembly with air conditioning

1. Control
2. Blower switch

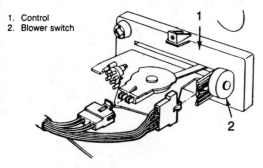

Blower switch replacement

17. Install the control screws.
18. Install the instrument panel bezel.
19. Install the headlamp switch control knob.
20. Connect the negative battery cable.

Evaporative Core

REMOVAL AND INSTALLATION

With Gasoline Engines

1. Disconnect the negative battery cable.
2. Purge the system of refrigerant. See Chapter 1.
3. Remove the coolant recovery tank and bracket.
4. Disconnect the electrical connectors from the core case assembly.
5. Remove the bracket at the evaporator case.
6. Remove the right marker lamp for access.
7. Disconnect the accumulator inlet and outlet lines, and the two brackets that attach the accumulator to the case.
8. Disconnect the evaporator inlet line.
9. Remove the three nuts and one screw that attaching the module to the dash panel.
10. Remove the core case assembly from the vehicle.

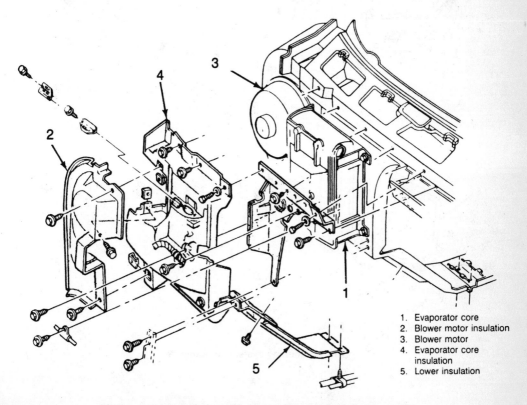

1. Evaporator core
2. Blower motor insulation
3. Blower motor
4. Evaporator core insulation
5. Lower insulation

Blower motor installation with air conditioning and diesel engine

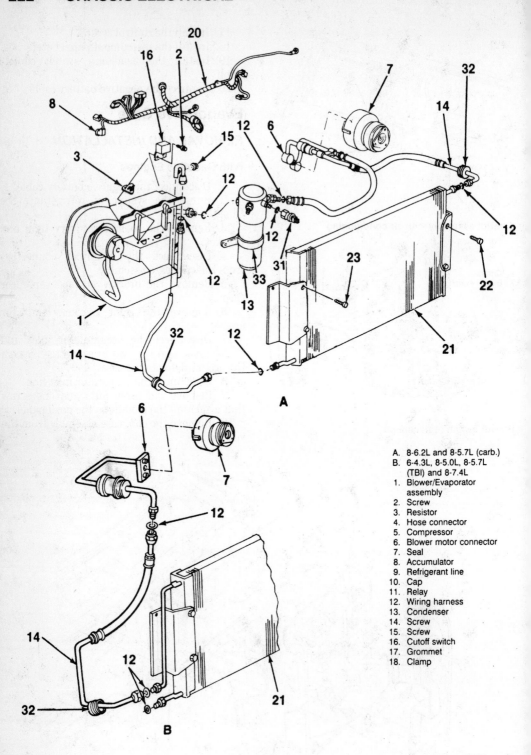

A. 8-6.2L and 8-5.7L (carb.)
B. 6-4.3L, 8-5.0L, 8-5.7L
   (TBI) and 8-7.4L
1. Blower/Evaporator
   assembly
2. Screw
3. Resistor
4. Hose connector
5. Compressor
6. Blower motor connector
7. Seal
8. Accumulator
9. Refrigerant line
10. Cap
11. Relay
12. Wiring harness
13. Condenser
14. Screw
15. Screw
16. Cutoff switch
17. Grommet
18. Clamp

Air conditioning system components

11. Remove the screws, separate the case sections and remove the evaporator core.

To install:

12. Add 3 ounces of 525 viscosity refrigerant oil to the condenser if a new one is installed.

13. Install the evaporator core.

14. Install the screws joining the case sections.

15. Install the core/case assembly.

16. Install the three nuts and one screw that attaching the module to the dash panel.

17. Connect the evaporator inlet line.

18. Connect the accumulator inlet and outlet lines, and the two brackets that attach the accumulator to the case.

19. Install the right marker lamp.

20. Install the bracket at the evaporator case.

21. Connect the electrical connectors at the core/case assembly.

22. Install the coolant recovery tank and bracket.

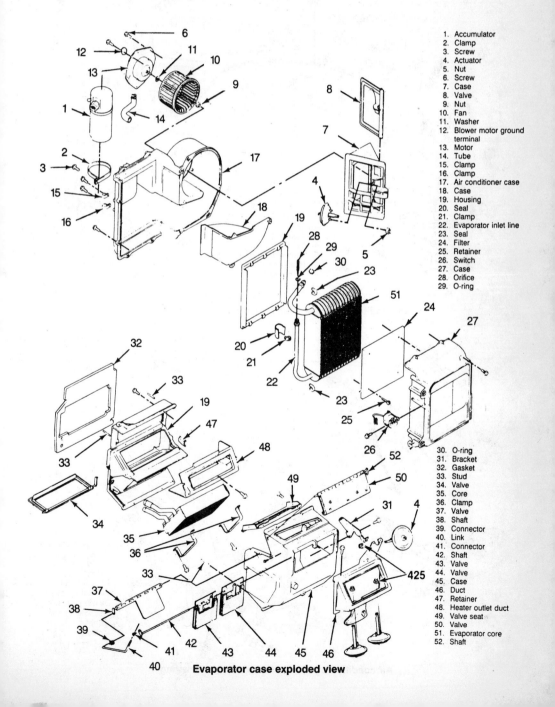

1. Accumulator
2. Clamp
3. Screw
4. Actuator
5. Nut
6. Screw
7. Case
8. Valve
9. Nut
10. Fan
11. Washer
12. Blower motor ground terminal
13. Motor
14. Tube
15. Clamp
16. Clamp
17. Air conditioner case
18. Case
19. Housing
20. Seal
21. Clamp
22. Evaporator inlet line
23. Seal
24. Filter
25. Retainer
26. Switch
27. Case
28. Orifice
29. O-ring
30. O-ring
31. Bracket
32. Gasket
33. Stud
34. Valve
35. Core
36. Clamp
37. Valve
38. Shaft
39. Connector
40. Link
41. Connector
42. Shaft
43. Valve
44. Valve
45. Case
46. Duct
47. Retainer
48. Heater outlet duct
49. Valve seat
50. Valve
51. Evaporator core
52. Shaft

Evaporator case exploded view

23. Charge the system. See Chapter 1.
24. Connect the negative battery cable.

With Diesel Engines

1. Discharge the system. See Chapter 1.
2. Disconnect the battery ground cable.
3. Remove the air intake.
4. Remove the hood latch assembly and cable retainer.
5. Remove the windshield solvent tank.

6. Disconnect the low pressure line and move it out of the way. Cap both openings at once!
7. Remove the accumulator. Cap all openings at once!
8. Disconnect the high pressure line at the evaporator. Cap both openings at once!
9. Disconnect the wiring at the case.
10. Remove the blower motor relay and the resistor.

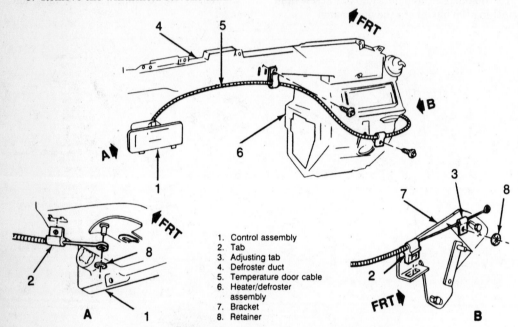

1. Control assembly
2. Tab
3. Adjusting tab
4. Defroster duct
5. Temperature door cable
6. Heater/defroster assembly
7. Bracket
8. Retainer

Air conditioning system temperature door control cable

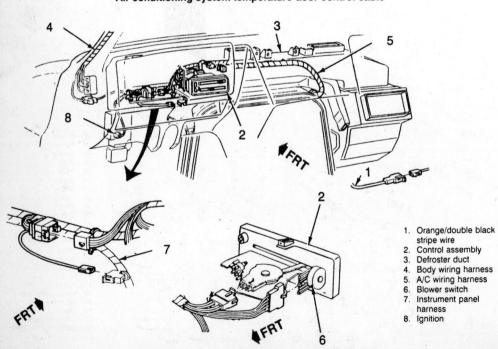

1. Orange/double black stripe wire
2. Control assembly
3. Defroster duct
4. Body wiring harness
5. A/C wiring harness
6. Blower switch
7. Instrument panel harness
8. Ignition

Air conditioning system instrument panel wiring

11. Remove the upper fan shroud.

12. Remove the radiator.

13. Remove the heater valve assembly bracket and move it out of the way.

14. Remove the upper screws of the lower insulation section, push the section down and remove the insulation.

15. Remove the three nuts and one screw that attaching the module to the dash panel.

16. Remove the core case assembly from the vehicle.

17. Remove the screws, separate the case sections and remove the evaporator core.

To install:

18. Add 3 ounces of 525 viscosity refrigerant oil to the condenser if a new one is installed.

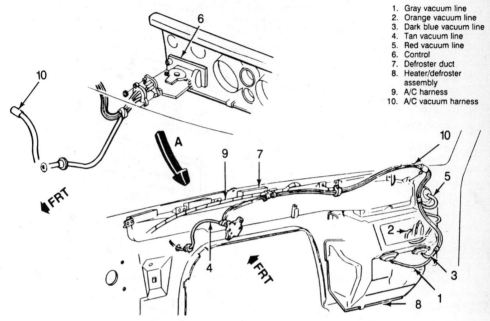

1. Gray vacuum line
2. Orange vacuum line
3. Dark blue vacuum line
4. Tan vacuum line
5. Red vacuum line
6. Control
7. Defroster duct
8. Heater/defroster assembly
9. A/C harness
10. A/C vacuum harness

Air conditioning system instrument panel vacuum routing

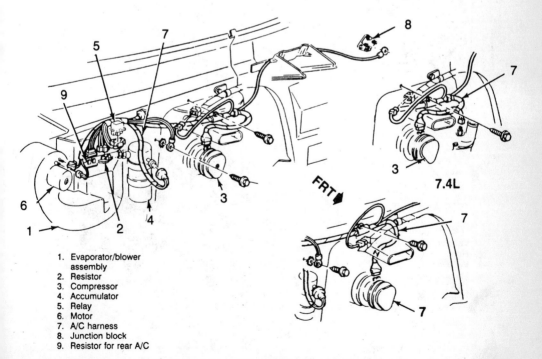

1. Evaporator/blower assembly
2. Resistor
3. Compressor
4. Accumulator
5. Relay
6. Motor
7. A/C harness
8. Junction block
9. Resistor for rear A/C

Air conditioning system engine compartment wiring

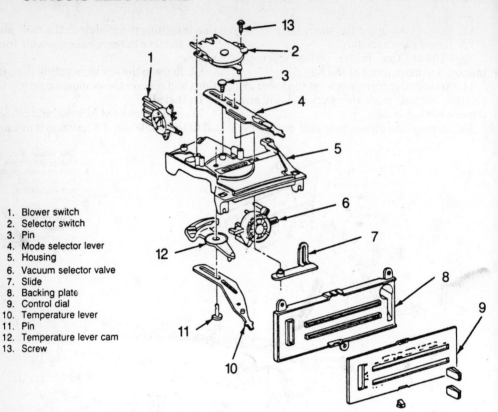

1. Blower switch
2. Selector switch
3. Pin
4. Mode selector lever
5. Housing
6. Vacuum selector valve
7. Slide
8. Backing plate
9. Control dial
10. Temperature lever
11. Pin
12. Temperature lever cam
13. Screw

Air conditioning system control assembly components

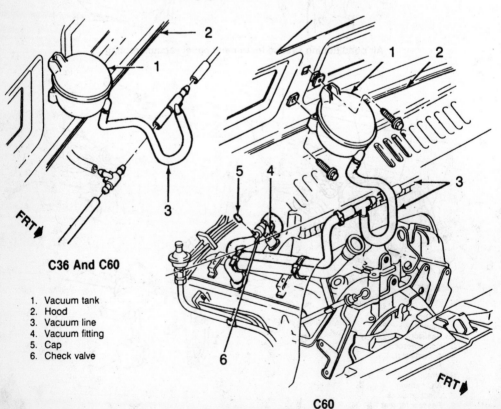

C36 And C60

1. Vacuum tank
2. Hood
3. Vacuum line
4. Vacuum fitting
5. Cap
6. Check valve

C60

Vacuum tank assembly with the 6-4.3L engine

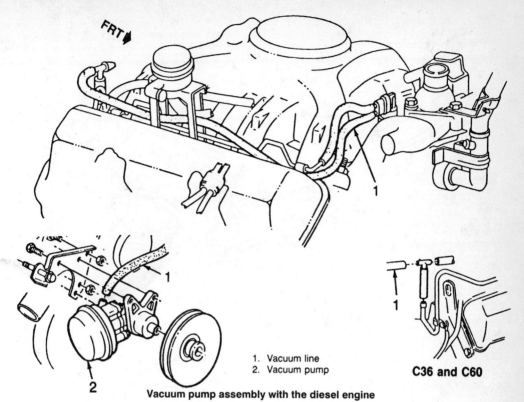

1. Vacuum line
2. Vacuum pump

C36 and C60

Vacuum pump assembly with the diesel engine

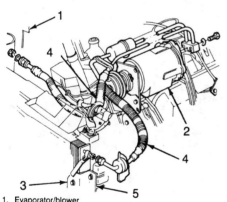

1. Evaporator/blower
2. Compressor
3. Condenser
4. Refrigerant hose
5. Radiator

Refrigerant hose routing with the diesel engine

19. Install the evaporator core in the case half.
20. Join the case sections and install the screws.
21. Position the core/case assembly in the vehicle.
22. Install the three nuts and one screw that attaching the case to the dash panel.
23. Install the insulation.
24. Install the heater valve assembly bracket.
25. Install the radiator.

26. Install the upper fan shroud.
27. Install the blower motor relay and the resistor.
28. Connect the wiring at the case.
29. Connect the high pressure line at the evaporator.
30. Install the accumulator.
31. Connect the low pressure line.
32. Install the windshield solvent tank.
33. Install the hood latch assembly and cable retainer.
34. Install the air intake.
35. Connect the battery ground cable.
36. Charge the system. See Chapter 1.

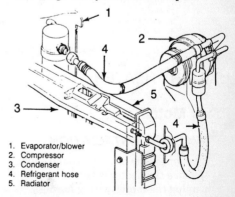

1. Evaporator/blower
2. Compressor
3. Condenser
4. Refrigerant hose
5. Radiator

Refrigerant hose routing with the 8-5.7L (carbureted) engines

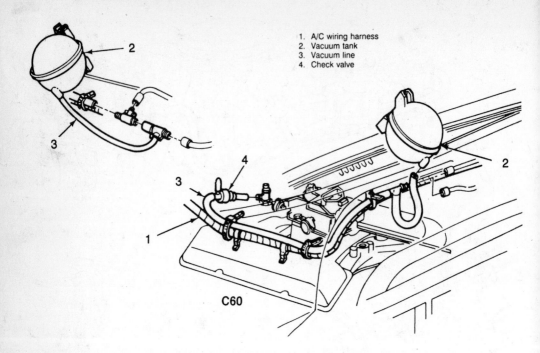

1. A/C wiring harness
2. Vacuum tank
3. Vacuum line
4. Check valve

C60

Vacuum tank assembly with the 8-5.0L and 8-5.7L engines

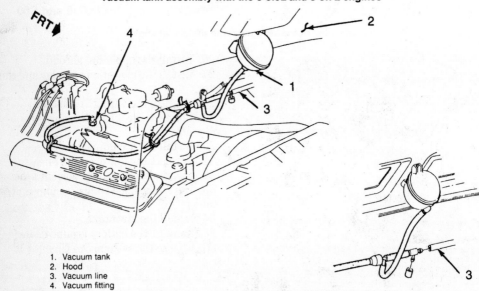

FRT

1. Vacuum tank
2. Hood
3. Vacuum line
4. Vacuum fitting

Vacuum tank assembly with the 8-7.4L engine

AUXILIARY HEATER

Blower Motor

REMOVAL AND INSTALLATION

1. Disconnect the battery ground cable.
2. Remove the heater cover.
3. Unplug the motor wiring harness.
4. Remove the attaching screws and lift out the motor.
5. Installation is the reverse of removal.

Heater Core

REMOVAL AND INSTALLATION

1. Drain the cooling system.

CAUTION: *When draining the coolant, keep in mind that cats and dogs are attracted by the ethylene glycol antifreeze, and are quite likely to drink any that is left in an uncovered container or in puddles on the ground. This will prove fatal in sufficient quantity. Always drain the coolant into a sealable con-*

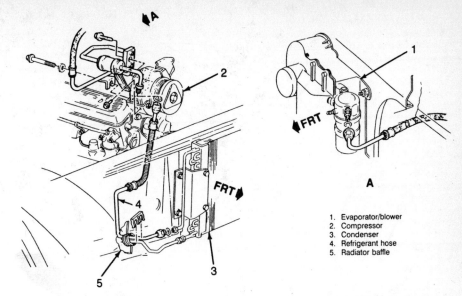

Refrigerant hose routing with the 6-4.3L, 8-5.0L, 8-5.7L (TBI) and 8-7.4L engines

1. Evaporator/blower
2. Compressor
3. Condenser
4. Refrigerant hose
5. Radiator baffle

tainer. Coolant should be reused unless it is contaminated or several years old.

2. Disconnect the battery ground cable.

3. Disconnect the heater hoses at the core tubes.

4. Remove the heater case-to-floor studs.

5. Remove the case cover.

6. Disconnect the wiring at the case.

7. Lift the case from the van.

8. Remove the core cover and lift the core and seal from the case.

To install:

9. Lower the core and seal into the case.

10. Install the core cover.

11. Install the case in the van.

12. Connect the wiring at the case.

13. Install the case cover.

14. Install the heater case-to-floor studs.

15. Connect the heater hoses at the core tubes.

16. Connect the battery ground cable.

17. Fill the cooling system.

AUXILIARY AIR CONDITIONING SYSTEM

Blower Motors

REMOVAL AND INSTALLATION

1987

1. Disconnect the battery ground cable.

2. Disconnect the drain tubes at the rear of the blower-evaporator shroud/duct.

3. Remove the screws securing the shroud to the roof and case.

4. Remove the shroud/duct.

5. Disconnect the blower motor ground straps at the center connector between the motors.

6. Disconnect the blower motor wires.

7. Support the case and remove the lower-to-upper case half screws and lower the case and motor assemblies.

8. Remove the motor retaining strap and remove the motor and wheels.

To install:

9. Install the motor and wheels.

10. Install the motor retaining strap.

11. Raise the case and Install the lower-to-upper case half screws.

12. Connect the blower motor wires.

13. Connect the blower motor ground straps at the center connector between the motors.

14. Install the shroud/duct.

15. Install the screws securing the shroud to the roof and case.

16. Connect the drain tubes at the rear of the blower-evaporator shroud/duct.

17. Connect the battery ground cable.

1988–90

1. Disconnect the battery ground cable.

2. Disconnect the drain tubes at the rear of the blower-evaporator duct.

3. Remove the screws securing the duct to the roof and case.

4. Remove the duct.

5. Discharge the system. See Chapter 1.

6. Disconnect the refrigerant lines at the case. Cap all openings at once!

NOTE: *You'll have to pull back the foam insulation to disconnect the high pressure line.*

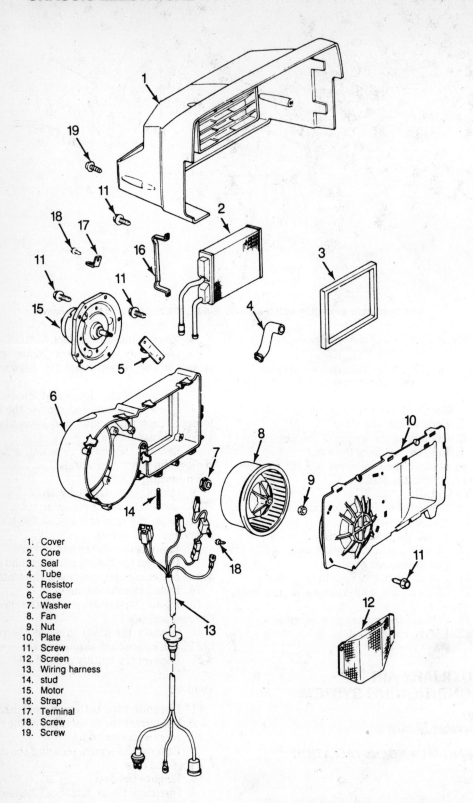

1. Cover
2. Core
3. Seal
4. Tube
5. Resistor
6. Case
7. Washer
8. Fan
9. Nut
10. Plate
11. Screw
12. Screen
13. Wiring harness
14. stud
15. Motor
16. Strap
17. Terminal
18. Screw
19. Screw

Auxiliary heater exploded view

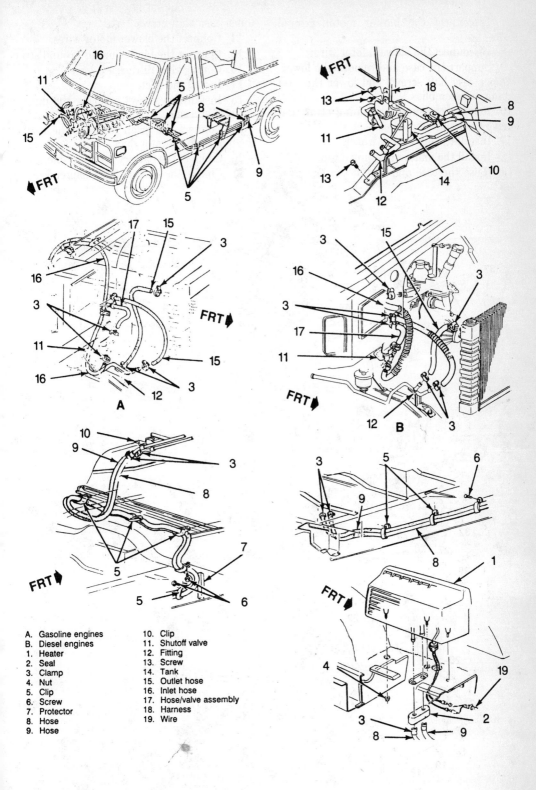

A. Gasoline engines
B. Diesel engines
1. Heater
2. Seal
3. Clamp
4. Nut
5. Clip
6. Screw
7. Protector
8. Hose
9. Hose
10. Clip
11. Shutoff valve
12. Fitting
13. Screw
14. Tank
15. Outlet hose
16. Inlet hose
17. Hose/valve assembly
18. Harness
19. Wire

Auxiliary heater plumbing components

7. Disconnect the blower motor ground strap.

8. Disconnect the blower motor wires.

9. Support the case and remove the lower-to-upper case half screws and lower the case and motor assemblies.

10. Remove the motor retaining strap and remove the motor and wheels.

11. Install the motor and wheels.

12. Install the motor retaining strap.

13. Raise the case and Install the lower-to-upper case half screws.

14. Connect the blower motor wires.

15. Connect the blower motor ground strap.

16. Connect the refrigerant lines.

17. Install the duct.

18. Install the screws securing the duct to the roof and case.

19. Connect the drain tubes at the rear of the blower-evaporator duct.

20. Connect the battery ground cable.

21. Charge the system. See Chapter 1.

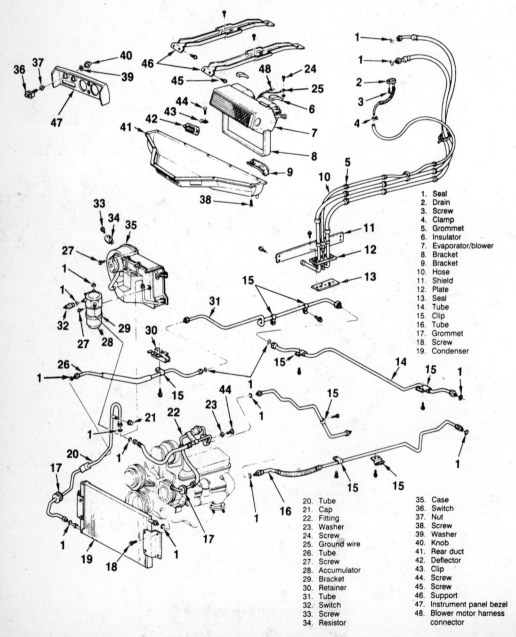

1. Seal
2. Drain
3. Screw
4. Clamp
5. Grommet
6. Insulator
7. Evaporator/blower
8. Bracket
9. Bracket
10. Hose
11. Shield
12. Plate
13. Seal
14. Tube
15. Clip
16. Tube
17. Grommet
18. Screw
19. Condenser

20. Tube
21. Cap
22. Fitting
23. Washer
24. Screw
25. Ground wire
26. Tube
27. Screw
28. Accumulator
29. Bracket
30. Retainer
31. Tube
32. Switch
33. Screw
34. Resistor

35. Case
36. Switch
37. Nut
38. Screw
39. Washer
40. Knob
41. Rear duct
42. Deflector
43. Clip
44. Screw
45. Screw
46. Support
47. Instrument panel bezel
48. Blower motor harness connector

Roof mounted heater components

Evaporator Core

REMOVAL AND INSTALLATION

1. Disconnect the battery ground cable.
2. Discharge the system. See Chapter 1.
3. Disconnect the drain tubes at the rear of the blower-evaporator shroud/duct.
4. Remove the screws securing the shroud/duct to the roof and case.
5. Remove the shroud/duct.
6. Disconnect the blower motor ground straps at the center connector between the motors.
7. Disconnect the blower motor wires.
8. Disconnect the refrigerant lines at the case. Cap all openings at once!
9. Support the case and remove the case-to-roof screws. Lower the case assembly.

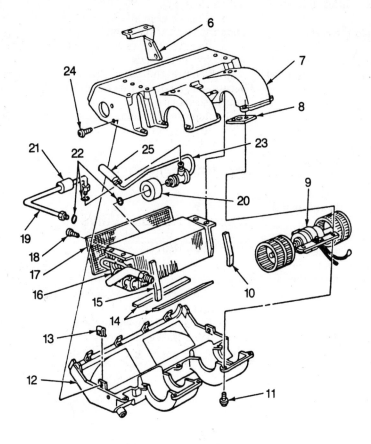

A. With Beauville option
B. Except Beauville option
1. Drain
2. Screw
3. Clamp
4. Evaporator/blower
5. Rear duct
6. Tube support bracket
7. Case upper half
8. Plate
9. Blower motor
10. Seal
11. Screw
12. Case lower half
13. U-nut
14. Seal
15. Seal
16. Evaporator core
17. Screen
18. Pin
19. Expansion tube
20. Insulator
21. Insulator
22. O-ring
23. Expansion valve
24. Screw
25. Bulb clamp
26. Insulation
27. Refrigerant hoses
28. Drain
29. Clamp

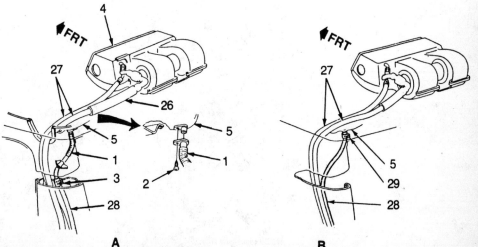

Roof mounted evaporator/blower components

10. Place the unit upside-down on a clean workbench.

11. Remove the screws and separate the case halves.

12. Remove the upper shroud and upper case from the evaporator core.

13. Disconnect the expansion valve lines and cap all openings at once!

14. Remove the expansion valve capillary bulbs from the evaporator outlet line and remove the valves.

15. Remove the screen from the core.

To install:

16. Always use new O-rings coated with clean refrigerant oil. Add 3 ounces of clean refrigerant oil to a new core.

17. Install the screen on the core.

18. Install the expansion valves.

19. Install the expansion valve capillary bulbs in the evaporator outlet line.

20. Connect the expansion valve lines.

21. Install the upper shroud and upper case.

22. Install the case screws.

23. Raise the case into position and install the case-to-roof screws.

24. Connect the refrigerant lines at the case.

25. Connect the blower motor wires.

26. Connect the blower motor ground straps at the center connector between the motors.

27. Install the shroud/duct.

28. Connect the drain tubes at the rear of the blower-evaporator shroud/duct.

29. Charge the system. See Chapter 1.

30. Connect the battery ground cable.

RADIO

REMOVAL AND INSTALLATION

1. Disconnect the ground cable from the battery.

2. Remove the engine cover.

3. Remove the air cleaner.

4. Cover the carburetor or throttle body with a clean rag.

5. Remove the knobs, washers and nuts from the front of the radio.

6. Remove the rear bracket screw and bracket from the radio.

7. Remove the radio through the engine access area. Lower the radio far enough to detach the wiring.

8. Remove the radio.

9. Installation is the reverse of removal.

CRUISE CONTROL

Vacuum Release Valve

REPLACEMENT

The valve is located on the brake pedal bracket.

1. Unplug the wiring connector (automatic transmission).

2. Disconnect the vacuum line.

3. Turn the retainer counterclockwise and slide out the valve.

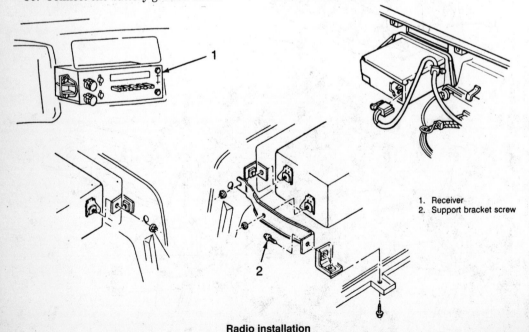

1. Receiver
2. Support bracket screw

Radio installation

To install:

4. Place the valve in the retainer and turn the retainer clockwise to seat the valve.

5. Slide the valve into the retainer, with the brake pedal fully depressed, as far as it will go. Clicking will be heard as the valve is pushed towards the pedal.

6. Pull the pedal fully rearward against its stop until the clicking stops.

7. Release the pedal and performs Steps 5 & 6 again to make sure the valve is correctly seated.

8. Connect the vacuum and wiring.

Clutch Release Switch

REPLACEMENT

The switch is located on the clutch pedal bracket.

1. Unplug the wiring connector.

2. Turn the retainer counterclockwise and slide out the switch.

To install:

3. Place the switch in the retainer and turn the retainer clockwise to seat the switch.

4. Slide the switch into the retainer, with the clutch pedal fully depressed, as far as it will go. Clicking will be heard as the switch is pushed towards the pedal.

5. Pull the pedal fully rearward against its stop until the clicking stops.

6. Release the pedal and performs Steps 5 & 6 again to make sure the valve is correctly seated.

7. Connect the vacuum and wiring.

Control Module

REPLACEMENT

The module is mounted on the left side of the brake pedal bracket.

1. Unplug the harness connector.

2. Remove the module by prying back the retaining clip on the bracket and sliding off the module.

3. Installation is the reverse of removal.

Servo

REPLACEMENT

The servo is mounted in the engine compartment. On gasoline engines, it is mounted on the driver's side, next to the distributor. On the diesel it is at the center, front of the engine.

1. Disconnect and tag the vacuum hoses.

2. Remove the actuator rod retainer and remove the rod.

3. Disconnect the control cable.

4. Remove the servo mounting bolts and lift off the servo.

To install:

5. Position the servo and tighten the bolts securely.

6. Connect the control cable.

7a. Gasoline engines: With the ignition switch OFF and the fast idle cam not engaged, and the throttle fully closed, hook the rod in the servo and position over the stud. Position the rod so that there is a gap of 1–5mm between the stud and the outer end of the slot in the rod. Install the retainer.

7b. Hook the rod in the servo and position the pin on the rod in the hole closest to the servo that allows 1mm of play at the throttle cable.

8. Connect the cruise control cable on the 3rd ball of the servo chain.

9. Turn the locknut until the cable sleeve at the throttle lever is tight, but not holding the throttle open.

10. Install the retainer.

11. Connect the hoses.

WINDSHIELD WIPERS

Blade and Arm

REMOVAL AND INSTALLATION

1. Pull the wiper arms away from the glass and release the clip underneath. The wiper arms are splined to the shafts and can be pulled off.

2. To remove the arm, pry underneath it with a screwdriver or similar tool. Be careful not to scratch the paint.

3. To install, position the arm over the shaft and press down. Make sure you install the arms in the same position on the windshield as they were when they were removed.

Wiper Motor

REMOVAL AND INSTALLATION

1. Be sure that the wiper motor arm is in PARK position. The wiper arms should be in their normal OFF position.

2. Open the hood and disconnect the battery ground cable.

3. Remove the exposed cowl cover screws with the hood up.

4. Remove the wiper arms. This can be done by pulling the wiper arms away from the glass to release the clip underneath. The wiper arms are splined to the shafts and can be pulled off.

5. Remove the remaining screws securing the cowl panel and remove it.

6. Loosen the nuts holding the transmis-

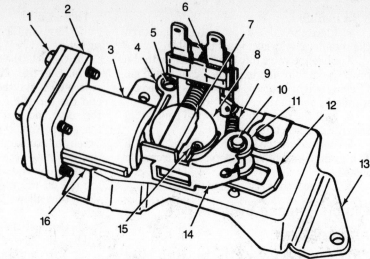

1. Valve assembly mounting screw
2. Valve assembly
3. Pump
4. Ratchet dog
5. Ratchet dog retaining screw
6. Solenoid coil
7. Solenoid plunger
8. Ratchet wheel
9. Ratchet pawl spring
10. Cam follower upper pin
11. E-ring
12. Cam follower
13. Frame
14. Ratchet pawl
15. Ratchet wheel spring
16. Retaining groove

Washer pump

sion linkage to the wiper motor crank arm.

7. Disconnect the power feed to the wiper arm at the connector next to the radio.

8. Remove the flex hose from the left defroster outlet to gain access to the wiper motor screws.

9. Remove the one screw holding the left hand heater duct to the engine shroud and move the heater duct down and out.

10. Remove the windshield washer hoses from the pump.

11. Remove the 3 screws holding the wiper motor to the cowl and lift the wiper motor out from under the dash.

To install:

12. Position the wiper motor in the PARK position.

13. Position the wiper motor under the dash.

14. Install the 3 screws holding the wiper motor to the cowl.

15. Install the windshield washer hoses at the pump.

16. Install the one screw holding the left hand heater duct to the engine.

17. Install the flex hose at the left defroster outlet.

18. Connect the power feed to the wiper arm at the connector next to the radio.

19. Tighten the nuts holding the transmission linkage to the wiper motor crank arm.

20. Install the cowl panel.

21. Install the wiper arms.

22. Install the cowl cover screws.

23. Connect the battery ground cable.

24. Be sure that the wiper motor arm is in PARK position. The wiper arms should be in their normal OFF position.

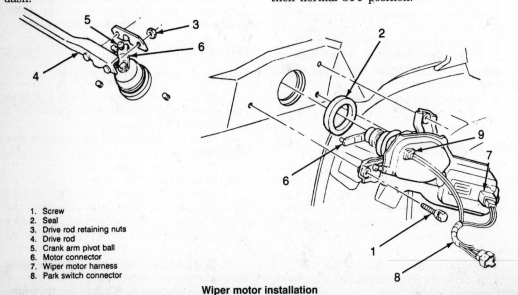

1. Screw
2. Seal
3. Drive rod retaining nuts
4. Drive rod
5. Crank arm pivot ball
6. Motor connector
7. Wiper motor harness
8. Park switch connector

Wiper motor installation

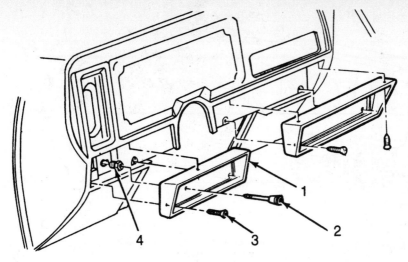

1. Trim plate
2. Knob
3. Screw
4. Bezel

Instrument panel trim plate

Wiper Linkage

REMOVAL AND INSTALLATION

1. Be sure that the wiper motor is in PARK position. The wiper arms should be in their normal OFF position.

2. Open the hood and disconnect the battery ground cable.

3. Remove the exposed cowl cover screws with the hood up.

4. Remove the wiper arms. This can be done by pulling the wiper arms away from the glass to release the clip underneath. The wiper arms are splined to the shafts and can be pulled off.

5. Remove the remaining screws securing the cowl panel and remove it.

6. Remove the screws and nuts securing the transmission linkage to the wiper motor crank arm. Disconnect the ball joint and remove the linkage.

To install:

7. Position the wiper motor in the PARK position.

8. Install the linkage.

9. Connect the ball joint.

10. Install the screws and nuts securing the transmission linkage to the wiper motor crank arm.

11. Install the cowl panel.

12. Install the wiper arms.

13. Install the cowl cover screws.

14. Connect the battery ground cable.

15. Be sure that the wiper motor is in PARK position. The wiper arms should be in their normal OFF position.

INSTRUMENTS AND SWITCHES

Instrument Cluster

The entire cluster may be removed from the vehicle for servicing the instruments and gauges. The illuminating and indicator lamps can be removed and replaced without removing the entire cluster. On earlier models, the lamps and bulbs are clip retained and can be easily snapped in or out. Later models use plastic bulb holders that are twist-locked through a laminated plastic printed circuit in the luster housing.

REMOVAL AND INSTALLATION

1. Disconnect the battery ground cable.

2. Reach up behind the cluster, depress the speedometer cable retaining tang and pull out the cable.

3. Remove the clock set stem knob.

4. Remove the cluster bezel retaining screws.

5. Remove the cluster bezel.

6. Remove the 2 lower cluster retaining screws.

7. Pull the top of the cluster away from the panel and lift out the bottom of the cluster. Pull the cluster out just far enough to unplug the wiring and remove the cluster.

8. Installation is the reverse of removal.

Wiper and Washer Switch

REMOVAL AND INSTALLATION

The wiper/washer switch is part of a multi-function switch mounted on the steering column. For service, see Chapter 8.

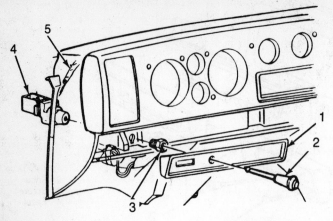

1. Trim plate
2. Knob
3. Bezel
4. Light switch
5. Light switch harness

Light switch

Head Light Switch

REMOVAL AND INSTALLATION

1. Disconnect the negative battery cable.
2. Remove the left instrument panel trim plate.

3. Remove the retaining nut securing the switch.

4. Disconnect the electrical connector from the back of the switch.

5. The switch can now be removed.

6. Reverse the procedure for installation.

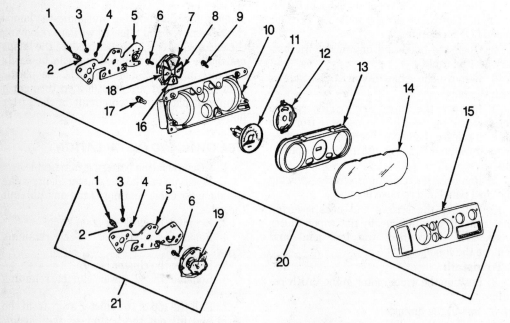

1. Bolt — 8-32 × $^{7}/_{16}$ in.
2. Speedometer mounting bushing
3. Nut
4. Flat washer
5. Laminated circuit
6. Screw — 8-18 × $^{7}/_{16}$ in.
7. Fuel gauge
8. Engine oil pressure gauge
9. Screw — 8-16 × $^{7}/_{16}$ in.
10. Retainer
11. Speedometer
12. Gauge mask
13. Lens retainer
14. Lens
15. Bezel
16. Voltmeter
17. Lamp
18. Engine coolant temperature gauge
19. Fuel gauge
20. Instrument cluster with gauges
21. Instrument cluster without gauges

Instrument panel components

Speedometer Cable

REMOVAL AND INSTALLATION

1. Reach up behind the speedometer and disconnect the speedometer cable from the rear of the speedometer head by depressing the clip.

2. Remove the old cable by pulling it out from the speedometer end of the cable housing. If the old cable is broken, the speedometer cable will have to be disconnected from the transmission and the cable removed from the other end.

3. Lubricate the lower $3/4$ of the new cable with speedometer cable lubricant and feed the cable into the cable housing.

4. Connect the speedometer cable to the speedometer head and to the transmission if disconnected there.

LIGHTING

Headlight

REMOVAL AND INSTALLATION

1. Remove the headlight bezel by releasing the attaching screws.

2. Remove the spring (if any) from the retaining ring and turn the unit to disengage it from the headlamp adjusting screws.

3. Disconnect the wiring harness connector.

NOTE: *Do not disturb the adjusting screws.*

4. Remove the retaining ring and the headlamp.

5. Position the new sealed beam unit in the retaining ring.

NOTE: *The number which is molded into the lens must be at the top.*

6. Attach the wiring connector.

7. Install the headlamp assembly, twisting the ring slightly to engage the adjusting screws.

8. Install the retaining ring spring and check the operation of the unit. Install the bezel.

HEADLIGHT AIMING

The headlights must be properly aimed to provide the best, safest road illumination. The lights should be checked for proper aim, and adjusted if necessary, after installing a new sealed beam unit or if the front end sheet metal has been replaced. Certain state and local authorities have requirements for headlight aiming and you should check these before adjusting.

NOTE: *The truck's fuel tank should be about half full when adjusting the headlights. Tires should be properly inflated, and*

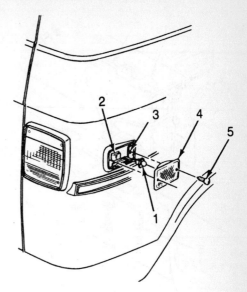

1. Bulb socket
2. Clip nut
3. Apply sealant
4. Lamp housing
5. Screw

Rear marker lamp

if a heavy load is carried, it should remain there.

Horizontal and vertical aiming of each sealed beam unit is provided by two adjusting screws, which move the mounting ring in the body against the tension of the coil spring. There is no adjustment for focus; this is done during headlight manufacturing.

Fog Lights

AIMING

1. Park the van on level ground, facing, perpendicular to, and about 25 ft. from a flat wall.

2. Remove any stone shields and switch on the fog lights.

3. Loosen the mounting hardware of the lights so you can aim them as follows:

   a. The horizontal distance between the light beams on the wall should be the same as between the lights themselves.

   b. The vertical height of the light beams above the ground should be 4 inches less than the distance between the ground and the center of the lamp lenses.

4. Tighten the mounting hardware.

Signal and Marker Lights

REMOVAL AND INSTALLATION

Front Turn Signal and Parking Lights

1. Disconnect the negative battery cable.
2. Remove the four bezel retaining screws.

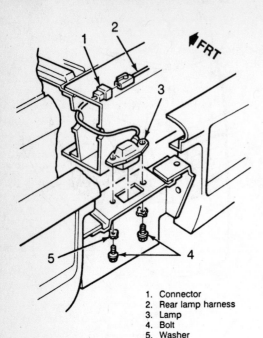

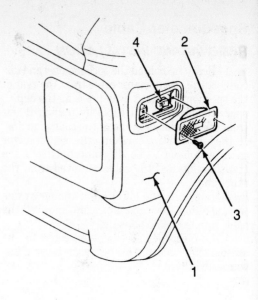

1. Connector
2. Rear lamp harness
3. Lamp
4. Bolt
5. Washer

1. Fender
2. Side marker lamp
3. Screw
4. Nut

License plate lamp

3. Remove the bezel.

4. Remove the three park lamp retaining screws.

5. Remove the parking lamp.

6. Disconnect the electrical connector from the parking lamp and install a new bulb.

7. Installation is the reverse of the removal procedure.

Front Side Marker Lights

1. Disconnect the negative battery cable.

2. Remove the two retaining screws.

3. Remove the side marker lamp.

4. Remove the bulb from the lamp and install a new bulb.

5. Installation is the reverse of the removal procedure.

Front side marker lamp

Rear Side Marker Lights

1. Disconnect the negative battery cable.

2. Remove the housing retaining screws.

3. Remove the housing.

4. Gently pull out the bulb socket.

5. Remove the bulb.

6. Installation is the reverse of the removal procedure.

Rear Turn Signal, Brake and Parking Lights

1. Disconnect the negative battery cable.

2. Remove the lens housing retaining screws.

3. Remove the lamp housing.

4. Remove the bulb socket by squeezing the retention lock and rotating the socket counterclockwise.

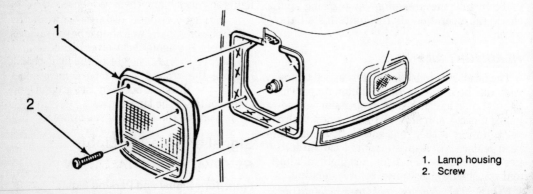

1. Lamp housing
2. Screw

Rear lamps

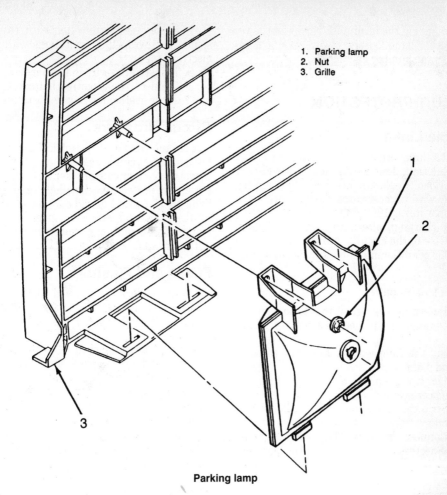

1. Parking lamp
2. Nut
3. Grille

Parking lamp

5. Remove the bulb.

6. Installation is the reverse of the removal procedure.

Trailer Wiring

Wiring the van for towing is fairly easy. There are a number of good wiring kits available and these should be used, rather than trying to design your own. All trailers will need brake lights and turn signals as well as tail lights and side marker lights. Most states require extra marker lights for overly wide trailers. Also, most states have recently required back-up lights for trailers, and most trailer manufacturers have been building trailers with back-up lights for several years.

Additionally, some Class I, most Class II and just about all Class III trailers will have electric brakes.

Add to this number an accessories wire, to operate trailer internal equipment or to charge the trailer's battery, and you can have as many as seven wires in the harness.

Determine the equipment on your trailer and buy the wiring kit necessary. The kit will contain all the wires needed, plus a plug adapter

set which included the female plug, mounted on the bumper or hitch, and the male plug, wired into, or plugged into the trailer harness.

When installing the kit, follow the manufacturer's instructions. The color coding of the wires is standard throughout the industry.

One point to note: some domestic vehicles, and most imported vehicles, have separate turn signals. On most domestic vehicles, the brake lights and rear turn signals operate with the same bulb. For those vehicles with separate turn signals, you can purchase an isolation unit so that the brake lights won't blink whenever the turn signals are operated, or, you can go to your local electronics supply house and buy four diodes to wire in series with the brake and turn signal bulbs. Diodes will isolate the brake and turn signals. The choice is yours. The isolation units are simple and quick to install, but far more expensive than the diodes. The diodes, however, require more work to install properly, since they require the cutting of each bulb's wire and soldering in place of the diode.

One, final point, the best kits are those with a spring loaded cover on the vehicle mounted socket. This cover prevents dirt and moisture from corroding the terminals. Never let the vehicle socket hang loosely; always mount it securely to the bumper or hitch.

CIRCUIT PROTECTION

Fusible Links

Fusible links are sections of wire, with special insulation, designed to melt under electrical overload. Replacements are simply spliced into the wire in most cases. Circuits protected by fusible links, 1967–74, are: engine wiring, battery charging, alternator, and headlights. For 1975–86, the circuits are: high beam indicator, air conditioning hi-blower, horn, and ignition.

Fusible Link Repair

1. Determine the circuit that is damaged.
2. Disconnect the negative battery terminal.
3. Cut the damaged fuse link from the harness and discard it.
4. Identify and procure the proper fuse link and butt connectors.
5. Strip the wire about ¹/₂ in. (12.7mm) on each end.
6. Connect the fusible link and crimp the butt connectors making sure that the wires are secure.

7. Solder each connection with resin core solder, and wrap the connections with plastic electrical tape.
8. Reinstall the wire in the harness.
9. Connect the negative battery terminal and test the system for proper operation.

Circuit Breakers

A circuit breaker is a electrical switch which breaks the circuit in case of an overload. All models have a circuit breaker in the headlight switch to protect the headlight and parking light systems. An overload may cause the lights to flash on and off. All models with rear mounted air conditioners have a circuit breaker at the firewall.

Fuses and Flashers

The fuse block is mounted to the firewall, inside the truck, to the left of the steering column. The turn signal flasher and hazard warning flasher plug into the fuse block. Each fuse receptacle is marked as to the circuits it protects and the correct amperage. In-line fuses are also used to protect some circuits. These are: ammeter, rear air conditioner, and auxiliary heater.

NOTE: *A special heavy duty turn signal flasher is required to properly operate the turn signals when a trailer's lights are connected to the system.*

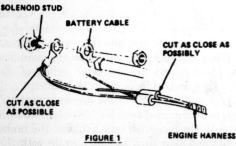

FIGURE 1
REMOVE BATTERY CABLE & FUSIBLE LINK FROM STARTER SOLENOID AND CUT OFF DEFECTIVE WIRE AS SHOWN TWO PLACES.

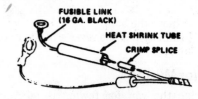

FIGURE 2
STRIP INSULATION FROM WIRE ENDS. PLACE HEAT SHRINK TUBE OVER REPLACEMENT LINK. INSERT WIRE ENDS INTO CRIMP SPLICE AS SHOWN. NOTE: PUSH WIRES IN FAR ENOUGH TO ENGAGE WIRE ENDS.

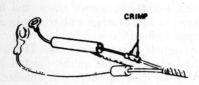

FIGURE 3
CRIMP SPLICE WITH CRIMPING TOOL TWO PLACES TO BIND BOTH WIRES.

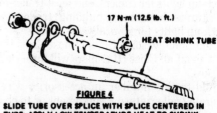

FIGURE 4
SLIDE TUBE OVER SPLICE WITH SPLICE CENTERED IN TUBE. APPLY LOW TEMPERATURE HEAT TO SHRINK TUBE AROUND WIRES & SPLICE. REASSEMBLE LINKS & BATTERY CABLE.

Fusible link repair

Drive Train

MANUAL TRANSMISSION

In 1987 the standard manual transmission for the 6-4.3L and 8-5.0L was the 3-speed Muncie. This transmission was discontinued after 1987.

The New Process 89mm 4-speed overdrive transmission was optional in 1987 and standard for 1988–90.

Back-Up Light Switch

REMOVAL AND INSTALLATION

The back-up light switch is located on the left side of the transmission case. See Chapter 6 for wiring details. To remove:

1. Disconnect the negative battery cable.
2. Disconnect the back-up switch harness.
3. Remove the back-up switch and the seal.
4. Installation is the reverse of the removal procedure.

Transmission

REMOVAL AND INSTALLATION

1. Raise and support the van.
2. Drain the transmission.
3. Disconnect the speedometer cable, back-up light and TCS switch.
4. Remove the shift controls from the transmission.
5. Disconnect the driveshaft and remove it from the vehicle.
6. Support the transmission with a floor jack.
7. Inspect the transmission to be sure that all necessary components have been removed or disconnected.

8. Mark the front of the crossmember to be sure that it is installed correctly.
9. Support the clutch release bearing to prevent it from falling out of the flywheel housing when the transmission is removed.
10. Remove the flywheel housing under pan and transmission mounting bolts.
11. Move the transmission slowly away from the engine, keeping the mainshaft in alignment with the clutch disc hub. Be sure that the transmission is supported.
12. Remove the transmission from under the vehicle.

To install:
13. Lightly coat the mainshaft with high temperature grease. Do not use much grease, since, under normal operation, the grease will be thrown onto the clutch, causing it to fail.
14. Raise the transmission into position under the vehicle.
15. Roll the unit forward, engaging the spline of the mainshaft with the splines in the clutch hub. Continue pushing forward until the transmission mates with the bell housing.
16. Install and tighten the transmission-to-bell housing bolts to 75 ft. lbs.
17. Install the flywheel housing under pan.
18. Install the crossmember. Torque the bolts to 50 ft. lbs.
19. Inspect the transmission to be sure that all necessary components have been installed or connected.
20. Connect the driveshaft.
21. Install the shift controls.
22. Connect the speedometer cable.
23. Connect the back-up light switch.
24. Connect the TCS switch.
25. Fill the transmission with lubricant.
26. Road test the vehicle.

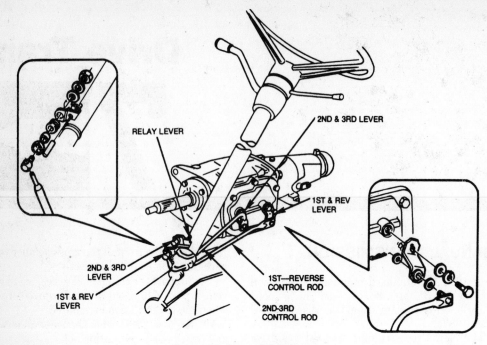

3-speed column shift linkage

Shift Linkage

ADJUSTMENT

3-Speed Column Shift

NOTE: *The gearshift linkage should be adjusted each time it is disturbed or removed. The 1st/reverse rod must be adjusted before the 2nd/3rd rod.*

1. Loosen the shift rod-to-transmission lever bolt.
2. Move the 1st/reverse transmission lever to the front detent, or, the 2nd/3rd transmission lever to the front detent, then back 1 detent.
3. Put the 1st/reverse column lever into reverse and lock the column, or, put the 2nd/3rd column lever into neutral.
4. Using a 1/4 in. (6mm) drill bit as a gauge pin, place the bit through the holes in the column levers and the relay lever. All should align.
5. Hold the shift rod down tightly in the swivel and tighten the bolt. Remove the gauge pin.

REMOVAL AND INSTALLATION

3-Speed Column Shift

1. Raise and support the front end on jackstands.

2. Remove the rod-to-column clips.
3. Disconnect the linkage at the column levers.
4. Disconnect the linkage at the transmission levers by removing the swivel bolts.
5. Unbolt the rods at the cross lever.
6. Remove the cross lever and linkage rods.
7. Installation is the reverse of removal. Lightly grease all moving parts.

Extension Housing Rear Seal

REPLACEMENT

3-Speed Transmission

1. Raise and support the rear end on jackstands.
2. Matchmark and remove the driveshaft.
3. Centerpunch the seal to distort it and pry it from the housing. Take care to avoid damage to the housing bore.
4. Coat the outside edge of the new seal with sealer.
5. Fill the gap between the seal lips with chassis grease.
6. Position the seal in the bore and carefully drive it into place. A seal installer tool is VERY helpful.
7. Coat the end of the driveshaft with grease and install it.

Rear Retainer Seal

REPLACEMENT

4-Speed Transmission

1. Raise and support the van on jackstands.
2. Matchmark and remove the driveshaft.
3. Drain the transmission.
4. Disconnect the speedometer cable.
5. Remove the flange nut and washer.
6. Pull the flange off the shaft.
7. Support the transmission with a floor jack.
8. Remove the transmission mount.
9. Unbolt and remove the rear bearing retainer and gasket.
10. Drive out the seal.

To install:

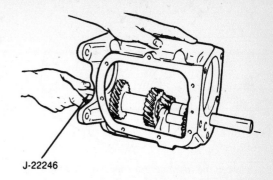

J-22246

Removing the countershaft - 3-speed

11. Coat the outside rim of the new seal with sealer.
12. Fill the gap between the seal lips with chassis grease.
13. Install the retainer and new gasket. Torque the top bolts to 20 ft. lbs.; the bottom bolts to 30 ft. lbs.
14. Install the transmission mount. Torque the bolts to 40 ft. lbs.
15. Install the flange, washer and nut. Torque the nut to 100 ft. lbs.
16. Connect the speedometer cable.
17. Install the driveshaft.
18. Refill the transmission.

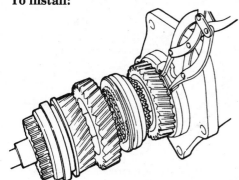

Removing the rear extension - 3-speed

Muncie 76mm 3-Speed Overhaul

The Muncie 76mm is a synchromesh three-speed transmission using helical constant mesh

1. Drive gear
2. Bearing retainer
3. Pilot bearings
4. Case
5. Rear extension
6. Vent
7. Mainshaft
8. Rear oil seal
9. Retainer oil seal
10. Bearing-to-gear snapring
11. Drive gear bearing
12. Bearing-to-case snapring
13. Front thrust washer
14. Rear thrust washer
15. Bearing-to-extension snapring
16. Countergear roller bearings
17. Countergear
18. Countershaft
19. Reverse idler shaft
20. Reverse idler retaining ring
21. Reverse idler gear
22. Woodruff key
23. Gasket
24. Spring washer
25. Screw
26. Rear extension bushing
27. Speedometer driven gear
28. Seal
29. Sleeve
30. Adapter
31. Screw
32. Spring washer
33. Gasket
34. Retaining washer
35. Reverse idler shaft spacer
36. Detent pin
37. Screw
38. Spring washer
39. Side cover
40. Gasket
41. Top gear blocker ring

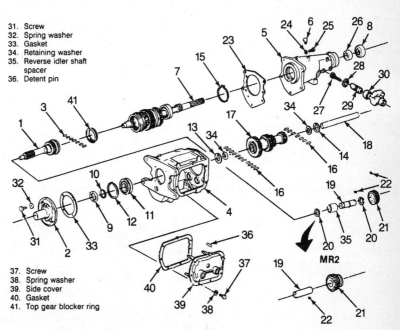

3-speed transmission exploded view

Removing the rear bearing snapring - 3-speed

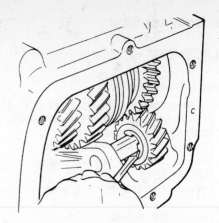

Removing the reverse idler retaining ring - 3-speed

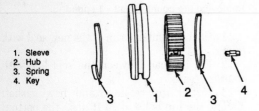

1. Sleeve
2. Hub
3. Spring
4. Key

Synchronizer components - 3-speed

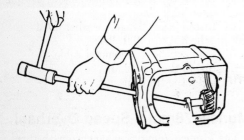

Removing the reverse idler shaft - 3-speed

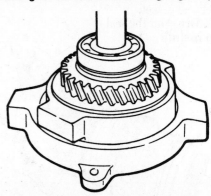

Pressing the mainshaft through the ring bearing -3-speed

gears. The engagement of all gears except reverse is assisted by synchronizers.

CASE DISASSEMBLY

1. Remove side cover assembly and shift forks.

2. Remove clutch gear bearing retainer.

3. Remove clutch gear bearing to gear stem snapring. Pull clutch gear outward until a screwdriver can be inserted between bearing and case. Remove clutch gear bearing.

4. Remove speedometer driven gear and extension bolts.

5. Remove reverse idler shaft snapring. Slide reverse idler gear forward on shaft.

Removing the synchronizer snapring - 3-speed

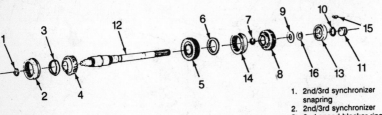

1. 2nd/3rd synchronizer snapring
2. 2nd/3rd synchronizer
3. 2nd speed blocker ring
4. 2nd gear
5. 1st gear
6. 1st gear blocker ring
7. 1st gear synchronizer snapring
8. Reverse gear
9. Reverse gear thrust washer
10. Rear bearing snapring
11. Speedometer drive gear
12. Mainshaft
13. Rear bearing
14. 1st/reverse synchronizer
15. Retaining clip
16. Wave washer

Mainshaft components - 3-speed

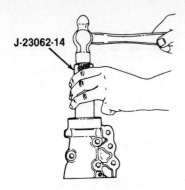

Install the rear extension bushing - 3-speed

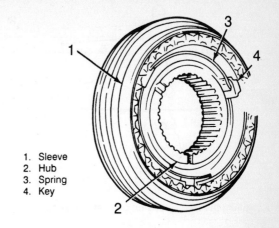

1. Sleeve
2. Hub
3. Spring
4. Key

Synchronizer assembly - 3-speed

6. Remove mainshaft and extension assembly.

7. Remove clutch gear and 3rd-speed blocker ring from inside case. Remove 14 roller bearings from clutch gear.

8. Expand the snapring which retains the mainshaft rear bearing. Remove the extension.

9. Using a dummy shaft, drive the countershaft and key out the rear of the case. Remove the gear, two tanged thrust washers, and dummy shaft. Remove bearing washer and 27 roller bearings from each end of countergear.

10. Use a long drift to drive the reverse idler shaft and key through the rear of the case.

11. Remove reverse idler gear and tanged steel thrust washer.

MAINSHAFT DISASSEMBLY

1. Remove 2nd and 3rd speed sliding clutch hug snapring from mainshaft. Remove clutch assembly, 2nd speed blocker ring, and 2nd speed gear from front of mainshaft.

2. Depress speedometer drive gear retaining clip. Remove gear. Some units have a metal speedometer drive gear which must be pulled off.

3. Remove rear bearing snapring.

4. Support reverse gear. Press on rear of mainshaft. Remove reverse gear, thrust

washer, spring washer, rear bearing, and snapring. When pressing off the rear bearing, be careful not to cock the bearing on the shaft.

5. Remove 1st and reverse sliding clutch hub snapring. Remove clutch assembly, 1st speed blocker ring, and 1st gear.

CLUTCH KEYS & SPRINGS

NOTE: *Keys and springs may be replaced if worn or broken, but the hubs and sleeves are matched pairs and must be kept together.*

1. Mark hub and sleeve for reassembly.

2. Push hub from sleeve. Remove keys and springs.

3. Place three keys and two springs, one on each side of hub, in position, so all three keys are engaged by both springs. The tanged end of the springs should not be installed into the same key.

4. Slide the sleeve onto the hub, aligning the marks.

NOTE: *A groove around the outside of the synchronizer hub marks the end that must be opposite the fork slot in the sleeve when assembled.*

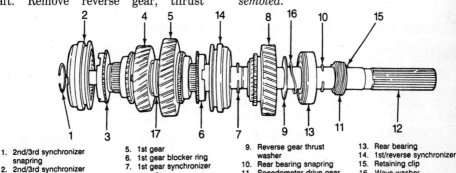

1. 2nd/3rd synchronizer snapring
2. 2nd/3rd synchronizer
3. 2nd speed blocker ring
4. 2nd gear
5. 1st gear
6. 1st gear blocker ring
7. 1st gear synchronizer snapring
8. Reverse gear
9. Reverse gear thrust washer
10. Rear bearing snapring
11. Speedometer drive gear
12. Mainshaft
13. Rear bearing
14. 1st/reverse synchronizer
15. Retaining clip
16. Wave washer
17. Flange (part of the mainshaft)

Mainshaft assembly - 3-speed

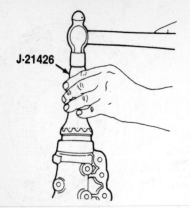

J-21426

Installing the rear extension oil seal - 3-speed

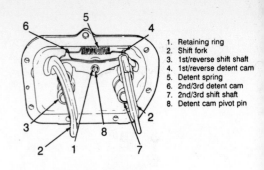

1. Retaining ring
2. Shift fork
3. 1st/reverse shift shaft
4. 1st/reverse detent cam
5. Detent spring
6. 2nd/3rd detent cam
7. 2nd/3rd shift shaft
8. Detent cam pivot pin

Side cover assembled - 3-speed

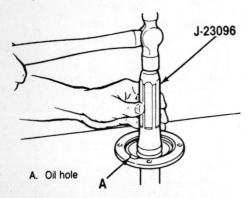

J-23096

A. Oil hole

Installing the bearing retainer oil seal - 3-speed

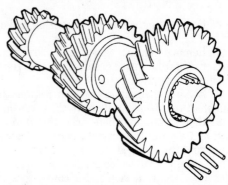

Installing the countergear bearings - 3-speed

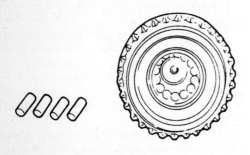

Drive gear gatherings - 3-speed

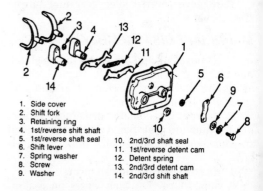

1. Side cover
2. Shift fork
3. Retaining ring
4. 1st/reverse shift shaft
5. 1st/reverse shaft seal
6. Shift lever
7. Spring washer
8. Screw
9. Washer
10. 2nd/3rd shaft seal
11. 1st/reverse detent cam
12. Detent spring
13. 2nd/3rd detent cam
14. 2nd/3rd shift shaft

Side cover - 3-speed

EXTENSION OIL SEAL & BUSHING

1. Remove seal.
2. Using bushing remover and installer tool, or other suitable tool, drive bushing into extension housing.
3. Drive new bushing in from the rear. Lubricate inside of bushing and seal. Install new oil seal with extension seal installer tool or other suitable tool.

CLUTCH BEARING RETAINER OIL SEAL

1. Pry old seal out.
2. Install new seal using seal installer or suitable tool. Seat seal in bore.

ASSEMBLY

1. Turn front of mainshaft up.
2. Install 2nd gear with clutching teeth up; the rear face of the gear butts against the flange on the mainshaft.
3. Install a blocker ring with clutching teeth down. All three blocker rings are the same.
4. Install 2nd and 3rd speed synchronizer assembly with fork slot down. Press it onto mainshaft splines. Both synchronizer assemblies are the same. Be sure that blocker ring notches align with synchronizer assembly keys.
5. Install synchronizer snapring. Both synchronizer snaprings are the same.

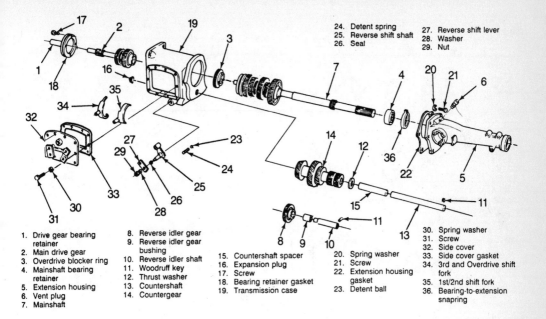

1. Drive gear bearing retainer
2. Main drive gear
3. Overdrive blocker ring
4. Mainshaft bearing retainer
5. Extension housing
6. Vent plug
7. Mainshaft
8. Reverse idler gear
9. Reverse idler gear bushing
10. Reverse idler shaft
11. Woodruff key
12. Thrust washer
13. Countershaft
14. Countergear
15. Countershaft spacer
16. Expansion plug
17. Screw
18. Bearing retainer gasket
19. Transmission case
20. Spring washer
21. Screw
22. Extension housing gasket
23. Detent ball
24. Detent spring
25. Reverse shift shaft
26. Seal
27. Reverse shift lever
28. Washer
29. Nut
30. Spring washer
31. Screw
32. Side cover
33. Side cover gasket
34. 3rd and Overdrive shift fork
35. 1st/2nd shift fork
36. Bearing-to-extension snapring

4-speed transmission exploded view

6. Turn rear of shaft up.

7. Install 1st gear with clutching teeth up; the front face of the gear butts against the flange on the mainshaft.

8. Install a blocker ring with clutching teeth down.

9. Install 1st and reverse synchronizer assembly with fork slot down. Press it onto mainshaft splines. Be sure blocker ring notches align with synchronizer assembly keys.

10. Install snapring.

11. Install reverse gear with clutching teeth down.

12. Install steel reverse gear thrust washer and spring washer.

13. Press rear ball bearing onto shaft with snapring slot down.

14. Install snapring.

15. Install speedometer drive gear and retaining clip. Press on metal speedometer drive gear.

CASE ASSEMBLY

1. Using dummy shaft load a row of 27 roller bearings and a thrust washer at each end of countergear. Hold in place with grease.

2. Place countergear assembly into case through rear. Place a tanged thrust washer, tang away from gear at each end. Install countershaft and key, making sure that tangs align with notches in case.

3. Install reverse idler gear thrust washer, gear, and shaft with key from rear of case. Be sure thrust washer is between gear and rear of case with tang toward notch in case.

NOTE: *The reverse idler gear bushing may not be replaced separately, only as a unit with the gear.*

4. Expand snapring in extension. Assemble extension over rear of mainshaft and onto rear bearing. Seat snapring in rear bearing groove.

5. Install 14 mainshaft pilot bearings into clutch gear cavity. Assemble 3rd speed blocker ring onto clutch gear clutching surface with teeth toward gear.

6. Place clutch gear, pilot bearings, and 3rd speed blocker ring assembly over front of main-

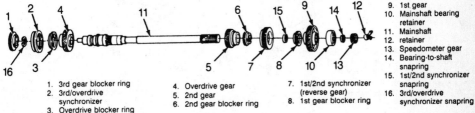

1. 3rd gear blocker ring
2. 3rd/overdrive synchronizer
3. Overdrive blocker ring
4. Overdrive gear
5. 2nd gear
6. 2nd gear blocker ring
7. 1st/2nd synchronizer (reverse gear)
8. 1st gear blocker ring
9. 1st gear
10. Mainshaft bearing retainer
11. Mainshaft
12. retainer
13. Speedometer gear
14. Bearing-to-shaft snapring
15. 1st/2nd synchronizer snapring
16. 3rd/overdrive synchronizer snapring

Mainshaft and components - 4-speed

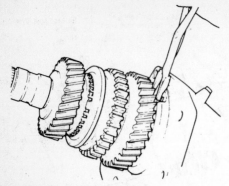

Removing the mainshaft - 4-speed

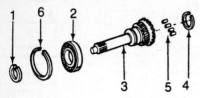

1. Bearing-to-shaft snapring	4. Snapring
2. Main drive gear bearing	5. Pilot bearings
3. Main drive gear	6. Bearing-to-case snapring

Main drive gear components - 4-speed

Removing the reverse idler shaft - 4-speed

1. Thrust washer
2. Countershaft bearings
3. Counter gear
4. Countershaft spacer
5. Bearing spacers

Countergear and components - 4-speed

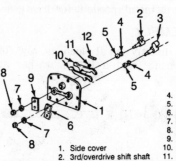

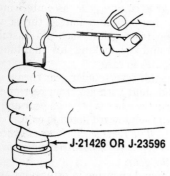

— J·21426 OR J·23596

Installing the rear extension bushing and seal - 4-speed

Pressing the mainshaft through the bearing - 4-speed

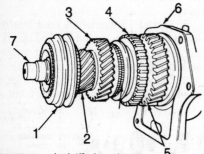

1. 3rd/overdrive synchronizer	4. 1st/2nd synchronizer (reverse gear)
2. Overdrive gear	5. 1st gear
3. 2nd gear	6. Extension housing
	7. Mainshaft

Mainshaft assembled - 4-speed

1. Side cover	4. Shift shaft seal
2. 3rd/overdrive shift shaft	5. Retainer
3. 1st/2nd shift shaft	6. 1st/2nd shift lever
	7. Washer
	8. Nut
	9. 3rd/4th shift lever
	10. Detent cam
	11. Retaining clip
	12. Detent spring

Side cover and components - 4-speed

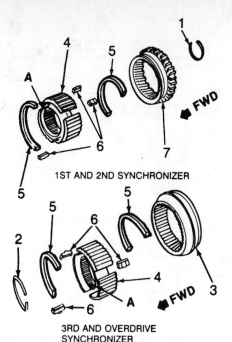

1ST AND 2ND SYNCHRONIZER

3RD AND OVERDRIVE
SYNCHRONIZER

A. Forward
1. 1st/2nd synchronizer
    snapring
2. 3rd/overdrive
    synchronizer snapring

3. Sleeve
4. Hub
5. Spring
6. Key
7. Reverse gear

Synchronizer components - 4-speed

shaft assembly. Be sure blocker rings align with keys in 2nd-3rd synchronizer assembly.

7. Stick extension gasket to case with grease. Install clutch gear, mainshaft, and extension together. Be sure clutch gear engages teeth of countergear anti-lash plate. Torque extension bolts to 45 ft. lbs.

8. Place bearing over stem of clutch gear and into front case bore. Install front bearing to clutch gear snapring.

9. Install clutch gear bearing retainer and

gasket. The retainer oil return hole must be at the bottom. Torque to 10 ft. lbs.

10. Install reverse idler gear shaft E-ring.

11. Shift synchronizer sleeves to neutral positions. Install cover, gasket, and forks, aligning forks with synchronizer sleeve grooves. Torque side cover bolts to 10 ft. lbs.

12. Install speedometer driven gear.

New Process 89mm 4-Speed Overhaul

CASE DISASSEMBLY

1. Mount the transmission in a holding fixture. Remove the parking brake assembly, if one is installed.

2. Shift the gears into neutral by replacing the gear shift lever temporarily, or by using a bar or screw driver.

3. Remove the cover screws, the 2nd screw from the front on each side is shouldered with a split washer for installation alignment.

4. While lifting the cover, rotate slightly counterclockwise to provide clearance for the shift levers. Remove the cover.

5. Lock the transmission in two gears and remove the output flange nut, the yoke, and the parking brake drum as a unit assembly.

NOTE: *The drum and yoke are balanced and unless replacement of parts are required, it is recommended that the drum and yoke be removed as a assembly.*

6. Remove the speedometer drive gear pinion and the mainshaft rear bearing retainer.

7. Before removal and disassembly of the drive pinion and mainshaft, measure the end play between the synchronizer stop ring and the 3rd gear. Clearance should be within 0.050–0.070 in. (1.27–1.78mm). If necessary, add corrective shims during assembly.

NOTE: *Record this reading for reference during assembly.*

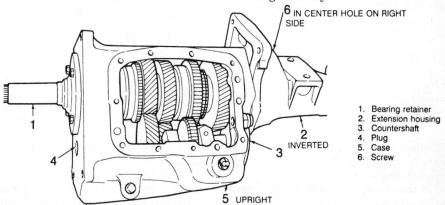

1. Bearing retainer
2. Extension housing
3. Countershaft
4. Plug
5. Case
6. Screw

Turning the extension housing - 4-speed

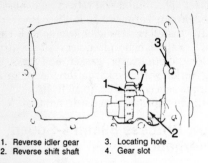

1. Reverse idler gear
2. Reverse shift shaft
3. Locating hole
4. Gear slot

Reverse idler gear and case - 4-speed

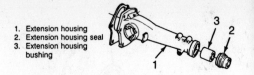

1. Extension housing
2. Extension housing seal
3. Extension housing bushing

Extension housing and components - 4-speed

1. Drive gear bearing retainer
2. Seal

Bearing retainer and seal - 4-speed

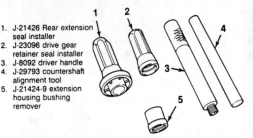

1. J-21426 Rear extension seal installer
2. J-23096 drive gear retainer seal installer
3. J-8092 driver handle
4. J-29793 countershaft alignment tool
5. J-21424-9 extension housing bushing remover

Special tools - 4-speed

8. Remove the drive pinion bearing retainer.

9. Rotate the drive pinion gear to align the space in the pinion gear clutch teeth with the countershaft drive gear teeth. Remove the drive pinion gear and the tapered roller bearing from the transmission by pulling on the pinion shaft, and rapping the face of the case lightly with a brass hammer.

10. Remove the snapring, washer, and the pilot roller bearings from the recess in the drive pinion gear.

11. Place a brass drift in the front center of the mainshaft and drive the shaft rearward.

12. When the mainshaft rear bearing has cleared the case, remove the rear bearing and the speedometer drive gear with a suitable gear puller.

13. Move the mainshaft assembly to the rear of the case and tilt the front of the mainshaft upward.

14. Remove the roller type thrust washer.

15. Remove the synchronizer and stop rings separately.

16. Remove the mainshaft assembly.

17. Remove the reverse idler lock screw and lock plate.

18. Using a brass drift held at an angle, drive the idler shaft to the rear while pulling.

19. Lift the reverse idler gear out of the case.

NOTE: *If the countershaft gear does not show signs of excessive side play or end play and the teeth are not badly worn or chipped, it may not be necessary to replace the countershaft gear.*

20. Remove the bearing retainer at the rear end of the countershaft. The bearing assembly will remain with the retainer.

21. Tilt the cluster gear assembly and work it out of the transmission case.

22. Remove the front bearings from the case with a suitable driver.

MAINSHAFT

1. Remove the clutch gear snapring.

2. Remove the clutch gear, the synchronizer outer stop ring to 3rd gear shim, and the 3rd gear.

3. Remove the special split lock ring with two screw drivers. Remove the 2nd gear and synchronizer.

4. Remove the 1st-reverse sliding gear.

5. Drive the old seal out of the bearing retainer.

6. Place the mainshaft in a soft-jawed vise with the rear end up.

7. Install the 1st-reverse gear. Be sure the two spline springs, if used, are in place inside the gear as the gear is installed on the shaft.

8. Place the mainshaft in a soft-jawed vise with the front end up.

9. Assemble the 2nd speed synchronizer spring and synchronizer brake on the 2nd gear. Secure the brake with a snapring making sure that the snapring tangs are away from the gear.

10. Slide the 2nd gear on the front of the mainshaft. Make sure that the synchronizer brake is toward the rear. Secure the gear to the shaft with the two piece lock ring. Install the 3rd gear.

11. Install the shim between the 3rd gear and the 3rd-4th synchronizer stop ring. Refer to the measurements of end play made during disassembly to determine if additional shims are needed.

NOTE: *The exact determination of end-play must be made after the complete assembly of the mainshaft and the main drive pinion is installed in the transmission case.*

REVERSE IDLER GEAR

Do not disassemble the reverse idler gear. If it is no longer serviceable, replace the assembly complete with the integral bearings.

COVER & SHIFT FORK UNIT

NOTE: *The cover and shift fork assembly should be disassembled only if inspection shows worn or damaged parts, or if the assembly is not working properly.*

1. Remove the roll pin from the 1st-2nd shift fork and the shift gate with a screw extractor.

NOTE: *A square type or a closely wound spiral screw extractor mounted in a tap is preferable for this operation.*

2. Move the 1st-2nd shift rail forward and force the expansion plug out of the cover. Cover the detent ball access hole in the cover with a cloth to prevent it from flying out. Remove the rail, fork, and gate from the cover.

3. Remove the 3rd-4th shift rail, then the reverse rail in the manner outlined in Steps 1 and 2 above.

4. Compress the reverse gear plunger and remove the retaining clip. Remove the plunger and spring from the gate.

5. Install the spring on the reverse gear plunger and hold it in the reverse shift gate. Compress the spring in the shift gate and install the retaining clip.

6. Insert the reverse shift rail in the cover and place the detent ball and spring in position. Depress the ball and slide the shift rail over it.

7. Install the shift gate and fork on the reverse shift rail. Install a new roll pin in the gate and the fork.

8. Place the reverse fork in the neutral position.

9. Install the two interlock plungers in their bores.

10. Insert the interlock pin in the 3rd-4th shift rail. Install the shift rail in the same manner as the reverse shift rail.

11. Install the 1st-2nd shift rail in the same manner as outlined above. Make sure the interlock plunger is in place.

12. Check the interlocks by shifting the reverse shift rail into the Reverse position. It should be impossible to shift the other rails with the reverse rail in this position.

13. If the shift lever is to be installed at this point, lubricate the spherical ball seat and place the cap in place.

14. Install the back-up light switch.

15. Install new expansion plugs in the bores of the shift rail holes in the cover. Install the rail interlock hole plug.

DRIVE PINION & BEARING RETAINER

1. Remove the tapered roller bearing from the pinion shaft with a suitable tool.

2. Remove the snapring, washer, and the pilot rollers from the gear bore, if they have not been previously removed.

3. Pull the bearing race from the front bearing retainer with a suitable puller.

4. Remove the pinion shaft seal with a suitable tool.

6. Position the drive pinion in an arbor press.

7. Place a wood block on the pinion gear and press it into the bearing until it contacts the bearing inner race.

8. Coat the roller bearings with a light film of grease to hold the bearings in place, and insert them in the pocket of the drive pinion gear.

9. Install the washer and snapring.

10. Press a new seal into the bearing retainer. Make sure that the lip of the seal is toward the mounting surface.

11. Press the bearing race into the retainer.

ASSEMBLY

1. Press the front countershaft roller bearings into the case until the cage is flush with the front of the transmission case. Coat the bearings with a light film of grease.

2. Place the transmission with the front of the case facing down. If uncaged bearings are used, hold the loose rollers in place in the cap with a light film of grease.

3. Lower the countershaft assembly into the case placing the thrust washer tangs in the slots in the case, and inserting the front end of the shaft into the bearing.

4. Place the roller thrust bearing and race on the rear end of the countershaft. Hold the bearing in place with a light film of grease.

5. While holding the gear assembly in alignment, install the rear bearing retainer gasket, retainer, and bearing assembly. Install and tighten the cap screws.

6. Position the reverse idler gear and bearing assembly in the case.

7. Align the idler shaft so that the lock plate groove in the shaft is in position to install the lock plate.

8. Install the lock plate, washer, and cap screw.

9. Make sure the reverse idler gear turns freely.

10. Lower the rear end of the mainshaft assembly into the case, holding the 1st gear on

the shaft. Maneuver the shaft through the rear bearing opening.

NOTE: *With the mainshaft assembly moved to the rear of the case, be sure the 3rd-4th synchronizer and shims remain in position.*

11. Install the roller type thrust bearing.

12. Place a wood block between the front of the case and the front of the mainshaft.

13. Install the rear bearing on the mainshaft by carefully driving the bearing onto the shaft and into the case, snapring flush against the case.

14. Install the drive pinion shaft and bearing assembly. Make sure that the pilot rollers remain in place.

15. Install the spacer and speedometer drive gear.

16. Install the rear bearing retainer and gasket.

17. Place the drive pinion bearing retainer over the pinion shaft, without the gasket.

18. Hold the retainer tight against the bearing and measure the clearance between the retainer and the case with a feeler gauge.

NOTE: *End play in Steps 19 and 20 below allows for normal expansion of parts during operation, preventing seizure and damage to bearings, gears, synchronizers, and shafts.*

19. Install a gasket shim pack 0.010–0.015 in. thicker than measured clearance between the retainer and case to obtain the required 0.007–0.017 in. (0.178–0.432mm) pinion shaft end play. Tighten the front retainer bolts and recheck the end play.

20. Check the synchronizer end play clearance (0.050–0.070 in. or 1.27–1.78mm) after all mainshaft components are in position and properly tightened. Two sets of feeler gauges are used to measure the clearance. Care should be used to keep both gauges as close as possible to both sides of the mainshaft for best results.

NOTE: *In some cases, it may be necessary to disassemble the mainshaft and change the thickness of the shims to keep the end play clearance within the specified limits, 0.050–0.070 in. (1.27-1.78mm). Shims are available in two thicknesses.*

21. Install the speedometer drive pinion.

22. Install the yoke flange, drum, and drum assembly.

23. Place the transmission in two gears at once, and tighten the yoke flange nut.

24. Shift the gears and/or synchronizers into all gear positions and check for free rotation.

25. Cover all transmissions components with a film of transmission oil to prevent damage during start up after initial lubricant fill-up.

26. Move the gears to the neutral position.

27. Place a new cover gasket on the transmission case, and lower the cover over the transmission.

28. Carefully engage the shift forks into their proper gears. Align the cover.

29. Install a shouldered alignment screw with split washer in the screw hole 2nd from the front of the cover. Try out gear operation by shifting through all ranges. Make sure everything moves freely.

30. Install the remaining cover screws.

CLUTCH

Adjustments

CLUTCH PEDAL FREE PLAY

This adjustment is for the amount of clutch pedal free travel before the throwout bearing contacts the clutch release fingers. It is required periodically to compensate for clutch lining wear. Incorrect adjustment will cause gear grinding and clutch slippage or wear.

1. Disconnect the clutch fork return spring at the fork on the clutch housing.

2. Loosen the outer locknut on the adjusting rod.

3. Move the clutch fork back until clutch spring pressure is felt.

4. Hold the clutch pedal against its bumper and turn the inner adjusting nut until it is 0.28 in. (7mm) from the cross lever.

5. Tighten the locknut against the cross lever.

6. Install the return spring.

6. Check the free travel at the pedal and readjust as necessary. It should be $1^3/8$ in. (34mm).

Clutch Cross Lever

REMOVAL AND INSTALLATION

1. Disconnect the battery ground cable.

2. Disconnect the springs and adjusting rod.

3. Disconnect the pedal rod.

4. Unbolt the cross lever bracket.

5. Remove the bracket and cross lever.

6. Replace the ball studs if they are excessively worn or if at all damaged.

7. Clean all metal parts with a non-flammable solvent. Clean all plastic parts with a dry, clean rag. Coat all moving parts with lithium-based grease.

To install:

8. Install the bracket and cross lever. Torque the ball stud to 20 ft. lbs. on the bracket side; 40 ft. lbs. on the engine side.

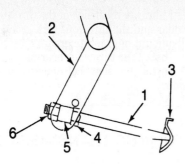

1. Adjusting rod
2. Cross lever
3. Clutch fork
4. Nut
5. Swivel
6. Nut

Clutch linkage adjustments

9. Connect the pedal rod.
10. Connect the springs and adjusting rod.
11. Connect the battery ground cable.

Clutch Pedal

REMOVAL AND INSTALLATION

1. Disconnect the battery ground cable.
2. Remove the cotter pin and washers from the pedal rod at the arm.
3. Remove the neutral start switch.
4. Remove the pedal arm retaining nut and washer.
5. Remove the pedal arm retaining bolt.
6. Remove the pedal arm
7. Disconnect the pedal rod.
8. Disconnect the return spring.
9. Remove the pedal.

CHILTON TIP: *Slide a long bolt or rod through the bracket while removing the pedal, to hold the brake pedal in place.*

10. Clean all metal parts with a non-flammable solvent. Clean all plastic parts with a dry,

clean rag. Coat all moving parts with lithium-based grease.
   To install:
11. Install the pedal.
12. Connect the return spring.
13. Connect the pedal rod.
14. Install the pedal arm
15. Install the pedal arm retaining bolt.
16. Install the pedal arm retaining nut and washer.
17. Install the neutral start switch.
18. Install the cotter pin and washers from the pedal rod at the arm.
19. Connect the battery ground cable.

Driven Disc and Pressure Plate

REMOVAL AND INSTALLATION

CAUTION: *The clutch driven disc contains asbestos, which has been determined to be a cancer causing agent. Never clean clutch surfaces with compressed air! Avoid inhaling any dust from any clutch surface! When cleaning clutch surfaces, use a commercially available brake cleaning fluid.*

1. Remove the transmission as previously outlined.
2. Disconnect the fork pushrod and remove the flywheel housing. Remove the clutch throwout bearing from the fork.
3. Remove the clutch fork by pressing it away from the ball mounting with a screwdriver until the fork snaps loose from the ball or remove the ball stud from the clutch housing.
4. Install a pilot tool (an old mainshaft makes a good pilot tool) to hold the clutch while you are removing it.

NOTE: *Before removing the clutch from the flywheel, matchmark the flywheel, the clutch cover and one of the pressure plate lugs. These parts must be reassembled in their orig-*

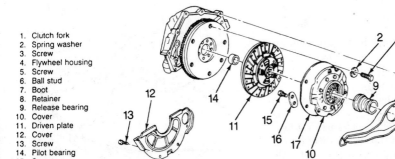

1. Clutch fork
2. Spring washer
3. Screw
4. Flywheel housing
5. Screw
6. Ball stud
7. Boot
8. Retainer
9. Release bearing
10. Cover
11. Driven plate
12. Cover
13. Screw
14. Pilot bearing
15. Screw
16. Strap
17. Pressure plate

R and V series clutch components

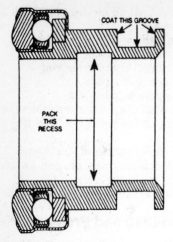

Lubrication points on the clutch throwout bearing

inal positions as they are a balanced assembly.

5. Loosen the clutch attaching bolts one turn at a time to prevent distortion of the clutch cover until the tension is released.

6. Remove the clutch pilot tool and the clutch from the vehicle.

7. Inspect the flywheel and pressure plate for discoloration, scoring or wear marks. The flywheel can be refaced if necessary, otherwise replace the parts. Also inspect the clutch fork and throwout bearing for looseness or wear. Replace if either is evident.

To install:

8. Install the pressure plate in the cover assembly, aligning the notch in the pressure plate with the notch in the cover flange.

9. Install the pressure plate retracting spring, lock washers, and the drive strap to the pressure plate bolts. Torque to 11 ft. lbs.

10. Turn the flywheel until the **X** mark is at the bottom.

11. Install the clutch disc, pressure plate and cover, using an old mainshaft as an aligning tool.

12. Turn the clutch until the **X** mark on the clutch cover aligns with the **X** mark on the flywheel.

13. Install the attaching bolts and tighten them a little at a time in a crisscross pattern until the spring pressure is taken up.

14. Remove the aligning tool.

15. Pack the clutch ball fork seat with a small amount of high temperature grease. Too much grease will cause slippage. Install a new retainer in the groove of the clutch fork, if necessary. Install the retainer with the high side up and the open end on the horizontal.

16. If the clutch fork ball was removed, reinstall it in the clutch housing and snap the clutch fork onto the ball.

17. Lubricate the inside of the throwout bearing collar and the throwout fork groove with a small amount of graphite grease.

18. Install the throwout bearing.

19. Install the flywheel housing and transmission.

20. Adjust the clutch.

AUTOMATIC TRANSMISSION

Two transmission are available depending on selected drivetrain combinations and GVW packages. They are the Turbo Hydra-Matic 400 3-speed and the Turbo Hydra-Matic 700R4 4-speed overdrive.

In 1990 the designations were changed, while the transmissions remained essentially the same. The THM 400 3-speed became the 3L80; the THM 700R4 became the 4L60.

Fluid Pan and Filter

REMOVAL AND INSTALLATION

The fluid should be drained with the transmission warm. It is easier to change the fluid if the truck is raised somewhat from the ground, but this is not always easy without a lift. The transmission must be level for it to drain properly.

1. Place a shallow pan underneath to catch the transmission fluid (about 5 pints). Loosen all the pan bolts, then pull one corner down to drain most of the fluid. If it sticks, VERY CAREFULLY pry the pan loose. You can buy aftermarket drain plug kits that makes this operation a bit less messy, once installed.

NOTE: *If the fluid removed smells burnt, serious transmission troubles, probably due to overheating, should be suspected.*

2. Remove the pan bolts and empty out the pan. On some models, there may not be much room to get at the screws at the front of the pan.

3. Clean the pan with solvent and allow it

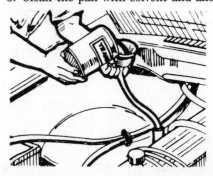

Transmission fluid is added through the dipstick tube

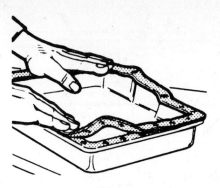

Install the new gasket on the pan

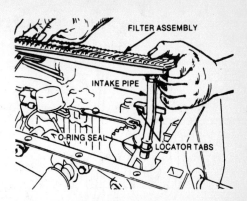

The Turbo Hydra-Matic 400 filter has an O-ring on the intake pipe; check the condition of this O-ring, and replace it as necessary

to air dry. If you use a rag to wipe it out, you risk leaving bits of lint and threads in the transmission.

4. Remove the filter or strainer retaining bolts. On the Turbo Hydra-Matic 400, there are two screws securing the filter or screen to the valve body. A reusable strainer may be found on some models. The strainer may be cleaned in solvent and air dried thoroughly. The filter and gasket must be replaced.

5. Install a new gasket and filter.

6. Install a new gasket on the pan, and tighten the bolts evenly to 12 foot pounds in a criss-cross pattern.

7. Add or DEXRON®II transmission fluid through the dipstick tube. The correct amount is in the Capacities Chart. Do not overfill.

8. With the gearshift lever in **PARK**, start the engine and let it idle. Do not race the engine.

9. Move the gearshift lever through each position, holding the brakes. Return the lever to **PARK**, and check the fluid level with the engine idling. The level should be between the two dimples on the dipstick, about $1/4$ in. (6mm) below the **ADD** mark. Add fluid, if necessary.

10. Check the fluid level after the truck has been driven enough to thoroughly warm up the transmission. Details are given under Fluid Level Checks earlier in the Chapter. If the transmission is over filled, the excess must be drained off. Overfilling causes aerated fluid, resulting in transmission slippage and probable damage.

Adjustments

SHIFT LINKAGE

1. Raise and support the front end on jackstands.

2. Loosen the shift lever bolt or nut at the transmission lever so that the lever is free to move on the rod.

3. Set the column shift lever to the Neutral gate notch, by rotating it until the shift lever

drops into the Neutral gate. Do not use the indicator pointer as a reference to position the shift lever, as this will not be accurate.

4. Set the transmission lever in the neutral position by moving it clockwise to the Park detent, then counterclockwise 2 detents to Neutral.

5. Hold the rod tightly in the swivel and tighten the nut or bolt to 17 ft. lbs.

6. Move the column shifter to Park and check that the engine starts. Check the adjustment by moving the selector to each gear position.

Neutral Start Switch

This switch prevents the engine from being started unless the transmission is in Neutral or Park. It is located on the shift linkage on the left side of the transmission. The switch is also used for the back-up lights.

REMOVAL, INSTALLATION AND ADJUSTMENT

1. Loosen the switch mounting screws.

2. Make sure the transmission is in Neutral.

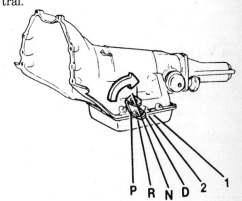

Shift positions

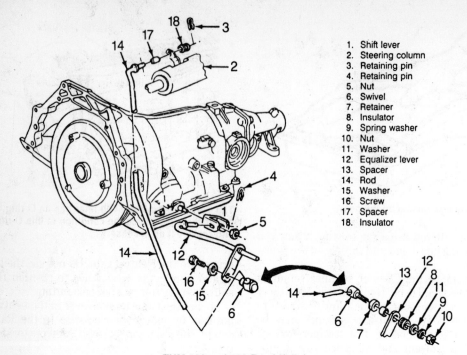

1. Shift lever
2. Steering column
3. Retaining pin
4. Retaining pin
5. Nut
6. Swivel
7. Retainer
8. Insulator
9. Spring washer
10. Nut
11. Washer
12. Equalizer lever
13. Spacer
14. Rod
15. Washer
16. Screw
17. Spacer
18. Insulator

THM 400 and 700-R4 shift linkage

3. Insert a pin through the hole in the switch actuating arm into the switch body to hold the switch in the Neutral position. Adjust as necessary to make the pin fit.

4. Tighten the adjustment. Remove the pin.

5. Check that the engine can be started only in Park and Neutral and that the backup lights go on only in Reverse. Adjust as necessary.

DOWNSHIFT ADJUSTMENT

Turbo Hydra-Matic 400

When installing a new downshift switch, press the plunger as far forward as possible. The switch will adjust itself the first time the accelerator is floorboarded.

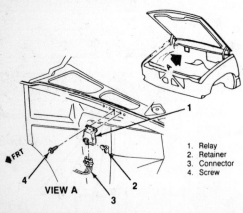

1. Relay
2. Retainer
3. Connector
4. Screw

VIEW A

Downshift relay

Back-Up Light Switch

The back-up light switch is located on the left side of the transmission case. To remove:

1. Disconnect the negative battery cable.

2. Disconnect the back-up switch assembly harness.

3. Place the gear selector in neutral.

4. Squeeze the switch tangs together and lift out the switch assembly.

5. Installation is the reverse of the removal procedure.

Throttle Valve Cable

REMOVAL AND INSTALLATION

THM 700R4

1. Remove the air cleaner.

2. Disconnect the cable from the throttle lever.

3. Compress the locking tangs and disconnect the cable housing from the bracket.

4. Remove all cable brackets and straps.

5. Remove the cable lower end retaining screw.

6. Disconnect the cable from the transmission link.

7. Installation is the reverse of removal. Take great care to avoid kinking the cable. Tighten the lower end retaining screw to 84 inch lbs. When connecting the cable to the throttle lever it should have a small amount of travel

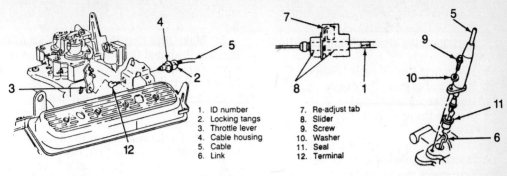

1.	ID number	7.	Re-adjust tab
2.	Locking tangs	8.	Slider
3.	Throttle lever	9.	Screw
4.	Cable housing	10.	Washer
5.	Cable	11.	Seal
6.	Link	12.	Terminal

TV cable replacement

against the return spring and should easily return under spring pressure.

8. Adjust the cable.

ADJUSTMENT

THM 700R4

The adjustment is made at the engine end of the cable with the engine off, by rotating the throttle lever by hand. DO NOT use the accelerator pedal to rotate the throttle lever.

1. Remove the air cleaner.
2. Depress and hold down the metal adjusting tab at the end of the cable.
3. Move the slider until it stops against the fitting.
4. Release the adjusting tab.
5. Rotate the throttle lever to the full extent of it travel.
6. The slider must move towards the lever when the lever is at full travel. Make sure that the cable moves freely.

CHILTON TIP: *The cable may appear to function properly with the engine cold. Recheck it with the engine hot.*

7. Road test the van.

Vacuum Modulator

REMOVAL AND INSTALLATION

THM 400

1. Raise and support the front end on jackstands.

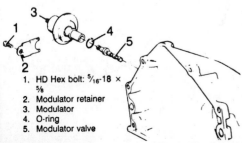

1. HD Hex bolt: $5/16$-18 × 5/8
2. Modulator retainer
3. Modulator
4. O-ring
5. Modulator valve

Vacuum modulator

2. Disconnect the vacuum line at the modulator.
3. Remove the screw and retaining clamp.
4. Remove the modulator. Be careful! Some fluid may run out.
5. Installation is the reverse of removal. Don't kink the vacuum line. Replace any lost fluid.

Speedometer Driven Gear or Vehicle Speed Sensor

REMOVAL AND INSTALLATION

1. Raise and support the front end on jackstands.
2. Disconnect the speedometer cable
3. Remove the retaining screw and retainer.
4. Remove the sleeve and seal.
5. Remove the driven gear or speed sensor.
6. Installation is the reverse of removal.

Extension Housing Rear Seal

REPLACEMENT

1. Raise and support the van on jackstands.
2. Matchmark and remove the driveshaft. Be careful! Some fluid may run out. You can avoid this by raising only the rear of the van.
3. Centerpunch the seal to distort it and carefully pry it out.
4. Coat the outer edge of the new seal with non-hardening sealer.
5. Place the seal in the bore and carefully drive it into place. A seal installer makes this job easier.
6. Install the driveshaft. It's a good idea to coat the driveshaft end with grease to avoid damaging the seal.
7. Lower the van and replace any lost fluid.

Transmission

REMOVAL AND INSTALLATION

NOTE: *It would be best to drain the transmission before starting.*

1. Disconnect the battery ground cable.
2. Remove the air cleaner.
3. Disconnect the downshift cable and throttle linkage.
4. Disconnect the TV cable (700R4).
5. Raise and support the van.
6. Drain the transmission.
7. Remove the driveshaft, after matchmarking its flange.
8. Disconnect the speedometer cable.
9. Disconnect the downshift cable.
10. Disconnect the TV cable.
11. Disconnect the vacuum modulator line.
12. Disconnect the shift linkage.
13. Disconnect the fluid cooler lines at the transmission.
14. Disconnect the support bracket at the catalytic converter.
15. Support the transmission and unbolt the rear mount from the crossmember.
16. Remove the crossmember.
17. Remove the converter underpan, matchmark the flywheel and converter, and remove the converter bolts.
18. Support the engine and lower the transmission slightly for access to the upper transmission to engine bolts.
19. Remove the transmission to engine bolts and pull the transmission back. Remove the filler tube. Rig up a strap or keep the front of the transmission up so the converter doesn't fall out.

To install:

20. Lubricate the internal yoke splines at the transmission end of the driveshaft with lithium based grease. The grease should seep out through the vent hole.
21. Raise the transmission into place and in-stall the engine bolts. Torque the bolts to 35 ft. lbs.
22. Make sure that the converter attaching lugs are flush and that the converter can turn freely before installing the bolts. Torque the bolts to 50 ft. lbs.
23. Install the converter underpan.
24. Install the crossmember. Torque the bolts to 60 ft. lbs.
25. Attach the rear mount to the crossmember. Torque the bolts to 25 ft. lbs.
26. Connect the support bracket at the catalytic converter.
27. Connect the fluid cooler lines at the transmission.
28. Connect the shift linkage.
29. Connect the vacuum modulator line.
30. Connect the TV cable.
31. Connect the downshift cable.
32. Connect the speedometer cable.
33. Install the driveshaft.
34. Connect the TV cable (700R4).
35. Connect the downshift cable and throttle linkage.
36. Install the air cleaner.
37. Connect the battery ground cable.
38. Refill the transmission.

DRIVELINE

Tubular driveshafts are used on all models incorporating needle bearing U-joints. An internally splined sleeve at the forward end compensates for variation in distance between the rear axle and the transmission.

Long wheelbase models use a 2-piece driveshaft with a center support bearing. The front section is supported at the rear end by a rubber

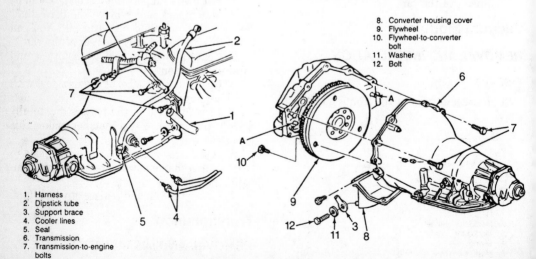

8. Converter housing cover
9. Flywheel
10. Flywheel-to-converter bolt
11. Washer
12. Bolt

1. Harness
2. Dipstick tube
3. Support brace
4. Cooler lines
5. Seal
6. Transmission
7. Transmission-to-engine bolts

THM 400 transmission and related components

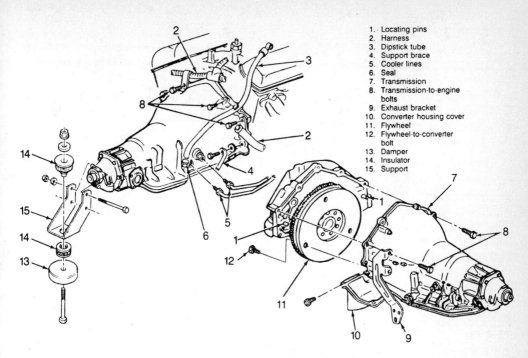

1. Locating pins
2. Harness
3. Dipstick tube
4. Support brace
5. Cooler lines
6. Seal
7. Transmission
8. Transmission-to-engine bolts
9. Exhaust bracket
10. Converter housing cover
11. Flywheel
12. Flywheel-to-converter bolt
13. Damper
14. Insulator
15. Support

THM 700-R4 transmission and related components

cushioned ball bearing mounted in a bracket attached to the frame crossmember. The ball bearing is permanently sealed and lubricated.

Driveshaft and U-Joints

REMOVAL AND INSTALLATION

1. Raise the vehicle and support it on jackstands. There is less chance of lubricant leakage from the rear of the transmission if the rear is raised.

2. Matchmark the driveshaft and rear

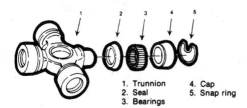

1. Trunnion   4. Cap
2. Seal   5. Snap ring
3. Bearings

Snapring type U-joint

pinion flange and both halves of 2-piece driveshaft. Remove the U-bolts or straps at the rear axle. Tape the bearing cups to the trunnions.

3. On models with 2-piece driveshaft, remove the bolts attaching the bearing support to the frame crossmember.

4. Slide the driveshaft forward and lower it. Slide the driveshaft toward the rear of the vehicle and disengage the splined sleeve from the output shaft of the transmission.

5. Remove the driveshaft from under the van.

6. Installation is the reverse of removal. Use the matchmarks made previously to help facilitate alignment. For models with 2-piece driveshaft, install the front half into the transmission and install the support to the crossmember. Rotate the shaft so that the front U-joint trunnions so that all are vertical. Rotate the rear shaft 4 splines to the left of the vehicle and connect the front and rear shaft. Some 2-piece

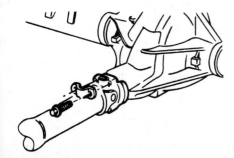

Rear driveshaft strap attachment

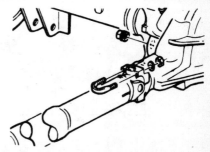

Rear driveshaft U-bolt attachment

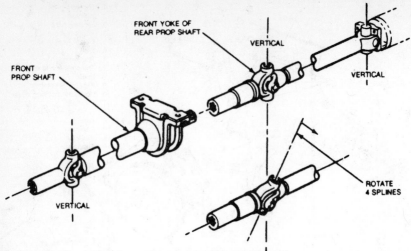

FRONT YOKE OF
REAR PROP SHAFT

VERTICAL

FRONT
PROP SHAFT

VERTICAL

VERTICAL

ROTATE
4 SPLINES

2-piece driveshaft alignment

driveshafts can only be assembled one way, in which case these instructions can be ignored. Attach the rear U-joint to the axle. On automatic transmission models, lubricate the internal yoke splines at the transmission end of the shaft with lithium base grease. The grease should seep out through the vent hole.

CHILTON TIP: *A thump in the rear driveshaft sometimes occurs when releasing the brakes after braking to a stop, especially on a downgrade. This is most common with automatic transmission. It is often caused by the* driveshaft splines binding and can be cured by removing the driveshaft, inspecting the splines for rough spots or sharp edges, and carefully lubricating.

U-JOINT OVERHAUL

U-Joint is mechanic's jargon for universal joint. U-joints should not be confused with U-bolts, which are U-shaped bolts used to hold U-joints in place to the axle or transfer case.

There are two types of U-joints used in these trucks. The first is held together by wire snapr-

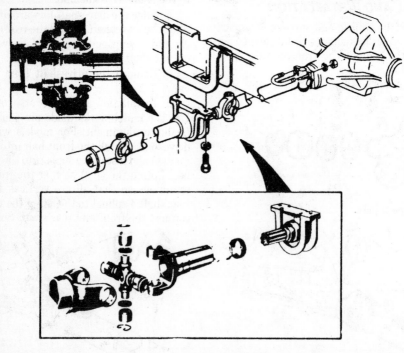

2-piece driveshaft

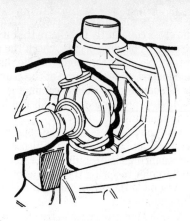

Installing the trunnion on the driveshaft yoke

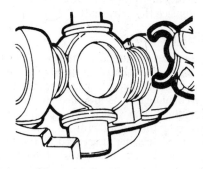

Installing the snapring

ings in the yokes. The second type is held together with injection molded plastic retainer rings. This type cannot be reassembled, once disassembled. Repair kits are available, however.

Snapring Type

These U-joints may be found on all model years.

1. Remove the driveshaft(s) from the truck.
2. Support the lockrings from the yoke and remove the lubrication fitting.
3. Support the yoke in a bench vise. Never clamp the driveshaft tube.
4. Use a socket to press against one trunnion bearing to press the opposite bearing from the yoke.
5. Grasp the cap and work it out.
6. Support the other side of the yoke and press the other bearing cap from the yoke and remove as in Steps 4 and 5.
7. Remove the trunnion from the driveshaft yoke.
8. If equipped with a sliding sleeve, remove the trunnion bearings from the sleeve yoke in the same manner as above. Remove the seal retainer from the end of the sleeve and pull the seal and washer from the retainer.
9. Disassemble the other U-joint. Clean and check the condition of all parts. You can buy

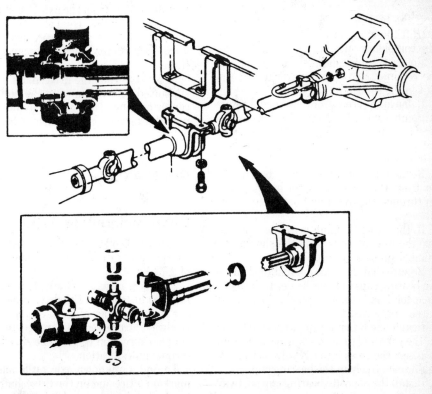

Driveshaft, U-joint and bearing support

U-joint repair kits to replace all the wearing parts.

To assemble the trunnion bearings:

10. Repack the bearings with grease and replace the trunnion dust seals after any operation that requires disassembly of the U-joint. Be sure that the lubricant reservoir at the end of the trunnion is full of lubricant. Fill the reservoirs with lubricant from the bottom.

11. Install the trunnion into the driveshaft yoke and press the bearings into the yoke over the trunnion hubs as far as it will go.

12. Install the lockrings.

13. Hold the trunnion in one hand and tap the yoke slightly to seat the bearings against the lockrings.

14. Replace the driveshaft.

Molded Retainer Type

NOTE: *Don't disassembly these joints unless you have a repair kit. The factory installed joints cannot be reassembled.*

1. Remove the driveshaft.

2. Support the driveshaft in a horizontal position. Place the U-joint so that the lower ear of the shaft yoke is supported by a $1^1/8$ in. socket. Press the lower bearing cup of the yoke ear. This will shear the plastic retaining the lower bearing cup.

NOTE: *Never clamp the driveshaft tubing in a vise.*

3. If the bearing cup is not completely removed, lift the cross, insert a spacer and press the cup completely out.

4. Rotate the driveshaft, shear the opposite plastic retainer, and press the other bearing cup out in the same manner.

5. Remove the cross from the yoke. Production U-joints cannot be reassembled. There are no bearing retainer grooves in the cups. Discard all parts that were removed and substitute those in the overhaul kit.

6. Remove the sheared plastic bearing retainer from the yoke. Drive a small pin or punch through the injection holes to aid in removal.

7. If the other U-joint is to be serviced, remove the bearing cups from the slip yoke in the manner previously described.

8. Be sure that the seals are installed on the service bearing cups to hold the needle bearings in place for handling. Grease the bearings if they aren't pregreased.

9. Install one bearing cup partway into one side of the yoke and turn this ear to the bottom.

10. Insert the cross into the yoke so that the trunnion seats freely in the bearing cup.

11. Install the opposite bearing cup partway. Be sure that both trunnions are started straight into the bearing cups.

12. Press against opposite bearing cups, working the cross constantly to be sure that it is free in the cups. If binding occurs, check the needle rollers to be sure that one needle has not become lodged under and end of the trunnion.

13. As soon as one bearing retainer groove is exposed, stop pressing and install the bearing retainer snapring.

14. Continue to press until the opposite bearing retainer can be installed. If difficulty installing the snaprings is encountered, rap the yoke with a hammer to spring the yoke ears slightly.

15. Assemble the other half of the U-joint in the same manner.

16. Check that the cross is free in the cups. If it is too tight, rap the yoke ears again to help seat the bearing retainers.

17. Replace the driveshaft.

Center Bearing

Center bearings support the drive line when two or more driveshafts are used. The center bearing is a ball type bearing mounted in a rubber cushion that is attached to the frame crossmember. The bearing is pre-lubricated and sealed by the manufacturer.

The center bearing is secured to the frame crossmember by two bolts, washers and nuts. Support the driveshafts properly and remove the bolts from the center bearing. Remove the rear driveshaft from the axle housing and separate the two shafts. Then slide the center bearing off. Reverse the procedure to install. Torque the center bearing attaching bolts to 24 ft. lbs.

Make sure that the driveshafts are properly supported before removing the bolts from the center bearing. The shafts may fall if not supported properly, once the center bearing is unbolted.

REAR AXLE

Determining Axle Ratio

Axle ratios offered in these trucks vary from a heavy duty ratio of 4.57:1 to an economy ratio of 2.73:1.

The axle ratio is obtained by dividing the number of teeth on the drive pinion gear into the larger number of teeth on the ring gear. It is always expressed as a proportion and is a simple expression of gear speed reduction and torque multiplication.

To find a unknown axle ratio, make a chalk mark on a tire and on the driveshaft. Move the truck ahead (or back) slowly for one tire rotation and have an observer note the number of driveshaft rotations. The number of driveshaft rotations if the axle ratio. You can get more accuracy by going more than one tire rotation and dividing the result by the number of tire rotations. This can also be done by jacking up both rear wheels and turning them by hand.

The axle ration is also identified by the axle serial number prefix on Chevrolet (GMC) axles. See Chapter 1 for serial number locations; the prefixes are listed in parts books. Dana axles usually have a tag under one of the cover bolts, giving either the ratio or the number of pinion ring gear teeth.

Axle Shaft, Bearing, and Seal

REMOVAL AND INSTALLATION

All Semi-Floating Axles Except Locking Differential

1. Support the axle on jackstands.
2. Remove the wheels and brake drums.
3. Clean off the differential cover area, loosen the cover to drain the lubricant, and remove the cover.
4. Turn the differential until you can reach the differential pinion shaft lock screw. Remove the lock screw and the pinion shaft.
5. Push in on the axle end. Remove the C-lock from the inner (button) end of the shaft.
6. Remove the shaft, being careful of oil seal.
7. You can pry the oil seal out of the housing by placing the inner end of the axle shaft behind the steel case of the seal, then prying it out carefully.
8. A puller or a slide hammer is required to remove the bearing from the housing.
9. Pack the new or reused bearing with wheel bearing grease and lubricate the cavity between the seal lips with the same grease.
10. The bearing has to be driven into the housing. Don't use a drift, you might cock the bearing in its bore. Use a piece of pipe or a large socket instead. Drive only on the outer bearing race. In a similar manner, drive the seal in flush with the end of the tube.
11. Slide the shaft into place, turning it slowly until the splines are engaged with the differential. Be careful of the oil seal.
12. Install the C-lock on the inner axle end. Pull the shaft out so that the C-lock seats in the counterbore of the differential side gear.
13. Position the differential pinion shaft through the case and the pinion gears, aligning the lock screw hole. Install the lock screw.
14. Install the cover with a new gasket and tighten the bolts evenly in a criss-cross pattern.
15. Fill the axle with lubricant as specified in Chapter 1.
16. Replace the brake drums and wheels.

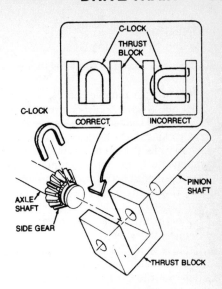

C-lock and thrust block installation

Removing the differential pinion lockscrew

Semi-Floating Locking Differential Axles

This axle uses a thrust block on the differential pinion shaft.

1. Follow Steps 1–3 of the preceding procedure.
2. Rotate the differential case so that you can remove the lock screw and support the pinion shaft so it can't fall into the housing. Remove the differential pinion shaft lock screw.
3. Carefully pull the pinion shaft partway out and rotate the differential case until the shaft touches the housing at the top.
4. Use a screwdriver to position the C-lock with its open end directly inward. You can't push in the axle shaft till you do this.
5. Push the axle shaft in and remove the C-lock.
6. Follow Steps 6–11 of the preceding procedure.
7. Keep the pinion shaft partway out of the differential case while installing the C-lock on the axle shaft. Put the C-lock on the axle shaft and carefully pull out on the axle shaft until the C-lock is clear of the thrust block.
8. Follow Steps 13–16 of the previous procedure.

Full-Floating Axles
with 9³/₄ and 10¹/₂ in. Ring Gear

The procedures are the same for locking and non-locking axles.

The best way to remove the bearings from the wheel hub is with an arbor press. Use of a press reduces the chances of damaging the bearing races, cocking the bearing in its bore, or scoring the hub walls. A local machine shop is probably equipped with the tools to remove and install bearings and seals. However, if one is not available, the hammer and drift method outlined can be used.

1. Support the axles on jackstands.
2. Remove the wheels.
3. Remove the bolts and lock washers that attach the axle shaft flange to the hub.
4. Rap on the flange with a soft faced hammer to loosen the shaft. Grip the rib on the end of the flange with a pair of locking pliers and twist to start shaft removal. Remove the shaft from the axle tube.
5. The hub and drum assembly must be removed to remove the bearings and oil seals. You will need a large socket to remove and later adjust the bearing adjustment nut. There are also special tools available.
6. Disengage the tang of the locknut retainer from the slot or slat of the locknut, then remove the locknut from the housing tube.
7. Disengage the tang of the retainer from the slot or flat of the adjusting nut and remove the retainer from the housing tube.
8. Remove the adjusting nut from the housing tube.
9. Remove the thrust washer from the housing tube.
10. Pull the hub and drum straight off the axle housing.
11. Remove the oil seal and discard.
12. Use a hammer and a long drift to knock the inner bearing, cup, and oil seal from the hub assembly.
13. Remove the outer bearing snapring with a pair of pliers. It may be necessary to tap the bearing outer race away from the retaining ring slightly by tapping on the ring to remove the ring.
14. Drive the outer bearing from the hub with a hammer and drift.
15. To reinstall the bearings, place the outer bearing into the hub. The larger outside diameter of the bearing should face the outer end of the hub. Drive the bearing into the hub using a washer that will cover both the inner and outer races of the bearing. Place a socket on top of this washer, then drive the bearing into place with a series of light taps. If available, an arbor press should be used for this job.

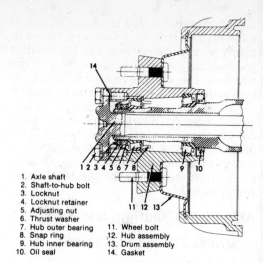

1. Axle shaft
2. Shaft-to-hub bolt
3. Locknut
4. Locknut retainer
5. Adjusting nut
6. Thrust washer
7. Hub outer bearing
8. Snap ring
9. Hub inner bearing
10. Oil seal
11. Wheel bolt
12. Hub assembly
13. Drum assembly
14. Gasket

Full-floating axle bearing and hub

16. Drive the bearing past the snapring groove, and install the snapring. Then, turning the hub assembly over, drive the bearing back against the snapring. Protect the bearing by placing a washer on top of it. You can use the thrust washer that fits between the bearing and the adjusting nut for the job.
17. Place the inner bearing into the hub. The thick edge should be toward the shoulder in the hub. Press the bearing into the hub until it seats against the shoulder, using a washer and socket as outlined earlier. Make certain that the bearing is not cocked and that it is fully seated on the shoulder.
18. Pack the cavity between the oil seal lips with wheel bearing grease, and position it in the hub bore. Carefully press it into place on top of the inner bearing.
19. Pack the wheel bearings with grease, and lightly coat the inside diameter of the hub bearing contact surface and the outside diameter of the axle housing tube.
20. Make sure that the inner bearing, oil seal, axle housing oil deflector, and outer bearing are properly positioned. Install the hub and drum assembly on the axle housing, being careful so as not to damage the oil seal or dislocate other internal components.
21. Install the thrust washer so that the tang on the inside diameter of the washer is in the keyway on the axle housing.
22. Install the adjusting nut. Tighten to 50 ft. lbs. while rotating the hub. Back off the nut and retighten to 35 ft. lbs., then back off ¹/₄ turn.
23. Install the tanged retainer against the inner adjusting nut. Align the adjusting nut so that the short tang of the retainer will engage the nearest slot on the adjusting nut.

24. Install the outer locknut and tighten to 65 ft. lbs. Bend the long tang of the retainer into the slot of the outer nut. This method of adjustment should provide 0.001–0.010 in. (0.0254–0.254mm) end play.

25. Place a new gasket over the axle shaft and position the axle shaft in the housing so that the shaft splines enter the differential side gear. Position the gasket so that the holes are in alignment, and install the flange-to-hub attaching bolts. Torque to 115 ft. lbs.

NOTE: *To prevent lubricant from leaking through the flange holes, apply a non-hardening sealer to the bolt threads. Use the sealer sparingly.*

26. Replace the wheels.

Pinion Seal

REPLACEMENT

Semi-Floating Axles

1. Raise and support the van on jackstands. It would help to have the front end slightly higher than the rear to avoid fluid loss.
2. Matchmark and remove the driveshaft.
3. Release the parking brake.
4. Remove the rear wheels. Rotate the rear wheels by hand to make sure that there is absolutely no brake drag. If there is brake drag, remove the drums.
5. Using a torque wrench on the pinion nut, record the force needed to rotate the pinion.
6. Matchmark the pinion shaft, nut and flange. Count the number of exposed threads on the pinion shaft.
7. Install a holding tool on the pinion. A very large adjustable wrench will do, or, if one is not available, put the drums back on and set the parking brake as tightly as possible.
8. Remove the pinion nut.
9. Slide the flange off of the pinion. A puller may be necessary.
10. Centerpunch the oil seal to distort it and pry it out of the bore. Be careful to avoid scratching the bore.

To install:
11. Pack the cavity between the lips of the seal with lithium-based chassis lube.
12. Position the seal in the bore and carefully drive it into place. A seal installer is VERY helpful in doing this.
13. Pack the cavity between the end of the pinion splines and the pinion flange with Permatex No.2® sealer, or equivalent non-hardening sealer.
14. Place the flange on the pinion and push it on as far as it will go.
15. Install the pinion washer and nut on the

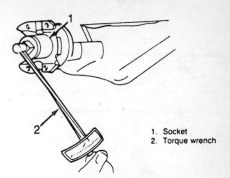

1. Socket
2. Torque wrench

Measuring pinion rotating torque

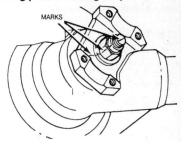

MARKS

Scribed marks

shaft and force the pinion into place by turning the nut.

WARNING: *Never hammer the flange into place!*

16. Tighten the nut until the exact number of threads previously noted appear and the matchmarks align.
17. Measure the rotating torque of the pinion under the same circumstances as before. Compare the two readings. As necessary, tighten the pinion nut in VERY small increments until the torque necessary to rotate the pinion is 3 inch lbs. higher than the originally recorded torque.
18. Install the driveshaft.

Full Floating Axle
with 9³/₄ and 10¹/₂ inch Ring Gear

1. Raise and support the van on jackstands. It would help to have the front end slightly higher than the rear to avoid fluid loss.
2. Matchmark and remove the driveshaft.
3. Matchmark the pinion shaft, nut and flange. Count the number of exposed threads on the pinion shaft.
4. Install a holding tool on the pinion. A very large adjustable wrench will do, or, if one is not available, set the parking brake as tightly as possible.
5. Remove the pinion nut.
6. Slide the flange off of the pinion. A puller may be necessary.
7. Centerpunch the oil seal to distort it and pry it out of the bore. Be careful to avoid scratching the bore.

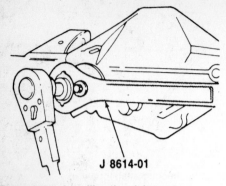

J 8614-01

Removing or installing the pinion nut

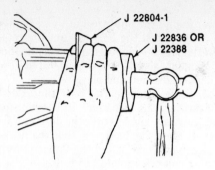

J 22804-1

J 22836 OR
J 22388

Installing the pinion seal

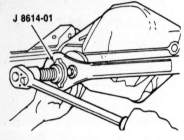

J 8614-01

Removing the pinion flange

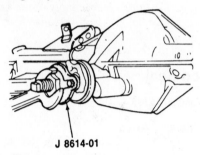

J 8614-01

Installing the pinion flange

To install:

8. Pack the cavity between the lips of the seal with lithium-based chassis lube.

9. Position the seal in the bore and carefully drive it into place. A seal installer is VERY helpful in doing this.

10. Place the flange on the pinion and push it on as far as it will go.

11. Install the pinion washer and nut on the shaft and force the pinion into place by turning the nut.

WARNING: *Never hammer the flange into place!*

12. Tighten the nut until the exact number of threads previously noted appear and the matchmarks align.

13. Install the driveshaft.

Axle Housing

REMOVAL AND INSTALLATION

1. Raise and support the rear end on jackstands.

2. For the $9^3/_4$ in. ring gear and the $10^1/_2$ in. ring gear axles, place jackstands under the frame side rails for support.

3. Drain the lubricant from the axle housing and remove the driveshaft.

4. Remove the wheel, the brake drum or hub and the drum assembly.

5. Disconnect the parking brake cable from the lever and at the brake flange plate.

6. Disconnect the hydraulic brake lines from the connectors.

7. Disconnect the shock absorbers from the axle brackets.

8. Remove the vent hose from the axle vent fitting (if used).

9. Disconnect the height sensing and brake proportional valve linkage (if used).

10. Support the stabilizer shaft assembly with a hydraulic jack and remove (if used).

11. Remove the nuts and washers from the U-bolts.

12. Remove the U-bolts, spring plates and spacers from the axle assembly.

13. Lower the jack and remove the axle assembly.

To install:

14. Raise the axle assembly into position.

15. Install the U-bolts, spring plates and spacers.

16. Install the nuts and washers on the U-bolts. Torque the nuts to 130 ft. lbs for 30/3500 series; 120 series for all other models.

17. Install the stabilizer shaft.

18. Connect the height sensing and brake proportional valve linkage.

19. Install the vent hose at the axle vent fitting.

20. Connect the shock absorbers at the axle brackets. Torque the nuts to 80 ft. lbs.

21. Connect the hydraulic brake lines.

22. Connect the parking brake cable.

23. Install the wheels.

24. Install the driveshaft.

25. Fill the axle housing.

Suspension and Steering

8

WHEELS

REMOVAL AND INSTALLATION

Single Wheels

1. Raise the truck on a jack just enough to take up the weight of the truck, leaving the tire on the ground.
2. Using a lug wrench or breaker bar and socket, break loose the lug nuts in a crisscross pattern.
3. Raise and safely support the truck, remove the lug nuts and remove the wheel.

To install:

4. Lift the wheel onto the lugs. Snug down the topmost nut, then snug down the rest of the nuts in a crisscross pattern. When all nuts are snugged, torque them, in a crisscross pattern, to:

Trucks with single front and rear wheels

• G10/1500 w/5 studs and steel or aluminum wheels: 100 ft. lbs.

• All G Series with 8 studs: 120 ft. lbs.

Trucks with single front and dual rear wheels

• All G Series: 140 ft. lbs.

FRONT SUSPENSION

Vans use an independent coil spring front suspension. This system consists of upper and lower control arms pivoting on bushings on shafts. which are attached to the crossmember. The control arms are attacked to the steering knuckle with ball joints and a coil spring is located between the lower control arm and the suspension crossmember.

A stabilizer (sway) bar is optional to minimize body lean and sway in curves. Heavy duty shock absorbers and springs have been optional on most models.

Springs

REMOVAL AND INSTALLATION

CAUTION: *The spring is under a great deal of tension! It's best to use a coil spring compressor when removing the spring. Mishandling the spring could cause it to fly out of its mounting, causing a great deal of personal damage!*

1. Raise and support the van under the frame rails. The control arms should hang free.
2. Disconnect the shock absorber at the lower end and move it aside. Disconnect the stabilizer bar (if any) from the lower control arm.
3. Support the cross-shaft with a jack and install a spring compressor or chain the spring to the control arm as a safety precaution.
4. Raise the jack to remove the tension from the lower control arm cross-shaft and remove the 2 U-bolts securing the cross-shaft to the crossmember.

NOTE: *The cross-shaft and lower control arms keeps the coil spring compressed. Use care when you lower the assembly.*

5. Slowly release the jack and lower the control arm until spring can be removed. Be sure that all compression is relieved from spring.

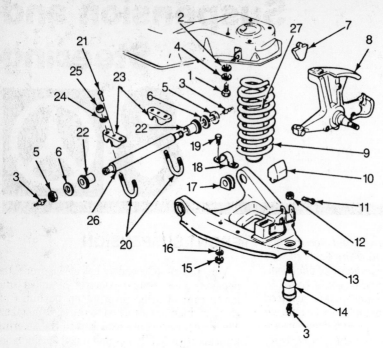

1.	Bolt
2.	Washer
3.	Fitting
4.	Washer
5.	Nut
6.	Washer
7.	Bumper
8.	Knuckle
9.	Spring
10.	Bumper
11.	Cotter pin
12.	Nut
13.	Lower control arm
14.	Lower ball joint
15.	Nut
16.	Washer
17.	Bushing
18.	Bracket
19.	Bolt
20.	U-bolt
21.	Rivet
22.	Bushing
23.	Bracket
24.	Washer
25.	Nut
26.	Pivot shaft
27.	Air cylinder

Lower control arm and related components

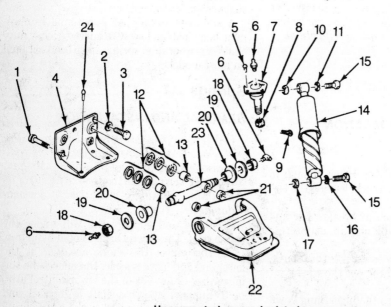

1.	Bolt
2.	Washer
3.	Bolt
4.	Bracket
5.	Rivet
6.	Fitting
7.	Upper ball joint
8.	Nut
9.	Cotter pin
10.	Nut
11.	Washer
12.	Shim pack
13.	Spacer
14.	Shock absorber
15.	Bolt
16.	Washer
17.	Nut
18.	Nut
19.	Washer
20.	Bushing
21.	Nut
22.	Upper control arm
23.	Pivot shaft
24.	Rivet

Upper control arm and related components

6. Remove the spring.

7. To install, position the spring on the control arm and jack it into position. Use the spring compressor again as a precaution.

8. Position the control arm cross-shaft on crossmember and install U-bolts. Be sure that the front indexing hole in cross-shaft is aligned with crossmember attaching saddle stud.

To install:

9. Raise the jack to apply tension to the lower control arm cross-shaft and install the 2 U-bolts securing the cross-shaft to the crossmember. Torque the U-bolts to 65 ft. lbs. for 10/1500 and 20/2500 series; 85 ft. lbs. for 30/3500 series.

10. Remove the spring compressor or chain.

11. Connect the shock absorber at the lower end. Torque the bolt to 80 ft. lbs.

12. Connect the stabilizer bar to the lower control arm. Torque the fasteners to 25 ft. lbs.

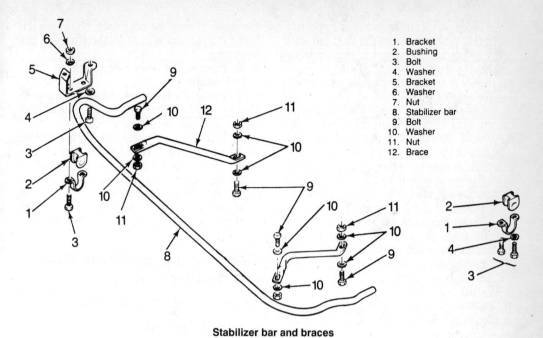

1. Bracket
2. Bushing
3. Bolt
4. Washer
5. Bracket
6. Washer
7. Nut
8. Stabilizer bar
9. Bolt
10. Washer
11. Nut
12. Brace

Stabilizer bar and braces

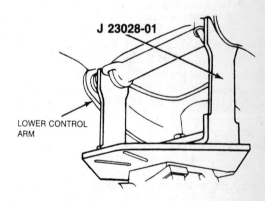

1. Nut
2. Washer
3. Shock absorber
4. Bolt
5. Washer
6. Nut

Shock absorber installation

Removing the coil spring

Shock Absorbers

TESTING

Adjust the tire pressure before testing the shocks. If the van is equipped with heavy duty equipment, this can sometimes be misleading. A stiff ride normally accompanies a stiff or heavy duty suspension. Be sure that all weight in the truck is distributed evenly.

Each shock absorber can be tested by bouncing the corner of the van until maximum up and down movement is obtained. Let go of the van. It should stop bouncing in 1-2 bounces. If not, the shock should be replaced.

REMOVAL AND INSTALLATION

The usual procedure is to replace shock absorbers in axle pairs, to provide equal damping. Heavy duty replacements are available for firmer control.

1. Raise and support the front end as necessary.
2. Remove the bolt and nut from the lower shock end.
3. Remove the upper bolt and nut.
4. Purge the new shock of air by extending it in its normal position and compressing it while inverted. Do this several times. It is normal for there to be more resistance to extension than to compression.
5. Install the shock absorber. Tighten the shock absorber bolts to 80 ft. lbs.

Upper Control Arm

REMOVAL AND INSTALLATION

1. Raise and support the van on jackstands.
2. Support the lower control arm with a floor jack.
3. Remove the wheel and tire.

4. Remove the cotter pin from the upper control arm ball stud and loosen the stud nut until the bottom surface of the nut is slightly below the end of the stud.

5. Install a spring compressor on the coil spring for safety.

6. Loosen the upper control arm ball stud in the steering knuckle using a ball joint stud removal tool. Remove the nut from the ball stud and raise the upper arm to clear the steering knuckle. It may be necessary to remove the brake caliper and wire it to the frame to gain clearance. Do not allow the caliper to hang by the brake hose.

7. Remove the nuts securing the control arm shaft studs to the crossmember bracket and remove the control arm.

8. Tape the shims and spacers together and tag for proper reassembly.

To install:

9. Place the control arm in position and install the nuts. Before tightening the nuts, insert the caster and camber shims in the same order as when installed.

10. Install the nuts securing the control arm shaft studs to the crossmember bracket. Tighten the nuts to 70 ft. lbs. for 10/1500 and 20/2500 series; 105 ft. lbs. for 30/3500 series.

11. Install the ball stud nut. Torque the nut to 90 ft. lbs. for 10/1500 series and 20/2500 series; 130 ft. lbs. for 30/3500 series. Install the cotter pin. Never back off the nut to install the cotter pin. Always advance it.

12. Install the brake caliper.

13. Remove the spring compressor.

14. Install the wheel and tire.

15. Have the front end alignment checked, and as necessary adjusted.

Lower Control Arm

REMOVAL AND INSTALLATION

1. Raise and support the van on jackstands.

2. Remove the spring (see Spring Removal and Installation).

3. Support the inboard end of the control arm after spring removal.

4. Remove the cotter pin from the lower ball stud and loosen the nut.

5. Loosen the lower ball stud in the steering knuckle using a ball joint stud removal tool. When the stud is loose, remove the nut from

the stud. It may be necessary to remove the brake caliper and wire it to the frame to gain clearance.

6. Remove the lower control arm.

To install:

7. Install the lower control arm. Torque the U-bolts to 65 ft. lbs. on 10/1500 and 20/2500 series; 85 ft. lbs. on 30/3500 series.

8. Install the ball stud nut. Torque the nut to 90 ft. lbs. for 10/1500 series and 20/2500 series; 130 ft. lbs. for 30/3500 series. Install the cotter pin. Never back off the nut to install the cotter pin. Always advance it.

9. Install the brake caliper.

10. Install the spring (see Spring Removal and Installation).

Lower Control Arm Pivot Shaft and Bushings

REMOVAL AND INSTALLATION

**10/1500 and 20/2500 Series
With Gasoline Engines**

1. Remove the lower control arm as explained earlier in this Chapter.

2. Remove the pivot shaft nuts and washers.

3. Place the control arm in a press and press on the front end of the pivot shaft to remove the rear bushing.

4. Remove the pivot shaft.

5. Remove the front bushing stakes with tool J–22717, or equivalent.

6. Assemble tool J–24435–7. J–24435–3, J–24435–2 and J–24435–6 on the control arm. Tighten the tool until the bushing is forced out.

To install:

7. Position the new front bushing in the

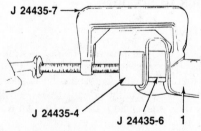

1. Lower control arm

Removing or installing the lower control arm bushings for G10/1500 and G20/2500 models

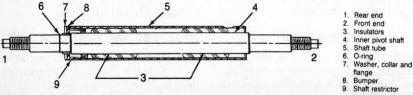

1. Rear end
2. Front end
3. Insulators
4. Inner pivot shaft
5. Shaft tube
6. O-ring
7. Washer, collar and flange
8. Bumper
9. Shaft restrictor

Lower control arm pivot shaft on G10/1500 and 20/2500 models with gasoline engines

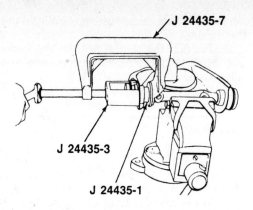

Removing the lower control arm bushing for G20/2500 models with the diesel engine

Installing the lower control arm bushing for G20/2500 models with the diesel engine

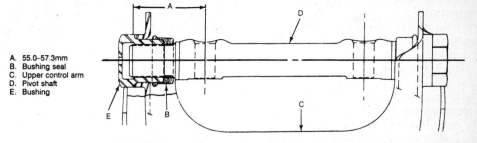

A. 55.0–57.3mm
B. Bushing seal
C. Upper control arm
D. Pivot shaft
E. Bushing

Centering the upper control arm shaft on G30/3500 models

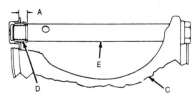

A.	29.96–31.9mm to properly center the pivot shaft	C.	Lower control arm
B.	Bushing seal	D.	Bushing
		E.	Pivot shaft

Centering the lower control arm shaft on G30/3500 models

arm and assemble tools J–24435–6, J–24435–4 and J–24435–7. Force the bushing into place until it is fully seated. The outer tube hole must be lined up so that it faces the front, towards the staked bushing.

8. Stake the bushing in at least 2 places.
9. Install the pivot shaft.
10. Install the rear bushing.
11. Install the washers and pivot shaft nuts. Torque the nuts to 115 ft. lbs.
12. Install the lower control arm.

20/2500 Series
With Diesel Engines

1. Remove the lower control arm as explained earlier in this Chapter.
2. Assemble tools J–24435–7, J–24435–3, and J–24435–1 on the control arm. Tighten the tool until the front bushing is forced out.

3. Remove the pivot shaft.
4. Repeat the forcing procedure for the other bushing.
To install:
5. Position the new front bushing in the arm and assemble tools J–24435–4, J–24435–5 and J–24435–7. Force the bushing into place until it is fully seated.
6. Install the pivot shaft.
7. Repeat the forcing procedure to install the rear bushing.
8. Install the lower control arm.

G30/3500

1. Remove the lower control arm.
2. Remove the grease fittings and unscrew the bushings.
3. Slide out the pivot shaft.
4. Discard the old seals.
To install:
5. Install new seals on the pivot shaft.
6. Slide the shaft into the arm.
7. Start the bushings into the arm and center the shaft in the bushings. Hand tighten the bushings to make sure shaft doesn't bind.
8. Tighten the bushings to 280 ft. lbs.
9. Check the pivot shaft for free rotation.
10. Install the grease fittings and lubricate the bushings.
11. Install the lower arm.

Upper Control Arm Pivot Shaft and Bushings

REMOVAL AND INSTALLATION

10/1500 and 20/2500 Series

1. Remove the upper control arm as explained earlier in this Chapter.
2. Remove the pivot shaft nuts and washers.
3. Assemble tool J–24435–1. J–24435–3, and J–24435–7 on the control arm. Tighten the tool until the front bushing is forced out.
4. Remove the pivot shaft.
5. Use the forcing procedure to remove the rear bushing.

To install:

6. Position the new front bushing in the arm and assemble tools J–24435–4, J–24435–5 and J–24435–7. Force the bushing into place until it is fully seated.
7. Install the pivot shaft.
8. Repeat the forcing procedure to install the rear bushing.
9. Install the lower control arm.
10. Install the nuts and washers. Torque the nuts to 115 ft. lbs.
11. Install the control arm.

G30/3500

1. Raise and support the front end on jackstands.
2. Take up the weight of the suspension with a floor jack positioned under the lower control arm as near to the ball joint as possible.
3. Loosen, but do not remove, the pivot shaft-to-frame nuts.
4. Tape together and matchmark each shim pack's position for exact installation.
5. Install a chain over the control arm, inboard of the stabilizer bar and outboard of the shock absorber to hold the control arm close to the crossmember.
6. Remove the pivot shaft nuts, bolts and spacers.
7. Remove the grease fittings and unscrew the bushings from the control arm.
8. Remove the pivot shaft. Discard the seals.

To install:

9. Install new seals on the pivot shaft.
10. Slide the shaft into the arm.
11. Start the bushings into the arm and center the shaft in the bushings. Hand tighten the bushings to make sure the shaft doesn't bind.
12. Tighten the bushings to 190 ft. lbs.
13. Check the pivot shaft for free rotation.

14. Install the grease fittings and lubricate the bushings.
15. Position the control arm on the frame and install the shim packs, spacers, nuts and bolts. Torque the nuts to 105 ft. lbs.
16. Remove the chain and install the wheel.
17. Have the alignment checked.

Ball Joints

INSPECTION

Excessive ball joint wear will usually show up as wear on the inside of the front tires. Don't jump to conclusions; front end misalignment can give the same symptom. The lower ball joint gets the most wear due to the distribution of suspension load. The wear limits given are the manufacturer's recommendation; they may not agree with your state's inspection law.

Upper

1. Raise and support the van so that the control arms hang free.
2. Remove the wheel.
3. Support the lower control arm with a jackstand and disconnect the upper ball stud from the steering knuckle.
4. The upper ball joint is spring loaded in its socket. If it has any perceptible lateral shake or can be twisted in its socket, it should be replaced.
5. If there are no defects, connect the steering knuckle to the upper stud and torque the nut to 50 ft. lbs. (90 ft. lbs. for G-30 and 3500). Tighten the nut further to install the cotter pin but don't exceed 90 ft. lbs. (130 for G-30 and 3500).

Lower

1. Support the weight of the control arm at the wheel hub.
2. Measure the distance between the tip of the ball joint stud and the grease fitting below the ball joint.
3. Move the support to the control arm and allow the hub and drum to hang free. Measure the distance again. If the variation between the 2 measurements exceeds $3/32$ in. (2.38mm) the ball joint should be replaced.

REMOVAL AND INSTALLATION

Upper

1. Raise and support the van.
2. Support the lower control arm with a floor jack.
3. Remove the cotter pin from the upper ball stud and loosen, but do not remove, the stud nut.
4. Using a ball joint stud removal tool,

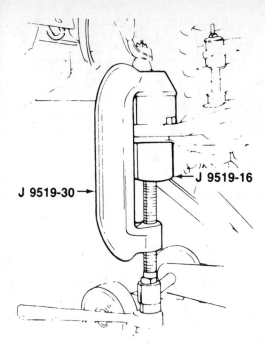

J 9519-30 →   ← J 9519-16

Installing the lower ball joint

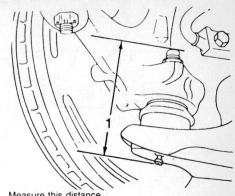

1. Measure this distance

Inspecting the lower ball joint

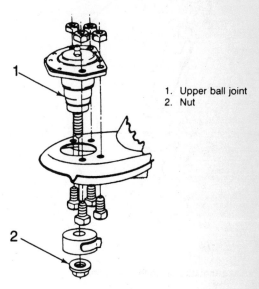

1. Upper ball joint
2. Nut

Installing the upper ball joint

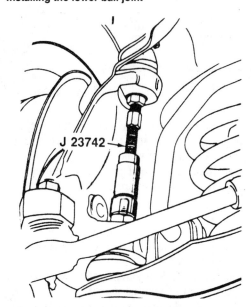

J 23742

Disconnecting the upper ball joint

loosen the ball stud in the steering knuckle. When the stud is loose, remove the tool and the stud nut. It may be necessary to remove the brake caliper and wire it to the frame to gain clearance. Do not allow the caliper to hang by the brake hose.

5. Drill out the rivets. Remove the ball joint assembly.

To install:

6. Install the service ball joint, using the nuts supplied. Torque the nuts to 18 ft. lbs.

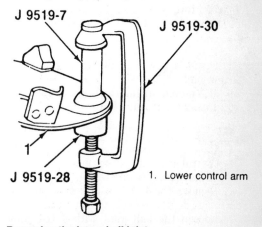

J 9519-7   J 9519-30

J 9519-28   1. Lower control arm

Removing the lower ball joint

7. Torque the ball stud nut as follows: 10 and 1500 Series: 50 ft. lbs. plus the additional torque to align the cotter pin. Do not exceed 90 ft. lbs. and never back the nut off to align the

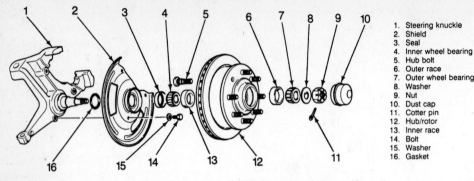

1.	Steering knuckle
2.	Shield
3.	Seal
4.	Inner wheel bearing
5.	Hub bolt
6.	Outer race
7.	Outer wheel bearing
8.	Washer
9.	Nut
10.	Dust cap
11.	Cotter pin
12.	Hub/rotor
13.	Inner race
14.	Bolt
15.	Washer
16.	Gasket

Steering knuckle and hub components

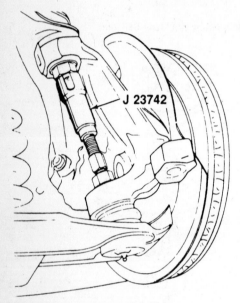

J 23742

Disconnecting the lower ball joint

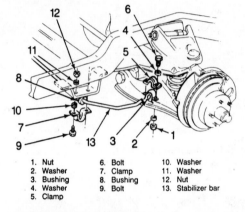

1.	Nut	6.	Bolt	10.	Washer
2.	Washer	7.	Clamp	11.	Washer
3.	Bushing	8.	Bushing	12.	Nut
4.	Washer	9.	Bolt	13.	Stabilizer bar
5.	Clamp				

Stabilizer bar attachment points

6. Install a spring compressor on the coil spring for safety.

7. Pull the brake disc and knuckle assembly up and off the ball stud and support the upper arm with a block of wood.

8. Remove the ball joint from the control arm with a ball joint tool. It must be pressed out.

To install:

9. Start the new ball joint into the control arm. Position the bleed vent in the rubber boot facing inward.

10. Seat the ball joint in the lower control arm. It must be pressed in.

11. Lower the upper arm and match the steering knuckle to the lower ball stud.

12. Install the brake caliper, if removed.

13. Install the ball stud nut and torque it to 80–100 ft. lbs. plug the additional torque necessary to align the cotter pin hole. Do not exceed 130 ft. lbs. or back the nut off the align the holes with the pin.

14. Install a new lube fitting and lubricate the new joint.

15. Install the tire and wheel.

16. Lower the van.

pin. 20, 2500, 30, 3500 Series: 90 ft. lbs. plus additional torque necessary to align the cotter pin. Do not exceed 130 ft. lbs. and never back off the nut to align the pin.

8. Install a new cotter pin.

9. Install a new lube fitting and lubricate the new joint.

10. If removed, install the brake caliper.

11. Install the tire and lower the van.

Lower

1. Raise and support the van. Support the lower control arm with a floor jack.

2. Remove the tire and wheel.

3. Remove the lower stud cotter pin and loosen, buy do not remove, the stud nut.

4. Loosen the ball joint with a ball joint stud removal tool. It may be necessary to remove the brake caliper and wire it to the frame to gain enough clearance.

5. When the stud is loose, remove the tool and ball stud nut.

Stabilizer Bar

REMOVAL AND INSTALLATION

1. Raise and support the front end on jackstands.
2. Remove the front wheels.
3. Unbolt the stabilizer bar from the frame.
4. Unbolt the stabilizer bar from the control arms.
5. Check the bushings for wear or damage and replace them as necessary.
6. Installation is the reverse of removal. Tighten all bolts to 24 ft. lbs.; all nuts to 21 ft. lbs.

Steering Knuckle

REMOVAL AND INSTALLATION

1. Raise and support the front end on jackstands.
2. Remove the wheels.
3. Dismount the caliper and suspend it out of the way without disconnecting the brake lines.
4. Remove the hub/rotor assembly.
5. Unbolt the splash shield and discard the old gasket.
6. Using a ball joint separator, disconnect the tie rod end from the knuckle. The procedure is explained later in this Chapter.
7. Position a floor jack under the lower control arm, near the spring seat. Raise the jack until it *just* takes up the weight of the suspension, compressing the spring. Safety-chain the coil spring to the lower arm.
8. Remove the upper and lower ball joint nuts.
9. Using tool J–23742, or equivalent, break loose the upper ball joint from the knuckle.
10. Raise the upper control arm just enough to disconnect the ball joint.
11. Using the afore-mentioned tool, break loose the lower ball joint.
12. Lift the knuckle off of the lower ball joint.
13. Inspect and clean the ball stud bores in the knuckle. Make sure that there are no cracks or burrs. If the knuckle is damaged in any way, replace it.
14. Check the spindle for wear, heat discoloration or damage. If at all damaged, replace it.
To install:
15. Maneuver the knuckle onto both ball joints.
16. Install both nuts. On 10/1500 series and 20/2500 series, torque the upper nut to 50 ft. lbs. and the lower nut to 90 ft. lbs. On 30/3500 series, torque both nuts to 90 ft. lbs.
17. Install the cotter pins. Always advance the nut to align the cotter pin hole. NEVER back it off! On the upper nut which was originally torque to 50 ft. lbs., don't exceed 90 ft. lbs. when aligning the hole. On nuts torqued originally to 90 ft. lbs., don't exceed 130 ft. lbs. to align the hole.
18. Remove the floor jack.
19. Install a new gasket and the splash shield. Torque the bolts to 10 ft. lbs.
20. Connect the tie rod end.
21. Install the hub/rotor assembly.
22. Install the caliper.
23. Adjust the wheel bearings.
24. Install the wheels.
25. Have the alignment checked.

Complete Front Suspension Unit

REMOVAL AND INSTALLATION

The front suspension and frame crossmember can be removed as a unit if extensive service is required.

1. Disconnect the battery ground cable.
2. Raise and support the van on jackstands placed under the frame rails.
3. Remove the front wheels.
4. Remove the brake hoses and discard the special washers. Cap the open pipes.
5. Disconnect the tie rod ends at knuckles.
6. Disconnect the stabilizer bar at the control arms.
7. Disconnect the shock absorbers at the control arms.
8. Remove the brake line clip bolts from the crossmember.
9. Support the engine with a floor jack and disconnect the crossmember from the engine mounts.
10. Disconnect the crossmember at the frame rails.
11. Place a floor jack under the crossmember and chain it in place.
12. Unbolt the upper control arm brackets from the frame.

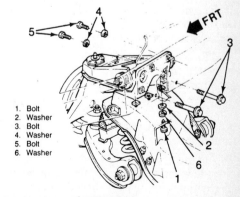

1. Bolt
2. Washer
3. Bolt
4. Washer
5. Bolt
6. Washer

Suspension unit installation

13. Lower the suspension unit until it is clear and roll it out from under the van.

To install:

14. Raise the suspension unit into position.

15. Connect the crossmember at the frame side rails. Torque the bolts to 65 ft. lbs.

16. Bolt the upper control arm brackets to the frame. Torque the bolts to 92 ft. lbs.

17. Install the crossmember-to-frame bottom bolts through the re-enforcement. Torque the bolts to 92 ft. lbs.

18. Connect the crossmember to the engine mounts. Torque the bolts to 60 ft. lbs.

19. Remove the floor jacks.

20. Install the brake line clip bolts from the crossmember.

21. Connect the shock absorbers at the control arms. Torque the bolts to 80 ft. lbs.

22. Connect the stabilizer bar at the control arms. Torque the nuts to 21 ft. lbs.; the bolts to 24 ft. lbs.

23. Connect the tie rod ends at the knuckles.

24. Install the brake hoses and new special washers. Bleed the brakes.

25. Install the front wheels.

26. Connect the battery ground cable.

Front End Alignment

Correct alignment of the front suspension is necessary to provide optimum tire life and for proper and safe handling of the vehicle.

CASTER AND CAMBER

Positive caster is the amount, in degrees, of the rearward tilt of the steering knuckle. Camber is the amount, in degrees, of the outward tilt from the vertical of the front wheels.

Caster and camber adjustments are made by placing shims between the upper control arm shaft and the mounting bracket.

TOE-IN ADJUSTMENT

Toe-in is the amount, measured in inches, that the centerlines of the wheels are closer together at the front than at the rear. Virtually all vehicles are set with toe-in.

NOTE: *Some alignment specialists set toe-in to the lower specified limit on vehicles with radial tires. The reason is that radial tires have less drag, and therefore a lesser tendency to toe-out at speed. By the same reasoning, off-road tires would require the upper limit of toe-in.*

Toe-in must be checked after caster and camber have been adjusted, but it can be adjusted without disturbing the other two settings. You can make this adjustment without special equipment, if you make careful measurements. The adjustments is made at the tie rod sleeves. The wheels must be straight ahead.

1. Toe-in can be determined by measuring the distance between the centers of the tire treads, front and rear. If the tread pattern of your tires makes this impossible, you can measure between the edges of the wheel rims, but make sure to move the van forward and measure in a couple of places to avoid errors caused by bent rims or wheel runout.

2. Loosen the clamp bolts on the tie rod sleeves.

3. Rotate the sleeves equally (in opposite directions) to obtain the correct measurement. If the sleeves are not adjusted equally, the steering wheel will be crooked.

NOTE: *If your steering wheel is already crooked, it can be straightened by turning the sleeves equally in the same direction.*

4. When the adjustment is complete, tighten the clamps.

STEERING AXIS INCLINATION

Steering axis inclination is the tilt of the steering knuckle. If it is not within specifications, the steering knuckle is bent and must be replaced.

REAR SUSPENSION

These vans have leaf spring rear suspension. Staggered rear shock absorbers are used to control axle hop on acceleration and braking. Heavy duty shock absorbers and springs have been available on most models.

Springs

REMOVAL AND INSTALLATION

1. Raise and support the van.

2. Support the axle so that the weight is taken off the springs.

3. Loosen, buy do not remove the spring-to-shackle retaining nut.

4. Remove the nut and bolt securing the shackle to the spring hanger.

5. Remove the nut and bolt securing the spring to the front hanger.

6. Remove the U-bolt retaining nuts and remove the U-bolts and spring plate.

7. Remove the spring.

To install:

8. Install the spring.

9. Install the U-bolts and spring plate. Install the nuts. Tighten the U-bolt nuts to 120 ft. lbs. (G-10, 1500, 20, and 2500) or 150 ft. lbs. (G-30 and 3500).

10. Be sure that the spring is in position at

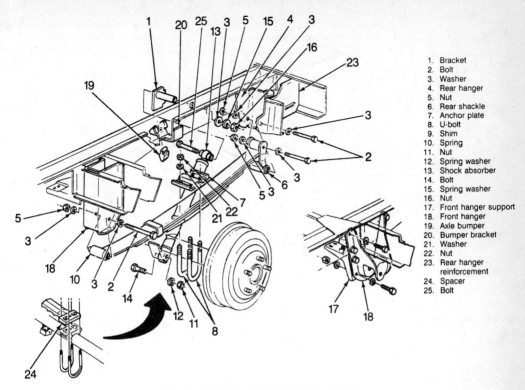

Rear suspension, except cutaway chassis

1. Bracket
2. Bolt
3. Washer
4. Rear hanger
5. Nut
6. Rear shackle
7. Anchor plate
8. U-bolt
9. Shim
10. Spring
11. Nut
12. Spring washer
13. Shock absorber
14. Bolt
15. Spring washer
16. Nut
17. Front hanger support
18. Front hanger
19. Axle bumper
20. Bumper bracket
21. Washer
22. Nut
23. Rear hanger reinforcement
24. Spacer
25. Bolt

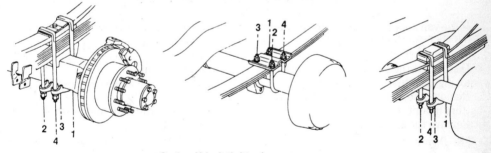

Spring U-bolt tightening sequence

both hangers. The shackle assembly must be attached to the rear spring eye before installing the shackle to the rear hanger. Torque the front eye bolt and rear shackle bolt to 135 ft. lbs.

NOTE: *Aftermarket kits, consisting of longer axle U-bolts and blocks to be placed between the spring and axle, are available to adjust the rear side height. If this modification is carried to extremes, the front end caster angle and rear end stability will be affected.*

Shock Absorbers

The usual procedure for testing shock absorbers is to stand on the bumper at the end nearest the shock being tested and start the vehicle bouncing up and down. Step off; the vehicle should come to rest within one bounce cycle. The stiffness of the suspension on some models makes this rather difficult unless you are a very substantial individual indeed. Another good test is to drive the vehicle over a bumpy road. Bouncing over bumps is normal, the shock absorbers should stop the bouncing, after the bump is passed, within one or two cycles.

REMOVAL AND INSTALLATION

The usual procedure is to replace shock absorbers in axle pairs, to provide equal damping. Heavy duty replacements are available for firmer control. Air adjustable shock absorbers can be used to maintain a level rid with heavy loads or when towing.

1. Raise and support the van.
2. Support the rear axle with a floor jack.

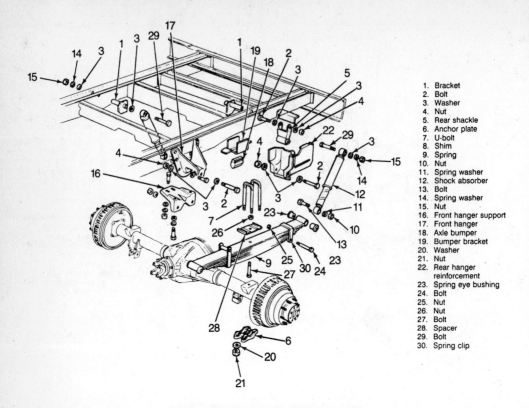

1. Bracket
2. Bolt
3. Washer
4. Nut
5. Rear shackle
6. Anchor plate
7. U-bolt
8. Shim
9. Spring
10. Nut
11. Spring washer
12. Shock absorber
13. Bolt
14. Spring washer
15. Nut
16. Front hanger support
17. Front hanger
18. Axle bumper
19. Bumper bracket
20. Washer
21. Nut
22. Rear hanger reinforcement
23. Spring eye bushing
24. Bolt
25. Nut
26. Nut
27. Bolt
28. Spacer
29. Bolt
30. Spring clip

Rear suspension on 30/3500 cutaway chassis

3. If the van is equipped with air lift shocks, bleed the air from the lines and disconnect the line from the shock absorber.

4. Disconnect the shock absorber at the top by removing the nuts, washer and bolt.

5. Remove the nut, washer, and bolt from the bottom mount.

6. Remove the shock from the van.

NOTE: *Before installation, purge the new shock of air by repeatedly extending it in its normal position and compressing it while inverted. It is normal for there to be more resistance to extension than to compression.*

7. Installation if the reverse of removal. If the van is equipped with air lift shock absorbers, inflate them to 10–15 psi minimum air pressure. Torque the shock absorber mounting nuts to 75 ft. lbs.

STEERING

Steering Wheel

REMOVAL AND INSTALLATION

1. Disconnect the battery ground cable.
2. Remove the horn button cap. On some models, it may be necessary to disconnect the horn wire on some models.

3. Mark the steering wheel-to-steering shaft relationship.

4. Remove the snapring from the steering shaft.

5. Remove the nut and washer from the steering shaft.

6. Remove the steering wheel with a puller.

7. Installation is the reverse of removal. The turn signal control assembly must be in the Neutral position to prevent damaging the canceling cam and control assembly. Torque the nut to 30 ft. lbs.

Turn Signal Switch

REMOVAL AND REPLACEMENT

Non-Tilt Columns

1. Disconnect the battery ground cable.
2. Remove the steering wheel.
3. Remove the column-to-instrument panel trim plate.
4. Place a screwdriver in the steering shaft lock plate cover slot. Pry up and out to free the cover from the lock plate.
5. Using tool J–23653–A, or equivalent, compress the lock plate and pry the retaining snapring off the shaft.

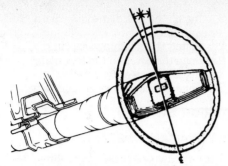

Steering wheel alignment. Dimension A is 1 inch to either side of the centerline

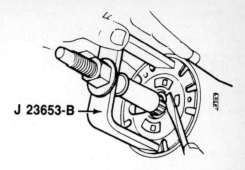

J 23653-B

Retaining ring removal

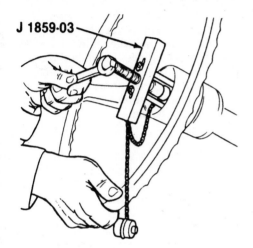

J 1859-03

Steering wheel removal

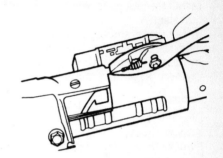

Turn signal wire protector removal

6. Remove the lock plate.

7. Remove the turn signal lever screw and the lever.

8. Remove the hazard warning knob by pressing it inward and unscrewing it.

9. Remove the switch screws and pull up on the switch, guiding the wiring harness through the opening.

10. Remove the wire protector by pulling it downward with a pliers.

11. Continue pulling up on the switch and remove it.

To install:

12. Be sure that the wiring harness is on the protector. Feed the connector and cover down through the housing and under the mounting bracket.

13. Install the switch screws.

14. Install the column-to-instrument panel trim plate.

15. Install the hazard warning knob.

16. Install the turn signal lever.

17. Install the lock plate.

18. Put the turn signal switch in the neutral position and pull out on the hazard knob.

19. Install the washer, spring and canceling cam.

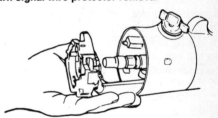

Turn signal switch removal

J 23653-B

Retaining ring installation

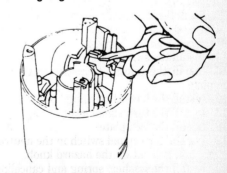

Ignition switch actuator sector removal

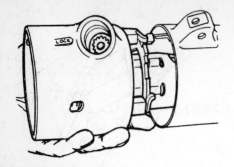

Turn signal housing removal

20. Install the lock plate using tool J–23653–A, or equivalent.
21. Install the retaining snapring.
22. Snap the cover on the lock plate.
23. Install the steering wheel.
24. Connect the battery ground cable.

Tilt Columns

1. Disconnect the battery ground cable.
2. Remove the steering wheel.
3. Remove the column-to-instrument panel trim plate.
4. Place a screwdriver in the steering shaft lock plate cover slot. Pry up and out to free the cover from the lock plate.
5. Using tool J–23653–A, or equivalent, compress the lock plate and pry the retaining snapring off the shaft.
6. Remove the lock plate.
7. Remove the turn signal lever screw and the lever.
8. Remove the hazard warning knob by pressing it inward and unscrewing it.
9. Remove the switch screws and pull up on the switch, guiding the wiring harness through the opening.
10. Remove the wire protector by pulling it downward with a pliers.
11. Put the turn signal and shifter housing in the "low" position, and remove the harness cover.
12. Continue pulling up on the switch and remove it.
   To install:
13. Feed the connector down through the housing and under the mounting bracket. Install the cover on the harness.
14. Install the switch screws.
15. Install the column-to-instrument panel trim plate.
16. Install the hazard warning knob.
17. Install the turn signal lever.
18. Install the lock plate.
19. Put the turn signal switch in the neutral position and pull out on the hazard knob.
20. Install the washer, spring and canceling cam.

21. Install the lock plate using tool J–23653–A, or equivalent.
22. Install the retaining snapring.
23. Snap the cover on the lock plate.
24. Install the steering wheel.
25. Connect the battery ground cable.

Ignition Switch

REMOVAL AND INSTALLATION

The switch is on the steering column, behind the instrument panel.
1. Lower the steering column, making sure that it is supported.
CAUTION: *Extreme care is necessary to prevent damage to the collapsible column.*
2. Make sure the switch is in the Lock position. If the lock cylinder is out, pull the switch rod up to the stop, then go down 1 detent.
3. Remove the two screws and the switch.
4. Before installation, make sure the switch is in the Lock position.
5. Install the switch using the original screws.
CAUTION: *Use of screws that are too long could prevent the column from collapsing on impact.*
6. Replace the column.

Lock Cylinder

REMOVAL AND INSTALLATION

1. Remove the steering wheel.
2. Remove the turn signal switch. It is not necessary to completely remove the switch from the column. Pull the switch rearward far enough to slip it over the end of the shaft, but do not pull the harness out of the column.
3. Turn the lock to Run.
4. Remove the lock retaining screw and remove the lock cylinder.
CHILTON TIP: *If the retaining screw is dropped on removal, it may fall into the column, requiring complete disassembly of the column to retrieve the screw.*
5. To install, rotate the key to the stop while holding onto the cylinder.
6. Push the lock all the way in.
7. Install the screw. Tighten the screw to 40 inch lbs. for regular columns, 22 inch lbs. for adjustable columns.
8. Install the turn signal switch and the steering wheel.

Steering Column

REMOVAL AND INSTALLATION

1. Disconnect the battery ground.
2. Disconnect the transmission control linkage at the column. See Chapter 7.

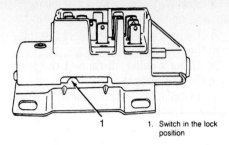

1. Switch in the lock position

Ignition switch

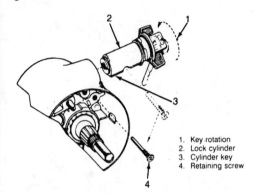

1. Key rotation
2. Lock cylinder
3. Cylinder key
4. Retaining screw

Lock cylinder installation

3. Matchmark the intermediate shaft upper yoke and the steering shaft.

4. Remove the upper yoke pinch bolt.

5. Remove the column-to-instrument panel bolts and nuts and carefully lower the column to the seat.

6. Remove the column toe-plate screws.

7. Disconnect all the wiring harness connectors at the column.

8. Carefully lift the column from the van.

To install:

9. Carefully position the column in the van.

10. Loosely install the column-to-instrument panel bolts.

11. Guide the steering shaft into the yoke, aligning the matchmarks.

12. Install the pinch bolt, making sure it passes through the undercut in the shaft. Torque the bolt to 35 ft. lbs. Make sure that the angle of the yoke does not exceed 39° or be less than 34°.

13. Torque the column bolts to 22 ft. lbs.

14. Install the toe-plate screws.

15. Connect all wiring harness connectors.

16. Connect the transmission linkage.

17. Connect the battery ground cable.

Idler Arm

REMOVAL AND INSTALLATION

1. Remove the idler arm frame bracket bolts.

2. Remove nut from the idler arm ball stud.

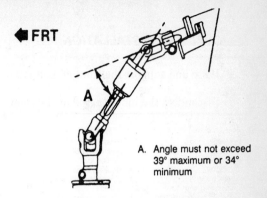

◀ FRT

A. Angle must not exceed 39° maximum or 34° minimum

Cardan joint angle

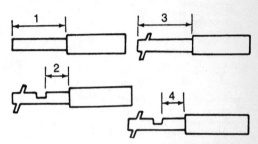

1. 87.7mm with tilt column, column shift
2. 144.9mm with tilt column and 4-speed
3. 192mm with standard column and column shift
4. 80mm with tilt column and floor shift

Steering column collapse inspection

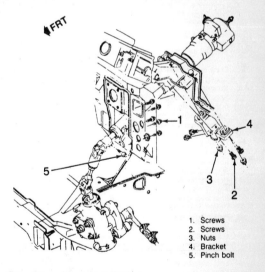

◀ FRT

1. Screws
2. Screws
3. Nuts
4. Bracket
5. Pinch bolt

Steering column installation

3. Disconnect the idler arm using a puller. Don't separate the idler arm using a fork-type separator. Damage could result to the seal or bushing.

4. Installation is the reverse of removal. Observe the following torques:
- Idler arm frame bracket: 35 ft. lbs.
- Idler arm ball stud nut: 66 ft. lbs.

Relay Rod

REMOVAL AND INSTALLATION

1. Raise and support the front end on jackstands.

2. Disconnect the inner tie rod at the relay rod.

3. Remove the nuts from the idler arm and pitman arm ball studs at the relay rod.

4. Using a puller, disconnect the relay rod from the idler arm.

5. Using a puller, disconnect the relay rod from the pitman arm.

6. Installation is the reverse of removal. Tighten all nuts to 66 ft. lbs.

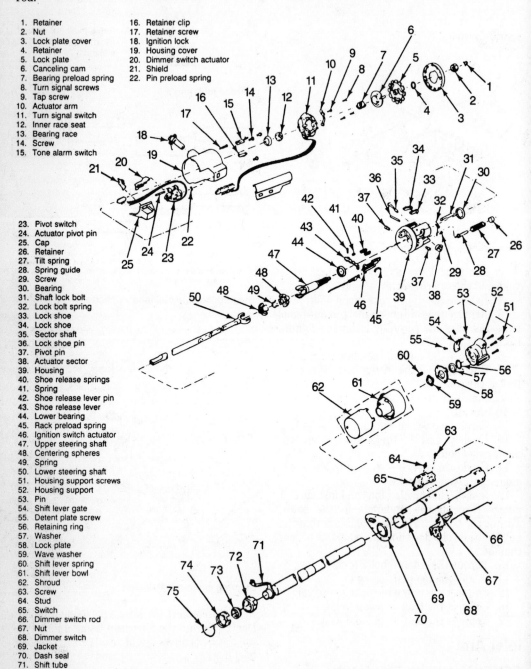

1. Retainer
2. Nut
3. Lock plate cover
4. Retainer
5. Lock plate
6. Canceling cam
7. Bearing preload spring
8. Turn signal screws
9. Tap screw
10. Actuator arm
11. Turn signal switch
12. Inner race seat
13. Bearing race
14. Screw
15. Tone alarm switch
16. Retainer clip
17. Retainer screw
18. Ignition lock
19. Housing cover
20. Dimmer switch actuator
21. Shield
22. Pin preload spring
23. Pivot switch
24. Actuator pivot pin
25. Cap
26. Retainer
27. Tilt spring
28. Spring guide
29. Screw
30. Bearing
31. Shaft lock bolt
32. Lock bolt spring
33. Lock shoe
34. Lock shoe
35. Sector shaft
36. Lock shoe pin
37. Pivot pin
38. Actuator sector
39. Housing
40. Shoe release springs
41. Spring
42. Shoe release lever pin
43. Shoe release lever
44. Lower bearing
45. Rack preload spring
46. Ignition switch actuator
47. Upper steering shaft
48. Centering spheres
49. Spring
50. Lower steering shaft
51. Housing support screws
52. Housing support
53. Pin
54. Shift lever gate
55. Detent plate screw
56. Retaining ring
57. Washer
58. Lock plate
59. Wave washer
60. Shift lever spring
61. Shift lever bowl
62. Shroud
63. Screw
64. Stud
65. Switch
66. Dimmer switch rod
67. Nut
68. Dimmer switch
69. Jacket
70. Dash seal
71. Shift tube
72. Adapter
73. Lower bearing
74. Reinforcement
75. Adapter clip

Tilt steering column with column shift

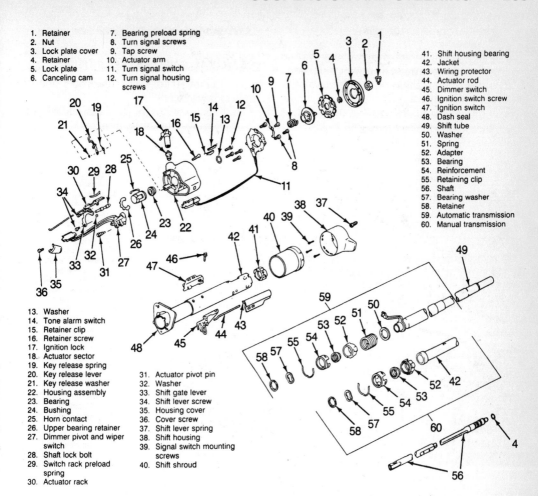

1. Retainer
2. Nut
3. Lock plate cover
4. Retainer
5. Lock plate
6. Canceling cam
7. Bearing preload spring
8. Turn signal screws
9. Tap screw
10. Actuator arm
11. Turn signal switch
12. Turn signal housing screws
13. Washer
14. Tone alarm switch
15. Retainer clip
16. Retainer screw
17. Ignition lock
18. Actuator sector
19. Key release spring
20. Key release lever
21. Key release washer
22. Housing assembly
23. Bearing
24. Bushing
25. Horn contact
26. Upper bearing retainer
27. Dimmer pivot and wiper switch
28. Shaft lock bolt
29. Switch rack preload spring
30. Actuator rack
31. Actuator pivot pin
32. Washer
33. Shift gate lever
34. Shift lever screw
35. Housing cover
36. Cover screw
37. Shift lever spring
38. Shift housing
39. Signal switch mounting screws
40. Shift shroud
41. Shift housing bearing
42. Jacket
43. Wiring protector
44. Actuator rod
45. Dimmer switch
46. Ignition switch screw
47. Ignition switch
48. Dash seal
49. Shift tube
50. Washer
51. Spring
52. Adapter
53. Bearing
54. Reinforcement
55. Retaining clip
56. Shaft
57. Bearing washer
58. Retainer
59. Automatic transmission
60. Manual transmission

Standard steering column

Pitman Arm

REMOVAL AND INSTALLATION

1. Raise and support the front end on jackstands.

2. Remove the relay rod nut and cotter pin.

3. Disconnect the relay rod from the pitman arm using a puller. Do not hammer on

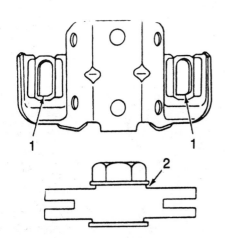

1. Capsules must be within ¹/₁₆ in. from bottom of slots. If not, replace the bracket assembly

2. The bolt head must not contact the surface "2". If contact is made, the capsule shear load will be increased. Replace the bracket

Steering column collapse inspection

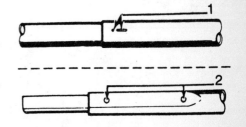

1. Inspect for sheared plastic in the shift tube

2. Inspect for sheared plastic in the steering shaft

Steering column collapse inspection

the pitman arm. Damage could result to the steering gear.

4. Remove the pitman arm nut and washer.

5. Remove the pitman arm with a puller.

6. Installation is the reverse of removal. Observe the following torques:

- Pitman arm-to-gear: 184 ft. lbs.
- Relay rod-to-pitman arm: 66 ft. lbs.

Steering Shock Absorber

REMOVAL AND INSTALLATION

1. Remove the shock absorber mounting nuts and washers.

2. Remove cotter pin and castellated nut.

3. Remove the shock absorber.

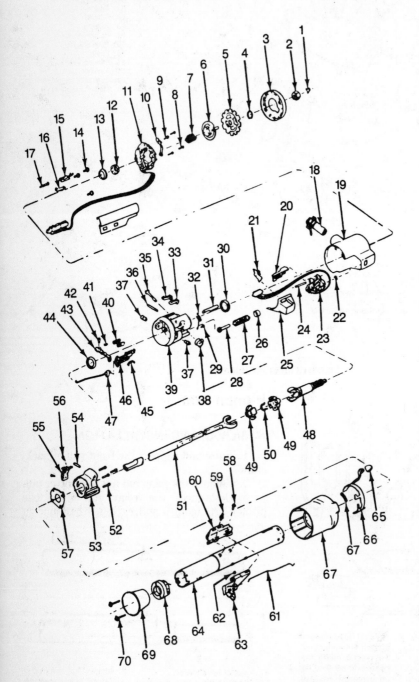

1. Retainer
2. Nut
3. Lock plate cover
4. Retainer
5. Lock plate
6. Canceling cam
7. Bearing preload spring
8. Turn signal screws
9. Tap screw
10. Actuator arm
11. Turn signal switch
12. Inner race seat
13. Bearing race
14. Screw
15. Tone alarm switch
16. Retainer clip
17. Retainer screw
18. Ignition lock
19. Housing cover
20. Dimmer switch actuator
21. Shield
22. Pin preload spring
23. Pivot switch
24. Actuator pivot pin
25. Cap
26. Retainer
27. Tilt spring
28. Spring guide
29. Screw
30. Bearing
31. Shaft lock bolt
32. Lock bolt spring
33. Lock shoe
34. Lock shoe
35. Sector shaft
36. Lock shoe pin
37. Pivot pin
38. Actuator sector
39. Housing
40. Shoe release springs
41. Spring
42. Shoe release lever pin
43. Shoe release lever
44. Lower bearing
45. Rack preload spring
46. Actuator rack
47. Ignition switch actuator
48. Upper steering shaft
49. Centering spheres
50. Spring
51. Lower steering shaft
52. Housing support screws
53. Housing support
54. Pin
55. Shift lever gate
56. Detent plate screw
57. Lock plate
58. Screw
59. Stud
60. Switch
61. Dimmer switch rod
62. Nut
63. Dimmer switch
64. Jacket
65. Key release lever
66. Key release spring
67. Shroud
68. Lower bearing
69. Retainer
70. Screws

Tilt steering column with floor shift

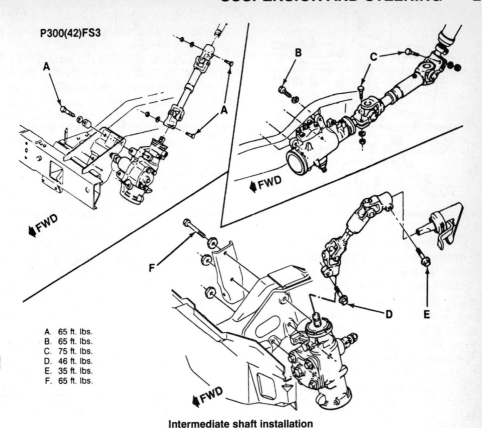

P300(42)FS3

A. 65 ft. lbs.
B. 65 ft. lbs.
C. 75 ft. lbs.
D. 46 ft. lbs.
E. 35 ft. lbs.
F. 65 ft. lbs.

Intermediate shaft installation

4. Installation is the reverse of removal. Tighten all nuts to 46 ft. lbs.

Tie Rod Ends

REPLACEMENT

1. Loosen the tie rod adjuster sleeve clamp nuts.

2. Remove the tie rod end stud cotter pin and nut.

3. You can use a tie rod end ball joint removal tool to loosen the stud, or you can loosen it by tapping on the steering arm with a hammer while using a heavy hammer as a backup.

4. Remove the inner stud in the same way.

5. Unscrew the tie rod end from the threaded sleeve. The threads may be left or right hand threads. Count the number of turns required to remove it.

6. To install, grease the threads and turn the new tie rod end in as many turns as were needed to remove it. This will give approximately correct toe-in. Tighten the clamp bolts.

7. Tighten the stud nuts and install new cotter pins. You may tighten the nut to align the cotter pin, buy don't loosen it.

8. Adjust the toe-in.

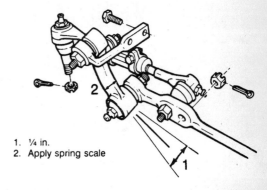

1. ¼ in.
2. Apply spring scale

Checking idler arm movement

Manual Steering Gear

ADJUSTMENT

Before any steering gear adjustments are made, it is recommended that the front end of the van be raised and a thorough inspection be made for stiffness or lost motion in the steering gear, steering linkage and front suspension. Worn or damaged parts should be replaced, since a satisfactory adjustment of the steering gear cannot be obtained if bent or badly worn parts exist.

It is also very important that the steering gear be properly aligned in the van. Misalign-

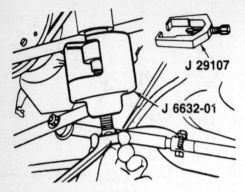

Removing the pitman arm

ment of the gear places a stress on the steering worm shaft, therefore a proper adjustment is impossible. To align the steering gear, loosen the steering gear-to-frame mounting bolts to permit the gear to align itself. Check the steering gear to frame mounting seat. If there is a gap at any of the mounting bolts, proper alignment may be obtained by placing shims where excessive gap appears. Tighten the steering gear-to-frame bolts. Alignment of the gear in the van is very important and should be done

carefully so that a satisfactory, trouble-free gear adjustment may be obtained.

The steering gear is of the recirculating ball nut type. the ball nut, mounted on the worm gear, is driven by means of steel balls which circulate in helical grooves in both the worm and nut. Ball return guides attached to the nut serve to recirculate the two sets of balls in the grooves. As the steering wheel is turned to the right, the ball nut moves upward. When the wheel is turned to the left, the ball nut moves downward.

Before doing the adjustment procedures given below, ensure that the steering problem is not caused by faulty suspension components, bad front end alignment, etc. Then, proceed with the following adjustments.

Bearing Drag

1. Disconnect the pitman arm from the gear.
2. Disconnect the battery ground cable.
3. Remove the horn cap.
4. Turn the steering wheel gently to the left stop, then back 1/2 turn.
5. Position an inch-pound torque wrench

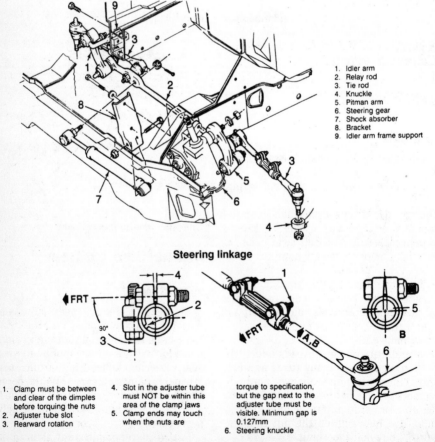

1. Idler arm
2. Relay rod
3. Tie rod
4. Knuckle
5. Pitman arm
6. Steering gear
7. Shock absorber
8. Bracket
9. Idler arm frame support

Steering linkage

1. Clamp must be between and clear of the dimples before torquing the nuts
2. Adjuster tube slot
3. Rearward rotation

4. Slot in the adjuster tube must NOT be within this area of the clamp jaws
5. Clamp ends may touch when the nuts are

torque to specification, but the gap next to the adjuster tube must be visible. Minimum gap is 0.127mm
6. Steering knuckle

Tie rod clamp and adjuster tube positioning

on the steering wheel nut and rotate it through a 90° arc. Note the torque. Proper torque is 5–8 inch lbs.

6. If the torque is incorrect, loosen the adjuster plug locknut and back off the plug 1/4 turn, then tighten the plug to give the proper torque.

7. Hold the plug and tighten the adjuster plug locknut to 85 ft. lbs.

Overcenter Preload

1. Turn the steering wheel lock-to-lock counting the total number of turns. Turn the wheel back 1/2 the total number of turns to center it.

2. Turn the lash (sector shaft) adjuster screw clockwise to remove all lash between the ball nut and sector teeth. Tighten the locknut to 25 ft. lbs.

3. Using a torque wrench on the steering wheel nut, observe the highest reading while the gear is turned through the center position. It should be 16 inch lbs. or less.

4. If necessary repeat adjust the preload with the adjuster screw. Tighten the locknut to 25 ft. lbs.

REMOVAL AND INSTALLATION

1. Set the front wheels in straight ahead position by driving vehicle a short distance on a flat surface.

2. Matchmark the relationship of the universal yoke to the wormshaft.

3. Remove the universal yoke pinch bolt.

4. Mark the relationship of the pitman arm to the pitman shaft.

5. Remove the pitman shaft nut and then remove the pitman arm from the pitman shaft, using puller J–6632.

6. Remove the steering gear to frame bolts and remove the gear assembly.

To install:

7. Place the steering gear in position, guiding the steering gear shaft into the universal yoke.

8. Install the steering gear to frame bolts and torque to 75 ft. lbs.

9. Install the yoke pinch bolt. Torque the pinch bolt to 45 ft. lbs.

10. Install the pitman arm onto the pitman shaft, lining up the marks made at removal. Install the pitman shaft nut torque to 185 ft. lbs.

Power Steering Gear

The procedures for maintaining, adjusting, and repairing the power steering system and its components are to be done only after determining that the steering linkages and front suspension systems are correctly aligned and in good condition. All worn or damaged parts should be replaced before attempting to service the power steering system. After correcting any condition that could affect the power steering, do the preliminary test of the steering system components.

PRELIMINARY TESTS

Proper lubrication of the steering linkage and the front suspension components is very important for the proper operation of the steering systems of vans equipped with power steering.

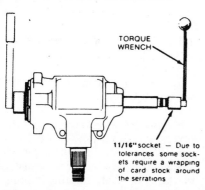

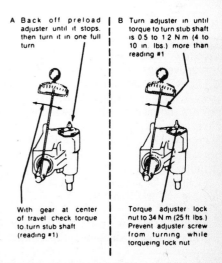

Manual steering gear adjustments

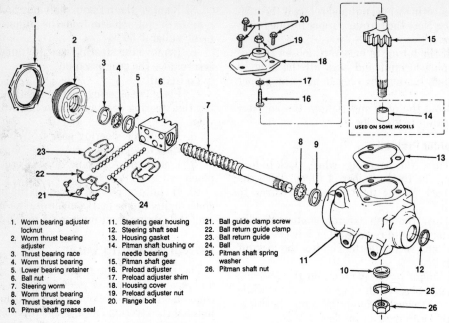

1. Worm bearing adjuster locknut	11. Steering gear housing	21. Ball guide clamp screw
2. Worm thrust bearing adjuster	12. Steering shaft seal	22. Ball return guide clamp
	13. Housing gasket	23. Ball return guide
3. Thrust bearing race	14. Pitman shaft bushing or needle bearing	24. Ball
4. Worm thrust bearing	15. Pitman shaft gear	25. Pitman shaft spring washer
5. Lower bearing retainer	16. Preload adjuster	26. Pitman shaft nut
6. Ball nut	17. Preload adjuster shim	
7. Steering worm	18. Housing cover	
8. Worm thrust bearing	19. Preload adjuster nut	
9. Thrust bearing race	20. Flange bolt	
10. Pitman shaft grease seal		

Manual steering gear exploded view

Most all power steering systems use the same lubricant in the steering gear box as in the power steering pump reservoir, and the fluid level is maintained at the pump reservoir.

With power cylinder assist power steering, the steering gear is of the standard mechanical type and the lubricating oil is self contained within the gear box and the level is maintained by the removal of a filler plug on the gear box housing. The control valve assembly is mounted on the gear box and is lubricated by power steering oil from the power steering pump reservoir, where the level is maintained.

REMOVAL AND INSTALLATION

1. Set the front wheels in the straight ahead position.
2. Matchmark the relationship of the universal yoke to the wormshaft.
3. Remove the universal yoke pinch bolt.
4. Place a drain pan under the gear and disconnect the fluid lines. Cap the openings.
5. Mark the relationship of the pitman arm to the pitman shaft.
6. Remove the pitman shaft nut and then remove the pitman arm from the pitman shaft, using puller J–6632.
7. Remove the steering gear to frame bolts and remove the gear assembly.

To install:

8. Place the steering gear in position, guiding the steering gear shaft into the universal yoke.
9. Install the steering gear to frame bolts and torque to 75 ft. lbs.

10. Install the yoke pinch bolt. Torque the pinch bolt to 45 ft. lbs.
11. Install the pitman arm onto the pitman shaft, lining up the marks made at removal. Install the pitman shaft nut torque to 185 ft. lbs.
12. Connect the fluid lines and refill the reservoir. Bleed the system.

ADJUSTMENTS

For proper adjustment, remove the gear from the van, drain all the fluid from the gear and place the gear in a vise.

It is important that the adjustments be made in the order given.

Worm Bearing Preload

1. Remove the adjuster plug locknut.
2. Turn the adjuster plug in clockwise until firmly bottomed. Then, tighten it to 20 ft. lbs.
3. Place an index mark on the gear housing in line with one of the holes in the adjuster plug.
4. Measure counterclockwise from the mark about 1/4 inch and make another mark on the housing.
5. Rotate the adjuster plug counterclockwise until the hole is aligned with the second mark.
6. Install the locknut. Hold the plug and tighten the locknut to 81 ft. lbs.
7. Place an inch pound torque wrench and 12-point deep socket on the stub shaft and measure the stub shaft rotating torque, starting with the torque wrench handle in a vertical position to a point 1/4 turn to either side. Note

your reading. The proper torque should be 4-10 inch lbs. If the reading is incorrect, wither your adjustment was done incorrectly or there is gear damage.

Overcenter Preload

1. Loosen the locknut and turn the pitman shaft adjuster screw counterclockwise until it is all the way out. Then, turn it in ½ turn.

2. Rotate the stub shaft from stop to stop, counting the total number of turns, then turn it back ½ that number to center the gear.

3. Place the torque wrench in a vertical position on the stub shaft and measure the torque necessary to rotate the shaft to a point 45° to either side of center. Record the highest reading. On gears with less than 400 miles, the reading should be 6-10 inch lbs. higher than the worm bearing preload torque previously recorded, but not to exceed 18 inch lbs. On gears with more than 400 miles, the reading should be 4–5 inch lbs. higher, but not to exceed 14 inch lbs.

4. If necessary, adjust the reading by turning the adjuster screw.

5. When the adjustment is made, hold the screw and tighten the locknut to 35 ft. lbs.

6. Install the gear.

Power Steering Pump

CHECKING

Air Bleeding

Air bubbles in the power steering system must be removed from the fluid. Be sure the reservoir is filled to the proper level and the fluid is warmed up to operating temperature. Then, turn the steering wheel through its full travel three or four times until all the air bubbles are removed. Do not hold the steering wheel against its stops. Recheck the fluid level.

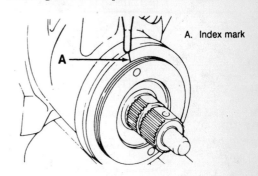

A. Index mark

Mark the housing even with the adjuster plug

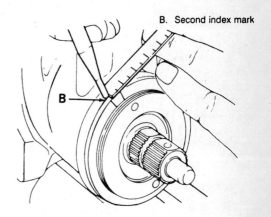

B. Second index mark

Remarking the housing

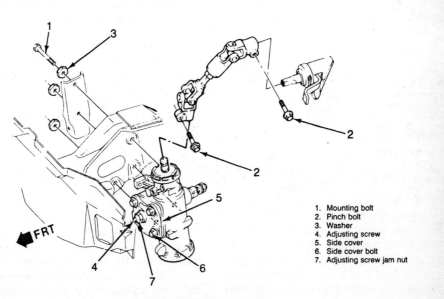

1. Mounting bolt
2. Pinch bolt
3. Washer
4. Adjusting screw
5. Side cover
6. Side cover bolt
7. Adjusting screw jam nut

Steering gear installation

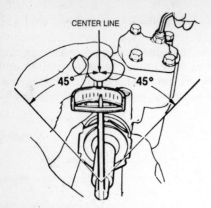

Checking over-center rotational torque

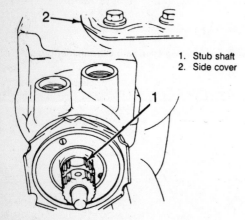

1. Stub shaft
2. Side cover

Aligning the stub shaft

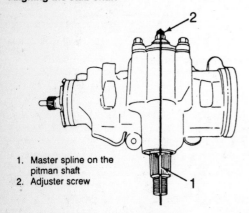

1. Master spline on the pitman shaft
2. Adjuster screw

Aligning the pitman shaft master spline

Fluid Level Check

1. Run the engine until the fluid is at the normal operating temperature. Then, turn the steering wheel through its full travel three or four times, and shut off the engine.

2. Check the fluid level in the steering reservoir. If the fluid level is low, add enough fluid to raise the level to the Full mark on the dipstick or filler tube.

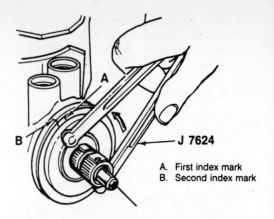

A. First index mark
B. Second index mark

Aligning the adjuster plug and the second mark

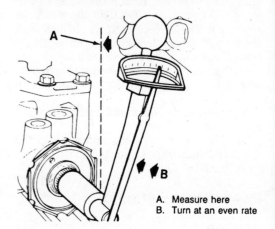

A. Measure here
B. Turn at an even rate

Checking rotational torque

Pump Belt Check

Inspect the pump belt for cracks, glazing, or worn places. Using a belt tension gauge, check the belt tension for the proper range of adjustment. The amount of tension varies with the make of truck or van and the condition of the belt. New belts (those belts used less than 15 minutes) require a higher figure. The belt deflection method of adjustment may be used only if a belt tension gauge is not available. The belt should be adjusted for a deflection of $1/4$–$3/8$ in. (6.35–9.53mm).

Check all possible leakage points (hoses, power steering pump, or steering gear) for loss of fluid. Turn engine on and rotate the steering wheel from stop to stop several times. Tighten all loose fittings and replace any defective lines or valve seats.

Check the turning effort required to turn the steering wheel after aligning the front wheels and inflating the tires to the proper pressure.

1. With the vehicle on dry pavement and the front wheel straight ahead, set the parking brake and turn the engine on.

2. After a short warmup period for the engine, turn the steering wheel back and forth several times to warm the steering fluid.

3. Attach a spring scale to the steering wheel rim and measure the pull required to turn the steering wheel one complete revolution in each direction. The effort needed to turn the steering wheel should not exceed the limits specified.

NOTE: *This test may be done with the steering wheel removed and a torque wrench applied on the steering wheel nut.*

Power Steering Hose Inspection

Inspect both the input and output hoses of the power steering pump for worn spots, cracks, or signs of leakage. Replace hose if defective, being sure to reconnect the replacement hose properly. Many power steering hoses are identified as to where they are to be connected by special means, such as fittings that will only fit on the correct pump fitting, or hoses of special lengths.

Test Driving Van to Check the Power Steering

When test driving to check power steering, drive at a speed between 15 and 20 mph. Make several turns in each direction. When a turn is completed, the front wheels should return to the straight ahead position with very little help from the driver.

If the front wheels fail to return as they should and yet the steering linkage is free, well oiled and properly adjusted, the trouble is probably due to misalignment of the power cylinder or improper adjustment of the spool valve.

The power steering pump supplies all the power assist used in power steering systems of all designs. There are various designs of pumps used by the truck and van manufacturers but all pumps supply power to operate the steering systems with the least effort. All power steering pumps have a reservoir tank built onto the oil pump. These pumps are driven by belt turned by pulleys on the engine, normally on the front of the crankshaft.

During operation of the engine at idle speed, there is provision for the power steering pump to supply more fluid pressure. During driving speeds or when the van is moving straight ahead, less pressure is needed and the excess is relieved through a pressure relief and flow control valve. The pressure relief part of the valve is inside the flow control and is basically the same for all pumps. The flow control valve regulates, or controls, the constant flow of fluid from the pump as it varies with the demands of the steering gear. The pressure relief valve limits the hydraulic pressure built up when the steering gear is turned against its stops.

REMOVAL AND INSTALLATION

1. Disconnect the hoses at the pump. When the hoses are disconnected, secure the ends in a raised position to prevent leakage. Cap the ends of the hoses to prevent the entrance of dirt.

2. Cap the pump fittings.

3. Loosen the bracket-to-pump mounting nuts.

4. Remove the pump drive belt.

5. Remove the bracket-to-pump bolts and remove the pump from the van.

6. Installation is the reverse of removal. Fill the reservoir and bleed the pump by turning the pulley counterclockwise (as viewed from the front) until bubbles stop forming. Bleed the system as outlined following.

BLEEDING THE HYDRAULIC SYSTEM

1. Fill the reservoir to the proper level and let the fluid remain undisturbed for at least 2 minutes.

2. Start the engine and run it for only about 2 seconds.

3. Add fluid as necessary.

4. Repeat Steps 1–3 until the level remains constant.

5. Raise the front of the vehicle so that the front wheels are off the ground. Set the parking brake and block both rear wheels front and rear. Manual transmissions should be in Neutral; automatic transmissions should be in Park.

6. Start the engine and run it at approximately 1500 rpm.

7. Turn the wheels (off the ground) to the right and left, lightly contacting the stops.

8. Add fluid as necessary.

9. Lower the vehicle and turn the wheels right and left on the ground.

10. Check the level and refill as necessary.

11. If the fluid is extremely foamy, let the van stand for a few minutes with the engine off and repeat the procedure. Check the belt tension and check for a bent or loose pulley. The pulley should not wobble with the engine running.

12. Check that no hoses are contacting any parts of the van, particularly sheet metal.

13. Check the oil level and refill as necessary. This step and the next are very important. When willing, follow Steps 1–10 above

14. Check for air in the fluid. Aerated fluid appears milky. If air is present, repeat the above operation. If it is obvious that the pump will not respond to bleeding after several attempts, a pressure test may be required.

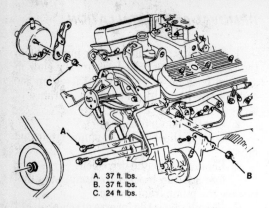

A. 37 ft. lbs.
B. 37 ft. lbs.
C. 24 ft. lbs.

Power steering pump mounting on the 6-4.3L engine

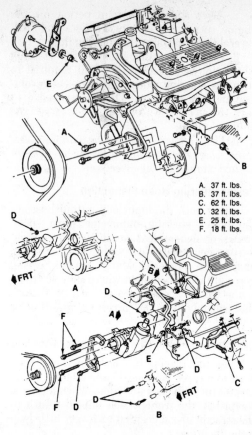

A. 37 ft. lbs.
B. 37 ft. lbs.
C. 62 ft. lbs.
D. 32 ft. lbs.
E. 25 ft. lbs.
F. 18 ft. lbs.

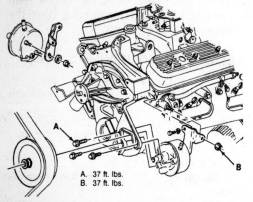

A. 37 ft. lbs.
B. 37 ft. lbs.

Power steering pump mounting on the 8-5.0L engine

Power steering pump mounting on the 8-5.7L engine

1.  J 6627-A

2. J 6632-01

3. J 29107

4.  J 24319-01

5.  J 29193

6.  J 29194

1. Tie rod puller/wheel stud remover
2. Pitman arm puller
3. Pitman arm puller
4. Universal steering linkage puller
5. Steering linkage installer (12mm)
6. Steering linkage installer (14mm)

Special tools

WHEEL ALIGNMENT SPECIFICATIONS

Year	Models	Caster (deg.)		Camber (deg.)		Toe-in (in.)	King Pin Incl. (deg.)
		Range	Pref.	Range	Pref.		
1987	G100, 200	See Chart Below		0 to 1P	½P	3/16	8½
	G300	See Chart Below		¼N to ¾P	¼P	3/16	8½
1988	G100, 200	See Chart Below		0 to 1P	½P	3/16	8½
	G300	See Chart Below		¼N to ¾P	¼P	3/16	8½
1989	G100, 200	See Chart Below		¼P to 1¼P	½P	0	8½
	G300	See Chart Below		½N to 1P	¼P	0	8½
1990	G100, 200	See Chart Below		¼P to 1¼P	½P	0	8½
	G300	See Chart Below		½N to 1P	¼P	0	8½

Caster is determined by ride height. Ride height is measured as the distance between the bumper stop bracket on the axle, and the frame. Use the following charts to determine caster. Caster tolerance is plus or minus 1 degree.

G100, 200

Ride height (in.)	1.5	1.75	2.0	2.25	2.5	2.75	3.0	3.25	3.5	3.75	4.0	4.25	4.5
Caster (deg.)	3.4P	3.2P	3P	2.9P	2.7P	2.5P	2.3P	2.2P	2P	1.8P	1.7P	1.5P	1.4P

G300

Ride height (in.)	1.5	1.75	2.0	2.25	2.5	2.75	3.0	3.25	3.5	3.75	4.0	4.25	4.5
Caster (deg.)	3.1P	3P	2.7P	2.4P	2.1P	1.8P	1.5P	1.2P	1P	0.7P	0.5P	0.2P	0.03N

Brakes

BRAKE SYSTEM

Systems Operations

All Chevrolet and GMC vans are equipped with a split hydraulic braking system. The system is designed with separate systems for the front and rear brakes using a dual master cylinder with separate reservoirs. If a hydraulic component should fail in either the front or the rear system, the van can still be stopped with reasonable control.

Vans are equipped with disc brakes at the front and drum brakes at the rear. The drum brakes are still of the duo-servo anchor pin self-adjusting type, while the front disc brakes are single piston sliding caliper types. The front disc brakes are inherently self-adjusting.

Rear Wheel Anti-Lock Brake System (ABS)

NOTE: *Service on components peculiar to the ABS system will be found at the end of this Chapter*

Beginning with the 1990 models, these vans have an optional Rear Wheel Anti-lock Brake System.

Essentially, this system controls the lock-up of the rear wheels during braking by electronically monitoring wheel rotational speed and vehicle momentum. The actual regulation process is directly controlled by regulating the brake hydraulic pressure at the rear wheel brakes.

Main system operating components are:
- A control valve, made up of a dump valve which releases pressure into an accumulator and an isolation valve which maintains rear brake pressure. The control valve is located near the combination valve master cylinder.
- An Electronic Control Unit (ECU), which controls the control valve. The ECU is located next to the master cylinder and is operated by signals received from the speed sensor located in the transmission, and the brake light switch. If the tire size and/or axle ratio are changed, the speed sensor must be changed.

The ABS system is wired into the existing brake warning light on the dash.

Brake Adjustments

DRUM BRAKES

These brakes are equipped with self-adjusters and no manual adjustment is necessary, except when brake linings are replaced.

DISC BRAKES

These brakes are inherently self-adjusting and no adjustment is ever necessary or possible.

BRAKE SPECIFICATIONS
(All specifications in inches)

| Years | Brake Disc | | | | Brake Drum | |
	Original Thickness	Minimum Thickness	Maximum Run-out	Diameter	Original Inside Diameter	Maximum Wear Limit
1987–90	1.290	1.230	0.004	11.86	11.00	11.060

Brake Pedal

ADJUSTMENT

The stop light switch provides for an automatic adjustment for the brake pedal when it is returned to its stop. With pedal in fully released position, the stop light switch plunger should be fully depressed against the pedal shank. Adjust the switch by moving in or out as necessary.

1. Make certain that the tubular clip is in brake pedal mounting bracket.

2. With brake pedal depressed, insert switch into tubular clip until switch body seats on clip. Audible clicks can be heard as the threaded portion of the switch is pushed through the clip toward the brake pedal.

3. Pull brake pedal fully rearward against pedal stop until audible clicking sounds can no longer be heard. Switch will be moved in tubular clip providing adjustment.

4. Release brake pedal and then repeat Step 3 to assure that no audible clicking sounds remain.

REMOVAL AND INSTALLATION

1. Remove the retaining pin and disconnect the pushrod from the pedal arm.

2. Disconnect return spring at pedal arm.

3. Remove the brake pedal shaft retaining clip or, on manual transmission models, the clutch pedal retaining bracket.

4. Remove the clutch pedal or brake pedal retaining pin.

5. Remove the brake pedal.

6. Installation is the reverse of removal.

Master Cylinder

REMOVAL AND INSTALLATION

WARNING: *Clean any master cylinder parts in alcohol or brake fluid. Never use mineral based cleaning solvents such as gasoline, kerosene, carbon tetrachloride, acetone, or paint thinner as these will destroy rubber parts.   Do not allow brake fluid to spill on the vehicle's finish, it will remove the paint. Flush the area with water.*

1. Using a clean cloth, wipe the master cylinder and its lines to remove excess dirt and then place cloths under the unit to absorb spilled fluid.

2. Remove the hydraulic lines from the master cylinder and plug the outlets to prevent the entrance of foreign material. On vans with ABS, disconnect the lines at the isolation/dump valve.

3. Remove the master cylinder attaching

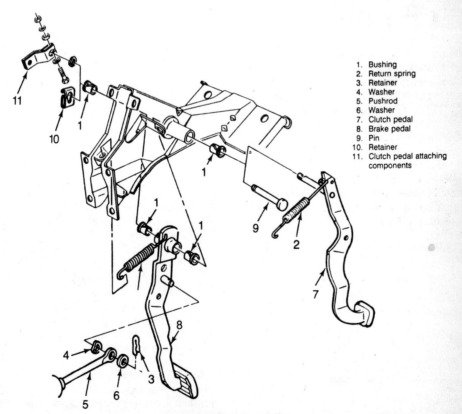

1. Bushing
2. Return spring
3. Retainer
4. Washer
5. Pushrod
6. Washer
7. Clutch pedal
8. Brake pedal
9. Pin
10. Retainer
11. Clutch pedal attaching components

Brake pedal components

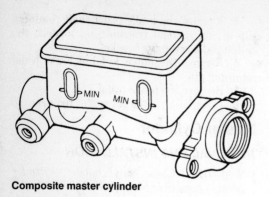

Composite master cylinder

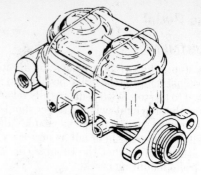

Cast iron master cylinder

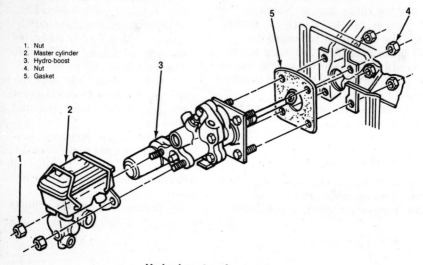

1. Nut
2. Master cylinder
3. Hydro-boost
4. Nut
5. Gasket

Hydro-boost replacement

bolts or, on vans with ABS, the attaching bolts from the isolation/dump valve, and remove the master cylinder from the brake booster.

CAUTION: *On vans with ABS: Never let brake fluid or your skin touch the ECU electrical connections! Also, never let the isolation/dump valve hang by it wiring!*

To install:

5. Position the master cylinder or, on vans with ABS the master cylinder and isolation/dump valve, on the booster. Torque the nuts to 21 ft. lbs.

Removing the reservoir

6. Connect the brake lines and fill the master cylinder reservoirs to the proper levels.

7. Bleed the brakes.

OVERHAUL

NOTE: *It is much easier to purchase a rebuilt master cylinder than to try to rebuild yours, yourself.*

Composite Bodied Master Cylinders

These units are identified by a cylinder body with a separate reservoir mounted on top of the cylinder.

1. Remove the cover and drain all the fluid from the reservoir.

2. Clamp the cylinder in a vise on its mounting flange.

3. Using a small prybar, pry off the reservoir and remove the grommets.

4. Remove the snapring and pull out the primary piston assembly.

5. Position the cylinder so that the bore is towards a padded surface about an inch away. Plug the rear port and direct low pressure compressed air into the front port. This will force out the secondary piston assembly.

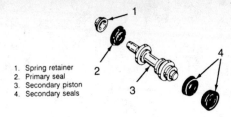

1. Spring retainer
2. Primary seal
3. Secondary piston
4. Secondary seals

Secondary piston

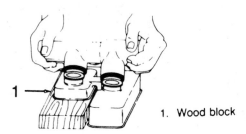

1. Wood block

Installing the reservoir

CAUTION: *The piston may come out with considerable force! Shield your eyes!*

6. Remove the seals, spring retainer and spring from the secondary piston.

7. Clean all metal parts in denatured alcohol. Clean all rubber parts with clean brake fluid.

WARNING: *Inspect the cylinder bore carefully. If there is any sign of rust, corrosion, scratching, nicking or any surface irregularity, the master cylinder MUST be discarded. It cannot be honed to correct surface irregularities. Any attempt to refinish the cylinder bore by honing will destroy the original finish and lead to rapid wear of the rubber components, resulting in early failure of the master cylinder!*

8. Lubricate all parts with clean brake fluid prior to assembly.

9. Using the new parts provided in the rebuilding kit, reassemble the secondary piston. The primary piston is not repairable.

10. Install the secondary piston in the bore.

11. Install the primary piston in the bore and, holding it inward, install the snapring.

12. Install the grommets and reservoir. The reservoir is easily installed by rocking it into place with firm hand pressure.

13. Bench-bleed the master cylinder.

Delco Cast Iron Master Cylinder

The cast iron Deco unit is a one-piece body with an integral reservoir/cylinder assembly made entirely of cast iron.

1. Position the master cylinder in a vise covering the jaws with cloth to prevent damage. (Do not tighten the vise too tightly).

2. Remove the snapring from the inside of

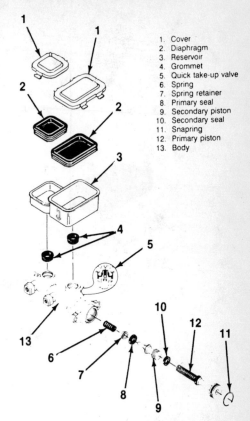

1. Cover
2. Diaphragm
3. Reservoir
4. Grommet
5. Quick take-up valve
6. Spring
7. Spring retainer
8. Primary seal
9. Secondary piston
10. Secondary seal
11. Snapring
12. Primary piston
13. Body

Composite master cylinder exploded view

the piston bore. Once this is done, the primary piston assembly may be removed.

3. Position the cylinder so that the bore is towards a padded surface about an inch away. Plug the rear port and direct low pressure compressed air into the front port. This will force out the secondary piston assembly.

CAUTION: *The piston may come out with considerable force! Shield your eyes!*

4. Remove the secondary seals, spring retainer, spring, and secondary seal from the secondary piston.

5. Remove the tube seats, if necessary, by threading a self-tapping screw into each seat any pulling the seat out with locking pliers.

6. Clean all metal parts in denatured alcohol. Clean all rubber parts with clean brake fluid.

WARNING: *Inspect the cylinder bore carefully. If there is any sign of rust, corrosion, scratching, nicking or any surface irregularity, the master cylinder MUST be discarded. It cannot be honed to correct surface irregularities. Any attempt to refinish the cylinder bore by honing will destroy the original finish and lead to rapid wear of the rubber components, resulting in early failure of the master cylinder!*

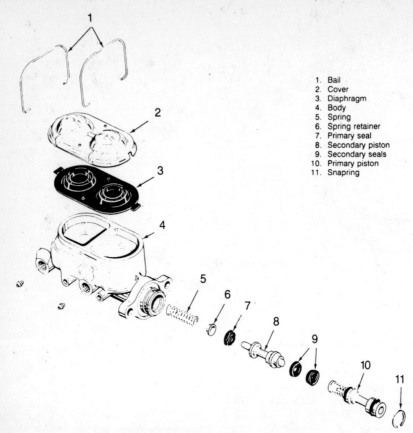

1. Bail
2. Cover
3. Diaphragm
4. Body
5. Spring
6. Spring retainer
7. Primary seal
8. Secondary piston
9. Secondary seals
10. Primary piston
11. Snapring

Cast iron master cylinder exploded view

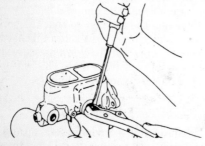

Removing the tube seats

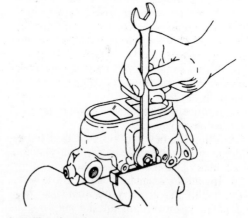

Installing the tube seats

7. Lubricate all parts with clean brake fluid prior to assembly.

8. Using the new parts provided in the rebuilding kit, reassemble the secondary piston. The primary piston is not repairable.

9. Install the secondary piston in the bore.

10. Install the primary piston in the bore and, holding it inward, install the snapring.

11. Install new tube seats, seating them using a nut the same size as a brake line nut.

12. Bench-bleed the master cylinder.

Bendix Master Cylinder

This unit is identified by the separate reservoir secured to the top of the cylinder by 4 bolts. The unit is used with the Hydro-boost hydraulic booster.

1. Unbolt the reservoir from the cylinder body.

2. Remove the reservoir O-rings and seals.

3. Depress the primary piston and remove the valve poppets and springs from the top of the cylinder body.

4. Remove the piston retaining snapring.

5. Remove the primary piston and return spring.

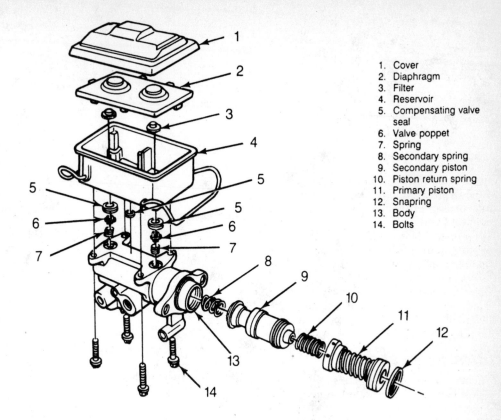

1. Cover
2. Diaphragm
3. Filter
4. Reservoir
5. Compensating valve seal
6. Valve poppet
7. Spring
8. Secondary spring
9. Secondary piston
10. Piston return spring
11. Primary piston
12. Snapring
13. Body
14. Bolts

Bendix master cylinder exploded view

6. Plug the front port, aim the cylinder at a close, padded surface (about an inch away) and apply low pressure compressed air to the rear port. This will force out the secondary piston. Remove the spring, also.

7. Clean all metal parts thoroughly with denatured alcohol and discard all rubber parts.

WARNING: *Inspect the cylinder bore carefully. If there is any sign of rust, corrosion, scratching, nicking or any surface irregularity, the master cylinder MUST be discarded. It cannot be honed to correct surface irregularities. Any attempt to refinish the cylinder bore by honing will destroy the original finish and lead to rapid wear of the rubber components, resulting in early failure of the master cylinder!*

8. Install all new rubber parts coated with clean brake fluid.

9. Install the secondary piston and spring.

10. Install the primary piston and spring.

11. Install the snapring.

12. Install new O-rings and springs.

13. Install new poppets and seals.

14. Install the reservoir. Torque the bolts to 13 ft. lbs.

Vacuum Booster

REMOVAL AND INSTALLATION

1. Unbolt the master cylinder from the booster and pull it off the studs, CAREFULLY! It is not necessary to disconnect the brake lines.

2. Disconnect the vacuum hose from the check valve.

3. Disconnect the booster pushrod at the brake pedal.

4. Remove the booster mounting nuts, located on the inside of the firewall.

5. Lift off the booster.

6. Installation is the reverse of removal. Torque the booster mounting nuts to 20 ft. lbs.; the master cylinder nuts to 20 ft. lbs.

Combination Valve

This valve is used on all models. It is non-adjustable and non-serviceable. It can be found by following the lines from the master cylinder. The combination valve itself contains a metering valve that restricts flow to the front brakes until the rear brakes overcome the force of their retracting springs to prevent front brake lockup, a pressure differential warning switch which activates a warning light if either the

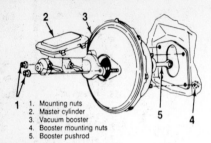

1. Mounting nuts
2. Master cylinder
3. Vacuum booster
4. Booster mounting nuts
5. Booster pushrod

Vacuum booster installation

front or rear hydraulic circuit is losing pressure, and a proportioning valve which limits hydraulic pressure to the rear brakes to prevent rear wheel lockup.

The pressure differential warning switch will reset itself automatically when the brakes are used after a malfunction causing the warning light to go on has been corrected.

When the brake hydraulic system is bled of air, the metering valve pin on the end of the combination valve must be hold in a slight amount to allow fluid flow to the front brakes.

CENTERING THE SWITCH

Whenever work on the brake system is done it is possible that the brake warning light will come on and refuse to go off when the work is finished. In this event, the switch must be centered.

1. Raise and support the truck.
2. Attach a bleeder hose to the rear brake bleed screw and immerse the other end of the hose in a jar of clean brake fluid.
3. Be sure that the master cylinder is full.
4. When bleeding the brakes, the pin in the end of the metering portion of the combination valve must be hold in the open position (with the tool described in the brake bleeding section installed under the pin mounting bolt). Be sure to tighten the bolt after removing the tool.
5. Turn the ignition key ON. Open the bleed screw while an assistant applies heavy pressure on the brake pedal. The warning lamp should light. Close the bleed screw before the helper releases the pedal.
6. To reset the switch, apply heavy pressure to the pedal. This will apply hydraulic pressure to the switch which will recenter it.
7. Repeat Step 5 for the front bleed screw.
8. Turn the ignition OFF and lower the truck.

NOTE: *If the warning lamp does not light during Step 6, the switch is defective and must be replaced.*

REMOVAL AND INSTALLATION

1. Raise and support the front end on jackstands.

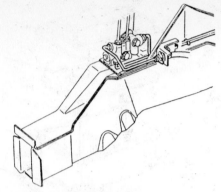

Combination valve location

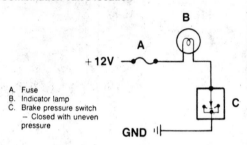

A. Fuse
B. Indicator lamp
C. Brake pressure switch
— Closed with uneven pressure

Brake pressure warning circuit

2. Clean the brake pipe connection thoroughly.
3. Disconnect the brake pipes at the valve.
4. Remove the valve retaining bolts.
5. Installation is the reverse of removal. Torque the mounting bracket bolts to 12 ft. lbs. Torque the brake pipe connections to 18 ft. lbs.
6. Bleed the system.

Brake Hoses

REPLACEMENT

1. Clean the connection thoroughly before opening it.
2. Unscrew the connection at the steel pipe or junction block and/or remove the bolt at the caliper. Discard any copper washers.
3. Remove any retaining clips and/or brackets securing the hose to the frame or control arm.
4. Cap all openings.
5. Installation is the reverse of removal. Always use new copper washers. The hose should not be twisted or in contact with any suspension component. Observe the following torques:
   • Brake hose-to-caliper bolt: 32 ft. lbs.
   • Front brake hose-to-frame nut: 58 inch lbs.
   • Front brake hose bracket bolt: 12 ft. lbs.
   • Rear brake hose-to-rear axle junction block: 12 inch lbs.

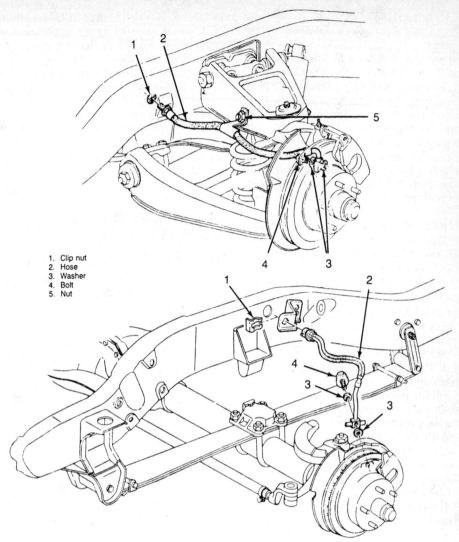

1. Clip nut
2. Hose
3. Washer
4. Bolt
5. Nut

Front brake flexible hoses

Brake Pipes

REMOVAL AND INSTALLATION

CAUTION: *When replacing a steel brake pipe, always use steel tubing of the same pressure rating and corrosion resistance. The replacement pipe must be of the same diameter. Copper tubing must never be used as a replacement for steel brake pipes! Brake pipes running parallel must be separated by at least $1/4$ in. along their common run.*

1. Clean the pipe fittings and disconnect the pipe at each end. Where necessary, always use a back-up wrench. Cap all openings.
2. Cut the new pipe to length, adding $1/8$ inch for each flare.
3. Always double-flare the pipe ends. Single flaring cannot withstand the pressure.

4. Always use a tubing bender when bending the pipe.
5. All brake pipe nuts should be torqued to 12 ft. lbs.

Hydro-Boost

Diesel engined vans and some 30/3500 series vans such as motor home chassis are equipped with the Bendix Hydro-boost system. This power brake booster obtains hydraulic pressure from the power steering pump, rather than vacuum pressure from the intake manifold as in most gasoline engine brake booster systems.

HYDRO-BOOST SYSTEM CHECKS

1. A defective Hydro-Boost cannot cause any of the following conditions:
   a. Noisy brakes
   b. Fading pedal

c. Pulling brakes.

If any of these occur, check elsewhere in the brake system.

2. Check the fluid level in the master cylinder. It should be within $1/4$ in. (6.35mm) of the top. If is isn't add only DOT-3 or DOT-4 brake fluid until the correct level is reached.

3. Check the fluid level in the power steering pump. The engine should be at normal running temperature and stopped. The level should register on the pump dipstick. Add power steering fluid to bring the reservoir level up to the correct level. Low fluid level will result in both poor steering and stopping ability.

CAUTION: *The brake hydraulic system uses brake fluid only, while the power steering and Hydro-Boost systems use power steering fluid only. Don't mix the two!*

4. Check the power steering pump belt tension, and inspect all the power steering/Hydro-Boost hoses for kinks or leaks.

5. Check and adjust the engine idle speed, as necessary.

6. Check the power steering pump fluid for bubbles. If air bubbles are present in the fluid, bleed the system:

a. Fill the power steering pump reservoir to specifications with the engine at normal operating temperature.

b. With the engine running, rotate the steering wheel through its normal travel 3 or 4 times, without holding the wheel against the stops.

c. Check the fluid level again.

7. If the problem still exists, go on to the Hydro-Boost test sections and troubleshooting chart.

HYDRO-BOOST TESTS

Functional Test

1. Check the brake system for leaks or low fluid level. Correct as necessary.

2. Place the transmission in Neutral and stop the engine. Apply the brakes 4 or 5 times to empty the accumulator.

3. Keep the pedal depressed with moderate (25–40 lbs.) pressure and start the engine.

4. The brake pedal should fall slightly and then push back up against your foot. If no movement is felt, the Hydro-Boost system is not working.

Accumulator Leak Test

1. Run the engine at normal idle. Turn the steering wheel against one of the stops; hold it there for no longer than 5 seconds. Center the steering wheel and stop the engine.

2. Keep applying the brakes until a hard pedal is obtained. There should be a minimum of 1 power assisted brake application when pedal pressure of 20–25 lbs. is applied.

3. Start the engine and allow it to idle. Rotate the steering wheel against the stop. Listen for a light hissing sound; this is the accumulator being charged. Center the steering wheel and stop the engine.

4. Wait one hour and apply the brakes without starting the engine. As in step 2, there should be at least 1 stop with power assist. If not, the accumulator is defective and must be replaced.

TROUBLESHOOTING THE HYDRO-BOOST SYSTEM

High Pedal and Steering Effort (Idle)

1. Loosen/broken power steering pump belt
2. Low power steering fluid level
3. Leaking hoses or fittings
4. Low idle speed
5. Hose restriction
6. Defective power steering pump

High Pedal Effort (Idle)

1. Binding pedal/linkage
2. Fluid contamination
3. Defective Hydro-Boost unit

Poor Pedal Return

1. Binding pedal linkage
2. Restricted booster return line
3. Internal return system restriction

Pedal Chatter/Pulsation

1. Power steering pump drive belt slipping
2. Low power steering fluid level
3. Defective power steering pump
4. Defective Hydro-Boost unit

Brakes Overly Sensitive

1. Binding linkage
2. Defective Hydro-Boost unit

Noise

1. Low power steering fluid level
2. Air in the power steering fluid
3. Loose power steering pump drive belt
4. Hose restrictions

REMOVAL AND INSTALLATION

CAUTION: *Power steering fluid and brake fluid cannot be mixed. If brake seals contact the steering fluid or steering seals contact the brake fluid, damage will result.*

1. Turn the engine off and pump the brake pedal 4 or 5 times to deplete the accumulator inside the unit.

2. Remove the two nuts from the master cylinder, and remove the cylinder keeping the brake lines attached. Secure the master cylinder out of the way.

3. Remove the hydraulic lines from the booster.

4. Remove the booster unit from the firewall.

5. To install, reverse the removal procedure. Torque the nuts to 25 ft. lbs. Bleed the Hydro-Boost system.

Bleeding the Brakes

Without Hydro-Boost

The brake system must be bled when any brake line is disconnected or there is air in the system.

NOTE: *Never bleed a wheel cylinder when a drum is removed.*

1. Clean the master cylinder of excess dirt and remove the cylinder cover and the diaphragm.

2. Fill the master cylinder to the proper level. Check the fluid level periodically during the bleeding process, and replenish it as necessary. Do not allow the master cylinder to run dry, or you will have to start over.

3. Before opening any of the bleeder screws, you may want to give each one a shot of penetrating solvent. This reduces the possibility of breakage when they are unscrewed.

4. Attach a length of vinyl hose to the bleeder screw of the brake to be bled. Insert the other end of the hose into a clear jar half full of clean brake fluid, so that the end of the hose is beneath the level of fluid. The correct sequence for bleeding is to work from the brake farthest from the master cylinder to the one closest; right rear, left rear, right front, left front.

5. The combination valve must be held open during the bleeding process. A clip, tape, or other similar tool (or an assistant) will hold the metering pin in.

6. Depress and release the brake pedal three or four times to exhaust any residual vacuum.

7. Have an assistant push down on the brake pedal and hold it down. Open the bleeder valve slightly. As the pedal reaches the end of its travel, close the bleeder screw and release the brake pedal. Repeat this process until no air bubbles are visible in the expelled fluid.

NOTE: *Make sure your assistant presses the brake pedal to the floor slowly. Pressing too fast will cause air bubbles to form in the fluid.*

8. Repeat this procedure at each of the brakes. Remember to check the master cylinder level occasionally. Use only fresh fluid to refill the master cylinder, not the stuff bled from the system.

9. When the bleeding process is complete, refill the master cylinder, install its cover and

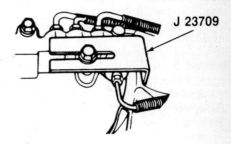

Using the combination valve depressor on the R/V series

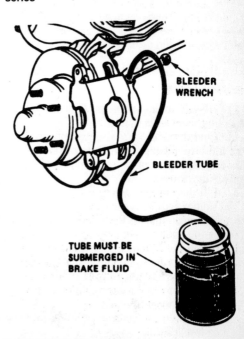

Brake bleeding equipment

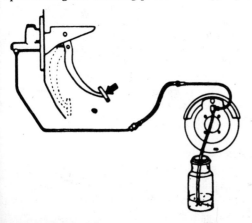

Have an assistant pump, then hold in the brake pedal, while you bleed each wheel

diaphragm, and discard the fluid bled from the brake system.

Hydro-boost System Bleeding

The system should be bled whenever the booster is removed and installed.

1. Fill the power steering pump until the fluid level is at the base of the pump reservoir neck. Disconnect the battery lead from the distributor.

NOTE: *Remove the electrical lead to the fuel solenoid terminal on the injection pump before cranking the engine.*

2. Jack up the front of the car, turn the wheels all the way to the left, and crank the engine for a few seconds.

3. Check steering pump fluid level. If necessary, add fluid to the Add mark on the dipstick.

4. Lower the car, connect the battery lead, and start the engine. Check fluid level and add fluid to the Add mark is necessary. With the engine running, turn the wheels from side to side to bleed air from the system. Make sure that the fluid level stays above the internal pump casting.

5. The Hydro-Boost system should now be fully bled. If the fluid is foaming after bleeding, stop the engine, let the system set for one hour, then repeat the second part of Step 4.

The preceding procedures should be effective in removing the excess air from the system, however sometimes air may still remain trapped. When this happens the booster may make a gulping noise when the brake is applied. Lightly pumping the brake pedal with the engine running should cause this noise to disappear. After the noise stops, check the pump fluid level and add as necessary.

Bench Bleeding the Master Cylinder

This procedure should be performed prior to installing the master cylinder.

1. Plug the outlet ports to prevent pressurized fluid from escaping and mount the master cylinder in a vise with the front end tilted slightly downward.

2. Fill the reservoir with clean brake fluid.

3. Using a dowel, either wood or metal, with a rounded, smooth end, depress the primary piston about 1 inch, several times. As air is bled from the cylinder, the resistance at the piston will increase to the point that you won't be able to depress the piston the full inch.

4. Reposition the master cylinder with the end slight up. Repeat Step 3.

5. Reposition the master cylinder in the vise in a level position.

6. Slightly loosen one plug. Slowly depress the piston and hold it depressed. Tighten the plug. Repeat this until no air, just fluid, is expelled at the plug.

7. Repeat this procedure at the other plug.

8. Fill the reservoir.

9. Install the master cylinder and connect the lines. Repeat Steps 6 and 7 at each line.

10. Once the master cylinder is bled and installed, bleed the entire system.

FRONT DISC BRAKES

Two different caliper designs are used. A Delco disc brake system is used on all models except G-30 and 3500 motorhome chassis. The motorhome chassis use the Bendix disc brake system. The difference will be noted in the following procedures.

Brake Pads

INSPECTION

Support the front suspension on jackstands and remove the wheels. Look in at the ends of the caliper to check the lining thickness of the outer pad. Look through the inspection hole in the top of the caliper to check the thickness of the inner pad. Minimum acceptable pad thickness is $\frac{1}{32}$ in. (0.79mm) from the rivet heads on original equipment riveted linings and $\frac{1}{2}$ in. (12.7mm) lining thickness on bonded linings.

NOTE: *These manufacturer's specifications may not agree with your state inspection law.*

All original equipment pads are the riveted type; unless you want to remove pads to measure the actual thickness from the rivet heads, you will have to make the limit for visual inspection $\frac{1}{16}$ in. (1.6mm) or more. The same applies if you don't know what kind of lining you have. Original equipment pads and GM replacement pads have an integral wear sensor. This is a spring steel tab on rear edge of inner pad which produces a squeal by rubbing against the rotor to warn that the pads have reached their wear limit. They do not squeal when brakes are applied.

The squeal will eventually stop if worn pads aren't replaced. Should this happen, replace the pads immediately to prevent expensive rotor (disc) damage.

REPLACEMENT

Delco System

1. Remove the cover on the master cylinder and siphon out $\frac{2}{3}$ of the fluid. This step prevents spilling fluid when the piston is pushed back.

2. Raise and support the front end on jackstands.

3. Remove the wheels.

4. Push the brake piston back into its bore using a C-clamp to pull the caliper outward.

5. Remove the two bolts which hold the caliper and then lift the caliper off the disc.

CAUTION: *Do not let the caliper assembly hang by the brake hose.*

6. Remove the inboard and outboard shoe.

NOTE: *If the pads are to be reinstalled, mark them inside and outside.*

7. Remove the pad support spring from the piston.

To install:

8. Position the support spring and the inner pad into the center cavity of the piston. The outboard pad has ears which are bent over to keep the pad in position while the inboard pad has ears on the top end which fit over the caliper retaining bolts. A spring which is inside the brake piston hold the bottom edge of the inboard pad.

9. Push down on the inner pad until it lays

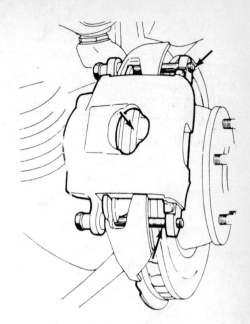

Lining inspection points

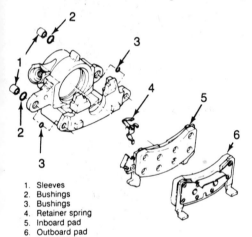

1. Sleeves
2. Bushings
3. Bushings
4. Retainer spring
5. Inboard pad
6. Outboard pad

Delco brake pads

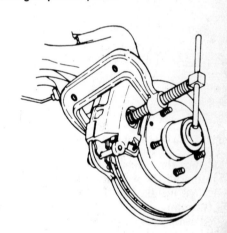

Compressing the Delco caliper piston

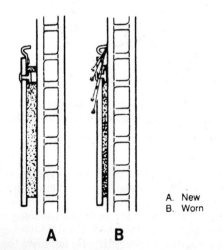

A. New
B. Worn

A   **B**

Brake pad wear indicators

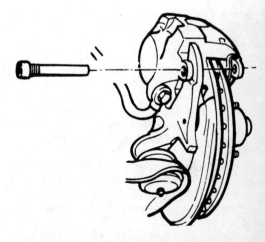

Removing the Delco caliper mounting bolts

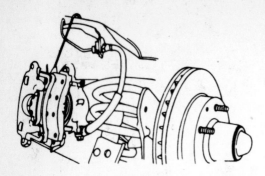

Suspend the caliper out of the way

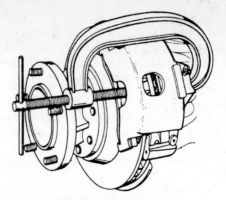

Compressing the Bendix caliper piston

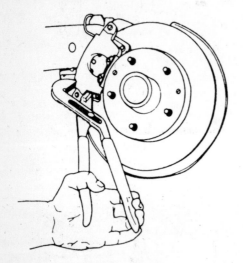

Compressing the Delco brake pad ears

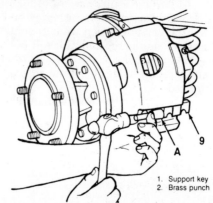

1. Support key
2. Brass punch

Removing the Bendix caliper support key

flat against the caliper. It is important to push the piston all the way into the caliper if new linings are installed or the caliper will not fit over the rotor.

10. Position the outboard pad with the ears of the pad over the caliper ears and the tab at the bottom engaged in the caliper cutout.

11. With the two pads in position, place the caliper over the brake disc and align the holes in the caliper with those of the mounting bracket.

CAUTION: *Make certain that the brake hose is not twisted or kinked.*

12. Install the mounting bracket bolts through the sleeves in the inboard caliper ears and through the mounting bracket, making sure that the ends of the bolts pass under the retaining ears on the inboard pad.

13. Tighten the mounting bolts to 35 ft. lbs. Pump the brake pedal to seat the pad against the rotor. Don't do this unless both calipers are in place. Use a pair of channel lock pliers to bend over the upper ears of the outer pad so it isn't loose.

NOTE: *After tightening the mounting bolts, there must be clearance between the caliper*

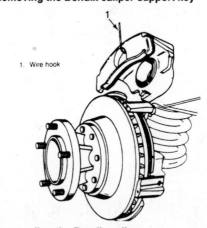

1. Wire hook

Suspending the Bendix caliper

and knuckle at both the upper and lowe edge. The clearance must be 0.06–0.26mm.

14. Install the front wheel and lower th truck.

15. Add fluid to the master cylinder reser voirs so that they are 1/4 in. (6.35mm) from th top.

16. Test the brake pedal by pumping it t obtain a hard pedal. Check the fluid level agai and add fluid as necessary. Do not move the ve hicle until a hard pedal is obtained.

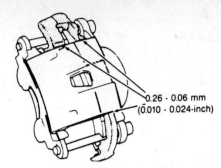

0.26 - 0.06 mm
(0.010 - 0.024-inch)

R/V series caliper-to-knuckle clearance

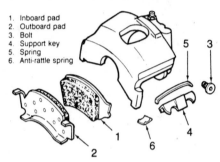

1. Inboard pad
2. Outboard pad
3. Bolt
4. Support key
5. Spring
6. Anti-rattle spring

Bendix caliper brake pads and related parts

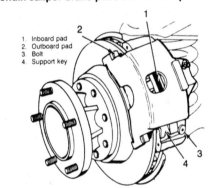

1. Inboard pad
2. Outboard pad
3. Bolt
4. Support key

Bendix disc brake assembly

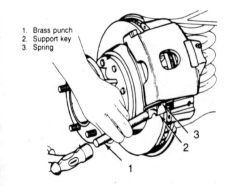

1. Brass punch
2. Support key
3. Spring

Installing the Bendix caliper support key

Bendix System

1. Remove approximately ⅓ of the brake fluid from the master cylinder. Discard the used brake fluid.

2. Jack up your vehicle and support it with jackstands.

3. Push the piston back into its bore. This can be done by suing a C-clamp.

4. Remove the bolt at the caliper support key. Use a brass drift pin to remove the key and spring.

5. Rotate the caliper up and forward from the bottom and lift it off the caliper support.

6. Tie the caliper out of the way with a piece of wire. Be careful not to damage the brake line.

7. Remove the inner shoe from the caliper support. Discard the inner shoe clip.

8. Remove the outer shoe from the caliper.

To install:

9. Lubricate the caliper support and support spring, with silicone.

10. Install a NEW inboard shoe clip on the shoe.

11. Install the lower end of the inboard shoe into the groove provided in the support. Slide the upper end of the shoe into position. Be sure the clip remains in position.

10. Position the outboard shoe in the caliper with the ears at the top of the shoe over the caliper ears and the tab at the bottom of the shoe engaged in the caliper cutout. If assembly is difficult, a C-clamp may be used. Be careful not to mar the lining.

11. Position the caliper over the brake disc, top edge first. Rotate the caliper downward onto the support.

12. Place the spring over the caliper support key, install the assembly between the support and lower caliper groove. Tap into place until the key retaining screw can be installed.

13. Install the screw and torque to 12–18 ft. lbs. The boss must fit fully into the circular cutout in the key.

14. Install the wheel and add brake fluid as necessary.

Caliper

REMOVAL AND INSTALLATION

Delco System

1. Remove the cover on the master cylinder and siphon enough fluid out of the reservoirs to bring the level to ⅓ full. This step prevents spilling fluid when the piston is pushed back.

2. Raise and support the vehicle. Remove the front wheels and tires.

3. Push the brake piston back into its bore using a C-clamp to pull the caliper outward.

4. Remove the two bolts which hold the caliper and then lift the caliper off the disc.

CAUTION: *Do not let the caliper assembly hang by the brake hose.*

5. Remove the inboard and outboard shoe.

NOTE: *If the pads are to be reinstalled, mark them inside and outside.*

6. Remove the pad support spring from the piston.

7. Remove the two sleeves from the inside ears of the caliper and the 4 rubber bushings from the grooves in the caliper ears.

8. Remove the hose from the steel brake line and tape the fittings to prevent foreign material from entering the line or the hoses.

9. Remove the retainer from the hose fitting.

10. Remove the hose from the frame bracket and pull off the caliper with the hose attached.

11. Check the inside of the caliper for fluid leakage; if so, the caliper should be overhauled.

CAUTION: *Do not use compressed air to clean the inside of the caliper as this may unseat the dust boot.*

12. Connect the brake line to start re-installation. Lubricate the sleeves, rubber bushings, bushing grooves, and the end of the mounting bolts using silicone lubricant.

13. Install new bushing in the caliper ears along with new sleeves. The sleeve should be replaced so that the end toward the shoe is flush with the machined surface of the ear.

14. Position the support spring and the inner pad into the center cavity of the piston. The outboard pad has ears which are bent over to keep the pad in position while the inboard pad has ears on the top end which fit over the caliper retaining bolts. A spring which is inside the brake piston hold the bottom edge of the inboard pad.

15. Push down on the inner pad until it lays flat against the caliper. It is important to push the piston all the way into the caliper if new linings are installed or the caliper will not fit over the rotor.

16. Position the outboard pad with the ears of the pad over the caliper ears and the tab at the bottom engaged in the caliper cutout.

17. With the two pads in position, place the caliper over the brake disc and align the holes in the caliper with those of the mounting bracket.

CAUTION: *Make certain that the brake hose is not twisted or kinked.*

18. Install the mounting bracket bolts through the sleeves in the inboard caliper ears and through the mounting bracket, making sure that the ends of the bolts pass under the retaining ears on the inboard pad.

19. Tighten the mounting bolts to 35 ft. lbs. Pump the brake pedal to seat the pad against the rotor. Don't do this unless both calipers are in place. Use a pair of channel lock pliers to

bend over the upper ears of the outer pad so it isn't loose.

NOTE: *After tightening the mounting bolts, there must be clearance between the caliper and knuckle at both the upper and lower edge. The clearance must be 0.06–0.26mm. If not, loosen the bolts and reposition the caliper.*

20. Install the front wheel and lower the truck.

21. Add fluid to the master cylinder reservoirs so that they are $1/4$ in. (6.35mm) from the top.

22. Test the brake pedal by pumping it to obtain a hard pedal. Check the fluid level again and add fluid as necessary. Do not move the vehicle until a hard pedal is obtained.

G-30/3500 Series Motorhomes

1. Remove approximately $1/3$ of the brake fluid from the master cylinder. Discard the used brake fluid.

2. Raise and support the front end on jackstands.

3. Push the piston back into its bore. This can be done by suing a C-clamp.

4. Remove the bolt at the caliper support key. Use a brass drift pin to remove the key and spring.

5. Rotate the caliper up and forward from the bottom and lift it off the caliper support.

6. Unscrew the brake line at the caliper. Plug the opening. Discard the copper washer. Be careful not to damage the brake line.

7. Remove the outer shoe from the caliper.

To install:

8. Using a new copper washer, connect the brake line at the caliper. Torque the connector to 32 ft. lbs.

9. Lubricate the caliper support and support spring with silicone.

10. Position the outboard shoe in the caliper with the ears at the top of the shoe over the caliper ears and the tab at the bottom of the shoe engaged in the caliper cutout. If assembly is difficult, a C-clamp may be used. Be careful not to mar the lining.

11. Position the caliper over the brake disc, top edge first. Rotate the caliper downward onto the support.

12. Place the spring over the caliper support key, install the assembly between the support and lower caliper groove. Tap into place until the key retaining screw can be installed.

13. Install the screw and torque to 12–18 ft. lbs. The boss must fit fully into the circular cutout in the key.

14. Install the wheel and add brake fluid as necessary.

OVERHAUL

The following procedure applies to both the Delco and Bendix types of calipers.

CAUTION: *Use only denatured alcohol or brake fluid to clean caliper parts. Never use any mineral based cleaning solvents such as gasoline or kerosene as these solvents will deteriorate rubber parts.*

1. Remove the caliper, clean it and place it on a clean and level work surface.

2. Remove the brake hose from the caliper and discard the copper gasket. Check the brake hose for cracks or deterioration. Replace the hose as necessary.

3. Drain the brake fluid from the caliper.

4. Pad the interior of the caliper with cloth and then apply compressed air to the caliper inlet hose.

CAUTION: *Do not place your hands or fingers in front of the piston in an attempt to catch it! Use just enough air pressure to ease the piston out of the bore.*

5. Remove the piston dust boot by prying it out with a screwdriver. Use caution when performing this procedure.

6. Remove the piston seal from the caliper piston bore using a small piece of wood or plastic. DO NOT use any type of metal tool for this procedure.

7. Remove the bleeder valve from the caliper.

IMPORTANT *Dust boot, piston seal, rubber bushings, and sleeves are included in every rebuilding kit. These should be replaced at every caliper rebuild.*

8. Clean all parts in the recommended solvent and dry them completely using compressed air if possible.

NOTE: *The use of shop air hoses may inject oil film into the assembly; use caution when using such hoses.*

9. Examine the mounting bolts for rust or corrosion. Replace them as necessary.

10. Examine the piston for scoring, nicks, or worn plating. If any of these conditions are present, replace them as necessary.

CAUTION: *Do not use any type of abrasive on the piston.*

11. Check the piston bore. Small defects can be removed with crocus cloth. If the bore cannot be cleaned in this manner, replace the caliper.

12. Lubricate the piston bore and the new piston seal with brake fluid. Place the seal in the caliper bore groove.

13. Lubricate the piston in the same manner and position the new boot into the groove in the piston so that the fold faces the open end of the piston.

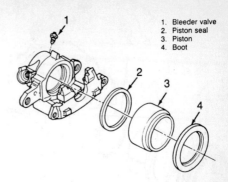

1. Bleeder valve
2. Piston seal
3. Piston
4. Boot

Delco caliper components

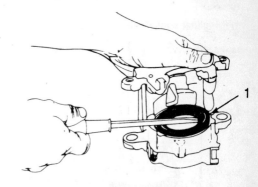

1. Boot

Removing the Delco piston boot

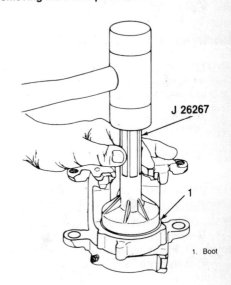

J 26267

1. Boot

Installing the Delco piston boot

14. Place the piston into the caliper bore using caution not to unseat the seal. Force the piston to the bottom of the bore.

15. Place the dust boot in the caliper counterbore and seat the boot. Make sure that the boot in positioned correctly and evenly.

16. Install the brake hose in the caliper inlet using a new copper gasket.

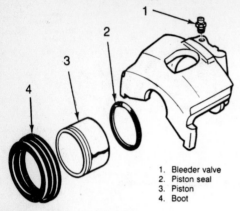

1. Bleeder valve
2. Piston seal
3. Piston
4. Boot

Bendix caliper components

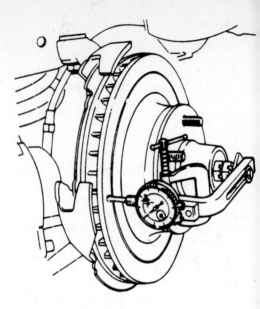

Checking rotor lateral runout

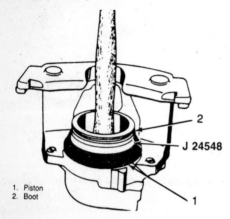

1. Piston
2. Boot

Installing the Bendix caliper piston

NOTE: *The hose must be positioned in the caliper locating gate to assure proper positioning of the caliper.*

17. Replace the bleeder screw.
18. Bleed the system.

Disc (Rotor)

REMOVAL AND INSTALLATION

1. Follow the procedures outlined for removing the caliper assembly.
2. Remove the bearing dust cap, cotter pin, center nut, and outer bearings.
3. Pull the rotor off the spindle and service it, as necessary.
4. To install the unit, reverse the removal procedure. Check the rotor before install it. Pack the inner and outer bearing to the proper specifications. (See Wheel Bearings).

The minimum wear thickness is cast into each disc hub. This is a minimum wear dimension and not a refinish dimension.

If the thickness of the disc after refinishing will be 1.230 in. (31.242mm) or less, it must be replaced. Refinishing is required whenever the disc surface shows scoring or severe rust scale.

Scoring not deeper than 0.015 in. (0.381mm) in depth can be corrected by refinishing.

NOTE: *Some discs have an anti-squeal groove. This should not be mistaken for scoring.*

DRUM BRAKES

Drum

REMOVAL AND INSTALLATION

Semi-Floating Axles

1. Raise and support the rear end on jackstands.
2. Remove the wheel.
3. Pulling the drum from the brake assembly. If the brake drums have been scored from worn linings, the brake adjuster must be backed off so that the brake shoes will retract from the drum. The adjuster can be backed off by inserting a brake adjusting tool through the access hole provided. In some cases the access hole is provided in the brake drum. A metal cover plate is over the hole. This may be removed by using a hammer and chisel.
4. To install, reverse the removal procedure.

Full Floating Axles

To remove the drums from full floating rear axles, use the Axle Shaft Removal and Installation procedure in Chapter 7. Full floating rear axles can readily be identified by the bearing

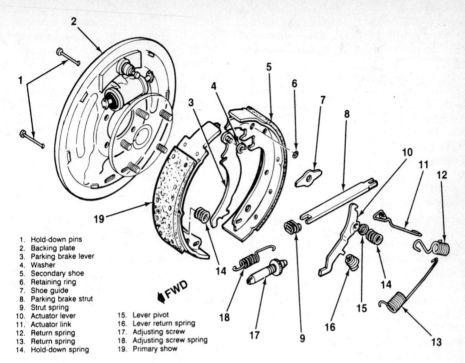

1. Hold-down pins
2. Backing plate
3. Parking brake lever
4. Washer
5. Secondary shoe
6. Retaining ring
7. Shoe guide
8. Parking brake strut
9. Strut spring
10. Actuator lever
11. Actuator link
12. Return spring
13. Return spring
14. Hold-down spring

15. Lever pivot
16. Lever return spring
17. Adjusting screw
18. Adjusting screw spring
19. Primary show

FWD

Drum brake components

housing protruding through the center of the wheel.

NOTE: *Make sure all metal particles are removed from the brake drum before reassembly.*

INSPECTION

Lining

Remove the drum and inspect the lining thickness on both brake shoes. A front brake lining should be replaced if it is less than $1/8$ in. (3mm) thick at the lowest point on the brake shoe. The wear limit for rear brake linings is $1/16$ in. (1.5875mm).

NOTE: *Brake shoes should always be replaced in axle sets. The wear specifications given may disagree with your state inspection rules.*

Drum

When the drum is removed, it should be inspected for cracks, scores, or other imperfections. These must be corrected before the drum is replaced.

CAUTION: *If the drum is found to be cracked, replace it. Do not attempt to service a cracked drum.*

Minor drum score marks can be removed with fine emery cloth. Heavy score marks must be removed by turning the drum. This is removing metal from the entire inner surface of the drum on a lathe in order to level the surface.

Automotive machine shops and some large parts stores are equipped to perform this operation.

If the drum is not scored, it should be polished with fine emery cloth before replacement. If the drum is resurfaced, it should not be enlarged more than 0.060 in. (1.524mm).

NOTE: *Your state inspection law may disagree with this specification.*

It is advisable, while the drums are off, to check them for out-of-round. An inside micrometer is necessary for an exact measurement, therefore unless this tool is available, the drums should be taken to a machine shop to be checked. Any drum which is more than 0.006 in. (0.1524mm) out-of-round will result in an inaccurate brake adjustment and other problems, and should be refinished or replaced.

NOTE: *Make all measurements at right angles to each other and at the open and closed edges of the drum machined surface.*

Brake Shoes

REMOVAL AND INSTALLATION

CAUTION: *Brake shoes contain asbestos, which has been determined to be a cancer causing agent. Never clean the brake surfaces with compressed air! Avoid inhaling any dust from any brake surface! When cleaning brake surfaces, use a commercially available brake cleaning fluid.*

1. Jack up and securely support the vehicle.

2. Loosen the parking brake equalizer enough to remove all tension on the brake cable.

3. Remove the brake drums.

WARNING: *The brake pedal must not be depressed while the drums are removed.*

4. Using a brake tool, remove the shoe springs. You can do this with ordinary tools, buy it isn't easy.

5. Remove the self-adjuster actuator spring.

6. Remove the link from the secondary shoe by pulling it from the anchor pin.

7. Remove the holddown pins. These are the brackets which run though the backing plate. They can be removed with a pair of pliers. Reach around the rear of the backing plate and hold the back of the pin. Turn the top of the pin retainer 45° with the plier. This will align the elongated tang with the slot in the retainer. Be careful, as the pin is spring loaded and may fly off when released. Use the same procedure for the other pin assembly.

8. Remove the adjuster actuator assembly.

NOTE: *Since the actuator, pivot, and override spring are considered an assembly it is not recommended that they be disassembled.*

9. Remove the shoes from the backing plate. Make sure that you have a secure grip on the assembly as the bottom spring will still exert pressure on the shoes. Slowly let the tops of the shoes come together and the tension will decrease and the adjuster and spring may be removed.

NOTE: *If the linings are to be reused, mark them for identification.*

10. Remove the rear parking brake lever from the secondary shoe. Using a pair of plier, pull back on the spring which surrounds the cable. At the same time, remove the cable from the notch in the shoe bracket. Make sure that the spring does not snap back or injury may result.

11. Use a brake cleaning fluid to remove dirt from the brake drum. Check the drums for scoring and cracks. Have the drums checked for out-of-round and service the drums as necessary.

12. Check the wheel cylinders by carefully pulling the lower edges of the wheel cylinder boots away from the cylinders. If there is excessive leakage, the inside of the cylinder will be moist with fluid. If there is any leakage at all, a cylinder overhaul is in order. DO NOT delay, as a brake failure could result.

NOTE: *A small amount of fluid will be present to act as a lubricant for the wheel cylinder pistons.*

13. Check the flange plate, which is located around the axle, for leakage of differential lubricant. This condition cannot be overlooked as the lubricant will be absorbed into the brake linings and brake failure will result. Replace the seals as necessary. See Chapter 7 for details.

NOTE: *If new linings are being installed, check them against the old units for length and type.*

14. Check the new linings for imperfections.

CAUTION: *It is important to keep your hands free of dirt and grease when handling the brake shoes. Foreign matter will be absorbed into the linings and result in unpredictable braking.*

15. Lightly lubricate the parking brake and cable and the end of the parking brake lever where it enters the shoe. Use high temperature, waterproof, grease or special brake lube.

16. Install the parking brake lever into the secondary shoe with the attaching bolt, spring washer, lock washer, and nut. It is important that the lever move freely before the shoe is attached. Move the assembly and check for proper action.

17. Lubricate the adjusting screw and make sure that it works freely. Sometimes the adjusting screw will not move due to lack of lubricant or dirt contamination and the brakes will not adjust. In this case, the adjuster should be disassembled, thoroughly cleaned, and lubricated before installation.

18. Connect the brake shoe spring to the bottom portion of both shoes. Make certain that the brake linings are installed in the correct manner, the primary and secondary shoe in the correct position. If you are not sure remove the other brake drum and check it.

19. Install the adjusting mechanism below the spring and separate the top of the shoes.

Make the following checks before installation:

   a. Be certain that the right hand thread adjusting screw is on the left hand side of the vehicle and the left hand screw is on the right hand side of the vehicle.

   b. Make sure that the star adjuster is aligned with the adjusting hole.

   c. The adjuster should be installed with the starwheel nearest the secondary shoe and the tension spring away from the adjusting mechanism;

   d. If the original linings are being reused, put them back in their original locations.

20. Install the parking brake cable.

21. Position the primary shoe (the shoe with the short lining) first. Secure it with the holddown pin and with its spring by pushing the pin through the back of the backing plate and, while holding it with one hand, install the spring and the retainer using a pair of needle

nose pliers. Install the adjuster actuator assembly.

22. Install the parking brake strut and the strut spring by pulling back the spring with pliers and engaging the end of the cable onto the brake strut and then releasing the spring.

23. Place the small metal guide plate over the anchor pin and position the self-adjuster wire cable eye.

CAUTION: *The wire should not be positioned with the conventional brake installation tool or damage will result. It should be positioned on the actuator assembly first and then placed over the anchor pin stud by hand with the adjuster assembly in full downward position.*

24. Install the actuator return spring. DO NOT pry the actuator lever to install the return spring. Position it using the end of a screwdriver or another suitable tool.

NOTE: *If the return springs are bent or in any way distorted, they should be replaced.*

25. Using the brake installation tool, place the brake return springs in position. Install the primary spring first over the anchor pin and then place the spring from the secondary show over the wire link end.

26. Pull the brake shoes away from the backing plate and apply a thin coat of high temperature, waterproof, grease or special brake lube in the brake shoe contact points.

CAUTION: *Only a small amount is necessary. Keep the lubricant away from the brake linings.*

27. Once the complete assembly has been installed, check the operation of the self-adjusting mechanism by moving the actuating lever by hand.

28. Adjust the brakes.

a. Turn the star adjuster until the drum slides over the brakes shoes with only a slight drag. Remove the drum:

b. Turn the adjuster back $1\frac{1}{4}$ turns.

c. Install the drum and wheel and lower the vehicle.

CAUTION: *Avoid over tightening the lug nuts to prevent damage to the brake drum. Alloy wheels can also be cracked by over tightening. Use of a torque wrench is highly recommended.*

d. If the adjusting hole in the drum has been punched out, make certain that the insert has been removed from the inside of the drum. Install a rubber hole cover to keep dirt out of the brake assembly. Also, be sure that the drums are installed in the same position as they were when removed, with the locating tang in line with the locating hole in the axle shaft flange.

e. Make the final adjustment by backing

the vehicle and pumping the brakes until the self-adjusting mechanisms adjust to the proper level and the brake pedal reaches satisfactory height.

29. Adjust the parking brake. Details are given later.

Wheel Cylinders

REMOVAL AND INSTALLATION

1. Raise and support the axle.
2. Remove the wheel and tire.
3. Back off the brake adjustment if necessary and remove the drum.
4. Disconnect and plug the brake line.
5. Remove the brake shoe pull-back springs.
6. Remove the screws securing the wheel cylinder to the backing plate. Later models have their wheel cylinders retained by a round retainer. To release the locking tabs, insert two awls (see illustration) into the access slots to bend the tabs back. Install the new retainer over the wheel cylinder abutment using a $1\frac{1}{8}$ in., 12-point socket and socket extension.
7. Disengage the wheel cylinder pushrods from the brake shoes and remove the wheel cylinder.
8. Installation is the reverse of removal. Bleed the system.

OVERHAUL

As with master cylinders, overhaul kits for wheel cylinders are readily available. When rebuilding and installing wheel cylinders, avoid getting any contaminants into the system. Always install clean, new high quality brake fluid. If dirty or improper fluid has been used, it will be necessary to drain the entire system, flush the system with proper brake fluid, replace all rubber components, refill, and bleed the system.

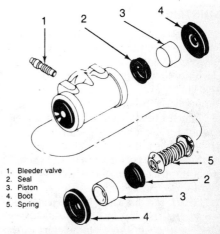

1. Bleeder valve
2. Seal
3. Piston
4. Boot
5. Spring

Wheel cylinder exploded view

1. Remove the rubber boots from the cylinder ends with pliers. Discard the boots.

2. Remove and discard the pistons and cups.

3. Wash the cylinder and metal parts in denatured alcohol or clean brake fluid.

CAUTION: *Never use a mineral based solvent such as gasoline, kerosene, or paint thinner for cleaning purposes. These solvents will swell rubber components and quickly deteriorate them.*

4. Allow the parts to air dry or use compressed air. Do not use rags for cleaning since lint will remain in the cylinder bore.

5. Inspect the piston and replace it if it shows scratches.

6. Lubricate the cylinder bore and counterbore with clean brake fluid.

7. Install the rubber cups (flat side out) and then the pistons (flat side in).

8. Insert new boots into the counterbores by hand. Do not lubricate the boots.

Brake Backing Plate

REMOVAL AND INSTALLATION

1. Remove the brake shoes and wheel cylinder as previously outlined.

2. Remove the axles as outlined in Chapter 7.

3. Remove the attaching bolts and pull off the backing plate.

4. Install all parts as outlined and torque the backing plate retaining bolts to 25–30 ft. lbs.

PARKING BRAKE

Cable

ADJUSTMENT

Before attempting parking brake adjustment, make sure that the rear brakes are fully adjusted by making several stops in reverse.

1. Raise and support the rear axle. Release the parking brake.

2. Apply the pedal 4 clicks.

3. Adjust the cable equalizer nut under the truck until a moderate drag can be felt when the rear wheels are turned forward.

4. Release the parking brake and check that there is no drag when the wheels are turned forward.

NOTE: *If the parking brake cable is replaced, prestretch it by applying the parking brake hard about three times before attempting adjustment.*

CABLE REPLACEMENT

Front Cable

1. Raise vehicle on hoist.

2. Remove adjusting nut from equalizer.

3. Remove retainer clip from rear portion of front cable at frame and from lever arm.

4. Disconnect front brake cable from parking brake pedal. Remove front brake cable. On some models, it may assist installation of new cable if a heavy cord is tied to other end of cable in order to guide new cable through proper routing.

5. Install cable by reversing removal procedure.

6. Adjust parking brake.

Center Cable

1. Raise vehicle on hoist.

2. Remove adjusting nut from equalizer.

3. Unhook connector at each end and disen-

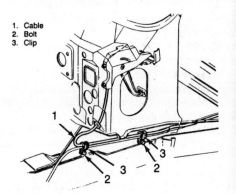

1. Cable
2. Bolt
3. Clip

Front brake cable components

gage hooks and guides.

4. Install new cable by reversing removal procedure.

5. Adjust parking brake.

6. Apply parking brake 3 times with heavy pressure and repeat adjustment.

Rear Cable

1. Raise vehicle on hoist.

2. Remove rear wheel and brake drum.

3. Loosen adjusting nut at equalizer.

4. Disengage rear cable at connector.

5. Bend retainer fingers.

6. Disengage cable at brake shoe operating lever.

7. Install new cable by reversing removal procedure.

8. Adjust parking brake.

ABS SYSTEM SERVICE

Electronic Control Unit

REPLACEMENT

The ECU is located next to the master cylinder.

1. Disconnect the wiring connector.
2. Pry on the tab at the rear of the ECU and pull it forward to remove it.
3. Installation is the reverse of removal.

CAUTION: *Never let brake fluid come in contact with the electrical connection and pins, nor should your skin touch them! Damage to the ECU will result.*

Isolation/Dump Valve

REPLACEMENT

The valve is located next to the master cylinder.

1. Disconnect the brake lines at the valve. Cap the openings.
2. Remove the attaching nuts from the valve.
3. Disconnect the bottom electrical connector at the ECU.

CAUTION: *Never let brake fluid come in con-*

tact with the electrical connection and pins, nor should your skin touch them! Damage to the ECU will result.

4. Remove the valve.
5. Installation is the reverse of removal. Torque the mounting nuts to 21 ft. lbs. Torque the brake lines to 18 ft. lbs. Bleed the system.

Speed Sensor

REPLACEMENT

The sensor is located at the left rear of the transmission. Before replacing a suspected defective sensor, check its resistance with an ohmmeter. Resistance should be 900–2000Ω.

1. Unplug the wiring connector.
2. Remove the attaching bolt and pull the sensor from the transmission.

NOTE: *Some fluid may spill from the transmission.*

3. Remove and discard the O-ring.
To install:
4. Install a new O-ring coated with clean transmission fluid.
5. Install the sensor and torque the bolt to 96 inch lbs. for automatics; 108 inch lbs for manuals.
6. Plug in the connector.

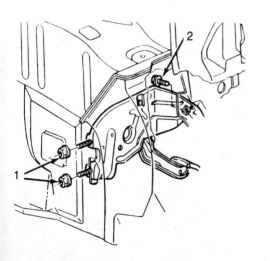

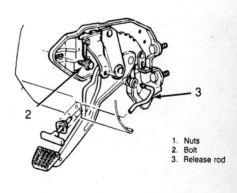

1. Nuts
2. Bolt
3. Release rod

R/V series parking brake pedal

1. Master cylinder
2. Isolation/dump valve
3. Control module
4. Bolts

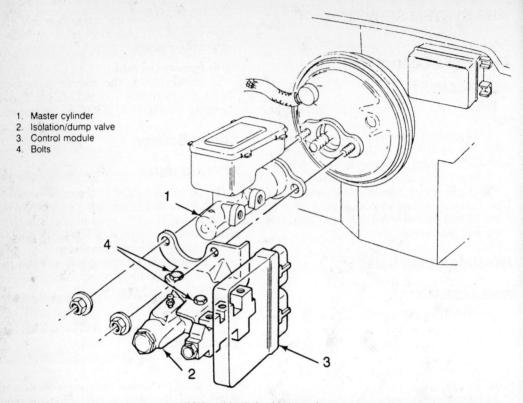

ECU and isolation/dump valve

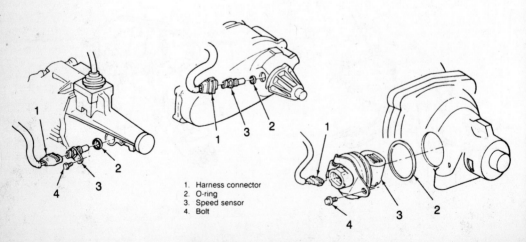

1. Harness connector
2. O-ring
3. Speed sensor
4. Bolt

Transmission speed sensor

Troubleshooting the Brake System

Problem	Cause	Solution
Low brake pedal (excessive pedal travel required for braking action.)	• Excessive clearance between rear linings and drums caused by in-operative automatic adjusters	• Make 10 to 15 alternate forward and reverse brake stops to adjust brakes. If brake pedal does not come up, repair or replace adjuster parts as necessary.
	• Worn rear brakelining	• Inspect and replace lining if worn beyond minimum thickness specification
	• Bent, distorted brakeshoes, front or rear	• Replace brakeshoes in axle sets
	• Air in hydraulic system	• Remove air from system. Refer to Brake Bleeding.
Low brake pedal (pedal may go to floor with steady pressure applied.)	• Fluid leak in hydraulic system	• Fill master cylinder to fill line; have helper apply brakes and check calipers, wheel cylinders, differential valve tubes, hoses and fittings for leaks. Repair or replace as necessary.
	• Air in hydraulic system	• Remove air from system. Refer to Brake Bleeding.
	• Incorrect or non-recommended brake fluid (fluid evaporates at below normal temp).	• Flush hydraulic system with clean brake fluid. Refill with correct-type fluid.
	• Master cylinder piston seals worn, or master cylinder bore is scored, worn or corroded	• Repair or replace master cylinder
Low brake pedal (pedal goes to floor on first application—o.k. on subsequent applications.)	• Disc brake pads sticking on abutment surfaces of anchor plate. Caused by a build-up of dirt, rust, or corrosion on abutment surfaces	• Clean abutment surfaces
Fading brake pedal (pedal height decreases with steady pressure applied.)	• Fluid leak in hydraulic system	• Fill master cylinder reservoirs to fill mark, have helper apply brakes, check calipers, wheel cylinders, differential valve, tubes, hoses, and fittings for fluid leaks. Repair or replace parts as necessary.
	• Master cylinder piston seals worn, or master cylinder bore is scored, worn or corroded	• Repair or replace master cylinder
Decreasing brake pedal travel (pedal travel required for braking action decreases and may be accompanied by a hard pedal.)	• Caliper or wheel cylinder pistons sticking or seized	• Repair or replace the calipers, or wheel cylinders
	• Master cylinder compensator ports blocked (preventing fluid return to reservoirs) or pistons sticking or seized in master cylinder bore	• Repair or replace the master cylinder
	• Power brake unit binding internally	• Test unit according to the following procedure: (a) Shift transmission into neutral and start engine (b) Increase engine speed to 1500 rpm, close throttle and fully depress brake pedal (c) Slow release brake pedal and stop engine (d) Have helper remove vacuum check valve and hose from power unit. Observe for backward movement of brake pedal. (e) If the pedal moves backward, the power unit has an internal bind—replace power unit

Troubleshooting the Brake System (cont.)

Problem	Cause	Solution
Spongy brake pedal (pedal has abnormally soft, springy, spongy feel when depressed.)	· Air in hydraulic system · Brakeshoes bent or distorted · Brakelining not yet seated with drums and rotors · Rear drum brakes not properly adjusted	· Remove air from system. Refer to Brake Bleeding. · Replace brakeshoes · Burnish brakes · Adjust brakes
Hard brake pedal (excessive pedal pressure required to stop vehicle. May be accompanied by brake fade.)	· Loose or leaking power brake unit vacuum hose · Incorrect or poor quality brakelining · Bent, broken, distorted brakeshoes · Calipers binding or dragging on mounting pins. Rear brakeshoes dragging on support plate.	· Tighten connections or replace leaking hose · Replace with lining in axle sets · Replace brakeshoes · Replace mounting pins and bushings. Clean rust or burrs from rear brake support plate ledges and lubricate ledges with molydisulfide grease. **NOTE:** If ledges are deeply grooved or scored, do not attempt to sand or grind them smooth—replace support plate.

	· Caliper, wheel cylinder, or master cylinder pistons sticking or seized
	· Power brake unit vacuum check valve malfunction
		· Repair or replace parts as necessary
		
		· Test valve according to the following procedure:
		  (a) Start engine, increase engine speed to 1500 rpm, close throttle and immediately stop engine
		  (b) Wait at least 90 seconds then depress brake pedal
		  (c) If brakes are not vacuum assisted for 2 or more applications, check valve is faulty

	· Power brake unit has internal bind	· Test unit according to the following procedure:
		  (a) With engine stopped, apply brakes several times to exhaust all vacuum in system
		  (b) Shift transmission into neutral, depress brake pedal and start engine
		  (c) If pedal height decreases with foot pressure and less pressure is required to hold pedal in applied position, power unit vacuum system is operating normally. Test power unit. If power unit exhibits a bind condition, replace the power unit.

	· Master cylinder compensator ports (at bottom of reservoirs) blocked by dirt, scale, rust, or have small burrs (blocked ports prevent fluid return to reservoirs). · Brake hoses, tubes, fittings clogged or restricted · Brake fluid contaminated with improper fluids (motor oil, transmission fluid, causing rubber components to swell and stick in bores · Low engine vacuum	· Repair or replace master cylinder **CAUTION:** Do not attempt to clean blocked ports with wire, pencils, or similar implements. Use compressed air only. · Use compressed air to check or unclog parts. Replace any damaged parts. · Replace all rubber components, combination valve and hoses. Flush entire brake system with DOT 3 brake fluid or equivalent. · Adjust or repair engine

Troubleshooting the Brake System (cont.)

Problem	Cause	Solution
Grabbing brakes (severe reaction to brake pedal pressure.)	• Brakelining(s) contaminated by grease or brake fluid	• Determine and correct cause of contamination and replace brakeshoes in axle sets
	• Parking brake cables incorrectly adjusted or seized	• Adjust cables. Replace seized cables.
	• Incorrect brakelining or lining loose on brakeshoes	• Replace brakeshoes in axle sets
	• Caliper anchor plate bolts loose	• Tighten bolts
	• Rear brakeshoes binding on support plate ledges	• Clean and lubricate ledges. Replace support plate(s) if ledges are deeply grooved. Do not attempt to smooth ledges by grinding.
	• Incorrect or missing power brake reaction disc	• Install correct disc
	• Rear brake support plates loose	• Tighten mounting bolts
Dragging brakes (slow or incomplete release of brakes)	• Brake pedal binding at pivot	• Loosen and lubricate
	• Power brake unit has internal bind	• Inspect for internal bind. Replace unit if internal bind exists.
	• Parking brake cables incorrrectly adjusted or seized	• Adjust cables. Replace seized cables.
	• Rear brakeshoe return springs weak or broken	• Replace return springs. Replace brakeshoe if necessary in axle sets.
	• Automatic adjusters malfunctioning	• Repair or replace adjuster parts as required
	• Caliper, wheel cylinder or master cylinder pistons sticking or seized	• Repair or replace parts as necessary
	• Master cylinder compensating ports blocked (fluid does not return to reservoirs).	• Use compressed air to clear ports. Do not use wire, pencils, or similar objects to open blocked ports.
Vehicle moves to one side when brakes are applied	• Incorrect front tire pressure	• Inflate to recommended cold (reduced load) inflation pressure
	• Worn or damaged wheel bearings	• Replace worn or damaged bearings
	• Brakelining on one side contaminated	• Determine and correct cause of contamination and replace brakelining in axle sets
	• Brakeshoes on one side bent, distorted, or lining loose on shoe	• Replace brakeshoes in axle sets
	• Support plate bent or loose on one side	• Tighten or replace support plate
	• Brakelining not yet seated with drums or rotors	• Burnish brakelining
	• Caliper anchor plate loose on one side	• Tighten anchor plate bolts
	• Caliper piston sticking or seized	• Repair or replace caliper
	• Brakelinings water soaked	• Drive vehicle with brakes lightly applied to dry linings
	• Loose suspension component attaching or mounting bolts	• Tighten suspension bolts. Replace worn suspension components.
	• Brake combination valve failure	• Replace combination valve
Chatter or shudder when brakes are applied (pedal pulsation and roughness may also occur.)	• Brakeshoes distorted, bent, contaminated, or worn	• Replace brakeshoes in axle sets
	• Caliper anchor plate or support plate loose	• Tighten mounting bolts
	• Excessive thickness variation of rotor(s)	• Refinish or replace rotors in axle sets
Noisy brakes (squealing, clicking, scraping sound when brakes are applied.)	• Bent, broken, distorted brakeshoes	• Replace brakeshoes in axle sets
	• Excessive rust on outer edge of rotor braking surface	• Remove rust

Troubleshooting the Brake System (cont.)

Problem	Cause	Solution
Noisy brakes (squealing, clicking, scraping sound when brakes are applied.) (cont.)	• Brakelining worn out—shoes contacting drum of rotor	• Replace brakeshoes and lining in axle sets. Refinish or replace drums or rotors.
	• Broken or loose holdown or return springs	• Replace parts as necessary
	• Rough or dry drum brake support plate ledges	• Lubricate support plate ledges
	• Cracked, grooved, or scored rotor(s) or drum(s)	• Replace rotor(s) or drum(s). Replace brakeshoes and lining in axle sets if necessary.
	• Incorrect brakelining and/or shoes (front or rear).	• Install specified shoe and lining assemblies
Pulsating brake pedal	• Out of round drums or excessive lateral runout in disc brake rotor(s)	• Refinish or replace drums, re-index rotors or replace

Body 10

EXTERIOR

Front Doors

REMOVAL AND INSTALLATION

1. Remove the door trim pad and disconnect the electrical wiring harness from the door (if equipped).
2. Remove the kick panel (if equipped).
3. Remove the hinge bolt cover plate. Mark the position of the hinges on the door and the door pillar.
4. Support the door and remove the door frame to hinge bolts.
5. Remove the door from the vehicle.
6. Remove the hinge to door bolts and remove the hinges from the door.
7. Installation is the reverse of the removal procedure.

ADJUSTMENT

Special tool J–23457–A #50 Torx® Wrench, or its equivalent is required to perform this procedure.
1. Remove the lock striker protector screw.
2. Remove the lock striker protector.
3. Remove the spring.
4. Remove the door striker using tool J–23457–A.
5. Remove the spacer.
6. Remove the kick panel (if equipped).
7. Remove the hinge bolt cover screw.
8. Remove the hinge bolt cover.
9. Loosen the door hinge bolts as needed to adjust the door. Adjust the door up or down, forward or rearward, and in or out at the door hinges.
10. Adjust the door to obtain a gap of 0.18 in. ± 0.02 in. (4.6mm ± 0.51mm) between the front door and the roof panel.
11. The gap between the rocker panel and

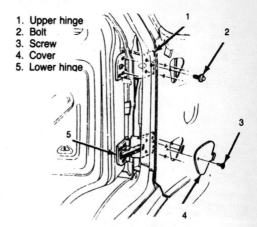

1. Upper hinge
2. Bolt
3. Screw
4. Cover
5. Lower hinge

Door hinge components

the front door at its base should be 0.25 in. ± 0.02 in. (6.35mm ± 0.51mm).
12. Adjust the door to obtain a gap of 0.18 in. ± 0.02 in. (4.6mm ± 0.51mm) between the doors rear edge and the rear door pillar.
13. The gap between the door's front edge and the rear edge of the fender should be 0.18 in. ± 0.02 in. (4.6mm ± 0.51mm).
14. Tighten the door hinge bolts that were loosened.
15. Reverse the removal procedure of the remaining component parts for installation.

Sliding Side Door

REMOVAL AND INSTALLATION

1. Remove the upper track cover and the hinge cover.
2. Open the door completely. Mark the position of the roller assembly on the door and remove the upper front roller assembly.
3. Remove the upper rear hinge retainer from the hinge.
4. Lift the upper rear hinge off of the track and remove the hinge.

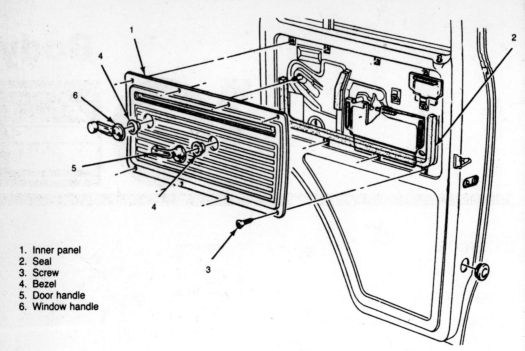

1. Inner panel
2. Seal
3. Screw
4. Bezel
5. Door handle
6. Window handle

Door trim inner panel

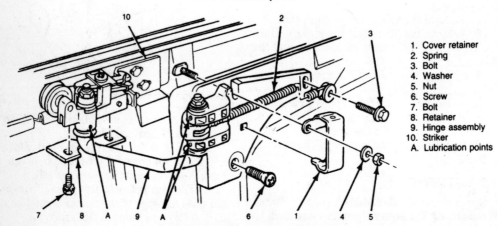

1. Cover retainer
2. Spring
3. Bolt
4. Washer
5. Nut
6. Screw
7. Bolt
8. Retainer
9. Hinge assembly
10. Striker
A. Lubrication points

Upper rear hinge components

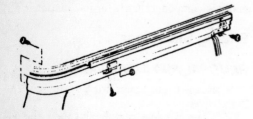

Upper track cover

5. Pivot the door away from the vehicle to disengage the rollers and lower the front roller from the track.

6. Remove the door from the vehicle.

7. Installation is the reverse of the removal procedure.

ADJUSTMENTS

Up and Down

Special tool J–23457 #50 Torx® Wrench, or its equivalent is required to perform this procedure.

1. Remove the upper rear hinge cover.
2. Remove the front lock striker.
3. Remove the rear lock striker using tool J–23457.
4. Remove the rear door wedge assembly.
5. Adjust the rear edge of the door to obtain

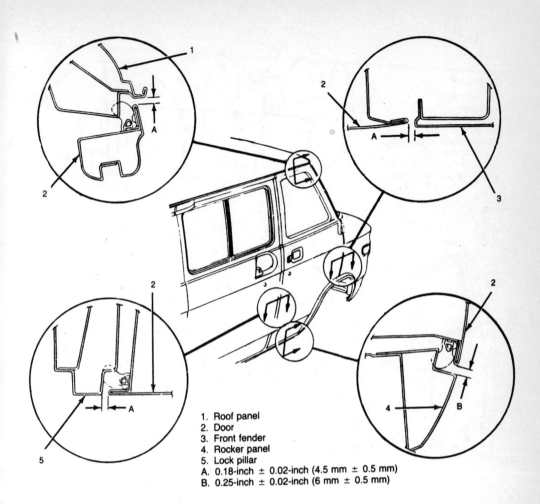

1. Roof panel
2. Door
3. Front fender
4. Rocker panel
5. Lock pillar
A. 0.18-inch ± 0.02-inch (4.5 mm ± 0.5 mm)
B. 0.25-inch ± 0.02-inch (6 mm ± 0.5 mm)

Door adjustments

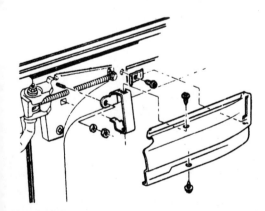

Upper hinge cover

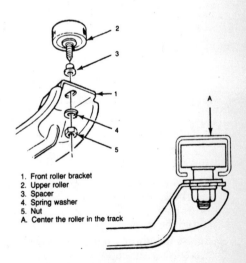

1. Front roller bracket
2. Upper roller
3. Spacer
4. Spring washer
5. Nut
A. Center the roller in the track

Upper front roller components

a gap of 0.18 in. ± 0.02 in. (4.6mm ± 0.51mm) between the top of the door and the roof side rail. This adjustment should provide a gap of 0.25 in. ± 0.02 in. (6.35mm ± 0.51mm) between the bottom of the door and the rocker panel. To accomplish this adjustment, loosen the upper rear hinge to door bolts and align the

rear edge of the door up and down. Next, tighten the upper rear hinge to door bolts.

6. Adjust the front edge of the door by loos-

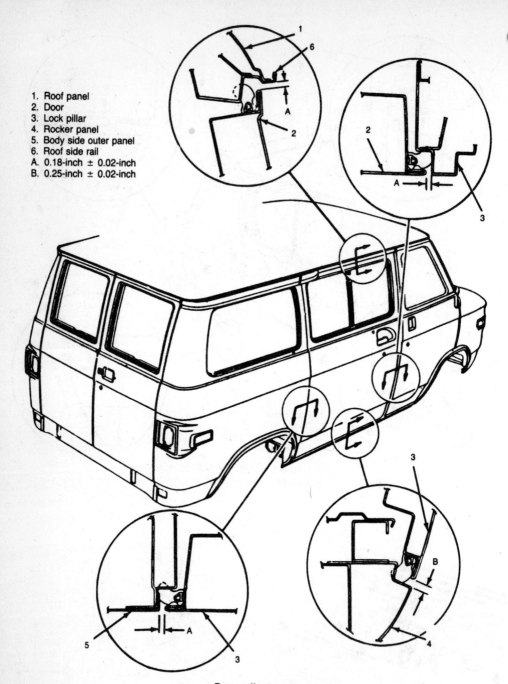

1. Roof panel
2. Door
3. Lock pillar
4. Rocker panel
5. Body side outer panel
6. Roof side rail
A. 0.18-inch ± 0.02-inch
B. 0.25-inch ± 0.02-inch

Door adjustments

ening the upper front roller bracket to door bolts and the lower hinge to door bolts. Align the door to obtain the same gap as in step 5, then tighten the lower hinge to door bolts.

7. Adjust the upper front roller bracket up and down so that the roller is centered in the track. The roller must not touch the top or bottom of the track. Tighten the upper front roller bracket to door bolts.

8. Install the previously removed components in the reverse order of their removal.

In-and-Out

1. Remove the front lock striker.

2. Loosen the nut retaining the upper front roller to the upper roller bracket.

3. Loosen the lower front roller assembly to roller assembly bracket bolts.

4. Loosen the rear door lock striker.

5. Adjust the door in or out until the surface of the door is flush with the surface of the body.

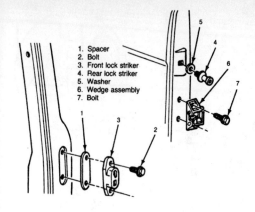

1. Spacer
2. Bolt
3. Front lock striker
4. Rear lock striker
5. Washer
6. Wedge assembly
7. Bolt

Front and rear lock striker

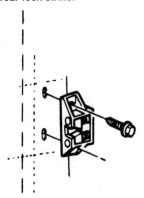

Rear wedge adjustment

6. Tighten the rear door lock striker.
7. Tighten the lower front roller assembly to roller assembly bracket bolts.
8. Tighten the nut retaining the upper front roller to the upper roller bracket.
9. Install the front lock striker.

Forward-and-Rearward

1. Mark the position of the front and rear latch strikers on the body pillars.
2. Remove the front and rear lock strikers.
3. Remove the upper front track cover.
4. Loosen the upper rear hinge striker.
5. Adjust the door forward or rearward to obtain a gap of 0.18 in. ± 0.02 in. (4.6mm ± 0.51mm) between the left and right door edge and the door pillars.
6. Tighten the upper rear hinge striker.
7. Install the upper front track cover.
8. Install the front and rear lock strikers at the position previously marked.

Front Striker

1. Loosen the front latch striker bolts.
2. Slide the door toward the striker.
3. The guide on the door must fit snugly into the rubber lined opening in the striker assembly.

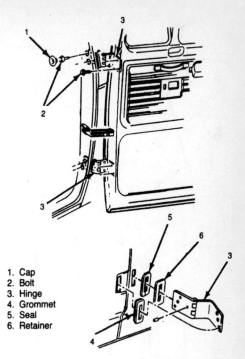

1. Cap
2. Bolt
3. Hinge
4. Grommet
5. Seal
6. Retainer

Door hinge components

4. Check that the latch fully engages the striker. Add or delete shims behind the striker to accomplish this adjustment.
5. Tighten the striker bolts.

Rear Striker

Tool J–23457 Wrench is required to make this adjustment.
1. Loosen the striker using J–23457.
2. Loosen the rear wedge assembly.
3. Center the striker vertically so that the striker properly engages the door lock. Mark the vertical position of the striker.
4. Adjust the striker in or out to align the surface of the door flush with the body surface. Mark the position of the striker.
5. Tighten the striker using tool J–23457.
6. Open the door and apply grease to the striker.
7. Close the door and make an impression of the lock on the striker.
8. Open the door and measure the distance from the rear of the striker head to the impression. The distance should be 0.20–0.30 in. (5.1–7.6mm).
9. Adjust the striker by adding or deleting shims. Align the striker to the previously made marks.
10. Tighten the striker using J–23457.

Upper Rear Hinge

1. The lower hinge lever should have a gap of 0.10–0.16 in. (2.54–4.06mm) between the

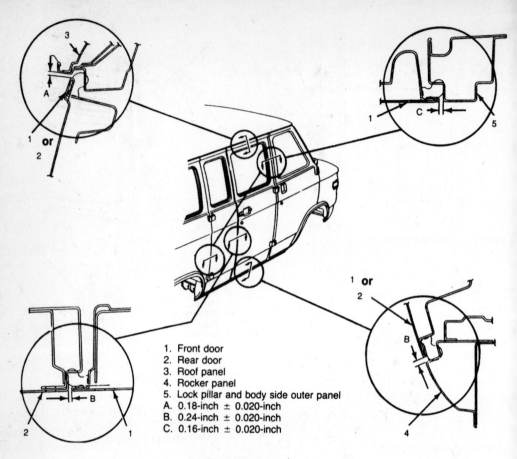

1. Front door
2. Rear door
3. Roof panel
4. Rocker panel
5. Lock pillar and body side outer panel
A. 0.18-inch ± 0.020-inch
B. 0.24-inch ± 0.020-inch
C. 0.16-inch ± 0.020-inch

Door adjustments

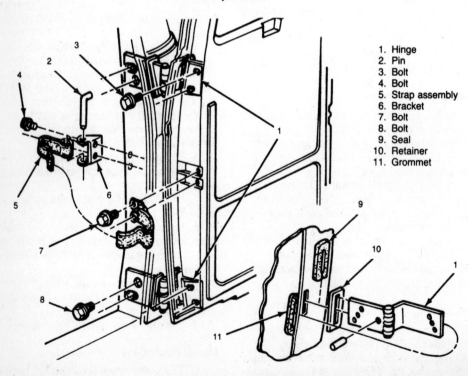

1. Hinge
2. Pin
3. Bolt
4. Bolt
5. Strap assembly
6. Bracket
7. Bolt
8. Bolt
9. Seal
10. Retainer
11. Grommet

Hinge components

outer edge of the lower hinge lever and the striker latch edge. This adjustment is made by adding an equal amount of shims between the guide block and the hinge assembly, and between the roller and the hinge assembly.

2. Adjust the striker up or down to obtain a gap of 0.06 in. (1.5mm) between the lower edge of the striker plate and the lower edge of the lower hinge lever.

3. Adjust the guide up or down to obtain a gap of 0.02 in. (0.51mm) between the track and the guide.

Door Hold Open Catch

1. Mark the position of the lower roller assembly to the bracket.

2. Loosen the lower roller assembly bolts.

3. Pivot the lower roller assembly to properly engage the latch striker.

4. Tighten the lower roller assembly bolts.

Rear Wedge Assembly

1. Loosen the rear wedge assembly screws.

2. Completely close the door.

3. From inside the vehicle, center the wedge assembly onto the door wedge.

4. Mark the position of the wedge assembly.

5. Open the door, and move the wedge assembly forward $3/16$ in. (4.76mm).

6. Tighten the rear wedge assembly screws.

Intermediate Door and Hinge

REMOVAL AND INSTALLATION

1. Open the door, remove the door trim panel and disconnect the electrical wiring harness (if equipped). Then mark the position of the door on the hinges using a wax pencil.

2. Remove the hinge hole plugs on the body side pillar.

3. Remove the strap pin from the bracket, then remove the snapring from the pin, and pull the pin.

4. Support the door safely, and remove the hinge to body pillar bolts.

5. Remove the door from the vehicle.

6. Remove the hinge to door bolts.

7. Remove the hinges from the door.

8. Remove the retainers, seals, and grommets from the door or the hinges.

9. Installation is the reverse of the removal procedure. Make sure to align the hinges with the previously made marks.

ADJUSTMENT

Tool J–23457–A Wrench is required to perform the following adjustments.

1. Remove the door lock striker from the rear intermediate door using J23457–A.

2. Remove the upper and lower rear intermediate door strikers.

3. Loosen the hinge bolts as necessary to adjust the doors.

4. Each of the two doors must first be adjusted in the door opening before adjusting the door to door clearance.

5. Adjust the door up and down, forward and rearward, and in and out, at the door hinges.

6. Adjust the door height so that there is a gap of 0.18 in. ± 0.020 in. (4.6mm ± 0.51mm) between the door and the roof panel.

7. Adjust the gap between the door and the rocker panel to 0.24 in. ± 0.020 in. (6.1mm ± 0.51mm).

8. Adjust the gap between the doors and the body at the hinge pillars to 0.16 in. ± 0.020 in. (4.1mm ± 0.51mm).

9. Adjust the gap between the front and rear intermediate doors to 0.25 in. ± 0.020 in. (6.35mm ± 0.51mm).

10. Tighten the hinge bolts that were loosened.

11. Install the upper and lower rear intermediate door strikers to the body.

12. Install the door lock striker to the rear intermediate door using J–23457–A.

13. Adjust the upper and lower intermediate door striker to door clearance so that there is 0.172 in. (4.37mm) between the striker and the door latch when the door is in the secondary latch position. (The door is latched but not fully closed.) An $11/16$ in. diameter drill bit may be used to gauge this clearance.

14. Adjust the front intermediate striker on the rear door so that the front door lock properly engages the rear door, and so that the front door is flush with the rear door.

Rear Door

REMOVAL AND INSTALLATION

1. Open the door, remove the door trim panel and disconnect the electrical wiring harness (if equipped). Then mark the position of the door on the hinges using a wax pencil.

2. Remove the hinge hole plugs on the body side pillar.

3. Remove the strap pin from the bracket, then remove the snapring from the pin, and pull the pin.

4. Support the door safely, and remove the hinge to body pillar bolts.

5. Remove the door from the vehicle.

6. Remove the hinge to door bolts.

7. Remove the hinges from the door.

8. Remove the retainers, seals, and grommets from the door or the hinges.

9. Installation is the reverse of the removal

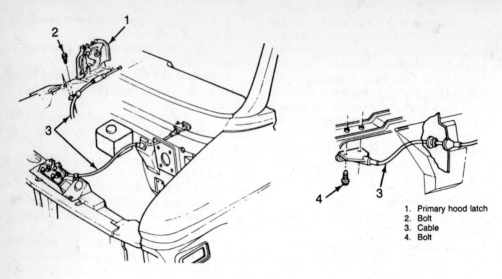

1. Primary hood latch
2. Bolt
3. Cable
4. Bolt

Hood release cable

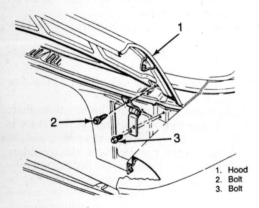

1. Hood
2. Bolt
3. Bolt

Hood hinge

procedure. Make sure to align the hinges with the previously made marks.

ADJUSTMENT

Each of the two doors must first be adjusted in the door opening before adjusting the door to door clearance.

1. Adjust the door height so that there is a gap of 0.25 in. ± 0.02 in. (6.35mm ± 0.51mm) between the roof panel and the rear door panel.

2. Adjust the gap between the bottom of the door panel (not the bottom of the outer panel) and the platform panel should be 0.25 in. ± 0.02 in. (6.35mm ± 0.51mm). This measurement should be taken on each door individually from the side of the door. The door should be in

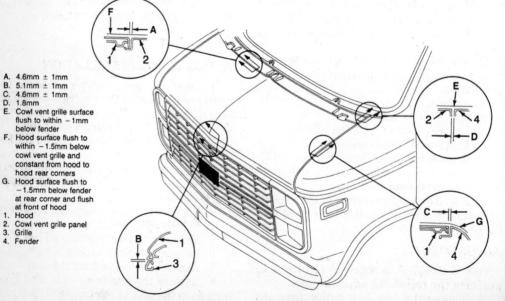

A. 4.6mm ± 1mm
B. 5.1mm ± 1mm
C. 4.6mm ± 1mm
D. 1.8mm
E. Cowl vent grille surface flush to within −1mm below fender
F. Hood surface flush to within −1.5mm below cowl vent grille and constant from hood to hood rear corners
G. Hood surface flush to −1.5mm below fender at rear corner and flush at front of hood
1. Hood
2. Cowl vent grille panel
3. Grille
4. Fender

Hood sheet metal gap specifications

its normal closed position. The outer rear door panel is 0.60 in. ± 0.02 in. (15.24mm ± 0.51mm) away from the rear platform panel when normally closed.

3. Adjust the rear door outer panel to the body side outer panel gap to 0.16 in. ± 0.02 in. (4.1mm ± 0.51mm).

4. The door to door clearance between the left and right outer door panels should be 0.25 in. ± 0.02 in. (6.35mm ± 0.51mm).

Rear Door Striker

REMOVAL AND INSTALLATION

1. Remove the striker to door frame bolts.
2. Remove the striker from the door frame.
3. Remove the spacer (if equipped).
4. Install in the reverse order of removal.

ADJUSTMENT

Adjust the striker to door latch clearance so that there are 0.172 in. (4.37mm) between the striker and the door latch when the door is in the secondary latch position. (The door is latched but not fully closed.) An $^{11}/_{16}$ in. diameter drill bit may be used to gauge this clearance.

Door Locks

REMOVAL AND INSTALLATION

1. Raise the window completely.
2. Remove the door trim panel and the door lock knob.
3. Remove the control assembly.
4. Remove the rear glass run panel.
5. Remove the door lock screws.
6. Remove the lock from the door.
7. Lower the lock in the door far enough to provide clearance for the inside lock rod and install the lock by reversing the removal procedure.

Hood

REMOVAL AND INSTALLATION

1. Mark the area around the hinges to make installation easier.
2. Support the hood and remove the hinge to hood frame bolts.
3. Remove the hood from the truck.
4. Installation is the reverse of the removal procedure.

Bumpers

REMOVAL AND INSTALLATION

Front Bumper

1. Remove the bracket-to-cross sill bolts.
2. Support the bumper and remove the brace-to-bumper nuts and bolts.
3. Installation is the reverse of removal. Torque the bracket-to-cross sill bolts to 30 ft. lbs.; the brace-to-bumper nuts to 21 ft. lbs.; the brace-to-bumper bolts to 30 ft. lbs.

Rear Standard Bumper

1. Remove the outer brace-to-bumper nuts and bolts.

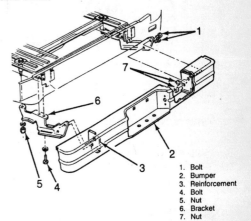

1. Bolt
2. Bumper
3. Reinforcement
4. Bolt
5. Nut
6. Bracket
7. Nut

Rear step bumper

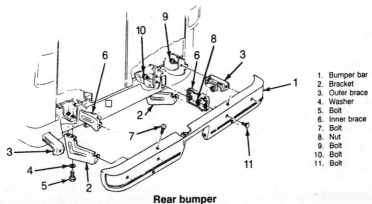

1. Bumper bar
2. Bracket
3. Outer brace
4. Washer
5. Bolt
6. Inner brace
7. Bolt
8. Nut
9. Bolt
10. Bolt
11. Bolt

Rear bumper

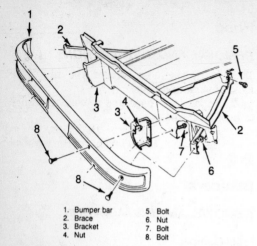

1. Bumper bar 5. Bolt
2. Brace 6. Nut
3. Bracket 7. Bolt
4. Nut 8. Bolt

Front bumper components

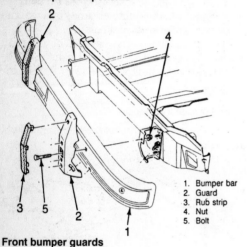

1. Bumper bar
2. Guard
3. Rub strip
4. Nut
5. Bolt

Front bumper guards

2. Remove the inner brace-to-cross sill bolts.

3. Support the bumper and remove the bracket-to-frame bolts and washers.

4. Installation is the reverse of removal. Assemble all fasteners loosely. When all are in place tighten the fasteners to:

- Outer brace-to-bumper bolts: 50 ft. lbs.
- Inner brace-to-cross sill nuts: 21 ft. lbs.

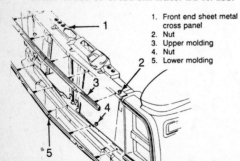

1. Front end sheet metal cross panel
2. Nut
3. Upper molding
4. Nut
5. Lower molding

Radiator grille molding attachments

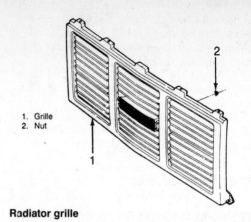

1. Grille
2. Nut

Radiator grille

- Outer bracket-to-bumper nuts: 50 ft. lbs.

Rear Step Bumper

1. Remove the reinforcement-to-bracket bolts.

2. Remove the bumper and reinforcements from the brackets.

3. Installation is the reverse of removal. Torque all bolts and nuts to 49 ft. lbs.

Grille

REMOVAL AND INSTALLATION

1. Raise and support the hood.

2. Remove the headlamp bezels.

3. Remove the sheet metal cross panel-to-grille bolts.

4. Remove the grille-to-lower front end panel bolts.

5. Lift the grille from the van.

6. Installation is the reverse of removal. Tighten all fasteners snugly.

Outside Mirrors

REMOVAL AND INSTALLATION

Below Eye Level Mirror

1. Lift the mirror cover, pivot the mirror towards the door and remove the mirror cover screw.

2. Remove the mirror-to-door bolts.

3. Remove the mirror and seal.

4. Installation is the reverse of removal.

West Coast Mirrors

1. Remove the mirror bracket-to-door bracket nuts, bolts and bushings.

2. Remove the mirror bracket from the door.

3. Remove the door bracket nuts and bolts.

4. Remove the brackets from the door.

5. Installation is the reverse of removal.

CHILTON'S
AUTO BODY REPAIR TIPS

Tools and Materials • Step-by-Step Illustrated Procedures
How To Repair Dents, Scratches and Rust Holes
Spray Painting and Refinishing Tips

With a little practice, basic body repair procedures can be mastered by any do-it-yourself mechanic. The step-by-step repairs shown here can be applied to almost any type of auto body repair.

TOOLS & MATERIALS

You may already have basic tools, such as hammers and electric drills. Other tools unique to body repair — body hammers, grinding attachments, sanding blocks, dent puller, half-round plastic file and plastic spreaders — are relatively inexpensive and can be obtained wherever auto parts or auto body repair parts are sold. Portable air compressors and paint spray guns can be purchased or rented.

Auto Body Repair Kits

The best and most often used products are available to the do-it-yourselfer in kit form, from major manufacturers of auto body repair products. The same manufacturers also merchandise the individual products for use by pros.

Kits are available to make a wide variety of repairs, including holes, dents and scratches and fiberglass, and offer the advantage of buying the materials you'll need for the job. There is little waste or chance of materials going bad from not being used. Many kits may also contain basic body-working tools such as body files, sanding blocks and spreaders. Check the contents of the kit before buying your tools.

BODY REPAIR TIPS

Safety

Many of the products associated with auto body repair and refinishing contain toxic chemicals. Read all labels before opening containers and store them in a safe place and manner.
- Wear eye protection (safety goggles) when using power tools or when performing any operation that involves the removal of any type of material.
- Wear lung protection (disposable mask or respirator) when grinding, sanding or painting.

Sanding

1 Sand off paint before using a dent puller. When using a non-adhesive sanding disc, cover the back of the disc with an overlapping layer or two of masking tape and trim the edges. The disc will last considerably longer.

2 Use the circular motion of the sanding disc to grind *into* the edge of the repair. Grinding or sanding away from the jagged edge will only tear the sandpaper.

3 Use the palm of your hand flat on the panel to detect high and low spots. Do not use your fingertips. Slide your hand slowly back and forth.

WORKING WITH BODY FILLER

Mixing The Filler

Cleanliness and proper mixing and application are extremely important. Use a clean piece of plastic or glass or a disposable artist's palette to mix body filler.

1 Allow plenty of time and follow directions. No useful purpose will be served by adding more hardener to make it cure (set-up) faster. Less hardener means more curing time, but the mixture dries harder; more hardener means less curing time but a softer mixture.

2 Both the hardener and the filler should be thoroughly kneaded or stirred before mixing. Hardener should be a solid paste and dispense like thin toothpaste. Body filler should be smooth, and free of lumps or thick spots.

Getting the proper amount of hardener in the filler is the trickiest part of preparing the filler. Use the same amount of hardener in cold or warm weather. For contour filler (thick coats), a bead of hardener twice the diameter of the filler is about right. There's about a 15% margin on either side, but, if in doubt use less hardener.

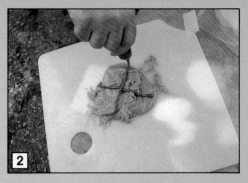

3 Mix the body filler and hardener by wiping across the mixing surface, picking the mixture up and wiping it again. Colder weather requires longer mixing times. Do not mix in a circular motion; this will trap air bubbles which will become holes in the cured filler.

Applying The Filler

1 For best results, filler should not be applied over ¼″ thick.

Apply the filler in several coats. Build it up to above the level of the repair surface so that it can be sanded or grated down.

The first coat of filler must be pressed on with a firm wiping motion.

Apply the filler in one direction only. Working the filler back and forth will either pull it off the metal or trap air bubbles.

REPAIRING DENTS

Before you start, take a few minutes to study the damaged area. Try to visualize the shape of the panel before it was damaged. If the damage is on the left fender, look at the right fender and use it as a guide. If there is access to the panel from behind, you can reshape it with a body hammer. If not, you'll have to use a dent puller. Go slowly and work the metal a little at a time. Get the panel as straight as possible before applying filler.

1 This dent is typical of one that can be pulled out or hammered out from behind. Remove the headlight cover, headlight assembly and turn signal housing.

2 Drill a series of holes ½ the size of the end of the dent puller along the stress line. Make some trial pulls and assess the results. If necessary, drill more holes and try again. Do not hurry.

3 If possible, use a body hammer and block to shape the metal back to its original contours. Get the metal back as close to its original shape as possible. Don't depend on body filler to fill dents.

4 Using an 80-grit grinding disc on an electric drill, grind the paint from the surrounding area down to bare metal. Use a new grinding pad to prevent heat buildup that will warp metal.

5 The area should look like this when you're finished grinding. Knock the drill holes in and tape over small openings to keep plastic filler out.

6 Mix the body filler (see Body Repair Tips). Spread the body filler evenly over the entire area (see Body Repair Tips). Be sure to cover the area completely.

7 Let the body filler dry until the surface can just be scratched with your fingernail. Knock the high spots from the body filler with a body file ("Cheesegrater"). Check frequently with the palm of your hand for high and low spots.

8 Check to be sure that trim pieces that will be installed later will fit exactly. Sand the area with 40-grit paper.

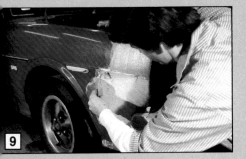

9 If you wind up with low spots, you may have to apply another layer of filler.

10 Knock the high spots off with 40-grit paper. When you are satisfied with the contours of the repair, apply a thin coat of filler to cover pin holes and scratches.

11 Block sand the area with 40-grit paper to a smooth finish. Pay particular attention to body lines and ridges that must be well-defined.

12 Sand the area with 400 paper and then finish with a scuff pad. The finished repair is ready for priming and painting (see Painting Tips).

Materials and photos courtesy of Ritt Jones Auto Body, Prospect Park, PA.

REPAIRING RUST HOLES

There are many ways to repair rust holes. The fiberglass cloth kit shown here is one of the most cost efficient for the owner because it provides a strong repair that resists cracking and moisture and is relatively easy to use. It can be used on large and small holes (with or without backing) and can be applied over contoured areas. Remember, however, that short of replacing an entire panel, no repair is a guarantee that the rust will not return.

1 Remove any trim that will be in the way. Clean away all loose debris. Cut away all the rusted metal. But be sure to leave enough metal to retain the contour or body shape.

2 Grind away all traces of rust with a 24-grit grinding disc. Be sure to grind back 3-4 inches from the edge of the hole down to bare metal and be sure all traces of paint, primer and rust are removed.

3 Block sand the area with 80 or 100 grit sandpaper to get a clear, shiny surface and feathered paint edge. Tap the edges of the hole inward with a ball peen hammer.

4 If you are going to use release film, cut a piece about 2-3″ larger than the area you have sanded. Place the film over the repair and mark the sanded area on the film. Avoid any unnecessary wrinkling of the film.

5 Cut 2 pieces of fiberglass matte to match the shape of the repair. One piece should be about 1″ smaller than the sanded area and the second piece should be 1″ smaller than the first. Mix enough filler and hardener to saturate the fiberglass material (see Body Repair Tips).

6 Lay the release sheet on a flat surface and spread an even layer of filler, large enough to cover the repair. Lay the smaller piece of fiberglass cloth in the center of the sheet and spread another layer of filler over the fiberglass cloth. Repeat the operation for the larger piece of cloth.

7 Place the repair material over the repair area, with the release film facing outward. Use a spreader and work from the center outward to smooth the material, following the body contours. Be sure to remove all air bubbles.

8 Wait until the repair has dried tack-free and peel off the release sheet. The ideal working temperature is 60°-90° F. Cooler or warmer temperatures or high humidity may require additional curing time. Wait longer, if in doubt.

12 Block sand the topcoat smooth with finishing sandpaper (200 grit), and 400 grit. The repair is ready for masking, priming and painting (see Painting Tips).

Materials and photos courtesy Marson Corporation, Chelsea, Massachusetts

PAINTING TIPS

Preparation

1 SANDING — Use a 400 or 600 grit wet or dry sandpaper. Wet-sand the area with a ¼ sheet of sandpaper soaked in clean water. Keep the paper wet while sanding. Sand the area until the repaired area tapers into the original finish.

2 CLEANING — Wash the area to be painted thoroughly with water and a clean rag. Rinse it thoroughly and wipe the surface dry until you're sure it's completely free of dirt, dust, fingerprints, wax, detergent or other foreign matter.

3 MASKING — Protect any areas you don't want to overspray by covering them with masking tape and newspaper. Be careful not get fingerprints on the area to be painted.

4 PRIMING — All exposed metal should be primed before painting. Primer protects the metal and provides an excellent surface for paint adhesion. When the primer is dry, wet-sand the area again with 600 grit wet-sandpaper. Clean the area again after sanding.

Painting Techniques

Paint applied from either a spray gun or a spray can (for small areas) will provide good results. Experiment on an

9 Sand and feather-edge the entire area. The initial sanding can be done with a sanding disc on an electric drill if care is used. Finish the sanding with a block sander. Low spots can be filled with body filler; this may require several applications.

10 When the filler can just be scratched with a fingernail, knock the high spots down with a body file and smooth the entire area with 80-grit. Feather the filled areas into the surounding areas.

11 When the area is sanded smooth, mix some topcoat and hardener and apply it directly with a spreader. This will give a smooth finish and prevent the glass matte from showing through the paint.

old piece of metal to get the right combination before you begin painting.

SPRAYING VISCOSITY (SPRAY GUN ONLY) — Paint should be thinned to spraying viscosity according to the directions on the can. Use only the recommended thinner or reducer and the same amount of reduction regardless of temperature.

AIR PRESSURE (SPRAY GUN ONLY) — This is extremely important. Be sure you are using the proper recommended pressure.

TEMPERATURE — The surface to be painted should be approximately the same temperature as the surrounding air. Applying warm paint to a cold surface, or vice versa, will completely upset the paint characteristics.

THICKNESS — Spray with smooth strokes. In general, the thicker the coat of paint, the longer the drying time. Apply several thin coats about 30 seconds apart. The paint should remain wet long enough to flow out and no longer; heavier coats will only produce sags or wrinkles. Spray a light (fog) coat, followed by heavier color coats.

DISTANCE — The ideal spraying distance is 8″-12″ from the gun or can to the surface. Shorter distances will produce ripples, while greater distances will result in orange peel, dry film and poor color match and loss of material due to overspray.

OVERLAPPING — The gun or can should be kept at right angles to the surface at all times. Work to a wet edge at an even speed, using a 50% overlap and direct the center of the spray at the lower or nearest edge of the previous stroke.

RUBBING OUT (BLENDING) FRESH PAINT — Let the paint dry thoroughly. Runs or imperfections can be sanded out, primed and repainted.

Don't be in too big a hurry to remove the masking. This only produces paint ridges. When the finish has dried for at least a week, apply a small amount of fine grade rubbing compound with a clean, wet cloth. Use lots of water and blend the new paint with the surrounding area.

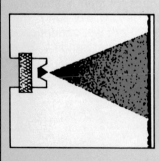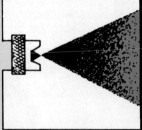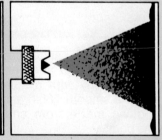

WRONG	**CORRECT**	**WRONG**
Thin coat. Stroke too fast, not enough overlap, gun too far away.	*Medium coat. Proper distance, good stroke, proper overlap.*	*Heavy coat. Stroke too slow, too much overlap, gun too close.*

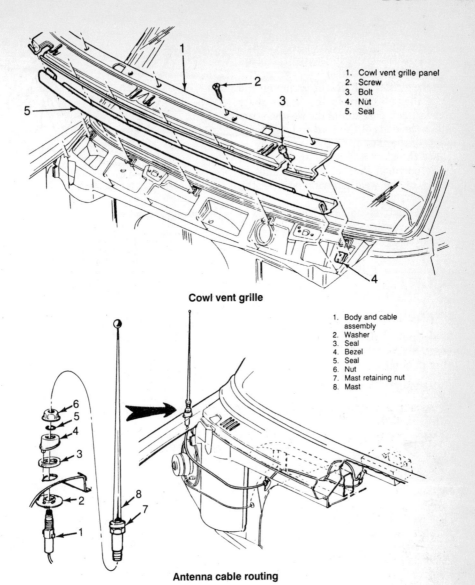

1. Cowl vent grille panel
2. Screw
3. Bolt
4. Nut
5. Seal

Cowl vent grille

1. Body and cable assembly
2. Washer
3. Seal
4. Bezel
5. Seal
6. Nut
7. Mast retaining nut
8. Mast

Antenna cable routing

Antenna

REMOVAL AND INSTALLATION

1. Disconnect the battery ground cable.
2. Unplug the antenna lead from the back of the radio.
3. Remove the mast retaining nut and lift the mast from the base.
4. Remove the antenna base nut and remove the bezel and seal.
5. Pull the antenna base and cable assembly down and out of the fender. At this point the cable can be unscrewed from the base. If the cable is being removed, carefully remove it from any under-dash clamps and thread it slowly through the firewall and out.
6. Installation is the reverse of removal.

Windshield

Bonded windshields require special tools and special removal procedures which are beyond the capability of most do-it-yourselfers. For this reason we recommend that you refer all removal and installation to a qualified technician.

Stationary Window Glass

REMOVAL AND INSTALLATION

1. Remove the interior trim moldings from around the window. On the rear doors, it may be necessary to drill out the weatherstripping rivets. Use a 1/4 inch bit.
2. Break loose the seal between the weatherstripping and the body panels.
3. Have someone outside push inward on the glass while you catch it.

4. Clean all old sealer from the glass and weatherstripping.

5. Fill the glass cavity in the weatherstripping with a $\frac{3}{16}''$ bead of sealer.

6. Fit the glass in the weatherstripping and place a $\frac{1}{4}''$ diameter cord in the frame cavity around the outside diameter of the weatherstripping. Allow the ends of the cord to hang down the outside of the glass from the top center.

7. Place the glass and weatherstripping in the vehicle opening. Pull on the cord ends to pull the lip of the weatherstripping over the body panel.

8. Install the trim molding. If the trim was held by rivets, replace them with $\frac{3}{16}$ in. blind rivets and a rivet gun.

INTERIOR

Door Panels

Special tool J–9886–01, Door Handle Clip Remover, is required to perform the following procedure.

REMOVAL AND INSTALLATION

1. Remove the window regulator handle using tool J–9886–01.

2. Remove the window regulator handle bezel.

3. Remove the door lock assembly handle using J–9886–01.

4. Remove the control assembly handle bezel.

5. Remove the assist handle (if equipped).

6. Remove the arm rest (if equipped).

7. Remove the door trim outer panel screws and pull the panel away from the retainer.

8. Remove the door trim inner panel screws and remove the trim inner panel.

9. Installation is the reverse of the removal.

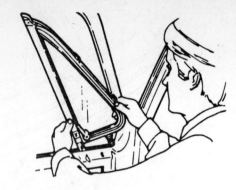

Removing vent window

Adjusting tension

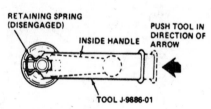

Inside handle removal

Door Vent/Window Run Channel Assembly

The door vent and the window run channel are one assembly. This assembly is fit into the front of the door frame.

REMOVAL AND INSTALLATION

1. Place the window in the lowered position and remove the door trim panel.

2. Remove the run channel molding. Pull the molding out of the vent assembly only.

3. Remove the door panel to run channel bolt.

4. Remove the door to ventilator screws.

5. Remove the door vent/window run channel assembly from the vehicle by pulling the top of the vent backwards away from the door frame. Then lift and rotate the assembly out of the door.

6. Installation is the reverse of the removal.

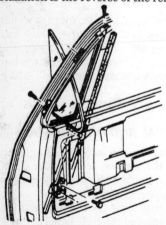

Door vent window

ADJUSTMENT

1. Remove the door trim panel.
2. Bend the tabs on the adjustment nut away from the nut.
3. Adjust the vent by placing a wrench on the adjusting nut, and then turning the vent window to the proper tension.
4. Bend the tabs over the adjusting nut and install the door trim panel.

Door Glass and Regulator

REMOVAL AND INSTALLATION

CAUTION: *Always wear heavy gloves when handling glass to minimize the risk of injury.*

Door Glass

1. Lower the glass to the bottom of the door and remove the door trim panel.
2. Remove the door vent/window channel run assembly.

NOTE: *Mask or cover any sharp edges that could scratch the glass.*

3. Slide the glass forward until the front roller is in line with the notch in the sash channel.
4. Disengage the roller from the channel.
5. Push the window forward, then tilt it up until the rear roller is disengaged.
6. Place the window in a level position, and raise it straight up and out of the door.
7. Installation is the reverse of the removal procedure.

Regulator

1. Raise the window and tape the glass in the full up position using cloth body tape.
2. Remove the door trim panel and the door panel to regulator bolts.
3. Slide the regulator rearward to disengage the rear roller from the sash channel. Then disengage the lower roller from the regulator rail.
4. Disengage the forward roller from the

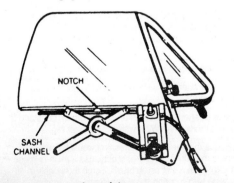

Door window and regulator

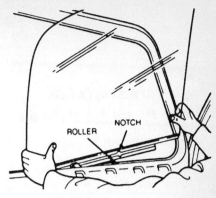

Removing door glass

sash channel at the notch in the sash channel.
5. Collapse the regulator and remove it through the access hole in the door.
6. Lubricate the regulator and the sash channel and regulator rails with Lubriplate® or its equivalent.
7. Install the regulator in the reverse of the removal procedure.

Electric Window Motor

REMOVAL AND INSTALLATION

1. Disconnect the negative battery cable.
2. Remove the door panel as described in the above procedure.
3. Remove the window regulator for clearance (if necessary).
4. Disconnect the wiring connector to the window motor.
5. Remove the motor to door frame bolts.
6. Remove the window motor.
7. Installation is the reverse of the removal procedure.

Headliner

REMOVAL AND INSTALLATION

1. Remove the upper window trim that supports the headliner.
2. Pull the headliner bow from the retainer
3. Remove the retainer bolts and the retainers.
4. Shift the headliner from side to side to disengage the headliner from the clips.

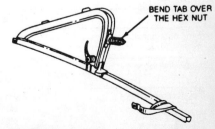

Bend tabs over hex nut

5. Remove the headliner from the vehicle.

6. Install in the reverse order of the removal procedure.

Front Seats

REMOVAL AND INSTALLATION

1. Remove the seat belt anchor plate-to-roof side rail bolt.

2. Disconnect the seat belt warning wire.

3. Remove the retractor-to-seat riser bolt.

4. Remove the retractor and anchor plate.

5. Remove the plug from the seat belt buckle arm.

6. Remove the buckle arm-to-seat riser bolt and washer.

7. From under the van, remove the seat riser-to-floor panel nuts and washers.

8. Lift the seat from the van.

9. Installation is the reverse of removal. Observe the following torques
- Seat-to-floor nuts to 47 ft. lbs.
- Buckle arm-to-seat riser bolt: 37 ft. lbs.
- Retractor-to-seat riser bolt: 37 ft. lbs.
- Anchor plate bolt: 37 ft. lbs.

Center and Rear Seats

REMOVAL AND INSTALLATION

To remove the center and rear seats, simply unlatch them and pull them rearward.

How to Remove Stains from Fabric Interior

For best results, spots and stains should be removed as soon as possible. Never use gasoline, lacquer thinner, acetone, nail polish remover or bleach. Use a 3′ x 3″ piece of cheesecloth. Squeeze most of the liquid from the fabric and wipe the stained fabric from the outside of the stain toward the center with a lifting motion. Turn the cheesecloth as soon as one side becomes soiled. When using water to remove a stain, be sure to wash the entire section after the spot has been removed to avoid water stains. Encrusted spots can be broken up with a dull knife and vacuumed before removing the stain.

Type of Stain	How to Remove It
Surface spots	Brush the spots out with a small hand brush or use a commercial preparation such as K2R to lift the stain.
Mildew	Clean around the mildew with warm suds. Rinse in cold water and soak the mildew area in a solution of 1 part table salt and 2 parts water. Wash with upholstery cleaner.
Water stains	Water stains in fabric materials can be removed with a solution made from 1 cup of table salt dissolved in 1 quart of water. Vigorously scrub the solution into the stain and rinse with clear water. Water stains in nylon or other synthetic fabrics should be removed with a commercial type spot remover.
Chewing gum, tar, crayons, shoe polish (greasy stains)	Do not use a cleaner that will soften gum or tar. Harden the deposit with an ice cube and scrape away as much as possible with a dull knife. Moisten the remainder with cleaning fluid and scrub clean.
Ice cream, candy	Most candy has a sugar base and can be removed with a cloth wrung out in warm water. Oily candy, after cleaning with warm water, should be cleaned with upholstery cleaner. Rinse with warm water and clean the remainder with cleaning fluid.
Wine, alcohol, egg, milk, soft drink (non-greasy stains)	Do not use soap. Scrub the stain with a cloth wrung out in warm water. Remove the remainder with cleaning fluid.
Grease, oil, lipstick, butter and related stains	Use a spot remover to avoid leaving a ring. Work from the outisde of the stain to the center and dry with a clean cloth when the spot is gone.
Headliners (cloth)	Mix a solution of warm water and foam upholstery cleaner to give thick suds. Use only foam—liquid may streak or spot. Clean the entire headliner in one operation using a circular motion with a natural sponge.
Headliner (vinyl)	Use a vinyl cleaner with a sponge and wipe clean with a dry cloth.
Seats and door panels	Mix 1 pint upholstery cleaner in 1 gallon of water. Do not soak the fabric around the buttons.
Leather or vinyl fabric	Use a multi-purpose cleaner full strength and a stiff brush. Let stand 2 minutes and scrub thoroughly. Wipe with a clean, soft rag.
Nylon or synthetic fabrics	For normal stains, use the same procedures you would for washing cloth upholstery. If the fabric is extremely dirty, use a multi-purpose cleaner full strength with a stiff scrub brush. Scrub thoroughly in all directions and wipe with a cotton towel or soft rag.

Mechanic's Data

11

1":254mm
TAX
10.16mm
Liter
Parts
Overhaul

General Conversion Table

Multiply By	To Convert	To	
LENGTH			
2.54	Inches	Centimeters	.3937
25.4	Inches	Millimeters	.03937
30.48	Feet	Centimeters	.0328
.304	Feet	Meters	3.28
.914	Yards	Meters	1.094
1.609	Miles	Kilometers	.621
VOLUME			
.473	Pints	Liters	2.11
.946	Quarts	Liters	1.06
3.785	Gallons	Liters	.264
.164	Cubic inches	Liters	61.02
16.39	Cubic inches	Cubic cms.	.061
28.32	Cubic feet	Liters	.0353
MASS (Weight)			
28.35	Ounces	Grams	.035
.4536	Pounds	Kilograms	2.20
—	To obtain	From	Multiply by

Multiply By	To Convert	To	
AREA			
6.45	Square inches	Square cms.	.155
.836	Square yds.	Square meters	1.196
FORCE			
4.448	Pounds	Newtons	.225
.138	Ft. lbs.	Kilogram/meters	7.23
1.356	Ft. lbs.	Newton-meters	.737
.113	In. lbs.	Newton-meters	8.844
PRESSURE			
.068	Psi	Atmospheres	14.7
6.89	Psi	Kilopascals	.145
OTHER			
1.104	Horsepower (DIN)	Horsepower (SAE)	.9861
.746	Horsepower (SAE)	Kilowatts (KW)	1.34
1.609	Mph	Km/h	.621
.425	Mpg	Km/L	2.35
—	To obtain	From	Multiply by

Tap Drill Sizes

National Coarse or U.S.S.		
Screw & Tap Size	Threads Per Inch	Use Drill Number
No. 5	.40	.39
No. 6	.32	.36
No. 8	.32	.29
No. 10	.24	.25
No. 12	.24	.17
1/4	.20	8
5/16	.18	F
3/8	.16	5/16
7/16	.14	U
1/2	.13	27/64
9/16	.12	31/64
5/8	.11	17/32
3/4	.10	21/32
7/8	9	49/64

National Coarse or U.S.S.		
Screw & Tap Size	Threads Per Inch	Use Drill Number
1	8	7/8
1 1/8	7	63/64
1 1/4	7	1 7/64
1 1/2	6	1 11/32

National Fine or S.A.E.		
Screw & Tap Size	Threads Per Inch	Use Drill Number
No. 5	.44	.37
No. 6	.40	.33
No. 8	.36	.29
No. 10	.32	.21

National Fine or S.A.E.		
Screw & Tap Size	Threads Per Inch	Use Drill Number
No. 12	.28	.15
1/4	.28	3
6/16	.24	1
3/8	.28	Q
7/16	.20	W
1/2	.20	29/64
9/16	.18	33/64
5/8	.18	37/64
3/4	.16	11/16
7/8	.14	13/16
1 1/8	.12	1 3/64
1 1/4	.12	1 11/64
1 1/2	.12	1 27/64

Drill Sizes In Decimal Equivalents

Inch	Dec-imal	Wire	mm	Inch	Dec-imal	Wire	mm	Inch	Dec-imal	Wire & Letter	mm	Inch	Dec-imal	Let-ter	mm	Inch	Dec-imal	mm
1/64	.0156		.39		.0730	49			.1614		4.1		.2717		6.9		.4331	11.0
	.0157		.4		.0748		1.9		.1654		4.2		.2720	I		7/16	.4375	11.11
	.0160	78			.0760	48			.1660	19			.2756		7.0		.4528	11.5
	.0165		.42		.0768		1.95		.1673		4.25		.2770	J		29/64	.4531	11.51
	.0173		.44	5/64	.0781		1.98		.1693		4.3		.2795		7.1	15/32	.4688	11.90
	.0177		.45		.0785	47			.1695	18			.2810	K			.4724	12.0
	.0180	77			.0787		2.0	11/64	.1719		4.36	9/32	.2812		7.14	31/64	.4844	12.30
	.0181		.46		.0807		2.05		.1730	17			.2835		7.2		.4921	12.5
	.0189		.48		.0810	46			.1732		4.4		.2854		7.25	1/2	.5000	12.70
	.0197		.5		.0820	45			.1770	16			.2874		7.3		.5118	13.0
	.0200	76			.0827		2.1		.1772		4.5		.2900	L		33/64	.5156	13.09
	.0210	75			.0846		2.15		.1800	15			.2913		7.4	17/32	.5312	13.49
	.0217		.55		.0860	44			.1811		4.6		.2950	M			.5315	13.5
	.0225	74			.0866		2.2		.1820	14			.2953		7.5	35/64	.5469	13.89
	.0236		.6		.0886		2.25		.1850	13		19/64	.2969		7.54		.5512	14.0
	.0240	73			.0890	43			.1850		4.7		.2992		7.6	9/16	.5625	14.28
	.0250	72			.0906		2.3		.1870		4.75		.3020	N			.5709	14.5
	.0256		.65		.0925		2.35	3/16	.1875		4.76		.3031		7.7	37/64	.5781	14.68
	.0260	71			.0935	42			.1890		4.8		.3051		7.75		.5906	15.0
	.0276		.7	3/32	.0938		2.38		.1890	12			.3071		7.8	19/32	.5938	15.08
	.0280	70			.0945		2.4		.1910	11			.3110		7.9	39/64	.6094	15.47
	.0292	69			.0960	41			.1929		4.9	5/16	.3125		7.93		.6102	15.5
	.0295		.75		.0965		2.45		.1935	10			.3150		8.0	5/8	.6250	15.87
	.0310	68			.0980	40			.1960	9			.3160	O			.6299	16.0
1/32	.0312		.79		.0981		2.5		.1969		5.0		.3189		8.1	41/64	.6406	16.27
	.0315		.8		.0995	39			.1990	8			.3228		8.2		.6496	16.5
	.0320	67			.1015	38			.2008		5.1		.3230	P		21/32	.6562	16.66
	.0330	66			.1024		2.6		.2010	7			.3248		8.25		.6693	17.0
	.0335		.85		.1040	37		13/64	.2031		5.16		.3268		8.3	43/64	.6719	17.06
	.0350	65			.1063		2.7		.2040	6		21/64	.3281		8.33	11/16	.6875	17.46
	.0354		.9		.1065	36			.2047		5.2		.3307		8.4		.6890	17.5
	.0360	64			.1083		2.75		.2055	5			.3320	Q		45/64	.7031	17.85
	.0370	63		7/64	.1094		2.77		.2067		5.25		.3346		8.5		.7087	18.0
	.0374		.95		.1100	35			.2087		5.3		.3386		8.6	23/32	.7188	18.25
	.0380	62			.1102		2.8		.2090	4			.3390	R			.7283	18.5
	.0390	61			.1110	34			.2126		5.4		.3425		8.7	47/64	.7344	18.65
	.0394		1.0		.1130	33			.2130	3		11/32	.3438		8.73		.7480	19.0
	.0400	60			.1142		2.9		.2165		5.5		.3445		8.75	3/4	.7500	19.05
	.0410	59			.1160	32		7/32	2188		5.55		.3465		8.8	49/64	.7656	19.44
	.0413		1.05		.1181		3.0		.2205		5.6		.3480	S			.7677	19.5
	.0420	58			.1200	31			.2210	2			.3504		8.9	25/32	.7812	19.84
	.0430	57			.1220		3.1		.2244		5.7		.3543		9.0		.7874	20.0
	.0433		1.1	1/8	.1250		3.17		.2264		5.75		.3580	T		51/64	.7969	20.24
	.0453		1.15		.1260		3.2		.2280	1			.3583		9.1		.8071	20.5
3/64	.0465	56			.1280		3.25		.2283		5.8	23/64	.3594		9.12	13/16	.8125	20.63
	.0469		1.19		.1285	30			.2323		5.9		.3622		9.2		.8268	21.0
	.0472		1.2		.1299		3.3		.2340	A			.3642		9.25	53/64	.8281	21.03
	.0492		1.25		.1339		3.4	15/64	.2344		5.95		.3661		9.3	27/32	.8438	21.43
	.0512		1.3		.1360	29			.2362		6.0		.3680	U			.8465	21.5
	.0520	55			.1378		3.5		.2380	B			.3701		9.4	55/64	.8594	21.82
	.0531		1.35		.1405	28			.2402		6.1		.3740		9.5		.8661	22.0
	.0550	54		9/64	.1406		3.57		.2420	C		3/8	.3750		9.52	7/8	.8750	22.22
	.0551		1.4		.1417		3.6		.2441		6.2		.3770	V			.8858	22.5
	.0571		1.45		.1440	27			.2460	D			.3780		9.6	57/64	.8906	22.62
	.0591		1.5		.1457		3.7		.2461		6.25		.3819		9.7		.9055	23.0
	.0595	53			.1470	26			.2480		6.3		.3839		9.75	29/32	.9062	23.01
	.0610		1.55		.1476		3.75	1/4	.2500	E	6.35		.3858		9.8	59/64	.9219	23.41
1/16	.0625		1.59		.1495	25			.2520		6.		.3860	W			.9252	23.5
	.0630		1.6		.1496		3.8		.2559		6.5		.3898		9.9	15/16	.9375	23.81
	.0635	52			.1520	24			.2570	F		25/64	.3906		9.92		.9449	24.0
	.0650		1.65		.1535		3.9		.2598		6.6		.3937		10.0	61/64	.9531	24.2
	.0669		1.7		.1540	23			.2610	G			.3970	X			.9646	24.5
	.0670	51		5/32	.1562		3.96		.2638		6.7		.4040	Y		31/32	.9688	24.6
	.0689		1.75		.1570	22		17/64	.2656		6.74	13/32	.4062		10.31		.9843	25.0
1/16	.0700	50			.1575		4.0		.2657		6.75		.4130	Z		63/64	.9844	25.0
	.0709		1.8		.1590	21			.2660	H			.4134		10.5	1	1.0000	25.4
	.0728		1.85		.1610	20			.2677		6.8	27/64	.4219		10.71			

AIR/FUEL RATIO: The ratio of air to gasoline by weight in the fuel mixture drawn into the engine.

AIR INJECTION: One method of reducing harmful exhaust emissions by injecting air into each of the exhaust ports of an engine. The fresh air entering the hot exhaust manifold causes any remaining fuel to be burned before it can exit the tailpipe.

ALTERNATOR: A device used for converting mechanical energy into electrical energy.

AMMETER: An instrument, calibrated in amperes, used to measure the flow of an electrical current in a circuit. Ammeters are always connected in series with the circuit being tested.

AMPERE: The rate of flow of electrical current present when one volt of electrical pressure is applied against one ohm of electrical resistance.

ANALOG COMPUTER: Any microprocessor that uses similar (analogous) electrical signals to make its calculations.

ARMATURE: A laminated, soft iron core wrapped by a wire that converts electrical energy to mechanical energy as in a motor or relay. When rotated in a magnetic field, it changes mechanical energy into electrical energy as in a generator.

ATMOSPHERIC PRESSURE: The pressure on the Earth's surface caused by the weight of the air in the atmosphere. At sea level, this pressure is 14.7 psi at 32°F (101 kPa at 0°C).

ATOMIZATION: The breaking down of a liquid into a fine mist that can be suspended in air.

AXIAL PLAY: Movement parallel to a shaft or bearing bore.

BACKFIRE: The sudden combustion of gases in the intake or exhaust system that results in a loud explosion.

BACKLASH: The clearance or play between two parts, such as meshed gears.

BACKPRESSURE: Restrictions in the exhaust system that slow the exit of exhaust gases from the combustion chamber.

BAKELITE: A heat resistant, plastic insulator material commonly used in printed circuit boards and transistorized components.

BALL BEARING: A bearing made up of hardened inner and outer races between which hardened steel balls roll.

BALLAST RESISTOR: A resistor in the primary ignition circuit that lowers voltage after the engine is started to reduce wear on ignition components.

BEARING: A friction reducing, supportive device usually located between a stationary part and a moving part.

BIMETAL TEMPERATURE SENSOR: Any sensor or switch made of two dissimilar types of metal that bend when heated or cooled due to the different expansion rates of the alloys. These types of sensors usually function as an on/off switch.

BLOWBY: Combustion gases, composed of water vapor and unburned fuel, that leak past the piston rings into the crankcase during normal engine operation. These gases are removed by the PCV system to prevent the buildup of harmful acids in the crankcase.

BRAKE PAD: A brake shoe and lining assembly used with disc brakes.

BRAKE SHOE: The backing for the brake lining. The term is, however, usually applied to the assembly of the brake backing and lining.

BUSHING: A liner, usually removable, for a bearing; an anti-friction liner used in place of a bearing.

BYPASS: System used to bypass ballast resistor during engine cranking to increase voltage supplied to the coil.

CALIPER: A hydraulically activated device in a disc brake system, which is mounted straddling the brake rotor (disc). The caliper contains at least one piston and two brake pads. Hydraulic pressure on the piston(s) forces the pads against the rotor.

CAMSHAFT: A shaft in the engine on which are the lobes (cams) which operate the valves. The camshaft is driven by the crankshaft, via a belt, chain or gears, at one half the crankshaft speed.

CAPACITOR: A device which stores an electrical charge.

CARBON MONOXIDE (CO): A colorless, odorless gas given off as a normal byproduct of combustion. It is poisonous and extremely dangerous in confined areas, building up slowly to toxic levels without warning if adequate ventilation is not available.

CARBURETOR: A device, usually mounted on the intake manifold of an engine, which mixes the air and fuel in the proper proportion to allow even combustion.

CATALYTIC CONVERTER: A device installed in the exhaust system, like a muffler, that converts harmful byproducts of combustion into carbon dioxide and water vapor by means of a heat-producing chemical reaction.

CENTRIFUGAL ADVANCE: A mechanical method of advancing the spark timing by using fly weights in the distributor that react to centrifugal force generated by the distributor shaft rotation.

CHECK VALVE: Any one-way valve installed to permit the flow of air, fuel or vacuum in one direction only.

CHOKE: A device, usually a movable valve, placed in the intake path of a carburetor to restrict the flow of air.

CIRCUIT: Any unbroken path through which an electrical current can flow. Also used to describe fuel flow in some instances.

CIRCUIT BREAKER: A switch which protects an electrical circuit from overload by opening the circuit when the current flow exceeds a predetermined level. Some circuit breakers must be reset manually, while most reset automatically

COIL (IGNITION): A transformer in the ignition circuit which steps up the voltage provided to the spark plugs.

COMBINATION MANIFOLD: An assembly which includes both the intake and exhaust manifolds in one casting.

COMBINATION VALVE: A device used in some fuel systems that routes fuel vapors to a charcoal storage canister instead of venting

them into the atmosphere. The valve relieves fuel tank pressure and allows fresh air into the tank as the fuel level drops to prevent a vapor lock situation.

COMPRESSION RATIO: The comparison of the total volume of the cylinder and combustion chamber with the piston at BDC and the piston at TDC.

CONDENSER: 1. An electrical device which acts to store an electrical charge, preventing voltage surges.
2. A radiator-like device in the air conditioning system in which refrigerant gas condenses into a liquid, giving off heat.

CONDUCTOR: Any material through which an electrical current can be transmitted easily.

CONTINUITY: Continuous or complete circuit. Can be checked with an ohmmeter.

COUNTERSHAFT: An intermediate shaft which is rotated by a mainshaft and transmits, in turn, that rotation to a working part.

CRANKCASE: The lower part of an engine in which the crankshaft and related parts operate.

CRANKSHAFT: The main driving shaft of an engine which receives reciprocating motion from the pistons and converts it to rotary motion.

CYLINDER: In an engine, the round hole in the engine block in which the piston(s) ride.

CYLINDER BLOCK: The main structural member of an engine in which is found the cylinders, crankshaft and other principal parts.

CYLINDER HEAD: The detachable portion of the engine, fastened, usually, to the top of the cylinder block, containing all or most of the combustion chambers. On overhead valve engines, it contains the valves and their operating parts. On overhead cam engines, it contains the camshaft as well.

DEAD CENTER: The extreme top or bottom of the piston stroke.

DETONATION: An unwanted explosion of the air/fuel mixture in the combustion chamber caused by excess heat and compression, advanced timing, or an overly lean mixture. Also referred to as "ping".

DIAPHRAGM: A thin, flexible wall separating two cavities, such as in a vacuum advance unit.

DIESELING: A condition in which hot spots in the combustion chamber cause the engine to run on after the key is turned off.

DIFFERENTIAL: A geared assembly which allows the transmission of motion between drive axles, giving one axle the ability to turn faster than the other.

DIODE: An electrical device that will allow current to flow in one direction only.

DISC BRAKE: A hydraulic braking assembly consisting of a brake disc, or rotor, mounted on an axle, and a caliper assembly containing, usually two brake pads which are activated by hydraulic pressure. The pads are forced against the sides of the disc, creating friction which slows the vehicle.

DISTRIBUTOR: A mechanically driven device on an engine which is responsible for electrically firing the spark plug at a predetermined point of the piston stroke.

DOWEL PIN: A pin, inserted in mating holes in two different parts allowing those parts to maintain a fixed relationship.

DRUM BRAKE: A braking system which consists of two brake shoes and one or two wheel cylinders, mounted on a fixed backing plate, and a brake drum, mounted on an axle, which revolves around the assembly. Hydraulic action applied to the wheel cylinders forces the shoes outward against the drum, creating friction, slowing the vehicle.

DWELL: The rate, measured in degrees of shaft rotation, at which an electrical circuit cycles on and off.

ELECTRONIC CONTROL UNIT (ECU): Ignition module, amplifier or igniter. See Module for definition.

ELECTRONIC IGNITION: A system in which the timing and firing of the spark plugs is controlled by an electronic control unit, usually called a module. These systems have no points or condenser.

ENDPLAY: The measured amount of axial movement in a shaft.

ENGINE: A device that converts heat into mechanical energy.

EXHAUST MANIFOLD: A set of cast passages or pipes which conduct exhaust gases from the engine.

FEELER GAUGE: A blade, usually metal, of precisely predetermined thickness, used to measure the clearance between two parts. These blades usually are available in sets of assorted thicknesses.

F-HEAD: An engine configuration in which the intake valves are in the cylinder head, while the camshaft and exhaust valves are located in the cylinder block. The camshaft operates the intake valves via lifters and pushrods, while it operates the exhaust valves directly.

FIRING ORDER: The order in which combustion occurs in the cylinders of an engine. Also the order in which spark is distributed to the plugs by the distributor.

FLATHEAD: An engine configuration in which the camshaft and all the valves are located in the cylinder block.

FLOODING: The presence of too much fuel in the intake manifold and combustion chamber which prevents the air/fuel mixture from firing, thereby causing a no-start situation.

FLYWHEEL: A disc shaped part bolted to the rear end of the crankshaft. Around the outer perimeter is affixed the ring gear. The starter drive engages the ring gear, turning the flywheel, which rotates the crankshaft, imparting the initial starting motion to the engine.

FOOT POUND (ft.lb. or sometimes, ft. lbs.): The amount of energy or work needed to raise an item weighing one pound, a distance of one foot.

FUSE: A protective device in a circuit which prevents circuit overload by breaking the circuit when a specific amperage is present. The device is constructed around a strip or wire of a lower amperage rating than the circuit it is designed to protect. When an amperage higher than that stamped on the fuse is present in the circuit, the strip or wire melts, opening the circuit.

GEAR RATIO: The ratio between the number of teeth on meshing gears.

GENERATOR: A device which converts mechanical energy into electrical energy.

HEAT RANGE: The measure of a spark plug's ability to dissipate heat from its firing end. The higher the heat range, the hotter the plug fires. **HUB:** The center part of a wheel or gear.

HYDROCARBON (HC): Any chemical compound made up of hydrogen and carbon. A major pollutant formed by the engine as a byproduct of combustion.

HYDROMETER: An instrument used to measure the specific gravity of a solution.

INCH POUND (in.lb. or sometimes, in. lbs.): One twelfth of a foot pound.

INDUCTION: A means of transferring electrical energy in the form of a magnetic field. Principle used in the ignition coil to increase voltage.

INJECTION PUMP: A device, usually mechanically operated, which meters and delivers fuel under pressure to the fuel injector.

INJECTOR: A device which receives metered fuel under relatively low pressure and is activated to inject the fuel into the engine under relatively high pressure at a predetermined time.

INPUT SHAFT: The shaft to which torque is applied, usually carrying the driving gear or gears.

INTAKE MANIFOLD: A casting of passages or pipes used to conduct air or a fuel/air mixture to the cylinders.

JOURNAL: The bearing surface within which a shaft operates.

KEY: A small block usually fitted in a notch between a shaft and a hub to prevent slippage of the two parts.

MANIFOLD: A casting of passages or set of pipes which connect the cylinders to an inlet or outlet source.

MANIFOLD VACUUM: Low pressure in an engine intake manifold formed just below the throttle plates. Manifold vacuum is highest at idle and drops under acceleration.

MASTER CYLINDER: The primary fluid pressurizing device in a hydraulic system. In automotive use, it is found in brake and hydraulic clutch systems and is pedal activated, either directly or, in a power brake system, through the power booster.

MODULE: Electronic control unit, amplifier or igniter of solid state or integrated design which controls the current flow in the ignition primary circuit based on input from the pickup coil. When the module opens the primary circuit, the high secondary voltage is induced in the coil.

NEEDLE BEARING: A bearing which consists of a number (usually a large number) of long, thin rollers.

OHM:(Ω) The unit used to measure the resistance of conductor to electrical flow. One ohm is the amount of resistance that limits current flow to one ampere in a circuit with one volt of pressure.

OHMMETER: An instrument used for measuring the resistance, in ohms, in an electrical circuit.

OUTPUT SHAFT: The shaft which transmits torque from a device, such as a transmission.

OVERDRIVE: A gear assembly which produces more shaft revolutions than that transmitted to it.

OVERHEAD CAMSHAFT (OHC): An engine configuration in which the camshaft is mounted on top of the cylinder head and operates the valves either directly or by means of rocker arms.

OVERHEAD VALVE (OHV): An engine configuration in which all of the valves are located in the cylinder head and the camshaft is located in the cylinder block. The camshaft operates the valves via lifters and pushrods.

OXIDES OF NITROGEN (NOx): Chemical compounds of nitrogen produced as a byproduct of combustion. They combine with hydrocarbons to produce smog.

OXYGEN SENSOR: Used with the feedback system to sense the presence of oxygen in the exhaust gas and signal the computer which can reference the voltage signal to an air/fuel ratio.

PINION: The smaller of two meshing gears.

PISTON RING: An open ended ring which fits into a groove on the outer diameter of the piston. Its chief function is to form a seal between the piston and cylinder wall. Most automotive pistons have three rings: two for compression sealing; one for oil sealing.

PRELOAD: A predetermined load placed on a bearing during assembly or by adjustment.

PRIMARY CIRCUIT: Is the low voltage side of the ignition system which consists of the ignition switch, ballast resistor or resistance wire, bypass, coil, electronic control unit and pick-up coil as well as the connecting wires and harnesses.

PRESS FIT: The mating of two parts under pressure, due to the inner diameter of one being smaller than the outer diameter of the other, or vice versa; an interference fit.

RACE: The surface on the inner or outer ring of a bearing on which the balls, needles or rollers move.

REGULATOR: A device which maintains the amperage and/or voltage levels of a circuit at predetermined values.

RELAY: A switch which automatically opens and/or closes a circuit.

RESISTANCE: The opposition to the flow of current through a circuit or electrical device, and is measured in ohms. Resistance is equal to the voltage divided by the amperage.

RESISTOR: A device, usually made of wire, which offers a preset amount of resistance in an electrical circuit.

RING GEAR: The name given to a ring-shaped gear attached to a differential case,or affixed to a flywheel or as part a planetary gear set.

ROLLER BEARING: A bearing made up of hardened inner and outer races between which hardened steel rollers move.

ROTOR: 1. The disc-shaped part of a disc brake assembly, upon which the brake pads bear; also called, brake disc.
2. The device mounted atop the distributor shaft, which passes current to the distributor cap tower contacts.

SECONDARY CIRCUIT: The high voltage side of the ignition system, usually above 20,000 volts. The secondary includes the ignition coil, coil wire, distributor cap and rotor, spark plug wires and spark plugs.

SENDING UNIT: A mechanical, electrical, hydraulic or electromagnetic device which transmits information to a gauge.

SENSOR: Any device designed to measure engine operating conditions or ambient pressures and temperatures. Usually electronic in nature and designed to send a voltage signal to an on-board computer, some sensors may operate as a simple on/off switch or they may provide a variable voltage signal (like a potentiometer) as conditions or measured parameters change.

SHIM: Spacers of precise, predetermined thickness used between parts to establish a proper working relationship.

SLAVE CYLINDER: In automotive use, a device in the hydraulic clutch system which is activated by hydraulic force, disengaging the clutch.

SOLENOID: A coil used to produce a magnetic field, the effect of which is to produce work.

SPARK PLUG: A device screwed into the combustion chamber of a spark ignition engine. The basic construction is a conductive core inside of a ceramic insulator, mounted in an outer conductive base. An electrical charge from the spark plug wire travels along the conductive core and jumps a preset air gap to a grounding point or points at the end of the conductive base. The resultant spark ignites the fuel/air mixture in the combustion chamber.

SPLINES: Ridges machined or cast onto the outer diameter of a shaft or inner diameter of a bore to enable parts to mate without rotation.

TACHOMETER: A device used to measure the rotary speed of an engine, shaft, gear, etc., usually in rotations per minute.

THERMOSTAT: A valve, located in the cooling system of an engine, which is closed when cold and opens gradually in response to engine heating, controlling the temperature of the coolant and rate of coolant flow.

TOP DEAD CENTER (TDC): The point at which the piston reaches the top of its travel on the compression stroke.

TORQUE: The twisting force applied to an object.

TORQUE CONVERTER: A turbine used to transmit power from a driving member to a driven member via hydraulic action, providing changes in drive ratio and torque. In automotive use, it links the driveplate at the rear of the engine to the automatic transmission.

TRANSDUCER: A device used to change a force into an electrical signal.

TRANSISTOR: A semi-conductor component which can be actuated by a small voltage to perform an electrical switching function.

TUNE-UP: A regular maintenance function, usually associated with the replacement and adjustment of parts and components in the electrical and fuel systems of a vehicle for the purpose of attaining optimum performance.

TURBOCHARGER: An exhaust driven pump which compresses intake air and forces it into the combustion chambers at higher than atmospheric pressures. The increased air pressure allows more fuel to be burned and results in increased horsepower being produced.

VACUUM ADVANCE: A device which advances the ignition timing in response to increased engine vacuum.

VACUUM GAUGE: An instrument used to measure the presence of vacuum in a chamber.

VALVE: A device which control the pressure, direction of flow or rate of flow of a liquid or gas.

VALVE CLEARANCE: The measured gap between the end of the valve stem and the rocker arm, cam lobe or follower that activates the valve.

VISCOSITY: The rating of a liquid's internal resistance to flow.

VOLTMETER: An instrument used for measuring electrical force in units called volts. Voltmeters are always connected parallel with the circuit being tested.

WHEEL CYLINDER: Found in the automotive drum brake assembly, it is a device, actuated by hydraulic pressure, which, through internal pistons, pushes the brake shoes outward against the drums.

A: Ampere

AC: Alternating current

A/C: Air conditioning

A–h: Amper hour

AT: Automatic transmission

ATDC: After top dead center

μA: Microampere

bbl: Barrel

BDC: Bottom dead center

bhp: Brake horsepower

BTDC: Before top dead center

BTU: British thermal unit

C: Celsius (Centigrade)

CCA: Cold cranking amps

cd: Candela

cm^2: Square centimeter

cm^3, cc: Cubic centimeter

CO: Carbon monoxide

CO_2: Carbon dioxide

cu.in., in^3: Cubic inch

CV: Constant velocity

Cyl.: Cylinder

DC: Direct current

ECM: Electronic control module

EFE: Early fuel evaporation

EFI: Electronic fuel injection

EGR: Exhaust gas recirculation

Exh.: Exhaust

F: Farenheit

F: Farad

pF: Picofarad

μF: Microfarad

FI: Fuel injection

ft.lb., ft. lb., ft. lbs.: foot pound(s)

gal: Gallon

g: Gram

HC: Hydrocarbon

HEI: High energy ignition

HO: High output

hp: Horsepower

Hyd: Hydraulic

Hz: Hertz

ID: Inside diameter

in.lb; in. lbs.; in. lbs.: inch pound(s)

Int: Intake

K: Kelvin

kg: Kilogram

kHz: Kilohertz

km: Kilometer

km/h: Kilometers per hour

kΩ: Kilohm

kPa: Kilopascal

kV: Kilovolt

kW: Kilowatt

l: Liter

l/s: Liters per second

m: Meter

mA: Milliampere

mg: Milligram

mHz: Megahertz

mm: Millimeter

mm^2: Square millimeter

m^3: Cubic meter

MΩ: Megohm

m/s: Meters per second

MT: Manual transmission

mV: Millivolt

μm: Micrometer

N: Newton

N–m: Newton meter

NOx: Nitrous oxide

OD: Outside diameter

OHC: Over head camshaft

OHV: Over head valve

Ω: Ohm

PCV: Positive crankcase ventilation

psi: Pounds per square inch

pts: Pints

qts: Quarts

rpm: Rotations per minute

rps: Rotations per second

R–12: refrigerant gas (Freon)

SAE: Society of Automotive Engineers

SO$_2$: Sulfur dioxide

T: Ton

t: Megagram

TBI: Throttle Body Injection

TPS: Throttle Position Sensor

V: 1. Volt; 2. Venturi

μV: Microvolt

W: Watt

∞: Infinity

$<$: Less than

$>$: Greater than

CHILTON'S REPAIR MANUAL MODEL INDEX
Car and truck model names are listed in alphabetical and numerical order

Part No.	Model	Repair Manual Title
6980	Accord	Honda 1973-88
7747	Aerostar	Ford Aerostar 1986-90
7165	Alliance	Renault 1975-85
7199	AMX	AMC 1975-86
7163	Aries	Chrysler Front Wheel Drive 1981-88
7041	Arrow	Champ/Arrow/Sapporo 1978-83
7032	Arrow Pick-Ups	D-50/Arrow Pick-Up 1979-81
6637	Aspen	Aspen/Volare 1976-80
6935	Astre	GM Subcompact 1971-80
7750	Astro	Chevrolet Astro/GMC Safari 1985-90
6934	A100, 200, 300	Dodge/Plymouth Vans 1967-88
5807	Barracuda	Barracuda/Challenger 1965-72
6844	Bavaria	BMW 1970-88
5796	Beetle	Volkswagen 1949-71
6837	Beetle	Volkswagen 1970-81
7135	Bel Air	Chevrolet 1968-88
5821	Belvedere	Roadrunner/Satellite/Belvedere/GTX 1968-73
7849	Beretta	Chevrolet Corsica and Beretta 1988
7317	Berlinetta	Camaro 1982-88
7135	Biscayne	Chevrolet 1968-88
6931	Blazer	Blazer/Jimmy 1969-82
7383	Blazer	Chevy S-10 Blazer/GMC S-15 Jimmy 1982-87
7027	Bobcat	Pinto/Bobcat 1971-80
7308	Bonneville	Buick/Olds/Pontiac 1975-87
6982	BRAT	Subaru 1970-88
7042	Brava	Fiat 1969-81
7140	Bronco	Ford Bronco 1966-86
7829	Bronco	Ford Pick-Ups and Bronco 1987-88
7408	Bronco II	Ford Ranger/Bronco II 1983-88
7135	Brookwood	Chevrolet 1968-88
6326	Brougham 1975-75	Valiant/Duster 1968-76
6934	B100, 150, 200, 250, 300, 350	Dodge/Plymouth Vans 1967-88
7197	B210	Datsun 1200/210/Nissan Sentra 1973-88
7659	B1600, 1800, 2000, 2200, 2600	Mazda Trucks 1971-89
6840	Caballero	Chevrolet Mid-Size 1964-88
7657	Calais	Calais, Grand Am, Skylark, Somerset 1985-86
6735	Camaro	Camaro 1967-81
7317	Camaro	Camaro 1982-88
7740	Camry	Toyota Camry 1983-88
6695	Capri, Capri II	Capri 1970-77
6963	Capri	Mustang/Capri/Merkur 1979-88
7135	Caprice	Chevrolet 1968-88
7482	Caravan	Dodge Caravan/Plymouth Voyager 1984-89
7163	Caravelle	Chrysler Front Wheel Drive 1981-88
7036	Carina	Toyota Corolla/Carina/Tercel/Starlet 1970-87
7308	Catalina	Buick/Olds/Pontiac 1975-90
7059	Cavalier	Cavalier, Skyhawk, Cimarron, 2000 1982-88
7309	Celebrity	Celebrity, Century, Ciera, 6000 1982-88
7043	Celica	Toyota Celica/Supra 1971-87
8058	Celica	Toyota Celica/Supra 1986-90
7309	Century FWD	Celebrity, Century, Ciera, 6000 1982-88
7307	Century RWD	Century/Regal 1975-87
5807	Challenger 1965-72	Barracuda/Challenger 1965-72
7037	Challenger 1977-83	Colt/Challenger/Vista/Conquest 1971-88
7041	Champ	Champ/Arrow/Sapporo 1978-83
6486	Charger	Dodge Charger 1967-70
6845	Charger 2.2	Omni/Horizon/Rampage 1978-88

Part No.	Model	Repair Manual Title
6739	Cherokee 1974-83	Jeep Wagoneer, Commando, Cherokee, Truck 1957-86
7939	Cherokee 1984-89	Jeep Wagoneer, Comanche, Cherokee 1984-89
6840	Chevelle	Chevrolet Mid-Size 1964-88
6836	Chevette	Chevette/T-1000 1976-88
6841	Chevy II	Chevy II/Nova 1962-79
7309	Ciera	Celebrity, Century, Ciera, 6000 1982-88
7059	Cimarron	Cavalier, Skyhawk, Cimarron, 2000 1982-88
7049	Citation	GM X-Body 1980-85
6980	Civic	Honda 1973-88
6817	CJ-2A, 3A, 3B, 5, 6, 7	Jeep 1945-87
8034	CJ-5, 6, 7	Jeep 1971-90
6842	Colony Park	Ford/Mercury/Lincoln 1968-88
7037	Colt	Colt/Challenger/Vista/Conquest 1971-88
6634	Comet	Maverick/Comet 1971-77
7939	Comanche	Jeep Wagoneer, Comanche, Cherokee 1984-89
6739	Commando	Jeep Wagoneer, Commando, Cherokee, Truck 1957-86
6842	Commuter	Ford/Mercury/Lincoln 1968-88
7199	Concord	AMC 1975-86
7037	Conquest	Colt/Challenger/Vista/Conquest 1971-88
6696	Continental 1982-85	Ford/Mercury/Lincoln Mid-Size 1971-85
7814	Continental 1982-87	Thunderbird, Cougar, Continental 1980-87
7830	Continental 1988-89	Taurus/Sable/Continental 1986-89
7583	Cordia	Mitsubishi 1983-89
5795	Corolla 1968-70	Toyota 1966-70
7036	Corolla	Toyota Corolla/Carina/Tercel/Starlet 1970-87
5795	Corona	Toyota 1966-70
7004	Corona	Toyota Corona/Crown/Cressida/Mk.II/Van 1970-87
6962	Corrado	VW Front Wheel Drive 1974-90
7849	Corsica	Chevrolet Corsica and Beretta 1988
6576	Corvette	Corvette 1953-62
6843	Corvette	Corvette 1963-86
6542	Cougar	Mustang/Cougar 1965-73
6696	Cougar	Ford/Mercury/Lincoln Mid-Size 1971-85
7814	Cougar	Thunderbird, Cougar, Continental 1980-87
6842	Country Sedan	Ford/Mercury/Lincoln 1968-88
6842	Country Squire	Ford/Mercury/Lincoln 1968-88
6983	Courier	Ford Courier 1972-82
7004	Cressida	Toyota Corona/Crown/Cressida/Mk.II/Van 1970-87
5795	Crown	Toyota 1966-70
7004	Crown	Toyota Corona/Crown/Cressida/Mk.II/Van 1970-87
6842	Crown Victoria	Ford/Mercury/Lincoln 1968-88
6980	CRX	Honda 1973-88
6842	Custom	Ford/Mercury/Lincoln 1968-88
6326	Custom	Valiant/Duster 1968-76
6842	Custom 500	Ford/Mercury/Lincoln 1968-88
7950	Cutlass FWD	Lumina/Grand Prix/Cutlass/Regal 1988-90
6933	Cutlass RWD	Cutlass 1970-87
7309	Cutlass Ciera	Celebrity, Century, Ciera, 6000 1982-88
6936	C-10, 20, 30	Chevrolet/GMC Pick-Ups & Suburban 1970-87

Chilton's Repair Manuals are available at your local retailer or by mailing a check or money order for **$14.95** per book plus **$3.50** for 1st book and **$.50** for each additional book to cover postage and handling to:

Chilton Book Company
Dept. DM
Radnor, PA 19089

NOTE: When ordering be sure to include your name & address, book part No. & title.

CHILTON'S REPAIR MANUAL MODEL INDEX
Car and truck model names are listed in alphabetical and numerical order

Part No.	Model	Repair Manual Title	Part No.	Model	Repair Manual Title
8055	C-15, 25, 35	Chevrolet/GMC Pick-Ups & Suburban 1988-90	7593	Golf	VW Front Wheel Drive 1974-90
			7165	Gordini	Renault 1975-85
6324	Dart	Dart/Demon 1968-76	6937	Granada	Granada/Monarch 1975-82
6962	Dasher	VW Front Wheel Drive 1974-90	6552	Gran Coupe	Plymouth 1968-76
5790	Datsun Pickups	Datsun 1961-72	6552	Gran Fury	Plymouth 1968-76
6816	Datsun Pickups	Datsun Pick-Ups and Pathfinder 1970-89	6842	Gran Marquis	Ford/Mercury/Lincoln 1968-88
			6552	Gran Sedan	Plymouth 1968-76
7163	Daytona	Chrysler Front Wheel Drive 1981-88	6696	Gran Torino 1972-76	Ford/Mercury/Lincoln Mid-Size 1971-85
6486	Daytona Charger	Dodge Charger 1967-70			
6324	Demon	Dart/Demon 1968-76	7346	Grand Am	Pontiac Mid-Size 1974-83
7462	deVille	Cadillac 1967-89	7657	Grand Am	Calais, Grand Am, Skylark, Somerset 1985-86
7587	deVille	GM C-Body 1985			
6817	DJ-3B	Jeep 1945-87	7346	Grand LeMans	Pontiac Mid-Size 1974-83
7040	DL	Volvo 1970-88	7346	Grand Prix	Pontiac Mid-Size 1974-83
6326	Duster	Valiant/Duster 1968-76	7950	Grand Prix FWD	Lumina/Grand Prix/Cutlass/Regal 1988-90
7032	D-50	D-50/Arrow Pick-Ups 1979-81			
7459	D100, 150, 200, 250, 300, 350	Dodge/Plymouth Trucks 1967-88	7308	Grand Safari	Buick/Olds/Pontiac 1975-87
			7308	Grand Ville	Buick/Olds/Pontiac 1975-87
7199	Eagle	AMC 1975-86	6739	Grand Wagoneer	Jeep Wagoneer, Commando, Cherokee, Truck 1957-86
7163	E-Class	Chrysler Front Wheel Drive 1981-88			
6840	El Camino	Chevrolet Mid-Size 1964-88	7199	Gremlin	AMC 1975-86
7462	Eldorado	Cadillac 1967-89	6575	GT	Opel 1971-75
7308	Electra	Buick/Olds/Pontiac 1975-90	7593	GTI	VW Front Wheel Drive 1974-90
7587	Electra	GM C-Body 1985	5905	GTO 1968-73	Tempest/GTO/LeMans 1968-73
6696	Elite	Ford/Mercury/Lincoln Mid-Size 1971-85	7346	GTO 1974	Pontiac Mid-Size 1974-83
			5821	GTX	Roadrunner/Satellite/Belvedere/GTX 1968-73
7165	Encore	Renault 1975-85			
7055	Escort	Ford/Mercury Front Wheel Drive 1981-87	5910	GT6	Triumph 1969-73
			6542	G.T.350, 500	Mustang/Cougar 1965-73
7059	Eurosport	Cavalier, Skyhawk, Cimarron, 2000 1982-88	6930	G-10, 20, 30	Chevy/GMC Vans 1967-86
			6930	G-1500, 2500, 3500	Chevy/GMC Vans 1967-86
7760	Excel	Hyundai 1986-90	8040	G-10, 20, 30	Chevy/GMC Vans 1987-90
7163	Executive Sedan	Chrysler Front Wheel Drive 1981-88	8040	G-1500, 2500, 3500	Chevy/GMC Vans 1987-90
7055	EXP	Ford/Mercury Front Wheel Drive 1981-87	5795	Hi-Lux	Toyota 1966-70
			6845	Horizon	Omni/Horizon/Rampage 1978-88
6849	E-100, 150, 200, 250, 300, 350	Ford Vans 1961-88	7199	Hornet	AMC 1975-86
			7135	Impala	Chevrolet 1968-88
6320	Fairlane	Fairlane/Torino 1962-75	7317	IROC-Z	Camaro 1982-88
6965	Fairmont	Fairmont/Zephyr 1978-83	6739	Jeepster	Jeep Wagoneer, Commando, Cherokee, Truck 1957-86
5796	Fastback	Volkswagen 1949-71			
6837	Fastback	Volkswagen 1970-81	7593	Jetta	VW Front Wheel Drive 1974-90
6739	FC-150, 170	Jeep Wagoneer, Commando, Cherokee, Truck 1957-86	6931	Jimmy	Blazer/Jimmy 1969-82
			7383	Jimmy	Chevy S-10 Blazer/GMC S-15 Jimmy 1982-87
6982	FF-1	Subaru 1970-88			
7571	Fiero	Pontiac Fiero 1984-88	6739	J-10, 20	Jeep Wagoneer, Commando, Cherokee, Truck 1957-86
6846	Fiesta	Fiesta 1978-80			
5996	Firebird	Firebird 1967-81	6739	J-100, 200, 300	Jeep Wagoneer, Commando, Cherokee, Truck 1957-86
7345	Firebird	Firebird 1982-90			
7059	Firenza	Cavalier, Skyhawk, Cimarron, 2000 1982-88	6575	Kadett	Opel 1971-75
			7199	Kammback	AMC 1975-86
7462	Fleetwood	Cadillac 1967-89	5796	Karmann Ghia	Volkswagen 1949-71
7587	Fleetwood	GM C-Body 1985	6837	Karmann Ghia	Volkswagen 1970-81
7829	F-Super Duty	Ford Pick-Ups and Bronco 1987-88	7135	Kingswood	Chevrolet 1968-88
7165	Fuego	Renault 1975-85	6931	K-5	Blazer/Jimmy 1969-82
6552	Fury	Plymouth 1968-76	6936	K-10, 20, 30	Chevy/GMC Pick-Ups & Suburban 1970-87
7196	F-10	Datsun/Nissan F-10, 310, Stanza, Pulsar 1976-88			
			6936	K-1500, 2500, 3500	Chevy/GMC Pick-Ups & Suburban 1970-87
6933	F-85	Cutlass 1970-87			
6913	F-100, 150, 200, 250, 300, 350	Ford Pick-Ups 1965-86	8055	K-10, 20, 30	Chevy/GMC Pick-Ups & Suburban 1988-90
7829	F-150, 250, 350	Ford Pick-Ups and Bronco 1987-88	8055	K-1500, 2500, 3500	Chevy/GMC Pick-Ups & Suburban 1988-90
7583	Galant	Mitsubishi 1983-89			
6842	Galaxie	Ford/Mercury/Lincoln 1968-88	6840	Laguna	Chevrolet Mid-Size 1964-88
7040	GL	Volvo 1970-88	7041	Lancer	Champ/Arrow/Sapporo 1977-83
6739	Gladiator	Jeep Wagoneer, Commando, Cherokee, Truck 1962-86	5795	Land Cruiser	Toyota 1966-70
			7035	Land Cruiser	Toyota Trucks 1970-88
6981	GLC	Mazda 1978-89	7163	Laser	Chrysler Front Wheel Drive 1981-88
7040	GLE	Volvo 1970-88	7163	LeBaron	Chrysler Front Wheel Drive 1981-88
7040	GLT	Volvo 1970-88	7165	LeCar	Renault 1975-85

Chilton's Repair Manuals are available at your local retailer or by mailing a check or money order for **$14.95** per book plus **$3.50** for 1st book and **$.50** for each additional book to cover postage and handling to:

Chilton Book Company
Dept. DM
Radnor, PA 19089

NOTE: When ordering be sure to include your name & address, book part No. & title.

CHILTON'S REPAIR MANUAL MODEL INDEX
Car and truck model names are listed in alphabetical and numerical order

Part No.	Model	Repair Manual Title	Part No.	Model	Repair Manual Title
5905	LeMans	Tempest/GTO/LeMans 1968-73	5790	Patrol	Datsun 1961-72
7346	LeMans	Pontiac Mid-Size 1974-83	6934	PB100, 150, 200,	Dodge/Plymouth Vans 1967-88
7308	LeSabre	Buick/Olds/Pontiac 1975-87		250, 300, 350	
6842	Lincoln	Ford/Mercury/Lincoln 1968-88	5982	Peugeot	Peugeot 1970-74
7055	LN-7	Ford/Mercury Front Wheel Drive 1981-87	7049	Phoenix	GM X-Body 1980-85
			7027	Pinto	Pinto/Bobcat 1971-80
6842	LTD	Ford/Mercury/Lincoln 1968-88	6554	Polara	Dodge 1968-77
6696	LTD II	Ford/Mercury/Lincoln Mid-Size 1971-85	7583	Precis	Mitsubishi 1983-89
			6980	Prelude	Honda 1973-88
7950	Lumina	Lumina/Grand Prix/Cutlass/Regal 1988-90	7658	Prizm	Chevrolet Nova/GEO Prizm 1985-89
			8012	Probe	Ford Probe 1989
6815	LUV	Chevrolet LUV 1972-81	7660	Pulsar	Datsun/Nissan F-10, 310, Stanza, Pulsar 1976-88
6575	Luxus	Opel 1971-75			
7055	Lynx	Ford/Mercury Front Wheel Drive 1981-87	6529	PV-444	Volvo 1956-69
			6529	PV-544	Volvo 1956-69
6844	L6	BMW 1970-88	6529	P-1800	Volvo 1956-69
6844	L7	BMW 1970-88	7593	Quantum	VW Front Wheel Drive 1974-87
6542	Mach I	Mustang/Cougar 1965-73	7593	Rabbit	VW Front Wheel Drive 1974-87
6812	Mach I Ghia	Mustang II 1974-78	7593	Rabbit Pickup	VW Front Wheel Drive 1974-87
6840	Malibu	Chevrolet Mid-Size 1964-88	6575	Rallye	Opel 1971-75
6575	Manta	Opel 1971-75	7459	Ramcharger	Dodge/Plymouth Trucks 1967-88
6696	Mark IV, V, VI, VII	Ford/Mercury/Lincoln Mid-Size 1971-85	6845	Rampage	Omni/Horizon/Rampage 1978-88
			6320	Ranchero	Fairlane/Torino 1962-70
7814	Mark VII	Thunderbird, Cougar, Continental 1980-87	6696	Ranchero	Ford/Mercury/Lincoln Mid-Size 1971-85
6842	Marquis	Ford/Mercury/Lincoln 1968-88	6842	Ranch Wagon	Ford/Mercury/Lincoln 1968-88
6696	Marquis	Ford/Mercury/Lincoln Mid-Size 1971-85	7338	Ranger Pickup	Ford Ranger/Bronco II 1983-88
			7307	Regal RWD	Century/Regal 1975-87
7199	Matador	AMC 1975-86	7950	Regal FWD 1988-90	Lumina/Grand Prix/Cutlass/Regal 1988-90
6634	Maverick	Maverick/Comet 1970-77			
6817	Maverick	Jeep 1945-87	7163	Reliant	Chrysler Front Wheel Drive 1981-88
7170	Maxima	Nissan 200SX, 240SX, 510, 610, 710, 810, Maxima 1973-88	5821	Roadrunner	Roadrunner/Satellite/Belvedere/GTX 1968-73
6842	Mercury	Ford/Mercury/Lincoln 1968-88	7659	Rotary Pick-Up	Mazda Trucks 1971-89
6963	Merkur	Mustang/Capri/Merkur 1979-88	6981	RX-7	Mazda 1978-89
6780	MGB, MGB-GT, MGC-GT	MG 1961-81	7165	R-12, 15, 17, 18, 18i	Renault 1975-85
			7830	Sable	Taurus/Sable/Continental 1986-89
6780	Midget	MG 1961-81	7750	Safari	Chevrolet Astro/GMC Safari 1985-90
7583	Mighty Max	Mitsubishi 1983-89			
7583	Mirage	Mitsubishi 1983-89	7041	Sapporo	Champ/Arrow/Sapporo 1978-83
5795	Mk.II 1969-70	Toyota 1966-70	5821	Satellite	Roadrunner/Satellite/Belvedere/GTX 1968-73
7004	Mk.II 1970-76	Toyota Corona/Crown/Cressida/ Mk.II/Van 1970-87	6326	Scamp	Valiant/Duster 1968-76
6554	Monaco	Dodge 1968-77	6845	Scamp	Omni/Horizon/Rampage 1978-88
6937	Monarch	Granada/Monarch 1975-82	6962	Scirocco	VW Front Wheel Drive 1974-90
6840	Monte Carlo	Chevrolet Mid-Size 1964-88	6936	Scottsdale	Chevrolet/GMC Pick-Ups & Suburban 1970-87
6696	Montego	Ford/Mercury/Lincoln Mid-Size 1971-85	8055	Scottsdale	Chevrolet/GMC Pick-Ups & Suburban 1988-90
6842	Monterey	Ford/Mercury/Lincoln 1968-88	5912	Scout	International Scout 1967-73
7583	Montero	Mitsubishi 1983-89	8034	Scrambler	Jeep 1971-90
6935	Monza 1975-80	GM Subcompact 1971-80	7197	Sentra	Datsun 1200, 210, Nissan Sentra 1973-88
6981	MPV	Mazda 1978-89			
6542	Mustang	Mustang/Cougar 1965-73	7462	Seville	Cadillac 1967-89
6963	Mustang	Mustang/Capri/Merkur 1979-88	7163	Shadow	Chrysler Front Wheel Drive 1981-88
6812	Mustang II	Mustang II 1974-78	6936	Siera	Chevrolet/GMC Pick-Ups & Suburban 1970-87
6981	MX6	Mazda 1978-89			
6844	M3, M6	BMW 1970-88	8055	Siera	Chevrolet/GMC Pick-Ups & Suburban 1988-90
7163	New Yorker	Chrysler Front Wheel Drive 1981-88	7583	Sigma	Mitsubishi 1983-89
6841	Nova	Chevy II/Nova 1962-79	6326	Signet	Valiant/Duster 1968-76
7658	Nova	Chevrolet Nova/GEO Prizm 1985-89	6936	Silverado	Chevrolet/GMC Pick-Ups & Suburban 1970-87
7049	Omega	GM X-Body 1980-85			
6845	Omni	Omni/Horizon/Rampage 1978-88	8055	Silverado	Chevrolet/GMC Pick-Ups & Suburban 1988-90
6575	Opel	Opel 1971-75			
7199	Pacer	AMC 1975-86	6935	Skyhawk	GM Subcompact 1971-80
7587	Park Avenue	GM C-Body 1985	7059	Skyhawk	Cavalier, Skyhawk, Cimarron, 2000 1982-88
6842	Park Lane	Ford/Mercury/Lincoln 1968-88			
6962	Passat	VW Front Wheel Drive 1974-90	7049	Skylark	GM X-Body 1980-85
6816	Pathfinder	Datsun/Nissan Pick-Ups and Pathfinder 1970-89			

Chilton's Repair Manuals are available at your local retailer or by mailing a check or money order for **$14.95** per book plus **$3.50** for 1st book and **$.50** for each additional book to cover postage and handling to:

Chilton Book Company
Dept. DM
Radnor, PA 19089

NOTE: When ordering be sure to include your name & address, book part No. & title.

Part No.	Model	Repair Manual Title	Part No.	Model	Repair Manual Title
7675	Skylark	Calais, Grand Am, Skylark, Somerset 1985-86	7040	Turbo	Volvo 1970-88
7657	Somerset	Calais, Grand Am, Skylark, Somerset 1985-86	5796	Type 1 Sedan 1949-71	Volkswagen 1949-71
7042	Spider 2000	Fiat 1969-81	6837	Type 1 Sedan 1970-80	Volkswagen 1970-81
7199	Spirit	AMC 1975-86	5796	Type 1 Karmann Ghia 1960-71	Volkswagen 1949-71
6552	Sport Fury	Plymouth 1968-76			
7165	Sport Wagon	Renault 1975-85	6837	Type 1 Karmann Ghia 1970-74	Volkswagen 1970-81
5796	Squareback	Volkswagen 1949-71			
6837	Squareback	Volkswagen 1970-81	5796	Type 1 Convertible 1964-71	Volkswagen 1949-71
7196	Stanza	Datsun/Nissan F-10, 310, Stanza, Pulsar 1976-88	6837	Type 1 Convertible 1970-80	Volkswagen 1970-81
6935	Starfire	GM Subcompact 1971-80	5796	Type 1 Super Beetle 1971	Volkswagen 1949-71
7583	Starion	Mitsubishi 1983-89			
7036	Starlet	Toyota Corolla/Carina/Tercel/Starlet 1970-87	6837	Type 1 Super Beetle 1971-75	Volkswagen 1970-81
7059	STE	Cavalier, Skyhawk, Cimarron, 2000 1982-88	5796	Type 2 Bus 1953-71	Volkswagen 1949-71
5795	Stout	Toyota 1966-70	6837	Type 2 Bus 1970-80	Volkswagen 1970-81
7042	Strada	Fiat 1969-81	5796	Type 2 Kombi 1954-71	Volkswagen 1949-71
6552	Suburban	Plymouth 1968-76			
6936	Suburban	Chevy/GMC Pick-Ups & Suburban 1970-87	6837	Type 2 Kombi 1970-73	Volkswagen 1970-81
8055	Suburban	Chevy/GMC Pick-Ups & Suburban 1988-90	6837	Type 2 Vanagon 1981	Volkswagen 1970-81
6935	Sunbird	GM Subcompact 1971-80	5796	Type 3 Fastback & Squareback 1961-71	Volkswagen 1949-71
7059	Sunbird	Cavalier, Skyhawk, Cimarron, 2000 1982-88	7081	Type 3 Fastback & Squareback 1970-73	Volkswagen 1970-70
7163	Sundance	Chrysler Front Wheel Drive 1981-88			
7043	Supra	Toyota Celica/Supra 1971-87	5796	Type 4 411 1971	Volkswagen 1949-71
8058	Supra	Toyota Celica/Supra 1986-90	6837	Type 4 411 1971-72	Volkswagen 1970-81
6837	Super Beetle	Volkswagen 1970-81	5796	Type 4 412 1971	Volkswagen 1949-71
7199	SX-4	AMC 1975-86	6845	Turismo	Omni/Horizon/Rampage 1978-88
7383	S-10 Blazer	Chevy S-10 Blazer/GMC S-15 Jimmy 1982-87	5905	T-37	Tempest/GTO/LeMans 1968-73
7310	S-10 Pick-Up	Chevy S-10/GMC S-15 Pick-Ups 1982-87	6836	T-1000	Chevette/T-1000 1976-88
7383	S-15 Jimmy	Chevy S-10 Blazer/GMC S-15 Jimmy 1982-87	6935	Vega	GM Subcompact 1971-80
			7346	Ventura	Pontiac Mid-Size 1974-83
7310	S-15 Pick-Up	Chevy S-10/GMC S-15 Pick-Ups 1982-87	6696	Versailles	Ford/Mercury/Lincoln Mid-Size 1971-85
7830	Taurus	Taurus/Sable/Continental 1986-89	6552	VIP	Plymouth 1968-76
6845	TC-3	Omni/Horizon/Rampage 1978-88	7037	Vista	Colt/Challenger/Vista/Conquest 1971-88
5905	Tempest	Tempest/GTO/LeMans 1968-73			
7055	Tempo	Ford/Mercury Front Wheel Drive 1981-87	6933	Vista Cruiser	Cutlass 1970-87
7036	Tercel	Toyota Corolla/Carina/Tercel/Starlet 1970-87	6637	Volare	Aspen/Volare 1976-80
			7482	Voyager	Dodge Caravan/Plymouth Voyager 1984-88
7081	Thing	Volkswagen 1970-81			
6696	Thunderbird	Ford/Mercury/Lincoln Mid-Size 1971-85	6326	V-100	Valiant/Duster 1968-76
			6739	Wagoneer 1962-83	Jeep Wagoneer, Commando, Cherokee, Truck 1957-86
7814	Thunderbird	Thunderbird, Cougar, Continental 1980-87	7939	Wagoneer 1984-89	Jeep Wagoneer, Comanche, Cherokee 1984-89
7055	Topaz	Ford/Mercury Front Wheel Drive 1981-87	8034	Wrangler	Jeep 1971-90
6320	Torino	Fairlane/Torino 1962-75	7459	W100, 150, 200, 250, 300, 350	Dodge/Plymouth Trucks 1967-88
6696	Torino	Ford/Mercury/Lincoln Mid-Size 1971-85			
			7459	WM300	Dodge/Plymouth Trucks 1967-88
7163	Town & Country	Chrysler Front Wheel Drive 1981-88	6842	XL	Ford/Mercury/Lincoln 1968-88
6842	Town Car	Ford/Mercury/Lincoln 1968-88	6963	XR4Ti	Mustang/Capri/Merkur 1979-88
7135	Townsman	Chevrolet 1968-88	6696	XR-7	Ford/Mercury/Lincoln Mid-Size 1971-85
5795	Toyota Pickups	Toyota 1966-70			
7035	Toyota Pickups	Toyota Trucks 1970-88	6982	XT Coupe	Subaru 1970-88
7004	Toyota Van	Toyota Corona/Crown/Cressida/Mk.II/Van 1970-87	7042	X1/9	Fiat 1969-81
			6965	Zephyr	Fairmont/Zephyr 1978-83
7459	Trail Duster	Dodge/Plymouth Trucks 1967-88	7059	Z-24	Cavalier, Skyhawk, Cimarron, 2000 1982-88
7046	Trans Am	Firebird 1967-81			
7345	Trans Am	Firebird 1982-90	6735	Z-28	Camaro 1967-81
7583	Tredia	Mitsubishi 1983-89	7318	Z-28	Camaro 1982-88
			6845	024	Omni/Horizon/Rampage 1978-88
			6844	3.0S, 3.0Si, 3.0CS	BMW 1970-88
			6817	4-63	Jeep 1981-87

Chilton's Repair Manuals are available at your local retailer or by mailing a check or money order for **$14.95** per book plus **$3.50** for 1st book and **$.50** for each additional book to cover postage and handling to:

**Chilton Book Company
Dept. DM
Radnor, PA 19089**

NOTE: When ordering be sure to include your name & address, book part No. & title.

CHILTON'S REPAIR MANUAL MODEL INDEX
Car and truck model names are listed in alphabetical and numerical order

Chilton's Repair Manuals are available at your local retailer or by mailing a check or money order for **$14.95** per book plus **$3.50** for 1st book and **$.50** for each additional book to cover postage and handling to:

Chilton Book Company
Dept. DM
Radnor, PA 19089

NOTE: When ordering be sure to include your name & address, book part No. & title.

CHILTON'S REPAIR MANUAL MODEL INDEX
Car and truck model names are listed in alphabetical and numerical order

Part No.	Model	Repair Manual Title	Part No.	Model	Repair Manual Title
6844	1500	DMW 1970-88	6844	2000	BMW 1970-88
6936	1500	Chevy/GMC Pick-Ups & Suburban 1970-87	6844	2002, 2002Ti, 2002Tii	BMW 1970-88
8055	1500	Chevy/GMC Pick-Ups & Suburban 1988-90	6936	2500	Chevy/GMC Pick-Ups & Suburban 1970-87
6844	1600	BMW 1970-88	8055	2500	Chevy/GMC Pick-Ups & Suburban 1988-90
5790	1600	Datsun 1961-72			
6982	1600DL, 1600GL, 1600GLF	Subaru 1970-88	6844	2500	BMW 1970-88
6844	1600-2	BMW 1970-88	6844	2800	BMW 1970-88
6844	1800	BMW 1970-88	6936	3500	Chevy/GMC Pick-Ups & Suburban 1970-87
6982	1800DL, 1800GL, 1800GLF	Subaru 1970-88	8055	3500	Chevy/GMC Pick-Ups & Suburban 1988-90
6529	1800, 1800S	Volvo 1956-69	7028	4000	Audi 4000/5000 1978-81
7040	1800E, 1800ES	Volvo 1970-88	7028	5000	Audi 4000/5000 1978-81
5790	2000	Datsun 1961-72	7309	6000	Celebrity, Century, Ciera, 6000 1982-88
7059	2000	Cavalier, Skyhawk, Cimarron, 2000 1982-88			